SIR WILLIAM LAIRD CLOWES was born in 1865 and made his reputation as naval correspondent of *The Times* between 1890 and 1895. He was a member of the Navy League and involved in the agitation for greater naval resources, and his anonymous articles which appeared in the *Daily Graphic* in 1893 undoubtedly influenced the naval Estimates.

He wrote and compiled this seven-volume history of the Royal Navy between 1897 and 1903, involving a number of distinguished contemporary writers to assist him. From America he employed Captain Mahan, author of *The Influence of Sea Power upon History*, and Theodore Roosevelt who covered the history of the war with the United States. Sir Clements Markham, President of the Royal Geographical Society, dealt with the history of voyages and discoveries, and H W Wilson, author of *Battleships in Action*, described many of the minor naval operations.

Vice Admiral Sir Horatio Nelson, Viscount Nelson, K.B.

From the oil painting in the possession of W. Pugin Thornton, Canterbury.

The Royal Navy

A History

From the Earliest Times to the Present

By

Wm. Laird Clowes

Fellow of King's College, London; Gold Medallist U.S. Naval Institute; Hon. Member of the Royal United Service Institution

Assisted by

Sir Clements Markham, K.C.B., P.R.G.S.
Captain A. T. Mahan, U.S.N.
Mr. H. W. Wilson
Col. Theodore Roosevelt, Governor of New York
Mr. L. Carr Laughton
etc.

Vol. IV.

Chatham Publishing

LONDON

PUBLISHER'S NOTE

In the original edition the four photogravure plates and three full-page illustrations faced the text pages as listed on page XI. In this edition these illustrations are collected at the back of the book after page 572, in the order in which they appeared in the first edition.

Published in 1997 by
Chatham Publishing,
1 & 2 Faulkner's Alley, Cowcross Street,
London EC1M 6DD

Chatham Publishing is an imprint of
Gerald Duckworth and Co Ltd

First published in 1899 by
Sampson Low, Marston and Company

ISBN 1 86176 013 2

A catalogue record for this book is available from the British Library

Printed and bound in Great Britain by Biddles Ltd, Guildford, Surrey

INTRODUCTION TO VOLUME IV.

THE present volume contains the record of the Minor Operations of the Royal Navy between 1763 and 1792, by Mr. H. W. Wilson; the story of Naval Voyages and Discoveries during the same period, by Sir Clements Markham; the Civil History of the Navy from 1793 to 1802, and an account of the Major Maritime Operations during the war of the French Revolution, by myself; a summary of the Minor Operations of that war, by Mr. H. W. Wilson; and a notice of Naval Voyages and Discoveries, 1793–1802, by Sir Clements Markham.

Mr. Wilson, while illustrating his subject with much fresh matter derived from hitherto unexplored sources, has, as will be seen, utilised Beatson as the canvas on which to do the main part of the work dealing with the operations of 1763 to 1792. Similarly, both he and I have, almost perforce, taken James's invaluable volumes as the canvas for the period from 1793 to 1802. James, in common with the most painstaking and conscientious of chroniclers, occasionally falls into error; but it is impossible to be as familiar as I now am with his monumental work, and with the authorities on which it is based, without marvelling at his extraordinary accuracy and carefulness. It is not often, assisted though one is to-day by many aids which were not at his disposal, that one is able successfully to challenge either his statements or his conclusions. For example, his judgment on the conduct of Nelson at Naples in 1799 is, I think, the judgment which must still be come to by every fair-minded man who has before him the large volume of additional evidence which has become available since James wrote. James had no blind dislike to the French, and no unreasonable prejudices against the other nationalities with which Great Britain found herself at issue during the period under review; and, almost invariably, he does even-handed justice to all. It is not until he has to describe the events of the American War of 1812 that he suffers himself to be misled by indefensible, and indeed unavowable, bias, and becomes to any serious extent untrustworthy. I make no apology, therefore, for having used James as the substructure for the whole of Chapter XXXV., and for having, in numerous passages, adopted almost his own words in telling the story. But I should add that I have never done this without, so far as possible, first satisfying myself, by independent research, that his version is in accordance with the facts. Minutes of courts-martial, admirals' dispatches, captains' letters, private logs and letters, ships' logs—used, however, with discretion—and my own large collections of original documents [1] relating to the affairs of the time, have enabled me to make, of course, some emendations, and many additions, to James's narrative; yet, as a rule, I have found that it calls for singularly little correction. It is only in the matter of criticism, and of application of the story of the past to the circumstances of the present and the future, that his work seems to leave much to be desired.

Owing to a misconception, for which I was, I fear, partly to blame, Mr. Wilson's contribution to the history of the events of 1793–1802 is somewhat briefer and less detailed than it might have been. Mr. Wilson unwittingly devoted some of the space allotted to him to the consideration of events which had been already dealt with in other chapters; and, with regret, I found myself obliged to delete all such passages as involved any repetition.

For help in the preparation of the present volume, or for the loan of documents and illustrative material, I have to express my thanks to, among many others, the late Lord Vernon, the Rev. A. G. Kealy, R.N., Mr. C. Constable, Mrs. Nelson Ward, Mr. E. W. H. Fyers, Mr. Henry Carey Baird, of Philadelphia, and, for further use of his unrivalled collection of naval medals, H.S.H. Captain Prince Louis of Battenberg, R.N., G.C.B., who has throughout taken a most kindly interest in the progress of the work. I have also received invaluable aid from the Right Hon. G. J. Goschen, M.P., First Lord of the Admiralty, by whose special direction information which I could scarcely have obtained elsewhere has been carefully compiled for me by an Admiralty official, to whom, though his name

[1] Inclusive of the voluminous collection made by Rear-Admiral Sir Home Riggs Popham.

remains unknown to me, I would tender my heartfelt thanks. As usual, Mr. R. B. Marston has combined the offices of a friend with those of a publisher, and has been indefatigable in keeping me informed of all such fresh publications, newly-published correspondence, and out-of-the-way entries in booksellers' catalogues as he has thought would interest me and benefit the work. He has also charged himself with the forwarding to me in Switzerland from time to time of consignments of books from my own library in London. I would, moreover, take this opportunity of expressing my indebtedness to Mr. Alfred Harmsworth, to whom the steady progress of my labours, in spite of my continued ill health, has of late owed much.

I would call attention to the unpublished portrait of Lord Nelson, which forms the frontispiece of this volume. I possess some scores of portraits of the great seaman, and I have seen hundreds of others; but I know of no picture of him which is at the same time so characteristic and so beautiful. I am greatly obliged to the gentleman who has allowed me the use of the original painting.

Although in the present volume, and in the one which is to follow it, Nelson occupies the leading place, I have not thought it either necessary or wise to say much about that great hero's private life. I have thus made but few references to the very interesting batch of Nelson letters printed, with a running comment, in 'Literature,' during the months of February, March, and April, 1898. Those letters, written by Nelson to his wife between 1794 and 1801, throw much new light upon the domestic relations of the pair, and, incidentally, enable one to correct certain errors of Clarke and M'Arthur, Morrison, Southey, Pettigrew, Laughton, and Mahan; but the papers thus tardily made public in 'Literature' upset little that is important in the generally accepted view of Nelson's service career. Those who are now responsible for bringing them to light have added to our knowledge of Nelson's treatment of his wife, and, it may be, afford grounds for the conclusion that the hero behaved to her with even greater duplicity than has been hitherto supposed; but their papers scarcely touch the military aspect of Nelson's genius; and it is with that that I have almost exclusively busied myself. That documents of such a character should have been kept in darkness for nearly a century is surprising.

At my urgent instance, the Publishers have most generously agreed to allow me to extend the size of this History from five to six volumes. I am fully aware of the disadvantages of bulky books; and, until quite recently I was as desirous as anyone else could have been to see the work completed in the five volumes which were originally contemplated. But so much fresh matter bearing upon the naval events and developments of the present century, and especially of the last half of it, has come into my possession, that I now unwillingly come to the conclusion that if the work is to be a well-proportioned whole, and is to do justice as much to the services of the living as to those of the dead, a sixth volume is absolutely necessary. I trust, however, that the completion of the History will not, in consequence, suffer more than a slight delay, much of the material for the fifth volume being already in type.

W. L. C.

DAVOS-AM-PLATZ, SWITZERLAND.
June, 1899.

ERRATA.

The reader is requested to make the following corrections of errors which escaped notice while the volume was passing through the press:—

P. 108, line 11. *For* Costy, *read* Cosby.
P. 189. Thomas Totty was made a Post-Captain not on 31–1–1781, but on 31–1–1782.
P. 280, line 14. *For* Charles, *read* James.
P. 529, first line of note. *For* Goelan, *read* Goélan.

CONTENTS.

VOLUME IV.

CHAPTER XXXII.

CHAPTER XXXIII.

CHAPTER XXXIV.

CHAPTER XXXV.

CHAPTER XXXVI.

CHAPTER XXXVII.

PUBLISHER'S NOTE
The photogravure plates and three full-page illustrations listed below appear in this edition at the back of the book, after page 572.

LIST OF ILLUSTRATIONS.

VOLUME IV.

PHOTOGRAVURE PLATES.

FULL-PAGE ILLUSTRATIONS.

ILLUSTRATIONS IN THE TEXT.

NAVAL HISTORY.

CHAPTER XXXII.

MINOR OPERATIONS OF THE ROYAL NAVY, 1763–1792.

H. W. Wilson.

Dispute with Spain—Spanish armament—Actions on North American coast—Capture of *Fox*—Her recapture—*Raleigh* attacks a convoy—*Lexington* and *Alert*—*Yarmouth* and *Randolph*—Paul Jones takes *Drake*—*Licorne* captured—*Arethusa* and *Belle Poule*—*Languedoc* and *Renown*—*Preston* and *Marseillais*—*Isis* and *César*—*Minerva* and *Concorde*—*Fox* taken by *Junon*—Capture of *Raleigh*—*Apollo* takes *Oiseau*—Attempt on Jersey—*Diligent's* fierce action with *Providence*—Sir Geo. Collier at Penobscot—Franco-Spanish fleet captures *Ardent*—Causes of her loss—D'Estaing at Savannah—*Pearl* takes *Sta. Monica*—Paul Jones meets *Serapis*—Furious battle—*Serapis* taken—*Quebec* fights *Surveillante*—Heroism of Capt. Farmer—Force of the ships—Capture of Omoa—*Jackal* carried off—British squadron fires on the Dutch—Arbuthnot at Charleston—Capture of the *Protée*—Mutiny in *Invincible*—Cowardice of two Captains—Capture of *Capricieuse*—Of *Belle Poule*—Respect for neutrals—Moutray's convoy taken—*Flora* and *Nymphe*—Hurricanes and disasters—Capture of *Rotterdam*—Of *Minerve*—Capture of Dutch ships—*Cerberus* and *Grana*—*Canada* takes *Sta. Leocadia*—*Actif* and *Nonsuch*—Loss of *Atalanta* and *Trepassey*—*Flora* and *Crescent* against *Castor* and *Briel*—West Indian actions—*Iris* takes *Trumbull*—*Helena* at Gibraltar—*Chatham* and *Magicienne*—Loss of *Hannibal*—Hughes takes Trincomale—*Success* captures *Sta. Catalina*—*Foudroyant* and *Pégase*—*Sta. Margarita* reads *Amazone* a lesson—La Pérouse in Hudson's Bay—*Rainbow* captures *Hébé*—*Hector's* glorious defence—She sinks—Heavy losses caused by a high gale—Capt. Inglefield deserts *Centaur*—*Torbay* and *London* chase *Scipion*—*Leander* and an unknown ship of the line—*Hussar* and *Sibylle*—*Argo* taken by French frigates—General remarks—Untrustworthiness of logs—Armaments—Weight of metal tells—Review of ship actions—Nautical qualities—Privateers—Riou and the *Guardian*—His heroism—Spanish armament—Russian armament—Bligh and the *Bounty*—*Pandora's* voyage.

PITCH POT, 1750.

IN 1766, Captain the Hon. John Byron returned from a voyage of discovery round the world, and reported so favourably of the Falkland Isles, that the Government determined to take effective possession of Port Egmont, in West Falkland.[1]

[1] Beatson, iv. 11, 20 ff.

Accordingly Captain John Macbride, with the *Jason*, 32, and three smaller vessels, was despatched to carry out this purpose. Not long after[1] his arrival the French established a settlement on East Falkland, at Port Louis, but soon abandoned it and handed it over to Spain. Port Louis was renamed La Solidad by its new owners.

Captain Macbride having returned to England, the duty of maintaining the rights of Great Britain devolved upon Commander Anthony Hunt (1), of the *Tamar*, 14, Commander George Farmer, of the *Swift*, 14, and Commander William Maltby, of the *Favourite*, 16. The commander of a Spanish vessel, discovered by Commander Hunt surveying the islands during 1769, was warned to leave, and did so; but two days later he reappeared with a protest from the governor of La Solidad, requiring the British to depart within six

DUTCH MEDAL COMMEMORATIVE OF THE SIEGE OF GIBRALTAR AND THE WRECK OF THE "ROYAL GEORGE."

(From an original lent by H.S.H. Capt. Prince Louis of Battenberg, R.N.)

months. On this Hunt sailed home for instructions. The *Swift* was wrecked, without serious loss of life, and thus the *Favourite* alone was left to guard the settlement. In June, 1770, five Spanish frigates or corvettes appeared in Port Egmont, fired at the *Favourite*, compelled the small garrison to surrender and embark in the sloop, and detained her for twenty days by taking possession of her rudder and several sails. At the expiration of that period Commander Maltby sailed for England, where he arrived on September 22nd.

The high-handed proceedings of the Spanish authorities caused great indignation in England, and strong representations were at once made to the court of Madrid. More effectual than any

[1] According to Beatson. Other authorities place the date of the French settlement in 1764.

representations, however, was the display of force by commissioning a "Spanish armament." First sixteen, and then an additional force of twenty-five ships of the line, ten frigates, and numerous smaller vessels were prepared for sea. France, after secretly instigating Spain to war, changed her policy, and advised Spain to keep peace with Great Britain, or, if she went to war, to expect no aid. On January 22nd, 1771, the Spanish ambassador was authorised to promise the restitution of Port Egmont, and the dispute terminated. The *Juno*, 32, Captain John Stott, *Hound*, 14, and *Florida*, store-ship, were sent out to receive the surrender of Port Egmont.

On July 4th, 1774, a terrible explosion occurred on board the *Kent*, 74, Captain Charles Feilding (1), whilst lying at Plymouth. A quantity of powder had been carelessly left on the poop whilst the guns were being scaled. This took fire from some wads, and forty-five men were killed or injured.

Throughout the years 1765–1775, the Navy on the North American station was constantly employed in police work and petty expeditions against the disaffected colonists. That it did not effect more than it did must be ascribed largely to the indifferent state of too many of the ships and the extreme weakness of the crews. The *Somerset*, 68, Captain Edward Le Cras, during 1775 co-operated with General Gage at Boston. On May 28th, the armed schooner *Diana*, 6, Lieut. Thomas Graves (3), had to be abandoned and burnt by her crew, in face of the colonists near Boston.[1] In the battle of Bunker's Hill on June 17th, the *Glasgow*, 20, Captain William Maltby, cannonaded the American position. The senior naval officer who was present on land in the action ordered the ships to fire red-hot shot to burn the village of Charlestown.

On July 15th, 1777, the schooner *Diligent*, Lieutenant John Knight (2), was surprised and captured by the people of Machias, whither she had gone on a visit.

The first naval action of the American War was the capture of the *Hunter* and a brig by two American privateers off Boston on November 23rd, 1775.[2] The British vessels were, however, almost immediately retaken by Lieut. John Bourmaster in an armed transport.

Early in 1776, on April 6th, the British 20-gun ship *Glasgow*,

[1] Beatson, iv. 72.

[2] Beatson, 'Naval and Military Memoirs,' iv. 113.

Captain Tyringham Howe, sailed into the midst of an American squadron under the command of Commodore Esek Hopkins, and composed of the *Alfred,* 24, *Columbus,* 20, *Andrea Doria,* 14, *Cabot,* 14,[1] and *Providence,* 12.[2] The British vessel engaged for over two hours with this very superior force, but succeeded in escaping, as the Americans were afraid that the noise of the firing would bring to the rescue a British squadron, which was lying at Newport. The *Glasgow* lost one killed and three wounded; the Americans, twenty-three or twenty-four killed and wounded.

On October 18th, Lieut. Henry Mouatt, with a small squadron of four ships, mounting thirty-six guns,[3] burnt the town of Falmouth,[4] owing to the refusal of the inhabitants to deliver up four guns and disarm. On December 5th, the American brig *Washington,* 10, was captured by the *Fowey,* 24, Captain George Montagu. Late in December, the American *Andrea Doria,* 14, captured the British *Racehorse,* 12, Lieut. James Jones, after a desperate action of two hours.[5] On March 26th, 1777, the American brig *Cabot,* 14, after a forty-eight hours' chase, was driven ashore and captured by the *Milford,* 28, Captain John Burr.[6] On April 16th, the British tender *Edward* was captured by the *Lexington,* 16, off the coast of Virginia. On May 2nd, the Harwich packet *Prince of Orange* was taken in the Channel by the American *Surprise,* 10, Captain Gustavus Conyngham,. The latter vessel had been bought at Folkestone, and, with glaring disregard of French neutrality, had been equipped at Dunkirk. On the *Surprise's* return to Dunkirk, the prize was seized and restored to Britain, though it was believed at the time, not without some reason, that the British Government, anxious to avoid a dispute with France, had purchased from Conyngham his capture. As showing the ubiquity of American privateers, it may be noticed that in June the British *Levant,* 28, fell in with and captured, after a short action, the American *Vigilant,* 14, in the Mediterranean. In the year 1777 there were attacks by American privateers on the shipping at Dublin and Penzance.[7]

[1] Rated "12" in the List Books and borne as a "12" in the Navy.

[2] Beatson, 134. This action caused great dissatisfaction in America. One of the American captains was at once cashiered; and Commodore Hopkins was shortly afterwards dismissed the service.

[3] Beatson, 227, 228.

[4] United States.

[5] I can find no reference to this action in the courts-martial.

[6] Beatson, 248. Log of *Milford* gives the *Cabot* 16 guns and 182 men.

[7] Ann. Reg. 1777, 192], 195].

On May 21st, 1777,[1] the American ships *Hancock*, 32, Captain John Manly, *Boston*, 30, Captain Hector McNeil, *Mifflin* and *Tartar*, 22, *Hawke*, 18, and five schooners, each of 14 guns, put to sea for a cruise. They were scattered by a gale, and only the *Hancock* and *Boston* were left in company. These two, on June 7th, off Boston, sighted a sail and gave chase. As both of them were exceptionally fast, they speedily overhauled the stranger, which proved to be the British frigate *Fox*, 28, Captain Patrick Fotheringham. The latter was a little slow in clearing for action, and, according to American accounts, she was not ready to open when the *Hancock* got in her first broadside. Captain Fotheringham managed to return the fire, and fought a sharp action for half an hour, until, noting that the *Boston* was coming down fast, and that she was a ship of formidable force, he made sail to draw the Americans apart, firing on the *Hancock*, meanwhile, with his stern-chasers. His ship, however, was an indifferent sailer, and the *Hancock* was not to be shaken off. The *Hancock* came up with the *Fox* a second time about noon, and engaged her closely till 1.15. At that point the *Boston* arrived on the *Fox's* starboard quarter, and opened a most galling fire. The *Fox's* main yard was shot away; the maintopmast was on the point of falling; the mainmast was badly wounded; the wheel had been shattered, and the ship would no longer answer her helm. The *Hancock* lay on the port bow, the *Boston* on the starboard quarter, so that they could scarcely be touched by a single one of the *Fox's* guns. At 1.45 Captain Fotheringham hauled down his colours. The injury to the hull and loss of life on board his ship had been small, because the Americans fired chiefly at the rigging. As an interesting episode, it is recorded that one of the *Boston's* burning gun-wads had lodged in the *Fox's* mizen chains, and was starting a fire there, when the captain of the *Boston* hailed the *Fox's* men with a speaking-trumpet and desired them to put out the fire. According to the evidence given at the court-martial, the *Fox* was weakly manned, having only 140 men fit to go to quarters, or 33 men short of her complement. From the same source we gather that the *Hancock* carried twenty 12's and twelve 6's[2]; the *Boston* five 12's, nineteen 9's, two 6's, and

[1] Cooper [J. F.], i. 79; Beatson, iv. 278; Courts Martial (Record Office MS.), vol. 50, Mar. 3rd; Maclay, i. 88 ff.; Clark, T., 'Naval History,' i. 53.

[2] Cf. Log of *Rainbow*. 'A Detail of some Particular Services' (B.M. 1447, c. 15, a journal kept in the *Rainbow*) gives the *Hancock* 34 guns.

four 4's. The usual tendency for the defeated to exaggerate the victor's strength must, however, be allowed for. Still, the above figures have been used in the estimate of comparative force.

—	Tons.	Guns.	Broadside.	Men.	Killed.	Wounded.	Total.
			Lbs.				
Hancock . .	730	32	156	270	?	?	8[1]
Boston . .	514	30?	131?	246	?	?	?
Fox . . .	585	28	114	150	2	10	12

Time, 120 minutes.

[1] Maclay. Burn, master of *Fox* stated at C. M. that *Hancock* threw ten dead men overboard. *Boston* seems to have suffered no loss.

The *Hancock* and *Boston* took a number of prisoners on board from their prize, and sent others in a captured fishing vessel to Newfoundland. The three then stood away for Boston, but on July 6th were sighted by the British 44-gun ship *Rainbow*, Captain Sir George Collier, and the 18-gun brig *Victor*. The Americans, mistaking the *Rainbow* for a vessel of the line, at once destroyed a prize that was in their company, and took to flight, forming in line of battle. The *Hancock* delayed the squadron. She was foul, and had been lightened too much forward, so that she did not sail well. During the 6th and 7th the pursuit continued, and early in the morning of the 8th a strange sail was seen from the *Rainbow*. She failed to answer the private signal, and was at first taken for another American; but as she joined in the pursuit and presently fired at the Americans, it was obvious that she was a friend. She was, in fact, the British frigate *Flora*, 32, Captain John Brisbane. At noon the *Rainbow* fired several shots, whereupon the Americans parted company and scattered. The *Boston* made off unmolested; the *Hancock* was followed by the *Rainbow*, and the *Fox* by the *Flora*. The brig *Victor* had now dropped behind. At 4 P.M. the *Rainbow* was close enough to her enemy to open fire with her broadside; a little later the report of distant guns told her that the *Flora* was also engaged. The *Hancock* was left by a sudden calm at the mercy of the *Rainbow's* powerful broadside, and struck at 8.30 P.M.[1]

The *Flora* sighted the enemy on the 7th, and at once gave chase.[2] On the 8th she ran the *Fox* to earth, and raked her as the

[1] Log of *Rainbow*. [2] Log of *Flora*.

enemy attempted to tack. A hot action followed before, about 4.30 in the afternoon, the *Fox* struck. The *Flora* had her foretop-mast wounded and much of her running rigging shot away. For their conduct on this occasion the American captains, Manly and McNiel, were court-martialled, and the latter, who in the *Boston* had deserted his commodore, was dismissed the American service. The comparative force of the ships was as follows :—

—	Tons.	Guns.	Broadside.	Men.	Killed.	Wounded.	Total.
			Lbs.				
Rainbow	831	44	285	211	?	?	?
Hancock	730	32	158	229	?	?	?
Flora	698	32	174	220	?	?	?
Fox	585	28	114	?	?	?	?

The *Hancock*[1] was purchased into the British service under the name of *Iris*. On board her were Captain Fotheringham of the *Fox* and forty of his men. On his arrival in England Captain Fotheringham was tried by court-martial for the loss of his ship, and honourably acquitted, as he had not struck till she was un-manageable and defenceless, when further resistance would have meant mere aimless waste of life.

In the course of the year the *Beaver*, 14, Commander James Jones, captured a large American privateer of 14 guns, with a loss of only 2 wounded. The American loss was 20 killed and as many wounded.

On September 4th, 1777, the *Camel*, 22, Captain the Hon. William Clement Finch, the *Weazel*, 16, Commander Samuel Warren (1), and the *Druid*, 14, Commander Peter Carteret, were convoying the homeward bound trade from the Leeward Islands, when a sudden attack was made upon the *Druid* by an enemy who had stolen into the fleet.[2] This was the 32-gun American frigate *Raleigh*, Captain Thomas Thompson. On September 2nd, cruising in the company of the *Alfred*, 24, she had captured a vessel of the convoy, and ascertained from her master the order of sailing and the signals used. On September 3rd, the Americans were in sight of the

[1] Dimensions: Charnock, 'Mar. Architecture,' iii. 257: length, 137 ft. 1 in.; beam, 34 ft. 3¾ in.; draught, 10 ft. 11 in.

[2] Allen, i. 245; Cooper, i. 153; Beatson, iv. 284; Log of *Druid* missing.

convoy, and managed to get near without exciting any suspicion; they were unable, however, to cut off any of the merchantmen, as the *Alfred* was a very bad sailer. Finally Captain Thompson decided to leave his consort behind; ran into the midst of the British fleet; exchanged signals with the British ships; and bore down upon the unsuspecting *Druid,* till, having selected his position, he ran out his guns and gave her for twenty minutes broadside after broadside. Taken completely by surprise she could make but feeble reply. Her Commander, Carteret, was mortally wounded at the first fire; her Master was killed; the command passed to Lieut. John Bourchier. The convoy had meantime fallen into great confusion, each ship suspecting her neighbour to be a disguised enemy. But, as it was seen that the surprise had proceeded from one solitary ship and that other enemies did not appear, the British warships, supported by several armed merchantmen, made all sail to come up with the *Raleigh.* She had therefore to draw off when the British vessels neared her. She left the *Druid* in a terribly damaged state; with masts, yards, and rigging much shattered; several shot-holes betwixt wind and water; five feet of water in the hold, and six men killed and sixteen wounded. On her part the *Raleigh* is said to have only lost three men. She was chased after the action by the *Camel* and *Weazel,* but, being clean, could not be overtaken. The engagement is instructive as showing the difficulty of concentrating against a bold assailant the ships engaged in protecting a convoy. The *Raleigh* and the *Alfred* did not, however, succeed in capturing a single ship. The *Alfred* appears throughout to have held back.

As this was a surprise action, and therefore no fair test of either ship, the relative force of the two combatants is unimportant. The *Raleigh* was, of course, a far more powerful ship than the *Druid,* and, singly, should have been more than a match for the *Druid, Weazel,* and *Camel* combined.

On September 19th, a sharp action took place in the Channel between the American brig, *Lexington,* 16, Captain H. Johnston, and the British cutter, *Alert,* 10, Lieut. John Bazely (1).[1] The American was caught unprepared and brought to action early in the morning. She had a short supply of ammunition, and no match ready. After more than two hours' fighting the *Lexington* crippled the *Alert's* rigging, and managed to draw off, with scarcely a shot left in her magazines. The *Alert,* however, was very smartly

[1] Log of *Alert.* Emmons, 'U.S. Navy,' 42; 'Gent.'s Magazine,' xlvii. 458.

repaired, and renewed the chase. She came up again with the enemy about 1.30, and, an hour later, was in a position to reopen fire. The Americans could now make no reply, and, after passively enduring the broadsides of the *Alert* for an hour, were compelled to strike. Cruising in the Channel in company with the *Reprisal* and *Dolphin*,

ADMIRAL JOHN BAZELY (1).

(From an engraving by Ridley, after the miniature by T. Langdon.)

the *Lexington* had in five days captured fourteen prizes. The force of each ship was as follows :—

—	Tons.	Guns.	Broadside.	Men.	Killed.	Wounded.	Total.
			Lbs.				
Alert . . .	205	10	20	60	2	3	5
Lexington .	..	16	34	84	7	11	18

Time, 3 hours 30 minutes.

Amongst the *Lexington's* killed and wounded were the master, first lieutenant, lieutenant of marines, and gunner. It should be noted that the victory of so inferior a vessel as the *Alert* was probably due to surprise.

In October the American ship *Lexington,* 16, was captured by the *Pearl,* 32, in West Indian waters, but the Americans rose on the prize crew and retook the ship.[1]

On March 7th, 1778, the British 64, *Yarmouth,* Captain Nicholas Vincent, fell in with a squadron of American ships cruising off Barbados. She gave chase, and overtaking the 32-gun frigate *Randolph,* Captain Nicholas Biddle, engaged with her in a running fight. This had and could have had but one issue—defeat to the smaller and weaker vessel. The *Randolph* blew up and all her crew of 315 perished with her, except four who were rescued five days later by the British ship from some wreckage to which they had clung. At the explosion, burning spars and timbers six feet long fell upon the *Yarmouth's* deck, and with these an undamaged American ensign. The British loss was 5 killed and 12 wounded; the damage to the *Yarmouth* was trivial.[2] She was of course vastly superior in weight of metal and strength of hull.

On March 9th, 1778, the British ships *Ariadne,* 24, Captain Thomas Pringle, and *Ceres,* 18, Commander James Richard Dacres (1), cruising in West Indian waters, saw two sail.[3] Giving chase, they speedily came up with the sternmost, which struck after receiving a few broadsides. She proved to be the American cruiser *Alfred,* Captain Elisha Hinman, armed with twenty long 9's and carrying 180 men. The other vessel, the *Raleigh,* of 32 guns, ignominiously escaped.

Early in 1777, the American Marine Committee decided to despatch ships to attack British trade in British waters.[4] The unprotected state of our commercial ports and coastline had been represented to Congress by the United States' Commissioners in Paris, and, as far back as 1776, plans had been matured for the destruction of Bristol and other important places. Captain John Paul Jones was selected for the important enterprise, and putting to sea in the *Ranger,* 18, on November 1st, arrived at Nantes in

[1] Probably the date should be 1776, but I can find no trace of the capture in the *Pearl's* log for October 1776 or 1777.

[2] *London Gazette,* May 23rd; Log of *Yarmouth.*

[3] *London Gazette,* May 23rd; Navy List Book.

[4] Laughton, 'Studies in Naval History,' 376–387; 'Life of Paul Jones from . . . manuscript of Miss J. Taylor,' 69–88; Hutchinson, W., 'History of Cumberland,' 1794, ii. 86; Beatson, iv. 439; Cts. Martial (MSS. Record Office), vol. 53.

December, with two prizes. Thence he convoyed some American ships to La Motte-Piquet's fleet, and from the French admiral obtained a salute for the new American flag. Having refitted at Brest, he sailed on April 10th, 1778, for the Irish Sea. On the 14th, north of the Scillies, he captured a brigantine; on the 17th, off Dublin, a vessel laden with porter. On the 18th, off the Scotch coast, he chased a revenue wherry unsuccessfully; on the 19th, he

CAPTAIN JOHN PAUL JONES, U.S.N.

(From J. B. Longacre's engraving, after the portrait by C. W. Peale.)

destroyed two more ships. On the 21st, learning that the British sloop *Drake*, 20, Commander George Burdon, was at anchor in Carrickfergus Bay, he determined to run in at night with his ship and board her. His plan, though bold and well-conceived, miscarried; he entered the bay, but did not anchor quickly enough, and, a gale springing up, he was obliged to run out again. On the 22nd, he decided to burn the shipping at Whitehaven, which place he knew well. At midnight two boats with thirty-two men left the

Ranger, and reached the land as the day was dawning. One party set the ships in the harbour on fire; the other entered a dilapidated fort, which was supposed to protect the town, and spiked the guns. One of his men, however, had slipped away, misliking the work, and given the alarm; and, though the harbour was dry, Jones found on returning from a second battery,[1] a little way further off, whither he had gone with the men to spike the guns, that the shipping was not burning. With some trouble he kindled a blaze in the steerage of a large vessel, which lay in the midst of 150 other ships, poured some tar on the flames, and re-embarked. The cannon in the fort were easily unspiked and fired at him by the fast-gathering inhabitants, as he made off; and the fire which he had so laboriously kindled was put out. He rowed across to the Scotch coast, hoping to seize Lord Selkirk as a hostage, for the better treatment of the American prisoners, but the nobleman was away. The American sailors carried off some of the family plate, which Captain Jones afterwards returned.

On April 24th, the *Ranger* was again off Carrickfergus, hoping for an action with the *Drake*. A boat, in charge of a Midshipman and six sailors, was sent out by the latter ship to reconnoitre the privateer and was captured. There must have been some carelessness on the part of the British commander, Burdon, as news of the doings at Whitehaven had already arrived. A little later the sloop was seen by the Americans to be working her way out against the wind and tide, whilst numbers of the inhabitants could be perceived on the high land ashore. The *Ranger* retired before the *Drake* to mid-channel, and when hailed replied: "The American Continental ship *Ranger* . . . it is time to begin." Accordingly her helm was sharply put up, she passed across the *Drake's* bows and raked her. Captain Jones quickly obtained the upper hand. The *Drake* was very short of officers: she had neither Lieutenant, Gunner, Boatswain, nor Master's Mate; her crew, though large in number, was composed mainly of volunteers or freshly pressed men, who were not at all to be trusted in action; her scantling was weak; her battery feeble and exposed; her twenty 4-pounders were no match for the *Ranger's* eighteen 6-pounders,[2] let alone the eight swivels which that

[1] Probably the "Half Moon" battery.

[2] Jones complains of the crankness and weakness of the *Ranger*. Originally she carried 26 guns, but 8 had been removed. Of the 18 carried he complained that they were all three calibres too short. The *Drake's* Master (Cts. Martial, 53) states that the *Ranger's* 6-prs. were "double fortified," *i.e.*, extra heavy.

ship carried; the powder was bad, the match was bad, and, as there was no paper on board, cartridges were not prepared either for the great guns or for the small arms. For the heavy guns only twenty rounds were ready. In short, the ship had been taken by surprise and was at the greatest disadvantage. Seventy-four minutes after the first shot, the *Drake* struck to her skilfully-handled and well-fought enemy.

—	Guns.	Broadside.	Men.	Killed.	Wounded.	Total.
		Lbs.				
Ranger	18	54	135	2	6	8
Drake	20	40	154	5	20	25

Time, 74 minutes.

After this action Jones sailed round the north of Ireland with his prize, and on May 8th arrived safely at Brest. The quality of the *Drake's* crew is shown by the fact that twenty of them enlisted in the American service. They were probably Irishmen who had been pressed for the Navy.

On May 6th, the *Hussar* galley, under the orders of Captain John Henry, with a small flotilla and a battalion of infantry, ascended the Delaware from Philadelphia, the object being to destroy various works and vessels which the Americans possessed high up the river on the New Jersey shore.[1] A landing was effected at Bordentown; a battery was destroyed, and 44 American sail were burnt or sunk. The expedition then returned to Philadelphia without the loss of a man. Towards the end of May a combined expedition, covered by the *Flora*, 32, destroyed a number of American boats and ships high up in Narragansett Bay, and carried off several guns without any loss. A similar expedition, but with less success, was made up the Taunton River. On June 1st, the town of Banff, in Scotland, was alarmed by the landing, from an American privateer, of a party of raiders, who plundered some of the inhabitants of their plate and portable effects.[2]

On June 15th, when the French Government was on the verge of hostilities with Great Britain, but before any declaration of war had been issued by either side, the frigates, *Belle Poule*, 30, *Licorne*, 32, the corvette, *Hirondelle*, 16, and the lugger *Coureur*, 10,

[1] *Lond. Gazette*, June 13; Beatson, iv. 314.

[2] 'Gent.'s Magazine,' xlviii. 282.

left Brest, under the orders of Lieut. de La Clocheterie[1] of the *Belle Poule*, to cruise in the Channel.[2] On the 17th, they fell in with Admiral Keppel's fleet of twenty sail of the line, four frigates and three smaller craft, which had put to sea on the 12th and which was cruising to the west of the Lizard. A general chase was signalled by the British Admiral, and by the evening the *Milford*, 28, Captain Sir William Burnaby, had closely approached one of the French vessels, the *Licorne*, commanded by Lieut. de Belizal. It was Admiral Keppel's wish that the chase should be brought to him, but M. de Belizal was not to be so easily caught. He attempted to escape and was only brought to by the *Hector*, 74, firing a shotted gun at him. Meanwhile, the *Arethusa*, 32, Captain Samuel Marshall (2), and two ships of the line were seen to be in pursuit of another French ship, and as evening came on the *Arethusa* was engaged. The *Licorne* was led through the fleet to the Commander-in-Chief's flagship, *Victory*. On the morning of the 18th she made one more bid for freedom, but was at once fired upon by one of the British sail of the line. On this she discharged her broadside into the 64, *America;* though M. de Belizal was, at the moment when the broadside was fired, talking in a friendly way to the *America's* captain. Having done this and wounded four men on board the *America*, she struck. The *Licorne* was probably armed with twenty-six 12's and six 6's; though some French accounts give her only 26 guns. She carried 230 men.

The *Arethusa* came up with *Belle Poule* soon after 6 P.M. on the 17th. Captain Marshall requested M. de La Clocheterie to bring to and follow the *Arethusa* to the British Admiral, and, on the French captain's absolute refusal to do any such thing, opened fire at a pistol shot's distance. The wind was very slight and would scarcely allow the two ships to steer. The frigates fought broadside to broadside, from 6.30 to 11.30 P.M.,[3] when they parted. The other ships of the British squadron were several miles behind the *Arethusa* and could give her no aid. According to the French account she retired towards them with her masts and rigging much damaged. According to the British account, which is, on the whole, the more

[1] Louis Chadeau de La Clocheterie, the son of a French naval officer who fell in the action of May 14th, 1747, was born about 1736. For his action with the *Arethusa* he was made a captain. He fought in the battles off Cape Henry and St. Kitts, in 1781, and was killed in the battle of Apr. 12th, 1782.—W. L. C.

[2] *Lond. Gazette*, June 26th; *Gazette de France*, June 23rd; Troude, ii. 23; Chevalier, 72; Allen, i. 263.

[3] Two hours, according to Capt. Marshall of the *Arethusa*.

probable, it was the *Belle Poule* that made off in the direction of the French coast. The French official version admits that, if the *Arethusa* retreated, it was impossible to pursue her, and that the *Belle Poule* anchored amidst the rocks of Plouascat. There, it says, next day she was blockaded by two British vessels, which, finding that they could not get at her, presently withdrew. The action was a very fiercely fought one. In the French ship the second in command was killed; whilst M. de La Clocheterie and several other officers were wounded. M. Bouvet, who was severely wounded, refused to leave the deck to have his injuries attended to. The *Arethusa* was a good deal cut up. The comparative force of the two ships was as follows:—

—	Tons.	Guns.	Broadside.	Men.	Killed.	Wounded.	Total.
			Lbs.				
Arethusa . .	700	28[1]	114	198	8	36	44
Belle Poule .	902	30[1]	168	230	45	57	102

Time, 2 hours?

[1] The armament of these two ships is a little doubtful. The French account gives the *Arethusa* twenty-eight 12's, but there do not appear to have been any British frigates of twenty-eight so armed. The *Belle Poule* was taken in 1780 and appears as a 32 when captured. Chevalier, p. 76, gives her twenty-six 12's and two 9's; Beatson, v. 137, gives her thirty-two 12's; Troude, whom I have followed, twenty-six 12's and four 6's (ii. 23); Charnock, 'Hist. Mar. Arch.' iii. 255, makes her a 36 in the British Navy. As such she appears in all Steel's Lists.

Whilst the *Belle Poule* and *Arethusa* were busy, the British cutter *Alert*, Lieut. William George Fairfax, attacked the French lugger *Coureur*.[1] The *Alert* carried eighty men, twelve 6's, and as many swivels: the *Coureur* had fifty men, two 3's, eight 2's, and six swivels; she was commanded by Enseigne de Rosily. She was ordered, like the *Belle Poule*, to go to the British Admiral; refused; and was at once fired upon. The two fought at pistol-shot range for nearly an hour and a half, until the *Coureur* struck. She hit the *Alert* several times on the water-line and cut up her rigging. The following are the particulars of the ships:—

—	Tons.	Guns.	Broadside.	Men.	Killed.	Wounded.	Total.
			Lbs.				
Alert . . .	205	12	36	80	0	4	4
Coureur . .	..	10	11?	50	5	7	12

Time, 90 minutes.

[1] Log of *Alert*.

On the 19th, the French 32-gun frigate *Pallas* was sighted and chased by Keppel's fleet. She was overtaken and her captain was invited to repair to the flagship, where it was decided to detain her. Her crew of two hundred and twenty were taken out of her and distributed throughout the British fleet, and she was carried into port as a prize.

Charges of treachery have been brought by French writers against Admiral Keppel, for the way in which he captured these ships. France, however, having in February signed a treaty of alliance with the revolted Colonists, was virtually at war with Great Britain, and though Keppel was not, probably, over particular, the behaviour of the *Licorne* and *Belle Poule* was so unfriendly as to justify his proceedings. It should be remembered that a formal declaration of war seldom precedes the commencement of hostilities. If it did not suit France to declare war at that moment, Great Britain, as the power plotted against, was perfectly justified in striking at her secret enemy, as she did.

On June 24th, the British cutter *Folkestone*, Lieut. William Smith (1), fell in with five French frigates, and was captured.

On July 8th, the *Mermaid*, 28, Captain James Hawker, was chased ashore in Delaware Bay by d'Estaing's squadron. Her crew threw overboard her guns and their arms ere she struck to a small American ship which hailed her.

On July 9th, the British 20-gun ship, *Lively*, Captain Robert Biggs, whilst cruising off Brest, was unlucky enough to be overtaken by the Count d'Orvilliers's fleet.[1] She was chased first of all by the cutter *Curieuse* of 10 guns, and ordered to lie to. The British Captain refused to obey, on which the large frigate *Iphigénie*, 32, stood close up to him and opened on the *Lively*. After one broadside the British ship struck her flag, and was conducted into Brest. On July 17th, the 12-gun cutter *Alert*, Lieut. W. G. Fairfax, was overtaken by the French frigate *Junon* and captured in the channel.[2]

The operations in Narragansett Bay, in July and August, 1778, have been described in Chapter XXI.

On the evening and night of August 13th, two separate actions

[1] C. M. (MS.), 53.

[2] An action between the *Rose* and *Engageante* is given in Troude (ii. 24), as occurring in July, but is not referred to in Beatson, Schomberg, or the *London Gazette*. From Chevalier (123), it appears that this *Rose* was a privateer of 22 guns, and was only taken after a most desperate resistance. She had to be sunk by her captors.

took place between isolated line-of-battle ships of Lord Howe's and d'Estaing's squadrons.[1] The ships of both fleets had been much scattered and damaged by the great storm of the 11–12th: which explains a somewhat singular occurrence. The first action was fought between the *Languedoc,* 80, Captain de Boulainvilliers, and the *Renown,* 50, Captain George Dawson (actg.). On board the *Languedoc* was d'Estaing himself. His ship was totally dismasted and the tiller had been broken, so that in spite of her immense advantage in weight of metal the odds were against her. The *Renown* made her attack about sunset. She opened on the *Languedoc* with her 12-prs., and then wore under the enemy's stern to rake with her lower deck 24-prs. At half a cable's length, she battered the *Languedoc,* which could make no reply, except from two guns which were run out through her stern gallery. The French, despairing of their safety, were throwing their dispatches overboard, when darkness came on and the *Renown* hauled off. Captain Dawson intended to renew the action next day, but when at dawn he reopened, he found six ships of the line coming down upon him and had to retreat. As the *Languedoc* could not sail or steer, it was only by this accident that she escaped capture.

The action between the *Preston,* 50, Commodore William Hotham, Captain Samuel Uppleby and the *Marseillais,*[2] 74, Captain de La Poype-Vertrieux, was very similar. The *Marseillais* had lost her foremast and bowsprit, and had barely rigged a jury-mast when the *Preston* attacked her. After some hours of steady fighting the approach of other members of the French squadron compelled Commodore Hotham to retire. On August 16th, yet another of these combats occurred; this time between the *Isis,* 50, Captain John Rayner, and the *César,* 74, Captain de Raymondis, or, as it was supposed at the time, the *Zélé,* Captain de Barras.[3] In this case the French ship was intact, and chased and brought to action the British vessel. The French, however, made the great mistake of clearing for action only on one side, and had stowed between the guns on the other side the lumber which should have been thrown overboard. It must have been a habit of theirs, for the *Isis's* Captain guessed what they were doing, let his ship drop to leeward,

[1] *Lond. Gazette;* Howe's dispatch; Beatson, iv. 348. The date is also given as the 18th, wrongly.

[2] Troude, ii. 15, makes the French ship the *Marseillais;* Chevalier, 118, the *César,* and Beatson, iv. 349, the *Tonnant.*

[3] *Lond. Gazette,* Oct. 27th.

and then engaged them on the encumbered side, at very close quarters. The French were confused by this manœuvre, and, being to windward, had some difficulty in opening their lower deck ports. After a short but furious fight the *César* retired, because—according to French accounts—the rudder had been injured and two other British ships were in sight. The *Isis* was unable to pursue, since, as usual, the French had aimed at the masts and rigging. In any case she was fortunate to escape from a ship of twice her weight of metal. Her crew, amongst whom was the Duke of Ancaster serving as a volunteer, behaved with great bravery. The *César's* captain had his arm shattered; the first lieutenant lost a leg; and from fifty to seventy men were killed or wounded.[1]

—	Tons.	Guns.	Broadside.	Men.	Killed.	Wounded.	Total.
Isis . . .	976	50	Lbs. 414	350 n.	1	15	16
César . . .	..	74	828 [1]	{ 500 n. / 700 }	?	?	50? [2]

n = nominal complement.

[1] French 74's were of two types; both carried twenty-eight 36's and sixteen 8's, but the first had thirty 24's and the second thirty 18's as well. I suppose *César* to have been of the second-class.

[2] The reported loss in the *Gazette* is given as fifty, but this estimate is obviously untrustworthy.

On August 14th, the French squadron captured the British 18-gun ship *Senegal*, the *Thunder*, bomb, and another small vessel. About the same time the *César* captured the British 10-gun brig *Stanley*.

On August 22nd, the British 32-gun frigate *Minerva*, Captain John Stott, whilst on a cruise in the West Indies, and unaware that war had broken out, met the *Concorde*, 32, Captain de Tilly.[2] Captain Stott, taking her for a harmless merchantman, was approaching to speak her, when the *Concorde* fired a broadside, and followed this up with a second before the *Minerva* could reply. The ships were of equal force, and the British crew, though caught off their guard, made a brave resistance. But luck was against them: an explosion of powder under the half-deck dismounted three guns, killed or wounded eighteen men, and caused great confusion. Another gun was put out of action by an accident. The seamen, intimidated by the explosion, began to bolt from the guns. Captain Stott, twice

[1] The above three encounters are briefly referred to in vol. iii., p. 409.

[2] Troude, ii. 25; *Gazette de France*, 726; C. M., 53. According to French accounts, the *Concorde* carried twenty-six 12's and six 6's.

severely wounded in the head, had been carried below. The mizen-mast went overboard; the other masts were tottering; the wheel was shot away; and the officers had lost control of the men. The battle lasted two and a half hours and then at last the *Minerva* struck. Her loss was very heavy, though exact figures cannot be given. Both Captain Stott and the first Lieutenant died of their wounds, aggravated by grief at the loss of their ship. On the other hand, the *Concorde* lost few men and suffered but little damage. Her captain's brother, who was serving on board, died of his wounds.

The defeat of the *Minerva* cannot be ascribed to any want of valour or skill on the part of her crew. It was due simply to the fact that she was undermanned and unprepared. She was retaken later, and named *Recovery*.

—	Tons.	Guns.	Broadside.	Men.	Killed.	Wounded.	Total.
			Lbs.				
Concorde . .	..	32	174	200 250 n.	4	11	15
Minerva . .	664	32	174	217 n.	?	?	?

Time, 2 hours 30 minutes.

On August 23rd, the British sloop *Zephyr*, 14, Commander Thomas West, was taken in the Mediterranean by a French frigate.

In East Indian waters the *Sartine*, 32, which had been detached from the squadron of M. Tronjoly, was sighted on August 25th, and chased and captured by the *Seahorse* and *Coventry*. According to Barras, her captain displayed great cowardice, surrendering without firing a shot. Troubridge, then a lieutenant in the *Seahorse*, is said to have distinguished himself in boarding her. She was purchased into the British service.[1]

On September 1st, the *Active*, 28, Captain William Williams, was captured off the San Domingo coast by the *Charmante*, 38, and the *Dédaigneuse*, 26.[2] In a previous storm, the *Active* had thrown eleven of her guns overboard, lost her topmasts, and sprung her mainmast, and so, when her enemies came up to her, she had no resource but to strike, which she did at the second broadside. Captain Williams is said by Nelson to have died of mortification at his capture.[3]

[1] She mounted twenty-six 9's. Barras, 'Mémoires,' i. 313.

[2] C. M., 53.

[3] Nicolas, 'Nelson Dispatches,' i. 25.

On September 10th, whilst the British frigate *Fox*, 28, Captain the Hon. Thomas Windsor, was cruising off Brest, she saw and chased a ship and a sloop.[1] The weather was so dark and squally that she did not for some time observe a frigate chasing her, but when she did, she shortened sail and waited for the enemy. It was the French frigate *Junon*, 32, Captain Vicomte de Beaumont, of far greater weight of metal. After some preliminary manœuvres to gain an advantageous position, the two frigates passed on opposite tacks, exchanging broadsides, and then the French captain attempted to rake his enemy, but with indifferent success. He next tacked and took up a position on the *Fox's* quarter, but to windward; and yet, even there, found that he could do little. Once again he attempted to rake, and was thwarted, but succeeded in closing with his enemy. At musket range the heavy guns of the *Junon*, trained with skill and deliberation, did what they ought to have done far sooner and got the *Fox's* fire under. The British ship lost all her masts and had several of her guns disabled. The *Junon's* gunners had been ordered to fire at the enemy's hull, not at her masts after the usual French fashion. Having offered a protracted and heroic resistance to overwhelming odds, Captain Windsor, who had been severely wounded in the arm, waved with his hat that he surrendered. The *Fox*, during the last period of the action, could only fire a few shots, and was terribly injured. The *Junon*, on the other hand, suffered little of either damage or loss.

—	Tons.	Guns.	Broadside.	Men.	Killed.	Wounded.	Total.
			Lbs.				
Junon[1] . .	..	32	174	330	4	15	19
Fox . . .	585	28	114	198 n.	11	38	49

Time, 3 hours 30 minutes.

1 According to Capt. Windsor's letter, the *Junon* fought on each side fourteen 12's and six 6's. The *Junon* is also described as an 18-pr. frigate. I have given her only the broadside of a 12-pr. 32, and therefore my figures are probably an underestimate.

On September 26th, the British ships *Experiment*, 50, Captain Sir James Wallace,[2] and *Unicorn*, 20, Commander Matthew Squire, cruising off Boston, made out a large sail, and gave chase. The vessel thus discovered was the American 32-gun frigate *Raleigh*,

[1] Beatson, iv. 431, Sept. 18th; *Gazette de France*, 691, Sept. 10th; Troude, ii. 27; C. M., 53.

[2] Maclay, i. 92 ff.; Cooper, i. 92 ff.; Beatson, iv. 379; Log of *Unicorn*.

Captain John Barry. The weather was thick, and by changing her course the American hoped that she had avoided the British ships; but in the course of the morning of the 27th, they again hove in sight. The *Raleigh* was a fast sailer, and was leaving them behind, when suddenly the wind dropped, enabling her enemies to come up. The *Unicorn* attacked first. Her fire brought down the *Raleigh's* fore-topmast and mizen-topmast, but the British ship was compelled by damage to her own rigging to haul off and refit. Meantime, the *Experiment* came up and opened on the *Raleigh*. Captain Barry, thus situated, determined to run his ship on some low-lying islands, which were in sight, and to abandon her. The first he was able to do, but before all his crew had got away, the *Experiment's* boats boarded the *Raleigh* and captured her with one hundred and thirty-six officers and men. She was got off without much difficulty and added to the British Navy. The presence of the *Experiment*, though she took but small part in the fighting, was doubtless the determining feature in the action. The details, so far as they are known, of the two ships are:

—	Tons.	Guns.	Men.	Broadside.	Killed.	Wounded.	Total.
				Lbs.			
Unicorn . .	581?	20[1]	198	114	10	many	?
Experiment .	923	50	345	414	?	?	?
Raleigh . .	697	32	235	174	?	?	25

1 In the MSS. Navy Lists *Unicorn* appears as a 20-gun ship, but the tonnage is that of a 28-gun ship, and she is given 28 guns in the account of the action. The *Raleigh*, by the *U.'s* log, carried twenty-six 12's and six 6's She was 131 ft. long, 34 ft. in beam, and 11 ft. in draught.

On October 20th, the *Jupiter*, 50, Captain Francis Reynolds, and the *Medea*, 28, Captain James Montagu (1), whilst cruising off Finisterre, fell in with the French line-of-battle ship, *Triton*, 64, Captain Comte de Ligondès.[1] The *Jupiter* ranged up on one board, the *Medea* on the other, about nightfall, and cannonaded the *Triton* hotly. The French captain succeeded in turning the same broadside to both his assailants, but after about an hour's fighting was wounded in either arm and had to hand over the command to Lieut. de Roquart. The engagement lasted two hours, before a squall of wind and rain, and the impenetrable darkness of the night separated the combatants. The *Triton* had thirteen killed and about twenty

1 Troude, ii. 27; *Gazette de France*, 840 ff.; Log of *Jupiter*; Log of *Medea*; Charnock, vi. 476.

wounded: she had fifty shot in her hull or masts; and her sails and rigging were much cut up. According to Captain Reynolds, she stood off and abandoned the battle, though the *Medea* had been struck by a 36-pound shot on the bows below the water-line and was virtually out of action after the first half-hour. The *Jupiter's* loss was three killed and seven wounded; the *Medea's* loss was one killed and three wounded.

On November 3rd, whilst cruising in the West Indies, the *Maidstone*, 28, Captain Alan Gardner, chased and came up with the 40-gun French armed ship *Lion*.[1] She was beaten off once, by damage to her masts and rigging, but, after refitting, came up again. The French ship struck an hour later. Captain Gardner was amongst the wounded.

—	Tons.	Guns.	Broadside.	Men.	Killed.	Wounded.	Total.
			Lbs.				
Maidstone .	593	28	114	198 n.	4	9	13
Lion . . .	..	40	198	216	8	18	22

On December 17th, 1778, the British sloop *Ceres*, 18, Commander James Richard Dacres (1), was chased by several French ships and finally captured by the frigate *Iphigénie*, 32, off the coast of St. Lucia.[2] The *Ceres* was in charge of a convoy from which she succeeded in diverting the attention of the French.

On January 13th, 1779, the *Weazel*, 16, Commander Lewis Robertson, whilst carrying Admiral Barrington's dispatches from the West Indies to England, was chased by the French *Boudeuse*, 32, and captured near St. Eustatius.[3] She struck at the second broadside.

On January 31st, the British frigate *Apollo*, 32, Captain Philemon Pownall, was cruising off the Breton coast, when she came in sight of ten vessels.[4] On giving chase she overtook them, and made out one of the ten to be a frigate. She steered for her, whilst the other French ships, which were merchantmen under convoy, scattered and sought the land. Soon after noon the *Apollo* was close enough to fire upon the strange frigate, which was the *Oiseau*, 32,[5] Lieut.

[1] *Lond. Gazette*, '79, Mar. 24th; *Lion* had probably been hired from the king, a fairly common practice in France, though she may have been an ordinary privateer.

[2] C. M., 52.

[3] *Lond. Gazette*, Mar. 24th; Troude, ii. 46; C. M.

[4] *Gazette de France*, 77; Beatson, iv. 555; Troude, ii. 47. Captain Pownall signed his name "Pownoll," but the spelling given is the one employed in the Navy Lists.

[5] *Gazette de France*, twenty-six 8's.

de Tarade, and which as yet had hoisted no colours. The first broadside of the *Apollo* did the Frenchman some damage and led him to hoist his flag. The two ships were upon opposite tacks, when the *Apollo* luffed and came round on the same tack as the *Oiseau*. After some skilful manœuvring on either side the *Apollo* got within pistol shot, but to leeward. The ships engaged very closely; so closely that more than once the *Apollo's* bowsprit all but caught in the *Oiseau's* foremast shrouds. The wind had fallen, and the *Oiseau's* advantage in speed had gone with it. The superior fire of the British sailors cleared the enemy's deck till Lieut. de Tarade and four men were all who were left on the quarter-deck; the main-deck battery was dismounted and silent; and finally a shot carried away the French flag. The *Apollo's* men cheered and hailed to know if the French had struck. No answer was made, but their fire had ceased, and so the English took possession. The *Oiseau* had lost her main-topmast and mizen-mast: her hull was terribly riddled, as many of the *Apollo's* shots had passed right through her; and if it had not been for the calm weather she could scarcely have been taken to Great Britain. The armament of both ships is given differently in the French and British accounts. It is not probable that the *Apollo* carried carronades, though "obusiers" are mentioned in the French version, where she is credited with 38 guns. The minimum of force has been allowed for the *Oiseau*, but Troude gives her 32 guns and in the British Navy she carried that number.

—	Tons.	Guns.	Broadside.	Men.	Killed.	Wounded.	Total.
Apollo[1] . .	679	32	Lbs. 174	220	6	22	28
Oiseau . .	783	26	104	224	30–35	?	?

Time, 1½–3½ hours.

[1] Dimensions:—	Length.	Beam.	Draught.
Apollo	125 ft.	35 ft. 2 in.	12 ft.
Oiseau	146 ft.	34 ft. 1 in.	9 ft. 10¾ in.

Both commanders were wounded in this action. The French fought very bravely against what was perhaps a superior force, and Lieutenant de Tarade was, for his courage, treated with unusual deference when a prisoner.[1]

[1] According to Troude (ii. 47), and *Gazette de France* (91) a British frigate, called the *Congress*, encountered the *Concorde*, a French 32, off Brest on Feb. 18th. Though the Frenchman had been damaged in a storm and had thrown twelve of her guns over-

In January a small French squadron captured the British settlements in Sénégal, and some weeks later those on the Gold Coast.

On March 7th, an indecisive brush took place in the West Indies, between the *Ruby*, 64, and *Niger*, 32, on the one hand, and the French frigate *Minerve*, 32, on the other.[1] The Frenchman fired at the *Niger's* rigging, and thus disabling her, escaped, though the British ships *Bristol* and *Æolus* were in sight.

On March 14th the *Rattlesnake*, 10, Lieut. William Knell, gave chase to two French privateer-cutters off the Isle of Wight.[2] She came up with them and fought them for over three hours, when the larger one struck, and the other sheered off. Lieut. Knell, however, instantly pursued her, bore down upon her, fired three broadsides into her, and then boarded. She was the *Frelon*, of Dunquerque, carrying twelve guns and eighty-two men, of whom

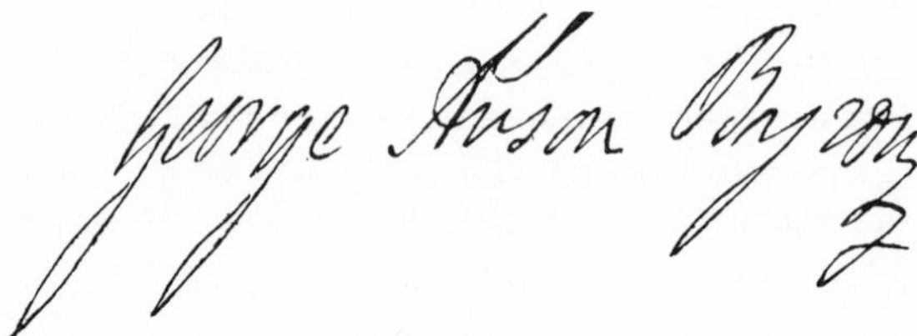

SIGNATURE OF CAPT. GEORGE ANSON BYRON (1), R.N., 1758–93.

twelve had been killed and thirty severely wounded. The other privateer succeeded in escaping. The loss of the *Rattlesnake* was twelve wounded, including Lieut. Knell.

Whilst cruising off Ushant the French frigate *Aigrette*, 32, Captain La Bretonnière, about nightfall of March 19th, sighted a frigate which was taken to be a friend.[3] The stranger was really the British 32-gun ship *Arethusa*, Captain Charles Holmes Everitt,[4] who lost no time in attacking the *Aigrette*. After a sharp action of two hours the two separated, as a line-of-battle ship was

board, she is said to have beaten off the British attack with the loss of four killed and twenty-three wounded. The name *Congress*, however, does not appear in our Navy Lists of the time, and the action is noticed by no British authority. Probably the British ship was a privateer.

[1] Troude, ii. 48.

[2] *Gazette*, 18th Mar.

[3] Troude, ii. 49; C. M., 54.

[4] So Schomberg, v. 46; Beatson, iv. 564.

made out, coming to the help of the *Aigrette*; but the British vessel was so unfortunate as to strike a rock during the night off the island of Molène. Her crew were rescued and made prisoners, with the exception of thirteen men who got away in a cutter.

Towards the close of April a flotilla of fishing boats, carrying fifteen hundred men, and escorted by the French warships *Danaé*, 26, *Diane*, 26, *Écluse*, 8, *Valeur*, 6, and *Guêpe*, 6, left St. Malo with the intention of effecting a descent on Jersey.[1] The wind, however, was so unfavourable that the flotilla was forced to return, and could not again put to sea till May 1st, when it suddenly appeared in St. Ouen's Bay, and attempted a debarkation. The Jersey militia at once stood to arms, and, with the soldiers of the Seaforth Highlanders, arrived in time to repulse the French. A fast ship was despatched to Portsmouth for help, and by good luck fell in with Admiral Marriot Arbuthnot, who was in charge of a convoy, with a considerable force of ships. The French fell back to St. Malo, but on the 10th moved out and anchored off Coutances. Thence the British senior officer, Captain Sir James Wallace (1), of the *Experiment*, 50, resolved to cut them off. With his own ship, the *Pallas*, 36, *Unicorn*, 20, *Cabot*, 14, *Fortune*, 14, and another, he sailed round the west of Jersey, whilst the *Richmond*, 32, and seven others steered straight for the French. On May 13th the British squadrons had the enemy between them. Only one French frigate escaped by running past Sir J. Wallace; the rest made for the shore in Cancale Bay under the shelter of a small battery, and drove aground. Wallace followed them, silenced the battery, boarded the stranded ships, and, as the enemy's land forces were mustering fast, set three, the *Valeur*, *Écluse*, and *Guêpe* on fire, and carried off the *Danaé*, a brig, and a sloop. The *Guêpe* was saved by the French after the British had retired. Troude complains of the cowardice of the *Danaé's* crew, who, when attacked, fled ashore in a panic.

On May 1st the two French 74's *Bourgogne* and *Victoire* were on their way from Toulon to Brest when, just outside the Strait of Gibraltar, they sighted the British frigate *Montreal*, 32, Captain Stair Douglas (1), and *Thetis*, 32, Captain John Gell.[2] The *Thetis*, being a very fast sailer, got away, but the *Montreal* was not so lucky. Overtaken by so superior an enemy, she struck her flag after a few

[1] Beatson, iv. 538; Troude, ii. 49.
[2] Beatson, iv. 536; Troude, ii. 50; C. M., 53.

shots. The British Captain and crew were carried into Alicante and there released.

On May 7th the British brig *Diligent*, 12, Lieut. Thomas Walbeoff, fought a most desperate action with the United States' brig *Providence*, 14, Captain Hacker.[1] The contest was a very unequal one, as the *Diligent's* guns were all 3-prs., whilst the *Providence* carried six 6-prs., six 4-prs., and two 2-prs. The British crew was only fifty-three; the American, eighty-three. The *Diligent* cleared for action only on her larboard side and was attacked by her enemy on her starboard side; her timbers were so thin that musket shot came through; she lay very low in the water, and the seas washed on to her deck. When they realised the heavy odds against them, thirteen or fourteen of her crew skulked and went below. None the less the heroic Walbeoff held out for three hours, when, with every officer but himself disabled, and with eleven dead and nineteen wounded, he struck. The *Providence's* sides were proof to grape, yet she lost fourteen, of whom eleven were killed or died of their wounds.

In May, Commodore Sir George Collier,[2] then in command on the North American station, with the *Raisonnable*, 64, *Rainbow*, 44, *Otter*, 14, *Diligent*,[3] 8, *Haarlem*, 14, and *Cornwallis*, 8, galley, embarked 2500 British troops, under Major-General Matthew, for an expedition to Hampton Roads and the neighbouring estuaries, where the Americans were known to be accumulating naval stores. On May 10th, the troops were disembarked at Portsmouth, Virginia, which place they captured, destroying stores and magazines. The Americans, before evacuating the place, had set fire to a frigate which was building, and to several other vessels. The American ships *Elizabeth* and *Chesapeake* were secured by boat parties, and when Collier returned to New York on May 28th he could report one hundred and thirty vessels captured or destroyed.

On June 1st, a combined expedition captured a fort on Strong Point, commanding the Hudson, and, next day, a second on Verplanks Point. Similar expeditions to Long Island Sound and Huntingdon Bay followed.

The *Jupiter*, 50, Captain Francis Reynolds, was cruising off

[1] C. M., 52; *Lond. Gazette*, Sept. 24th; Maclay, i. 98; Cooper, i. 118.

[2] *Lond. Gazette*, June 22nd; Allen, i. 275.

[3] It is probable that the *Diligent's* name is given by mistake; unless, indeed, she was captured on this very expedition. But then there is no notice of soldiers on board her.

Finisterre on May 21st, when she sighted a large convoy in charge of La Motte-Piquet's division of ships of the line.[1] Anxious to discover whither the convoy was proceeding, Captain Reynolds ran into the midst of it, and was boldly attacked by the large French frigate *Blanche*, 32. In spite of her onslaught he captured one of the convoy, took eighteen Frenchmen from her, and put five of his own men on board, before he was forced to retire by the movements of the French ships, which were stretching out on either flank to cut him off. He was obliged to abandon his prize, and was himself wounded by flying splinters.

The British ships *Ruby*, 64, Captain Michael John Everitt, *Æolus*, 32, and the sloop *Jamaica*, 18, were cruising off Hayti,[2] when on June 2nd, in the Bay of Gonave, they fell in with the French frigate *Prudente*, 36,[3] Captain d'Escars. The *Ruby* chased her for some hours, and was much annoyed by the well-directed fire of the enemy's stern-chasers, by which Captain Everitt and a sailor lost their lives. When within easy range of her, at about sunset, the *Ruby* compelled her to strike, with the loss of two killed and three wounded. She was purchased into the British Navy under the same name.

On June 22nd, the French 16-gun brig *Hélène*, Captain de Montguyot, was captured by the British 32-gun ship *Ambuscade*,[4] Captain the Hon. Charles Phipps, in the Channel. On July 21st the British frigate *King George*, 26,[5] is said by Troude to have been captured by the *Concorde*, 32, Captain de Tilly. On the 21st, according to the Paris *Gazette*,[6] the British frigate *Pelican*, 24, fought a seventy-five minutes' action with a French frigate and lost twenty-three killed or wounded. Five days earlier the British sloop *Haarlem*, 14, Lieutenant Josias Rogers, was chased ashore by an American flotilla and captured.

On July 14th, the British schooner *Egmont*, 10, Lieut. John Gardiner, was captured on the Banks of Newfoundland by the American privateer brig *Wild Cat*, 14.[7] The powder in the

[1] *Jupiter's* Log; Beatson, iv. 559; Troude, ii. 51.

[2] *Gazette de France*, 80, 45; Beatson, iv. 488; Troude; Log of *Ruby*.

[3] Troude, 26 guns. She was rated 36 in the British Navy.

[4] Troude, ii. 52. Not noticed in Beatson or Schomberg. She seems to have been the British *Helena*, which had been taken by the French *Sensible* in 1778.

[5] No such ship appears in the Navy Lists; probably a privateer. There was a famous Bristol privateer of that name.

[6] *Gazette de France*, 308. Not noticed in Beatson, nor in Log of *Pelican*.

[7] C. M., 52.

British ship was wet; her crew numbered only twenty-six, and was not sufficiently strong to work her sails and guns; and she was in consequence boarded and easily overpowered by the American.

Early in August Sir G. Collier received information that a British force was besieged in Penobscot by American troops and ships.[1] Accordingly, he left New York on August 3rd with the

VICE-ADMIRAL SIR GEORGE COLLIER, KT.

(From a lithographed portrait by Blood, in the 'Naval Chronicle,' 1814.)

Raisonnable, 64, *Blonde* and *Virginia*, 32's, *Greyhound*, *Camilla*, and *Galatea*, 20's, and *Otter*, 14. In spite of thick fogs, which scattered the squadron, all except the *Otter* were off the mouth of the Penobscot on the evening of August 13th. The ships immediately proceeded up the river, and next morning the rebel fleet came into sight. It consisted of one 32-gun ship, the *Warren*, two 24-gun, two 22-gun, two 20-gun, two 18-gun, four 16-gun, three 14-gun, and one 12-gun ships, with twenty-four transports and

[1] *Lond. Gazette*, Sept. 24th; Beatson, iv. 513.

other vessels, a total of forty-one,[1] and was drawn up in a crescent. Before the British came to close quarters, however, it took to flight, on which Collier made the signal for a general chase, and the British ships rushed on their enemies. The *Hunter*, 18, attempted to run round to the west of Long Island,[2] but was boarded and captured; the *Defence*, 16, was fired by her crew and blew up; the *Hampden*, 20, hard pressed by the British, struck; and the *Warren*, with the rest of the flotilla, was burnt. In this action the *Albany*, 14, *Nautilus*, 16, and *North*, 14, which had been stationed at Penobscot to support the garrison, joined with great effect. All the loss in killed and wounded was on board them. The total loss of the Navy was four killed, nine wounded, and three missing, whilst the enemy is stated to have lost 474.

In the month of August a combined Franco-Spanish fleet of fifty-six sail of the line and thirty frigates cruised in the Channel, and the British admiral, Sir Charles Hardy (2), too weak to offer any resistance, could only observe its movements.[3] On August 14th, the British warships *Marlborough*, 74, and *Ardent*, 64, Captain Philip Boteler, left Plymouth to join Hardy's fleet, and were so unlucky as to fall in with the French fleet on the 17th. No intimation of the presence of such an enemy had been given to either of the British Captains, and they were naturally quite unprepared for battle. The *Ardent* had been hurried out of port with a raw crew, but she had spent twenty-six hours in Torbay setting up her rigging. "There must have been time to send an express by land," said her Captain in his defence before the court-martial. On August 16th, the British Commander-in-Chief at Plymouth, having ascertained the presence of the enemy in the Channel, sent out the *Kingfisher* to warn not only the *Ardent* but also the *Stag*, which, with a convoy, was proceeding westwards. The *Stag* was turned back, but the *Ardent*, though sighted and signalled, paid no attention whatsoever to the *Kingfisher*. Either she did not see the latter or the signals were mistaken.

The *Marlborough* in some way divined that the strange fleet was hostile; the *Ardent*, however, fell into a trap. Her private signal was twice answered; and, all unsuspectingly, she steered to join the

[1] Many of these vessels did not belong to the U.S. Navy, nor to any of the regular Colonial marines.—W. L. C.

[2] Not the New York Long Island, but the Long Island in Maine.

[3] C. M., 54; *Gazette de France*, 332, 361; Charnock, vi. 466–7; Troude, ii. 52; Beatson, iv. 545.

supposed British Admiral. Presently a large frigate—the 32-gun *Junon*, Captain de Marigny—came up with her, and, as she discovered her mistake, fired two broadsides into her. Captain Boteler had not hoisted his colours. It was only after he had received this fire that he showed them. His ship was quite unprepared. There were few cartridges filled and scarcely any wads ready. The decks had to be cleared in a desperate hurry. On the starboard side the lower-deck ports had to be closed as soon as the guns were cast loose, because the water poured in. Noticing this, the *Junon* passed under the British ship's stern, giving her a raking fire, and ranged up on the starboard beam. Almost at the same time the *Gentille*, another French 32, came to the *Junon's* help. The British ship had now opened, but her fire was extremely ill-directed, slow, and ineffective. It was at this point that some unauthorised person lowered the *Ardent's* colours, and the French imagined she had struck. As she did not shorten sail the frigates *Bellone* and *Surveillante*, which had come up, one on either quarter, joined in the attack; and two large French line-of-battle ships neared her beam. Thus surrounded, and persuaded that further resistance was futile, Captain Boteler struck his colours. It cannot be supposed that he surrendered to two, or even four, frigates; the presence of the French battleships must be taken into account. The comparative force was as follows:—

—	Tons.	Guns.	Broadside.	Men.	Killed.	Wounded.	Total.
			Lbs.				
Junon . .	..	32	174	257?			
Gentille . .	..	32	174	257?			
Ardent . .	1376	64	600	500	5	8	13

A stouter resistance and a heavier percentage of loss would certainly have been expected from a British battleship. The *Ardent's* crew was, however, weak and of inferior quality. If Captain Boteler's defence can be believed, of the 500, 400 were landsmen, mostly pressed, not one of whom had ever seen a gun fired. The 100 seamen, destitute of clothing and of every necessary, were mutinously inclined. There had not been time even to make up the quarter-bill, much less to drill the raw hands. "The whole force of the objection against sending ships to sea with men so totally unformed, lies in the danger of their falling in with an enemy before there is time to exercise them and discipline them," as he urged. Nevertheless, Captain Boteler was sentenced to be dismissed the service. Remembering a very similar mistake on the part of a man so great as Boscawen, and the subsequent loss of the *Pégase* by France under identical circumstances, it would appear that the sentence was unjust.[1]

The *Ardent* and the *Active*, a 12-gun cutter, captured in the Channel by the 14-gun cutter *Mutine*, Captain de Roquefeuil, were, with a number of merchantmen, the only trophies that this immense fleet carried home.

In August, on the Jamaica station, the British frigate *Boreas*,[2] 28, Captain Charles Thompson (1), captured a French *flûte*,[3] the *Compas*, of 18 guns, laden with sugar. The *Compas's* loss was nine killed or wounded. Early in September, the French 32-gun frigate *Amphitrite*, Captain de Langan-Boisfévrier, fell in with the British *Sphinx*, 20, Captain Robert Manners Sutton. The *Amphitrite* opened; her superior weight of metal soon brought down the *Sphinx's* main-topmast and cut her sails and rigging to pieces; and after a two hours' fight Captain Sutton hauled down his flag.

—	Tons.	Guns.	Broadside.	Men.	Killed.	Wounded.	Total.
Amphitrite .	?	32	Lbs. 174	257 n.	?	?	?
Sphinx . .	431	20	90	138 n.	?	?	?

On December 29th, the *Sphinx* was recaptured from the French by the *Proserpine*, 32, in the West Indies.[4]

On October 20th, the *Proserpine*, with a 44-gun ship in company, fell in with the French frigate *Alcmène*, 26, dismasted and disabled by a storm.[5] The *Alcmène*, incapable of any resistance to such a force, struck her flag at once.

In September, d'Estaing's fleet on the American coast took two valuable prizes. The first was the *Ariel* of 20 guns, Captain Thomas Mackenzie.[6] She was chased by the 26-gun frigate *Amazone* and overtaken on September 10th. An action of ninety

[1] *Vide* also 'Nelson Dispatches,' i. 36, and Capt. Evelyn Sutton's defence in the case of the *Isis*. C. M., 56.

[2] Troude, ii. 33.

[3] A *flûte*, or a vessel armed *en flûte*, carried her lower deck guns in her hold.

[4] Log of *Proserpine* does not name the *Sphinx* and calls her a French 32.

[5] Troude, ii. 54; *Gazette de France*, 80, 50.

[6] C. M., 54.

minutes followed, in which the *Ariel* lost one of her masts and had another wounded, before she struck, with four killed and twenty wounded. On the 24th, the *Experiment*, 50, Captain Sir James Wallace, was captured. She was bound with a convoy from New York to Savannah, and the French, discovering this, detached the *Fendant*, 74, *Zélé*, 74, and *Sagittaire*, 50, Captain de Rions, to look for her. The *Experiment* had lost her masts in a storm, and could not get away, though she did her best, and gave the *Sagittaire* some trouble. She struck after a short resistance.[1] She had 150,000 piastres on board; and two store-ships in her company fell victims with her.

On September 9th, the French admiral, d'Estaing, with twenty ships of the line and thirteen smaller craft, anchored at Tybee. at the mouth of the Savannah river.[2] The island of Tybee was seized, and between the 9th and 16th a large force of French troops numbering over three thousand, who had been drawn from the garrisons of the French West India islands, were landed at Beaulieu, thirteen miles from Savannah, and the town of Savannah was summoned to surrender. The British ships, *Fowey*, 20, Captain John Henry, *Rose*, 20, Captain John Brown, *Vigilant*, 20, Commander Brabazon Christian, *Keppel*, 12, *Germaine*, 12, *Savannah*, 14, and seven galleys, were lying at that place. They landed men and guns as soon as d'Estaing's arrival was known, and the *Rose*, being old, dilapidated, and worm-eaten, was sunk in the channel. General Prevost, the British commander on land, brought up troops from Port Royal; and the place, which might have been carried by d'Estaing by an immediate attack, was, by the delays and shortsightedness of the French, allowed time to develop its resistance. A truce of twenty-four hours gave Colonel Maitland time to come up from Port Royal. The French and Americans broke ground, and on the night of October 3rd–4th, bombarded the town. On the night of the 9th, they delivered an assault. D'Estaing was filled with alarm for his ships, which on that exposed coast were suffering much from storms; and his attack was on that occasion as rash as his abstention from attack had previously been timid. The assault was repulsed with heavy loss, amounting to about 750 in the case of the French alone. The loss of the British Navy was

[1] C. M., 54.

[2] 'Ann. Register,' 1779, [207; Troude, ii. 43; Captain Henry's letter in Admirals Dispatches, N. American Station, vol. 7.

four killed and sixteen wounded. The siege was abandoned on the 18th, and d'Estaing re-embarked his diminished force.[1]

The *Pearl*, 32, Captain George Montagu, was cruising off Fayal in the Azores, when at 6 A.M. on the morning of September 14th, she saw and chased a sail.[2] At 9.30 A.M. she brought the stranger to action, and two hours later compelled her to strike, herself sustaining only damage to her rigging. The captured ship was the *Santa Monica*, Don M. de Nunes, a Spanish frigate of twenty-eight guns. The comparative force and loss of the two were as follows :—

——	Tons.	Guns.	Weight of Metal.	Men.	Killed.	Wounded.	Total.
[1] *Pearl* . . .	683	32	Lbs. 174	220	12	19	31
Sta. Monica .	956	28	160	271	38	45	83

Time, 2 hours.

[1] DIMENSIONS :—	Length.	Beam.	Draught.
Sta. Monica	145 ft.	38 ft. 8 in.	11 ft. 10 in.
Pearl	125 ft.	35 ft. 3 in.	12 ft.

The *Santa Monica* was a finer and larger ship than the *Pearl*, though more feebly armed. She was bought into the British Navy and rated as a 36.

In spite of his successes in the spring of 1778, Captain Paul Jones could not get another squadron to sea before June 1779, and then it was composed of very indifferent material.[3] Captain Jones's ship was the *Bonhomme Richard*, a former East Indiaman, equipped in singular fashion. As her sides were very high she carried guns on her lower deck—six long, old-fashioned 18-prs., which could all be fought on the same side. On her main deck she mounted twenty-eight 12-prs., and on the forecastle and quarter-deck eight 9-prs. Her crew was a medley of all races and nationalities,[4] and even her officers were not all Americans. As consorts she had the *Alliance*, a 32-gun frigate[5] commanded by Captain Landais; the *Pallas*, of thirty guns,[6] an ex-merchantman; the *Vengeance*, also an armed

[1] These operations have been very briefly touched upon in vol. iii. 442.

[2] *Lond. Gazette*, Sept. 28; Log of *Pearl*; Beatson, iv. 559.

[3] *See* authorities already cited for the *Ranger's* cruise. Add also Capts. Pearson and Piercy's Official Letters, London *Chronicle*, Oct. 12th; the court martial [C. M., 54]; Maclay, 'Hist. U.S.N.,' i. 104–136; 'Century,' vol. 49, 873; Beatson, iv. 548.

[4] A number of American sailors were taken on board the *Bonhomme Richard* whilst she was undergoing repairs.

[5] Laughton calls *Alliance* a 36-gun ship, with 9-prs. on the main deck.

[6] Laughton says, thirty-two 6-prs.

merchantman, of twelve guns, and the 18-gun cutter *Cerf*. Landais was at the best contumacious and insubordinate. At the worst he was a violent madman, more dangerous to friends than to enemies. The only tie which united these five ships was a paper agreement to act together. This was certain to be broken as soon as it was to any one's interest to break it.

Leaving Lorient on June 19th, 1779, the *Bonhomme Richard* and

CAPTAIN WILLIAM LOCKER, R.N., 1732–1800.
(*Lieut.-Govr. of Greenwich Hospital*, 1793–1800.)
(*From a lithograph by Ridley.*)

Alliance collided, and sustained so much damage that they were compelled to return to port. On their way back they chased three supposed British frigates, and the *Cerf* fought a sharp engagement with an unknown British vessel, which is said to have struck, but had to be abandoned on other British ships coming up. The repairs were completed by August 14th, when the squadron again put out, with two French privateers. These, however, soon quarrelled with Captain Jones, and parted company. Off the south coast of Ireland two prizes were captured; but, on the other hand, twenty-three Englishmen of the *Bonhomme Richard's* crew escaped to the Kerry coast in two of the ship's boats. At the same time Landais began to show such insubordination as convinced Captain Jones of the man's madness. He practically asserted his entire independence, and followed this up by parting company when he chose. The *Cerf* and *Pallas* vanished from sight on August 26th. Sailing north round the west coast of Ireland to Cape Wrath, Jones was rejoined by the *Pallas*. Some time was spent in waiting for the *Alliance*, and in endeavouring to persuade Landais to show some obedience when she arrived, but all in vain. The *Bonhomme Richard*, *Pallas*, and *Vengeance* doubled Cape Wrath and sailed down the east coast of Scotland, whilst the *Alliance* followed, joining or deserting the squadron according to her captain's fancy. On September 13th, the ships were off the Firth of Forth; and Jones, hearing that a British 20-gun ship was lying at anchor off Leith, and anxious to lay Edinburgh and Leith under contribution, wished to run up the estuary. The captains of the *Pallas* and *Vengeance*, however, had no stomach for any such bold moves, and it was not till the 14th that Jones could overcome their reluctance. The wind was then adverse. Laboriously the ships beat their way up the firth, whilst the alarmed inhabitants gathered to make what resistance they could, and threw up a battery at Leith. Jones had picked up a pilot from a collier, and would have had the town at his mercy, had not the unfavourable wind freshened suddenly to a gale on the 17th, and swept the motley squadron out to sea. Thereupon he determined to try in the Tyne what he had purposed to accomplish in the Forth. His conceptions were, as usual, accurate and judicious, but again the cowardice and insubordination of his captains balked him. On September 21st, three ships were taken or destroyed off Flamborough Head; on the 22nd, the *Bonhomme Richard* and *Vengeance* being in company, pilots were seized off the Humber, and from them Jones learnt that the wildest alarm prevailed in Great Britain. Up to that date the squadron had taken seventeen ships. On the morning of the 23rd, the *Pallas* and *Alliance* rejoined. Very little later, in the afternoon, a great fleet came into sight. It was the Baltic trade, convoyed by his Majesty's frigate *Serapis* of forty-four guns, Captain Richard Pearson, and the armed ship *Countess of Scarborough* of twenty, Commander Thomas Piercy. The warships at once placed themselves between their convoy and the American squadron, whilst the merchant ships went off on the other tack. Captain Jones signalled to form line of battle, to which signal neither the *Alliance* nor *Pallas* paid much attention. On shore, the cliffs of Scarborough and the coast of Flamborough Head were crowded with spectators, who were to be rewarded by the sight of one of the fiercest fights in history.

At dusk the *Bonhomme Richard* and the *Serapis* were within musket-shot, both standing for the land on the port tack. The two hailed one another, each summoning the other to surrender. Almost at the same moment, at 7.20 P.M., the *Bonhomme Richard* opened fire, and was replied to by the *Serapis*. At the first round two of the *Bonhomme Richard's* lower-deck 18 prs. burst, killing several men and doing great damage to the ship. The other four were abandoned, and the American had to fall back upon her thirty-six 12- and 9-prs. Against her was the *Serapis*, a man-of-war, handy, a better sailer, with a homogeneous crew and a far more powerful armament.[1] In leadership alone had the American any advantage. Her captain, if not superior in sheer courage to Captain Pearson, hopelessly outdistanced him in audacity, resource, and inspiration. Whilst these two closed in desperate encounter, the *Pallas* engaged the *Countess of Scarborough*, and the *Alliance* sailed round and round, firing at random on British and Americans alike.

The heavy shot of the *Serapis* quickly began to tell. The *Bonhomme Richard* received several hits between wind and water; and she had her fourteen 12-prs. disabled or dismounted, and seven of her deck guns put out of action, so that she was left with a battery of only three 9-prs., one of which had to be shifted over from the starboard side. In these circumstances Jones determined, as his only hope of safety, to close with his enemy; and Captain Pearson of the *Serapis* was foolish enough to allow his half-beaten opponent to lay himself alongside. The *Serapis* evaded the *Bonhomme Richard's* first attempt to grapple. At the second the *Bonhomme Richard's* mizen-shrouds caught the *Serapis's* jib-boom, which was promptly lashed fast by the American captain himself. The boom broke, but the *Serapis's* spare anchor hooked the *Bonhomme Richard's* quarter, and held the two combatants side by side, bow to

[1] Laughton, 'Studies in Naval Hist.' 398, states that she carried 18-prs. on her lower and 12-prs. on her upper deck. Cooper, and Maclay, 'Hist. U.S.N.' i. 129, give her twenty 18's, twenty 9's, and ten 6's. The regular 44-gun frigate carried twenty 18's, twenty-two 9's, and two 6's; see James, 'Naval History,' i. 445, and Derrick, 279; but a MS. of Capt. Pearson, refers to the age and bad condition of the *Serapis's* 12-prs., which makes it evident that she had 12's and not 9's.

stern, starboard to starboard, with the muzzles of the guns touching. This happened at about 8.30 in the evening. The *Serapis* let go her other anchor in the hope that the American would be swept clear by the tide; but, owing to this entanglement, the manœuvre did not succeed in its object. Meantime the *Bonhomme Richard's* men, driven from the 18 and 12-prs. below, had swarmed to the deck and the tops, whence they swept the *Serapis* with a steady musketry fire, and from time to time pitched hand-grenades on board her. Below, the port lids of the *Serapis's* 18-pr. battery had been closed when the two ships swung alongside, from fear of boarders. The guns were fired through them, and speedily reduced to splinters the hull of the American. Their fire, however, though it ultimately sank the

MEDAL COMMEMORATIVE OF CAPT. PAUL JONES, U.S.N.

(From an original lent by H.S.H. Capt. Prince Louis of Battenberg, R.N.)

enemy's ship, did not kill his men, since these had been withdrawn from the lower battery. The 18-prs. thus failed to exercise a decisive influence on the fate of the action. Already the *Serapis's* starboard side had taken fire in seven or eight places, and was blazing fiercely. Yet, in spite of this, victory was decidedly inclining to her when a terrible mischance befell her. An American seaman climbed out on the *Bonhomme Richard's* main-yard, which overhung the *Serapis's* deck, and dropped a hand grenade down the main-hatchway into the *Serapis's* gun-room, where a number of 12-pr. cartridges had been placed. The grenade fired the cartridges, and the explosion ran aft between the row of guns, scorching or killing officers and men, and disabling five of the guns. Thirty-eight were killed or wounded at this one blow. Amongst those injured was Lieutenant the Hon. Henry Edwyn Stanhope, who in his agony leapt overboard, but, climbing back, had his wounds dressed and returned to his quarters A minute later the *Alliance* hove in sight and was seen to fire a broadside. The fire was directed on the *Bonhomme Richard,* and not on the British ship, though Captain Pearson could hardly know this. The *Serapis* still fought on, her men by that time recovering from the shock of the explosion; and at ten there was a call for quarter from the American. It came from her gunner, and was promptly silenced by Jones, who rapped him on the head with a pistol. But at the shout the British prisoners in the hold of the *Bonhomme Richard,* taken from the various prizes, had been released. The ship was sinking: her lower deck ports were completely shattered, and she was on fire in more than one place. The prisoners poured up on deck: the fate of the battle was in their hands. With astounding coolness Captain Jones set them to work the pumps, and thus converted them from a source of danger into a source of strength. They seem without question to have obeyed him, perhaps dumbfounded by his assurance. Each ship was now at her last gasp; each crew had fought fairly to a standstill; the men on either side had done their best; the issue rested with the captains. A refugee crawled through the ports of the *Bonhomme Richard* and told Captain Pearson of his enemy's condition. He ordered the boarders away, but they could do nothing in face of the small arms' fire from the rigging of the American. The last effort of the British crew had failed: the *Alliance* could be seen passing across the *Serapis's* stern, and preparing to rake her, whilst the *Serapis* could not fire a gun. Her mainmast was tottering, and the bold face of Captain Jones made the British hopeless of success. At 10.30 Captain Pearson hauled down his flag, just as the mainmast went overboard. The Americans took possession of their prize, transferred to her the crew of the *Bonhomme Richard,* and saw the latter sink a day later. As the battle had been fought with unusual obstinacy, the loss on board each ship was very heavy.[1]

[1] Many American writers deny that the *Alliance* exercised any influence on the issue of the action. I think, however, that any unprejudiced man will allow, with Professor Laughton, that her mere presence had a very discouraging effect on the crews of the *Serapis* and *Countess of Scarborough.*

—	Tons.	Guns.	Broadside.	Crew.	Killed.	Wounded.	Total.
			Lbs.				
Bonhomme Richard	..	42	312	347	49[1]	67[1]	116
Serapis . .	886	44	324	264	54	75	129

Time, 3½ hours.

1 The American losses are variously given and range from 317 (Capt. Pearson's estimate) to that given in the text. Cooper estimates the loss at 150, viz., 42 seamen killed or died of wounds, and 41 wounded; the others marines or soldiers serving as marines. The number of the crew is variously given, the above being Cooper's figures.

The inferiority of the *Bonhomme Richard's* armament should be taken into account. If her 18-prs., which scarcely fired a shot, are subtracted, her broadside falls to 204 lbs.

Captain Pearson was outwitted, and threw his advantage away. The action, however, has an interesting bearing upon a point which is much debated at the present day:—whether the guns should attack the enemy's water-line or his men. It seems to show that the efforts of the gunners should be directed to the killing of their opponents rather than to the disabling of the hostile ship. Captain Jones had paid great attention to his top-fire, and his marksmen cleared the *Serapis's* deck of all but Captain Pearson, whom they spared for his gallantry.

The *Countess of Scarborough* fought the *Pallas* for two hours, when Commander Piercy struck to the French-American, with heavy damage to his rigging, seven guns disabled, and twenty-four out of a crew of one hundred and fifty killed or wounded. He appears, like the *Serapis*, to have been fired upon by the *Alliance*. Owing to the vigorous resistance of the British ships the convoy was enabled to escape without any loss, and the Americans were left unfit for any further depredation. Captain Pearson was deservedly rewarded for his determined resistance with a knighthood. After the battle Jones proceeded to the Texel, and thence, after some weeks' blockade, sailed with his usual audacity down the Channel to Lorient under the very noses of the British cruisers. There his squadron was broken up, and though liberal promises were made to him, and though the consternation and rage in England testified to the success of his methods of making war, he was not given another command, but seems to have been distrusted by the American commissioners.

The French cutters, of 14 guns, *Mutine* and *Pilote*, fell in, on

October 2nd,[1] with the British ships *Jupiter*, 50, *Apollo*, 32, and *Crescent*, 28, and were captured after a short cannonade, in which the *Mutine* was dismasted.

On October 6th, the *Quebec*, 32, Captain George Farmer, in company with the *Rambler*, 10, Lieutenant Rupert George, was cruising off Ushant to watch for a squadron which was reported to be leaving Brest, when at dawn she sighted the French frigate, *Surveillante*, 32,

CAPTAIN SIR RICHARD PEARSON KT., R.N.
Lieut.-Govr. of Greenwich Hospital.
(From an engraving by H. R. Cook.)

Lieut. Du Couëdic de Kergoualer, and the cutter, *Expédition*, 10, Lieut. de Roquefeuil.[2] These vessels had put out from Brest to observe a British squadron, which was supposed to be on the point of sailing for Brest. Du Couëdic was a man of ebullient courage, and had vowed to the king that the *Surveillante* should be his

[1] Troude, ii. 55.

[2] *Lond. Chronicle*, xlvi. 354, 363, 381; 'Dict. Nat. Biogr.': "Farmer, G."; Hennequin, 'Biogr. Nav.' i. 98; *Gazette de France*, 401, 424, 435, 448; Beatson, iv. 561; Troude, ii. 55: *Lond. Gazette*, Oct. 12; C. M. missing.

chariot of triumph, or his tomb. His enemy, Captain Farmer, was fully worthy of him, though of a temper less demonstrative. The spirit of their captains inspired the crews of the two ships. An encounter between such antagonists was certain to be desperate and bloody. Neither shirked the combat; they stood eagerly towards one another; hoisted their respective flags, and fired each a long range shot as a signal of defiance. Du Couëdic sailed as close to the wind as possible, whilst Farmer rapidly bore down upon him. Some time after ten in the morning the two frigates were within close range. The *Surveillante* had already been firing for some time, but at long range, and without inflicting much injury. Not till she was within musket range did the *Quebec* reply. The two then settled down to a furious battle, broadside to broadside. An hour passed and neither ship had the advantage, when Captain Farmer determined to rake his opponent. He tried to drop astern, with this object in view, but was foiled by Du Couëdic's promptness and judgment. Once more the two closed. They could no longer hug the wind, but had to go before it; the masts of both ships were tottering; the fire on each side was murderous; and yet neither showed any sign of yielding. Twice, indeed, the *Quebec's* officers saw, or thought they saw, the French crew running from their guns, but for all that the *Surveillante* maintained her fire. In the *Quebec* the crew was dwindling fast; from seven men to each gun it had fallen to three; Captain Farmer was wounded in the finger, and his collar bone was shattered. He did not leave the deck, but bandaged his wounds as best he could, and called to his men, "My lads, this is warm work, and therefore keep up your fire with double spirit. We will conquer or die." Beside him stood his first Lieutenant, Francis Roberts, who had lost an arm. Most of the other officers were killed or disabled.

It was verging upon noon when the masts of the *Surveillante* went overboard. They fell to port, and did not mask her battery, nor encumber and endanger the ship. A few minutes before this Du Couëdic had been twice wounded in the head by bullets. He did not, however, leave the deck. Just after the fall of the *Surveillante's* masts, the *Quebec's* masts came down. Unfortunately for her, they did not clear the ship, but, falling fore and aft, blocked the gangways, and impeded the service of the forecastle and quarter-deck guns. The mizen-mast sails hung down on the engaged side, and were almost instantly set on fire by the flash of the guns. Du Couëdic at that moment is said, in the French accounts, to have attempted to board. His dispositions for that end were made, and his bowsprit was fast entangled in the wreckage of the *Quebec's* masts, when he was wounded a third time, just as he had ordered his three nephews to lead the boarding party. Smoke was already pouring up from the *Quebec's* sails, and her quarter-deck was beginning to blaze. The French captain, for all his wounds, directed the fire of his guns to cease, and his boats to be lowered, whilst the *Surveillante's* bowsprit was cut away, and the *Quebec* was pushed off with spars: not any too soon, for the French ship's rigging was already beginning to burn. The heat was intense. On board the *Quebec*, Farmer still kept his station, and refused to leave the ship whilst there was a man on board. The pumps were by his orders directed on the magazine, and thus there was no apparent danger of an explosion. The first Lieutenant was by him: the crew at his orders were jumping into the sea or saving themselves as best they could; whilst the cutter *Rambler* had come up to the aid of the men in the water, though the constant explosion of the *Quebec's* guns made the work of rescue very dangerous. Of the *Surveillante's* boats, only one would float, and that one was damaged in getting it out. The French crew, however, threw oars and ropes to the drowning men. At six in the evening the *Quebec*, with her colours still flying, blew up. When last seen, her Captain was sitting calmly on the fluke of the anchor.

His splendid gallantry was rewarded by his country in the way it deserved. His eldest son was made a baronet, and pensions were granted to his widow and his children, "to excite an emulation in other officers to distinguish themselves in the same manner, and render Captain Farmer's fate rather to be envied than pitied, as it would give them reason to hope that, if they should lose their lives with the same degree of stubborn gallantry, it would appear to posterity that their services had met with the approbation of their sovereign."[1] Thus died in the flower of his age a great and accomplished officer;[2] and one of those who may be said to have made and moulded our Navy for the next French war. Under him Nelson and Troubridge served, and the master was worthy of his disciples.

[1] Admiralty Minute.

[2] Capt. George Farmer had been posted on Jan. 10th, 1771.—W. L. C.

Du Couëdic died in port some months later.[1] His family were as splendidly rewarded, and a handsome monument was erected at Brest to his memory, to be defaced and destroyed in the shameful excesses of the Revolution.

The loss of both ships was terribly heavy. Of the *Quebec's* 195 men only 68 were saved; 17 by the *Rambler*, 13 by a passing Russian ship, and 38 by the *Surveillante*; and of these again two died of their injuries. The French behaved with a magnanimous humanity to their prisoners. Men who had so fought and suffered, they said, must be released; and accordingly they sent them back to a British port. They are stated in one British account to have fired upon a British boat engaged in saving life. We may indignantly reject this malicious libel. The fire probably came from the *Quebec's* own heated guns. In the *Surveillante* 30 were killed and 85 wounded. In one or other category were nearly all the officers. The ship herself was in a sinking condition. She had been frequently hulled between wind and water, and was leaking heavily. She was taken in tow by the *Expédition*: in time jury-masts were rigged; and she succeeded in returning to Brest.

The comparative force of the two ships is disputed. According to Farmer's own letters the *Quebec* carried twenty-six 9-prs., and six 6-prs. This anomalous armament was due to the fact that she had struck a rock some months before; and, being compelled to throw all her 12-prs. overboard, she could only replace them with the smaller 9-prs. on reaching a British port. French writers give her thirty-six guns, but are obviously untrustworthy, as they had no means of knowing accurately. The *Surveillante*, by the official British version, carried twenty-eight 18-prs. and twelve small guns—probably in the writer's imagination 8 or 6 prs. To get the truth, however, we must go to the French accounts, and they differ strangely. M. de Lostanges, who fought on board, gives her thirty-six guns—probably twenty-six 18-prs. and ten 8-prs.: Troude and the official French account give twenty-six 12-prs. and six 6-prs. It was the impression of the *Quebec's* survivors that the *Surveillante* was greatly their superior in power and weight of metal, but men who have fought a desperate battle are naturally prone to exalt the strength of their enemy. We have, therefore, accepted Troude's

[1] Du Couëdic was instantly promoted to be *capitaine de vaisseau*, and, for a time, his recovery seemed probable; but he died of his wounds, three months after the action, aged forty.

statement, though even then the disparity is quite sufficient to explain the result:—

—	Tons.	Guns.	Broadside.	Men.	Killed.	Wounded.	Total.
			Lbs.				
Surveillante .	..	32	174	255	30	85	115
Quebec . .	685	32	125	195	127	?[1]	127[1]

[1] At least three of the sixty-eight survivors were "greatly wounded," besides the two who actually died. No wounded or men dying from their wounds have been included in the above total. Troude gives the survivors as eighty-one.

The *Rambler* and *Expédition*,[1] whilst the fight between the *Quebec* and *Surveillante* was raging, were just as hotly engaged, from eleven o'clock onwards. At about two, however, the *Expédition* made off—either to aid the *Surveillante* or because she had had enough. She had, by the French account, suffered severely from the *Rambler's* musketry. The *Rambler* was much cut up in her rigging, her gaff, topmast, and topsail halyards being shot through, and her mainsail rendered useless. She stood at once to the help of the *Quebec*, and with her boat rescued seventeen people—of whom two were Midshipmen, and one the Master's Mate.

—	Tons.	Guns.	Broadside.	Men.	Killed.	Wounded.	Total.
			Lbs.				
Rambler . .	139	10[1]	?	50	0	2	2[2]
Expédition .	..	12	68	?	3	14	17

[1] Navy List gives her eight guns.
[2] Several slightly wounded (these as usual not being included in the return or estimate).

A brilliant episode of the autumn of 1779 was the capture of Omoa and two Spanish treasure ships by Captain the Hon. John Luttrell, with a small squadron, and a few armed "Baymen" from British Honduras.[2] The squadron consisted of the *Charon*, 44, Captain Luttrell, *Lowestoft*, 32, Captain Christopher Parker (2), *Pomona*, 28, Captain Charles Edmund Nugent, *Porcupine*, 20, Commander John Pakenham, *Racehorse*, schooner, and some other schooners and smaller craft. These arrived on the Honduras coast on September 15th. After some skirmishing in the Gulfs of

[1] Log of *Rambler*.
[2] Beatson, iv. 475; Cf. also C. M., 53; Court of inquiry on conduct of Capt. Luttrell.

Honduras and Dolce, and after an attempt to capture the town of Omoa by a purely naval attack from the sea had failed through the remissness of the pilots, a landing was effected at Puerto Caballo, and a force composed of seamen, 250 Baymen, a number of Mosquito Indians, and detachments of the Royal Irish Regiment and Marines, began the march on Omoa, nine miles distant, on the night of October 16th. It was hoped to surprise the fort, but the allowance of time was not sufficient and the difficulties of the march were enormous. The landing force had to make its way through mangrove swamps and across mountains, and, when day dawned, it was in great disorder and still six miles off the town. After some hours' halt the march was resumed.

When the force was near Omoa it met with a party of 50 or 60 Spaniards, who fired upon it, inflicting trivial loss, and then fled. The British sailors carried and fired the town ; but the fort they could not take, as the Baymen, who were carrying the scaling ladders, had dropped them in their eagerness to fight. Meantime the British ships had stood in to the support of the assaulting party. The *Lowestoft* and *Charon* opened fire, but at somewhat long range. The *Lowestoft* then tried to run in closer, and grounded, but luckily got off again, though not without considerable damage. On the 18th the sailors landed some of the *Pomona's* guns and opened with them on the fort; but this was rather to hide the real plan of attack than to breach the walls.

It was decided to assault the fort on the night of the 19th-20th, while the ships covered and aided the storming party. Accordingly, on the night of the 19th, the squadron attacked the fort. When the garrison was busy, four storming parties of seamen, Marines, and Royal Irish dashed forward and were in the fort before the Spaniards were aware of their presence, with a loss of only six killed and wounded. The treasure taken in the galleons and the fort was estimated at 3,000,000 dollars. The fort was garrisoned by British troops till November 28th, when it was abandoned on a Spanish force threatening it. In the assault only two Spaniards were wounded by the British seamen. A story is told of a sailor who, with a cutlass in each hand, met an unarmed Spaniard, presented him with one of his cutlasses, and challenged him with these words, "I scorn to take any advantage : you are now upon a footing with me."

On November 11th, the Spanish 28-gun frigate *Santa Margarita* was sighted in the afternoon by Commodore George Johnstone off Finisterre.[1] The *Tartar*, 28, Captain Alexander Græme, was ordered to give chase, and came up with her at four o'clock, when, after a broadside or two, seeing that escape was hopeless in the face of the British squadron, she struck with four killed or wounded. The *Tartar* did not lose a man; but she suffered some damage, as, during the action, the Spaniard fell on board her, carrying away her mizen topsail yard. The *Santa Margarita* carried twenty-six 12-prs. and two 6-prs., with two hundred and seventy men. She was purchased into the British service under the same name.[2]

On November 19th, the *Hussar*, 28, Captain Elliot Salter, in company with the *Chatham*, 50, and convoying the trade home from Lisbon, saw a two-decked ship standing out of the convoy, and at once gave chase. She came up with the ship next day and, on the Spanish flag being hoisted, attacked, when, after a short engagement, the Spaniard struck. She was the *Nuestra Señora del Buen Confeso*, armed *en flûte*, and mounting only twenty-six 12-prs., though pierced for sixty-four guns. She carried a valuable cargo. The force of the two was:—

—	Tons.	Guns.	Broadside.	Men.	Killed.	Wounded.	Total.
			Lbs.				
Hussar	586	28	114	198 n.	4	10	14
Nuestra Señora del Buen Confeso . .	..	28	168	120	27	8	35

Time, 45 minutes.

On November 27th, the cutter *Jackal*, 14, whilst lying in the Downs, was seized by seventeen of her crew and carried off to a French port. Her officers were mostly ashore; several of the mutineers were smugglers impressed on the Irish coast.[3] Some of them were afterwards taken and executed for this act of mutiny. The ships lying near the *Jackal* had no idea of the intentions of her crew, or they could easily have brought her to. The *Jackal* was

[1] Beatson, iv. 561; *Tartar's* Log; Johnstone's squadron included one 50, three frigates and two sloops; Schomberg, iv. 359.

[2] Often spelt at that time *Sta. Margaretta*. She was rated as a 36.

[3] Beatson, iv. 565; C. M., 53, 61; Captains' Letters, 1781, 1782, Napier. She was renamed the *Boulogne*, and was re-captured by the *Prudente* in 1781, with many of her original crew.

sold at Calais, and turned into a privateer; and she proceeded to plunder and harass British trade off the coast of Scotland.

On December 21st, the French frigates *Fortunée* and *Blanche*, 32's,[1] and *Elise*, 28, were off Guadeloupe, when they fell in with four large vessels flying the French flag. These were the British ships *Magnificent*, 74, *Suffolk*, 74, *Vengeance*, 74, and *Stirling Castle*, 64, under Rear-Admiral Joshua Rowley. The French ships were in bad order; their crews were excessively weak; and thus they could not escape the vastly superior British force. The *Blanche* was overtaken and captured on the evening of the 21st; the *Fortunée*, by throwing her quarter-deck guns overboard, kept away a little longer, but was captured at last in the early morning of December 22nd, an hour before the *Elise*.

In the course of the year the French made themselves masters of the West Indian islands of St. Bartholomew, St. Vincent, and Cariacou.

On the last day of the year[2] 1779 a British squadron[3] under Captain Charles Feilding (1) came up with a large Dutch convoy in charge of the Dutch Rear-Admiral van Bylandt, who had with him two sail of the line and two frigates. It was notorious that the Dutch ships were laden with naval stores and other contraband of war for the French. Captain Feilding requested permission to search these ships, but it was refused him; and van Bylandt declared that he would fire if any such search were attempted. Next day, however (January 1st), boats were sent from the British ships, on which the Dutch fired, and the British warships replied by opening on the Dutch. His honour being now satisfied, van Bylandt struck, though no blood had been shed in the interchange of compliments. Captain Feilding refused to accept the surrender, and returned to port with nine prizes, which were all condemned in due course.

On December 26th, 1779, as soon as the departure of d'Estaing's French fleet from the coast of North America had been ascertained, Vice-Admiral Marriot Arbuthnot[4] left New York with a squadron of

[1] Beatson, iv. 473; *Gazette*, 80, Feb. 29th; English accounts give the *F.*, 42 guns, and the *B.*, 36.

[2] Beatson, iv. 573. Some allusion to the legal aspects of this affair will be found in vol. iii. 351.

[3] *Namur*, 90; *Centaur*, *Courageux*, *Thunderer*, *Valiant*, 74's; *Buffalo*, 60; *Portland*, 50; *Emerald*, 32; *Seaford*, *Camel*, 20; *Hawk*, 12; *Wolf*, 8.

[4] *See* vol. iii. 472.

warships and transports—in which were embarked 7550 troops under General Sir H. Clinton—for Charleston.[1] The following were the warships :—

Ships.	Guns.	Captains.	Ships.	Guns.	Captains.
Russell .	74	F. S. Drake, Commod.	*Richmond* .	32	Chas. Hudson.
Robust .		Phillips Cosby.	*Blonde* .		And. Barkley.
Europe .	64	M. Arbuthnot, V.-Ad.	*Raleigh* .		Ja. Gambier (2).
		Wm. Swiney (1).	*Virginia*[1] .	28	Jno. Orde (1).
Defiance .		Max. Jacobs.	*Perseus* .	20	Hon. G. K. Elphinstone.
Raisonnable		T. Fitzherbert.	*Camilla* .		Jno. Collins.
Renown .	50	Geo. Dawson.			
Roebuck .	44	Sir And. S. Hamond(1).	Armed ships, *Sandwich* and *Germaine*.		
Romulus .		Geo. Gayton.			

[1] Reached Charleston after the rest of the fleet.

Putting into Savannah in January, and capturing Port Royal, the armament proceeded to North Edisto Inlet, near Charleston, on February 10th, and the troops quickly made themselves masters of James Island, which shuts in Charleston Harbour to the south and south-west. Four hundred and fifty Marines and seamen, with guns from the ships, were landed under Captain the Hon. Geo. Keith Elphinstone, and on March 29th the siege was duly formed. Meantime, the smaller ships were lightened and carried over the bar on March 20th; the 74's and 64's were sent back to New York; and Arbuthnot's flag was hoisted in the *Roebuck*.

A 44-gun ship, seven frigates and sloops, and a French frigate and polacca—of which, however, there is no mention in French authorities—had been moored by the Americans in the mouth of the harbour off Fort Moultrie. This work protected the entrance; it mounted about forty guns; and its fire had some years before repulsed Sir Peter Parker's attack. When Arbuthnot crossed the bar the American flotilla was retired and sunk in the channel between Charleston and the island of Shute's Folly.[2] On April 9th, Arbuthnot led his fleet, consisting of the *Roebuck*, *Romulus*, *Blonde*, *Virginia*, *Raleigh*, *Sandwich*, and *Renown*, through the entrance, past Fort Moultrie. The ships gave and received a heavy fire, the loss to the British being twenty-seven killed or wounded, and

[1] Beatson, v. 16; Colomb, 'Naval Warfare,' 417; Schomberg, ii. 16, iv. 359; 'Ann. Register,' 1780, [218; Log of *Roebuck*; Admirals' Dispatches, North American Station, vol. vii.; Allardyce, 'Lord Keith.'

[2] On the capture of Charleston the American frigate *Boston*, which was one of the vessels sunk, was raised, and, under the name *Charleston* (spelt *Charles-Town* by Steel), added to the Navy.

a good deal of damage to masts and rigging. The fleet anchored off James Island, out of range, it was hoped, of the American batteries at Charleston. These presently opened fire on the *Roebuck* at the head of the British line. Every shot went through her, but, with admirable judgment, she made no reply; and the Americans, in consequence, jumped to the conclusion that their shots were falling short and ceased their cannonade, when they might have destroyed her. The coolness of the *Roebuck's* captain, Sir Andrew Snape Hamond, deserves a word of praise. The boats of the fleet endeavoured, unsuccessfully, to force their way up Cooper River; but landing-parties of Marines and seamen stormed a work at Mount Pleasant, and compelled the surrender of Fort Moultrie on May 7th. This fort fell, as did the works at Mobile in 1864, when isolated by Farragut's fleet. On May 11th, Charleston capitulated. The loss to the Navy in these operations was twenty-three killed or wounded.

In January, 1780, a small expedition of five hundred men was sent against the Spanish forts on the river San Juan, controlling the approach to Lake Nicaragua in Central America.[1] Captain Horatio Nelson, in the *Hinchinbroke*, 28, convoyed the transports to Greytown, where the troops landed. Nelson himself took part in the expedition, which succeeded in capturing Castillo Viejo on April 29th, though only after he had left, invalided. The climate was so unhealthy that the men died like flies; the transports at Greytown were left without a man in charge; and very few of the troops returned, though large reinforcements had been sent in the meanwhile. The survivors were withdrawn, defeated by the climate. The expedition was grievously mismanaged, and moreover it was sent at the wrong time of the year.

A French convoy of two storeships and thirteen other vessels, bound for Mauritius under the care of the 64's *Protée* and *Ajax*, the frigate *Charmante*, and the corvette *Argus*, was unlucky enough to be sighted to the south of Madeira on February 23rd by a British squadron under Rear-Admiral the Hon Robert Digby.[2] The French at once scattered, and, darkness coming on, altered course, with the exception of the *Protée*, *Charmante*, and two of the smallest ships. At one in the morning of February 24th, some hours after this change had been made, the *Protée's* captain came to the conclusion that the safety of his consorts was assured, and decided to look

[1] Nicolas, 'Nelson,' i. 9; Collingwood's Correspondence (1 vol.), 7; Beatson, v. 96.
[2] Beatson v. 130; Troude, ii. 66; *Gazette de France*, 125.

to that of his own ship. Hitherto he had been sailing large; now it was necessary to sail nearer the wind. In altering course, however, his main topgallant mast came down, injuring the sails of the foremast, and hindering the working of the ship. In consequence, the *Protée* was quickly overtaken. At about two, the *Resolution*, 74, Captain Lord Robert Manners, opened upon her. A little later the *Bedford* and *Marlborough*, both 74's, joined in the cannonade. Resistance was perfectly hopeless from the first, but Captain Vicomte Du Chilleau did not strike till his wheel had been shattered, his sails riddled, and his ship rendered incapable of movement. He surrendered at 3.15 A.M., having lost thirty-two killed and a great number of wounded. The *Resolution* had not lost a man. On board the *Protée* was a large sum of money. Of the rest of the convoy, three sail only were taken. The *Charmante* was hotly pursued, but she got away.

In April a serious mutiny occurred on board the *Invincible*, 74, Captain Charles Saxton, at Portsmouth.[1] She had been ordered to the West Indies, but as the seamen had six months' wages due, reckoning by lunar months, they refused to weigh anchor till they were paid. It had frequently happened before that crews refused to proceed to sea without receiving their arrears of wages;[2] and the men could point to an Act of Parliament enjoining prompt payment of all wages, leaving always, however, six months' wages due. On the other hand, the Articles of War decreed death to those who delayed the service and demanded arrears of wages. The mutineers were well behaved and obedient, but no threats or promises would induce them to go to sea. The *Alexander*, 74, was warped alongside the *Invincible*, and ostentatious preparations were made for battle, but the mutineers did not turn a hair. They effected their purpose, as they were not sent to the West Indies till November, and the only punishment dealt out to them was the trial of four men by court-martial, and the infliction upon two of those four of

[1] Minutes of C. M. wanting; Beatson, v. 5.

[2] In C. M., 52 (MSS. Record Office), will be found a similar instance. Seven seamen of the *Egmont*, on Sept. 29th, 1779, demanded their pay. They were severely punished. Three were condemned to death and petitioned for mercy in moving words. "We, the unhappy condemned objects never willing to offend, now posterate ourselves imploring mercy, strangers to mutiny, or dissatisfaction, always ready to obey, but now led away through error, misguided by insinuating men, fall a victim to the martial law. Pity our misconduct and be merciful to us. Take not away our lives but spare us from the approaching and gloomy day, being young in the service, that we may live to be an honour to our Sovereign and help to our country."

five hundred lashes. It was not till the mutiny of 1797 that the Act for the better payment of the Navy reformed one of the worst abuses in the service. Till that Act it was extraordinarily difficult for the seaman to get his pay.

On April 26th, the British sloop *Fortune*, 18, Commander Lewis Robertson, was captured by the French frigates *Iphigénie* and *Gentille* in the West Indies.[1]

At about that time, within ten days, the *Iris* and *Galatea*, cruising on the American coast, took nine privateers, manned by eight hundred men.

On the 30th of the same month, a small British squadron, composed of the *Ariadne*, 20, Captain Matthew Squire, the *Fury*, 16, Commander Alexander Agnew, and the armed ships, each of 20 guns, *Queen* and *Loudoun*, Commanders Richard Trotten and Stephen Rains (1), was cruising off Flamborough Head, when three French privateers of from 20 to 24 guns each were sighted.[2] These were chased and attacked by the *Ariadne* and *Queen*, whilst the *Fury* and *Loudoun* held aloof and gave no assistance. The *Queen* suffered considerably. Seven men were wounded in her and every running rope cut away. After a sharp action, the privateers got away by using sweeps. The conduct of two of the British Commanders was so unsatisfactory that Agnew and Rains were cashiered by court-martial. Commander Rains was a very old and infirm officer, which, perhaps, explains his indifferent behaviour. Captain Squire, on the other hand, was honourably acquitted.

On May 1st the cartel ship *Sartine*, John Dallis, master, with the French officers and soldiers who had surrendered at Pondicherry, after a ten months' voyage arrived off Cape St. Vincent, where she was sighted and fired upon by the *Romney*, 50, Captain Roddam Home. She carried a French flag and a cartel flag. At once she lowered her French flag, but she was again fired upon, with the result that Dallis and two French soldiers were killed and twelve wounded. Strong complaint was made by the French of the *Romney's* conduct, but as it appeared at the court of inquiry that the *Sartine* had hoisted a broad pennant, contrary to the custom of cartels, and failed to lower it, Captain Home was acquitted of all blame.[3]

[1] Troude, ii. 78. The *Iphigénie* carried twenty-six 12-prs. and eight 6-prs.; the *Gentille*, thirty-four 12-prs. and six 6 prs., according to evidence to be found in C. M., 56.

[2] Beatson, v. 147; C. M., 57.

[3] Chevalier, 105; C. M., 55, July 17th.

On June 6th, in West Indian waters, the *Iris*, 32, Captain James Hawker, engaged for eighty minutes the French 32 of equal force, *Hermione*,[1] Captain de La Touche. Each side accuses the other of breaking off the engagement, but as the *Hermione* was coppered, and therefore presumably the fastest sailer, it is probable that she, rather than the *Iris*, retired. The British loss was seven killed and nine wounded; the French lost ten killed and thirty-seven wounded; which bears out the account of the *Iris's* log, and leads us to think that the *Hermione* had all the worst of it.

On June 15th, the British 32-gun frigate *Apollo*, Captain Philemon Pownall, chased, and fought an indecisive action with, the French privateer *Stanislas*, 26, in the Channel. The *Apollo* lost her Captain and five other men killed, and twenty wounded. The *Stanislas* ran aground off Ostend in neutral waters, but soon got off, was taken into port, and was there eventually sold to the British Government.[2]

On June 26th, in the West Indies, the French cutter *Sans Pareil* was captured by the British 44-gun *Phœnix* and two other frigates. On July 1st, the *Romney*, 50, cruising off Finisterre under the command of Captain Roddam Home, fell in with and captured the French "frigate" *Artois* of 40 guns and four hundred and sixty men.[3] The *Artois's* battery is stated to have been composed of 24-, 18-, and 9-prs. She was a new ship and much was expected from her. In spite of this she struck after a short action, having lost very heavily.

—	Guns.	Broadside.	Men.	Killed,	Wounded.	Total.
		Lbs.				
Romney . .	50	416	365	0	2	2
Artois . .	40	?	460	20	40	60

Time, 45 minutes.

A few days later, on July 5th, the *Romney* made another prize; this time the *Perle*, of 18 guns and one hundred and thirty-eight men, commanded by the Chevalier de Breignon. The *Perle* merely fired a broadside, and then struck. On July 5th, the British

[1] Troude, ii. 78–9; Beatson, v. 46–7; Log of *Iris*.

[2] *Lond. Gazette*, Aug. 8th.

[3] Not in Troude. The *Artois* was possibly a privateer or a ship hired from the French king.

frigates *Prudente*, 36,[1] Captain the Hon. William Waldegrave, and *Licorne*, 32, Captain the Hon. Thomas Cadogan, captured off Cape Ortegal the *Capricieuse*, 32, a French frigate commanded by Captain Le Breton de Ranzanne. The *Prudente* saw and gave chase to the Frenchman at 10 A.M. of the 4th; at midnight she was able to bring her enemy to close action, and attacked the *Capricieuse* yardarm to yardarm, inflicting heavy loss upon her. The action had lasted an hour before the *Licorne* could come up. She then stood across the *Capricieuse's* quarter. The French ship, nevertheless, prolonged her determined resistance to overpowering odds till 4.30 A.M., when she struck, with five feet of water in her hold. The *Capricieuse* was a new frigate of 1100 tons, pierced for forty-four guns and mounting thirty-two, and was reduced to such a terrible condition by the British fire that no attempt was made to bring her into port. She was destroyed and her crew transferred to the British vessels. The loss of life on board her during the action was very heavy. Her captain and first lieutenant were killed, and all but two of the officers were wounded. Her crew displayed the greatest intrepidity in offering so stubborn a resistance to so superior a force.

—	Tons.	Guns.	Broadside.	Men.	Killed.	Wounded.	Total.
Prudente . .	897	40?	Lbs. 228?	247 n.	17	31	48
Licorne . .	679	32	174 n.	220 n.	3	7	13
Capricieuse .	1,100	32[1]	174?	308	..	..	"at least 100"

Time, 4½–5½ hours.

[1] So Troude, though British authorities say forty. I have reckoned her as an ordinary French 32 (12-pr.).

A third French ship fell a victim to the English on this day. This was the *Hussard*, 18, which struck to the *Nonsuch*, 64, Captain Sir James Wallace, off Ushant.

On the night of July 11th, the *Nonsuch*, Captain Sir James Wallace, cruising off Croisic, came up with the French frigate *Belle Poule*, 32, commanded by the Chevalier de Kergariou-Coatlès.[2] Against a line-of-battle ship, such as the *Nonsuch*, a frigate could

[1] Of 44 guns according to Troude; *Gazette de France*, 297, gives her twenty-eight 12's, eight 6's, and four 18's = "obusiers." *Lond. Gazette*, July 18th; Troude, ii. 81. She was officially rated a 32.

[2] *Gazette de France*, 303; Beatson, v. 137; Troude, ii. 81; Log of *Nonsuch*.

hope to effect little; but, notwithstanding the great disparity of force, the Frenchman offered a brave resistance. For about twenty minutes a running fight was maintained, in which Captain de Kergariou in vain endeavoured to dismast or cripple the rigging of his opponent. Just after midnight he yawed three times, and fired as many broadsides at the *Nonsuch*'s masts, but without success. The *Nonsuch* closed him fast; her musketry fire cut down the men exposed on the poop and forecastle, which were not barricaded, or the barricades of which had been thrown overboard; and her heavy guns quickly deprived the *Belle Poule* of all manœuvring power. Then the line-of-battle ship placed herself on the frigate's port bow, and held this advantageous position for a quarter of an hour. Soon after two the French captain was mortally wounded; but the French did not strike till three. Half their guns were dismounted; the masts and rigging were much cut up; the sea was pouring in through the shot-holes on the water line; and from below the cry was coming up, "We are sinking." The British took possession about four o'clock. They had suffered very slight loss, probably owing to the greater strength of the line-of-battle ship's sides.

—	Tons.	Guns.	Broadside.	Men.	Killed.	Wounded.	Total.
			Lbs.				
Nonsuch . .	1,372	72[1]	648	491 n.	3	10	13
Belle Poule .	902	32	192	275	21	47	68

[1] Eight 12-pr. carronades, [cf. *Gazette de France*, 304] included.

The *Belle Poule* was bought into the British Navy and rated as a 36.

An action, which is interesting as showing the British respect for a strong neutral, is that between the *Porcupine*, 24, Captain Sir Charles Henry Knowles, and *Minorca*, 18, xebec, Lieutenant Hugh Lawson, on the one hand, and the French *Montréal*, 32, on the other.[1] The *Montréal* had under her charge a convoy of six ships. On July 30th, she was attacked by the two British ships on the Algerian coast; but these did not venture inshore to rake her owing to the risk of running aground. The three ships fought at long range for an hour and forty minutes, when the *Porcupine* and *Minorca* hauled off. The French lost four killed, including their

[1] *Gazette de France*, 326; Troude, ii. 82; Beatson, v. 116.

captain; the English had five killed and two wounded. They retired because, had the *Montréal* struck, they could not have carried her off from Algerian waters, and because three other ships had appeared above the horizon. The French version represents the British as employing three frigates, three "corsaires,' a "senau" (snow), and a schooner. There is no mention of these craft in the British reports; the names of their captains, as given by the French, are suspiciously un-English, and their existence seems to have been due to a vivid imagination. Some days before this action the *Porcupine* had fought an indecisive action with two Spanish polaccas.

On July 29th, a convoy of sixty-three valuable ships, bound for the East and West Indies, left Great Britain under the care of Captain John Moutray in the *Ramillies*, 74, with the frigates *Thetis* and *Southampton*, both of 36 guns.[1] On August 8th, in lat. 36° 40′ N., long. 15° W., strange sails were seen, and Captain Moutray signalled his ships to alter course and follow him close to the wind. They paid no attention to his orders, and by daylight of the 9th the bulk of the convoy found themselves close to the enormous combined Franco-Spanish fleet. The warships, with eight of the convoy, alone escaped; the other fifty-five merchantmen, with 2865 prisoners, and cargo worth a million and a half, were captured. It was a terrible blow to British commerce, and especially to the forces in the West Indies, which lost a vast quantity of military stores. The merchants at home were so enraged that Captain Moutray had to be made a scapegoat. He was tried by court-martial and dismissed his ship, but was again employed before long. Early in July, the outward-bound Quebec fleet was attacked on the Newfoundland Banks by privateers, and about fourteen of its richest ships were carried off.[2]

On August 10th was fought the famous action between the *Flora* and *Nymphe*, which demonstrated the value of the carronade, then newly introduced into the British Navy.[3] The *Flora*, 36, Captain William Peere Williams, was off Ushant, when, in the afternoon, she sighted and chased a cutter and a frigate. The former got away; the latter was overhauled and brought to action soon after

[1] *Gazette de France*, 334, 347; Beatson, v. 149 ff.; C. M., 56, Feb. 13th. During the earlier part of this war the French were exceedingly well informed of British proceedings. Cf. 'Annual Register,' 1781, [239, for the trial of a French spy named Lamotte, who appears to have sent them intelligence.

[2] 'Ann. Register,' 1781, 3.

[3] *Gazette de France*, 323–4; Troude, ii. 82; James, i. 39; Log of *Flora*; Beatson, v. 138. For an account of the introduction of the carronade, see vol. iii., 330-333.

five, when she proved to be the French 32-gun *Nymphe*, Captain Du Rumain. The two fought yardarm to yardarm from 5.45 to 6.15 P.M., during which time the *Flora's* wheel was shot away and her shrouds and rigging were greatly cut up. On the other side the French captain was mortally wounded by four musket-shot, a magazine of cartridges exploded, the ship was twice on fire, and terrible havoc was wrought on deck by one of the *Flora's* 18-pr. forecastle carronades, handled by only the boatswain and a boy. At 6.15 the ships fell on board one another. The French sounded "boarders away," abandoned their guns, and endeavoured to carry the *Flora*. The attempts of the French to board having been easily repulsed, it was now the turn of the British. They dashed on to the *Nymphe's* deck, which presented a horrible scene of slaughter, and quickly were masters of the ship.

—	Tons.	Guns.	Broadside.	Men.	Killed.	Wounded.	Total.
			Lbs.				
Flora . . .	868	42[1]	333	259	9	17	26
Nymphe . .	937	32	174	291	55	81	139

Time, about 50 minutes.

[1] In the text above I have described the *Flora* by her official rating as a 36-gun ship. But the official rating is wholly misleading as it does not include carronades, nor does it give any real idea of the great superiority of force on the British side. The French have always complained—and justly—of these fictions. According to the account of the (French) Lieut. Taillard in the *Gazette de France*, the *Flora* had eight carronades, 18-prs. James ('Naval History,' i. 39), whom I have followed, gives her only six.

The number of the *Nymphe's* killed and wounded is given differently in all the accounts, but the substantial fact remains that she lost in less than an hour from 43 to 45 per cent. of her crew, whilst inflicting on her enemy a loss of just 10 per cent. Without doubt it was the superior weight of the *Flora's* metal, her 18-prs. against the *Nymphe's* 12-prs., her 9-prs. against the French 6-prs., and her carronades, which gave her the victory. The *Nymphe* was a larger ship, a longer ship, and a better sailer,[1] but she had not the battery. We cannot accuse the French of either lack of spirit or mismanagement.

On August 13th, the *Bienfaisant*, 64, Captain John Macbride, and *Charon*, 44, in charge of a convoy on the Irish coast, captured a French privateer of unusual size, the *Comte d'Artois*, of sixty-four

[1]	Length of gun-deck.	Beam.	Depth.	Tonnage.
	Ft.	Ft.	Ft.	
Flora . .	137	38	13¼	868
Nymphe .	141¼	38½	11¾	937

guns and 644 men. The French lost 57 killed or wounded, the English ships 26.

On September 13th, the British sloop *Rover*, 18, Commander Henry Savage, was captured by the French *Junon*, 32, in the West Indies.[1] At the second shot one of the *Rover's* masts fell. She was in a leaky condition, and had four feet of water in her hold, yet she offered a good resistance, though she suffered no loss. On the 4th, a French frigate and two ships of the line captured the *Unicorn*, 20, Captain Thomas Lenox Frederick, off Tortuga, after a bravely fought action in which she had two guns and two carronades dismounted, and lost 4 killed and 13 wounded.[2] Later in the same month, off San Domingo, the British 14-gun ship *Leveret* is said by Troude to have been captured by the French 18-gun cutter *Serpent*.[3] The *Leveret* must have been a privateer, or an armed ship, since the name does not occur in the Navy List.

On September 10th, a capture of great importance was made by Captain George Keppel in the *Vestal*, aided by the *Fairy*.[4] This was the American packet *Mercury* from Philadelphia, with the American minister to Holland, and important dispatches, on board. The dispatches, as usual, were thrown into the sea when capture was inevitable, but not being weighted they did not sink; and an English sailor leapt overboard and picked them up. Amongst them was a treaty between the United States and Holland, which betrayed the Dutch intentions of war. It is claimed that in October the French frigates *Aimable* and *Diligente* captured three British cutters, the *Alert*, *Tartar*, and *Jersey*, in the Bay of Biscay. As their names do not occur in the Navy Lists of 1780 these ships may have been privateers.

Between the 4th and 16th of October the West Indies were visited by an extraordinary series of violent hurricanes, which inflicted on the British Navy the severest losses. On October 5th Rear-Admiral Rowley was caught at sea to the N.E. of San Domingo with the *Grafton*, 74, *Thunderer*, 74, *Hector*, 74, *Berwick*, 74, *Ruby*, 64, *Trident*, 64, *Stirling Castle*, 64, and *Bristol*, 50. In the afternoon waterspouts were seen. Towards dark the wind rose steadily, till at midnight a furious hurricane blew. The *Thunderer* disappeared and was never seen again; the *Grafton* was dismasted, and the wreckage, dashing against her

1 C. M., 56, Jan. 18th.
2 *Ib.*
3 Troude, ii. 84.
4 Beatson, v. 52.

sides, was threatening to disable her, when twenty-five of her crew volunteered for the desperately dangerous work of cutting it away. In this they succeeded without suffering hurt or loss. That night the *Stirling Castle* struck on the San Domingo coast and quickly went to pieces, only fifty of her crew being saved. The *Berwick* was so much damaged that she had to part company and steer for Great Britain, and the *Trident, Ruby, Bristol,* and *Hector* were all dismasted. A day earlier the *Phœnix,* 44, was wrecked on the Cuban coast; the *Scarborough,* 20, *Barbados,* 14, and *Victor,* 10, foundered; and the *Ulysses,* 44, and *Pomona,* 28, were dismasted.

On October 10th, the *Ajax, Montagu, Egmont, Endymion, Amazon, Vengeance,* and several smaller ships at St. Lucia, were driven from their anchorage and dismasted. The *Andromeda* and *Laurel,* both of 28 guns, were swept ashore at Martinique and but few of their crews saved; the *Deal Castle,* 24, was lost at Puerto Rico; the *Cameleon,* 14, and *Blanche,* 32, foundered at sea with the loss of all hands; the *St. Vincent,* 14, and *Vengeance,* 74, drove ashore at St. Lucia, but got off again slightly damaged; the *Venus,* 36, and *Alcmene,* 32, were dismasted and carried to Antigua. Thus, in all, His Majesty's fleet lost through these storms one 74, one 64, one 44, a 32, and seven smaller ships.[1]

On November 2nd, the British ship *Zephyr,* 14, Commander John Inglis (1), engaged in trade protection on the coast of Africa, with the *Polly,* 16, privateer, entered the Gambia River, and attacked the French 18-gun ship *Sénégal,* which, under the name of *Racehorse,* had been captured from Great Britain.[2] There was a sharp action of five hours' duration, after which the enemy struck, with twelve killed and twenty-eight wounded. The British loss was two killed and four wounded. The *Sénégal* did not long survive her capture, but blew up on the 22nd, from some unexplained cause, killing twenty-three British officers and men who were on board at the time.

In November and December, Vice-Admiral Sir Edward Hughes gained some small successes against the armed ships of Hyder Ali.[3] One of the Madras Rajah's ships was cut out by the boats of the squadron at Calicut; a second was driven ashore; but the *Sartine,* 32, in covering these operations, was unfortunate enough to strike on

[1] Beatson, v. 80–1.; 'Ann. Register,' 1781, 30 ff.

[2] *Lond. Gazette,* Mar. 13th, 1781; Beatson, v. 93. This was the *Racehorse* of the Arctic expedition in which Nelson took part.

[3] *Lond. Gazette,* June 16th, 1781. C. M., 55.

a rock and sink on November 26th. Her Captain, Robert Simonton, had previously protested against being sent too close inshore.

The Spanish sloop *Real Carlos*, 20, on a voyage between Montevideo and Ferrol, met the British West Indiaman *Mary*, M. Stewards, master, of twenty-two guns and eighty-three men in the latitude of the West Indies on December 27th.[1] She fought the merchant ship for five hours, shooting away all her topmasts, hitting her three times between wind and water, dismounting seven guns and killing or wounding eight men. Each side claims to have driven off the other, but, be this as it may, it is wonderful that the merchant ship should have been able to escape from a man-of-war. The Spanish loss was fourteen. Unfortunately the *Mary*, in her disabled state, was attacked a little later by the American privateer *Pilgrim* and compelled to strike.

On December 30th, the *Marlborough*, 74, Captain Taylor Penny, and *Bellona*, 74, Captain Richard Onslow, overtook and engaged the Dutch warship *Prinses Carolina*, of fifty-four guns and three hundred men, in the Channel.[2] She could offer little resistance to a force so superior. After thirty minutes' fight she struck with sixteen killed or wounded to the British loss of three. She was purchased and added to the Navy as the *Princess Caroline*.

On the last day of the year 1780 the Dutch 50-gun ship *Rotterdam* was chased and attacked by the *Isis*, Captain Evelyn Sutton, of her own force, in the Channel. The British ship fired a broadside and came very precipitately to close quarters, when the crew, who were raw and undisciplined, fell into great confusion. The *Rotterdam* is said to have struck; but Captain Sutton failed to take possession of her. For his conduct he was court-martialled and reprimanded. His defence was that his men had deserted their quarters; that on the lower deck there was much disorder, and cartridges were left lying about; that of a total crew of 284, in place of 350, fifteen were sick, that of the rest many were undisciplined, had never been afloat before, and did not understand English; and, finally, that the men could not work the ship properly, but tacked slowly and awkwardly.[3] The *Isis* had been sent

[1] *Gazette de France* (1781), 77; Beatson, v. 205.

[2] Beatson, v. 148.

[3] Beatson, v. 419; C. M., 56, Jan. 19; Nicolas, 'Nelson's Dispatches,' i. 36. In view of the theory that Irish were not numerous in the fleet during this war, the mention of men who could not understand English, and who were almost certainly Irishmen, is interesting. Similar statements are not infrequent in the Mins. of C. M. during the period.

to sea in hot haste, and the hands had never been exercised. In these circumstances she was perhaps fortunate in escaping capture. Some days later, on January 5th, 1781, the *Rotterdam* was brought to action by the *Warwick*, 50, Captain the Hon. George Keith Elphinstone. Though the *Warwick's* crew had been weakened by detachments for the purpose of manning prizes, the Dutch ship struck to her without causing her the loss of a man. Prior to this action the *Rotterdam* had fought a British ship of the line and two cutters, but had got away from them through the aid of two French privateers.[1]

In January a weak French force landed in Jersey and seized St. Helier, but was quickly overpowered and captured.[2]

On January 4th, whilst the French ship *Minerve*, 32, Captain de Grimouard, was cruising with three other frigates in the Channel, she and her sisters were chased by the British 74's *Courageux*, Captain Lord Mulgrave, and *Valiant*,[3] Captain Samuel Granston Goodall. The *Courageux* was quickly within range of the *Minerve*, but, to the surprise of the British, the frigate did not, as was the custom, strike promptly to the line-of-battle ship. On the contrary she fought on for an hour at pistol-shot range. Then, on the *Valiant* coming up, the *Minerve*, reduced to a complete wreck, surrendered. Her captain was wounded; her crew had lost very heavily, two officers being amongst the killed; her guns had for the most part been dismounted; her masts had fallen or were threatening to fall; her rigging was terribly cut up; and her hold was filling with water. Nor had the *Courageux* escaped scatheless. She had seventeen killed or wounded, and had sustained grave injury to her foremast, mizenmast, and bowsprit. For a frigate to have offered such a resistance against such terrific odds, and to have inflicted so much loss and damage, was no mean achievement.

—	Guns.	Broadside.	Men.	Killed.	Wounded.	Total.
		Lbs.				
Courageux .	82[1]	829	590 n.	10	7	17
Minerve . .	32	174	316	51	23	74

Time, 1 hour.

[1] Eight carronades allowed.

[1] *Gazette de France*, 25.

[2] Beatson, v. 367.

[3] *Gazette de France*, 55; Troude, ii. 116; Beatson, v. 419.

The *Minerve* had to be towed into port, where she was purchased for the Navy and named *Recovery*. She was the same *Minerva* that had been captured by the French frigate *Concorde* on August 22nd, 1778.[1] A new *Minerva* of thirty-eight guns had been built for the British fleet in 1780.

On January 9th, 1781, the *Fairy*, 16 (6-pdrs.), Commander Joseph Browne, was captured by a large French privateer of 30 or 32 guns, ten leagues S.S.W. of the Scillies. Her loss was due to the fact that no private signals had been issued to the Plymouth cruisers. It was consequently impossible for her to discover an enemy at a distance.

On January 25th, a small combined expedition proceeded from Charleston to Cape Fear River.[2] Captain Andrew Barkley had under him the *Blonde*, 32, *Otter*, 14, Commander Richard Creyke (1), and *Delight*, 14, Commander John Inglis (1), and some smaller craft, and was the naval commander. On board were 300 soldiers under Major Craig. These, with 80 Marines were disembarked, and on the 28th occupied Wilmington and captured seven American ships. The object of this expedition was to open up sea communication with Lord Cornwallis, and to secure a base for his army, then moving northward. And here it may be mentioned that on March 20th General Phillips, with 2000 men, was convoyed from New York to the Chesapeake and James River by the *Ambuscade*, 32, *Chatham*, 50, *Orpheus*, 32, *Savage*, 16, *Halifax*, 18, *Bonetta*, 14, and *Vulcan*, fireship.

On Rodney's arrival at St. Eustatius, the Dutch frigate *Mars*, 38, and five other vessels of from 26 to 14 guns fell into his hands.[3] A day before his coming a rich convoy of thirty ships had sailed for Europe under the convoy of Rear-Admiral Willem Crul, in the Dutch line-of-battle ship *Mars*,[4] 60. Captain Francis Reynolds, with the *Monarch*, 74, *Panther*, 60, and *Sibyl*, 28, was despatched in chase. On February 4th, at ten in the morning, he was alongside the *Mars*. She refused to strike and a short action took place in which the Dutch flag-officer lost his life. On this the *Mars* surrendered, to be purchased into the Navy under the name of *Prince Edward*. All

[1] *Vide* pp. 18, 19.

[2] *Lond. Gazette*, Mar. 31st; Beatson, v. 236–7.

[3] See Chap. xxxi., (vol. iii. 481).

[4] The duplication of the name *Mars* is, at first, puzzling. No 60-gun *Mars* appears in the list of the Dutch Navy (Beatson, vi. 256). [But the account of the capture appears in its place in De Jonge, iv. 463 *et seq.*—W.L.C.]

the ships of the convoy were taken, and by four in the afternoon Captain Reynolds was on his way back to join Rodney.

False colours were kept flying at St. Eustatius, and in this way several merchant ships, American, French, and Dutch, were captured. The goods seized in the island were sold by auction—much below their real value—or shipped to Great Britain. It was found that many of the merchants, who had warehouses at St. Eustatius, were Englishmen. These were particularly detested by Rodney, and were treated with inexcusable severity by him.

In the month of February the sloop *Rover*, 18, which had been taken by the French on September 13th, 1780, was retaken by a privateer, but was lost at sea with her crew.[1] In the same month the *Romulus*, 44,[2] Captain George Gayton, was proceeding to the Chesapeake when she was captured by a squadron from Des Touches's squadron under the orders of Captain Le Gardeur de Tilly, composed of the *Eveillé*, 64, *Gentille*, 32, *Surveillante*, 32, and *Guêpe*, cutter.[3]

On the 25th, the *Cerberus*, 28, Captain Robert Man (3), whilst cruising off Finisterre, sighted, chased, and brought to action the Spanish 30-gun frigate *Grana*, Don N. de Medina. She was a month out from Ferrol on a cruise. Her armament was wretchedly light, consisting of twenty-two 6-prs. and eight 4-prs., and to this must probably be ascribed her easy capture.[4] She was purchased into the Navy under the same name, and rated as a 28.

—	Guns.	Broadside.	Men.	Killed.	Wounded.	Total.
		Lbs.				
Cerberus . .	28	126	176 n.	0	2	2
Grana . .	30	82	166	7	17	24

Time, 15 minutes.

Towards the end of February, a flotilla of six British privateers, of from thirty-two to four guns, entered the river Demerara,

[1] Troude, ii. 117.

[2] Troude, ii. 97; C. M., 58, Sept. 26.

[3] *Lond. Gazette*, Mar. 10th; *Cerberus*'s Log.

[4] The proportions of the *Grana* and *Cerberus* were these (Charnock, 'Mar. Arch.' iii. 258–9):—

	Length.	Beam.	Tonnage.
Cerberus	118 ft.	34	593
Grana	118 „	31	528

and on the 27th of the month captured fifteen Dutch ships of considerable value.[1] In the meantime the British governor of Barbados had sent an officer under a flag of truce to demand the surrender of Demerara and Essequibo on favourable terms. The governor, alarmed at the depredations of the privateers, at once acceded to this demand. On March 17th, the French island of St. Bartholomew surrendered to Commander Lawrence Græme, of the *Sylph*, 18.

On April 14th,[2] the 36-gun American frigate *Confederacy*, Captain Seth Harding, was captured by the British frigates *Roebuck*, 44, Captain John Orde (1), and *Orpheus*, 32, Captain John Colpoys, on a voyage from the West Indies to Washington. She was loaded with stores for the American army, and with colonial produce. She was purchased into the Navy under the name *Confederate*.[3]

On April 16th, the *George and Molly*, 8 (3-prs.), Lieutenant Richard Saunders, captured an American 16-gun privateer in the Channel.

The British 28-gun frigate *Resource*, Captain Bartholomew Samuel Rowley, was cruising in the West Indies, when, on April 20th, she sighted a large sail.[4] As the stranger bore down upon her, she cleared for action, and engaged at about 4.30 in the afternoon. The enemy struck at six; she proved to be the *Licorne*, a French frigate, commanded by Captain de St. Ture, and mounting twenty 9-prs. and eight 12-pr. carronades. The *Resource* had her Gunner killed and her second Lieutenant wounded. Her loss in killed and wounded was much heavier than that of the French ship. The gallantry of his crew was greatly commended by Captain Rowley, as was that of some soldiers of the Loyal American Rangers who were on board. The *Licorne* had passed through many vicissitudes, as she had been originally a British vessel, but had been taken by the French in September 1780, as has been shown.[5]

[1] Beatson, v. 172.

[2] Beatson, v. 303. Maclay, i. 147, gives the 22nd as the date, but he is wrong by the *Roebuck's* log.

[3] Charnock, 'Mar. Arch.,' iii. 256, gives these particulars of her: Length, 159 ft. 7½ in., beam, 36 ft. 9 in., draught, 12 ft. 1½ in., displacement, 959 tons. She was at the date of her capture the largest 36-gun ship in the Navy.

[4] Beatson, v. 209; Log of *Resource*. The *Licorne's* name was commonly anglicised as *Unicorn*.

[5] *See* p. 57.

—	Tons.	Guns.	Broadside.	Men.	Killed.	Wounded.	Total.
			Lbs.				
Resource . .	603	34[1]	150	194 n.	15	30	45
Licorne . .	581	28	138	197	8	30	38

[1] Possibly the *Resource* was armed as the *Licorne*, though the 28-gun ship properly carried twenty-four 9's, four 3's, and six 12-pr. carronades. There seems in the rating to be some confusion between ships carrying 20 guns + 8 carronades, and 28 guns + carronades. In Schomberg and the List Books, the *Licorne* is a 20-gun ship; in Charnock and Beatson a 28-gun; in Allen she is a 24. Log of *Resource* calls her a 28-gun frigate.

She was restored to the Navy as the *Unicorn*, 20.

On May 1st, the *Canada*, 74, Captain Sir George Collier, having been detached from Admiral Darby's fleet, then on the west coast of Spain, to scout, came in sight of the Spanish frigate *Sta. Leocadia*, 34, Captain Don F. Winthuysen, and a small sloop, standing towards a number of British merchantmen.[1] The sloop escaped, but the *Sta. Leocadia* was hotly chased all that day. At nightfall the ships were still some distance apart when the wind began to fall. The *Sta. Leocadia* endeavoured to make her escape by changing course. Unfortunately for her there was a bright moon and she failed in her attempt. It was now calm and the *Canada* had almost forged within pistol shot. The action was opened by the *Sta. Leocadia*, which offered a desperate resistance to the tremendous fire of the ship of the line. A heavy swell made the shooting difficult for the gunners on both sides, and prevented the *Canada* from opening her lower-deck ports. Some twenty minutes after the engagement had begun, Winthuysen's arm was broken by a cannon-ball and he had to give up the command. A little later his successor had also to retire —wounded in the tongue. After fighting for rather over half an hour the *Sta. Leocadia*, disabled and leaking heavily, struck her flag. Though pierced for forty guns, she carried only thirty-four.

—	Tons.	Guns.	Broadside.	Men.	Killed.	Wounded.	Total.
			Lbs.				
Canada . .	1,605	82[1]	829	590			
Sta. Leocadia	952	34	186?	250	20	10	30

Time, 35–45 minutes.

[1] Eight 12-pr. carronades included.

The *Sta. Leocadia* was purchased into the Navy and rated as a

[1] *Lond. Gazette*, June 5th; *Gazette de France*, 317 (1781); Log of *Canada*.

36-gun ship. In size and lines[1] she was little inferior to the *Confederate*.

On May 14th, the *Nonsuch*, 64, Captain Sir James Wallace, was scouting with Admiral Darby's fleet in the Bay of Biscay when she saw and chased a sail, looking like a French line-of-battle ship.[2] Soon after ten in the evening she was close enough to open on the strange vessel, which was the *Actif*, 74, Captain de Boades. The two interchanged broadsides and then the *Nonsuch* wore and raked her opponent. The fight lasted for an hour, during part of which time the ships were on board of one another, as the *Nonsuch's* anchor hooked the *Actif's* quarter. Getting free, the *Actif* made sail and stood away, and the *Nonsuch*, owing to injuries to her mizenmast yards and rigging, could not again overtake her for some hours. The British ship, however, having repaired her injuries, pursued and came up a second time about daylight on the 15th. A second and still hotter action of ninety minutes' duration followed, in which the *Nonsuch* sustained much damage. Her fore-yard fell, and her masts, yards, and rigging were badly cut up. She, therefore, hauled off and left the *Actif* free to retire to Brest. The latter ship made no attempt to pursue, as there was some risk of falling in with Admiral Darby's fleet. The *Nonsuch's* lighter metal and weaker hull were probably the cause of her comparatively heavy loss.

—	Tons.	Guns.	Broadside.	Men.	Killed.	Wounded.	Total.
			Lbs.				
Actif . . .	1	74 [2]	838	750	15	38	53
Nonsuch . .	1372	72 [3]	648	491 n.	26	64	90

Time, 2½ hours.

1 Probably of from 1680 to 1780 tons. We captured no French 74's of less displacement between 1750 and 1783.
2 Troude, *loc. cit.*, gives her only 64 guns, but Beatson, vi. 94, in his 'Correct List of the French Navy, 1778, makes her a 74; so also Capt. Wallace describes her; *Lond. Gazette, loc. cit.*
3 Sixty-four guns, and eight 12-pr. carronades which she most probably carried.

On May 27th, the British brigs *Atalanta*, 16, Commander Sampson Edwards, and *Trepassey*, 14, Commander James Smyth, saw and chased a strange vessel in the North Atlantic. As they closed with her, however, ascertaining that she was of great size, they hauled their wind, and made off, chased in turn.[3] The

[1] Length, 144 ft. 10 in., beam, 38 ft. 8 in., draught, 11 ft. 7¼ in.
[2] *Lond. Gazette*, May 22nd; Troude, ii. 118; Beatson, v. 384.
[3] Beatson, v. 308; C. M., 58, Oct. 15th; *Gazette*, Aug. 4th.

stranger came up with them on the 28th about noon, when they discovered that she was the American frigate *Alliance*, 36, Captain John Barry. The wind had fallen to a dead calm; the brigs had no chance of escape; they therefore turned, and with sweeps headed for the enemy. The *Trepassey*, endeavouring to take up a favourable position on the *Alliance's* quarter, unfortunately overshot the mark and came up on her broadside. Then the *Atalanta* gallantly stood in to the rescue, between the American and the British brig, but the *Trepassey* was so shattered that she could not get away. The American captain early in the action was struck by a grape shot on the shoulder; Commander Smyth of the *Trepassey* was killed. Lieutenants in each ship took up the command. The *Alliance*, with a freshening breeze, was able to use her heavy battery to the greatest advantage. Three and a half hours after the first shot the *Trepassey* struck with a loss of seventeen. The *Atalanta* had been in action an hour longer than her consort, and she still held out, but in the end struck with a loss of twenty-four. On board her Lieutenant Samuel Arden [1] lost an arm, but with heroic courage, as soon as the amputation had been performed, he returned to his quarters. All the ships were badly cut up in masts and rigging. If evidence given at the court-martial can be believed, the *Alliance* carried twenty-eight 12's and eight 9's.

—	Tons.	Guns.	Broadside.	Men.	Killed.	Wounded.	Total.
			Lbs.				
Alliance . .	..	36	204	300	6	26	32
{ *Trepassey* .	342	14	28	80	6	11	17
{ *Atalanta* .	..	16	32	125	6	18	24

Time, 4½–5 hours.

The *Trepassey* was sent to Halifax as a cartel; the *Atalanta* was shortly afterwards retaken off Boston by the *Assurance*, *Charleston*, and *Amphitrite*. Considering the immense disproportion between the two sides, the British must be held to have got off very lightly.

The British frigates *Flora*, 36, Captain William Peere Williams, and *Crescent*, 28, Captain the Hon. Thomas Pakenham, had been detached by Admiral Darby with a convoy to Minorca.[2] On

[1] He was promoted for his gallantry, and posted in 1783. In 1806 he retired.

[2] Beatson, v. 387; *Lond. Gazette*, June 30th, 1781; *Gazette de France*, p. 258, 1781; C. M., 57.

their return, early on May 23rd, when off the south-east coast of Spain, they were chased by a Spanish squadron, and only escaped after a sharp skirmish, in which the *Flora* lost a man killed and another badly injured, through loading a gun before it had been sponged out. The British frigates, having shaken off their pursuers by altering course, reached Gibraltar safely on the 29th. After communicating with the garrison, they stood over to Ceuta to look for two large ships which had been seen earlier in the morning. They discovered these to be Dutch frigates, and were preparing to attack when a storm compelled them to haul off. Next day the wind fell and they were able to attack the two Dutch vessels, which were the *Castor*, 36, Captain Pieter Melvill,[1] and the *Briel*, Captain Gerardus Oorthuijs, also of 36 guns. The ships paired off, the *Flora* engaging the *Castor*, and the *Crescent* the *Briel*.

The *Flora* was very much more heavily armed than the *Castor*,[2] but the Dutchman fought her, none the less, for two hours and a quarter before striking. The *Flora* lost her Lieutenant of Marines killed, as also did the *Castor*; of the British wounded eight, and of the Dutch eleven, died after the battle.

—	Tons.	Guns.	Broadside.	Men.	Killed.	Wounded.	Total.
			Lbs.				
Flora . . .	868	42	333	270	9	32	41
Castor . .	..	36	186	230	22	41	63

Time, 2 hours 15 minutes.

The *Crescent*, a far smaller and weaker ship, was less fortunate in her combat with the *Briel*, a vessel of equal if not superior force. The quarter-deck guns and four main-deck guns were disabled; the head-yards and sails were shot away early in the engagement; and a little later the wreck of the mainmast, mizenmast, and booms fell into the waist of the ship, fatally encumbering her deck, disabling all the guns before the mainmast, and rendering the ship

[1] Pieter Melvill, born at Dordrecht in 1743, entered the navy at the age of fourteen; lieutenant, 1762; commander, 1766; captain, 1777; Schout-bij-Nacht, 1789; quitted the service from 1795 to 1813; vice-admiral, 1814; died 1826.—W. L. C.

[2] *Flora* mounted twenty-six long 18-prs., six 18-pr. carronades, and ten 9-prs.; *Castor* only twenty-six 12-prs. and ten 6-prs.

unmanageable. The *Briel* was to windward and could not be boarded by the *Crescent,* and the Dutch frigate at once made use of her advantage and came round under the *Crescent's* stern, whence she began to rake the British ship. Captain Pakenham, as not a gun would bear, and not a yard of canvas was left standing on his frigate, was compelled to strike. The Dutch were not able to take possession, since by that time the victorious *Flora* was approaching. The *Briel,* therefore, made off to Cadiz in a very shattered condition, and though her mainmast fell, succeeded in reaching that port.

—	Tons.	Guns.	Broadside.	Men.	Killed.	Wounded.	Total.
			Lbs.				
Briel . . .	..	36[1]	178	230?	12	40	52
Crescent . .	611	34[1]	168	200n	26	67	93

Time, 2 hours, 30 minutes.

[1] *Briel* mounted twenty-six 12-prs., two 6-prs., eight 4-prs.; *Crescent's* establishment was twenty-four 9-prs. and four 3-prs., in addition to which she probably carried four to six 18-pr. carronades. She has been allotted therefore six carronades.

The *Crescent's* heavy loss was probably due to her weaker scantling and sides, and to the fact that she was raked more than once. That her crew faced a loss which probably exceeded 50 per cent.—for British ships were as often as not below their nominal establishment in number of men—speaks volumes for their obstinacy and courage. Captain Pakenham, when his ship had struck, refused to resume his command, considering that a court-martial was necessary to clear him of guilt. The first lieutenant of the *Flora,* John Bligh (1), was therefore appointed by Captain Williams to the command.

Beatson justly remarks that a want of combination between the British frigates is obvious. The evidence at the court-martial showed that a considerable time intervened between the *Castor's* striking to the *Flora,* and the *Crescent's* surrender, when the *Flora's* help would have decided the action in favour of the *Crescent.* Another British ship, the *Enterprise,* 28, Captain Patrick Leslie, was in sight and sound of the engagement, but gave absolutely no aid. She had a convoy in her charge, it is true, but her mere appearance would probably have decided the capture of the *Briel.* This action, again, appears to bear very strong testimony to the importance of a heavy battery. The men on either side were of equal courage and skill, and so it was the weight of metal which decided the day. Of course, if the *Crescent* carried no carronades—a point on which we cannot speak with absolute assurance—her weight of broadside would be only two-thirds that of the *Briel's*.

The three ships repaired their injuries as well as they could, and stood away for England.[1] On June 19th, however, while the *Flora* was chasing a privateer, a squall suddenly cleared and revealed to her two French frigates, which at once gave chase. The battered appearance of the three British vessels doubtless encouraged the French to confront such formidable odds. Captain Williams did not think it safe to risk an action after the heavy losses he had sustained. He had not much more than three hundred unwounded people to work and fight three ships requiring crews of seven hundred men. The three parted company and steered different courses. The *Castor* was overtaken by the *Friponne*, 32, and with only seventy-five British seamen on board, nearly all of whom were at the pumps or working the ship, struck at the first shot. The *Crescent* had only five men to each gun on her broadside, and but nine Marines to act as a small-arms' party. She offered some resistance, but she, too, had quickly to strike. The *Flora* alone succeeded in escaping.

On May 28th, the British ship *Champion*, 32, attacked the Dutch fort of Commendah, on the Gold Coast, and was repulsed.[2] At about the same time the Dutch captured Secondee, a British fort near Cape Three Points.

On June 5th, in West Indian waters, the *Ulysses*, 44, Captain John Thomas, had an indecisive action with the *Surveillante*, 40, Captain de Villeneuve Cillart.[3] The *Ulysses* laid the French frigate alongside. Captain Thomas was almost at once wounded, and had to be carried below, as also had the Master and one of the Lieutenants. The wheel and tiller ropes were shot away, the rigging was badly cut up, and the mainyard fell. At about midnight the *Surveillante* made off after a four hours' fight. She is said to have sustained severe damage. On July 28th, there was another indecisive action, between the *Fée*, 32, Captain de Boubée, and the

[1] Troude, ii. 119, and other authorities cited; Letter of Acting Capt. John Bligh in *Gazette*.

[2] *Gazette de France* (1782), 265; Log of *Champion*.

[3] Beatson, v. 208; Troude, ii. 119; Log of *Ulysses*.

Southampton, 32, Captain William Affleck (1).[1] The *Fée* is said by Troude to have had a previous engagement on June 2nd with the *Ulysses*,[2] but that ship's log proves him to have made a mistake. The vessel which the *Fée* fought cannot be discovered. The *Fée* had lost her topmasts and was carrying jury rigging when sighted by the *Southampton*. She was chased and closed by the British vessel late in the night of the 27th–28th. The action began at midnight at a cable's distance, and was maintained for ninety minutes, when the two ships, having received serious damage to masts and rigging, separated. Most of the *Southampton's* standing and running gear had been shot away, and her foresail came down just before the close of the action. She lost four killed and twenty-three wounded; the *Fée*, three killed and twenty-three wounded.

On June 13th, in the Atlantic, the *Snake* 12 (4-prs.), Lieutenant William Jackson, fell in with two American privateers of immensely superior force, the *Pilgrim* and *Rambler*, and was captured.

On July 21st, Commodore George Johnstone's squadron, on the way to the East Indies, captured five valuable prizes in Saldanha Bay.[3] These were the Dutch East Indiamen *Dankbaarheid*, 24, *Perel*, 20, *Schoonkoop*, 20, *Hoogcarspel*, 20, and *Middelburg*, 24.[4] Their masters were surprised and could not escape; they therefore cut their cables, loosed their fore-topsails, and drove on shore, where the ships were fired, and the men landed. The British boats, however, were smartly on the spot and checkmated the Dutch designs. The fires were got under on board all the ships except the *Middelburg*, which burnt furiously, floated off, and nearly drifted on board two of the other prizes. Finally she blew up. A hooker laden with the sails of the captured ships, was discovered hidden away, and captured. Two other hookers were taken, but restored to the Dutch inhabitants by the Commodore. The prizes were sent home, but it is noteworthy as showing the extreme insecurity of British waters at that time, that two of them had sharp fights in coming up the Channel.

[1] Log of *Southampton*; *Gazette de France*, 381.

[2] Troude, ii. 118.

[3] *Gazette*, Oct. 15th.

[4] The exact names of some of these ships are doubtful. They are suggested as above by the misspelt travesties in the British accounts. They are not given by De Jonge.—W. L. C.

The *Hoogcarspel* was chased by a French frigate, and had to retire to Mount's Bay, there to await an escort. The *Perel* was attacked by two privateers, which only retired when their ammunition was exhausted.

On July 21st, the two French frigates *Astrée*, 32, Captain de La Pérouse, and *Hermione*, 32, Captain de La Touche-Tréville, whilst cruising off Cape Breton Island, perceived several sail approaching.[1] They were a number of British merchant vessels escorted by the *Charleston*, 28, Captain Henry Francis Evans; *Allegiance*, 14, Commander David Phips; *Vulture*, 14, Commander Rupert George; *Vernon*, 14, and *Jack*,[2] 14. The two last were armed ships. After a long chase the French vessels came up with them. The British formed single line ahead, the *Charleston* in the centre, between their enemy and the convoy, and opened fire between 7 and 8 P.M. The heavy fire of the French frigates soon began to produce effect. The *Jack*—probably weakly built—had to strike, and the French assert that the *Charleston*, having lost her maintopmast, struck also, but that she took advantage of the darkness to steal away. The *Allegiance*, *Vulture*, and *Vernon* likewise made off, but the *Astrée* had been so damaged in her rigging during the action that she could not pursue. The British ships altered course and got safely away, whilst the French, after taking possession of their prize, returned to Boston. Since the French official account represents M. de La Pérouse as fighting against odds, it is well to remember that two large and heavily-armed frigates would have a great advantage against a number of weak and small frigates, sloops, and armed ships. The British ships, if they had carronades, no doubt carried a greater weight of metal, but their scantling would be weaker, and their force was scattered in several ships.

Amongst the British killed was Captain Henry Francis Evans of the *Charleston*.

[1] *Gazette de Paris*, 406; Beatson, v. 303; Troude, ii. 119; Allen, i. 317.

[2] In the Navy List Book for June, *Charleston* appears as a 32, *Allegiance* as a 16, *Vulture* as a 16; but Steel gives the ratings as above. Allen adds to the ships given the *Rupert*, armed ship, and wrongly names the *Vulture's* commander (William) Langhorne. The *Charleston* was the American *Boston*, renamed after her capture. *Charleston's* log is missing; *Allegiance's* log makes no reference to the action. There does not seem to have been a C. M. on the loss of the *Jack*, which was therefore probably a merchantman. Possibly the *Vernon* was also a merchantman, as she does not figure in Steel's contemporary lists.

—	Tons.	Guns.	Broadside.	Men.	Killed.	Wounded.	Total.
			Lbs.				
Astrée . .	..	32	174	255	6	15?	21[1]
Hermione .	..	32	174	255	6	15?	21
		64	348	510	12	30	42
Charleston .	514	34[2]	168[2]	..	8	29	37
Allegiance .	..	24	102	..	1	5	6
Vulture . .	..	24	102	..	1	2	3
Vernon . .	..	24?	102?	..	7	6	13
Jack . . .	..	14?	42?	..	?	?	?
		120	516		17	42	59

1 French losses from *Gazette de France*, p. 407.

2 Include carronades, viz., six 18-prs. for *Charleston*, and ten 12-prs. each for *Allegiance*, *Vulture*, and *Vernon*. It is possible that they carried these guns. In any case the armaments of these ships are quite uncertain. French accounts give the *Allegiance* and *Vernon*, 24 guns, and the *Vulture*, 26. If this *Vernon* be the same as the *V.* which on Mar. 16th, 1782, with the *Success* encountered the *Sta. Catalina*, she was a 22-gun (6-pr.) ship. But there is no *Vernon* in the Navy Lists of the time.

On July 29th, the French ships *Lively*, 26, and *Hirondelle*, 16, fell in with a British fleet in the Channel, and though the *Hirondelle* got away, the *Lively* had to strike to the 36-gun frigate *Perseverance*,[1] Captain Skeffington Lutwidge, after a short but desperate defence, in which she lost six killed and ten wounded.

On July 30th, when de Grasse's fleet was entering the Chesapeake, two British ships were seen off Cape Henry and chased by the *Glorieux*, 74, and *Diligente*, 26. The British vessels, which were the *Guadaloupe*, 28, Captain Hugh Robinson, and *Loyalist*, 16, Commander Morgan Laugharne, took to flight, and the *Guadaloupe* got safely into York River. The *Loyalist*, however, was run down and captured.

In August the crews of the British line-of-battle ships *Lion* and *Canada*, which had been ordered with Admiral Digby to escort a fleet to the West Indies, refused to go on foreign service till they had received their pay, then a year in arrear.[2] Thereupon the men received six months' pay, and no longer raised any difficulty.

On the 8th of that month the American frigate *Trumbull*, 32, Captain James Nicholson, off Delaware, was sighted and chased by the British *Iris*, 32, Captain George Dawson.[3] The American was badly manned; she had a weak crew on board, and of these

1 Troude, ii. 121; Log of *Perseverance*.

2 *Gazette de France*, 305.

3 *Lond. Gazette*, Sept. 25th; Maclay, i. 142, 143; Beatson, v. 304.

many were British deserters. What her normal crew could have been is difficult to conjecture, for American writers tell us with one accord that she was two hundred men short. On the 9th there was a heavy gale which brought down the American's fore topmast and main top-gallantmast. Late in the evening, while she was thus crippled, and before the wreckage had been cleared away, the *Iris* came up. The *Trumbull's* crew showed the greatest cowardice or disaffection; they put out the battle lanterns and flew from their quarters, whilst Captain Nicholson and Lieutenants Alexander Murray and Richard Dale, with a handful of American seamen, alone fought the ship. After an hour's engagement the *Trumbull* struck her flag.

—	Tons.	Guns.	Broadside.	Men.	Killed.	Wounded.	Total.
			Lbs.				
Iris . . .	730	32[1]	156	220n	1	6	7
Trumbull .	..	32	174?	200?	5	11	16

Time, 1 hour.

[1] Carronades not included, as it is doubtful whether she carried them.

On August 7th, a brilliant display of courage and seamanship was given by Commander Francis Roberts and the crew of the *Helena*, 14.[1] Roberts had served under a good master, as he had been first Lieutenant to Captain Farmer of the *Quebec*. He ran into Gibraltar in the face of fourteen Spanish gunboats, though the weather was so calm that the *Helena's* sails were useless, and sweeps had to be employed. From the rock the hostile boats could be seen close to her, "and," it is added, "the clouds of grape and other shot that seemed almost to bury her were astonishing." Presently the British gunboats *Repulse* and *Vanguard* went to her aid, and the Spaniards fell back. The *Helena* was dreadfully cut up, but, strange to say, only lost one man.

On August 14th, the British sloop *Cameleon*, 14, Commander Thomas Drury, cruising in the North Sea, came up with and engaged a Dutch dogger of 18 guns.[2] The *Cameleon*, which carried, in addition to her gun armament, four carronades, was probably of the heavier metal. The two fought furiously at the closest

[1] *Lond. Gazette*, Sept. 18th. [2] *Ib*, Aug. 21st.

quarters for forty-five minutes, when the Dutch ship blew up, setting the *Cameleon's* sails and rigging on fire, and covering her deck with human fragments. Not one of the dogger's crew survived the explosion. The British loss was thirteen, including Commander Drury, wounded.

On August 19th, an allied expedition, under the Duc de Crillon, laid siege to Port Mahon in Minorca.[1] Serving with the British garrison was, according to the official account, a small corps of Marines and sailors, who, "being more accustomed to live on salted provisions, kept their health much better than the other troops of the garrison did." They do not appear to have numbered more than one hundred or two hundred men.

On August 24th, the armed ship *Sandwich*, 20, Commander William Bett, and sloop *Cormorant*, 14, Commander Robert M'Evoy, were captured by de Grasse's fleet off Charleston Bar.

Early in the morning of September 2nd, the British 50-gun ship *Chatham*, Captain Andrew Snape Douglas, overtook, after a long chase, the French 32-gun frigate *Magicienne*, Captain de La Bouchetière.[2] The *Magicienne* endeavoured to regain Boston, from which port she was sailing to Portsmouth, New Hampshire; but, after a desultory cannonade, she found it impossible to escape, and turned to fight a broadside action. She engaged the *Chatham* in that way for thirty minutes. The weakness of her scantling and battery, however, brought inevitable defeat, and, as usual in cases where frigates fought sail of the line, she suffered very heavy loss and inflicted little upon her enemy.

—	Tons.	Guns.	Broadside.	Men.	Killed.	Wounded.	Total.
			Lbs.				
Chatham . .	1,052	60[1]	534	350	1	1	2
Magicienne .	..	32	174	280	32	54	86

Time, 90 minutes.

[1] Including ten 24-pr. carronades, which were probably carried. In the British Navy the *Magicienne* was rated 36.

The time as given in the British accounts is thirty minutes, but this probably does not include the desultory fire carried on before the two came to close quarters.

[1] Beatson, v. 309, 363. [2] Beatson, v. 304; Troude, ii. 121.

On the 6th of September, the British sloop *Savage*, 16, Commander Charles Stirling (1), whilst cruising off Charleston, was chased and brought to action by the American privateer *Congress*, 24, of vastly superior force.[1] The *Savage*, as the enemy was so much stronger, fired at the *Congress's* rigging, hoping thus to get away. She did, indeed, compel the privateer to lie to to make repairs, but not before her hull had been wrecked by the *Congress's* broadsides. The privateer came up afresh, and, after another hour's fighting, received the surrender of the *Savage*. According to American historians—on what authority does not appear—the *Congress's* crew was largely composed of landsmen. The *Savage*, on her way to an American port, was retaken by the *Solebay*.

—	Tons.	Guns.	Broadside.	Men.	Killed.	Wounded.	Total
			Lbs.				
Congress . .	..	24	132	215	11	30	41
Savage . .	302	24[1]	96	100?	8	31	39

Time, about 2 hours.

[1] Eight carronades, 12-prs., allowed.

Rear-Admiral Thomas Graves (2), when he appeared off the Chesapeake and the French fleet put to sea to meet him, had reason to suppose that the enemy's ships had slipped, and buoyed their cables.[2] He therefore despatched the *Iris*, 32, Captain George Dawson, and *Richmond*, 32, Captain Charles Hudson, to cut away the cables from their buoys. These ships were thus engaged when, on September 11th, they were surprised by M. de Barras' squadron and compelled to strike.

Early in October a number of British ships were destroyed by the American batteries before Yorktown. On the one side was Washington's army, on the other de Grasse's fleet, so that no escape was possible. Four vessels were set on fire by hot shot on October 10th, the *Charon*, 44, Captain Thomas Symonds, *Guadaloupe*, 28, Captain Hugh Robinson, *Fowey*, 24, Captain Peter Aplin, and *Vulcan*, fireship, Commander George Palmer, in addition to some transports. In this way they were saved from the indignity

[1] Beatson, v. 305; Maclay, i. 149; C. M. wanting; Ann. Register, 1781 [251.
[2] Beatson, v. 277; Troude, ii. 122.

of a surrender to the Americans and French. The *Bonetta*, 14, Commander Ralph Dundas, was taken, however, by the French when Yorktown fell.

On October 26th, the *Hannibal*, 50, Captain Alexander Christie, whilst cruising off the Cape of Good Hope, saw and chased a fleet of merchant ships under convoy of the French *Necker*, 28.[1] The *Necker* was captured, her mainmast, foremast, and mizen-topmast going overboard just as the *Hannibal* was closing her. With one other prize the *Hannibal* arrived at St. Helena. The *Necker* was purchased into the Navy and was sent to the East Indies. Though Beatson describes her as a frigate, Troude does not mention her, and thus it is probable rather that she was an armed merchantman, or a hired privateer, than a frigate of the Royal French navy.

A marked feature of the year 1781 was the growing audacity of the privateers, French, Dutch, and American, which infested British waters.[2] Aberbrothick was cannonaded and a ransom demanded; ships were carried off from Aberdeen; French privateers cruised off Dublin and Belfast; American off Wexford; and Dutch off Flamborough Head. Amongst the privateers taken this year was the *Jackal*, 14, captured by the *Prudente*, 36. The *Jackal*, it will be remembered, had been carried off from the Downs by her crew on November 27th, 1779. Amongst the brilliant achievements of British privateers was the capture by the *Tigress*, 22,[3] T. Hall, of Appledore, of a large Dutch ship, the *Tromp*, 46, which was escorting two merchant ships.[4] They also were taken.

On January 3rd, 1782, the *Bonetta*, 14, which had been captured by the French, was retaken by the *Amphion*, 32, Captain John Bazely (1), on the American coast.[5]

On January 4th, Vice-Admiral Sir Edward Hughes, with his fleet, arrived off Trincomale, the Dutch garrison of which place had been for some time blockaded by the frigate *Seahorse*, 24.[6] A force of five hundred sepoys, a battalion of sailors, and a detachment of Marines were landed; and on the evening of the 5th the Marines carried Trincomale fort. On the 11th, Fort Oostenburg, which commanded the town and anchorage, was stormed by the sailors and Marines. The British loss was considerable, as a Lieutenant of

[1] Beatson, v. 329.
[2] Beatson, v. 401 ff., 422 ff.
[3] Six-pounders.
[4] Beatson, v. 428, 429.
[5] Beatson, v. 553.
[6] Beatson, i. 560 ff.

the *Superb*, and twenty seamen were killed, and two officers and forty men were wounded. A garrison was left in the captured forts and the British squadron withdrew.

On January 11th, the British frigate *Coventry*, 28, Captain William Wolseley, cruising in the Bay of Bengal, sailed into the midst of a French squadron on the Orissa coast, mistaking it for a fleet of British merchantmen, and was captured.[1]

On January 18th, the *Hannibal*, 50, Captain Alexander Christie, which had been detached by Commodore Johnstone to the East Indies, was seen and chased by the French fleet in the Indian Ocean.[2] Calms and unfavourable winds prevented her from making her escape, and on the 21st she was overtaken, brought to action, and compelled to strike to the *Héros*, 74, and *Artésien*, 64. A month later, on February 25th, the British sloop *Chaser*, 18, Commander Thomas Parr, was captured by the *Bellone*, 32, in the Bay of Bengal, after an action of twenty minutes.[3]

At the end of January and the beginning of February the settlements in Guiana, which had been captured by the British from the Dutch, were recaptured by a French squadron of five ships, commanded by Captain de Kersaint, in the *Iphigénie*, 32.[4] With the Colony were surrendered the following ships of the Navy: *Oronoque*, 20, Commander William Tahourdin; *Barbuda*, 16, Commander Francis Pender; *Sylph*, 18, Commander Lawrence Græme; *Stormont*, 16, Commander Christmas Paul, and *Rodney*, brig, 16, Lieutenant John Douglas Brisbane.

On March 16th, off Cape Spartel, the British frigate *Success*, 32, Captain Charles Morice Pole, and the storeship *Vernon*, 22,[5] sighted a sail right ahead, which was presently made out to be a large frigate with a poop.[6] The stranger directed her course towards the British vessels, and at about five o'clock hoisted Spanish colours. The *Success*, as the enemy closed, raked her on the lee bow, passed to windward, pouring in a vigorous fire at very short range, wore, and renewed the attack on her lee quarter. The Spaniards,

[1] Troude, ii. 225; Chevalier, 452.

[2] Beatson, v. 568; Troude, ii. 167; *Gazette de France*, 1782, 300.

[3] Troude, ii. 203; Beatson, v. 569.

[4] *Gazette de France*, 185; Troude, i. 212–219; C. M., 59.

[5] The *Vernon* did not belong to the Navy. Her master's name was John Falconer.—W. L. C.

[6] *Lond. Gazette*, Mar. 30th; *Gazette de France*, 173; Log of *Success*.

who had expected the British ship to engage broadside to broadside, were taken aback by this manœuvre and fell into confusion. According to the Spanish accounts the British ships had made their approach under the Dutch flag,[1] and just as a Spanish officer was about to speak them, hauled down the false colours and sent the true ones, opening fire simultaneously. The *Vernon* gave the *Success* good support, and at about 8.20 A.M. the enemy struck. She

SIR CHARLES MORICE POLE, BART., ADMIRAL OF THE FLEET.

(*From H. R. Cook's engraving after the portrait by J. Northcote, R.A.*)

proved to be the *Santa Catalina*, 34, Captain Don Miguel Jacon.[2] He had been especially ordered to look out for the *Success*, and had already chased her twice. He complained no little of the behaviour of his crew. The details of the ships were as follows—for though the Spaniards made the *Success* out a 24-pr. 38-gun frigate, there

[1] This is corroborated by the log.

[2] The log calls him Joron; Schomberg, Jacen, and the *Gazette*, Jacon.

were then none such in the Navy, and their estimate was an exaggeration.[1]

—	Tons.	Guns.	Men.	Broadside.	Killed.	Wounded.	Total.
				Lbs.			
Success . .	683	40 [1]	290n	246 [1]	1	4	5
Vernon . .	?	22	100?	66	0	1	1
Sta. Catalina	?	34	339	180	25–30	8	33–38

[1] Carronades included.

The *Sta. Catalina* was a much larger and finer ship than the *Success*, as the following figures will show:—

	Length of Deck.	Beam.
Success	126 ft.	35 ft. 2 in.
Sta. Catalina	151 ft.	39 ft. 4 in.

but she was palpably under-armed. Her hull was terribly shattered, being, according to Captain Pole's letter, "like a sieve, the shot going thro' both sides." Her mizenmast fell before she struck, and her mainmast afterwards. So damaged was she that when, on the 18th, other supposed hostile sail were seen, Captain Pole decided to set her on fire. This was accordingly done, after the prize crew and prisoners had been removed. The strange sail, however, proved to be the British ships *Apollo*, 32, and *Cerberus*, 28, with a convoy. The *Success* underwent some danger on her voyage home in consequence of the great number of prisoners whom she had on board.

In the winter of 1871, and spring of 1782, the *Leander*, 50, Captain Thomas Shirley, and the *Alligator*, 14, Commander John Frodsham, were engaged in operations against the Dutch forts on the Gold Coast.[2] Between February 16th and 21st unsuccessful attacks were made on Elmina. Aided by troops who were disembarked from his ships Captain Shirley took Mouree (March 2nd), Commendah (March 6th), Apam (March 16th), Barracoe (March 23rd), and Accra (March 30th).[3]

[1] The 38-gun frigates of the time mounted 18, not 24-prs.

[2] *Lond. Gazette*, July 9th; Log of *Leander*.

[3] Mouree, near Cape Coast Castle; Commendah or Cormantyne, some miles to the west; Apam, east of Cape Coast Castle; Barracoe, between Apam and Accra further to the east again. They will all be found on an old map of West Africa: Brit. Museum, 63690.

On April 8th, the *General Monk*, 18, Commander Josias Rogers, whilst operating in Delaware Bay, was unfortunate enough to be captured. Aided by a 16-gun privateer she had driven a 16-gun American ship on shore, and had taken a brig of 14 guns, when she was engaged by the Pennsylvanian ship *Hyder Ali*, 18.[1] The *General Monk* was armed almost entirely with 9-pr. carronades, and those, at the range the *Hyder Ali* selected, were quite useless.

COMMEMORATIVE MEDAL OF THE DEFENCE OF GIBRALTAR, 1779–83.

(*From an original lent by Capt. H.S.H. Prince Louis of Battenberg, R.N.*)

Moreover they were badly mounted and upset on being fired. The British ship was compelled to strike.

—	Tons.	Guns.	Men.	Broadside.	Killed.	Wounded.	Total.
				Lbs.			
Hyder Ali .	?	18	130	78	4	11	15
General Monk	?	18[1]	110	78	8	29	37

[1] Sixteen 9-pr. carronades, two 6-pr. cannons.

On April 11th, the armed cutter *Jackal*, 20, Lieutenant Gustavus Logie, was captured in the West Indies by the American *Deane*, 32, otherwise known as the *Hague*.

On April 20th, Vice-Admiral the Hon. Samuel Barrington, who was cruising off Brest with twelve sail of the line and three frigates,

[1] Beatson, v. 555.

watching for a French convoy which was to sail for the East Indies, came within sight of a hostile squadron and signalled a general chase.[1] The 80-gun ship *Foudroyant*, which had the honour of being the largest two-decked vessel in the British Navy, and which was commanded by Captain John Jervis, quickly outstripped the rest of her consorts. By nightfall she got sufficiently close to discover that the French squadron consisted of "three or four warships, besides eighteen vessels under convoy." The warships were the 74's *Pégase* and *Protecteur*; the 32-gun frigate *Andromaque*; and another frigate and the *Actionnaire*, 64, equipped as storeships. The other vessels of the British fleet were almost out of sight, when Captain Jervis made up his mind to pursue the *Pégase*, the largest of the French ships. He cleared for action, and, as the night was dark and it was difficult to keep the chase in sight, ordered Midshipman Richard Bowen[2] to the forecastle with directions not to take his eyes off her. At midnight the *Foudroyant* was near enough to her enemy to make out that she was a ship of the line. The other French 74—the *Protecteur*—was too far off to give her consort any support, and the way was open for the *Foudroyant*. The Frenchman put his helm up, and endeavoured at the outset of the action to rake the British ship, but, owing to the smartness of young Bowen, the *Foudroyant* anticipated this manœuvre, put her helm to port, passed under the Frenchman's stern, and raked her with deadly effect. The French captain, de Sillans, had failed to make use of his stern-chasers, though for nearly four hours the *Foudroyant* had been within their range. He had not been able to place small-arms'-men in the rigging and tops, nor to get the grappling-irons into position. Though his crew had suffered heavily from the British fire, and though his ship had sustained considerable damage, he attempted to board his antagonist.[3] His attempt was made without sufficient preparation and determination; everyone was summoned on deck, the batteries between decks being thus abandoned; and the result was a repulse. The British then

[1] Tucker's 'Life of St. Vincent,' i. 71–76; 'Dictionary of National Biography,' article, 'John Jervis'; Chevalier, 330–334; Beatson, v. 656; Report of Barrington, *Lond. Gazette*, Apr. 27th, May 4th; *Gazette de France*, 189. This affair is briefly alluded to in chap. xxxi.

[2] Richard Bowen, born, 1761; Lieutenant, 1782; Commander and Captain, 1794; won great fame as a frigate captain; fell at Santa Cruz, July 24th, 1797.—W. L. C.

[3] One of the judges at the court-martial held M. de Sillans's manœuvres to be so bold, that with a better crew he would infallibly have captured his enemy. Chevalier, i. 333.

boarded, laying the *Foudroyant* along the French ship's port side, and, headed by Bowen, carried her easily, a little after one o'clock.

The action was in many ways surprising. The *Foudroyant* was, it is true, of superior metal, having an advantage of about one-eighth in weight of broadside, but that advantage would not be expected to give her the victory with such trifling loss as she actually sustained. No one was killed on board her; and the wounded, amongst whom was Captain Jervis, were only five. A desperate resistance was to be looked for from a French line-of-battle ship, at a time when France had, in single-ship actions, fairly held her own. But the truth was that the *Pégase* had been built and sent to sea in the extremest haste.[1] She had only been launched on April 11th; on the 13th M. de Sillans had taken command; on the 19th she had left Brest. She was very heavily laden and could not open her lower-deck ports. As a further disadvantage her personnel was exceedingly bad. A young sub-lieutenant of nineteen commanded her lower-deck battery, and her men were raw landsmen, as sailors could not be found. When she fought the *Foudroyant* her quarters' bill had not been drawn up. Her captain had doubtless made mistakes, but, though he was suspended from command by the sentence of the French court-martial, his superiors, who sent him out, must bear some part of the blame for the loss of the ship. A vessel sent to sea in war-time should be in a state to uphold the honour of her flag when she puts out, and should certainly not be manned by landsmen.

The comparative force of the two ships was as follows :—

—	Tons.	Guns.	Broadside.	Men.	Killed.	Wounded.	Total.
			Lbs.				
Foudroyant .	1,979	88	1,020[1]	719	0	5	5
Pégase . .	1,778	74	838[2]	700	80	40	120

Time, 45 minutes.[3]

[1] The *Foudroyant* is assumed to have carried the ordinary armament for 80-gun ships, viz., thirty 32's thirty-two 24's, and eighteen 12's. She had probably, in addition, four 12-pr. carronades.

[2] French shot were also one twelfth heavier than their nominal weight, which would bring the broadside of the *Pégase* to about 900 lbs. See James, 'Naval History,' i. 45.

[3] [According to Chevalier (i. 330) and M. de Sillans (*Gazette de France*, 189) the *Pégase* did not strike till 3 A.M. in which case the action lasted three hours. Barrington's letter gives the time as 45 minutes.

[1] The *Pégase* was laid down, built, completed, and at sea in three months and five days; thus surpassing the record of the *Couronne*, which was laid down on May 17, 1781, and was cruising with de Guichen in December. See 'Parliamentary History,

After the action the *Pégase's* mizen mast and fore topmast went overboard. On the morning of the 21st, other ships of the squadron came up, and Captain Jervis was able to put eighty men into his prize, and to withdraw forty from her. More he could not take on board owing to the heavy sea. The *Queen*, however, came to the assistance of the *Pégase*, took three hundred prisoners on board, and placed forty more men on the prize. Next morning a fresh sail was seen and chased by the *Queen*. After some hours the British ship came up with the stranger, which proved to be the store-ship *Actionnaire*. She received a broadside, and then struck, with thirty-four men killed or wounded. She was bound for Mauritius with masts, sails, rigging, and stores for the French squadron in the East Indies, and with five hundred and fifty soldiers. Of the convoy, ten were taken and sent safely into British ports.[1] In this ignominious rout ended the second attempt of the French to despatch a convoy to India; the *Protecteur* only, with three or four ships, succeeding in evading the vigilance of the British observing squadron.

For his victory Captain Jervis was rewarded with a K.B., and permitted to bear on his coat-of-arms a winged horse.

On May 8th, the British governor of the Bahamas was obliged to capitulate to an overwhelming Spanish force, which was aided also by a considerable number of Americans.

On June 26th, the *Alligator*, 14, Commander John Frodsham, whilst carrying dispatches home from West Africa, was chased off the Lizard by the French frigate *Fée*, 32, and taken.[2] The *Alligator* defended herself with great courage and held out to the last. She lost three killed and sixteen wounded.

On July 29th, whilst cruising on the American coast, the *Santa Margarita*, 36, Captain Elliot Salter, was chased by the French frigate *Amazone*, 36. The British frigate made all sail away,

---

xxii. 902. At Brest France had three thousand shipwrights at that time, whilst Portsmouth only employed eight hundred, and British ships were often three or four years on the stocks.

[1] The names were *Lion*, *Grand Sarpedon*, *Bellone*, *Fidelité*, *Duc de Chartres*, *Superbe*, *Honore*, *Villa Nova*, *Amphion* and *Chalnour*. The *Marquis of Castries*, which is included in some lists, was not taken with this convoy, but later: see Beatson, v. 659. Lapeyrouse, iii. 259, gives the transports captured as twelve in number.

[2] *Gazette de France*, 265; *Lond. Gazette*, July 9th; C. M., 59, Aug. 7th. According to evidence there given the *Fée* carried four 18-pr. carronades.

for astern of the Frenchman several other warships could be made out. About the middle of the afternoon these other ships were lost to sight; and at the request of the crew, Captain Salter tacked and stood to meet the *Amazone*, which did not decline the fight. The battle opened at five, the two ships closing gradually to within pistol shot. At that range they fought for an hour and a quarter before the *Amazone* struck, with her captain killed, half her men killed or wounded, four feet of water in the hold, and her masts and rigging very much cut up. The main and mizen masts fell just as the flag was hauled down. The force of the two ships was as follows:—

—	Tons.	Guns.	Broadside.	Men.	Killed.	Wounded.	Total.
			Lbs.				
Santa Margarita[1] . .	992	44	258	247	5	17	22
Amazone . .	..	36	186	301	70	70–80	150

[1] Troude gives the *Sta. Margarita*, 38 guns and 10 carronades and calls her an 18-pr. frigate. This is a ridiculous exaggeration, as the List Book shows her to have been a 36-gun ship, and James, i. 366, proves her a 12-pr. frigate. At the same time Troude probably understates the armament of the *Amazone*. He gives her no 6-prs. and only twenty-six 12's. Capt. Salter's letter gives her ten 6's, and these I have allowed in the table. The *Sta. Margarita* probably carried eight 18-pr. carronades.

The British frigate was severely wounded in masts and rigging, but otherwise suffered little injury. A lieutenant and sixty-eight men were sent to take possession of the prize, which was taken in tow. Although all possible sail had been made, Captain Salter was chagrined next morning to discover the enemy's fleet in sight. In these circumstances he had no alternative but to recall his men from the prize and abandon her to the enemy. This was done, and he safely effected his retreat.

On July 30th, the *Cormorant*, 16, Commander John Melcomb, captured the French sloop *Téméraire*, 10, some days out from Brest with dispatches.[1]

At the end of May a French expedition under M. de La Pérouse sailed from Hayti for Hudson's Bay, which it entered, after sustaining some damage and being in imminent danger in the ice, on July 17th.[2] It was composed of the *Sceptre*, 74, *Astrée*, 36, and *Engageante*, 36, with 290 soldiers on board. On August 8th,

[1] Beatson, v. 675.

[2] *Gazette de France*, 413; Beatson, v. 540; Troude, ii. 220; Annual Register, 1783, 116 ff.

it arrived off Fort Churchill. The governor of the fort, panic-stricken, surrendered without sending information of the coming of the French to the other stations. Having destroyed the fort, the French sailed for Fort York at the mouth of the Nelson, which they surprised and captured in the same way. There, too, the governor, who might have made a successful resistance, displayed only discreditable cowardice, and surrendered at the first parley. The French landing party had to wade ashore through nearly a mile of soft mud, far out of the reach of the covering squadron. They had then to enter the trackless forests and to cross a marsh six miles wide. The fort was burnt, and the troops re-embarked. M. de La Pérouse, with a kindness and humanity rare in the annals of war, left a certain quantity of ammunition and provisions for some of the British, who had fled to the woods. A Hudson's Bay Company's ship in those lonely waters was all but taken by the French, but succeeded in making her escape.

On August 11th, the British sloops *Swift* and *Speedy* were captured by the French frigates *Friponne* and *Résolue*,[1] according to Troude. British authorities do not notice this, and the *Speedy* appeared in the Navy List for long afterwards.

On August 12th, the British frigate *Coventry*, 28, Captain Andrew Mitchell (1), whilst on her way from Bombay to join Hughes's squadron of Ceylon, fell in with the French *Bellone* of 32 guns, Captain de Piervert.[2] The two closed and fought a desperate but indecisive action for two or two and a half hours, early in which the French captain fell. The second and third officers of the *Bellone* disputed as to the command, and meanwhile the French ship was paralysed. Each side accuses the other of retiring; the British Captain alleging that the *Bellone* was only saved by the arrival of the main French fleet. Both ships sustained severe damage and heavy loss.

—	Tons.	Guns.	Broadside.	Men.	Killed.	Wounded.	Total.
Coventry . .	599	28[1]	Lbs. 120?	200	15	29	44
Bellone . .	..	32	174?	..	?	?	?

[1] Troude calls her a 30-gun ship and gives her twenty-six 12's and four 6's. He gives her no carronades. But our 28's were usually 9-pr. ships and with carronades the broadside would be 174 lbs.: without, 120 lbs. British accounts give *Bellone* 48 guns; Troude, twenty-six 12's and six 6's.

[1] Troude, ii. 205. [2] *Ib.*; Beatson, v. 596.

On September 1st, the British 18-gun sloop *Duc de Chartres*, Commander John Child Purvis (1),[1] captured the 22-gun *Aigle*, described as a corvette in the French navy, off the American coast. As the only *Aigle* in the French navy which the author can trace was a 40-gun frigate, it is probable that this sloop was a hired craft.

On September 4th, the British ship *Rainbow*, 44, Captain Henry Trollope, cruising off the Ile de Bas, sighted and chased a large French frigate, the *Hébé*, 40, Captain de Vigny.[2] The *Rainbow* opened on her with her bow-chasers. The enemy responded from her stern-chasers, but as the *Rainbow* closed, the *Hébé* luffed, fired a broadside, and, to the great surprise of Captain Trollope, struck. It appeared that the 32-lb. shot from the *Rainbow's* bow-chaser carronades had fallen on board the *Hébê*, and that their size led Captain de Vigny to suppose he was dealing with a vessel of the line. The *Rainbow* was armed entirely with carronades, of which she had twenty 68-prs., twenty-two 42-prs., and six 32-prs., against the *Hébé's* twenty-eight long 18-prs. and twelve long 8-prs. At close quarters, therefore, the *Rainbow* would have had an enormous advantage.

—	Tons.	Guns.	Broadside.	Men.	Killed.	Wounded.	Total.
			Lbs.				
Rainbow . .	831	50	1,238	297n	1[1]	0	1
Hébé . . .	1,063	40[2]	335	360	5	?	5?

[1] Killed by accident.

[2] Troude, 38 guns, as also Charnock. The dimensions of the two ships were—

	Length.	Beam.	Depth.
Rainbow	133 ft.	37 ft. 10¼ in.	16 ft.
Hebé	150 ft.	39 ft. 11 in.	12 ft. 10 in.

Captain de Vigny was court-martialled for misbehaviour, and cashiered and sentenced to fifteen years' imprisonment for his conduct. The *Hébé's* only injury was a wound to her foremast and some damage to her wheel.

At the end of July, Rear-Admiral Graves, with the *Ramillies*, *Canada*, and *Centaur*, all 74's, and the *Pallas*, 32,[3] left Jamaica with a large convoy, consisting of the sail of the line captured on

[1] Capt. Purvis was, in consequence, posted as from Sept. 1.—W. L. C.

[2] Beatson, v. 675, vi. 379; James, i. 40; Troude, 206; Log of *Rainbow*.

[3] Annual Register, 1783, [121; Hood's Letters, 138; Beatson, v. 495–525; *Gazette de France*, 429; Troude, ii. 207.

April 12th from the French fleet by Rodney—*Ville de Paris*, 110, *Glorieux*, 74, *Hector*, 74, *Jason*, *Caton*, and *Ardent*, all 64's—and of some 180 homeward bound merchantmen. Both the *Ardent* and *Jason* had almost at once to put back owing to their very leaky condition. The others joined Rodney's fleet off Havana on August 14th, and lost it during the night. Part of the convoy was bound for New York, the rest for England, and so the course steered was a northerly one. On August 22nd, the *Hector*, Captain John Bourchier, being in a miserable state, shattered, leaky, and with a crew of but 223 men, of whom many were sickly, dropped astern. On September 4th, she was sighted by two very powerful French frigates, the *Aigle*, 40, Captain La Touche-Tréville, and *Gloire*, 32, Captain de Vallongue. They chased her during the night, and, noting that she only mounted fifty-two guns and that, from the want of men, she was very feebly handled, brought her to close action at about 2 A.M., one on the bow and the other on the quarter. A three or four hours' engagement followed, in which the *Hector*, in spite of her weakness, showed herself a formidable antagonist. Captain La Touche-Tréville made one attempt to board, but was repulsed. The resistance of the *Hector* was almost as creditable as was, years later, that of the *Leander*. Both ships were manned by seamen from a victorious fleet. At last the two French ships retired, leaving the *Hector* in a very battered condition, with all the masts wounded and the hull very leaky. The excuse for their retreat was that other British sails could be seen on the horizon. This, however, was incorrect.

—	Tons.	Guns.	Broadside.	Men.	Killed.	Wounded.	Total.
			Lbs.				
Hector . .	..	52	400?	223	9	33	42
Aigle . . .	1,002	40[1]	384	500	5	11	16
Gloire . .	..	32	174	255 n			

Time, 3 hours.

[1] Twenty-eight 24's and twelve 8's. She was the finest frigate in the French navy. Both frigates had many troops on board.

Amongst the severely wounded was the British captain, Bourchier. After the action the water gained so on the pumps that the hold filled and the provisions spoiled. A terrible scene followed. The officers with swords and pistols kept the failing seamen to the pumps, at which several men dropped dead. After incredible sufferings the remnant of this heroic crew was rescued by a gallant privateersman, Hill of the *Hawke*, a Dartmouth snow. At imminent risk to his own small craft, he embarked the *Hector's* men, and reached St. John's in safety with them.

The other warships of Graves's squadron were equally unfortunate. In a gale on September 8th the *Caton* sprang a leak, and, with the *Pallas*, was ordered to put back to Halifax, where both arrived. On September 16th, the fleet and convoy, then ninety sail strong, were off the Banks of Newfoundland, when a terrific E.S.E. gale caught them, rising steadily during the evening and night, till, early in the morning, a furious N.N.W. squall succeeded. The sudden shift of the wind was disastrous to the fleet. The *Ramillies* lost her main, mizen, and foretop masts. A perfect deluge of water descended; the seas swept the deck; on all sides signals of distress were flying; and there was scarcely a man-of-war which was not dismasted and foundering. At 10 A.M. of the 9th, the *Ramillies*, with fifteen feet of water in her hold, was abandoned and set on fire, her crew taking to the boats. The *Ville de Paris* and *Glorieux* were never seen again. A seaman, floating on a mass of wreckage, was picked up by a Danish merchant ship. He had been in the *Ville de Paris*, had seen the *Glorieux* sink, and could tell nothing more. Memory had left him. The *Centaur* lost all her masts and her rudder. When she heeled in the squall, the water in the hold burst up between decks, and the ship became a water-logged hulk, settling slowly. The tale of those who survived is one of the most piteous records of human agony—mental and physical. Her captain, John Nicholson Inglefield, untrue to the greatest traditions of our Navy, which ordain that the Captain shall be the last to quit his ship, at whatsoever peril to himself, left her in a pinnace with eleven others, and, after enduring incredible tortures, reached the Azores sixteen days later. The *Canada*—one suspects very skilfully handled by such a captain as Cornwallis—lost her mizenmast, but reached Great Britain, though leaking heavily. The *Jason* arrived in a similar condition.

That the men-of-war must have been in a dilapidated condition is evident from the fact that the losses of the convoy were by no means so heavy. The captured vessels would naturally be in bad order. The *Ramillies* was an old craft—built in 1763—and had been some time on the station; the *Centaur*, built in 1759, was even worse. But such was our want of ships that these vessels had to be employed.

On September 9th, four East Indiamen and "country ships" beat off the French frigate *Pourvoyeuse*, 40, in the Straits of Malacca.

On September 12th, the French frigates *Aigle* and *Gloire* chased and captured the British 14-gun brig *Racoon*, Lieut. Edmund Nagle.[1] On the same day they were chased by a British squadron under Captain the Hon. George Keith Elphinstone, composed of the *Warwick*, 50, *Lion*, 64, *Vestal*, 28, and *Bonetta*, 14. On the 13th, the two Frenchmen entered the Delaware by a shallow and difficult channel, whither Captain Elphinstone followed them. On the 14th, after a desperate pursuit, the *Aigle* ran aground in shallow water. The *Vestal* and *Bonetta* placed themselves on her quarter, the *Sophie*, a prize captured from the French, took station under her stern; and, unable to make any reply, the *Aigle* struck, not, however, without Captain La Touche-Tréville having cut away his masts and bored through the bottom of his ship. She was got off and repaired by her captors. The *Gloire*, of lighter draught, escaped up the river. La Touche-Tréville was made prisoner and taken to Great Britain.

On October 14th, Captain George William Augustus Courtenay of the *Eurydice*, 24, captured the French 14-gun brig *Samea* (*sic*), of one hundred and six men. At about the same time the *Jackal*, 14, captured the French lugger *Sylph*.[2]

On October 17th, the *London*, 98, Captain James Kempthorne, *Torbay*, 74, Captain John Lewis Gidoin, and the sloop *Badger*, 14, sighted and chased two strange sail off San Domingo.[3] These were the *Scipion*, 74, Captain de Grimoard, and the 40-gun frigate *Sibylle*, both French vessels. The *London*, in the course of the afternoon, drew up with the *Scipion*, and a running fight began, both ships using their chasers, and the *London* yawing from time to time to bring her broadside to bear. The *Sibylle* kept on the *London's* bows, and maintained a galling fire. At 8.30 P.M. the *London* got close enough to use her broadside with effect. For twenty minutes the two fought, and then fell on board one another,

[1] Beatson, v. 548 ff.; Troude, ii. 209; *Lond. Gazette*, Nov. 12th.

[2] *Lond. Gazette*, Oct. 19th. Not in Troude; probably the *Samea* and *Sylph* were privateers or armed ships. This *Jackal* was a cutter, commanded by Lieut. Daniel Dobrée.

[3] Beatson, v. 526 ff.; *Gazette de France*, 489; Troude, ii. 210; C. M., 60, Nov. 26th, which also gives extracts from logs.

the *Scipion's* larboard cathead being abreast of the *London's* starboard gangway. When the *Scipion* got clear, the small-arms' fire of both ships had, in the few minutes during which the ships were locked together, wrought terrible ravages amongst the men at the upper deck guns. The *Scipion* passed astern of the *London* and raked her, shooting away her weather tiller-rope and fore-yard arm, and wounding her mizenmast. Thus disabled, the *London* all but fell on board the *Torbay*, which had come up on the French ship's larboard quarter and opened fire. Both ships were much delayed, and the *Scipion* was given a start. The *Torbay* and the *London*, as soon as it was possible to wear her, resumed the pursuit, and exchanged some shots with her and with the *Sibylle* during the night, but the two-decker was able to get away. Closely pursued, she entered Samana Bay on the morning of the 18th, and was just anchoring there when she struck a rock and sank. Her behaviour in the action with, and her escape from, two such powerful ships as the *London* and *Torbay* were most creditable to her. The *Sibylle* easily effected her escape.

—	Tons.	Guns.	Broadside.	Men.	Killed.	Wounded.	Total.
			Lbs.				
London . .	1,894	98[1]	1018	743 n.	11	72	83
Torbay . .	1,572	82	828	594 n.	?	?	?
Scipion . .	..	74	828	734 n.	15	43	58
Sibylle . .	..	32	174	275 n.	?	?	?

[1] The *London* is described as a 90-gun ship, but Charnock, Steel, and the French authorities call her a 98. Here she has been reckoned as a 98 with 10 carronades.

A court of inquiry into Captain Kempthorne's behaviour acquitted him honourably.

Troude mentions the capture, during October, of the *Molly*, 18, off Madeira, by the French corvette *Sémillante*, 18.

On December 6th, Rear-Admiral Sir Richard Hughes (3) fell in with a small French squadron off Barbados; and the *Ruby*, 64, Captain John Collins, succeeded in bringing the *Solitaire*, 64, Captain Chevalier de Borda, to close action at about 1.30 P.M.[1] After a stout fight, the French ship struck, as a second vessel of the line was coming up to the help of the *Ruby*.

[1] Troude, 211; Beatson, v. 480.

—	Tons.	Guns.	Broadside.	Men.	Killed.	Wounded.	Total.
			Lbs.				
Ruby . . .	1,369	72	648	491 n.	..	2	2
Solitaire . .	1,521	64	510	589 n.	over 20	35	55

At the same time, the French 18-gun sloop *Amphitrite* was captured.[1] The *Solitaire* was purchased for the Navy, and kept her old name.

On December 12th, Captain the Hon. John Luttrell, in the *Mediator*, 44, sighted five French and American vessels, mostly storeships or vessels armed *en flûte*, and bound for the West Indies. They shortened sail and waited for him, on which he bore down, captured the *Alexandre*, mounting twenty-four 9-prs.; then, resuming the chase, got possession of two more large ships, the *Eugène* and *Menagère*, without the loss of a man in the *Mediator*. The *Alexandre's* captain, when a prisoner in the *Mediator*, attempted to foment a mutiny, for which he was placed in irons.

On December 20th, a British squadron, consisting of the *Diomede*, 44, Captain Thomas Lenox Frederick, *Quebec*, 32, and *Astræa*, 32, off the Delaware, fell in with the South Carolinan frigate *South Carolina*.[2] After an eighteen hours' chase, the *Diomede*, seconded by the *Quebec*, closed the American, which fought for two hours, and then, as the *Astræa* was coming up fast, struck. The *South Carolina* carried an extraordinarily heavy battery for a frigate—twenty-eight 32-prs., and twelve 12-prs.

—	Tons.	Guns.	Broadside.	Men.	Killed.	Wounded.	Total.
			Lbs.				
{ *Diomede* . .	891	54	438	297 n.	?	?	?
{ *Quebec* . .	699	40	246	217 n.	?	?	?
South Carolina	..	40	520	450	?	?	6

On January 2nd, 1783, the British ships *Endymion*, 44, and *Magicienne*, 36, Captain Thomas Graves (3), chased a French convoy, in charge of the *Sibylle*, 32, Captain Kergariou Locmaria,

[1] Possibly a privateer, as another *Amphitrite* appears in the French navy a few weeks later.

[2] Beatson, 551. He gives the *South Carolina*, 42-prs., not 32-prs. She was 160 ft. long. Logs of *Diomede* and *Quebec*.

and *Railleur*, 14, off San Domingo.[1] The *Magicienne* quickly outstripped her consort and overhauled the two French ships. She gave the *Railleur* two broadsides, and then closed with the *Sibylle*, at about 2 P.M. Almost at once she lost her foremast. The two frigates lay so close together that their sides touched, and the men fought from their ports with pikes and rammers. At 2.30 the *Magicienne's* remaining masts followed her foremast, and she was left helpless. At about the same time Captain Kergariou was wounded. The *Sibylle* drew ahead and made off, as the *Endymion* was fast coming up. She succeeded in escaping. The *Railleur* got away for the time, but was taken on January 11th by the *Cyclops*, 28, on the American coast. The armament of the *Sibylle* is disputed. British authorities describe her as a 36-gun ship,[2] French, as a 32. Accepting the French version her defence was exceedingly creditable.

—	Tons.	Guns.	Broadside.	Men.	Killed.	Wounded.	Total.
			Lbs.				
Sibylle . .	..	32	174	275 n.	13	38	51
Magicienne .	..	44	258	270 n.	18	31	49

Time, 90 minutes.

On January 19th, in the West Indies, the *Leander*, 50, Captain John Willett Payne, with a convoy in charge, fell in with a hostile 74-gun ship.[3] In spite of the weakness of his command, with a temerity that merits the epithet of glorious, Captain Payne pursued his enemy and closed with her early in the morning of the 19th. A desperate action of two hours' duration followed, in which the *Leander* was, as might be expected, reduced to a wreck, her rigging in particular being terribly cut up. Her crew, however, repulsed all attempts to board. The *Leander* was three times set on fire by burning wads from the stranger, but each time the fires were extinguished. Finally the two separated, and at

[1] Troude, ii. 257; Beatson, v. 531.

[2] Admiral Digby's letter describes her as a 36-gun ship, with 350 men. The *Hussar's* log makes her a 38.

[3] Beatson, v. 482; Log of *Leander*. No notice in French authorities. James, ii. 268, calls the French ship the *Pluton*, Capt. de Rions, a 74, and gives the French loss as five killed and eleven wounded. He states that the *Pluton* was partially disabled. My own belief is that the hostile ship of the line was, as asserted in the *Leander's* log, a Spaniard. Beatson gives no authority for his statement that she was the *Couronne*. French gunnery was capable of inflicting much more damage.

daybreak neither could discover the other. Beatson calls the stranger the *Couronne*.

—	Tons.	Guns.	Broadside.	Men.	Killed.	Wounded.	Total.
			Lbs.				
Leander . .	1,044	60[1]	534	350	7	12[2]	19
Stranger . .	?	80 ?	900 ?	940 ?	?	?	?

Time, 2 hours 20 minutes.

[1] Carronades included. The Stranger's broadside is calculated as that of an 18-pr. ship. In the *Leander's* log the enemy is said to have been a Spanish 74.

[2] Several mortally.

Most of the *Leander's* wounded died of their injuries.

On January 6th, as soon as the *Sibylle* had completed her repairs after her action with the *Magicienne*, she was caught by a storm and totally dismantled.[1] Jury masts had been rigged, and she was beating up the American coast, when, on January 22nd, the British frigate *Hussar*, 28, Captain Thomas Macnamara Russell, sighted her off the Chesapeake. Twelve of the *Sibylle's* guns had been thrown overboard, so that she was in no situation to resist her antagonist. She tried to escape by hoisting British over French colours, and also, it is alleged, by a misuse of the signals of distress. The *Hussar* closed her, supposing her disabled, when suddenly the *Sibylle* fired a broadside at the British frigate, and ran on board her. Before the French could board, however, the *Hussar* drew clear and opened fire. After an hour's action the *Sibylle* tried to make off, but was hotly pursued and again brought to action. Her magazine was flooded by shot-wounds below the water-line, so that further resistance became impossible, and she was forced to strike. Owing to Captain Kergariou's very questionable behaviour, Captain Russell broke his sword and placed him in close confinement. The British ships *Centurion*, 50, and *Harrier*, 18, were close at hand when the *Sibylle* surrendered; and the *Centurion* actually gave her a broadside. Twelve guns were thrown overboard during the chase, so that when she struck she had only eight pieces left.

—	Tons.	Guns.	Broadside.	Men.	Killed.	Wounded.	Total.
			Lbs.				
Hussar . .	586	34	168	200 n.	?	?	?
Sibylle . .	..	20	?	200 ?	?	?	?

[1] Troude, 238; Beatson, v. 553, vi. 349; *Gazette de Paris*, 177; Log of *Hussar*.

On January 30th, the Dutch 50-gun East Indiaman *Vrijheid* was captured under the guns of Cuddalore, on the Indian coast, by the boats of the *Medea*, 28, Captain Erasmus Gower.[1] The *Vrijheid* was unfortunately wrecked soon after her capture.

On February 16th, the *Argo*, 44, Captain John Butchart, was unfortunate enough to be discovered and chased by the French frigates *Nymphe*, 36, Captain Vicomte de Mortemart, and *Amphitrite*, 32, Captain de St. Ours, whilst attempting to replace a sprung main topmast.[2] At 10.30 A.M. the *Amphitrite* opened the action, and, a little later, gained a position on the *Argo's* starboard quarter. The *Argo's* lower deck ports could not be opened, owing to the sea that was running and to their small height above the water-line; and she was hard pressed. The *Amphitrite* next gained a position on her larboard quarter, and a steady fight continued until 5 P.M., when the *Nymphe* came up and the *Argo* struck. Her main topmast—a new one, it would appear—had been shot away, her rigging much cut up, and she had been badly hulled between wind and water. On February 19th, she was chased and recaptured by the *Invincible*, 74, Captain Charles Saxton, the *Amphitrite* and *Nymphe* effecting their escape. In the British accounts the *Concorde*, 40, is substituted for the *Amphitrite*.

—	Tons.	Guns.	Broadside.	Men.	Killed.	Wounded.	Total.
			Lbs.				
Amphitrite .	..	32	174	255 n	0	0	0
Nymphe . .	..	36	186?	301 n	?	?	?
Argo . . .	879	54	405	297 n	13	?	13?

On February 15th, the French frigate *Concorde*, 32,[3] Captain de Clesmeur, whilst in company with the *Triton*, 64, and *Amphion*, 50, was chased by a British squadron in the West Indies. The other two escaped, but the *Concorde* was overhauled and captured by the *St. Albans*, 64, Captain Charles Inglis (1).

On March 2nd, the *Resistance*, 44, Captain James King, and *Duguay Trouin*, 14, Captain John Fish, overtook and captured the

[1] Beatson, v. 606.

[2] Troude, ii. 240; Beatson, v. 483. The Log of the *Argo* was split to pieces by a shot, but a copy remains. C. M. missing.

[3] Troude, 242; Schomberg, ii. 136; Log of *St. Albans* gives her 44 guns and 399 men.

French frigate *Coquette*, 28,[1] Captain the Marquis de Grasse-Briançon.[2] Learning from his prisoners that the French had seized and occupied Turk's Island, Captain King informed Captain Horatio Nelson of the *Albemarle*, 28. Reinforced by the *Drake*, 14, the ships landed one hundred and sixty-seven men on the island under Commander Charles Dixon of the *Drake*, but the attack was repulsed, and the ships lost eight wounded.

On April 14th, the French corvette *Naïade*, 20, Captain de Villaret-Joyeuse, was chased in the East Indies by the British 64-gun ship *Sceptre*, Captain Samuel Graves (2), and captured after two hours' desperate resistance.[3] She lost two topmasts, her wheel shot away, and seven guns dismounted. According to Villaret-Joyeuse's report, the *Sceptre* had her mainmast damaged, her main topmast shot away, and twenty-four officers and men killed or wounded, whereas the *Naïade* lost not a man. The *Sceptre's* log, however, shows that only the mizenmast was wounded. This was a most honourable and creditable defence on the part of the French.

There is great difficulty in obtaining accurate and detailed information of many of the minor actions in the period of the American War. The Captains' letters, giving the official version, were usually published in the *Gazette*, and were thence transcribed almost literally by the writers Beatson and Schomberg. But these letters are often curiously unreliable, and almost invariably exaggerate the enemy's force. Both in letters and in ships' logs the number of men killed and wounded is, for the most part, omitted. We hear in the log if a topmast is wounded, or if a cask of pork is opened, but the loss of human life makes little or no impression.[4] Again, logs and letters frequently contradict one another, and it is a nice question which to believe. Courts-martial only took place when the British ship was beaten and surrendered, or when some officer behaved badly; but the full evidence recorded in them gives a most valuable and interesting picture. The French authority, Troude, is not, on the whole, much more trustworthy than Schom-

[1] Twenty-three mounted.

[2] Schomberg, ii. 137; Nicolas, 'Nelson Dispatches,' i. 73; Beatson, v. 534.

[3] Chevalier, 459; Beatson, v. 608; Hughes's letter describes the *Naïade* as of 30 guns and 160 men; Log of *Sceptre*.

[4] "I do not think that log-books, which are kept in the manner in which ships' log-books are, ought to be implicitly taken as evidence," said Capt. Alex. A. Hood at the C. M. on Keppel in 1779.

berg. He often misdates actions by days or weeks; he always exaggerates the force of the French ship, and depreciates that of the British ship; and it is difficult to suppose that he drew upon original French sources of information. Chevalier scarcely touches minor actions. The French *Gazette* gives the French captains' letters, and is usually as trustworthy as the London *Gazette*.

The armament of ships is a very puzzling subject during both this and the next war. The trouble is caused by the carronade, which appears, at first permissorily, in a few British ships in 1779, and quickly spreads. But it is always uncertain whether a particular British ship did or did not carry carronades. Many Captains had a great prejudice against them;[1] others wanted, and obtained, more than they were properly allowed. In regard to foreign ships, there is even more uncertainty. It appears, however, from a casual mention or two, that towards the close of the war, French ships may occasionally have carried caronnades. For example, if we can believe evidence given at the court-martial on Commander John Frodsham,[2] the French *Fée*, 32, carried four 18-pr. carronades in 1782. Still, we captured no prize that included carronades in her armament.[3]

A fact which does seem to emerge from the ship actions of this period is the extreme importance of weight of metal. Otherwise, why should each side endeavour to diminish its own weight of broadside, and exaggerate that of the enemy? In this war, the quality of both French officers and seamen was excellent. There was little to choose between them and our men for valour and skill; and if their operations on a grand scale so often miscarried, it was the faulty strategy imposed by the French Government that was in the main to blame. Instructed to avoid fighting, their action was timid. Even in ship to ship encounters we find this fatal plan of campaign exercising its paralysing effect. Discipline in the French fleet had not as yet been subjected to the rude shocks of the Revolution. There were no such actions as we find in the next war, when British frigates repeatedly captured enemies of equal force, suffering

[1] Thus the *Endymion's* Captain wants to get rid of his forecastle 18-prs. Capt. Tovey (Ordnance Board Letters, 1778–1783, MS., Record Office) reports against carronades; the wads blow back and set the ship on fire; the guns jump about and break the breeching.

[2] C. M., 59, Aug. 7th.

[3] Except, of course, vessels that had been British, such as the *Licorne*. There seems to be no positively trustworthy evidence that any foreign warships had carronades until after 1783.—W. L. C.

little or no loss themselves, but inflicting terrific slaughter. Hence, with men equal in quality on both sides, and with, as was usually the case, the better built ship on the French side, weight of metal won with a singular constancy in the actions between British and French ships. In fifteen cases, superior broadside gave a British ship the victory—omitting many instances where there was a great advantage on our side. I have not yet been able to discover a case of a French warship striking to a British ship of inferior broadside.[1] There may be error in the figures given in the text in one of two directions: (1), overstatement of the British ships' force through wrong inclusion of carronades; (2), understatement of French ships' force through usually accepting the French version. Still, I am disposed to think my figures the most accurate that can now be obtained, and in general correct.

Taking eight typical instances of British ships captured or destroyed by the French, in four cases (*Sphinx*,[2] *Unicorn*, *Rover*, and *Jack*), the French force was so very superior that we can feel no surprise at the result. The other four cases are of larger and more important ships—the *Minerva*, *Fox*, *Quebec*, and *Argo*. The *Minerva's* and *Quebec's* loss was due, in part, to accident. In the first there was an explosion of powder, in circumstances that remind us of that in the *Serapis* in her action with the *Bonhomme Richard*: the second was so unlucky as to catch fire. In each instance, the British ship was the weaker in broadside—the *Minerva* slightly (allowing for the extra weight of the French pound, which was one-twelfth heavier than the English), the *Quebec* very much so. The *Minerva* also was weakly manned, and was taken by surprise. The *Fox* was much inferior in weight of metal to the *Junon*, which beat her. The *Argo* was superior in broadside to the pair of French frigates that attacked her; but she was one of our wretched class of 44-gun ships with lower-deck ports only a few inches above the water, and was, owing to the swell, unable to open those ports, or to use her heavy guns. Her case, however, is all in favour of a heavy broadside perfectly mounted.

In actions with United States' ships, we lost seven ships and took six under conditions that illustrate the value of broadside. Two American vessels, the *Lexington* and the *Trumbull*, were

[1] The *Lion*, taken in 1778 by the *Maidstone*, a British ship of inferior broadside, was a privateer; and so of many other cases, which are apparent exceptions.

[2] *See* index for references to these actions.

captured by British ships of inferior force. The *Lexington* was surprised: the *Trumbull* is said to have been miserably manned. On the other hand, the British brigs *Trepassey* and *Atalanta* were captured by an American frigate whose force was just equal to theirs combined; and the *General Monk* was taken by a Yankee privateer of equal force. The *Trepassey* and *Atalanta*, however, were two weak ships against one strong one. The *General Monk* was armed almost entirely with carronades, and was attacked at ranges where these weapons were inefficient: moreover, the carronades were badly mounted. There remains the case of the *Serapis*, which was taken by Paul Jones in a ship nominally her superior in force, but actually, through the defective artillery carried, her inferior. Jones, however, was such an exceptionally able and skilful captain that, pitted against a commonplace, if brave, man, his victory was almost certain. The case illustrates the value of leadership, but it does not destroy the argument for a heavy broadside. Moreover, accidents played a certain part. A gun burst in the American, but there was also a serious explosion of powder in the *Serapis* with the most disastrous results. A feature of these minor actions is that such an explosion usually decides the fate of the day against the ship in which it occurs. This is natural when the shock to the confidence of the crew caused by such an incident is remembered. In the battle of Santiago (1898) the bad shooting of the Spaniards was probably due in part to the accidents which occurred when firing-pins were blown out of the gun-breeches.

In actions with Spanish ships, we took six and lost not one ship. But all through this century the Spanish navy was almost worthless as a fighting force. "A Spanish ship chased is a Spanish ship captured," was a French proverb of the time. The Spanish ships were wretchedly manned and officered. Of the six ships we took, two were of superior force to their captors, but in each case there were other British ships close at hand.

There were two actions with Dutch ships, both at the same time and place. The result is very instructive. The heavier broadside won in each case—a British ship winning one action and losing the other.

A few instances may next be examined where a very inferior ship fought a very superior one. In these cases it will generally be found that, unless the superior ship is crippled in some way, by loss of her rudder or masts, she inflicts very heavy punishment on her antagonist; though there are some very striking exceptions. Thus the British *Nonsuch*, 64, in an action with the French *Actif*, 74, loses 90 men to the enemy's 53, though she is not taken. The British *Flora* meets the French *Nymphe*, of half her weight of metal, and takes her, inflicting a loss of 136 to her own 26 incurred. The French *Capricieuse*, in action with two ships of more than twice her weight of broadside, loses 100 men against the loss of 58 which she inflicts. The *Belle Poule* and *Magicienne*, French 32's, meet, the first, a 64, suffering a loss of 68, and inflicting a loss of 13; the second, a 50, suffering a loss of 86, and inflicting a loss of only 2. Both were taken. Their fate shows the very great risk which is incurred by a ship if she assails a vessel of superior class. The *Leander*, a British 50, engaged a Spanish 74, and though her loss was not heavy, she was reduced to a wreck.

On the other hand, there are four or five instances where the weaker ship inflicts disproportionate loss on the stronger. The French *Belle Poule*, of 168 lbs. broadside, loses 102 men against the 44 men of the British *Arethusa*, of 114 lbs. No explanation can be given, except that the British gunnery was better, and that the French fired to dismast. The British *Isis*, of 414 lbs. broadside, is said to have inflicted on the French *César*, of 828 lbs., a loss of 50 men, as against her own loss of 16. Special circumstances, such as the clearing for action of the Frenchman on only one side, may account for this. Then there is the case of the French *Scipion*, of 828 lbs. broadside, engaged with the *London*, of 1018 lbs., or perhaps even more. The *Scipion* loses 58, and the *London* 83 men. Each ship had some assistance—the *Scipion* from a 32-gun frigate, and the *London* from a 74. Possibly the French 74, *Scipion*, was a stronger and stouter ship than the British 90, *London*.

Superior nautical qualities and size in ships, strangely enough, seem to go for very little in action. Again and again, short, small, heavily-armed British ships capture longer, larger, but less heavily-armed enemies. The Spaniards seem to have been the worst offenders in undergunning their ships. Thus the *Grana*, of 528 tons, carries thirty 6- and 4-pounders. Her captor, the *Cerberus*, of 593 tons, carries twenty-eight 9-pounders. So, again, the *Sta. Catalina*, though far larger than her captor, has an armament inferior by 25 per cent.

Actions with privateers were very numerous, but have, for the most part, been omitted. The want of discipline in those craft rendered them usually an easy prey to far smaller men-of-war. There were exceptions, however, when privateers captured British men-of-war. For instance, the *Egmont*, *Savage*, and *General Monk*, all three small vessels, were taken by American privateers. In the first the powder was wet; in the second the British crew was too small, and the ship too weak to stand up against her opponent. The loss of the *General Monk* has already been explained.

French, Dutch and American privateers swarmed in British seas. In May, 1777, there were five American privateers lying off Waterford, waiting for the Newfoundland fleet. In the same year, two privateers anchored in Solway Firth; off Kintyre there were two more, and others cruised between Jersey and Guernsey. "Fall, the Pirate," one of the most notorious, was chased, unsuccessfully, by Nelson, in 1781.[1] He had harried the coast of Scotland. The letters of Captain the Hon. Charles Napier (1) show the Firth of Forth to have been much troubled by such freebooters.[2] The *Jackal*, which had been carried off by her crew from Sheerness, under one Luke Ryan, an Irish outlaw, was particularly active. As the Navy, owing to the immense burdens which were imposed upon it, was unable to afford adequate protection against the inroads of these gentry, shipowners generally armed their ships; and several privateers discovered that an armed merchantman was quite capable of giving very nasty knocks. In the course of the war, Dublin, Penzance, Banff, Whitehaven, Aberbrothick, Leith, and Newcastle, were either actually attacked, or threatened by American privateers. There were practically no fixed defences at those places; but there usually were Navy tenders at Dublin and Leith on the impress service. Liverpool, however, had "two grand batteries of twenty-seven 18-pdrs."

Three actions illustrate the danger of sending ships to sea with raw crews when there is a chance of their falling in with the enemy. The cases are those of the *Ardent*, captured by the French, of the *Isis*, badly fought in an action with a Dutch ship, and of the *Pégase*, captured with ridiculous ease by Jervis in the *Foudroyant*.

Two instances show a very un-British respect for neutrals, the explanation being that the Navy was weak in this war, and unequal to all its work. A hostile privateer, the *Stanislas*, runs aground in

[1] Nicolas, i. 50.

[2] Captains' Letters, N. 1780, 1781, Record Office; Cf. also G. Williams, 'Liverpool Privateers,' p. 200 ff., where many curious and interesting details are given.

territorial waters off Ostend, and is not touched. A French frigate and a convoy, in Algerine waters, are spared. As against this, a Dutch convoy is fired upon on resistance being offered to an attempt to search it.

If, generally speaking, the minor actions issued favourably to England, it was because her ships were better armed, and because she had a plentiful supply of officers and seamen. In quality, it

E. Thompson

CAPT. EDWARD THOMPSON, R.N., AUTHOR OF 'A SEAMAN'S LETTERS,' ETC.[1]

(From Ridley's engraving after a miniature once in the possession of the Popham family.)

does not appear that her officers were better than those of the French.

The events of the peace, which lasted from 1783 to 1793, do not call for long description here.

[1] Capt. Thompson died Commodore on the West Coast of Africa, in 1786.

In the course of 1787, the interference of France in the affairs of Holland almost precipitated a fresh war between England and her old adversary. But as Frederick William II. of Prussia, whose sister was the wife of the Dutch Stadtholder, the Prince of Orange, supported the policy of Britain, France withdrew her assistance from the rebels, or "patriots" as they called themselves in Holland, and the crisis ended peacefully. Britain had given to Prussia an undertaking to place forty ships of the line in commission, and had commissioned in October a powerful squadron which included, with the guardships at the naval ports, thirty sail of the line and eleven frigates or 44-gun ships. As an answer to this, France equipped sixteen sail of the line at Brest, and recalled an evolutionary squadron from the coast of Portugal. On October 27th, however, a joint declaration was signed in Paris by which England and France agreed to disarm; and towards the close of the year a great part of the British squadron was paid off.[1]

On December 23rd, 1787, the *Bounty*, Lieutenant William Bligh, left Spithead on a voyage to the South Seas,[2] for the purpose of collecting bread-fruit plants, which were to be introduced into the West Indies. She was an armed transport of two hundred and fifteen tons, with a crew of forty-four officers and men, and two gardeners for the care of the plants. Her chief officers were, besides Bligh, John Fryer, Master; William Elphinstone, Master's Mate; Fletcher Christian, Lieutenant (actg.); and John Hallett, Thomas Hayward, Robert Tinkler, Peter Heywood, Edward Young, George Stewart, Midshipmen. Unfortunately the offices of Captain and Purser were combined in Bligh's person. He himself was a harsh and tyrannical officer, as his subsequent behaviour when governor of New South Wales proved.[3] From the very outset he behaved with great violence and brutality to his crew. The provisions issued were light in weight and defective in quality. At Tenerife he accused his men of stealing cheese, and stopped the rations of both officers and men till the deficiency was made good. When the crew remonstrated mildly he told them, "You damned infernal scoundrels, I'll make you eat grass or anything you can catch before I've done with you." On further complaints he threatened to flog

[1] *Ann. Reg.* 1787, 192 ff.]; Malmesbury, 'Memoirs'; Stanhope, 'Pitt,' i. 344.

[2] Bligh, 'Narrative of the Mutiny on board H.M.S *Bounty*'; Marshall, 'Naval Biography,' ii. 747, Supplement, i. 98; 'Courts-Martial,' vol. 70.

[3] He was deposed and deported for "harsh and despotic conduct" in that capacity, in 1806.

the first man who said a word. What with hard duty in the intemperate weather of the Southern Atlantic, confinement in a small ship usually battened down, and bad food, many of the crew fell ill. But the service was performed with alacrity, and all went well between the Cape and Tasmania, where the *Bounty* anchored in Adventure Bay on August 20th, 1788. There Bligh confined his Carpenter, William Purcell. Leaving Adventure Bay the *Bounty* anchored in Matavie Bay, Tahiti, on October 26th. Bligh's conduct now became more arbitrary than ever.[1] We read that—

"Lieutenant Bligh seized on all hogs that came to the ship, whether large or small, dead or alive, claiming them as his property, and serving them out as the ship's allowance in the proportion of one pound *per diem*. He also seized on those belonging to the Master, and slaughtered them for the use of the crew, although he had more than 40 of his own on board . . . When the Master remonstrated with him on the subject, he replied that he would convince him that everything became *his* as soon as it was brought on board; that he would take nine-tenths of any man's property."[2]

On various pretexts the crew's allowance of spirits was curtailed; Christian was bullied and abused; and a Midshipman who was on watch when three seamen deserted was put in irons and kept there for the greater part of three months, because he had slept on watch. To the natives Bligh behaved with most undiplomatic severity. On April 26th, 1789, the *Bounty* weighed for her homeward voyage. Next day Bligh pretended to miss some cocoanuts, and accused Christian of stealing them, abusing him in the presence of the other officers, and calling him a "damned hound," and them "scoundrels," "thieves," and "rascals." On the night of the 28th, Christian, exasperated, determined to leave the ship and swim ashore, but suddenly conceived the idea of seizing the vessel. He took into his confidence four seamen who had been flogged by Bligh, distributed

[1] John Adams, the sole survivor of the mutineers who fled to Pitcairn Island, spoke to Capt. Thomas Staines, in 1814, of Bligh's "harsh and severe treatment in terms of strong feeling." Marshall, Suppl., i. 103. He was living in 1826.

[2] From the diary of James Morrison, Boatswain's Mate in the *Bounty*. Marshall's account of the mutiny (*loc. cit.*) is based on this and not on Bligh's own version, which is a masterpiece of suppression and innuendo. The diary has never been published in full. Morrison was a man of good character. He was not one of the mutineers; and, though he was sentenced to death, was immediately pardoned and promoted. He served under Troubridge, as Gunner in the unhappy *Blenheim*, and was lost in her in 1807. He is therefore a witness who can be trusted. Bligh had obvious reasons for concealing the truth about his own brutalities and arbitrariness. He served afterwards with credit at Copenhagen, where he won Lord Nelson's praise, and appears to have been brave and capable as an officer. But he was a type of the worst kind of naval officer, such as we find gibbeted in Marryat and Smollett, and appearing from time to time in the records of the courts-martial, a man intoxicated with power.

arms to them from the arms'-chest, at which he got by stratagem, and then seized and secured Bligh, the Master, the Gunner (William Peckover), and the botanist (David Nelson). Bligh offered little or no resistance, and not one of his officers raised a hand; which is not, perhaps, to be wondered at in the circumstances. Other seamen joined Christian's party, either willingly or by compulsion. Bligh and eighteen officers and men were placed in the cutter. They were given food, spirits, tools, a sextant and charts, and turned adrift. The boat lay very low in the water, and this circumstance prevented three or four of the officers and men who were loyal to Bligh from going in her. There were left in the *Bounty* at the Friendly Islands, Christian, three Midshipmen,[1] and twenty-five other officers and men.

Enduring great hardships in his crowded boat, Bligh steered for Timor. Being unarmed—for the only weapons in the boat were four cutlasses—he did not venture to touch at any of the New Hebrides. His party landed on islands near the Australian coast, where they obtained quantities of oysters and much-needed rest after their sufferings. Leaving these islands on June 2nd, 1789, they proceeded towards Timor, which they reached on June 14th. Throughout this long and painful voyage in an open, undecked boat, Bligh's conduct and management were admirable. He showed firmness and character, and he succeeded in bringing his party to Timor without the loss of a life. From Timor he went to Batavia, and so home.

On his return the *Pandora*, 24, Captain Edward Edwards, was despatched in 1790 to search for and capture the mutineers. Bligh seems to have made no distinction between the innocent and the guilty, and naturally had suppressed all evidence of his own bad conduct. Edwards, who was entrusted with the task of avenging him, was, as subsequent events showed, a cruel and merciless man.

When the boat left the *Bounty*, the ship was steering W.N.W. She soon altered course and put into Tahiti, whence she proceeded to the small island of Toobouai, where a fort was built. Christian maintained strict discipline and placed offenders in irons. On September 11th, 1789, the *Bounty* returned to Tahiti, where sixteen of her crew wished to remain. Christian, with the other eight, who, we may suppose, were the really guilty, dreading vengeance, decided to retire to some unknown island. They

[1] Heywood, Stewart and Young. Stewart was drowned in irons when the *Pandora* was wrecked; Young died at Tahiti.

sailed, therefore, from Tahiti, and nothing more was heard of them for many years.

Of the sixteen men left at Tahiti, two were murdered. On March 23rd, 1791, the *Pandora* arrived at the island, and Midshipmen Heywood and Stewart came off and gave themselves up. The other twelve men surrendered or were captured. All were confined as "piratical villains," with both legs in irons, in a small box, eleven feet long, on the *Pandora's* deck. The only ventilation was through two gratings nine inches square. "The heat of the prison during calm weather was so intense that the perspiration ran in streams from their bodies." Every torture that Edwards could invent was applied. These men, most or all of them innocent of mutiny, were confined in this diminutive space until they were covered with filth. Their bedding was vermin-infested, and their food wretched. On August 28th, 1791, the *Pandora* struck a reef in Torres Strait and foundered. It will scarcely be believed that Edwards refused, though entreated by Heywood, to release his wretched prisoners. Fortunately for them there were more merciful hearts in the crew. As the *Pandora* sank the Master-at-Arms dropped the keys of the irons into the dreadful box. William Moulter, a boatswain's mate, at the risk of his own life, opened the small scuttle in the roof, which was the only means of entrance or exit, and ten of the fourteen escaped, though all had their wrists handcuffed. The other four were drowned. The survivors were landed on a small island, where Edwards left them without clothing or shelter under the scorching sun by day and the icy dew at night.[1] Finally, they were sent to the Cape in Dutch vessels and fed, by Edwards's orders, in this way: each man was to have 3 lbs. of bad meat, 1½ lbs. of stock fish, 1½ lbs. of tamarinds and sugar, ½ pint each of ghee and rancid oil, and 1 pint of vinegar a fortnight, with 2 drams of arrack and a scanty allowance of the very worst rice a day.

On June 19th, 1792, the so-called mutineers reached England and were tried by court-martial. Remembering the rigours of the tribunals which punished offences against discipline, it is not wonderful to learn that six of the ten survivors were found guilty, though it is probable that not one was really guilty, and though two of the men so condemned had taken up arms to rescue the ship

[1] It need scarcely be said that Edwards's own account of his voyage says nothing of all this quite unnecessary cruelty.

in Bligh's interest, whilst two more were mere boys when the mutiny occurred. Bligh had promised to make a distinction between the innocent and guilty, and had broken his promise. He was absent from England on a second voyage during the court-martial, but it is evident that he had condemned all alike in his reports to the Admiralty. The six were sentenced to death, and three were executed at Spithead, amongst them being two men who were undoubtedly innocent. Midshipman Heywood and Boatswain's Mate Morrison were pardoned, and a third man was respited. Heywood was employed in the subsequent war in Howe's flagship, and great interest was taken in him by both Howe and Hood. He served with marked distinction throughout the war.

It is strange that such men as Bligh and Edwards were in no way censured or punished. Both died after having attained flag-rank.

Nothing more was heard of Christian and the other mutineers till 1813, when the Admiralty was informed by an American trader, who had touched at the small and remote Pitcairn's Island in the Southern Pacific, that he had found it, to his great surprise, inhabited by survivors or descendants of the mutineers. On September 17th, 1814, Captain Thomas Staines, of the *Briton*, independently discovered the island and its inhabitants. After this lapse of time, John Adams, the sole survivor of the *Bounty* mutineers, was not molested.[1]

On December 24th, 1789, whilst on a voyage from the Cape of Good Hope to Australia, the *Guardian*, armed *en flûte*, Lieutenant Edward Riou, being in want of water, approached an immense iceberg, a little to the north-east of the (then unknown) Marion Isles, to obtain blocks of ice. Boats were lowered and a quantity of ice was collected; but on the ship attempting to stand off from the berg she was embayed by an indraught, and struck violently upon a submerged hummock, damaging her stern and rudder. With great difficulty she got off, after striking a second time abreast of the main chains. It was then found that the water in her well was rising fast. All hands manned the pumps, but at midnight of the 25th the water in the hold was 4 feet 6 inches; at 6 A.M. of the 26th, 7 feet deep. A furious sea was running, and this further embarrassed the crew. There were many convicts on board, and to

[1] The Pitcairn islanders have since been removed, at their own wish, to Norfolk Island, in the South Pacific.

keep order amongst them was by no means easy. Riou gave permission to his officers and crew to take to the boats, but for himself announced his absolute determination to remain in the ship. From this resolve he could not be moved by any entreaties. The launch, the large cutter and the jolly-boat were got out, and a certain number of officers and men jumped into them or swam to them when they put off, leaving Riou and sixty-one souls in the *Guardian*, as it seemed, to hopeless destruction. The jolly-boat, however, had not gone far when she foundered. The launch was picked up by a French merchantman on January 3rd, 1790, after her crew had suffered terrible privations. The cutter appears to have been lost.

Wonderful to relate, the *Guardian* did not founder. Her hold was full of casks which buoyed her up, and, on the other hand, the ballast washed out through the gaps in her bottom and lightened her. She drove before the wind and sea till, on February 21st, 1790, the coast of Cape Colony was sighted. She was beached in Table Bay, and all those who had remained on board her were saved. Riou, whose conduct rose to a height of courage above all praise, met an early and glorious death eleven years later in the battle of Copenhagen. His example will inspire men to heroic devotion and self-sacrifice so long as the annals of our Navy are read and studied.

The years 1790 and 1791 were chiefly famous for the Spanish and Russian armaments.[1] Spain had laid claim to Nootka Sound on the west coast of Vancouver, and had despatched a force to eject the British traders there established. Following the precedent of 1770, the British Government at once demanded restitution, and commissioned a powerful fleet under Admiral Lord Howe (W.). It included no fewer than twenty-nine ships of the line, with nine frigates, two sloops, four cutters, and two fireships. Under Howe were the flag-officers, Admiral the Hon. Samuel Barrington (B.), Vice-Admiral Sir Alexander Arthur Hood (W.), Rear-Admiral William Hotham (1) (R.), Rear-Admiral Sir John Jervis (B.), and Rear-Admiral Sir Richard Bickerton (B.). This great fleet, perhaps the most powerful ever assembled by England up to that time, cruised at sea during August and September. In October, Rear-Admiral Samuel Cornish (B.) was detached to the West Indies with six ships of the line. On the 28th of the same month Spain came to terms and agreed to surrender Nootka Sound and compensate the

[1] Schomberg, ii. 217–219, iv. 428; Stanhope, 'Pitt,' ii. 49.

dispossessed settlers and merchants. The specially commissioned ships were then paid off.

In 1791, difficulties with Russia, marking an important change in British policy, but hardly falling within the scope of a history of the British Navy, led to the commissioning of a squadron even more powerful.[1] This was composed of thirty-six ships of the line, one 50-gun ship, and nine frigates. The officers in command were Vice-Admirals Lord Hood (B.), the most able and capable flag-officer then serving in the Navy, and William Hotham (1) (B.), and Rear-Admirals Sir Richard King (1) (R.), Jonathan Faulknor (1) (R.), Phillips Cosby (W.), the Hon. John Leveson Gower (W.), and Samuel Granston Goodall (B.). In August the differences were settled, whereupon most of the ships were put out of commission.

[1] Stanhope, 'Pitt,' ii. 113 ff.; Schomberg, iv. 437.

A THREE-DECKER OF THE EIGHTEENTH CENTURY.

APPENDIX TO CHAPTERS XXXI. AND XXXII.

NAVAL LOSSES OF THE BELLIGERENT POWERS, 1775–1783.

A.—Vessels of H.M. Navy, or employed under Naval Officers, Taken, Destroyed, Burnt, Foundered or Wrecked, 1775–1783.

Year.	Date.	Name.	Guns.	Commander. * Lost his life.	Remarks.
1775	..	*Pomona*	18	Com. Thomas Eastwood.*	Foundered in the West Indies.
1775	..	*Savage*	8	,, Hugh Bromedge.	Lost near Louisbourg.
1775	July 15.	*Diligent*, schooner	..	Lieut. John Knight (2).	Taken at Machias.
1776	..	*Bolton*, brig. . .	12	,, Edward Sneyd.	Taken by the Americans.
1776	June 29	*Actæon*	28	Capt. Christopher Atkins.	Abandoned and destroyed at Charleston.
1776	Aug.	*Ferret*	14	Com. James Rodney.*	Foundered in the West Indies.
1776	Dec.	*Racehorse*, schooner	12	Lieut. James Jones.	Taken by the *Andrea Doria*, 14.
1777	..	*Repulse*	32	Capt. Henry Davies.*	Foundered off Bermuda.
1777	..	*Liverpool* . . .	28	,, Henry Bellew.	Wrecked off Long Island.
1777	..	*Earl of Bute*, armed ship	26	Com. Benjamin Hill.	Foundered in the Gulf of Florida.
1777	..	*Pegasus*	16	,, J— Hamilton Gore.*	Foundered off Newfoundland.
1777	..	*Sprightly*, cutter .	12	Lieut. Hills.*	Capsized off Guernsey.
1777	..	*Cruiser*	8	Com. Francis Parry (2).	Burnt off S. Carolina.
1777	..	*Vestal*	20	Capt. James Shirley.*	Foundered off Newfoundland.
1777	June 7	*Fox*	28	,, Patrick Fothering-ham.	Taken by the *Hancock*, 32, and *Boston* 24. Retaken, 1777.
1777	Oct. 23	*Merlin*	18	Com. Samuel Reeve.	Abandoned and burnt at Mud Island.
1777	,, 23	*Augusta* . . .	64	Capt. Francis Reynolds.	Accidentally burnt at Mud Island.
1777	Nov. 10	*Syren*	20	,, Tobias Furneaux.	Wrecked off Rhode Island.
1778	..	*Grampus*, armed transp. . . .	32	Com. John Frodsham.	Foundered off Newfoundland.
1778	..	*Mermaid* . . .	28	Capt. James Hawker.	Driven ashore by d'Estaing's fleet.
1778	..	*Mercury* . . .	24	,, James Montagu (1).	Wrecked near New York.
1778	..	*Swallow* . . .	16	Com. C— Warre.*	Foundered coming from the Cape of Good Hope.
1778	..	*Swift*	16	,, Joseph Tathwell.	Wrecked off Cape Henry, and burnt.
1778	..	*Cupid*	16	,, William Carlyon.	Foundered off Newfoundland.
1778	..	*Dispatch*. . . .	14	,, J— Botham.*	Capsized in the Gulf of St. Lawrence.
1778	..	*York*, tender . .	12	Lieut. Thomas Walbeoff.	Taken off the American coast.
1778	..	*Spy*	12	,, Thomas Lenox Frederick.	Wrecked off Newfoundland.
1778	..	*Hinchinbroke*, armed vessel . .	12	..	Taken by American privateers.
1778	..	*Helena*	12	,, Thomas Hicks.	Taken by the *Sensible*. Retaken, 1779.
1778	..	*Otter*.	10	,, John Wright.	Wrecked off Florida.
1778	..	*Enterprise*, tender .	10	..	Taken by the Americans, and burnt.
1778	Apr. 24	*Drake*	14	Com. George Burdon.*	Taken by the *Ranger*, 18, near Belfast.
1778	June 24	*Folkestone* . . .	8	Lieut. W— Smith (1).	Taken by the French, off the French coast.
1778	July 9	*Lively*	22	Capt. Robert Biggs.	Taken by *Iphigénie*, etc. Retaken.
1778	,, 17	*Alert*, cutter . .	12	Lieut. William George Fairfax.	Taken by the *Junon*.
1778	,, 30	*Kingfisher* . . .	16	..	Abandoned and burnt at Rhode Island.
1778	Aug.	*Stanley*	10	..	Taken by *César*, 74.
1778	,, 7	*Juno*	32	Capt. Hugh Dalrymple.	Abandoned and burnt at Rhode Island.
1778	,, 7	*Lark*	32	,, Richard Smith.	Abandoned and burnt at Rhode Island.
1778	,, 7	*Orpheus*	32	,, Charles Hudson.	Abandoned and burnt at Rhode Island.
1778	,, 7	*Flora*	32	,, John Brisbane.	Sunk at Rhode Island.
1778	,, 7	*Cerberus*. . . .	28	,, John Symons.	Abandoned and burnt at Rhode Island.
1778	,, 7	*Falcon*	16	Com. Harry Harmood.	Burnt at Rhode Island: weighed, and was lost.
1778	,, 14	*Senegal*, ex *Racehorse*	18	,, John Inglis (1).	Taken by d'Estaing: retaken, 1780, and blown up.
1778	,, 17	*Thunder*, bomb. .	8	,, James Gambier (2).	Taken by d'Estaing, in America.

Year.	Date.	Name.	Guns.	Commander. * Lost his life.	Remarks.
1778	Aug. 22	*Minerva* . . .	32	Capt. John Stott.*	Taken by the French in the West Indies. Retaken, 1781.
1778	,, 23	*Zephyr*	14	Com. Thomas West.	Taken by the French. Retaken, 1780, and burnt.
1778	Sept. 1	*Active*	28	Capt. William Williams.	Taken by the French in the West Indies.
1778	,, 10	*Fox*	28	,, Hon. Thomas Windsor.	Taken by the *Junon*.
1778	Oct.	*Somerset*. . . .	70	,, George Ourry.	Wrecked near Cape Cod.
1778	,,	*Zebra*	16	Com. Henry Colins.	Wrecked at Egg Island Harbour.
1778	Dec. 17	*Ceres*	18	,, James Richard Dacres (1).	Taken by the French. Retaken, 1782.
1779	..	*Supply*, storeship .	20	,, John Lockhart Nasmyth.	Accidentally burnt at St. Kitts.
1779	..	*Tortoise*, armed transp. . . .	32	,, Jahleel Brenton (1).	Foundered off Newfoundland.
1779	..	*North*, armed ship .	20	,, George Selby.*	Wrecked off Nova Scotia.
1779	..	*Thorn*	16	,, William Wardlaw.	Taken by an American frigate. Retaken.
1779	..	*Tapageur*, cutter .	14	Lieut. Lord Charles Fitzgerald.	Wrecked in the W. Indies.
1779	..	*Hope*	14	,, Michael Hindman.	Taken by an American privateer.
1779	..	*West Florida* . .	14	,, John Willett Payne.	Taken at Pensacola by the Americans.
1779	..	*York*.	12	,, Daniel Dobrée.	Taken by d'Estaing at Grenada.
1779	..	*Leviathan*, ex *Northumberland*. .	50	Capt. Robert Alexander Lambert.	Foundered returning from Jamaica.
1779	..	*Penelope*. . . .	24	,, James Jones.*	Lost in the W. Indies.
1779	Jan. 13	*Weazel*	16	Com. Lewis Robertson.	Taken by *Boudeuse* in W. Indies.
1779	Mar. 19	*Arethusa* . . .	32	Capt. Charles Holmes Everitt.	Wrecked off Ushant.
1779	May 1	*Montreal* . . .	32	,, Stair Douglas (1).	Taken by two French vessels in Mediterranean.
1779	,, 7	*Diligent*	12	Lieut. Thomas Walbeoff.	Taken by the *Providence*.
1779	June 19	*Glasgow*	24	Capt. Thomas Lloyd ( ).	Accidentally burnt at Jamaica.
1779	July 14	*Egmont*, schooner .	10	Lieut. John Gardiner.	Taken by *Wild Cat*, 14, off Newfoundland.
1779	,, 16	*Haarlem* . . .	14	,, Josias Rogers.	Taken by American privateers.
1779	..	*Holdernesse*, cutter.	8	..	Taken by the allied fleets in the Channel.
1779	Aug.	*Active*, cutter . .	12	..	Taken by the *Mutine* in the Channel.
1779	,,	*Ardent*	64	Capt. Philip Boteler.	Taken by the allied fleets. Retaken 1782.
1779	Sept.	*Sphinx*	20	,, Robert Manners Sutton	Taken by *Amphitrite*. Retaken.
1779	,,	*Rose*	20	,, John Brown.	Sunk to block Savannah Bar.
1779	,,	*Savannah*, brig .	14	Lieut. Richard Fisher.	Sunk at Savannah to block the Bar.
1779	,, 10	*Ariel*.	20	Capt. Thomas Mackenzie.	Taken by *Amazone* off Carolina.
1779	,, 23	*Serapis*	44	,, Richard Pearson.	Taken by *Bonhomme Richard*.
1779	,, 23	*Countess of Scarborough* . . .	20	Com. Thomas Piercy.	Taken by squadron of Paul Jones.
1779	,, 24	*Experiment*. . .	50	Capt. Sir James Wallace, Kt.	Taken by d'Estaing off Georgia.
1779	Oct. 6	*Quebec*	32	,, George Farmer.*	Blown up engaging *Surveillante*.
1779	Nov. 27	*Jackal*, cutter . .	14	Lieut. John Gibson.	Carried to France by mutineers. Retaken in 1781.
1779	,,	*Hussar*	28	Capt. Charles Maurice Pole.	Wrecked near Hell Gate, New York.
1780	..	*True Briton*, brig .	14	Lieut. Hon. Patrick Napier.	Taken by the French. Retaken.
1780	..	*Active*	14	,, William Quarme.	Taken by Americans, near New York.
1780	Feb. 18	*Defiance*. . . .	64	Capt. Maximilian Jacobs.	Wrecked on Savannah Bar.
1780	Oct. 11	*Viper*	16	,, John Augustus, Lord Hervey.	Wrecked in the Gulf of St. Lawrence.
1780	..	*Scorpion*. . . .	16	..	Wrecked in N. America.
1780	..	*Coureur*, schooner .	16	Lieut. C— Major.	Taken by the Americans off Newfoundland.
1780	..	*Cormorant* . . .	16	Robert M'Evoy.	Taken by de Grasse off Charleston.
1780	Apr. 26	*Fortune*	18	Com. Lewis Robertson.	Taken by the French in the W. Indies.
1780	Sept. 4	*Unicorn*	20	Capt. Thomas Lenox Frederick.	Taken by the French in the W. Indies. Retaken as the *Licorne*, in 1781.
1780	..	*Vigilant*, armed ship	20	Com. Thomas Goldesbrough.	Burnt at Beaufort, S. Carolina.
1780	Sept. 13	*Rover*	18	,, Henry Savage.	Taken by the French in the W. Indies. Retaken in 1781, but lost.
1780	..	*Bellona*, armed ship	18	,, Francis Tinsley.	Wrecked in the mouth of the Elbe.
1780	Oct.	*Endeavour*, brig .	14	Lieut. Francis Wooldridge.	Lost in the hurricane, W. Indies.
1780	..	*Nimble*, cutter . .	12	,, W. Furnival.*	Wrecked in Mount's Bay.
1780	Oct. 4	*Phœnix*	44	Capt. Sir Hyde Parker (2).	Lost in the hurricane, W. Indies.
1780	,, 5	*Victor*, brig. . .	10	..	Lost in the hurricane, W. Indies.
1780	..	*Incendiary*, fireship	8	Com. William Augustus Merrick.	Wrecked off the Isle of Wight.
1780	Oct. 5	*Scarborough* . .	20	Capt. Samuel Hood Walker.*	Lost in the hurricane, W. Indies.

Year.	Date.	Name.	Guns.	Commander. * Lost his life.	Remarks.
1780	Oct. 5	*Stirling Castle*	64	Capt. Robert Carkett.*	Lost in the hurricane, W. Indies.
1780	,, 5	*Barbados*	14	Com. Ralph Milbank.*	Lost in the hurricane, W. Indies.
1780	,, 5	*Thunderer*	74	Commod. Hon. Robert Boyle Walsingham.* Capt. Robert Boyle Nicholas.*	Lost in the hurricane, W. Indies.
1780	..	*Cornwall*	74	,, Timothy Edwards.	Sunk, being unserviceable, at St. Lucia.
1780	Oct. 11	*Laurel*	28	,, Thomas Lloyd (1).*	Lost in the hurricane, W. Indies.
1780		*Shark*	28	,, Howell Lloyd.*	Wrecked in North America.
1780	,, 11	*Andromeda*	28	,, Henry Bryne.*	Lost in the hurricane, W. Indies.
1780	,, 11	*Deal Castle*	24	,, James Hawkins.	Lost in the hurricane, W. Indies.
1780	,, 11	*Cameleon*	14	Com. James Johnstone.*	Lost in the hurricane, W. Indies
1780	,, 11	*Blanche*	32	Capt. Samuel Uppleby.*	Lost in the hurricane, W. Indies
1780	,, 11	*Beaver's Prize*	16	Com. John Auriol Drummond.*	Lost in the hurricane, W. Indies.
1780	Dec.	*Sartine*	32	,, Robert Simonton.	Wrecked in the E. Indies.
1781	Jan. 9	*Fairy*	14	Com. Joseph Browne.	Taken by the French. Retaken.
1781	,, 23	*Culloden*	74	Capt. George Balfour.	Wrecked off Long Island.
1781	..	*Terrible*	74	,, Hon. William Clement Finch.	Burnt in America as unserviceable.
1781	Feb.	*Romulus*	44	,, George Gayton.	Taken by the French.
1781	May 8	*Mentor*	20	,, Robert Deans (1).	Burnt at Pensacola.
1781	..	*Molly*, armed ship	20	Com. William Long.*	Accidentally burnt.
1781	..	*Germaine*, armed ship	20	,, George Augustus Keppel.	Taken by the Americans.
1781	..	*Echo*	18	,, John Manley (1).	Wrecked in Plymouth Sound.
1781	..	*Minorca*, xebec.	18	Lieut. H. Lawson.	Sunk at Mahon to save from capture.
1781	May 8	*Port Royal*	18	,, Kelly.	Taken by the Spaniards at Pensacola.
1781	..	*St. Firmin*	16	Com. Jonathan Faulknor (2).	Taken by the Spaniards off Gibraltar.
1781	May 28	*Atalanta*	16	,, Sampson Edwards.	Taken by the American *Alliance*. Retaken.
1781	,, 28	*Trepassey*	14	,, James Smyth.*	Taken by the American *Alliance*.
1781	..	*Hope*, cutter.	14	Lieut. L. Vickers.*	Taken by the French in America.
1781	..	*Antigua*	14	,, John Hutt.	Taken by the French in the W. Indies.
1781	..	*Fly*, armed cutter	14	Com. Milham Ponsonby.	Taken by the French in America.
1781	..	*Bonetta*	14	,, Ralph Dundas.	Taken by the French in the Chesapeake. Retaken 3.1.82.
1781	June 13	*Snake*	12	Lieut. William Jackson.	Taken by American privateers.
1781	,, 20	*Castor*	36		Taken by *Gloire* and *Friponne*.
1781	,, 20	*Crescent*	28	,, John Bligh (1), actg.	Taken by *Gloire* and *Friponne*.
1781	July 30	*Loyalist*	14	Com. Morgan Laugharne.	Taken by the French in the Chesapeake.
1781	..	*Rattlesnake*	14	,, Philip d'Auvergne.	Lost in the E. Indies.
1781	..	*Pigmy*, cutter	14	Lieut. Thomas Dyson.	Driven ashore and taken at Dunquerque.
1781	..	*Rover*	14	,, J. Duncan.	Wrecked in America.
1781	..	*Gibraltar*, armed brig	14	,, W. Anderson.	Taken by the Spaniards off Gibraltar.
1781	..	*Thunder*, bomb	8	Com. John Wallace.*	Foundered in the Channel.
1781	Aug. 1	*Pelican*	24	Capt. Cuthbert Collingwood.	Lost in a hurricane at Jamaica.
1781	,, 24	*Sandwich*, armed ship	20	Com. William Bett.	Taken by de Grasse's fleet.
1781	,, 24	*Cormorant*	14	,, Robert M'Evoy.	Taken by de Grasse's fleet.
1781	Sept. 6	*Savage*	16	,, Charles Stirling.	Taken by the privateer *Congress*, 24. Retaken by *Solebay*.
1781	..	*Swallow*	16	,, Thomas Wells (1).	Wrecked off Long Island.
1781	..	*Hope*	16	,, William Thomas.	Wrecked off Savannah.
1781	..	*Shelanagig*	16	,, James Keith Shepard.	Taken by the French in the W. Indies.
1781	..	*Duchess of Cumberland*	16	Lieut. Edward Marsh.	Wrecked off Newfoundland.
1781	..	*Delight*	16	Com. Francis Thomas Drake.*	Foundered going to N. America.
1781	..	*Racehorse*	14	Lieut. George Brisac.	Wrecked off Beachy Head.
1781	..	*Pheasant*, cutter	14	,, George Matthews.*	Capsized in the Channel.
1781	Sept. 11	*Iris*	32	Capt. George Dawson.	Taken by de Grasse.
1781	,, 11	*Richmond*	32	,, Charles Hudson.	Taken by de Grasse.
1781	Oct. 10	*Fowey*	24	,, Peter Aplin.	Sunk in the Chesapeake.
1781	..	*Sandwich*, armed ship	24	,, William Bett.	Taken by the Americans off Charleston.
1781	..	*Syren*	24	,, Isaac Vaillant.	Wrecked on the coast of Sussex.
1781	Oct. 10	*Guadaloupe*	28	,, Hugh Robinson.	Sunk in the Chesapeake to save from capture.
1781	..	*Greyhound*	28	,, William Fox.	Wrecked on South Sand Head.
1781	Oct. 10	*Charon*	44	,, Thomas Symonds.	Burnt in the Chesapeake to save from capture.
1781	..	*Thetis*	32	,, Robert Linzee.	Wrecked off St. Lucia.
1781	..	*Firebrand*, fireship	8	Com. Richard Hill.	Accidentally burnt near Falmouth.
1781	Oct. 10	*Vulcan*, fireship	8	,, George Palmer.	Burnt in the Chesapeake.
1781	..	*Conflagration*, fireship	8	,, J. Duncan.	Lost in N. America.

Year.	Date.	Name.	Guns.	Commander. * Lost his life.	Remarks.
1782	Jan. 21	*Hannibal* . . .	50	Capt. Alexander Christie.	Taken by the French off Sumatra.
1782	..	*Santa Monica* . .	36	" John Linzee.	Wrecked off Tortola.
1782	..	*Blonde*	32	" Edward Thornbrough.	Wrecked on Nantucket Shoals.
1782	Jan. 25	*Solebay*	28	" Charles Holmes Everitt.	Wrecked and burnt at Nevis.
1782	..	*Coventry* . . .	28	" William Wolseley.	Taken by the French in the Bay of Bengal.
1782	..	*Hinchinbroke* . .	20	..	Foundered off Jamaica.
1782	Feb.	*Oronoque* . . .	20	Com. William Tahourdin.	Taken at capitulation of Demerara.
1782	"	*Sylph*	18	" Lawrence Græme.	Taken at capitulation of Demerara.
1782	"	*Barbuda* . . .	16	" Francis Pender.	Taken at capitulation of Demerara.
1782	"	*Stormont* . . .	16	" Christmas Paul.	Taken at capitulation of Demerara.
1782	"	*Rodney*, brig . .	16	Lieut. John Douglas Brisbane.	Taken at the capitulation of Demerara.
1782	" 25	*Chaser*	18	Com. Thomas Parr.	Taken by the French in the Bay of Bengal.
1782	Apr. 8	*General Monk* . .	18	" Josias Rogers.	Taken by the Pennsylvanian ship, *Hyder Ali*, 16.
1782	" 11	*Jackal*, armed ship	20	" Gustavus Logie.	Taken by the *Deane* in the W. Indies.
1782		*Britannia*, armed ship	20	" M. Davis.*	Wrecked on the Kentish Knock.
1782	June 26	*Alligator* . . .	14	" John Frodsham.	Taken by the French at the mouth of the Channel.
1782	..	*Repulse*, cutter . .	14	Lieut. J. Atkinson.*	Wrecked off Yarmouth.
1782	..	*Swan*	14	Com. Lewis Robertson.	Capsized off Waterford.
1782	Aug. 29	*Royal George* . .	100	Rear-Adm. Richard Kempenfelt.* Capt. Martin Waghorn.	Capsized at Spithead.
1782	Sept.	*Ramillies* . . .	74	Rear-Adm. Thomas Graves (2). Capt. Sylverius Moriarty.	Burnt as unserviceable.
1782	"	*Hector*	74	" John Bourchier.	Sunk on the Banks of Newfoundland.
1782	"	*Glorieux* . . .	74	" Hon. Thomas Cadogan.*	Foundered returning from Jamaica.
1782	"	*Centaur*	74	Capt. John Nicholson Inglefield.	Foundered returning from Jamaica.
1782	"	*Ville de Paris* . .	104	" George Wilkinson.*	Foundered returning from Jamaica.
1782	" 12	*Racoon*, brig . .	14	Lieut. Edmund Nagle.	Taken by *Gloire* and *Aigle*.
1782	..	*Polecat*, brig . .	14	" Hon. Patrick Napier.	Taken by the French in N. America.
1782	..	*Allegiance* . . .	14	Com. David Phips.	Taken by the Americans.
1782	..	*Lively*, brig. . .	14	Lieut. M. Stanhope.	Captured by prisoners and taken to Havana.
1782	..	*Prince Edward*, brig	14	" Richard Simmonds.	Captured by her American prisoners.
1782	..	*Resolution*, armed transp. . . .	14	" R. F. Hassard.	Taken by the French in the E. Indies.
1782	..	*Raikes*, armed transp.	14	" Norris Thompson.	Taken by the French in the E. Indies.
1782	..	*Flying Fish*, cutter	14	" Charles Craven.	Wrecked near Calais.
1782	..	*Placentia*, brig . .	14	" Charles Anderson.*	Wrecked off Newfoundland.
1782	..	*Cornwallis*, armed ship	14	" R. T. Appleby.*	Foundered in the Atlantic.
1783	Feb. 16	*Argo*	44	Capt. John Butchart.	Taken by the *Nymphe*, 36, and *Amphitrite*, 32. Retaken, 19.2.83, by *Invincible*, 74.
1783	Nov. 5	*Superb*	74	Vice-Adm. Sir Edward Hughes. Capt. Henry Newcome.	Wrecked off Tellicherry, E. Indies.
1783	..	*Cato*	50	Vice-Adm. Sir Hyde Parker (1), Kt.* Capt. James Clark.*	Lost going to the E. Indies.
1783	..	*Pallas*	36	" Christopher Parker (2).	Run ashore on St. George's Isle.
1783	..	*Cerberus*. . . .	32	" Sir Jacob Wheate, Bt.	Wrecked near Bermuda.
1783	..	*Raven*	16	Com. John Wells.	Taken by two French frigates in W. Indies.
1783	..	*Mentor*	16	" R. Tullidge.	Wrecked near Bermuda.
1783	..	*Tickler*	14	" William O'Brien Drury.	Taken by a French frigate in W. Indies.

B.—VESSELS OF THE UNITED STATES NAVY, AND OF THE REGULAR COLONIAL MARINES TAKEN, DESTROYED, BURNT, FOUNDERED OR WRECKED DURING THE WAR OF AMERICAN REVOLUTION.

Year.	Date.	Name.	Guns.	Commander. * Lost his life.	Remarks.
1777	Mar. 26	*Cabot*[1]	16	Joseph Olney.	Chased ashore, taken, and got off by *Milford*, 28, Capt. John Ford.
1777	May	*Surprise*	10	Gustavus Conyngham.	Seized by the French, as a pirate.
1777	July 8	*Hancock*[2]	32	John Manly.	Taken by *Rainbow*, 44, Capt. Sir George Collier.
1777	„ 8	*Fox*	28	..	Retaken by *Flora*, 32, Capt. John Brisbane.
1777	..	*Andrea Doria*	14	..	Burnt to save her from capture in the Delaware.
1777	Sept. 22	*Lexington*	16	H. Johnston.	Taken by *Alert*, 10, Lieut. John Bazely (1), in Channel.
1777	„ 27	*Delaware*[1]	24	Charles Alexander.	Surrendered to British troops in the Delaware.
1777	Oct. 6	*Congress*	28	..	Destroyed to save her from capture in the Hudson.
1777	„ 6	*Montgomery*	24	..	Destroyed in the Hudson.
1777	Nov. 21	*Washington*	32	..	Destroyed in the Delaware.
1777	„ 21	*Effingham*	28	..	Destroyed in the Delaware.
1777	„ 21	*Sachem*	10	..	Destroyed in the Delaware.
1777	„ 21	*Independence*	10	..	Destroyed in the Delaware.
1777	„ 21	*Dolphin*	10	..	Destroyed in the Delaware.
1777	„ 21	*Wasp*	8	..	Destroyed in the Delaware.
1777	„ 21	*Mosquito*	4	..	Destroyed in the Delaware.
1778	Mar. 7	*Randolph*	32	Nicholas Biddle.*	Blew up in action with the *Yarmouth*, 64, Capt. Nich. Vincent.
1778	„ 9	*Alfred*	24	Elisha Hinman.	Taken by the *Ariadne*, 24, and *Ceres*, 18.
1778	..	*Reprisal*	16	Lambert Wickes.*	Foundered at sea.
1778	Mar. 30	*Virginia*[1]	28	James Nicholson.	Grounded, and was taken in the Chesapeake.
1778	Sept. 28	*Raleigh*[1]	32	John Barry.	Taken by *Experiment*, 50, and *Unicorn*, 20.
1779	Aug. 14	*Warren*	32	Dudley Saltonstall.	Burnt to save her from capture, in the Penobscot.
1779	„ 14	*Diligent*	14	Brown.	Burnt to save her from capture, in the Penobscot.
1779	„ 14	*Providence*[1]	12	Hacker.	Taken by Sir George Collier in the Penobscot.
1779	„ 14	*Hazard* (Massa.)	16	John Foster Williams (Mass.).	Burnt to save her from capture, in the Penobscot.
1779	„ 14	*Tyrannicide* (Massa.)	14	Cathcart (Mass.).	Burnt to save her from capture, in the Penobscot.
1779	Sept. 24	*Bonhomme Richard*	40	John Paul Jones.	Sank after action with the *Serapis*, 44.
1780	May 12	*Queen of France*	28	Rathburne.	Taken at Charleston, by Vice-Adm. Arbuthnot.
1780	„ 12	*Providence*	28	Abraham Whipple.	Taken at Charleston, by Vice-Adm. Arbuthnot.
1780	„ 12	*Boston*[3]	24	Tucker.	Taken at Charleston, by Vice-Adm. Arbuthnot.
1780	„ 12	*Ranger*[4]	18	Simpson.	Taken at Charleston, by Vice-Adm. Arbuthnot.
1780	..	*Protector*[5] (Massa.)	26	..	Taken by *Roebuck*, 44, and *Medea*, 28.
1780	May 12	*Bricole* (S. Car.)	44	..	Destroyed at Charleston, by Vice-Adm. Arbuthnot.
1780	„ 12	*General Moultrie* (S. Car.)	20	..	Destroyed at Charleston, by Vice-Adm. Arbuthnot.
1780	„ 12	*Notre Dame* (S. Car.)	16	..	Destroyed at Charleston, by Vice-Adm. Arbuthnot.
1781	..	*Saratoga*	16	John Young.	Supposed lost at sea.
1781	Apr. 14	*Confederacy*	32	Seth Harding.	Taken by *Orpheus*, 32, and *Roebuck*, 44.
1781	Aug. 9	*Trumbull*	28	James Nicholson.	Taken by the *Iris*, 32, and *General Monk*, 18.
1782	Dec. 23	*South Carolina* (S. Car.)	40	Joyner (S. Car.).	Taken by *Diomede*, 44, *Astræa*, 32, and *Quebec*, 32.

[1] Added to the Royal Navy under same name.
[2] Added to the Royal Navy as *Iris*.
[3] Added to the Royal Navy as *Charleston*, 28.
[4] Added to the Royal Navy as *Halifax*.
[5] Added to the Royal Navy as *Hussar*, 28.

C.—Vessels of the French Navy, Taken, Destroyed, or Burnt by H.M. Ships, and also, so far as can be Ascertained, Similar Vessels Lost or Wrecked during the War, 1778–1783.

Year.	Date.	Name.	Guns.	Remarks.
1778	June 17	*Coureur*[1]	14	Taken by the *Alert*, cutter, 10, Lieut. Wm. Geo. Fairfax, Channel.
1778	„ 18	*Licorne*[1]	32	Taken by the fleet under Lord Keppel, Channel.
1778	„ 19	*Pallas*[1]	32	Taken by the fleet under Lord Keppel, Channel. Renamed *Convert.*
1778	Aug. 25	*Sartine*[1]	32	Taken by the squadron of Vice-Adm. Sir E. Vernon. E. Indies.
1779	Jan. 31	*Oiseau*[1]	32	Taken by the *Apollo*, 32, Capt. Philemon Pownall, Channel.
1779	May 13	*Valeur*	6	Destroyed by the squadron of Sir James Wallace, Cancale Bay.
1779	„ 13	*Écluse*	8	Destroyed by the squadron of Sir James Wallace, Cancale Bay.
1779	..	*Sphinx*	20	Taken by the *Proserpine*, 28, Capt. George Anson Byron.
1779	May 13	*Dieppe*, cutter	16	Destroyed by the squadron of Sir James Wallace, Cancale Bay.
1779	..	*Fénelon*	14	Taken by the *Rattlesnake*, cutter, 10, Lieut. William Knell.
1779	May 13	*Danaé*[1]	26	Taken by the *Experiment*, 50, Capt. Sir Jas. Wallace.
1779	June 2	*Prudente*[1]	36	Taken by the *Ruby*, 64, Capt. Michael John Everitt.*
1779	„ 22	*Hélène*	16	Taken by the *Ambuscade*, 32, Capt Hon. Charles Phipps.
1779	Aug.	*Compas*, flûte	18	Taken by the *Boreas*, 28, Capt. Charles Thompson (1).
1779	Oct. 2	*Pilote*[1]	14	Taken by the *Jupiter*, 50, and consorts, Channel.
1779	„ 2	*Mutine*[1]	14	Taken by the *Apollo*, 32, and consorts, Channel.
1779	„ 20	*Alcmène*[1]	26	Taken by the *Proserpine*, 32, Capt. George Anson Byron.
1779	„ 21	*Blanche*[1]	32	Taken by the *Magnificent*, 74.
1779	Dec. 22	*Fortunée*[1]	32	Taken by the *Suffolk*, 74.
1779	„ 22	*Elise*	28	Taken by the *Magnificent*, 74, and *Stirling Castle*, 64.
1780	Feb. 24	*Protée*[1]	64	Taken by the squadron of Rear-Adm. Hon. Robt. Digby, Bay of Biscay.
1780	June 26	*Sans Pareil*, cutter	..	Taken in W. Indies by *Phœnix*, 44, etc.
1780	July 1	*Artois*[1]	40	Taken by the *Romney*, 50, Capt. Roddam Home, coast of Portugal.
1780	„ 5	*Hussard*	18	Taken off Ushant by *Nonsuch*, 64, Capt. Sir James Wallace.
1780	„ 5	*Capricieuse*	32	Taken and burnt by the *Prudente*, 36, and *Licorne*, 32.
1780	„ 5	*Perle*	18	Taken by the *Romney*, 50, Capt. Roddam Home, coast of Portugal.
1780	„ 12	*Belle Poule*[1]	32	Taken by the *Nonsuch*, 64, Capt. Sir Jas. Wallace, coast of France.
1780	..	*Légère*	36	Driven ashore and destroyed by the *Nonsuch*, 64.
1780	..	*Renard*[1]	18	Taken by the *Brune*, 32, Capt. Fras. John Hartwell, W. Indies.
1780	Aug. 10	*Nymphe*[1]	32	Taken by the *Flora*, 36, Capt. William Peere Williams, off Ushant.
1780	Oct.	*Intrepide*	74	Lost in the hurricane, W. Indies.
1780	..	*Palmier*	74	Lost.
1780	..	*Magnifique*	74	Lost.
1780	Oct.	*Junon*	40	Lost in the hurricane, W. Indies.
1780	Nov. 2	*Sénégal*, ex *Racehorse*	18	Taken by the *Zephyr*, 14, Com. John Inglis (1), coast of Africa.
1781	Jan. 4	*Minerve*[1]	32	Ex *Minerva*. Taken by the *Courageux*, 74, Capt. Lord Mulgrave, etc. Renamed *Recovery*.
1781	Feb.	*Rover* (ex-British)	18	Taken by a privateer, but lost at sea.
1781	..	*Alerte*	18	Taken by the *Perseverance*, 36, Capt. Skeffington Lutwidge, N. America.
1781	Apr. 20	*Licorne*[1]	20	Taken by the *Resource*, 28, Capt. Bar. Samuel Rowley, W. Indies.
1781	July 26	*Lively*	26	Taken by the *Perseverance*, Capt. S. Lutwidge, Channel.
1781	Sept. 2	*Magicienne*[1]	32	Taken by the *Chatham*, 50, Capt. And. Snape Douglas, N. America.
1781	Oct. 26	*Necker*,[1] armed ship	28	Taken by the *Hannibal*, 50, Cape of Good Hope.
1782	Apr. 12	*Ville de Paris*[1]	104	Taken in Lord Rodney's victory.
1782	„ 12	*Glorieux*[1]	74	Taken in Lord Rodney's victory.
1782	„ 12	*Hector*[1]	74	Taken in Lord Rodney's victory.
1782	„ 12	*César*	74	Burnt after Lord Rodney's victory.
1782	„ 12	*Ardent*[1]	64	Taken in Lord Rodney's victory.
1782	„ 19	*Caton*[1]	64	Taken by Lord Hood in the Mona Passage.
1782	..	*Bizarre*	64	Wrecked near Trincomale.
1782	Apr. 19	*Jason*[1]	64	Taken by Lord Hood in the Mona Passage.
1782	„ 19	*Aimable*[1]	32	Taken by Lord Hood in the Mona Passage.
1782	„ 19	*Cérès*[1]	18	Taken by Lord Hood in the Mona Passage.
1782	„ 21	*Pégase*[1]	74	Taken by the *Foudroyant*, 80, Capt. John Jervis, Bay of Biscay.
1782	..	*Orient*	74	Wrecked near Trincomale.
1782	Apr. 23	*Actionnaire*, flûte (24)	64	Taken by the *Queen*, 98, Capt. Hon. Fred. Lewis Maitland, Bay of Biscay.

[1] Added to H.M. Navy.

Year.	Date.	Name.	Guns.	Remarks.
1782	..	*Dauphin*, flûte (26) . .	64	Taken by the *Argo*, 44, Capt. John Butchart, W. Indies.
1782	July 29	*Amazone*	36	Taken, but abandoned, by *Santa Margarita*, 36, Capt. Elliot Salter, N. America.
1782	,, 30	*Téméraire*	10	Taken by the *Cormorant*, 16, Com. John Melcombe.
1782	Sept. 1	*Aigle*, hired	22	Taken by *Duc de Chartres*, 18, Capt. John Child Purvis, off Cape Henry.
1782	..	*Espion*, cutter . . .	16	Taken by the *Lizard*, 28, Capt. Edmund Dod, off St. Kitts.
1782	Sept. 4	*Hébé*[1]	40	Taken by the *Rainbow*, 44, Capt. Henry Trollope, Channel.
1782	,, 14	*Aigle*[1].	40	Taken by squadron of Capt. Hon. Geo. Keith Elphinstone, off the Delaware.
1782	Oct. 18	*Scipion*	74	Driven ashore by *London*, 98, and *Torbay*, 74, Hispaniola.
1782	Dec. 6	*Solitaire*	64	Taken by the *Ruby*, 64, Capt. John Collins, Atlantic.
1782	,, 6	*Amphitrite*	18	Taken by Sir R. Hughes's squadron.
1782	,, 12	*Menagère*, flûte (34). .	64	Taken by *Mediator*, 44, Capt. Hon. John Luttrell.
1783	Jan. 11	*Railleur*	14	Taken by the *Cyclops*, 28, American coast.
1783	,, 16	*Chasseur*	20	Taken by the *Medea*, 28, Capt. Erasmus Gower.
1783	,, 22	*Sibylle*	36	Taken by *Hussar*, 28, Capt. Thos. Macnamara Russell, N. America.
1783	Feb. 15	*Concorde*[1]	36	Taken by *St. Albans*, etc.
1783	Mar. 2	*Coquette*	28	Taken by the *Resistance*, 44, Capt. James King, off Turk's Island.
1783	Apr. 14	*Naïade*	20	Taken by the *Sceptre*, 64, Capt. Samuel Graves (2), East Indies.

[1] Added to H.M. Navy.

D.—Vessels of the Spanish Navy, Taken, Destroyed, or Burnt by H.M. Ships, and, so far as can be Ascertained, Similar Vessels Lost or Wrecked during the War, 1779–1782.

Year.	Date.	Name.	Guns.	Remarks.
1779	Sept. 14	*Santa Monica*[1] . . .	28	Taken by the *Pearl*, 32, Capt. Geo. Montagu, off the Azores.
1779	Nov. 11	*Santa Margarita*[1] . .	28	Taken by the *Tartar*, 28, Capt. Alex. Graeme, off Lisbon.
1780	Jan. 16	*Fenix*[1]	80	Taken in Lord Rodney's victory off St. Vincent. Renamed *Gibraltar*.
1780	,, 16	*Monarca*[1]	70	Taken in Lord Rodney's victory off St. Vincent.
1780	,, 16	*Princesa*[1]	70	Taken in Lord Rodney's victory off St. Vincent.
1780	,, 16	*Diligente*[1].	70	Taken in Lord Rodney's victory off St. Vincent.
1780	,, 16	*San Domingo* . . .	70	Blown up in action with Lord Rodney's fleet.
1780	,, 17	*San Juliano*	70	Drove ashore after capture in Lord Rodney's action.
1780	,, 17	*San Eugenio*	70	Drove ashore after capture in Lord Rodney's action.
1781	Feb. 25	*Grana*[1]	30	Taken by the *Cerberus*, 32, Capt. Robert Man (3), Bay of Biscay.
1781	May 2	*Santa Leocadia*[1] . .	34	Taken by the *Canada*, 74, Capt. Sir Geo. Collier Bay of Biscay.
1782	Mar. 16	*Santa Catalina* . . .	34	Taken and burnt by the *Success*, 32, Capt. Charles Morice Pole, Bay of Biscay.
1782	,, 16	*Santa Catalina* . . .	22	Taken by the *Fox*, 32, Capt. Geo. Stoney, off Jamaica.
1782	Sept. 14	*Pastor*	31	Burnt in action at Gibraltar.
1782	,, 14	*Paula Prima* . . .	31	Burnt in action at Gibraltar.
1782	,, 14	*Talla Piedra* . . .	31	Burnt in action at Gibraltar.
1782	,, 14	*Rosario*	29	Burnt in action at Gibraltar.
1782	..	*San Miguel*[1]. . . .	72	Driven ashore and taken by garrison of Gibraltar.
1782	Sept. 14	*San Cristóbal* . . .	28	Burnt in action at Gibraltar.
1782	,, 14	*Principe Carlos*. . .	15	Burnt in action at Gibraltar.
1782	,, 14	*Paula Segunda* . . .	13	Burnt in action at Gibraltar.
1782	,, 14	*San Juan*.	13	Burnt in action at Gibraltar.
1782	,, 14	*Santa Ana*	11	Burnt in action at Gibraltar.
1782	,, 14	*Dolores*	10	Burnt in action at Gibraltar.

[1] Added to H.M. Navy.

E.—Vessels of the Dutch Navy, Taken, Destroyed, or Burnt by H.M. Ships during the War, 1780–1782.

Year.	Date.	Name.	Guns.	Remarks.
1780	Dec. 30	*Prinses Carolina* [1]	54	Taken by the *Marlborough*, 74, Capt. T. Penny, etc., Channel.
1780	..	*Hollandia*	64	Sunk after the battle of the Doggersbank.
1781	Jan. 5	*Rotterdam* [1]	50	Taken by the *Warwick*, 50, Capt. Hon. Geo. Keith Elphinstone, etc.
1781	Feb. 4	*Mars* [1]	60	Taken by Lord Rodney's fleet, W. Indies. Renamed *Prince Edward*.
1781	,,	*Mars* [1]	38	Taken by Lord Rodney's fleet, W. Indies.
1781	..	*St. Eustatia* [1]	28	Taken by Lord Rodney's fleet, W. Indies.
1781	May 30	*Castor*	36	Taken by the *Flora*, 36, Capt. W. P. Williams, off Ceuta.
1781	Aug. 14	A dogger	18	Blew up in action with *Cameleon*, 14.
1782	..	A brig	16	Taken by *Defiance*, armed ship, 18, Lieut. George Cadman, N. Sea.

[1] Added to H.M. Navy.

CAPTAIN NICHOLAS BIDDLE, U.S.N.

Blown up in the U.S.S. *Randolph*, March 7th, 1778. (*See* p. 10.)

(*From an engraving by D. Edwin.*)

CHAPTER XXXIII.

VOYAGES AND DISCOVERIES, 1763–1792.

Sir Clements Markham, K.C.B., F.R.S.

Byron to the Pacific—Wallis and Carteret to the Pacific—Cook's first and second voyages—Phipps and Lutwidge to the Arctic—Abortive voyages to the Arctic—Cook's third voyage and death—Wilson at the Pelew Islands—McCluer at New Guinea—Bligh's expedition—Voyages of Vancouver.

AFTER the voyage of Anson, the British Government fully recognised that discovery and exploration formed an important part of the duties of the Navy. In the instructions to Captain Byron, the Lords Commissioner of the Admiralty declared that "nothing

MEDAL COMMEMORATIVE OF COOK'S SECOND VOYAGE.

(From an original lent by H.S.H. Capt. Prince Louis of Battenberg, R.N.)

can redound more to the honour of this nation as a maritime power, to the dignity of the Crown of Great Britain, and to the advancement of the trade and navigation thereof, than to make discoveries of countries hitherto unknown."

In accordance with these views, an expedition was fitted out for the circumnavigation of the globe, consisting of a sixth rate, the *Dolphin*, of 24 guns, with a complement of 150 men, and the

Tamar, 14, Commander Patrick Mouat. It was placed in command of Captain the Hon. John Byron, an officer then aged forty, who had been shipwrecked in the *Wager* during Anson's expedition, and whose narrative of hardships and sufferings on the coast of Chile is so well known.

Byron's expedition sailed from the Downs on the 21st of June, 1764. Before entering the Pacific Ocean, Byron had orders to examine the land that had been reported between the Cape of Good Hope and Magellan's Strait, and called Pepys Island. He was also to visit the Falkland Islands, which had not hitherto been sufficiently surveyed.

On leaving Rio de Janeiro on the 22nd of October, Captain Byron turned the hands up, and announced for the first time that they were on a voyage of discovery, and that they would receive double pay if their conduct was satisfactory. They all expressed great joy at the news, and declared that there was no danger or difficulty that they would not cheerfully face, in the service of their country. Byron encountered a furious "pampero" off the Patagonian coast, and, after resting his people at Port Desire, he commenced his search for Pepys Island on the 5th of December.

This land was reported to be in 47° S., and is shown in that parallel on Halley's chart; but the only person who pretended to have seen it was Cowley, and, in his narrative, he gave no longitude. The two ships of Byron's squadron spread, and, as the weather was clear, they could see, between them, over about twenty leagues. Having convinced himself that there was no such island, Byron shaped a course for Cape Virgins, at the entrance of Magellan's Strait, anchoring about four or five leagues up the Strait on the north shore. There took place the Commodore's interview with the Patagonians, whose stature excited his astonishment. He did not measure them, but thought that the height of the chief could not be much less than seven feet. Mr. James Cumming, the first lieutenant, who was the standard of measurement, was six feet two inches in height. Byron then proceeded up the Strait for wood and water, before complying with his instructions relating to the Falkland Islands. For that purpose the vessels were anchored first at Sandy Point and afterwards at Port Famine.

In January, 1765, Captain Byron left the Strait, and took formal possession of the islands by the name of the Falkland Islands, Captain Strong, in 1689, having given the name of Falkland to the Strait which divides them. Byron came to the conclusion that they were identical with the Pepys Island of Cowley. He named the bay in which he anchored Port Egmont, and another large bay was called Berkeley Sound. Having made a cursory examination of great part of the group, the squadron proceeded to Port Desire again, to meet a store ship sent out from England, which duly arrived and was sent on to Port Famine. There she filled up the discovery ships, and sailed on her return to England on February 25th, 1765.

Byron passed Cape Pilar and entered the Pacific Ocean, running at the rate of nine knots before a slashing, south-easterly gale. As yet all his men were free from scurvy, which immunity he attributed to the supply of fresh vegetables of various kinds obtained in the Strait. The passage had occupied seven weeks and two days, the vessels having encountered very severe weather during the greater part of the time. Wood, water, fresh fish and goats were obtained at the island of Masafuera on the 28th and following days, and the squadron proceeded on its voyage on May 1st.

During his voyage across the Pacific, although he passed through the Dangerous Archipelago and not far from the Society Islands, Byron succeeded in discovering nothing, a most difficult feat on his part. He appears to have shaped a course direct for Tinian, where Anson had recruited his scurvy-stricken people. He sighted a coral island on the 7th of June, and it was unavoidable that he should see several others, but he appears to have made no attempt at exploration. Reaching Tinian on the 30th of July, he put up tents for the sick, who soon recovered from the scurvy which had afflicted them during the voyage. Byron remained nine weeks at Tinian, and touched at Pulo Tiuman and Batavia, proceeding home round the Cape. He sent the *Tamar* to Antigua to be hove down and have her rudder newly hung, proceeding home in the *Dolphin*, and arriving in the Downs on May 9th, 1766. His voyage was not satisfactory, the results being so small, and it was decided to despatch another expedition almost immediately. Byron was Governor of Newfoundland in 1769, commanded a squadron in North America and the West Indies against d'Estaing in 1779, with no success, and died, a Vice-Admiral, in 1786. He was grandfather of Lord Byron, the poet.

Captain Samuel Wallis was selected to command the new expedition on board the *Dolphin*, 24, with Commander Philip

Carteret (2), who had served in Byron's voyage, under his command, in the *Swallow*. They left Plymouth on the 22nd of August, 1766, a little over three months after Byron's return. In December, the two ships anchored in the same place, inside Cape Virgins, where the former expedition had been, and where Captain Byron had roughly over-estimated the stature of the Patagonians. Captain Wallis made exact measurements, with the result that the tallest among them were found to be from six feet five inches to six feet seven inches in height; the average being from five feet ten to six feet.

On the 17th of December, 1766, Captain Wallis commenced the passage of Magellan's Strait, anchoring at Port Famine on the 27th, where the ships were refitted, and abundance of fish was caught. There also, owing to the diet of fresh vegetables, the scurvy entirely disappeared. But the expedition was detained in the Strait longer than that of Byron. It was not until April 11th, 1767, that the *Dolphin* passed Cape Pilar, and on the same day the *Swallow* parted company, never again rejoining her consort. Captain Wallis devoted a chapter of his work to some useful sailing directions, describing the best anchorages in the Strait. He made his way across the Pacific, sighted land on the 4th of June, 1767, and passed several islands of the Low Archipelago, to which he gave names. On the 19th he came in sight of the lofty mountains of Tahiti, anchoring in seventeen fathoms on the following day, and thus making a great and important discovery.

Captain Wallis had a very difficult game to play during his stay at Tahiti, especially in managing the intercourse of his people with the natives. On the whole he displayed sound judgment and considerable patience. Native encroachments were firmly and consistently resisted, open attacks were duly but not too severely punished, and in the end he established friendly relations both with the people and with the Queen Oberea. His difficulties were increased by ignorance of the language, and the absence of any interpreter. Wallis remained for seven weeks at Tahiti, which enabled him to land his sick and restore health to the crew, as well as to obtain stores of fresh provisions. He gave the name of George III. Island to his discovery. Sailing on the 27th of July he shaped a westward course, passed near the lovely island of Eimeo, and also discovered Sir Charles Saunders Island, which has a high hill in its centre.

But there the discoveries of the *Dolphin* ended, for, as an explorer, Wallis was only half-hearted. With very little excuse, either on the ground of his vessel being unseaworthy, or his people being exhausted, he made the best of his way to Tinian, and thence home by the Cape, arriving at Plymouth on May 20th, 1768. Captain Wallis was appointed a Commissioner of the Navy in 1782, and lived in Seymour Street for many years, where he became the friend of Major Rennell and other geographers of that time. He died in 1795.

Carteret, in the *Swallow*, was parted from his consort just outside Magellan's Strait, with no rendezvous assigned, while the principal stores were on board the *Dolphin*, to which vessel the *Swallow* was little more than a tender. It required considerable nerve on Carteret's part to continue the exploring work single handed; and, in the circumstances, he would have been justified in returning home. He steered for Juan Fernandez to take in wood and water, resolving to carry out the work entrusted to him to the best of his ability, with the insufficient means at his disposal. He found that Juan Fernandez was no longer a desert island, but that it had been fortified and occupied by Spanish troops. He beheld the fort and surrounding houses with astonishment, for no news of this measure of the Spanish government, which had been adopted eighteen years before, had reached England. The order was sent out to occupy Juan Fernandez in 1747, after the publication of Lord Anson's voyage by his chaplain: and the arrangements were made by the Conde de Superunda, Viceroy of Peru. In 1751 a terrible earthquake destroyed the settlement, the governor and all his family being submerged by a huge wave; but the new Viceroy, Don Manuel Amat, promptly sent another governor, succour and reinforcements. Thus it was that Carteret beheld guns pointed at him from a fort, instead of the lonely beach described by Anson's chaplain.

Disconcerted by this surprise, Carteret, who had the experience gained from his voyage with Byron, made for the less accessible island of Masafuera. By throwing his casks into the surf, and by recourse to swimming, the boat's crew succeeded in watering the ship, but not without some hairbreadth escapes and enduring great privations on the island. Three men swam on shore, and the weather became so boisterous that they could not return. Abandoned and naked they kept warmth in their bodies by each one taking turns to be sandwiched between the two others. Their postures must have been unlike those of the Three Graces of Canova, remarks the Chilian historian of Juan Fernandez.

All the men were got on board by the 19th of May, 1768, and Carteret then took a northerly course, wishing to solve the question of Davis's Land which had been placed on the chart in consequence of a report from Davis the buccaneer. He suggests that the land seen by Edward Davis in 1687, was the small isles of San Felix and San Ambrosio near the coast of South America. The description, in Wafer's voyage, makes this impossible, and Burney had little doubt that Davis's Land is identical with the Easter Island of Roggewein.

Steering westward across the ocean, Carteret discovered an island on July 2nd, which was named Pitcairn's Island, because it was first seen from the masthead of the *Swallow* by a midshipman of that name. Carteret then sighted several coral islands to the south of the Low Archipelago, and thus missed Tahiti. In August the crew began to be afflicted by scurvy, and land was anxiously looked out for; but none was reached until they fell in with an island of the Santa Cruz group. The attacks of the natives with poisoned arrows made it impossible to refit. Carteret, who was himself very ill with scurvy, could do no more than get in a supply of water, and the next land he sighted was the New Britain of Dampier. There he made the important discovery that this land consisted of two islands, and he sailed between them. He named the other island New Ireland, and the strait St. George's Channel. At last he was able to careen and caulk his vessel, and to get some fruit for his scurvy-stricken people; but he was again fiercely attacked by the savages. Reaching Macassar, he was treated most inhospitably by the Dutch, who refused to allow him any fresh provisions, and he was obliged to sail onwards to Batavia. Carteret brought the *Swallow* back to Spithead on the 20th of March, 1769, ten months after the return of Captain Wallis. He became a Superannuated Rear-Admiral and died at Southampton in 1796.

During the absence of Wallis's expedition, the Royal Society had addressed the Government with a view to a vessel being despatched to the South Pacific to observe the transit of Venus over the sun's disc, which was to occur in the year 1769. The enlightened Government of that day readily acceded to the request, and resolved to fit out and despatch an expedition mainly with the object of observing the transit, but also for exploration and discovery.

The selection of a leader for this famous expedition was the most fortunate that ever was made; and the honour appears to have been due to Mr. Philip Stephens, the Secretary of the Admiralty.

James Cook, the founder of modern marine surveying, possessed qualifications which are rarely combined in one man, and which place him first in the glorious roll of maritime discoverers, not only in his own time, but for all time. He has no equal, and stands alone. He excelled all others in resolute determination, in patience and reasonableness, in devotion to his work, and in the power of taking trouble and of attending to minute details as well as to important matters. Others have had one or more of those qualifications in equal degree. No other has ever combined them so pre-eminently as Cook did, in a way which amounted to genius. The son of a farm labourer near Guisborough, in the North Riding of Yorkshire, James Cook was born on October 27th, 1728. He was taught to read and cipher at a village school, and at the age of twelve was bound apprentice to a man who kept a general shop at the little fishing village of Staiths, near Whitby. At Staiths, he saw the sea for the first time, and before long he got his discharge from the shop and bound himself apprentice for seven years to Messrs. Walker of Whitby, who owned the *True Love* in the coal trade. After he had served his time, young Cook continued to work as a foremast hand, until at last he was made mate on board one of Mr. Walker's ships. In 1755, Cook was in the Thames when there was a great demand for seamen to man the fleet, and, to avoid being pressed, he volunteered as an able seaman on board H.M.S. *Eagle*. She sailed to North America under Captain Hugh Palliser and took part in the capture of Louisbourg. It appears that Palliser was so impressed with young Cook's intelligence and ability, that he used all his influence to get him made an officer, and so successfully that in 1759 Cook was appointed Master of the *Mercury*, 24, which ship was also sent to North America, at the time of the expedition against Quebec. Then followed a series of valuable services in sounding the St. Lawrence during the war, and in surveying the coasts of Newfoundland. Cook's work was so highly appreciated at the Admiralty that, when it was resolved to send out an expedition to observe the transit of Venus, he was selected for the command, at the recommendation of Mr. Stephens, and received a commission of Lieutenant in His Majesty's Navy. The transfer of a Master to the executive line in those days was most unusual, while such a rise, from the rating of able seaman, was almost unprecedented. It reflects the highest credit on the Admiralty of that day, for no selection could have been better in any respect. Cook was by that time an officer of experience, an accurate and conscientious surveyor; and he possessed those far higher qualifications which could only be developed when he was face to face with the responsibilities of his position, and with the innumerable difficulties which surrounded the commander of such an expedition.

Cook was allowed to select his vessel, and he chose a strongly built bark of 370 tons, and drawing little water, named the *Endeavour*. Built at Whitby, she was purchased into the Navy, brought round to the Thames, and fitted out at Deptford Dockyard. Besides the Lieutenant-commanding, her complement of officers consisted of two Lieutenants and a Master, three Master's Mates, seven Midshipmen, a Surgeon and Surgeon's Mate, a Clerk, and three warrant officers. Mr. Joseph Banks of Revesby Abbey, a scientific botanist as well as a Lincolnshire squire of large fortune, volunteered to accompany the expedition, taking with him a Swedish naturalist named Solander, and four artists. Mr. Charles Green, one of the assistants at Greenwich Observatory, was appointed astronomer. It was originally intended to proceed to the Marquesas Islands to observe the transit. But Captain Wallis returned before the expedition sailed and recommended his new discovery so strongly that Tahiti was finally selected. Harrison had completed his invention of the chronometer, but none were supplied to the *Endeavour*. The expedition had to rely entirely upon the observations of lunars for its longitudes. This was one of the special duties of the astronomer, constantly assisted by Cook himself; and the accuracy of these lunar observations is, as the present Hydrographer has pointed out, one of the most remarkable results of the voyage. The first Nautical Almanac was published by Dr. Nevil Maskelyne, the Astronomer Royal, 1767; but it then only contained tables of declination, and distances of the moon from the sun and fixed stars, computed for the meridian of Greenwich and expressly designed for finding the longitude at sea. It was quite a thin volume.

Mr. Banks and his scientific staff joined at Plymouth, the expedition finally sailing on the 26th of July, 1768. Besides twenty officers and seven members of the scientific staff, she had a crew of sixty-seven men; so that the little vessel must have been very closely packed. This of course necessitated constant attention to the sanitary conditions, and to the diet, if the crew of the *Endeavour* was not to be decimated by scurvy; a fate which had attended all previous expeditions of the kind.

Cook resolved to abandon the practice of his predecessors, who navigated through Magellan's Strait during many weary weeks, in the face of strong adverse winds. He saved much time and fatigue by rounding Cape Horn, arriving safely at Tahiti on the 13th of April, 1769. The *Endeavour* anchored in the "Port Royal" of Captain Wallis, called by the natives Matavai. Lieutenant Cook's first care was to establish friendly relations with the people, and with that object he drew up rules to be observed by the ship's company, "for the better establishing of a regular and uniform trade for provisions, with the inhabitants of King George's Island." An observatory was established on shore, and the transit of Venus across the sun's disc was successfully observed by Captain Cook, Mr. Green, and Dr. Solander on the 4th of June, 1769.

Having taken this important observation, the commander, accompanied by Mr. Banks, circumnavigated the island in the pinnace, with a view of mapping the coasts and harbours. A very full and interesting account was drawn up of the island of Tahiti, its physical aspects and products, the appearance of the people and their manners and customs, manufactures, implements, language, religion, and government, with detailed descriptions of their weapons and canoes. When Captain Cook prepared for his departure, one of the most influential men in the island, named Tupia, volunteered to accompany him. This was very desirable, chiefly as a means of acquiring the language, and Tupia was received on board with a native boy as his servant. The *Endeavour* sailed on the 13th of July after a stay of three months, during which time judicious measures were adopted for maintaining friendly relations with the people, and order was maintained in the regulation of the traffic, which was principally managed by Mr. Banks. The northern extremity of Tahiti was named Point Venus.

Tupia informed Captain Cook of the existence of several inhabited islands to the westward of Tahiti, which were visited by the *Endeavour*; and the excellent chart based on Cook's survey was the only guide to mariners for more than a century. Retaining the native names for the six islands, some of which he visited and surveyed, Cook gave the name of Society Islands to the whole group, in honour of the Royal Society.

Sailing from the Society Islands, Cook shaped a southerly course with the object of ascertaining whether the alleged southern continent existed. He went as far as 40° S., but, meeting with very tempestuous weather, he laid aside this design and stood to the northward. On the 7th of October the land of the North Island of New Zealand was sighted from the masthead, and on the 9th the *Endeavour* was anchored in the entrance of the small river of Tauranga nui. On the 15th, Cook was off Akuriri Cliff, at the back of which now stands the flourishing town of Napier. On the 5th of November, the *Endeavour* anchored in what is now known as Cook's Bay. Passing the harbour where Auckland now stands, which is hidden behind a number of islands, Cook reached Hauraki Gulf; and on the 27th he named a cape after Sir Piercy Brett, one of the Lords of the Admiralty, who had served in Anson's expedition. On the 29th he anchored in the Bay of Islands; and on the 14th of December he reached the northern extremity of the North Island. Cook then examined the west side of the island. On January 13th, 1770, he was off the lofty-peaked mountain which he named Mount Egmont, and on the 15th he anchored in Queen Charlotte Sound, in the north-east part of the Middle Island.

Sir William Wharton, in annotating this part of Cook's journal, remarks on the extraordinary accuracy of his positions, on the characteristic tenacity with which he stuck to the coast in order to complete his survey, and on the mingled audacity and caution of his navigation.

He next proceeded to examine the coasts of the Middle Island of New Zealand. He named the southernmost point of the North Island after his patron Sir Hugh Palliser, but was not near enough to see the entrance to Port Nicholson, within which Wellington, the present capital of New Zealand, is situated. On the 17th of February, Banks's Peninsula, which Cook believed to be an island, was sighted, with its harbours of Lyttleton and Akaroa. On the 5th of March the *Endeavour* was off the south point of the Middle Island, and on the 9th South or Stewart Island was sighted. Cook believed that it was part of the Middle Island, and proceeded to examine the mountainous western coast. Sir William Wharton remarks:—

"The astonishing accuracy of Cook's outline of New Zealand must be the admiration of all who understand the difficulties of laying down a coast; and when it is considered that this coast line is 2400 miles in extent, the magnitude of the task will be realised by everybody. Never has a coast been so well laid down by a first explorer, and it must have required unceasing vigilance and continual observation in fair weather and foul to arrive at such a satisfactory conclusion; and with such a dull sailer as the *Endeavour*, the six-and-a-half months occupied in the work must be counted as a short interval in which to do it."

Cook devotes a chapter to a full and interesting account of New Zealand and the Maoris. Cook then discusses the question of a southern continent, the routes of Quiros and Roggewein, and the position of the much disputed Davis's Land. His conclusion is that there could be no continental land to the north of 40° S. between New Zealand and Cape Horn.

On the 1st of April, Cook left New Zealand and steered to the westward, sighting the south-east coast of Australia on the 19th. A gale forced him to run to the northward, and on the 29th the *Endeavour* was anchored in Botany Bay. Leaving it in May, he passed a bay which he named Port Jackson, after one of the secretaries of the Admiralty, on the 6th, but did not detect the existence of the magnificent harbour of Sydney. Proceeding northwards, Cook steered the ship between the land and the Great Barrier Reef, of the existence of which he was not aware. Soon he got among numerous shoals and islands, "the whole sea in his track being strewn with dangers," and on the 11th of June the ship struck and stuck fast on the Endeavour reef. Upwards of fifty tons of guns, ballast, and old stores were thrown overboard to lighten her, and the two bower anchors were laid out astern. Meanwhile the leak gained considerably on the pumps. Nevertheless Cook resolved to heave her off, and at ten on June 12th she floated, the leak still gaining. The commander fully expected that the ship would sink. He knew that the boats could not convey all his people to the distant and inhospitable shore. But when the ship floated it was found, to his surprise and joy, that the pumps actually gained upon the leak. Once more the *Endeavour* was under sail and standing for the land. Yet it was impossible long to continue the labour by which the pumps were made to hold their own against the leak. As its exact position could not be found, there was no hope of stopping it from inboard. Cook determined to fother the ship, and as a young midshipman, named Monkhouse, had seen this done on board a merchant ship, the operation was entrusted to his superintendence. Taking a lower studding sail, he mixed together a large quantity of oakum and wool chopped pretty small, and stitched it down in handfuls upon the sail, which, thus prepared, was hauled under the ship's bottom. When it came over the leak, the suction which drew in the water also carried with it the oakum and wool from the surface of the sail. The leak was so far reduced, by this means, that it was easily kept under.

During the whole of this trying time every soul on board, having perfect confidence in the commander, behaved admirably. The ship was brought into a river on the coast, which was named Endeavour River, where the flourishing port of Cook-town has recently risen into importance. A monument to the memory of Captain Cook has been erected on the very spot where his ship was careened. Here the *Endeavour* was thoroughly refitted; and it was here that kangaroos were first seen by Europeans. The name was obtained from the natives by Mr. Banks. Cook found a safe passage through the Barrier Reef, 150 miles to the north, which led him into Torres Strait, and which he named "Providential Channel." Thus was the whole coast of New South Wales discovered by the great navigator.

The navigation of Torres Strait is difficult and very intricate. The passage discovered by Cook, through what he called Endeavour Strait, is now little used, the difficulty of finding a narrow pass among the reefs, so far from land, having caused it to be abandoned. Cook established the existence of the strait between Australia and New Guinea, for the fact that Luis Vaez Torres passed through it in 1606 was unknown, the detail of that voyage having been concealed by the Spanish Government. It was first made known by Dalrymple.

After a short detention to examine the coast of New Guinea, and to effect a landing, on its western side, Cook made the best of his way to Batavia, where he anchored on the 11th of October, 1770. Among the successful achievements of this gifted sailor the greatest was perhaps his preservation of his people from scurvy. The usual antiscorbutics were supplied such as *saur-kraut*, inspissated lemon juice, molasses, portable soup, and malt to be made into wort; but this had been done before. Cook's success was due to his constant vigilance, and close personal inspection. No opportunity was ever allowed to be missed of procuring supplies of green food; such as the wild celery of Tierra del Fuego. Wort was served out as a regular article of diet. Cold bathing was enforced, unusual attention was paid to cleanliness, stoves were used to keep the decks dry even in hot weather, and the commander personally saw that all his sanitary regulations were carried out. Three slight cases of scorbutic disorder occurred on the voyage to Tahiti, and were promptly cured; otherwise there was no scurvy on board during the expedition; a result which was entirely due to Cook's vigilance and close personal attention to the sanitation of the ship.

But two months in the sickly climate of Batavia, a detention which was unavoidable in order to refit and execute repairs, brought on diseases against which the commander was unprepared. Dysentery and fever broke out, and the return home was saddened by the loss of both the Lieutenants, the Master and Surgeon, two Midshipmen, the Boatswain and Carpenter, Mr. Green the astronomer, three of Mr. Banks's artists, Tupia the Tahitian, and his boy; while the ship's company was decimated before the *Endeavour* reached the Cape. Out of 94 persons who left England in her, only 54 were alive when she reached home on the 12th of June, 1771.

The beneficial effect of this memorable voyage on the Government and on public opinion immediately became evident. It was fully admitted in Byron's instructions that one of the duties of the Navy was the prosecution of voyages of discovery. But now that important duty was carried out with an amount of alacrity and zeal which is deserving of all praise. Cook was justly looked upon as a genius, and as possessing unrivalled qualifications for such service. The old *Endeavour* was sold, and she sailed for many years as a collier in the North Sea. But within three months of paying her off, James Cook was appointed to command a second expedition of discovery in the Pacific Ocean. He again selected two Whitby built colliers, the *Resolution*, of 462, and the *Adventure*, of 336 tons. Cook was promoted to the rank of Commander,[1] and Lieutenant Tobias Furneaux, who had served with Captain Wallis in the *Dolphin*, was appointed to the *Adventure*. Two officers who had been out as Master's Mates in the first voyage, Charles Clark and Richard Pickersgill, were selected by Commander Cook as second and third Lieutenants respectively of the *Resolution*. There were other old *Endeavours* among the junior officers and men. Mr. Wales sailed in the *Resolution* and Mr. Bagley in the *Adventure* as astronomers, and two German naturalists, father and son, named Forster, were taken. There were also Mr. Hodges an artist, and a Swedish

[1] Cook's Commander's commission was dated Aug. 29th, 1771, and his commission as Captain, Aug. 9th, 1775.—W. L. C.

botanist, shipped at the Cape, named Sparman. Among the Midshipmen were George Vancouver the future commander of a famous expedition, and James Burney (1),[1] who afterwards wrote the standard work on voyages to the Pacific Ocean.

This time the ships carried four chronometers; and close attention was given to the supply of antiscorbutics, the vigilant Commander redoubling his efforts to preserve his people from the scourge of scurvy.

The chief object of Cook's second voyage was to solve the question of the existence of a great southern continent; a subject which, during the first expedition, had engaged the attention of the accomplished navigator. He was well acquainted with the early Spanish and Dutch voyages through the translations of Dalrymple, and with the speculations of cartographers; and the importance of deciding the question was recognised alike by men of science and by statesmen. Thus the avowed object of Cook's second voyage was to complete the discovery of the southern hemisphere. He was to proceed to the Cape of Good Hope, and to sail thence in a southerly direction in search of Cape Circumcision, reported in 1739 by M. Bouvet, a French commander, as having been sighted in 54° S. and 11° 20′ E. If it proved to be part of a continent he was to use his best endeavours to explore it, and he was to continue prosecuting discoveries in high latitudes, penetrating as near to the south pole as possible. On the 13th of July, 1772, Captain Cook sailed from Plymouth, with the *Adventure* in company, arriving at the Cape of Good Hope on the 29th of October.

On the 22nd of November, the expedition sailed from the Cape and shaped a course to the alleged position of Bouvet's Cape Circumcision. On the 10th of December, they sighted one of the flat-topped Antarctic icebergs, passing six on the 12th, some of them near two miles in circumference; and next day there were upwards of twenty in sight. On the 14th, the ships were stopped by the great polar pack. Having ascertained that Cape Circumcision had no existence, Commander Cook continued to examine the edge of the ice, amidst very perilous navigation, until he had crossed the Antarctic Circle, and reached a latitude of 67° 15′ S. He then bore up, and, having searched the Antarctic seas from the

[1] James Burney (1) was made a Commander on Oct. 2nd, 1780, and a Post-Captain on June 18th, 1782. He retired in 1804, and died many years later, a Superannuated Rear-Admiral.—W. L. C.

meridian of the Cape of Good Hope to that of New Zealand, he anchored in Dusky Bay, in the Middle Island, on March 26th, 1773. The *Adventure* had parted company, during thick weather, in February. Commander Cook found her in May, when the *Resolution* went northward to Queen Charlotte Sound. Lieutenant Furneaux had examined the east coast of Van Diemen's Land. In June, the two vessels sailed for Tahiti, arriving there on the 16th of August. Friendly relations were renewed with the amiable natives of that lovely island, and with their King Otu, who afterwards took the name of Pomare I. and reigned until 1808. On September 1st, the ships left Tahiti, and proceeded to Huaheine, one of the Society Islands, where Furneaux consented to take on board his ship a young native named Omai, whose conduct was excellent throughout the voyage, and during his residence of two years in England. The Prince of Wales, in a letter to Archbishop Markham, described the visit of Omai to King George III. at Kew. The ships then visited Uliatea, another of the Society Islands, and Commander Cook took on board a youth named Uadidi, who was a native of Bolabola.

The expedition next shaped a course to the Friendly Islands, which had not been visited since their discovery by Tasman. Commander Cook touched at the islands of Tongatábu and Eua, and then returned to New Zealand. There very severe weather was encountered, gale succeeded gale, and the *Adventure* parted company never again to rejoin. Lieutenant Furneaux went home by Cape Horn, and arrived in England a year before his senior officer. Thus left alone, the *Resolution* proceeded to Queen Charlotte's Sound on November 2nd, and waited in vain for her consort until the 25th.

On November 25th, 1773, Commander Cook sailed from New Zealand on his second attempt to penetrate far to the south. The first iceberg was encountered on the 12th of December in 62° 10′, eleven degrees further south than the first ice they saw in the preceding year, after leaving the Cape of Good Hope. On the 14th, there was loose ice, with many bergs, which rapidly increased in number as the ship proceeded southwards. The pack ice appeared to be composed chiefly of calvings from the bergs. For six weeks Cook faced the stormy Antarctic seas, and braved the perils of the ice; until, on the 29th of January, 1774, he was stopped by a field of ice extending far beyond sight to east and west, with a strong ice bleak to the south. This was in 70° 23′ S. As many as ninety-seven icebergs were counted within the ice, many of them of great size, besides those outside. The Commander believed that there must be land beyond the ice-field. He had reached 71° 10′ S. before he resolved to turn his ship's head northwards. Cook had now complied with his instructions; but, with a good ship and healthy crew, he felt it to be his duty to continue his discoveries. His plan was to fix the position of the Easter Island of Roggewein, and then to go in search of the "Espiritu Santo" of Quiros, finally returning by Cape Horn, and examining the southern part of the Atlantic Ocean. All his officers heartily concurred in the plans of their leader, and were resolved zealously to carry out his orders.

In the morning of the 11th of March, 1774, land was sighted and was identified by Cook as Davis's Land or Easter Island. Indeed, with the help of a glass, he could make out the colossal stone statues, described by the authors of Roggewein's voyage. On the 13th, he anchored off the island, and during the next three days he made a thorough examination of the curious platforms and statues, and noted the products and the character and appearance of the inhabitants. Thence the *Resolution* shaped a course to the Marquesas Islands, and on the 6th of April a young Midshipman named Hood sighted land, which proved to be an undiscovered island of the Marquesas group. Cook gave it the name of Hood's Island. The others discovered by Mendana in 1595 soon came in sight, San Pedro, San Dominico and Santa Cristina; and the ship was anchored on the 7th at the entrance of Mendana's Bay in Santa Cristina's Island. It was in July, 1595, that Alvaro de Mendana had discovered the group, and four of the islands which compose it were described by his chief pilot, Pedro Fernandez de Quiros. On the 28th, the ships of Mendana anchored in a bay of the island of Santa Cristina, which was named Puerto del Madre de Dios, and on the 5th they left the group which received the name of "Las Marquesas de Mendoza," in honour of the Marquis of Cañete, Viceroy of Peru, whose surname was Mendoza. The British Commander sought for and anchored in Mendana's port. The *Resolution* left the Marquesas on the 11th of April, 1774, and Cook devotes a chapter of his narrative to a description of the islands and an account of the inhabitants. On the 21st of the same month the *Resolution* was once more anchored at Tahiti, in Matavai Bay. The chief object of this second visit was to obtain the error and rate of the chronometers, and Mr. Wales landed at once with his instruments. At that time there was no one on the sick list. Once more the friendly relations with King Otu and his people were renewed. The ship also underwent a thorough refit; and the naturalists made a botanical excursion into the mountains of the interior. In May, the Society Islands were revisited, and young Uadidi, an excellent and useful lad who had been nearly a year on board, remained at Uliatea.

Continuing the voyage from the Society to the Friendly Islands, Commander Cook discovered several islands on the way, anchoring at Anamoca on the 27th of June, 1774. Thence he shaped a course to the "Espiritu Santo," discovered by Quiros on the 30th of April, 1606, and supposed by him to be the "Australia" of which he was in search. On the 21st of July, 1774, the *Resolution* was anchored in a bay of the island of Malicolo, one of the largest of the New Hebrides group. Several other islands were afterwards discovered and surveyed, and on the 5th of August the *Resolution* was anchored in a bay of the island of Tanna. Cook explored the whole group of islands forming the New Hebrides, which extends over three hundred and fifty miles. Sir William Wharton says: "Cock's chart of the New Hebrides is still, for some of the islands, the only one; and, wherever superseded by more recent surveys, the general accuracy of his work, both in outline and position, is very remarkable. On several occasions, up to the present year (1893), Cook's recorded positions have saved the adoption of so-called amendments reported by passing ships, which would have been anything but amendments in reality." After leaving the New Hebrides, Captain Cook discovered the island of New Caledonia, exploring the eastern side three hundred miles long, and Norfolk Island.

The *Resolution* returned to New Zealand to refit, anchoring in Queen Charlotte Sound on October 19th, 1774. After three weeks the ship resumed her voyage across the Pacific Ocean to Tierra del Fuego, making the desolate looking land on the 17th of December. At Christmas the *Resolution* was anchored in a bay which received the name of Christmas Sound, with numerous islets and snowy mountains bounding the view. The voyage was continued round Cape Horn, and through the strait of Le Maire. On the 3rd of January, 1775, Captain Cook left Staten Island and steered S.E. to discover the extensive coast line laid down by Mr. Dalrymple on his chart, in which was "the Gulf of San Sebastian." On the 14th, snow-covered land was sighted, and received the name of South Georgia, in 54° 30′ S. Pressing southwards, the existence of Dalrymple's continent was disproved, and Sandwich Land was discovered amidst snow, fogs, gales of wind and icebergs, in 60° S. On March 23rd, the *Resolution* was anchored in Table Bay. There Cook heard of the discoveries of the French captains, Surville and Crozet.

The *Resolution* was safely anchored at Spithead on the 30th of July, 1775, after an absence of three years and eighteen days. During the whole of that time Cook lost only four men, and only one from sickness. This remarkable immunity was not due to antiscorbutics, or very slightly due to them, for the *Adventure* was supplied in exactly the same way, yet suffered much from scurvy. It was due to the untiring vigilance of the Commander. He personally saw that his orders were carried out, that the men shifted into dry clothes when wet; that their persons, bedding, and clothes were kept clean and dry; that the ship was always clean and dry between decks, and frequently aired with swinging stoves; the air purified; the ship's coppers always kept clean. Cook modestly ends his narrative with the remark that "without claiming any merit but that of attention to my duty, our having discovered the possibility of preserving health amongst a numerous ship's company for such a length of time, in such varieties of climate, and amidst such continued hardships and fatigues, will make this voyage remarkable when the disputes about a southern continent shall have ceased to engage the attention, and to divide the judgment of philosophers."

This certainly was an achievement deserving of the highest praise. It was a great and important service to the nation; and it should be remembered that the explorers and surveyors, in expelling the scurvy from their ship, set an example which was but slowly followed by the rest of the Navy. The healthful condition of the officers and crew of the *Resolution* ensured that efficiency which resulted in so many valuable discoveries, and in the examination of the whole circuit of the southern ocean in the highest latitudes ever reached.

Commander Cook was promoted to post rank on his return, and was elected a Fellow of the Royal Society. He communicated papers on the prevention of scurvy and on the tides of the Pacific to the

Society, and prepared his own narrative for the press. The Royal Society caused a fine portrait medal to be struck in his honour.

It may have been the instructions to Cook to endeavour to solve the question of a southern continent, which suggested to the mind of Mr. Daines Barrington the importance of a renewal of Arctic exploration. Certain it is that he urged the matter on the attention of the Council of the Royal Society immediately

CAPTAIN THE HON. CONSTANTINE JOHN PHIPPS, R.N. LATER LORD MULGRAVE.

(*From an engraved portrait by Ridley in the 'Naval Chronicle,'* 1802.)

after Cook's departure on his second voyage, representing that there was evidence to show that a near approach to the north pole was not impracticable. The Royal Society was convinced of the importance of despatching an expedition to make the attempt, and submitted a request to the First Lord of the Admiralty that such an enterprise might be undertaken by the Government. Lord Sandwich entered warmly into the project, which was brought before him at the end of February, 1773. Two bomb vessels, the *Racehorse* and *Carcass*, were selected for the service and specially strengthened, the command of the expedition being entrusted to Captain the Hon. Constantine John Phipps (afterwards Lord Mulgrave), who sailed in the *Racehorse*, while Commander Skeffington Lutwidge was appointed to the *Carcass*. In the *Racehorse* there were three Lieutenants and a Master, three Master's Mates, and six Midshipmen. The *Carcass* had three Lieutenants and a Master, three Master's Mates, and six Midshipmen. One of these six midshipmen was Horatio Nelson, who thus, like Hyde Parker, Saunders, Brett, Riou, and many others among his predecessors and contemporaries, prepared himself for his glorious naval career by the very best training that a sailor can possibly have—service in an exploring expedition.

Captain Phipps's expedition left the Thames on June 4th, 1773, and in a month the two vessels were off the north-west point of Spitzbergen. On the 9th, they were in latitude 80° 36′ N. Captain

SIGNATURE OF ADMIRAL SKEFFINGTON LUTWIDGE, AS CAPTAIN, 1789.

Phipps then stood into every opening he could find to the northward; but was stopped, at every attempt, by solid fields of ice. He forced the ships, by press of sail, as far as possible through the loose pack. His highest northern latitude was in 80° 48′ N.; and he examined the edge of the ice extending over 20° of longitude, finding no opening in the polar pack in any direction. The expedition returned to England in September, after a careful and persevering examination of the ice, and after having attempted to bore through it at every point that offered the remotest chance of success. To force a way through the drifting pack, away from the land, against the current, is an impossibility; and this is what Captain Phipps was trying to do. But he did all that energy and good seamanship could possibly achieve, and he was well supported by his officers.[1] He is entitled to a very honourable place in the roll of Arctic worthies.

On the return of Captain Phipps, the British Government

[1] Commander Lutwidge was posted on Oct. 15th, 1773. He died a full Admiral on Aug. 21st, 1814.—W. L. C.

turned its attention to the discovery of a passage, round the northern coast of America, from the Pacific to the Atlantic. After full consideration, an expedition had been determined upon, when Cook returned from his second voyage. He might well have rested on his laurels; but this loyal and indefatigable public servant considered it to be his duty to volunteer once more. The offer of his services was gladly accepted by Lord Sandwich, and he was entrusted with the conduct of the projected voyage. The *Resolution* was employed again, and a vessel of three hundred tons, named the *Discovery*, was purchased to act as her consort.

Cook's instructions were to proceed to the Cape of Good Hope, and thence to shape a southerly course in search of some islands reported by the French in 48° S. Touching at New Zealand, he was next to proceed to Tahiti and land Omai, who had come to England with Captain Furneaux.[1] From Tahiti Captain Cook was directed to proceed to the coast of New Albion in about 45° N., steering northward along the coast of North America to 65° N., or further, if not obstructed by land or ice, and then to seek for any inlet leading in the direction of Hudson's or Baffin's Bays, and, if there were such an opening, he was to use his utmost endeavour to pass through. If there were no passage he was to proceed to Petropaulovski, or some other port, to refresh his people; and, in the spring of 1778 he was to make another attempt. If his object were found impracticable, he was to return to England by such route as he might think best for the improvement of geography and navigation. Captain Cook's instructions were dated July 6th, 1776.

The Admiralty also resolved to cause an examination of the west coast of Baffin's Bay to be made, to ascertain whether there was any opening leading to the westward. With this object the brig *Lion* was commissioned, and Lieutenant Richard Pickersgill, who had been with Captain Cook during his second voyage, received the command. Pickersgill sailed to Davis Strait in July, 1776; but only went as far north as 68° 14′ N., and returned in the autumn. His conduct was not considered satisfactory, and in the following year Lieutenant Young was appointed to the *Lion*, but his proceedings were even less successful than those of Pickersgill. The two voyages, in 1776 and 1777, to find a western outlet to Baffin's Bay were abortive.

[1] Commander Tobias Furneaux had been posted on Aug. 10th, 1775.—W. L. C.

Meanwhile, Captain Cook proceeded on his last voyage. The *Discovery* was commanded by Commander Charles Clark, who had been with Captain Byron in the *Dolphin*, and a Lieutenant in Cook's second voyage. Lieutenants John Gore,[1] James King,[2] and John Williamson[3] were in the *Resolution*; Lieutenants James Burney,[4] who had been a Midshipman in the second voyage, and John Rickman[5] in the *Discovery*. The Master of the *Resolution* was William Bligh;[6] of the *Discovery*, Thomas Edgar;[7] and among the Midshipmen was Edward Riou, who afterwards fell gloriously at the battle of Copenhagen, in command of the *Amazon* frigate, and Vancouver. Mr. Bagley, the astronomer, who had been with Furneaux, now sailed in the *Discovery*, and chronometers were supplied to both ships. Dr. Anderson was surgeon and naturalist, and Mr. Webber joined as draftsman. Omai, the Society Islander, was loaded with presents, and embarked for a passage to his native country. The expedition sailed from Plymouth on July 14th, 1776.

Captain Cook's first duty, after sailing from the Cape, was to examine the discoveries, in high southern latitudes, reported by French vessels; but he was supplied with few details. He visited Kerguelen Island, made a survey of Christmas Harbour, and then shaped a course for Van Diemen's Land, remaining a few days in Adventure Bay, and having friendly intercourse with the natives—a race now extinct.

On February 10th, 1777, Captain Cook was at Queen Charlotte's Sound, in New Zealand, and, after staying there a fortnight to recruit and refresh his people, he resumed his voyage. During the passage to the Friendly Islands, Mangia and other islands were discovered. After a stay of nearly three months at the Friendly Islands, where the people were presented with several useful animals, the expedition arrived at Tahiti on August 12th, having discovered the Island of Tubuai on the 8th. The old friendly relations with the king and people were renewed, and useful animals and plants were imported. After leaving Tahiti on

[1] John Gore (1) became a Captain on Oct. 2nd, 1780, and died in 1790.—W. L. C.

[2] James King became a Captain on Oct. 3rd, 1780, and died in 1784.—W. L. C.

[3] John Williamson (1) became a Captain on June 11th, 1782, and died in 1799. —W. L. C.

[4] *See* note, p. 130, *antea.*

[5] John Rickman, a Lieutenant of 1776, was never further promoted.—W. L. C.

[6] William Bligh ("*Bounty* Bligh"), of whom later, died a Vice-Admiral in 1817. —W. L. C.

[7] Thomas Edgar was made a Lieutenant in 1781, and died in that rank.—W. L. C.

September 30th, the islands of Eimeo, Huaheine, Uliatea, and Bolabola were visited. Omai was landed, with his numerous presents, at his native island of Huaheine. In the narrative of his third voyage, Captain Cook devotes a chapter to another full account of the Tahitians, their customs and language, chiefly from information collected by Dr. Anderson, the surgeon and naturalist.

Captain Cook then steered northwards with a view to carrying out the most important part of his instructions. In January, 1778, he came in sight of the north-western islands of a previously unknown group which he named the Sandwich Islands. It was a most important discovery. He touched, on this occasion, at the islands of Atooi (Kauai) and Oneehow (Nihau), and then proceeded on his northern course. On March 6th, he sighted the coast of New

MEDAL COMMEMORATIVE OF COOK'S VOYAGES.

(From an original lent by Capt. H.S.H. Prince Louis of Battenberg, R.N.)

Albion, discovered by Sir Francis Drake nearly two hundred years before. Cook remained a month in Nootka Sound, on the west coast of what, in honour of one of his own Midshipmen, is now called Vancouver's Island. Continuing his voyage to the north, he looked out for any strait or outlet leading in the direction of Hudson's Bay. Prince William's Inlet and Cook's River were examined and the western extreme of North America was reached. Passing through Behring's Strait, Captain Cook proceeded to examine the ice on either side. On the American coast he went as far as Icy Cape; but he was in shoal water on a lee shore, with the ice to windward driving down upon his ship. An immense herd of walrus was seen on the ice. The ships reached a latitude of 70° 6′ N., and attention was then turned to the Asiatic side.

Captain Cook resolutely persevered in this hazardous navigation for several weeks, but on October 26th the ships' heads were turned to the south, as the illustrious commander of the expedition had resolved to winter at the Sandwich Islands. The islands of Maui and Hawaii were sighted on December 1st, and on January 16th, 1779, Mr. Bligh, the Master, was sent to examine the Bay of Karakakoa, on the west coast of Hawaii. Next day the ships were anchored in that bay, friendly relations being established with the natives; and there the narrative of Captain Cook ceased. His life-work was completed. The story is continued by his faithful lieutenant, James King.

The king of the island, named Tiriobu, who had been absent in Maui, returned a few days after the ships had anchored, and was cordial in his reception of the explorers, while an observatory established on shore was made *tabu* and placed under the protection of the priests. On the 7th of February, the ships put to sea, but returned on the 11th, having encountered a gale of wind, during which the head of the foremast of one of the ships was sprung. The foremast was got out and towed on shore for repair, and the sails were also sent on shore to be overhauled and repaired, near the observatory and the watering-place. Soon afterwards the conduct of the natives became suspicious, the watering parties were molested, and a cutter was stolen. On the 14th, Captain Cook ordered guard to be rowed to prevent canoes from leaving the bay, sent Lieutenant King to the watering-place, and went himself in the pinnace, with Lieutenant Phillips of the Marines and nine privates, to a village called Kowrowa, where the king resided, intending to take him on board as a hostage for the restoration of the cutter.

Captain Cook marched with the Marines into the village, where he was respectfully received. He invited Tiriobu to spend the day on board. He at once consented, and his two young sons ran down to the beach and got into the pinnace. The rest of the party had nearly reached the seaside when the king's wife ran after him and entreated him not to go on board. At the same time two of the chiefs laid hold of him and insisted upon his remaining, while an immense crowd assembled along the shore. He sat down perplexed and irresolute. Lieutenant Phillips formed the Marines on some rocks near the water's edge. After vainly urging the king to come with him Captain Cook abandoned his plan, and was walking down to the boat. The boats stationed across the bay had fired at some canoes, and, at this juncture, the news arrived that a chief had been killed. The women and children were at once sent away, and the men armed themselves. One of them flourished his spear and threatened the Captain with a stone. The man persisting in his insolence, the Captain fired a charge of small shot which fell harmlessly on the war mats. Stones were then thrown at the Marines, and Captain Cook at length fired his second barrel loaded with ball,

H.M.S. "DISCOVERY":
ONE OF THE VESSELS WHICH ACCOMPANIED COOK ON HIS LAST VOYAGE, 1776–79.

(From a drawing by E. W. Cooke, R.A., made when the "Discovery" lay at Deptford as a convict hulk, 1829.)

and a native fell. There was a general discharge of stones, answered by a volley from the Marines. The natives stood their ground, and rushed upon the Marines with shouts and yells before the men could reload. There was a scene of horror and confusion. Four Marines were cut off and slaughtered, while the rest swam to the boat. Captain Cook kept the savages at bay while he faced them. But, when at the water's edge, he turned round and hailed the boat to cease firing and pull in. This humanity proved fatal to him. He was stabbed in the back, and fell with his face in the water. The body was dragged on shore by the yelling savages and lost sight of in the crowd. A fire was opened from the boat, and some guns were directed at the crowd from the *Resolution*, which at length forced the savages to retire. Four young Midshipmen then manned a small boat and pulled in to rescue any survivor, but no one was to be seen. When Mr. Bligh brought the news to the observatory, the foremast, and the sails which were under repair, were brought off to the ships.

After some consultation, Captain Clark,[1] who now assumed the command, decided upon adopting a policy of extreme leniency, though there was difficulty in restraining the officers and men. He ordered no reprisals to be made, even when the watering parties were attacked. There was, however, a revulsion of feeling among the natives, and eventually all that could be recovered of the great navigator's body, including the skull and hands, with his shoes and the barrel of his gun, were given up. The remains were placed in a coffin and committed to the deep with military honours.

Lieutenant King truly said that "after a life of so much distinguished and successful enterprise, Captain Cook's death, as far as regards himself, could not be reckoned premature." His glorious career was suitably closed. He died in the midst of his discoveries, and in the very act of humanely striving to protect his murderers. It is not possible to conceive a more glorious end. Lieutenant King went on to say: "Perhaps no science ever received greater additions from the labours of a single man than geography has done from those of Captain Cook. As a navigator his services were not less splendid, certainly not less important and meritorious. The method which he discovered, and so successfully pursued, of preserving the health of seamen, forms a new era in navigation, and will transmit his name to future ages amongst the friends and benefactors of mankind."

On the 20th, the foremast was stepped, and on the 22nd peace was restored. The cutter had been broken up. The ships then left this fatal spot and, after a cruise among the Sandwich Islands, they made sail for Kamschatka on the 15th of March, 1779, arriving on the 28th of April at Petropaulovski. Another attempt was made to penetrate the ice beyond Behring Strait, but it was given up in July, and on August 22nd Captain Clark died. Lieutenant

[1] Com. Charles Clark had been posted on Feb. 10th, 1779.—W. L. C.

John Gore (1) then assumed command of the expedition on board the *Resolution*, and Lieutenant James King was given command of the *Discovery*. Captain Clark was buried on shore at Petropaulovski.

Passing along the east coast of Japan, and visiting Macao, the ships returned by the Cape. They were driven to the northward when approaching the Channel, and anchored at Stromness in the Orkney Islands, whence King was sent with dispatches to the Admiralty. The *Resolution* and *Discovery* reached the Nore on the 4th of October, 1780. There is a memorable fact connected with Cook's third voyage which ought to be borne in mind, especially at the present day. When the expedition sailed, the insurgents in the American colonies had broken out into open rebellion. The Declaration of Independence was on the 4th, the departure of Cook's expedition on the 14th of July, 1776. The French and Spaniards declared war in 1778, when Cook was making discoveries in the icy seas. Thus was Great Britain calmly employing her sons to explore the unknown regions of the earth, for the advancement of civilisation and the good of mankind, at the very time when rebels and powerful enemies were banded together for her destruction. When Captain Cook met his glorious death in the midst of his discoveries Elliot was defying the united forces of France and Spain on the rock of Gibraltar. The necessity for repelling the attacks of enemies in front and of rebels in rear, did not for a moment induce the country to abandon her work of exploration and discovery.

At that period the ships of the East India Company were making occasional discoveries. In August, 1783, the *Antelope*, commanded by Henry Wilson, ran on a rock near one of the Pelew Islands and became a wreck. The group had been sighted by the Spaniards and others but it had never been explored. This was done by Wilson. He was very hospitably treated by the natives, and the crew built a small vessel in which they returned to Macao, taking with them a son of the king of the Pelew Islands named Prince Libu. Wilson took him to England, and he died of small-pox at Rotherhithe in December, 1784. McCluer, an accomplished surveyor in the service of the East India Company, was sent, with the *Panther* and *Endeavour*, to announce the sad news to the father. He had with him two officers, Wedgborough and White, who had both been with Wilson in the *Antelope*. They had been educated at the navigation school of Christ's Hospital, an institution which did such useful work in training youths for the Navy and mercantile marine in those days. Leaving Bombay in August, 1790, McCluer reached the Pelew Islands in January, 1791, and performed his melancholy task. He then proceeded to carry out the other part of his instructions, which was to survey the north coast of New Guinea. He was engaged on that work from July to December, 1791, and he discovered the great inlet at the western extremity which is still known as McCluer's Inlet. Returning to the Pelew Islands he addressed a letter on service to Wedgborough, dated February, 1793, resigning his command of the *Panther*, asking for arms and ammunition, which were given to him, and announcing his intention to remain on shore. The *Panther* returned to Bombay under the command of Wedgborough, while McCluer had wives and children and lived happily for fifteen months. He then began to long for news, and went in an open boat to Macao. There he got a vessel, returned to the Pelew Islands, took his family on board, and went to Bencoolen. He sailed from thence and was never heard of again.

Commander William Bligh's voyage in the *Bounty* to collect plants of the bread-fruit tree at Tahiti, and convey them to the West Indies, does not come within the category of voyages of discovery; and has been described in the preceding chapter. Bligh's stern and austere character did not expose him to the risk of succumbing to those temptations to which McCluer fell a victim. But the majority of his people were much more susceptible. After the mutiny in April, 1789, when Bligh was turned adrift in an open boat with eighteen men, his wonderful voyage, conducted with such extraordinary skill, almost amounted to an expedition of discovery. For he sailed over more than 3600 miles in three months before he reached Timor, and sighted several islands which were previously unknown. Bligh reached England with twelve survivors in March, 1790, and in 1791 he went out again in the *Providence*, and at length successfully performed the service of transporting bread-fruit plants from Tahiti to the West Indies.

When the news arrived in England of the seizure of Nootka Sound by the Spaniards, negotiations were opened which ended in the Spanish Government consenting to its restitution. The British Government resolved to send a vessel to receive Nootka Sound from the Spanish officials, and to complete a survey of that part of the North American coast. The *Discovery* was commissioned, a new vessel of 350 tons, and the command was entrusted to Commander George Vancouver,[1] who had served as a Midshipman under Captain Cook in the two last voyages, and afterwards in the West Indies under Sir Alan Gardner. An armed tender named the *Chatham*, of 135 tons, under the command of Lieutenant William Robert Broughton,[2] was placed under his orders. Vancouver received a written order signed by the Count of Florida Blanca, Spanish Prime Minister, and addressed to the Spanish authorities, ordering them to deliver up Nootka Sound to the British officer who should present it to them. On the 1st of April, 1791, the *Discovery* and *Chatham* left England.

Leaving the Cape on July 10th, Commander Vancouver discovered King George's Sound, on the south-west coast of Australia, in September, 1791, and proceeded thence to Dusky Bay in New Zealand. He reached Tahiti in the end of December. The tender had parted company in thick weather, discovering Chatham Island in November, and rejoining the *Discovery* in December, 1791.

Vancouver, a man trained under the eye of Captain Cook, had considerable ability and resolution, was a good sailor, and an accomplished surveyor. But some other qualifications for command were wanting. He was austere and unsympathetic. The corporal punishments on board the *Discovery* were excessive, and some of the Midshipmen were treated with harshness and even cruelty. It must, however, be admitted that young gentlemen such as Lord Camelford[3] were not easy to manage.

In January, 1792, the *Discovery* left Tahiti and shaped a course for the Sandwich Islands. On March 7th, Vancouver anchored at Waititi Bay, near Honolulu, the present capital, in the island of Oahu. He afterwards visited Kauai (Atooi), and found that, although so short a time had elapsed since their discovery by Captain Cook, several British subjects had already made their way to the Sandwich Islands.

[1] George Vancouver was a Commander of Dec. 15th, 1790, and a Captain of Aug. 28th, 1794. He died in 1798.—W. L. C.

[2] William Robert Broughton became a Captain on Jan. 28th, 1797, and died in that rank on Mar. 12th, 1821.—W. L. C.

[3] Thomas Pitt, Lord Camelford, born in 1775, was an officer whose eccentricities bordered upon madness, and led him more than once into serious trouble. He attained the rank of Commander in 1797, but resigned his commission, and was killed in a duel in 1804.—W. L. C.

On the 17th of April, 1792, the expedition sighted the coast of New Albion, near Cape Mendocino, and on the 29th the vessels anchored within the strait of Juan de Fuca, on the southern shore. Proceeding up the strait Vancouver again anchored in a harbour which he named Port Discovery. During the month of May the exploration of the strait was continued, and a deep inlet received the name of Puget Sound, after one of the lieutenants.[1] In June the surveyors continued their discoveries within the strait to the northward, in boats. They went through very severe work, and their indefatigable exertions established the insularity of Vancouver's Island by the discovery of a narrow channel, which received the name of Johnstone's Strait, after the Master[2] of the *Chatham*. In July the ships passed through an archipelago which was called after Lieutenant Broughton, who commanded the *Chatham*, and entered Fitzhugh Sound, on the coast of the continent, to the north of Vancouver's Island. This part of the coast had been visited by English traders in 1786, who had given the names of Queen Charlotte Sound and Fitzhugh Sound. On the 6th of August, the *Discovery* suddenly grounded on a bed of sunken rocks in Queen Charlotte Sound at the northern end of Vancouver's Island. The *Chatham* sent all her boats, the stream anchor was laid out, and an attempt was made to heave the ship off, but without success. But when the tide rose the efforts of a well-directed crew were rewarded and the ship was hove off. Luckily the water was smooth and there was no swell. On the 28th of August, Commander Vancouver safely arrived in .Nootka Sound, and was cordially received by the Spanish commandant, Don Juan Francisco de la Bodega y Quadra. A storeship, the *Dædalus*, had also arrived, but she brought the unwelcome news that two of her officers[3] had been murdered by the people of Oahu.

Nootka Sound had been occupied by the Spaniards, under orders from the Viceroy of Mexico in 1789. Señor Quadra had instructions to deliver over the settlement, with all its buildings, to the British. He was very anxious that some place should receive the

[1] Peter Puget, a Captain of Apr. 29th, 1797, became a Rear-Adm. in 1821, and died in that rank.—W. L. C.

[2] James Johnstone (2) was promoted during his absence to be a Lieutenant, became a Commander on June 22nd, 1802, and was posted on Jan. 22nd, 1806. He was afterwards Commissioner at Bombay.

[3] Lieut. Richard Hergest, commanding, and Mr. William Gooch, astronomer. Hergest was a Lieut. of 1780.—W. L. C.

joint names of the British captain and himself. In compliance with this request the whole island, on September 5th, 1792, received the name of the Island of Quadra and Vancouver.

In October, Vancouver left Nootka Sound and proceeded to examine the Spanish survey of the west coast of the island as far as the strait of Juan de Fuca; and in November he proceeded to the port of San Francisco, containing "a variety of as excellent harbours as the known world affords." No habitations were visible, though the herds of cattle and flocks of sheep on the surrounding hills indicated their existence. The inhabitants, it was afterwards ascertained, consisted of thirty-five Spanish soldiers in the Presidio, with some Indian servants and a few Franciscan monks. What a marvellous change has since taken place! The Spanish settlement was only formed in 1775. Vancouver was enchanted with the scenery when he rode into the country over twenty miles of what he described as comparable only to an English park. From San Francisco Vancouver proceeded to Monterey, where he found the *Chatham*. Her commander, Lieutenant Broughton, had been engaged in examining the Columbia River. From Monterey the storeship *Dædalus*[1] sailed for Port Jackson; and in January, 1793, Lieutenant Broughton was sent home with dispatches by the overland route across Mexico. Lieutenant Puget succeeded him in command of the *Chatham*.

In February, 1793, Vancouver returned to the Sandwich Islands, anchoring in Karakakoa Bay on the 22nd. The new king was the famous Kamehameha I., who came on board in a magnificent feather cloak and helmet, bringing numerous presents. He received in return five cows, two ewes, and a ram; and he gave all possible facilities for refitting and provisioning the vessels. In March, Vancouver proceeded to Oahu, where the murderers of the officers of the *Dædalus* were given up, tried, and executed. The islands of Maui and Kauai were also visited, and in April Vancouver returned to Nootka Sound to resume the survey of the North American coast. The work was very intricate and laborious, and a great deal of it was done in boats away from the ship. It was continued until October, extending as far as 56° 30′ N.; and in November the *Discovery* went south, and revisited Monterey. In December, the coast of California was examined as far as San Diego

[1] Under Lieut. James Hanson, who became a Commander in 1795, and was lost in the *Brazen*, sloop, on Jan. 25th, 1800.—W. L. C.

in 34° 42′ N.; and Captain Vancouver gives a detailed account of all the Spanish settlements and missions.

In January, 1794, Vancouver's expedition paid a third visit to the Sandwich Islands, again anchoring in Karakakoa Bay, and receiving visits from King Kamehameha. His Majesty solemnly ceded the island of Hawaii to the King of Great Britain, a cession which Vancouver conceived it to be his duty to accépt. He then completed a survey of the other islands, and in March, 1794, directed his course northwards, and reached Cook's River in April. Prince William Sound was surveyed by the boats; and the survey was then connected with the work of the preceding year. In August, the surveys of the continental shores of north-western America were completed, and the *Discovery* and *Chatham* proceeded to Nootka Sound.

After a pleasant visit to Monterey, Captain Vancouver proceeded southwards, having completed his arduous surveys. On December 14th, he sighted Cape San Lucas, the southernmost point of the peninsula of California, and fixed its position. He then visited the Tres Marias Islands on the coast of Mexico, and passed Cape Corrientes on the 19th. Touching at the island of Cocos, he next sighted the Galapagos; and during the subsequent voyage to the Chilian coast, scurvy broke out in the ship. This was a great mortification to Vancouver, who had endeavoured to follow the precepts of Captain Cook; but not with the same vigilance, nor could he count upon the same obedience, incited by respect and affection. The blame was thrown on the cook, for allowing the men to have lard to mix with their peas. The *Discovery* and *Chatham* arrived at Valparaiso on March 25th, 1795. Vancouver had orders not to put into any Spanish port on the west coast of South America, except in a case of necessity, but he considered that the damaged state of his mainmast justified the course he adopted. He was received with the greatest hospitality by order of the enlightened Captain General of Chile, Don Ambrosio O'Higgins; and he at once proceeded to get the mainmast out, and haul it up on the beach near the Almendral. It proved to be sprung two-thirds through, a little below the hounds. The mast was fished, but Captain Vancouver felt that "it would be but a rotten stick to depend upon." The sails were repaired and the ship refitted, while the Captain, with five of his officers, went up to Santiago to pay his respects to the Captain General. Vancouver gives some very interesting particulars respecting the origin and services of Don Ambrosio, and describes the road to Santiago, and the condition of the city as it was in 1795. On his return to Valparaiso he found that his troubles had been increased in his absence by the discovery that the mainyard was rotten half through and unfit for service. His only resource was to use the spare topsail yard, lengthened by the yard arms of the condemned mainyard. The work was done on shore, while the Captain drew up sailing directions for the port. At length, on May 7th, 1795, the *Discovery* departed from Valparaiso on her homeward voyage; with the *Chatham* in company. The *Discovery* arrived in the Thames on the 20th of October, the *Chatham* having reached England three days earlier. Notwithstanding the outbreak of scurvy, the *Discovery* only lost six men, their deaths being all due to accidents, and the *Chatham* not one, during a prolonged service of four years and nine months.[1]

Captain Vancouver's narrative was published in 1798, in three quarto volumes. The survey of the intricate inlets and channels along the north-west coast of North America, the discovery of the straits and channels dividing Vancouver's Island from the continent, and the examination of Puget Sound, the Colombia river, and the Californian coast, form a service which reflects the highest credit on Vancouver and his officers. Much of the work was done in open boats, and in boisterous weather, privations and hardships of long continuance had to be endured, yet the surveys were worthy of the disciples of Captain Cook—they can receive no higher praise. It is to the credit of our Government that these exploring operations were steadily supported and continued through the first and most critical period of our struggle with revolutionary France.

[1] Among the officers, not already mentioned, of the *Discovery* and *Chatham*, were Lieut. Zachary Mudge (who died an Admiral in the fifties); Lieut. Joseph Baker (who died a Captain in 1817); Master's Mate Spelman Swaine (who died a retired Rear-Adm. in 1848); Master's Mate Thomas Manby (who died a Rear-Adm. in 1834); Midshipman Robert Barrie (who died Rear-Adm. Sir Robert Barrie in 1831); Midshipman Volant Vashon Ballard (who died a Rear-Adm. in 1832); Master's Mate John Sheriff (who was killed in 1806, Commander of the *Curieux*); and Midshipman John Sykes (1) (who died an Admiral in 1858).—W. L. C.

CHAPTER XXXIV.

CIVIL HISTORY OF THE ROYAL NAVY, 1793–1802.

Administration of the Navy—The succession of officials—Salaries of Commissioners—Expenditure on the Navy—Number of seamen and Marines—Strength of the effective fleet—Naval architecture—Some typical ships—Changes of armament—Naval works—Manning—Bounties—Impressment—Allotment of pay—Deserters—Officers—Half-pay—Servants—Conduct money—Surgeons' head-money—Widows' pensions—Poor Knights of Windsor—Character of the officers—Prevalent abuses—False certificates—Prize money—Points in prize law—Points in international law—The right of search—Contraband of war—Freight money—Discipline—Mutinies—In the *Culloden*—In the *Shark*—At Spithead—At the Nore and in the North Sea—Other examples—St. Vincent's sternness—The case of the *Hermione*—Mutiny at the Cape—Punishment of mutineers—The Marines—Naval uniform—Medals—The Army and naval law—Morality of the lower deck—Prisoners of war—Signal towers—Telegraphs—Sea Fencibles—The Hydrographer—The Royal Naval Hospitals—Various improvements—Admiralty fees—The Flag.

SIGNATURE OF THE EARL OF CHATHAM, FIRST LORD OF THE ADMIRALTY, 1788–97.

THE succession of the more important administrative officers of the Navy during the brief period 1793–1802 was as follows:—

FIRST LORD OF THE ADMIRALTY.

John, Earl of Chatham.
1797. Earl Spencer.
Feb. 19, 1801. John, Earl St. Vincent, K.B., Admiral.

SECRETARY OF THE ADMIRALTY.

Sir Philip Stephens, Bart.
(As Assistant) John Ibbetson.
Mar. 3, 1795. { Evan Nepean.
William Marsden (2nd. Sec.).

TREASURER OF THE NAVY.

Rt. Hon. Henry Dundas.
1800. Rt. Hon. Dudley Rider.
Nov. 21, 1801. Rt. Hon. Charles Bragge.

CONTROLLER OF THE NAVY.

Sir Henry Martin, Bart., Captain, R.N.
Aug. 30, 1794. Sir Andrew Snape Hamond, Bart., Captain, R.N.

Deputy Controller.

Aug. 1793. Edward Le Cras, Captain, R.N.
Feb. 1794. Sir Andrew Snape Hamond, Bart., Captain, R.N.
Oct. 1794. Sir Samuel Marshall, Kt., Captain, R.N.
1796. Charles Hope, Captain, R.N.
Jan. 1, 1801. Henry Duncan (1), Captain, R.N.

Surveyors of the Navy.

{Edward Hunt.
{John Henslow.
Jan. 26, 1793. {Sir John Henslow, Kt.
{William Rule.

Clerk of the Acts.

George Marsh.
This office ceased on Aug. 2, 1796.[1]

Controller of the Treasurer's Accounts.

George Rogers.
This office ceased on Aug. 2, 1796.[1]

Controller of the Victualling Accounts.

William Palmer.
This office ceased on Aug. 2, 1796.[1]

Controller of the Storekeeper's Accounts.

Sir William Bellingham, Kt.
This office ceased on Aug. 2, 1796.[1]

Extra Commissioners.

Samuel Wallis, Captain, R.N.
1793. Sir Andrew Snape Hamond, Bart., Captain, R.N.
Dec. 1793. Samuel Marshall, Captain, R.N.
1793. Harry Harmood, Captain, R.N.
July 1794. Charles Hope, Captain, R.N.
This office, as such, ceased on Aug. 2, 1796.[1]

Commissioners without Special Functions.

June 25, 1796. George Marsh.
June 25, 1796. George Rogers (omitted from patent of Nov. 23, 1801).
June 25, 1796. William Palmer.
June 25, 1796. Sir William Bellingham, Bart.
June 25, 1796. Harry Harmood, Captain, R.N.
June 25, 1796. Samuel Gambier, Captain, R.N.
Jan. 1, 1801. Francis John Hartwell, Captain, R.N.
Nov. 9, 1801. Benjamin Tucker.

Commissioners at H.M. Dockyards, etc.

Chatham.

Charles Proby, Captain, R.N.
1799. Francis John Hartwell, Captain, R.N.
Jan. 1, 1801. Charles Hope, Captain, R.N.
(Until 1796 Sheerness Yard was under the inspection of the Chatham Commissioner.)

Portsmouth.

March 13, 1790. Sir Charles Saxton, Kt. and Bart., Captain, R.N.

---

[1] When these offices ceased, Commissioners, having no special branch to attend to, were appointed. By Order in Council of June 8th, 1796, it had been directed that, instead of Commissioners presiding over distinct departments, Committees should be formed.

Plymouth.

Nov. 13, 1789. Robert Fanshawe, Captain, R.N.

Sheerness.

1796. Harry Harmood, Captain, R.N.
Sept. 1796. Francis John Hartwell, Captain, R.N.
June 28, 1799. Isaac Coffin, Captain, R.N.

Lisbon.

Sept. 1797. Isaac Coffin, Captain, R.N.

Gibraltar, Malta, etc.

1793. Harry Harmood, Captain, R.N.
Nov. 1794. Andrew Sutherland, Captain, R.N.
1796. John Nicholson Inglefield, Captain, R.N.
Jan. 1. 1801. Sir Alexander John Ball, Bart., Captain, R.N.

Corsica.

1795. John Nicholson Inglefield, Captain, R.N.
1796. Isaac Coffin, Captain, R.N.

Halifax, Nova Scotia.

Henry Duncan (1), Captain, R.N.
Jan. 1, 1801. John Nicholson Inglefield, Captain, R.N.

Commissioners of Transport.

Aug. 1794. { Hugh Cloberry Christian, Captain and Rear-Adm. Philip Patton, Captain and Rear-Adm. Ambrose Serle.

Sept. 1795. { Rupert George, Captain, R.N. John Schanck, Captain, R.N. William Albany Otway, Captain, R.N. John Marsh. Ambrose Serle.

Dec. 1798. Joseph Hunt (*vice* Marsh).

(At the Peace, Captain Schanck was retired on a pension of £500 and Mr. Hunt was transferred to the Ordnance Department, leaving but three Commissioners of Transport.)

Hydrographer.

Sept. 11, 1795. Alexander Dalrymple.

The salaries of the Commissioners at Chatham, Portsmouth, and Plymouth, which, until 1801, were in each case £500 a year, with £12 for paper and firing, were then increased to £1000. The Commissioner at Sheerness was paid £800 a year until 1801, and then £1000. The Lisbon Commissioner's pay was £1000. The Commissioner for Malta, etc., received first £1000, and, in 1801, £1200. The Commissioner at Corsica was paid £1000. The Commissioner at Halifax received £1000 until 1801, and, thenceforward, £1200. Each Commissioner of Transport received £1000 a year.

The total expenditure, as voted by Parliament for the Navy from year to year, and the number of seamen and Marines authorised, were :—

Year.	"Extra."	"Ordinary."	—	No. of Seamen and Marines.	Total Naval Supplies Granted.
	£	£			£
1793	387,710	669,205	..	45,000	4,003,984
1794	547,310	558,021	..	85,000	5,525,331
1795	525,840	589,683	..	100,000	6,315,523
1796	708,400	624,152	..	110,000	7,613,552
1797	768,100	653,573	..	120,000	13,133,673[1]
1798	639,530	689,858	..	120,000	13,449,388
1799	693,750	1,119,063	..	120,000	13,654,013
1800	772,140	1,169,439	2 mos. 11 mos.	120,000 110,000	13,619,079
1801	933,900	1,269,918	3 mos. 10 mos.	120,000 135,000	16,577,037
1802	773,500	1,365,524	5 mos. 1 mos. 7 mos.	130,000 88,000 70,000	11,833,570

1 Including £5,000,000 "for preventing the increase of the debt of the Navy," etc.

The fluctuations in the strength of the effective fleet are thus summarised from the annual abstracts compiled by Mr. James:—

CRUISING SHIPS, EXCLUSIVE OF HARBOUR AND STATIONARY VESSELS, TROOP AND STORESHIPS, SHIPS BUILDING, ETC., AT THE BEGINNING OF EACH YEAR.

Class.	1793	1794	1795	1796	1797	1798	1799	1800	1801	1802
First-rates . . .	5	6	6	6	6	6	6	6	6	6
Second-rates . . .	16	16	17	16	16	17	17	16	16	16
Third-rates . . .	92	95	91	94	94	97	102	101	105	104
Total of the line	113	117	114	116	116	120	125	123	127	126
Fourth-rates . . .	12	12	12	21	16	16	14	14	13	13
Fifth-rates . . .	79	84	102	106	115	123	117	112	113	120
Sixth-rates . . .	35	36	35	37	40	41	42	34	34	28
Sloops	40	53	62	84	91	94	98	107	104	98
Bombs	2	2	2	2	2	11	15	15	14	14
Fireships . . .	5	3	3	3	3	3	7	7	3	2
Brigs, cutters, etc. .	18	21	33	36	52	94	99	97	103	104
Grand total. .	304	328	363	405	435	502	517	509	511	505

The total tonnage of the vessels enumerated above was, in 1793, 295,409, and, in 1802, 416,566.

Concerning the shipbuilding of the period 1793–1802, there is little that needs saying. Naval architecture underwent but small changes. In 1794, the Admiralty directed that frigates, from the 18-pounder 32's upwards, should in future be constructed with four-inch instead of three-inch bottoms. It was also at about the same time decided to give ships of war greater length in proportion to their beam than had been customary in Great Britain, and to raise the lower batteries in new vessels of the higher rates. Fir, as a material for hulls, was reintroduced for sloops in 1796, after it had been disused since 1757; and in 1797 seven frigates, with hulls of the same wood, were under construction.

Details of some of the most typical and important ships added to the Navy in 1793–1802 are given in the accompanying table:—

Name.	Length of Gun Deck.		Length of Keel.		Beam.		Depth of Hold.		Tons.	Men.	Guns.	When and Where Built, or how Acquired, etc.
	Ft.	In.	Ft.	In.	Ft.	In.	Ft.	In.				
Ville de Paris	190	0	156	$1\frac{1}{8}$	53	0	22	4	2332	850	110	Built at Chatham, 1795: design by Henslow.
Commerce de Marseilles	208	4	172	$0\frac{1}{8}$	54	$9\frac{1}{2}$	25	$0\frac{1}{2}$	2747	875	120	Taken at Toulon, 1793.
San Josef	194	3	156	$11\frac{1}{2}$	54	3	24	3	2457	840	112	Taken from the Spaniards, 1797.
Dreadnought	185	0	152	$6\frac{5}{8}$	51	0	21	6	2111	750	98	Built at Portsmouth, 1801: design by Henslow.
Foudroyant	184	0	151	$5\frac{5}{8}$	50	6	22	6	2055	600	80	Built at Plymouth, 1798: design by Henslow.
Canopus	197	7	160	8	51	0	23	3	2223	718	80	Taken from the French, 1798: ex *Franklin*.
Mars	176	0	144	3	49	0	20	0	1842	600	74	Built at Deptford, 1794: design by Henslow.
Belleisle	184	5	149	$5\frac{1}{4}$	48	9	21	$7\frac{1}{2}$	1889	690	74	Taken from the French, 1795: ex *Formidable*.
San Isidro	176	0	144	1	48	11	20	1	1836	590	74	Taken from the Spaniards, 1797.
Vrijheid	167	7	138	5	46	3	18	9	1562	..	72	Taken from the Dutch, 1797.
Aboukir	185	5	150	5	48	4	21	0	1869	..	74	Taken from the French, 1798: ex *Aquilon*.
Courageux	181	1	150	$9\frac{1}{2}$	47	1	19	10	1772	590	74	Built at Deptford, 1800.
York	174	3	144	4	43	2	19	7	1433	..	64	Built in the Thames, 1796.
Admiral de Vries	157	5	128	0	44	8	36	2	1360	490	64	Taken from the Dutch, 1797.
Tromp	143	10	117	10	40	9	15	3	1040	420	60	Taken from the Dutch, 1797: ex *M. H. Tromp*.
Diomede	151	0	124	$7\frac{1}{2}$	41	0	17	8	1 14	350	50	Built at Deptford, 1798.
Pomone	159	$2\frac{3}{8}$	132	$4\frac{1}{4}$	41	$11\frac{3}{8}$	12	4	1239	300	44	Taken from the French, 1794.
Pandour	134	3	108	11	39	3	15	2	894	300	44	Taken from the Dutch, 1799: ex *Hector*.
Seine	156	9	131	4	40	6	12	4	1146	280	40	Taken from the French, 1798, as a 42.
Endymion	159	3	132	3	42	7	12	4	1277	320	40	Built in the Thames, 1797.
Révolutionnaire	157	2	131	10	40	$5\frac{1}{2}$	12	6	1148	290	38	Taken from the French, 1794.
Fishguard	160	0	134	2	40	8	13	3	1182	280	38	Taken from the French, 1797: ex *Résistance*.
Hussar	150	3	125	8	39	6	13	9	1043	280	38	Built at Woolwich, 1799.
Réunion	144	0	118	$4\frac{3}{8}$	38	$10\frac{1}{2}$	12	1	951	255	36	Taken from the French, 1793.
Penelope	150	0	125	4	39	8	13	0	1051	260	36	Built at Bursledon, 1798.
Immortalité	145	2	123	10	39	2	11	5	1010	260	35	Taken from the French, 1793, as a 42.
Ethalion	152	0	129	2	38	0	13	0	992	250	36	Built at Woolwich, 1802.
Janus	133	1	110	7	35	8	12	0	740	200	32	Taken from the Dutch, 1796: ex *Argo*.
Unité	142	5	118	5	37	8	11	0	893	250	32	Taken from the French, 1796, as a 38.
Pique	146	7	123	1	39	7	11	10	1028	270	32	Taken from the French, 1800: ex *Pallas*, 40.
Tartar	142	2	118	5	37	6	12	6	886	260	32	Built at Frindsbury, 1801: design by Henslow.
Braak	116	6	95	8	34	8	10	6	613	150	24	Taken from the Dutch, 1799: ex *Minerva*.
Bourdelais	138	6	116	6	31	9	15	1	625	190	24	Taken from the French, 1799 (a privateer).
Babet	119	3	99	$5\frac{3}{8}$	31	1	9	$4\frac{1}{2}$	511	170	20	Taken from the French, 1794.
Heureux	127	8	102	9	33	1	16	2	598	150	20	Taken from the French, 1799 (a privateer).
Swift	100	0	81	$11\frac{3}{4}$	27	6	13	6	3 9	100	16	Built at Portsmouth, 1793.
Hornet	108	4	90	$9\frac{5}{8}$	29	7	9	0	423	125	16	Built in the Thames, 1794.
Bonne Citoyenne	120	1	100	6	30	11	8	7	511	120	20	Taken from the French, 1796.
Arrow	128	8	..		30	0	7	11	386	120	18	Built at Redbridge, 1796.
Havik	101	10	83	5	25	8	12	9	365	1 0	18	Taken from the Dutch, 1796.
Lutine	145	2	121	8	39	0	11	6	332	120	18	Taken from the French, 1798.
Attack, gunboat	75	$0\frac{1}{2}$	62	$2\frac{1}{2}$	21	$1\frac{1}{4}$	7	$0\frac{1}{2}$	147	50	12	Built at Frindsbury, 1794.
Firm, gunboat	96	0	77	$8\frac{1}{8}$	31	0	7	4	397	100	16	Built at Deptford, 1794.
Hecate, gunboat	76	0	62	3	22	6	8	3	168	50	12	Built at Frindsbury, 1797.

More important changes were made in the arming of ships, especially in the direction of the increased employment of carronades. In 1794, when the *Albion*, 74, and *Nonsuch*, 64, were fitted as floating batteries, they were given, the one twenty-eight, and the other twenty 68-pounder carronades; and, at about the same time, many of the smaller vessels, which could have carried no bigger long guns than 3 or 4-pounders in equal numbers, were armed almost exclusively with 18-pounder carronades, to the great improvement of their fighting value at short range. On November 19th, 1794, indeed, a new establishment of carronades, superseding that of 1779, was adopted; but seeing that many Captains preferred, and were allowed to have, in lieu of long guns, more carronades than the establishment, and seeing also that many ships then in commission retained their old armament until long afterwards, it is of little use to give it at length. On August 28th, 1795, every ship bigger than a 16-gun brig was ordered to be supplied with a carronade for her launch; and on March 17th, 1798, it was further ordered that every line-of-battle ship coming forward to be fitted should be prepared to receive carronades all along her quarter-deck and forecastle, except in way of the shrouds. In the same year, six out of eight bomb-vessels, which had been purchased in 1797, were ordered to be fitted with eight 24-pounder carronades each, instead of with eight long 6-pounders as previously. In 1799 the carronade was made the general quarter-deck and forecastle gun in frigates. And on February 21st, 1800, it was directed that for the future all ships of twenty-four and twenty guns should be fitted on the main deck for 32-pounder carronades in place of the long 9-pounders, which up to that time had been carried.

To consider all suggestions with relation to building, fitting out, arming, navigating, and victualling H.M.'s ships, as well as with relation to docks, basins, buildings, etc., the office of Inspector-General of his Majesty's Naval Works was established on March 28th, 1796, and General Bentham was appointed to it, with a technical staff to assist him.

Very soon after the commencement of the war with revolutionary France, difficulty began to be experienced in obtaining the required number of seamen for the manning the fleet. Even in 1793, before war had been actually declared, the City of London deemed it desirable to supplement the usual royal bounty by offering forty shillings to every able seaman, and twenty shillings to every ordinary seaman who should voluntarily enter the service; and, when the war had been in progress for less than eighteen months, the Lord Mayor opened a subscription with the object of giving additional bounties as follows: to every able-bodied seaman, £10 10*s.*; to every ordinary seaman, £8 8*s.*; to every landsman, £6 6*s.*; and to boys, according to height, etc., £2 2*s.* and £1 1*s.* Yet these extra bounties, large though they were, were quickly exceeded, and in 1795 many seaport towns were offering as much as £30 a head to able seamen. Bounties alone failed, however, to attract all the men who were needed. Parliament had to take action, and the position of the seamen had to be in some measure improved ere those who were wanted could be secured; and this in spite of the press, of the engagement of numerous foreigners, especially Americans, and of the practice which obtained of permitting to certain offenders the option of joining the Navy or going to prison. On March 5th, 1795, an Act was passed for raising men in every county in England and Wales in proportion to its population, the quota rising from 23 in the case of Rutland, and 33 in the case of Flintshire, to 451 in the case of Middlesex, 589 in that of Lancashire, and 1081 in that of Yorkshire. And on April 16th following, another Act was passed for obliging the ports also to contribute, and for laying an embargo on all British shipping until the assigned quota should be provided. Under this Act there were demanded from Bristol, 666; from the Clyde, 683; from Newcastle, 1240; from Liverpool, 1711; and from London 5704 men. The Act which applied to the counties was designed to raise 9764, and the Act which applied to the ports, 20,354 men. To render the Navy more attractive than it had been, Acts were also passed in 1795 to enable men who had voluntarily entered the service to allot part of their pay[1] for the maintenance of their wives and families, this to be paid every lunar month upon production of a properly signed and witnessed ticket; to enable Boatswains, Gunners, and Carpenters to similarly allot; and to reduce the postage of letters to or from seamen on board men-of-war in all parts of the world to one penny. These concessions, no doubt, contributed to make the service a little less unpleasant than it had been previously; but they did not touch the more serious causes of discontent, which, as will be seen, led during the war

[1] An able seaman, 5*d.*; an ordinary seaman or a landsman, 4*d.*; and a Marine, 3*d.* per diem.

to graver and more frequent outbreaks of mutiny and insubordination than the Royal Navy has ever witnessed before or since. Nor did they, one may safely conclude, induce the right kind of men to flock on board his Majesty's ships in the large numbers which the exigencies of the times demanded; for, as late as 1801, a royal proclamation was issued, offering a pardon to all seamen or Marines who should surrender themselves as deserters before September 1st in that year, and assuring to all seamen who had deserted, but who had re-enlisted, and who were then borne in any of his Majesty's ships, the payment of wages due to them at the time of their desertion.

There seems never to have been any corresponding difficulty in obtaining as many officers as were needed; yet quite as much was done during the period to increase the attractiveness of the quarter-deck as was done to make the lower deck more tolerable. Indeed, upon the whole, the officers fared better than the men at the hands of the authorities. An Act of 1795 permitted all flag-officers, Captains, Commanders, Lieutenants, Masters, and Surgeons, upon being appointed to ships from half-pay, to apply for three months' pay in advance; and it entitled officers on half-pay to have their pay remitted to them free of expense. It also entitled pensioned widows of officers to have their pensions similarly remitted to them. An Order in Council, of September 21st, 1796, raised the pay and half-pay of the Lieutenants, and conceded other benefits to the same officers, as follows: Lieutenants of ships bearing a flag or a broad pennant, and having also a Captain, were given 5*s*. 6*d*. a day, and Lieutenants of other ships, 5*s*. a day, with one servant apiece as before; and Lieutenants commanding his Majesty's vessels were granted two servants. All these officers, moreover, were allowed conduct money at the rate of 6*d*. a mile, whenever called upon for service. The half-pay of the Lieutenants was settled at: for the first hundred, 5*s*. a day each; for the second hundred, 3*s*. 6*d*. a day each; and for the rest, 3*s*. a day each. It was at the same time directed that the first fifty Lieutenants on the list should be superannuated with the rank of Commander, and should receive 6*s*. a day, and that the widow of any such should be entitled to a pension of £45 a year.

The position of the Masters was improved in 1795, when, by an order of August 8th, they were granted half-pay, subject to their possession of certain qualifications, at the rate of from 2*s* to 4*s*. a day, according to their seniority. It was at the same time directed that those of them who were entitled to superannuation should receive pensions upon the scale of half-pay. Somewhat similar advantages were extended to the Surgeons, whose half-pay, subject to certain conditions, was fixed at from 2*s*. 6*d*. to 5*s*. a day, according to their seniority. Surgeons had, up to 1795, been allowed 15*s*. per patient for the cure of venereal diseases. In lieu of this, under regulations then introduced, £5 a year was allowed to a Surgeon for every hundred men borne in his ship; £5 a year in cases where the number borne was less than one hundred and exceeded fifty; and £4 a year in cases where the number borne was less than fifty. Widows of Masters and Surgeons were, under the same regulations, entitled to pensions of £30 a year, provided their husbands had been upon the half-pay list.

Under the will of Mr. Samuel Travers, who, in 1724, had left a residuary estate in trust for building or buying a house near Windsor Castle for the reception of superannuated or disabled Lieutenants, being single men of blameless character, the first seven Poor Knights of Windsor were appointed by the King on November 27th, 1795. These officers benefited to the extent of £60 a year each, £26 of that sum being applied to "keeping them a constant table." The seven officers thus chosen as the earliest recipients of the charity, and the dates of their commissions as Lieutenants, were: William Haygarth, 1757; George Trussell, 1761; John Bowen, 1762; Alexander Brown, 1765; Ambrose Warham, 1778; William Bampton, 1781; and William Elliott, 1781. There were then many older Lieutenants on the list; but the will of Mr. Travers did not contemplate the appointment of officers merely on the ground of length of service. It directed, on the contrary, that twenty-one names should be submitted by the Commissioners of the Navy to the Lords of the Admiralty, and that, of these, fourteen should be submitted by the Lords of the Admiralty to the King, who should be prayed to select the seven to be appointed.

The naval officers of the period were, as a rule, men of higher character and finer feelings than those of the early part of the eighteenth century; but a vast number of abuses still flourished among them; and the records of the courts-martial of the time seem to prove that the sense of honour throughout the higher ranks of the Navy was not nearly so keen as it afterwards became.

Lieutenant William Walker,[1] of the *Sparkler*, gun-vessel, who, on July 2nd, 1800, was dismissed the service, was a type of too many Lieutenants, Commanders, and Captains of his day. According to the verdict of the court-martial, he had repeatedly answered, at the time of muster, for men who had run, declaring that they were on liberty; he had answered for his own child, aged one year, whom he had rated as an A.B., saying that he was on duty ashore; he had sent a member of the ship's company, under the assumed name of William Walker, his aforesaid son, to receive £5 bounty money at Portsmouth; he had deprived his people of fresh provisions, and had himself drawn the provisions for his own table while he was on shore; and he had drawn provisions for his full complement of fifty men, when he had less than that number on board. Some, even among the most gallant officers in the service, were guilty of extraordinary brutality to their men. Captain Sir Edward Hamilton, the hero of the heroic recapture of the *Hermione*, was tried on board the *Gladiator*, on January 22nd, 1802, and sentenced to be dismissed the service, for having seized up William Bowman, gunner of the *Trent*, in the main rigging for an hour and a half in frosty weather until the man, who was old, fainted. Sir Edward was reinstated in his rank in the following June, it appearing that he had acted in the heat of passion, and that there had been some informality in the procedure; but there can be no doubt that cases of the sort were terribly common at the time, and that far too frequently they went entirely unpunished. A common abuse was struck at by an order of July 1st, 1801, which directed that for the future all naval officers who might come ashore on sick-quarter tickets, should go to the officers' wards in one of the Royal Naval Hospitals, and not to private lodgings.

Other prevalent abuses were the outcome of the regulations which existed as to officers' servants. An order of April 16th, 1794, ranged these servants in three classes, officers being allowed in respect of each servant £11 8*s.* 2*d.* a year, being the nett wages to which such servants were entitled. The classes were: (1), Young gentlemen, not under eleven years of age, who were intended for the sea-service, and who were styled volunteers; (2), boys of between fifteen and seventeen years of age, intended to become seamen; and (3), boys of between thirteen and fifteen years of age, intended to do actual duty as servants. It became a

[1] C. M. in *Gladiator*, at Portsmouth.

common practice to bear upon a ship's books young gentlemen who, besides being much under eleven years of age, were still in the nursery at home, or were at school; and to bear, nominally as seamen-boys or as working servants—and to the prejudice of those classes—youngsters who were designed for the quarter-deck.[1] Nor is it any exaggeration to say that very few naval officers of the period now under consideration considered it in the least dishonourable—unless they chanced to be found out and punished—to make, or to connive at the making of, false statements on certain subjects. False certificates of age were, indeed, generally winked at. Under the instructions which held good during the eighteenth century, no one was to be made a Lieutenant who had not passed his examination; and the examining officers were required to certify, among other things, that the candidate had served six years at sea, two of them being as Midshipman or Mate in his Majesty's ships, and was not under twenty years of age. These instructions were, as Professor Laughton says, systematically evaded, and little boys in the nursery or at school were borne on the books of a ship for a time, which was afterwards counted towards the stipulated six years.[2] It ultimately became the fashion for the candidate for examination to present a baptismal certificate as evidence of age; and then, if the age was not really sufficient, the certificate was unblushingly forged. Says Admiral the Hon. Sir George Elliot:—

> "In July, 1800, having completed my six years' servitude, I was sent, with nine other Midshipmen, to London, to pass the necessary examination for a Lieutenant's commission. Our examinations before the old Commissioners of the Navy were not severe; but we were called on to produce certificates that we were all twenty-one years of age—I was sixteen and four days. The old porter in the hall furnished them at 5*s.* apiece, which, no doubt, the old Commissioners knew; for, on our return with them, they remarked that the ink had not dried in twenty-one years."

Barrington had been certified as "more than twenty" in 1745, when, in fact, he was only sixteen; Nelson had been certified as "more than twenty" in 1777, when, in fact, he was less than nineteen; but there were many far more flagrant cases than these. The distinguished officer who afterwards became known as Sir

[1] Adm. Sir John Louis was borne as a first-class volunteer in the *Minotaur* before he was eleven; Adm. of the Fleet Sir Thomas John Cochrane was borne as a first-class volunteer in the *Thetis* when he was seven; and the name of the second Lord Radstock was borne in the *Courageux* when the boy, aged eight, was at home or at school. Instances of the kind may be multiplied almost to infinity.

[2] 'Study of Nav. Hist.' (Roy. U. S. Inst. 1896).

Thomas Boulden Thompson, Bart., was actually commissioned as a Lieutenant when, according to family records, he was six weeks less than sixteen years of age; and that undistinguished officer, the Hon. John Rodney, by the interest and connivance of his father, Lord Rodney, not only became a Lieutenant at the immature age of fifteen years and four months, but was a full-blown Post-Captain five weeks later.[1] There were examples almost as glaring in the period 1793–1802; and even Admiral of the Fleet Sir Provo William Parry Wallis, who died as recently as February 10th, 1892, was borne on more than one ship's books while he was still in the nursery, and was a Lieutenant long before he was twenty.

For seamen, and especially for officers, all questions connected with the distribution of prize-money possessed great interest during the French wars, for, although a seaman's share of prize-money came to him merely as a small, though welcome, addition to his wages, an officer's share not infrequently amounted to many times as much as his pay, and often, changing a poor man into a wealthy one, enabled him to buy an estate and found a family. The lower deck was chiefly anxious for prompt payment of whatever prize-money happened to be due to it. This was recognised, after the Battle of the Glorious First of June, by the King, who, with much forethought, ordered that the following proportion of prize-money should be immediately advanced in respect of the captures in that engagement, viz., to each warrant officer, £20; to each petty officer, £10 10*s.*; and to each seaman, Marine and soldier, £2 2*s.* But more difficult problems often arose to trouble the minds of officers whose interests were less superficially affected. A case in point arose in 1794, when Captain Francis Laforey, in the *Carysfort*, recaptured H.M.S. *Castor*, which had been taken nineteen days earlier, and commissioned by the French. Upon the arrival of the prize in port, she was claimed by the Commissioners of the Navy as belonging of right to the King. The French captain, upon being interrogated, said that he had been appointed to command the *Castor* by the French admiral, who had given him a commission to do so as commander of a man-of-war in the service of the Republic; and that the admiral in question had power and authority to condemn prizes, and to arm, equip, and commission such ships as he might capture, without first sending them to France to be formally condemned

[1] Hon. John Rodney. Born, May 10th, 1765. Lieutenant, September 10th, 1780. Post-Captain, October 14th, 1780.

there. The point for decision was, therefore, whether, in the circumstances, the re-captors had merely re-taken a British vessel, or whether they had, in effect, taken a French one; whether, in fact, they were entitled to salvage only,[1] or to the whole of the prize. Sir James Marriot, Judge of the High Court of Admiralty, relied upon a clause in the Prize Act, which declared that, "If any ship or vessel retaken shall appear to have been, after the taking of his Majesty's enemies, by them set forth as a ship of war, the said ship or vessel shall not be restored to the former owners or proprietors, but shall, in all cases, whether retaken by his Majesty's ships, or by any privateer, be adjudged a lawful prize for the benefit of the captors"; and he therefore adjudged the whole value of the *Castor* to the captors.

Another interesting point in prize law was decided in 1795. A very valuable French vessel had been taken without the firing of a shot by several East Indiamen, on board of which, at the time of the capture, there were many recruits and non-combatant passengers. The question for decision was whether these recruits and passengers were entitled to share in the prize. The right of the recruits was admitted with little demur, but although it was urged, on behalf of the passengers, that the East India Company and its commanders held all on board to be liable to the performance of duty in case of action, and that the passengers had, by their presence, assisted in overawing the foe, the judge decided against the passengers' claim, observing that it was certain that the women and children had not intimidated the French, and that it was unlikely that the gentlemen, who probably were looking through the cabin windows with their hair full dressed, struck any terror into the minds of the enemy.

Yet another point was decided in 1799. In 1781, Captain Evelyn Sutton had commanded the *Isis* in the squadron of Commodore Johnstone. After the action at Porto Praya, Johnstone had put Sutton under arrest, and had appointed Captain the Hon. Thomas Charles Lumley to command the *Isis* in his stead. The question was whether Captain Lumley was entitled to share the prize-money arising from captures made by the *Isis* while he was in command of her during the arrest of Captain Sutton. Lord Kenyon decided that, to all intents and purposes, Captain Sutton had been Captain of the

[1] At that time, men-of-war effecting recaptures were entitled to one-eighth, and privateers to one-sixth, of the value of ships so recaptured.

Isis so long as he remained entitled to pay as such, and had not been displaced either by the Admiralty, or by sentence of court-martial; and that the fact of arrest—apart from that arrest having been, as was proved, improper—had not displaced him. There could be but one Captain of a ship at a time, and the Captain of the *Isis*, at the moment of the making of the captures in question, was undoubtedly Captain Sutton. He gave judgment accordingly.

In the same year, 1799, several other interesting cases were determined. In January, it was decided that, when ships with cargo on board were captured, even though the ships were commissioned and armed, the captors were not entitled to head money.[1] A little later, Sir William Scott, in the case of the *Rebecca*, delivered an important judgment touching the *droits* of Admiralty. The *Rebecca*, having put into St. Marcou for safety, had been fired at from a work on shore, and had struck her colours; and she had then ridden there a whole day before possession had been taken of her, and until she had been boarded by a boat's crew from the fort, which was held by the Navy. The Admiralty, claiming under a grant confirmed by an Order in Council of 1665, urged that the law gave to the Lord High Admiral, as his *peculium*, the benefit of all captures made in roadsteads, creeks, or havens. The captors declared that the capture was made by naval officers in their naval character, and that, therefore, it was, *prima facie*, acquired to the King, and, through him, to the actual captors. They submitted that the place of capture was not a port or haven; and they contended that there was no proof that the vessel had anchored when she struck her colours. Sir William Scott admitted that the Lord High Admiral was entitled under the grant to the benefit of captures "of all ships and goods coming into ports, creeks or roads of England or Ireland, unless they came in voluntarily upon revolt, or were driven in by the King's cruisers," and that usage had extended the area of the Lord High Admiral's rights in that matter from England and Ireland to all the dominions thereunto belonging. But he could not admit that a road or roadstead within the meaning of the grant existed wherever a ship could find anchorage ground. "For," he continued, "if that be so, the Lord High Admiral would be entitled to all captures made within a moderate distance of most parts of the coasts of England and Ireland, and the foreign dominions belonging to them, which, assuredly, is not the case; for who would say that,

[1] 'Admlty. Reps.' i. 157.

if a ship at anchor in the channel of Dover be seized by a commissioned cruiser, the Lord High Admiral is entitled? Every anchorage ground is not a roadstead. A roadstead is a known general station for ships, *statio tutissima nautis*, notoriously used as such, and distinguished by the name, and not every spot where an anchor will find bottom and fix itself." The judge was inclined to think that St. Marcou possessed no road. He was not sure, moreover, that St. Marcou, occupied temporarily as a mere naval station for the convenience of a couple of small vessels, could be recognised as a possession of the Crown of England within the meaning of the grant; but, leaving those points undecided, he preferred to base his decision upon the consideration whether, at the time of her surrender, or *deditio*, the vessel had entered the alleged road or not. She had struck upon being fired at. She had not then anchored; but, ere being taken possession of, she had anchored. He must regard the effective *deditio* as dating from the moment of striking—a moment at which the vessel had, it was admitted, not taken up any anchorage. Nothing had occurred after the *deditio* to prejudice it. The French had not, for example, attempted to defeat the surrender. The formal submission had never been discontinued or reversed. Therefore, he must hold that the ship had not entered any road when she was captured. The Admiralty might claim that the capture had been made from the land, and by a land force. There might possibly be something to say in favour of such a contention in certain cases. A vessel compelled to strike by the fire from Dover Castle would be a *droit* of Admiralty.

"I likewise," he went on, "think that cases may occur in which naval persons, having a real authority to take upon the sea for their own advantage, may yet entitle the Admiralty and not themselves, by a capture made upon the sea by the use of a force stationed upon the land. Suppose the crew, or part of the crew of a man-of-war were landed, and descried a ship of the enemy at sea; and that they took possession of any battery or fort upon the shore, such as may be met with in many parts of the coast, and, by means of such battery or fort, compelled such a ship to strike; I have no doubt that such a capture, though made by persons having naval commissions, yet being made by means of a force upon the land, which they employed accidentally, and without any right under their commission, would be a *droit* of Admiralty, and nothing more."

But at St. Marcou there was no garrison or military establishment; it was occupied entirely as a temporary naval station. Everyone in it was borne upon some ship's books, and was victualled from a ship, and such defences as existed had been made by the Navy, and mounted with ships' guns, or with spare guns specially procured.

The judge, therefore, considered St. Marcou as a part or appendage of the Navy, as a sort of stationary tender, and he held that the capture was a regular maritime one, effected in a spot where the right of Admiralty had not begun. He consequently pronounced in favour of the captors.[1]

In the same year, Sir William Scott decided a case involving the right of the Army to share with the Navy in the distribution of prize-money arising out of the capture of Dutch men-of-war in Saldanha Bay, in August, 1796. He came to the conclusion that the case for the Army could not be sustained. With regard to a claim on behalf of several non-commissioned East India ships for an interest in the capture of the Cape of Good Hope, in June, 1795, Sir William Scott concluded a lengthy judgment with the following words :—

> "Upon the whole of these facts, I feel myself obliged to pronounce that it has not been shown that these ships set out in an original military character, or that any military character has been subsequently impressed upon them by the nature and course of their employment; and therefore, however meritorious their services may have been, and however entitled they may be to the gratitude of their country, it will not entitle them to share in this valuable capture."

Some important questions of international, as well as of prize law, arose during the period. In 1798, Captain Loring, of the *Carnatic*, exercised a right which was claimed and exercised by Great Britain for many years afterwards, and which was one of the causes of the war of 1812–15, and stopped and searched an American man-of-war off Havana for British sailors. This incident led to the issue of the following letter by the Secretary of the United States Navy :—

> "Sir,—It is the positive command of the President that, in no pretence whatever, you permit the public vessel of war under your command to be detained or searched, nor any of the officers or men belonging to her to be taken from her by the ships or vessels of any foreign nation, so long as you are in a capacity to repel such outrage on the honour of the American flag. If force should be exerted to compel your submission, you are to resist that force to the utmost of your power; and, when overpowered by superior force, you are to strike your flag, and thus yield your vessel as well as your men, but never your men without your vessel. You will remember, however, that your demeanour be respectful and friendly to the vessels and people of all nations in amity with the United States; and that you avoid as carefully the commission of, as the submission to, insult or injury. I have the honour to be your obedient servant,
>
> "Benjamin Stoddart.
>
> "Given at the Navy Department, Dec. 29, 1798.
>
> "To the Commanders of armed vessels in the service of the United States."

---

[1] Crews of the *Sandfly* and *Badger*.

In a message sent to Congress on January 7th, 1800, the President, after alluding to the same incident, concluded—

> "It is but justice to say that this is the first instance of misbehaviour of any of the British officers towards our vessels of war that has come to my knowledge. According to all the representations I have seen, the flag of the United States, and the officers and men, have been treated by the civil and military authority of the British nation, in Nova Scotia, the West India Islands, and on the ocean, with uniform civility, politeness, and friendship. I have no doubt but that this first instance of misconduct will be readily corrected."

A case arising out of the detention, and bringing into the Downs, by Commodore John Lawford, in January, 1798, of a Swedish frigate which had offered resistance to search for contraband of war, and of her convoy, the latter laden with pitch, tar, hemp, deals and iron, and bound, some to enemy's ports, and some elsewhere, was the subject of a lengthy and learned judgment of Sir William Scott, in 1799. The points in dispute were too numerous and complicated to be noticed here, but as the judgment is one which has since been often cited, it may be well to mention that it is to be found at length not only in the Admiralty Reports, but also in Schomberg.[1]

Yet another interesting question was decided by the Court of Common Pleas on June 12th, 1800. The point was whether junior Flag-officers were entitled to a share in the third of freight-money which was allowed by the regulation to Commanders-in-Chief. The case was brought before the court by Sir William Parker, on behalf of himself and the junior Admirals in the fleet of Lord St. Vincent. It was admitted that there was no law upon the subject; it was a point of usage and precedent. Admirals Wolseley, Lord Hotham, Caldwell, Bligh, and Pole, and Captain Caleb O'Brien, gave evidence in support of the alleged custom of the service as understood by Sir William Parker. Admiral Lord Hood, and Mr. Alford, agent for Lord St. Vincent, supported the opposite view. In the result, Lord Eldon held that the usage was fully established, and the jury found a verdict for the plaintiff. It would appear from the evidence given in the case, that it was the practice for a Commander-in-Chief to surrender one-third of his third to his junior, where he had but one Flag-officer under him, and to surrender one-half of his third for division among the juniors, when there happened to be two or more of them in the fleet. Lord Hood, in the course of the proceedings, appealed to Lord Hotham, who had served under him as junior

[1] 'Nav. Chronol.' iii. 264–284.

Admiral in the Mediterranean, whether he had ever paid him a shilling of freight-money. "I kept it all myself," said Hood. "You did, my lord," assented Hotham; "but I thought that I was entitled to a part of it." Howe seems to have invariably recognised the existence of the usage.

One of the most painful features of the period under review is the whole subject of the discipline of the Navy. Not only did nearly everyone of these eight eventful years witness mutinous outbreaks such as hardly ever before had disgraced the service; not only was mutiny more than once accompanied by murder and by treason; but also the disaffection became so general that, for a time, it threatened to imperil the very existence of the country. At first, the outbreaks were isolated ones. They occurred in ships commanded by Captains of the best reputation, as well as in those commanded by Captains of the worst; and, although there were undoubtedly many excuses for discontent upon the lower deck, it would almost seem as if the state of unrest among the seamen was rather of the nature of an epidemic, the germs of which were afloat in the air of the age, than the result of any more obvious causes. In France, there had been a revolt against all constituted authority. Britons, as a body, suffered little from the infection from across the Channel; but, in cases where there was already a *nidus* favourable to the reception and propagation of the germs, some Britons caught the contagion in a very severe form, and were as completely dominated by it as the most susceptible of Frenchmen.[1]

Symptoms of trouble manifested themselves very soon after the beginning of the war; but, perhaps, the first outbreak which indicated the existence of an abnormal state of affairs in the Navy, was a mutiny on board the *Culloden*, Captain Thomas Troubridge, in December, 1794. The ship's company refused to proceed to sea. Troubridge, who behaved with admirable firmness, seized the ringleaders, and brought them to trial by court-martial on the 15th.[2] Eight were sentenced to death, and, on January 13th following, five of these were executed on board the *Culloden* at Spithead, the remaining three receiving his Majesty's pardon. The outbreak in the *Windsor Castle* at San Fiorenzo, in November, 1794, is noticed

[1] There is a certain amount of evidence that some of the mutinies were assisted, if not actually fomented, by French agents. *See* the curious revelations in Moreau de Jonnès: 'Aventures de Guerre' (Ed. 1858), i. 424–461.

[2] The court first assembled in the *Cæsar* at Spithead, and then adjourned to the *Stately*, in Portsmouth Harbour.

in the following chapter. It is to be regarded as of an altogether different character from the mutiny in the *Culloden*, seeing that the *Windsor Castle's* crew assigned as the reason for their action their dislike to certain officers of the ship; but it was, in all probability, not without its effect upon the subsequent development of events, for the mutineers, instead of being met firmly, were humoured in the most extraordinary and indefensible way, and not only were given new officers in place of those objected to, but also were pardoned.

A very significant incident of 1795 was the mutiny of the crew of the Dutch hoy *Shark*, 4. The mutineers carried the little craft into La Hougue, and handed her over to the enemies of their country. During 1796 the slumbering evil manifested itself only in comparatively mild forms; but in 1797 there occurred several mutinies which were of an altogether unexampled character among British seamen.

In February of that year petitions, purporting to come from each of the line-of-battle ships at Portsmouth, were forwarded to Lord Howe. No attention was paid to them. Early in March the Channel Fleet put to sea for a cruise; and, on its return to port, the seamen, finding that their petitions had been ignored, began a correspondence among themselves. The result of this was a general agreement throughout the fleet that no ship belonging to it should again weigh anchor so long as the alleged grievances remained unredressed. The resolution bore its first fruit when, on April 15th, Admiral Lord Bridport ordered the fleet to prepare for sea. Thereupon the crew of the *Queen Charlotte* ran up the shrouds, and, giving three cheers, the signal for mutiny, were answered in like manner from every other ship.[1] Attempts were everywhere made to persuade the people to return to their duty; but in vain. On the 16th, two delegates from each ship were chosen as representatives of the fleet, and the Admiral's cabin of the *Queen Charlotte* was appointed as their place of meeting. On the 17th, every man in the fleet was solemnly sworn to adhere to the cause; unpopular officers were set ashore: and ropes were reeved at the fore-yardarm of many vessels, as a sign that the mutineers were ready to proceed to extremities, and also, it may be, that they were determined to preserve some sort of order among

[1] The ships of the line thus implicated were: *Royal George*, *Queen Charlotte*, *Royal Sovereign*, *London*, *Glory*, *Duke*, *Mars*, *Marlborough*, *Ramillies*, *Robust*, *Impétueux*, *Defence*, *Terrible*, *Pompée*, *Minotaur*, and *Defiance*.

themselves. On the 18th, a committee of the Board of Admiralty, consisting of Earl Spencer, Lord Arden, Rear-Admiral William Young (1), and Mr. William Marsden, reached Portsmouth from London, and made some ineffectual overtures to the mutineers. On the 21st, Vice-Admirals Sir Alan Gardner and John Colpoys, and Rear-Admiral Charles Morice Pole went out to the *Queen Charlotte*, and had an interview with the delegates, but were assured that no conclusive arrangement could be made unless it were duly sanctioned by Parliament and the King, and were accompanied by a proclamation of general pardon. This answer unfortunately led Sir Alan Gardner to lose his temper and to lay hold of one of the delegates, declaring that the man and all his associates, together with every fifth seaman throughout the fleet, should be hanged. The consequence was that only with difficulty did the Vice-Admiral escape alive. When the delegates from the *Royal George* returned to their ship and reported what had occurred, a council of the leaders of the mutiny was summoned on board that vessel, the signal being the hoisting of a red flag. Utterly disgusted at the conduct of the fleet, Bridport struck his flag, with the intention of never again hoisting it. Some kind of personal apology having, however, been made to him, he rehoisted his flag in the *Royal George* on the 23rd. In the meantime, the mutineers had caused all the guns of the fleet to be loaded; had confined the remaining officers to their respective ships; had ordered the keeping of watches on board as if the fleet were at sea; and had despatched an explanatory letter to the Admiralty. Before rehoisting his flag on April 23rd, Lord Bridport, addressing his ship's company, informed the mutineers that a redress of all grievances had been granted, and that he had with him the King's pardon for the offenders.

The grievances set forth in the petitions of the seamen were substantially as follows: that wages had not been raised since the time of Charles II., when the necessaries of life, and slops of all sorts, were 30 per cent. cheaper than in 1797; that the wages of the Army had been augmented while those of the Navy had not been increased; that provisions were served out of short weight and inferior quality; that no vegetables were issued to ships in port; that the sick were insufficiently attended to, and that luxuries intended for them were embezzled; that liberty, within reasonable and stipulated bounds, was not commonly enough granted to the crews of ships in harbour; and that men wounded in action were deprived of their wages, pending cure or discharge.[1] These grievances were set forth in moderate language, and with many professions of loyalty. The Committee of the Board of Admiralty promptly undertook to recommend an increase of wages by the addition of 4*s.* a lunar month to the pay of petty officers and able seamen, of 3*s.* a month to the pay of ordinary seamen, and of 2*s.* a month to the wages of landsmen; and determined also that seamen wounded in action should be continued in pay while their wounds were healing, or until, being declared unserviceable, they should be given a pension, or should be received into Greenwich Hospital.[2]

The seamen protested against the drawing of any distinction between ordinary seamen and landsmen—a distinction which, they declared, had never before existed in the Navy; and they pressed for the raising of an able seaman's wages to 1*s.* a day, and of Marines', other seamen's, and petty officers' wages in proportion. They asked, further, for the raising of Greenwich Hospital pensions from £7 to £10 a year, and suggested that, to make good the difference, merchant seamen should contribute 1*s.* instead of 6*d.* a head a month to the Hospital funds, adding, "and as this, in time of peace, must be paid by your petitioners, we trust it will give a convincing proof of our disinterestedness and moderation." They suggested, too, that the new advantages as to pensions should be granted as well to seamen of the East India Company as to those of the Royal Navy; and asked that the provisions issued should be at the rate of sixteen ounces to the pound of bread and meat, with cheese, butter, and liquors in proportion, and with vegetables as well, and that the quality should be better than in the past, and that no flour should be issued with fresh beef.[3]

The Commissioners finally conceded an addition of 5*s.* 6*d.* a month to the wages of petty officers and seamen, making an able seaman's pay 1*s.* a day; an addition of 4*s.* 6*d.* a month to the wages of ordinary seamen; an addition of 3*s.* 6*d.* a month to the wages of landsmen; the non-stoppage of shore allowances to Marines when embarked; the issue of full weight of provisions, without deduction for leakage or waste; and, pending the completion of arrangements to that end, the payment of short-allowance money in respect of deductions; and the payment of full wages

[1] Petition of April 18th, 1797. [2] Commrs. to Bridport, April 18th, 1797.
[3] Reply of April 19th, 1797.

to the wounded; and they promised pardon to every ship's company which, within an hour after being apprised of their Lordships' resolutions, should return to its duty and cease to hold intercourse with the mutineers.[1] The seamen received these concessions with satisfaction, but added: "But we beg to remind your Lordships that it is a firm resolution that, until the flour in port be removed, the vegetables and pensions augmented, the grievances of private ships redressed, an Act passed, and his Majesty's most gracious pardon for the fleet now lying at Spithead granted, the fleet will not lift an anchor; and this is the total and final answer." In spite of this threat the Government contented itself with proclaiming a pardon,[2] and with regarding the affair as at an end.

But it was not at an end. Part of the fleet dropped down to St. Helen's. When, however, on May 7th, Lord Bridport signalled to weigh and put to sea, every ship's company refused to obey. The men considered that the silence of the Government indicated that the grievances which had not been specifically dealt with by the Commissioners, were not to be redressed. They therefore resolved to hold another meeting of delegates on board the *London*, which still lay at Spithead; and for that purpose their boats proceeded alongside that ship. Vice-Admiral Colpoys, whose flag flew in her, refused to allow them on board, and declared that if they persisted he would order the Marines to fire at them. The delegates did persist; a scuffle ensued; a delegate fired at and wounded Lieutenant William Sims of the Marines; the Marines were ordered by the *London's* first Lieutenant to fire; and five seamen, including two delegates, were killed. An active mutiny immediately broke out on board the *London*, and the seamen obliged the officers and the Marines to surrender. They would have hanged the first Lieutenant had not Vice-Admiral Colpoys satisfied them that that officer had acted in pursuance of specific instructions from the Admiralty. All the officers were confined to their cabins, and the Marines were made prisoners. Similar violence was displayed in other ships; and most of the superior officers who were strict disciplinarians were sent ashore. So things went on until May 14th, when Lord Howe, armed with plenary powers, arrived from London, bringing with him an Act of Parliament, which had been passed on May 9th, in accordance

[1] Commrs. to Bridport, April 20th, 1797.
[2] Dated at Windsor, April 22nd, 1797.

with the desires of the seamen, and a new proclamation of pardon for all such as should return at once to their duty. The Act, the proclamation, and Lord Howe's popularity and tact restored order and discipline; on the 15th the mutiny ceased; and on the 16th the Channel Fleet put to sea.

It was generally hoped and expected that there would be no more trouble; but within a day or two a new and more serious mutiny broke out in the ships at the Nore and in the North Sea. As before, the mutineers chose two delegates from each ship. In addition, they appointed a man named Richard Parker[1] president of the delegates, and elected in every ship a committee of twelve to manage the affairs of the vessel. On May 20th, the delegates sent to Vice-Admiral Charles Buckner, Commander-in-Chief at the Nore, the following statement of demands:—

"1. That every indulgence granted to the fleet at Portsmouth be granted to his Majesty's subjects serving in the fleet at the Nore and places adjacent.

"2. That every man, upon a ship's coming into harbour, shall have liberty (a certain number at a time, so as not to injure the ship's duty) to go and see their friends and families; a convenient time to be allowed to each man.

"3. That all ships, before they go to sea, shall be paid all arrears of wages, down to six months, according to the old rules.

"4. That no officer that has been turned out of any of his Majesty's ships shall be employed in the same ship again without consent of the ship's company.

"5. That when any of his Majesty's ships shall be paid that may have been some time in commission, if there are any pressed men on board that may not be in the regular course of payment, they shall receive two months' advance to furnish them with necessaries.

"6. That an indemnification be made any man who ran, and may now be in his Majesty's service, and they shall not be liable to be taken up as deserters.

"7. That a more equal distribution be made of prize-money to the crews of his Majesty's ships and vessels of war.

"8. That the Articles of War, as now enforced, require various alterations, several of which ought to be expunged therefrom; and, if more moderate ones were held forth to the seamen in general, it would be the means of taking off that terror and prejudice against his Majesty's service, on that account too frequently imbibed by seamen, from entering voluntarily into the service."

The statement was forwarded to the Admiralty, which, on the 22nd, replied, refusing some of the demands, but promising forgiveness to the men if they would then return to duty. Vice-Admiral Buckner delivered the answer to the delegates, and allowed them ten minutes wherein to make up their minds concerning it. Instead of submitting, the mutineers went into harbour in their boats, and took thence all the gunboats which lay there. They then carried

[1] At one time a Midshipman in the Navy; court-martialled and reduced for misbehaviour, Dec. 12th, 1793; discharged the service as insane, 1794.

them to the Nore; and, as the boats passed the fort at Sheerness, each of them, in defiance, fired a gun at it. The delegates informed Vice-Admiral Buckner "that nothing could be settled until three of the Board of Admiralty came down to Sheerness." On May 23rd, they struck his flag on board the *Sandwich*, which was the head-quarters of Parker, and hoisted instead of it the red flag of mutiny. Moreover, they obliged every ship lying near Sheerness to drop down to the Nore, where they concentrated their forces. Among these ships was the *San Fiorenzo*, which had been fitted up for the conveyance of the Princess of Württemberg to Germany. Her crew, however, was loyal, and, although the frigate was ordered to lie close under the stern of the *Sandwich*, her captain, Sir Harry Burrard Neale, found means, a few days later, to carry her unmolested into Harwich.

On May 24th, the mutineers were again offered a conditional pardon by the Admiralty, but Richard Parker peremptorily refused the conditions. Up to about that time the delegates and committee-men were in the habit of landing daily at Sheerness, holding meetings, and parading the streets with flags and music; but the arrival on the spot of Admiral Lord Keith and General Sir Charles Grey, who were charged with enforcing naval and military measures of repression, put a stop to those proceedings, and thenceforth the mutineers visited the shore at their peril.

On May 26th, Admiral Duncan, whose orders were to watch the Dutch coast, succeeded in putting to sea with the whole of his squadron except the *Montagu*, 74, and *Nassau*, 64, which ships refused to get under way upon pretence that their crews were being paid at the time; but the evil example presently spread; and, by May 31st, the Admiral had been deserted by all his vessels except the *Venerable*, 74 (flag), and *Adamant*, 50. Mutiny actually broke out in the *Venerable*, but Duncan repressed it, largely by a personal exhibition of strength and determination; and, in spite of his isolation, he managed to keep his station until he was reinforced.

On May 27th, a number of delegates went up the river in order to tamper with the crews of some ships which were lying in Long Reach. Below Tilbury they were fired at from the shore, and, landing at Gravesend, they were arrested by the inhabitants; but they succeeded in regaining their liberty, and in corrupting the crew of the *Lancaster*, 64.

The same members of the Board of Admiralty as had gone to Portsmouth to deal with the mutiny there, now went to Sheerness, and, on May 27th, held a meeting at the house of Commissioner Francis John Hartwell, where they saw the delegates and tried in vain to bring them to reason. The only result was that the mutineers became more aggressive and insolent than ever; whereupon their Lordships returned to London, after announcing that no further concessions whatsoever were to be expected. It is tolerably clear, from the revelations of M. Moreau de Jonnès and other Frenchmen, that the leaders of the rebels, or some of them, were by that time in communication with the enemies of their country, and had formed projects for carrying the fleet across the Channel, though Parker resolutely denied any suggestion of the kind; but the general body of seamen revolted at the idea of so treasonable a proceeding. The situation of the mutineers had, however, become a desperate one. Success was hopeless; punishment was almost certain; and flight, either with or without the ships, seemed to promise the sole chance of safety. It is, upon the whole, astonishing, therefore, that the fleet did not desert. Instead of fleeing, the delegates attempted to coerce London into supporting their demands. They moored the *Standard*, 64, *Brilliant*, 28, *Inspector*, 16, and *Swan*, 16, across the river to block the traffic, and allowed no vessels to pass them without an order signed by Richard Parker, and then only neutral ships, colliers, and a few small craft. In the meantime, communication with the shore having been cut off, the rebels turned pirates, helping themselves to provisions and water from merchant ships which they detained, carrying off sheep from the Isle of Grain, and plundering the storeship *Grampus*, which had been fitted out to proceed to the fleet in the West Indies. They did not, nevertheless, omit to fire a royal salute on June 4th, the anniversary of the King's birthday, though they still kept the red flag flying at the main-topmasthead of the *Sandwich*. On June 6th, when the mutineers were joined by the last of the deserting vessels from Admiral Duncan's fleet, their total force consisted of the twelve ships of the line, two 50's, six frigates, and six smaller craft mentioned in the note.[1] That day sealed the fate of the rebellion.

[1] *Sandwich*, 90; *Montagu*, 74; *Agamemnon*, 64; *Ardent*, 64; *Inflexible*, 64; *Monmouth*, 64; *Director*, 64; *Nassau*, 64; *Repulse*, 64; *Belliqueux*, 64; *Standard*, 64; *Lion*, 64; *Leopard*, 50; *Isis*, 50; *Terpsichore*, 32; *Iris*, 32; *Brilliant*, 28; *Vestal*, 28; *Proserpine*, 28; *Champion*, 20; *Pylades*, 16; *Inspector*, 16; *Swan*, 16; *Comet*, fire-

It was on June 6th that two Acts of Parliament were hastily introduced, passed, and assented to. One was "for the better prevention and punishment of attempts to seduce persons serving in his Majesty's forces by sea or land from their duty and allegiance, or to entice them to mutiny or disobedience"; and the other was "for the more effectually restraining intercourse with the crews of certain of his Majesty's ships now in a state of mutiny and rebellion, and for the effectual suppression of such mutiny and rebellion." In pursuance of the intention of the authorities to crush the outbreak at all costs, new batteries were erected on both sides of the Thames; the buoys at its mouth were removed; furnaces for heating shot were prepared at various points; and the *Neptune*, 98, Commodore Sir Erasmus Gower, *Lancaster*, 64, *Agincourt*, 64, and several gunboats, which lay near Gravesend, were directed to drop down and attack the insurgents. The mutineers, feeling that the end was approaching, opened negotiations through the Earl of Northesk, Captain of the *Monmouth*; but still simulated an uncompromising demeanour. Their overtures were rejected; and the preparations for reducing them by force were almost complete when, on June 9th, it became apparent that the insurrection was about to collapse. On that day the *Repulse* and *Leopard* escaped from the fleet, the latter getting up the Thames, but the former, unfortunately, taking the ground, and being fired at by the *Monmouth* and *Director*. In the following night the *Ardent* also made off, though she, too, was fired at by the *Monmouth*. Both in her and in the *Repulse*[1] several people were hit. On the 10th, several vessels hauled down the red flag, and the river traffic was reopened. On the 12th, other ships struck the symbol of disaffection, and expressed a desire to submit; and on the evening of that day the rebels had only seven ships still adhering to them. Early on the 13th, the *Agamemnon*, *Standard*, *Nassau*, *Iris*, and *Vestal*, after there had been bloody struggles in most of them, took refuge either up the Thames or under the guns of Sheerness; and, later on the same day, the general body of

---

ship, 14; *Grampus*, storeship, 20; and *Serapis*, storeship, 20. The *Lancaster*, 64, had by that day returned to its duty. The *Serapis* appears on that day to have escaped into the Medway. The *Discovery*, bomb, had entered the Medway some days before.

[1] Lieutenant George Augustus Delanoe, of the *Repulse*, lost a leg on the occasion. He was in consequence promoted and given a pension of 2*s*. a day. He was also granted a pension by the City of London. He was promoted in the course of the year, and died, still a Commander, in 1802.

rebels, even including the crew of the *Sandwich,* announced an inclination to submit if a general pardon should be granted. On the morning of the 14th, the *Sandwich* was carried under the guns of Sheerness, and Vice-Admiral Buckner, sending a boat full of soldiers on board of her, effected the arrest of Richard Parker, of a man named Davies, who had acted as his flag-captain, and of about thirty other delegates. One delegate, named Wallace, to escape capture, committed suicide. Parker was tried by court-martial on board the *Sandwich* on June 22nd. The trial continued for several days, and resulted in the man's condemnation to death. He was executed on June 29th on board the *Sandwich,* and died acknowledging the justice of the sentence. Other mutineers were then tried. Many were executed; several were flogged from ship to ship; some were imprisoned in the Marshalsea; and a number remained under sentence on board the *Eagle,* 64, prison ship in the Medway, until after the battle of Camperdown, when, at the prayer of Admiral Duncan, the King was pleased to pardon them.

Yet the mutinies did not cease with the collapse of the great outbreak at the Nore. There were further outbreaks in the *Pompée,* 80, *Royal Sovereign,* 100, *Saturn,* 74, *Mars,* 74, *Marlborough,* 74, *Bedford,* 74, *Ardent,* 64, *Grampus,* storeship, *Beaulieu,* 40, *Phœnix,* 36, *Calypso,* 16, and other vessels, and, during the whole of the summer of 1797, courts-martial were sitting to try the offenders, many of whom were condemned to death, or to floggings so severe as to be scarcely preferable. In July, there was a mutiny of a particularly determined type on board the *St. George,* 98, in the Mediterranean. This was quelled by the personal gallantry and firmness of her commander, Captain Shuldham Peard, and punished with the sternness which, in such circumstances, always characterised Lord St. Vincent, the Commander-in-Chief. The Admiral, however, on that occasion, issued a general order in which, somewhat prematurely, as the issue proved, he expressed his high sense of "the loyalty, fidelity, and subordination of the rest of the fleet," which he would not "fail to make known to the Lords Commissioners of the Admiralty, and request their lordships to lay it before the King." St. Vincent had, very soon afterwards, to contend with the evil in many forms and in many vessels. The epidemic, after having broken out in the Mediterranean, was continually renewed by the arrival of ships and drafts from the home station. In England disaffection had, perhaps, been too tenderly dealt with in its inception. St. Vincent adopted a different method. It has been noted that the *Marlborough*, then commanded by Captain Henry Nicholls, had been concerned in the mutiny at Spithead. Under another Captain, she had subsequently given much trouble to her officers, when lying in Bantry Bay, and, being despatched in 1798 to join the fleet of Earl St. Vincent, some of her crew were again mutinous while she was on her passage. The Commander-in-Chief, aware of her character at the time, ordered her, as soon as she was within signalling range of him, to take up a berth between the lines of the fleet, which was then at anchor; and, immediately after her arrival, application was made to him for a court-martial to be held on a seaman. There was also trouble on board the *Lion*[1] and the *Centaur*[2]—a fact which St. Vincent may have accepted as a proof that the spirit of insubordination was not merely of a local character, though the evidence, as it now stands, does not altogether bear this out. Tucker, in his 'Memoirs of St. Vincent,' relates what followed in the case of the *Marlborough*; and the whole episode is sufficiently instructive to demand a full chronicle here. It is given in Tucker's words:—

"A court-martial on the principal mutineers was immediately assembled, and one was no sooner sentenced to die than the Commander-in-Chief ordered him to be executed on the following morning, 'and by the crew of the *Marlborough* alone, no part of the boats' crews from the other ships, as had been usual on similar occasions, to assist in the punishment'—his Lordship's invariable order on the execution of mutineers. On the receipt of the necessary commands for this execution, the captain of the *Marlborough*, Captain Ellison,[3] waited upon the Commander-in-Chief, and, reminding his Lordship that a determination that their shipmates should not suffer capital punishment had been the very cause of the ship's company's mutiny, expressed his conviction that the *Marlborough's* crew would never permit the man to be hanged on board that ship.

"Receiving the Captain on the *Ville de Paris's* quarter-deck, before the officers and ship's company, hearkening in breathless silence to what passed, and standing with his hat in his hand over his head, as was his Lordship's invariable custom during the whole time that any person, whatever were his rank, even a common seaman, addressed him on service, Lord St. Vincent listened very attentively till the Captain ceased to speak; and then, after a pause, replied: 'What; do you mean to tell me, Captain Ellison, that you cannot command his Majesty's ship the *Marlborough*? For, if that is the case, sir, I will immediately send on board an officer who can.

"The Captain then requested that, at all events, the boats' crews from the rest of the fleet might, as always had been customary in the service, on executions, attend at this also, to haul the man up; for he really did not expect the *Marlborough* would do

[1] Captain Manley Dixon.

[2] Captain John Markham

[3] Captain Joseph Ellison: born, 1753; Commander, 1782; Captain, 1783; retired, 1806; died, 1816.

it. Lord St. Vincent sternly answered: 'Captain Ellison; you are an old officer, sir; have served long, suffered severely in the service, and have lost an arm in action; and I should be very sorry that any advantage should be now taken of your advanced years. That man shall be hanged, at eight o'clock to-morrow morning, and by his own ship's company; for not a hand from any other ship in the fleet shall touch the rope. You will now return on board, sir; and, lest you should not prove able to command your ship, an officer will be at hand to you who can.'

"Without another word Captain Ellison instantly retired. After he had reached his ship, he received orders to cause her guns to be housed and secured, and that at daybreak in the morning her ports should be lowered. A general order was then issued to the fleet for all launches to rendezvous under the *Prince* at seven o'clock on the following morning, armed with carronades and twelve rounds of ammunition for service; each launch to be commanded by a Lieutenant, having an expert and trusty gunner's mate and four quarter-gunners, exclusive of the launch's crew; the whole to be under the command of Captain Campbell,[1] of the *Blenheim*. The written orders to the Captain will appear in their place. On presenting them, Lord St. Vincent said, 'he was to attend the execution, and, if any symptoms of mutiny appeared in the *Marlborough*, any attempt to open her ports, or any resistance to the hanging of the prisoner, he was to proceed close touching the ship, and to fire into her, and to continue to fire until all mutiny or resistance should cease; and that, should it become absolutely necessary, he should even sink the ship in face of the fleet.'

"Accordingly, at seven the next morning, all the launches, thus armed, proceeded from the *Prince* to the *Blenheim*, and thence, Captain Campbell having assumed the command, to the *Marlborough*. Having lain on his oars a short time alongside, the Captain formed his force in a line athwart her bows, at rather less than pistol-shot distance off; and then he ordered the tompions to be taken out of the carronades, and to load.

"At half-past seven, the hands throughout the fleet having been turned up to witness punishment, the eyes of all were bent upon a powerfully armed boat as it quitted the flag-ship; every one knowing that there went the provost-marshal conducting his prisoner to the *Marlborough* for execution. The crisis was come; now was to be seen whether the *Marlborough's* crew would hang one of their own men.

"The ship being in the centre between the two lines of the fleet, the boat was soon alongside, and the man was speedily placed on the cathead and haltered. A few awful minutes of universal silence followed, which was at last broken by the watch-bells of the fleet striking eight o'clock. Instantly the flagship's gun fired, and, at the sound, the man was lifted well up; but then, and visibly to all, he dropped back again; and the sensation throughout the fleet was intense. For, at this dreadful moment, when the eyes of every man in every ship were straining upon this execution, as the decisive struggle between authority and mutiny, as if it were destined that the whole fleet should see the hesitating unwillingness of the *Marlborough's* crew to hang their rebel, and the efficacy of the means taken to enforce obedience, by an accident on board the ship the men at the yard-rope unintentionally let it slip, and the turn of the balance seemed calamitously lost; but then they hauled him up to the yard-arm with a run,—the law was satisfied, and, said Lord St. Vincent at the moment, perhaps one of the greatest of his life, 'Discipline is preserved, sir.'

"When the sentence was executed, and not any disturbance appeared, that it might be again made perceptible to all the fleet that abundant force had been provided to overpower any resistance which a line-of-battle-ship could offer, Captain Campbell broke his line, and, rowing down, placed his launches as close alongside the *Marlborough* as

---

[1] Captain Robert Campbell (1): born, 1770; Commander and Captain, 1797; died, 1815.

their oars would permit; and then, re-forming them, resumed his station across her bows, continuing there until, the time for the body's hanging having expired, it was taken down, sewed up as usual in its own hammock with a shot, and carried in one of the *Marlborough's* boats to half a mile from the ship, and sunk; upon which Captain Campbell withdrew his force, and the *Marlborough's* signal was made to take her station in the line. . . . The dreadful sentence was again and again inflicted, and, in all cases of insubordination, the crews were invariably the executioners of their own rebels; but never again was the power of the law doubted by anyone."[1]

But the sequence of events has been anticipated. The many serious mutinies of 1797 have not yet all been enumerated, and some of the worst remain to be described.

The *Hermione*, 32, commanded by Captain Hugh Pigot (2), a courageous but very tyrannical officer, had begun what promised to be a distinguished commission on the Jamaica station, where, on September 22nd, off Puerto Rico, part of the crew rose in the night, seized those of their fellows who were not parties to the plot, and savagely murdered Captain Pigot in cold blood. It is admitted—although the fact does not in the least excuse their conduct—that some of them had been ill-treated by his orders; but that admission affords no shadow of explanation for the barbarity of their further procedure. After murdering Pigot, against whom they had personal grievances, they murdered two Lieutenants,[2] the Purser, Mr. Pacey, the Surgeon, Dr. Sansom, the Captain's Clerk, Mr. Mainwaring, a Midshipman named Smith, the Boatswain, William Martin, and Lieutenant M'Intosh, of the Marines, against the majority of whom they certainly had none; and not only did they murder them, but they also mangled their bodies. To complete their crime they carried the ship into La Guayra, and handed her over to the Spaniards, to be employed against their own countrymen. The splendid story of the frigate's recapture will be found in Chapter XXXVI. It is a further satisfaction to be able to say here that many of the mutineers were subsequently taken, and that they suffered for their villainy.[3]

On yet another station—that of the Cape of Good Hope—the

[1] 'Mems. of St. Vincent,' i. 303, etc.

[2] They had previously murdered the first Lieutenant, Samuel Read, who had bravely endeavoured to suppress the outbreak at its inception. The two Lieutenants killed after the death of the Captain were Archibald Douglas, and Henry Fanshawe.

[3] A somewhat analogous case of mutiny occurred in the West Indies in the same year on board the schooner, *Marie Antoinette*, 10, the crew of which murdered their commander, Lieutenant John M'Inerheny, and carried the ship into a French port. In the following year, an attempt, happily ineffectual, was made by her crew to seize the *Haughty*, 12, and deliver her to the enemy.

contagion from Spithead and the Nore broke out ere the close of the year. In October, a mutiny manifested itself in the *Tremendous*, 74, the crew of which attempted to try by a court, nominated by themselves, their captain, George Hopewell Stephens, for cruelty and misconduct. This initial outbreak was suppressed, and Captain Stephens demanded a court-martial, which was held on board the *Sceptre* in Table Bay, and which honourably acquitted him. In the course of the proceedings, some of the seamen witnesses grossly misbehaved themselves, and one of them was consequently punished. Soon afterwards, symptoms of mutiny appeared in several ships of the squadron, but, thanks to the prompt and determined measures of Lord Macartney, the governor of the Colony, Rear-Admiral Thomas Pringle, and General Dundas, the outbreak was quelled; the delegates who, as at the Nore, had been chosen, were given up; the leading offenders were executed or flogged, and discipline was restored.

For some time afterwards, mutiny was lamentably common in the Navy, but it never again reached the height to which it had attained in 1797. On September 18th, 1798, nineteen seamen of the *Defence* were sentenced to death, and six to flogging and imprisonment, and on October 9th following, eight seamen of the *Glory* were sentenced to death, two to receive one hundred lashes each, to be mulcted of all their pay, and to suffer twelve months' solitary confinement, and one to receive two hundred lashes, and to be fined and imprisoned. In March, 1800, the *Danae*, 32, Captain Lord Proby, was seized by her crew, while engaged in blockading Brest, and carried into that port; but the mutineers, to their no small astonishment, were imprisoned by the French, while Lord Proby and his officers were extremely well treated. Again, in November, 1800, another British vessel, the *Albanaise*, bomb, Commander Francis Newcombe, was taken possession of by her crew, and carried into a foreign port; but it appears that, in this case, many of the offenders were foreigners.[1] Yet cases of the kind became from year to year fewer and fewer, probably in consequence of the extremely severe punishments which it became the practice to deal out to mutineers. For example, for having written anonymous letters, endeavoured to make mutinous assemblies, and uttered

[1] C. M., June 17th, 1801. At this inquiry Lieutenant William Prosser Kent refused to give evidence upon oath, "from mistaken religious motives," and was thereupon adjudged to be unfit to hold his Majesty's commission.

seditious and mutinous words, King, a seaman of the *Active*, 38, was condemned, in April, 1801,[1] to receive five hundred lashes, and two of his shipmates, Beetham and Forrest, were condemned to receive three hundred apiece, from ship to ship. The last serious mutinous outbreak of the period under review occurred in December, 1801, in the *Téméraire*, 98, flagship of Rear-Admiral George Campbell, upon the ship being ordered from Bantry Bay to the West Indies. On January 6th, 1802, the trial of fourteen of the alleged offenders began at Spithead. Thirteen of them were condemned to death, and one was sentenced to receive two hundred lashes. On January 14th, the trial of six more began, and of these, five were condemned to death, and one was adjudged to receive two hundred lashes from ship to ship. On all these regrettable occasions, the Marines behaved with conspicuous discipline and loyalty, and, more than once, they were publicly thanked for their conduct. When the war was renewed, an almost equally good spirit reigned among the seamen, and there were but few outbreaks of serious insubordination. It may be that officers, as well as men, had learnt a lesson, and that the better treatment meted out to the latter was, as much as anything, responsible for their improved behaviour, for it is noticeable that, after 1797, prosecutions of officers for ill-treatment of their men became, for a time, more common than before, and then almost died out. Yet, at a considerably later date, we find the *Naval Chronicle* complaining that ill-treatment of seamen was still often overlooked or inadequately punished.

Not only in assisting to maintain discipline in the fleet, but also on nearly every possible occasion throughout the war, the behaviour of the Marines was admirable, and the good conduct of the corps was more than once officially recognised. In 1759, George II. had formed a new establishment of Marine officers of superior rank to be chosen from officers in the Royal Navy, viz., a General,[2] a Lieut.-General,[3] and three Colonels.[4] The first General was Admiral the Hon. Edward Boscawen, and among his successors up to the time of the Peace were Howe, Barrington, and Bridport. The first Lieut.-General was Vice-Admiral Sir Charles Saunders, and among his successors were Palliser, Barrington, Bridport, and St. Vincent. The first three Colonels were Captain Sir Piercy Brett (1), Kt.,

[1] C. M. in *Gladiator*, at Portsmouth, April 9th, 1801.

[2] Salary, £2000 a year. [3] Salary, £1200 a year. [4] Salary, £800 a year each.

Captain the Hon. Augustus Keppel,[1] and Captain Lord Howe. Among their successors, up to 1802, were Captains the Hon. Augustus Hervey,[2] the Hon. Samuel Barrington, Thomas Graves (2),[3] Joshua Rowley, the Hon. Robert Boyle Walsingham, William Hotham (1),[4] Sir John Lindsay, K.B., the Hon. William Cornwallis, Sir Hyde Parker (2), Sir Roger Curtis, Kt., James Gambier (2),[5] Lord Hugh Seymour, Horatio Nelson, the Hon. George Cranfield Berkeley, John Thomas Duckworth, Sir James Saumarez, Sir Edward Pellew, Bt.,[6] and Sir Thomas Troubridge, Bt. In June, 1794, a Major-General of Marines was also appointed, the first holder of the rank being Rear-Admiral Sir Alan Gardner, afterwards Lord Gardner. In 1802, after the close of the war, the King, to mark his satisfaction with the behaviour of the corps, signified his pleasure that it should be styled for the future the Royal Marines.

An alteration in the uniform of naval officers was effected by an order of June 1st, 1795. It was then that the wearing of epaulettes [7] —a French fashion, to which Nelson, for a time, most strongly objected—was first introduced into the service. Admirals were directed to wear two gold epaulettes, with three silver stars on each; Vice-Admirals the same, with two stars on each; Rear-Admirals the same, with one star on each; and Post-Captains of above three years' standing, two epaulettes without stars. A Post-Captain of under three years' standing was assigned one gold epaulette, to be worn on the right shoulder, and a Master and Commander the same, to be worn on the left. It was at the same time ordered that the lappels and cuffs of Captains' uniforms were to be blue instead of white, and that the lace was to be the same as before the previous alteration; but neither lace nor embroidery was to be worn on the undress coat. The only survival of the old white facing remained in the shape of the piping on the Lieutenant's coat, and both remained, and still remains, in the patch on the Midshipman's collar.

Medals continued to be very sparingly granted. As will be seen in the next chapter, medals for the battle of the Glorious First of June, 1794, were issued to certain selected flag-officers and Captains who

[1] Later, Viscount Keppel.
[2] Later, Earl of Bristol.
[3] Later, Lord Graves.
[4] Later, Lord Hotham.
[5] Later, Lord Gambier.
[6] Later, Lord Exmouth.

[7] Mr. Popham Lethbridge says that the wearing of epaulettes arose out of the fact that some British naval officers, while visiting France during the peace, observed that the sentries did not salute them, though they did salute British Marine officers, who then wore silver epaulettes. When one of the naval officers became a Lord of the Admiralty he procured the adoption of the new regulation.

had been present on that occasion. In addition, a gold chain, to which his medal was to be suspended, was given to Earl Howe. Concerning the manner in which these distinctions were conferred, Captain Isaac Schomberg[1] very sensibly says:—

> "The meritorious conduct of these officers was, no doubt, highly deserving of so distinguished a mark of royal favour. How far such selections may be consistent with the well-being of so important a service as that of the British Navy, in which every officer is supposed on like occasions to act to the best of his abilities, needs no comment. If, in the presence of an enemy, or in action, a commander appears deficient either in courage or conduct, it is more candid and decided in a Commander-in-Chief to have such conduct investigated before a public tribunal, rather than leave a doubt on the minds of his country by such oblique insinuations that some have fallen short in their duty."

Medals were again granted to the flag-officers and Captains—this time without exception[2]—present at Jervis's victory off Cape St. Vincent in 1797, at the battle off Camperdown in the same year, and at the battle of the Nile in 1798. These were all of gold, and all alike, and were directed to be worn with uniform, hanging from a neck-chain, by flag-officers, and, attached to a blue and white ribbon passed through the third and fourth buttonholes on the left side of the coat, by Captains. The gold medal was also given to Captain Edward Hamilton, of the *Surprise*, for his recapture of the *Hermione*, on October 25th, 1799. After the Nile, Lord Nelson's friend and agent, Mr. Alexander Davison, at his own expense, presented handsome medals, or "tributes of regard," in gold, silver, bronze-gilt and bronze, to the various ranks engaged; and, in commemoration of St. Vincent, Lord St. Vincent distributed to the seamen a medal which he styled "a testimony of approbation"; but these, of course, had no official significance. Not until very many years afterwards, when most of the participants were dead, were the services of the junior commissioned officers, warrant officers, seamen, and Marines, during the War of the French Revolution, recognised by the issue by Government to the survivors of a naval war medal with appropriate clasps.

On many occasions during the war, and especially in the earlier part of it, large numbers of troops were embarked in the fleet, to serve in lieu of Marines, and for other purposes.[3] This practice

[1] 'Nav. Chronol.' ii. 270.

[2] Save in the case of one of the Camperdown Captains.

[3] At the battle of St. Vincent, in 1797, part of the 69th Regiment served in Nelson's ship, the *Captain*. In consequence, the present Welsh Regiment, the 2nd Battalion of which was formerly the 69th Regiment, bears on its colour "St. Vincent." The Royal

quickly led to a conflict of authority between the Navy and the Army, and, in 1795, H.R.H. the Duke of York, then the military Commander-in-Chief, saw fit to issue an order that regular troops, serving on board men-of-war, should not be amenable to naval discipline, but, in case of misbehaviour, should be sent ashore for trial by a military court. A meeting of flag-officers and Captains was held at Portsmouth on November 3rd in that year to consider the situation thus created, and, in the meanwhile, certain vessels, having troops on board, and about to sail for abroad, were detained. In the event, it was very wisely decided by the Government that no alteration should be made in the naval Articles of War, and that officers and privates of the army, serving in his Majesty's ships, should be subject to the laws of naval discipline.

The morality of the lower deck remained, it must be feared, at a rather low ebb. Numerous allusions are to be found in the logs and journals of the time to the presence of women on board ship, not only in port, but also at sea. After the *Resistance*, 44, had blown up in the Strait of Banca on July 24th, 1798, Thomas Scott, one of the four survivors, deposed that, among those who perished in her, were three English women, married on board, and one Malay woman of Amboyna. And in the Rules and Orders to be observed by the mutinous crews of the ships at the Nore in 1797, occurs the significant paragraph, "No woman shall be permitted to go on shore from any ship, but as many may come in as please." But as it will be necessary to revert later to this subject, nothing further shall here be said about it.

It was, naturally, inevitable that, in the course of a gigantic struggle such as was waged from 1793 to 1802, questions connected with the maintenance and exchange of prisoners of war should often arise. Early in 1798, the problem of maintenance, and, in September of the same year, the numerous problems involved in the arrangement of a satisfactory scheme of exchange, appeared to be finally and equitably solved. It was agreed between Great Britain and France that the prisoners of each should be supported at the cost of their respective countries; that each country should send to the other an agent to superintend the furnishing of the prisoners of

---

Berkshire Regiment, the 1st Battalion of which was formerly the 49th Foot, and the Rifle Brigade, the 1st Battalion of which was then known as Col. Manningham's Corps of Riflemen, similarly bear "Copenhagen," on account of their services in Nelson's division in 1801.

his nationality with provisions; that the markets should be open to these agents; and that the prisoners should be concentrated in a few central localities, instead of being distributed over the two countries. The agents first appointed in pursuance of this convention were, on the part of Great Britain, Captain James Cotes, R.N., and, on the part of the French Republic, M. Niou.[1] As regards exchange, it was agreed that France should begin by returning in a French vessel a batch of British prisoners, including five per cent. of officers; that Great Britain would then return in a British vessel a corresponding batch of French prisoners, and that afterwards the two countries should take it in turns to commence the exchange. Prisoners for exchange were to be selected by their resident agents. A table showing the equivalent in men for an officer of every rank was drawn up, and the allowance of food to be provided daily by the surrendering government to prisoners while on board the cartels was fixed. Moreover, it was agreed that men incapacitated by wounds, age, or infirmities, and boys under twelve years of age, should be at once surrendered without equivalent, and that Surgeons, Pursers, Secretaries, Chaplains, Schoolmasters, and non-combatant passengers, should not be detained as prisoners of war. Provision was also made for the liberation, on parole not to serve again during the war until regularly exchanged, of combatant officers. But in 1799, when the balance of prisoners[2] was even more against France than it had been in 1798, the government of the Republic refused any longer to support or clothe its prisoners in Great Britain, the idea, no doubt, being that a captor could not well refuse to keep his captives alive, and that the expense of doing so would help to weaken his resources. There ceased also, for a time, to be any regular system of exchange. Remonstrance was made, but without effect, and, pending negotiations, the prisoners in Great Britain suffered great hardships. Eventually, so heavy was the mortality, that it was ordered, on January 1st, 1801, that the French prisoners in Great Britain should be supplied with warm clothing at the public expense.

Among the numerous improvements which were effected during the period, three of the most important were the construction of

[1] At that time there were in Britain 30,265 French prisoners, besides 300 officers on parole, confined at Portsmouth, Plymouth, Norman Cross, Liverpool, Edinburgh, Chatham, and Stapleton; and in France only about 4000 British prisoners.

[2] There were then in Great Britain 25,646 French prisoners, and in France only about 1470 British. 'Report to Transport Board' of December 21st, 1799.

signal towers along the coasts of England to facilitate the rapid transmission of intelligence from point to point; the creation of lines of telegraph stations between London and Deal, with a branch to Sheerness, and between London and Portsmouth; and the institution of the force known as the Sea Fencibles. The signal towers, to the number of eighty-seven, were built in 1795, and to each of them were allotted a Lieutenant at 7*s*. 6*d*. a day over and above his half-pay, a Midshipman at 2*s*. a day, with, in addition, the pay of a Midshipman of a fourth-rate, and two seamen at 2*s*. a day. This staff lodged in a house adjoining the tower, and was allowed coals and candles. The telegraph stations were erected in 1795 and 1796. The method whereby messages were transmitted was by semaphore, the invention of the Rev. Lord George Murray, later Bishop of St. David's, and the various stations were: (1), *Between London and Deal*, Admiralty, West Square, New Cross, Shooter's Hill, Swanscombe, Gadshill, Callum Hill, Beacon Hill, Shottenden, Barham Downs, Bettishanger, and Deal; (2), *Between Beacon Hill and Sheerness*, Tong, Barrow Hill, and Sheerness; and (3), *Between London and Portsmouth*, Admiralty, Chelsea, Putney, Cabbage Hill, Netley Heath, Hascombe, Blackdown, Beacon Hill, Portsdown, and Portsmouth. The Sea Fencibles were raised in the spring of 1798 at the instance of Captain Home Riggs Popham. The corps was composed of fishermen, sailors employed in coasters, and other persons engaged on the water; and the men were trained in the use of the pike, and, whenever possible, in gunnery also. For the purpose, the coast was divided into districts, to each of which a Post-Captain, and one, two or three Commanders were appointed, the Captains receiving £1 10*s*. a day as pay and allowance, besides 5*s*. for the expense of a clerk, stationery, and travelling, and the Commanders receiving £1 a day, besides 1*s*. 9*d*. for contingencies. The men were given protection against impressment, and were paid 1*s*. each at every muster or drill. About nine thousand were raised, chiefly in the southern counties and in Yorkshire; but, upon the signing of the preliminaries of peace, the Sea Fencibles were discontinued, and their officers were discharged. The corps was, in some respects, the prototype of the modern Coastguard.

In 1795 it was decided to establish a Hydrographical office at the Admiralty, and the post of Hydrographer was offered to, and accepted by, Mr. Alexander Dalrymple, who, since 1779, had been Hydrographer to the East India Company. For more than a hundred years previously there had been government hydrographers in France, but Dalrymple's appointment was the first of its kind in Great Britain. Dalrymple did good work for some years, but was dismissed from his post on May 28th., 1808, and died, it is said of a broken heart, on June 19th following.

Other improvements were; the appointment, in 1795, as governors of the Royal Naval Hospitals there, of Post-Captains, each with three Lieutenants under him, to Plymouth and Haslar, and of

ALEXANDER DALRYMPLE, 1733–1808.
FIRST HYDROGRAPHER TO THE ADMIRALTY, 1795–1808.

(*From Blood's engraving after a drawing by John Brown.*)

Lieutenants to Deal and Great Yarmouth; the allowance of servants, in 1799, to some of the principal shipwrights in the dockyards; the abolition, in 1801, of the ancient but iniquitous practice of permitting shipwrights to remove chips from the yards, and the allowance to them instead of 6*d*. a day; the creation of a Victualling Yard[1] at Deptford; and the adoption, about the year 1799, of

[1] The shipbuilding premises known as Dudman's Dock were purchased for that purpose.

appliances for filtering, before use, the water supplied to ships' companies. The fitting of locks to heavy guns for the purpose of firing them, in substitution of, or as alternative to, the firing-irons and smouldering ropes' ends then generally in use, was experimented with during the period, but was not generally adopted until some years later.

At the beginning of 1800, a new scale of fees was established for the issue of Admiralty commissions and warrants. The more important of these were: commission to a flag-officer, £5 7*s.* 6*d.*; to a Captain or Commander, £2 3*s.*; to a Lieutenant, £1 1*s.* 6*d.*; warrant to a Purser, Gunner, Boatswain, or Carpenter of a ship of one of the three higher rates, £2 3*s.*; to a Chaplain of a man-of-war, 10*s.* 6*d.*; warrant to admit a scholar into the Royal Naval Academy, £1 1*s.* 6*d.* Fees also had to be paid on orders for superannuation, on orders for pensions, on the granting of passes to protect against Moorish pirates and against impressment, on letters of leave, and on the issue of various certificates.

The national ensign had remained unchanged since the time of the union with Scotland, when, on January 1st, 1801, the accomplishment of the Union between Great Britain and Ireland necessitated an addition to the Union Flag of an emblem to represent Ireland. The emblem fixed upon was what is vulgarly called the cross of St. Patrick. A cross is the attribute only of a martyr, and St. Patrick, not having been a martyr, has no cross. But the saltire adopted, besides figuring in the coat armour of the Fitzgeralds, long one of the greatest of Irish families, seems to have been recognised before the Union as a badge of Ireland, and, though its origin as such is, perhaps, obscure, it was wisely made use of in preference to the harp or to the shamrock, neither of which would have readily lent itself to inclusion in the general heraldic scheme of the old Union Flag.[1] At the same time the Royal Ensign was altered,

[1] The Proclamation of January 1st, 1801, contained the following descriptive paragraph:—

"The Union Flag shall be: Azure, the crosses saltire of St. Andrew and St. Patrick quarterly per saltire, counterchanged Argent and Gules, the latter fimbriated of the second; surmounted by the cross of St. George of the third, fimbriated as the saltire."

According to the practice of the Royal Navy, the Union Flag has ever since been constructed of the following proportions: All British naval flags are of twice the length of their breadth. Assuming, therefore, that it be desired to construct a Union Flag 60 in. in length, then, the total breadth will be 30 in.; the breadth of the red St. George's cross, 6 in.; the breadth of the fimbriation, or white border, on each side

the arms of England figuring in the first and fourth quarters, those of Scotland in the second, those of Ireland in the third, and those of

---

of the St. George's cross, 2 in. (thus making the whole breadth of the upright cross and its borders 10 in.); the breadth of the visible part of the red Irish saltire, 2 in.; the breadth of its narrow fimbriation, 1 in.; and the breadth of the visible part of the white cross of St. Andrew, 3 in. (thus making the whole breadth of the composite diagonal cross, 6 in.).

The diagrams given herewith will help to make clearer the scheme of composition of the Union, which is very often improperly made, and which, in the British merchant service, as forming part of the Blue and Red Ensigns, is almost invariably incorrect. The diagrams will also explain the heraldic process known as "counterchanging,"—a process here applied with the object of giving equal prominence to the two saltires.

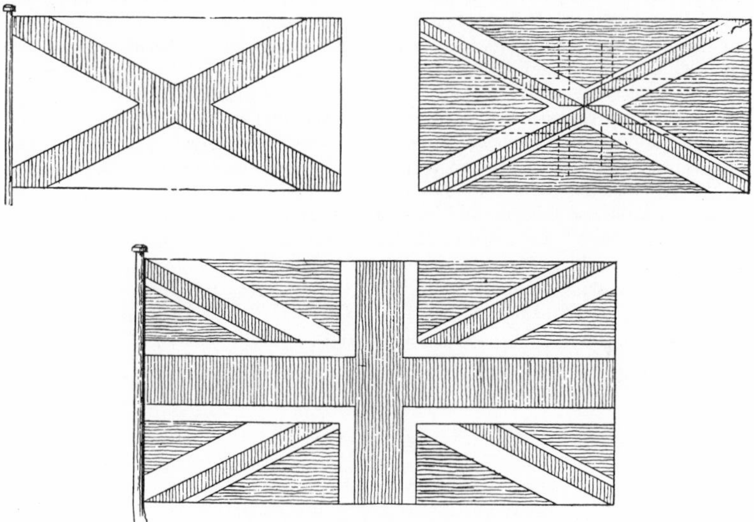

THE UNION FLAG OF JAN. 1ST, 1801.

The figures above show (1) the saltire introduced to represent Ireland; and (2) the method of "counterchanging" the saltires of Scotland and Ireland in the Union Flag as it has stood since 1801.

The Scots saltire, as representing an older member of the Union than the Irish, takes the superior position in the upper corner of the flag, next the staff; and the flag should not, of course, be hoisted so as to exhibit it in any other position.

On the same day (January 1st, 1801) it was further proclaimed that:—

"Whereas, according to ancient usage, the ensigns, flags, 'Jacks,' and pennants worn by our ships, and appointed as a distinction for the same, ought not to be worn on board any ship or vessel belonging to any of our subjects, so that our ships and those of our subjects may be easily distinguished and known, we have therefore thought fit, by and with the advice of our Privy Council, to order and appoint the ensign" (the Red Ensign), "described on the side or margin hereof, to be worn on board of all ships or vessels of any of our subjects whatsoever, and to issue this our Royal Proclamation to notify the same to all our loving subjects, hereby strictly charging and commanding the masters of all merchant ships and vessels belonging to

Hannover, etc., being borne on an escutcheon of pretence. From the new Royal Ensign, as from the arms of the United Kingdom, the arms of the Royal House of France, which had figured for centuries as a quartering in the arms of the Kings of England, were very sensibly expunged. The omission was made the more appropriately at a time when Great Britain was victorious over her hereditary foe, when the French Royal Family was in exile, and when the tricolour had become the flag of France.

---

our subjects, whether employed in our service or otherwise, to wear the said ensign on board their ships or vessels: And we do strictly charge and command all our subjects whatsoever that they do not presume to wear in any of their ships or vessels our 'Jack,' commonly called the 'Union Jack,' nor any pendants, nor any such colours as are usually borne by our ships, without particular warrant for their so doing from us or our High Admiral of Great Britain."

This proclamation gave the Red Ensign (a red flag with the Union in the upper canton next the staff) as the flag of the merchant service; but it did not remove it from the Royal Navy. On the contrary, until the distinction in the colours of flag-officers was abolished, more than half a century later, flag-officers of the Red, the White, and the Blue, and the ships of their divisions, continued, as before, to fly, respectively, the Red Ensign, the White or St. George's Ensign (which is now the flag of the Royal Navy), and the Blue Ensign, in order to indicate their rank and place. But, when several Flag-officers of different ranks and colours were together in a fleet, the senior officer often ordered the ships of all the squadrons to fly, for convenience, a single ensign. So it happened that, at the Glorious First of June, all ships fought under the Red, and that, at the Nile and Trafalgar, all fought under the White Ensign which was pre-eminently Nelson's favourite.

CAULKER'S IRON PITCH FURNACE.

APPENDIX TO CHAPTER XXXIV.

LIST, in continuation of the list in vol. iii. pp. 565–568, OF BRITISH FLAG-OFFICERS ON THE ACTIVE LIST AT THE OUTBREAK OF THE WAR WITH FRANCE IN 1793, and of all officers who were subsequently promoted to flag-rank on the active list up to the conclusion of the war in 1802.

NOTE.—*The promotions of the following officers are given in detail in the list above-mentioned. The names are repeated here only to show the complete list as it stood at the opening of the war.*

ADMIRAL OF THE FLEET.

Hon. John Forbes, General of Marines.

ADMIRALS OF THE WHITE.

Harry, Duke of Bolton.
Sir Francis Geary, Bart.
George, Earl Mount Edgcumbe.
John Montagu.
Richard, Earl Howe, Vice-Adm. of England (K.G., 1797).
Molyneux, Lord Shuldham.
Sir Hugh Palliser, Bart., Gov. of Greenwich Hospital.
Matthew Barton.

ADMIRALS OF THE BLUE.

Sir Peter Parker (1), Bart.
Hon. Samuel Barrington, Lieut.-General of Marines.
Marriot Arbuthnot.
Robert Roddam.[1]
William Lloyd (1).
Sir Edward Hughes, K.B.
John Evans.
Mark Milbanke.

VICE-ADMIRALS OF THE RED.

Nicholas Vincent.[1]
Sir Edward Vernon, Kt.
Richard Edwards.
Thomas Graves (2) (Lord Graves, 1794).
Hon. Robert Digby.[1]
Benjamin Marlow.
Sir Alexander Arthur Hood, K.B., Rear-Adm. of England (Lord Bridport, 1794).[1]
Sir Chaloner Ogle (2), Kt. (Bart., 1816).[1]
Samuel, Lord Hood (Viscount, 1796; G.C.B., 1815).[1]

VICE-ADMIRALS OF THE WHITE.

Sir Richard Hughes (3), Bart.[1]
John Elliot.[1]
William Hotham (Lord Hotham, 1797).[1]
Joseph Peyton (1).
John Carter Allen.
Sir Charles Middleton, Bart. (Lord Barham, 1805).[1]
Sir John Laforey, Bart.
John Dalrymple.

VICE-ADMIRALS OF THE BLUE.

Herbert Sawyer.
Sir Richard King, Bart.[1]
Jonathan Faulknor (1).
Philip Affleck.
Sir John Jervis, K.B. (Earl St. Vincent, 1797).[1]
Adam Duncan (Visct. Duncan, 1797).
Richard Brathwaite.
Phillips Cosby.[1]

REAR-ADMIRALS OF THE RED.

Thomas Fitzherbert.
Samuel Pitchford Cornish.[1]
John Brisbane.[1]
Charles Wolseley.[1]
Samuel Granston Goodall.
Hon. Keith Stewart.
H.R.H. William Henry, Duke of Clarence.[1]

---

[1] These officers were promoted to be Admirals of the Red at the creation of that rank on November 9th, 1805. The fact is noted here, as promotions to the rank of Admiral of the Red are not given in the list in vol. iii. pp. 565–568.

LIST OF BRITISH FLAG-OFFICERS ON THE ACTIVE LIST AT THE OUTBREAK OF THE WAR WITH FRANCE IN 1793—*continued.*

NAME AND TITLES.	BORN.	POST-CAPTAIN.	REAR-ADMIRAL.			VICE-ADMIRAL.			ADMIRAL.		ADMIRAL OF THE FLEET.	DIED.
			Blue.	White.	Red.	Blue.	White.	Red.	Blue.	White.		
Richard Onslow (Bart. 1797; G.C.B. 1815)	23-6-1741	14-4-1762	—	1-2-1793	12-4-1794	—	4-7-1794	1-6-1795	14-2-1799	23-4-1804 [1]	—	27-12-1817
Robert Brice Kingsmill (Bart. 1800)	*ca.* 1731	26-5-1762	—	1-2-1793	12-4-1794	—	4-7-1794	1-6-1795	14-2-1799	23-4-1804 [1]	—	23-11-1805
Sir George Collier, Kt.	1738	12-7-1762	—	1-2-1793	12-4-1794	4-7-1794	—	—	—	—	—	6-4-1799
George Bowyer (Bart. 1794)		28-10-1762	—	1-2-1793	12-4-1794	4-7-1794	—	1-6-1795	14-2-1799	—	—	6-12-1800
Sir Hyde Parker (2), Kt.	1739	18-7-1763	—	1-2-1793	12-4-1794	4-7-1794	—	1-6-1795	14-2-1799	23-4-1804 [1]	—	16-3-1807
Rowland Cotton		7-5-1764	—	1-2-1793	12-4-1794	4-7-1794	—	—	—	—	—	30-11-1794
Benjamin Caldwell (G.C.B. 1820)	31-1-1739	1-4-1765	—	1-2-1793	12-4-1794	4-7-1794	—	1-6-1795	14-2-1799	23-4-1804 [1]	—	1820
Hon. William Cornwallis (G.C.B. 1815)	20-2-1744	20-4-1765	—	1-2-1793	12-4-1794	4-7-1794	—	1-6-1795	14-2-1799	23-4-1804 [1]	—	1819
William Allen (2)		20-6-1765	1-2-1793	—	12-4-1794	4-7-1794	1-6-1795	—	14-2-1799	—	—	10-1804
John Macbride		20-6-1765	1-2-1793	—	12-4-1794	4-7-1794	1-6-1795	—	14-1-1799	—	—	17-2-1800
George Vandeput		20-6-1765	1-2-1793	—	12-4-1794	4-7-1794	1-6-1795	—	14-2-1799	—	—	1799
Charles Buckner		17-2-1766	1-2-1793	12-4-1794	—	4-7-1794	1-6-1795	—	14-2-4799	9-11-1805 [2]	—	1811
John Gell		4-3-1765	1-2-1793	12-4-1794	—	4-7-1794	1-6-1795	—	14-2-1799	9-11-1805	—	1806
William Dickson		2-5-1766	1-2-1793	12-4-1794	—	4-7-1794	1-6-1795	—	14-2-1799	—	—	1803
Alan Gardner (Bart. 1794; Lord Gardner, 1800)	12-4-1742	19-5-1766	1-2-1793	12-4-1794	—	4-7-1794	1-6-1795	—	14-2-1799	9-11-1805 [2]	—	1-1-1809
John Lewis Gidoin		26-5-1768	—	12-4-1794	4-7-1794	—	1-6-1795	—	—	—	—	1795
George Gayton		26-5-1768	—	12-4-1794	4-7-1794	—	1-6-1795	—	—	—	—	1797
Hon. George Murray (1)		26-5-1768	—	12-4-1794	4-7-1794	—	1-6-1795	—	—	—	—	28-12-1795
Robert Linzee		3-10-1770	—	12-4-1794	4-7-1794	—	1-6-1795	14-2-1799	1-1-1801	—	—	9-1805
Sir James Wallace, Kt.		10-1-1771	—	12-4-1794	4-7-1794	—	1-6-1795	14-2-1799	1-1-1801	—	—	6-3-1803
William Peere Williams (*later* Freeman)	1741	10-1-1771	—	12-4-1794	4-7-1794	—	1-6-1795	14-2-1799	1-1-1801	9-11-1805 [3]	28-6-1830	10-2-1832
Thomas Pasley (Bart. 1794)	2-3-1734	21-1-1771	—	12-4-1794	4-7-1794	—	1-6-1795	14-2-1799	1-1-1801	9-11-1805	—	29-11-1808
John Symons		28-1-1771	12-4-1794	—	4-7-1794	1-6-1795	—	14-2-1799	—	—	—	16-12-1799
Sir Thomas Rich, Bart.		14-2-1771	12-4-1794	—	4-7-1794	1-6-1795	—	14-2-1799	1-1-1801	—	—	6-4-1803
Charles Thompson (1) (Bart. 1797)		7-3-1772	12-4-1794	4-7-1794		1-6-1795	—	14-2-1799	—	—	—	17-3-1799
James Cumming	1738	30-7-1772	12-4-1794	4-7-1794		1-6-1795	—	14-2-1799	1-1-1801	9-11-1805	—	1808
John Ford		25-6-1773	12-4-1794	4-7-1794		1-6-1795	—	—	—	—	—	1796
John Colpoys (K.B. 1797)	1742	25-8-1773	12-4-1794	4-7-1794		1-6-1795	—	14-2-1799	1-1-1801	9-11-1805 [3]	—	1821
Skeffington Lutwidge	1736	15-10-1773	12-4-1794	4-7-1794		1-6-1795	—	14-2-1799	1-1-1801	9-11-1805 [4]	—	21-8-1814
Archibald Dickson (1) (Bart. 1802)		31-1-1774	12-4-1794	4-7-1794		1-6-1795	—	14-2-1799	1-1-1801	—	—	1803
George Montagu (G.C.B. 1815)	12-12-1750	15-4-1774	12-4-1794	4-7-1794		1-6-1795	—	14-2-1799	1-1-1801	9-11-1805 [4]	—	12-1828
Thomas Dumaresq	1728	23-1-1775	12-4-1794	4-7-1794		1-6-1795	—	14-2-1799	1-1-1801	—	—	18-7-1802
Hon. George Keith Elphinstone (K.B. 1794; Ir. Baron Keith, 1797; Baron of U. K. 1801; Visct. 1814)		12-3-1775	12-4-1794	4-7-1794		1-6-1795	—	14-2-1799	1-1-1801	9-11-1805 [4]	—	1823

James Pigott		22-2-1776	4-7-1794	—	—	1-6-1795	—	14-2-1799		9-11-1805 [4]	—	1822
Hon. William Waldegrave (1) (Lord Radstock, 1800; G.C.B. 1815)	9-7-1753	30-5-1776	4-7-1794	—	—	1-6-1795	—	14-2-1799		9-11-1805 [4]	—	20-8-1825
Thomas Mackenzie	1753	12-6-1776	4-7-1794	—	1-6-1795	—	14-2-1799	1-1-1801	23-4-1804	9-11-1805 [4]		20-9-1813
Thomas Pringle		25-11-1776	4-7-1794	—	1-6-1795	—	14-2-1799	1-1-1801	—	—	—	1803
Hon. William Clement Finch	1753	18-3-1777	4-7-1794	—	—	—		—	—	—	—	1794
Sir Roger Curtis, Kt. (Bart. 1794; G.C.B. 1815)	4-6-1746	30-4-1777	4-7-1794	—	1-6-1795	—	14-2-1799	1-1-1801	23-4-1804	9-11-1805 [4]	—	4-11-1816
Henry Harvey (1) (K.B. 1800)	1737	9-5-1777	4-7-1794	—	1-6-1795	—	14-2-1799	1-1-1801	23-4-1804	9-11-1805	—	28-12-1810
Robert Man (3)		30-5-1777	4-7-1794	—	1-6-1795	—	14-2-1799	1-1-1801	23-4-1804	28-4-1808 [5]		20-9-1813
William Parker (1) (Bart. 1797)	1743	28-8-1777	4-7-1794	—	1-6-1795	—	14-2-1799	1-1-1801	—	—	—	31-10-1802
Charles Holmes Everitt Calmady		7-9-1777	23-10-1794	—	1-6-1795	—	14-2-1799	1-1-1801	23-4-1804	—	—	3-1807
John Bourmaster	1736	9-9-1777	23-10-1794	—	1-6-1795	—	14-2-1799	1-1-1801	23-4-1804	—	—	1807
Sir George Young, Kt.	17-6-1732	7-11-1777	23-10-1794	—	1-6-1795	—	14-2-1799	1-1-1801	23-4-1804	28-4-1808		28-16-1810
John Henry	28-9-1731	22-11-1777	23-10-1794	—	1-6-1795	—	14-2-1799	1-1-1801	23-4-1804	28-4-1808 [5]	—	
Richard Rodney Bligh (G.C.B. 1820)	1737	6-12-1777	23-10-1794	—	1-6-1795	—	14-2-1799	1-1-1801	23-4-1804	28-4-1808 [6]	—	1821
Alexander Græme		24-1-1778	—	1-6-1795	20-2-1797	—	14-2-1799		23-4-1804	28-4-1808 [6]	—	1818
George Keppel		26-1-1778	—	1-6-1795	20-2-1797	—	14-2-1799		23-4-1804	—	—	
Samuel Reeve		1-2-1778	—	1-6-1795	20-2-1797	—	14-2-1799	—	—	—	—	
Robert Biggs		18-3-1778	—	1-6-1795	—	14-2-1799	1-1-1801	—	—	—	—	11-7-1803
Francis Parry (2)		7-4-1778	—	1-6-1795	—	14-2-1799	1-1-1801	—	—	—	—	18-12-1803
Isaac Prescott		8-4-1778	—	1-6-1795	—	14-2-1799	1-1-1801	23-4-1804	9-11-1805	25-10-1809 [7]	—	
John Bazely (1)	3-1741	15-4-1778	—	1-6-1795	—	14-2-1799	1-1-1801	23-4-1804	9-11-1805	—	—	6-4-1809
Christopher Mason		22-4-1778	—	1-6-1795	—	14-2-1799	1-1-1801	—	—	—	—	6-1802
Thomas Spry (1) (*previously* Thos. Davy)		5-5-1778	—	1-6-1795	—	14-2-1799	1-1-1801	23-4-1804	9-11-1805	25-10-1809 [7]	—	27-11-1828
Sir John Orde, Bart.	12-1752	19-5-1778	—	1-6-1795	—	14-2-1799	1-1-1801	23-4-1804	9-11-1805	25-10-1809 [7]	—	1824
William Young (1) (G.C.B. 1815)	1750	23-9-1778	—	1-6-1795	—	14-2-1799	1-1-1801	23-4-1804	9-11-1805	31-7-1810 [7]	—	25-10-1821
James Gambier (2) (Lord Gambier, 1807; G.C.B. 1815)	13-10-1756	9-10-1778	—	1-6-1795	—	14-2-1799	1-1-1801	23-4-1804	9-11-1805	31-7-1810 [7]	23-7-1830	19-4-1833
Andrew Mitchell (1) (K.B. 1799)	1757	28-10-1778	1-6-1795	20-2-1797	—	14-2-1799	1-1-1801	23-4-1804	9-11-1805	—	—	26-2-1806
Charles Chamberlayne		28-10-1778	1-6-1795	20-2-1797	—	14-2-1799		23-4-1804	9-11-1805	—	—	1810
Peter Rainier (1)		29-10-1778	1-6-1795	20-2-1797	—	14-2-1799		23-4-1804	9-11-1805	—	—	1808
Hugh Cloberry Christian (K.B. 1797)	1747	8-12-1778	1-6-1795	20-2-1797	—	—	—	—	—	—	—	11-1798
William Truscott	25-11-1734	14-12-1778	1-6-1795	20-2-1797	—	—	—	—	—	—	—	31-1-1798
Lord Hugh Seymour (*formerly* Hon. Hugh Seymour Conway)	29-4-1759	8-2-1779	1-6-1795	20-2-1797	—	14-2-1799	—	—	—	—	—	11-9-1801
John Stanhope	1744		1-6-1795	—	14-2-1799	—	—	—	—	—	—	11-12-1800
Christopher Parker (2)	1762	7-3-1779	1-6-1795	—	14-2-1799	1-1-1801	—	23-4-1804			—	26-5-1804
Philip Patton	1739	22-3-1779	1-6-1795	—	14-2-1799	1-1-1801	—	23-4-1804	9-11-1805	31-7-1810 [7]	—	31-12-1815
Charles Morice Pole (Bart. 1801; K.C.B. 1815; G.C.B. 1818)	18-1-1757	22-3-1779	1-6-1795	—	14-2-1799	1-1-1801	—	23-4-1804	9-11-1805	31-7-1810 [7]	23-7-1830	31-8-1830
John Brown	1751	25-3-1779	1-6-1795	—	14-2-1799	1-1-1801	23-4-1804	9-11-1805	28-4-1808	—	—	2-5-1808

[1] Promoted to be Admirals of the Red, 9-11-1805. [2] *Ib.*, 28-4-1808. [3] *Ib.*, 25-10-1809. [4] *Ib.*, 31-7-1810. [5] *Ib.*, 12-8-1812. [6] *Ib.*, 4-12-1813. [7] *Ib.*, 4-6-1814.

List of British Flag-Officers on the Active List at the outbreak of the War with France in 1793—*continued.*

Name and Titles.	Born.	Post-Captain.	Rear-Admiral.			Vice-Admiral.			Admiral.		Admiral of the Fleet.	Died.
			Blue.	White.	Red.	Blue.	White.	Red.	Blue.	White.		
John Leigh Douglas		5–4–1779	1–6–1795	—	14–2–1799	1–1–1801	23–4–1804	9–11–1805	28–4–1808	31–7–1810	—	13–11–1810
William Swiney (1)		2–5–1779	20–2–1797	—	14–2 1799	1–1–1801	23–4–1804	9–11–1805	28–4–1808	31–7–1810 [1]	—	
Charles **Edmund** Nugent (G.C.H. 1834)	*ca.* 1759	2–5–1779	20–2–1797	—	14–2–1799	1–1–1801	23–4–1804	9–11–1805	28–4–1808	31–7–1810 [1]	24–4–1833	7–1–1844
William Fooks		14–5–1779	20–2–1797	—	—	—	—	—	—	—	—	1798
Charles Powell Hamilton		18–5–1779	20–2–1797	—	14–2–1799	1–1–1801	23–4–1804	9–11–1805	28–4–1808	31–7–1810 [1]	—	12–3–1825
Edmund Dod	1734	18–5–1779	20–2–1797	—	14–2–1799	1–1–1801	23–4–1804	9–11–1805	28–4–1808	31–7–1810	—	18–12–1815
Horatio **Nelson** (**K**.B. 1797; Lord Nelson, 1798; Viscount, 1801)	29–9–1758	11–6–1779	20–2–1797	—	14–2–1799	1–1–1801	23–4–1804	—	—	—	—	Killed 21–10–1805
Thomas Lenox Frederick	3–1750	14–7–1779	20–2–1797	—	14–2–1799	—	—	—	—	—	—	8–11–1799
Sir George Home, Bart.		21–7–1779	20–2–1797	—	14–2–1799	—	—	—	—	—	—	2–5–1803
Sir Charles Cotton, Bart.	6–1753	10–8–1779	20–2–1797	—	14–2–1799		23–4–1804	9–11–1805	28–4–1808	31–7–1810	—	23–2–1812
Matthew Squire		6–11–1779	—	—	14–2–1799	—	—	—	—	—	—	1800
Roddam Home		6–11–1779	—	—	14–2–1799	—	—	—	—	—	—	13–2–1801
John Thomas		11–12–1779	—	—	14–2–1799	—	23–4–1804	9–11–1805	25–10–1809	31–7–1810	—	11–10–1810
James Brine		30–12–1779	—	14–2–1799	1–1–1801	—	23–4–1804	9–11–1805	25–10–1809	31–7–1810	—	1814
John Pakenham (1)	1743	1–1–1780	—	14–2–1799	1–1–1801	—	23–4–1804	9–11–1805	—	—	—	2–12–1807
Sir Erasmus Gower, Kt.	3–12–1742	9–1–1780	—	14–2–1799	1–1–1801	—	23–4–1804	9–11–1805	25–10–1809	31–7–1810	—	21–6–1814
John Holloway	*ca.* 1747	17–1–1780	—	14–2–1799	1–1–1801	—	23–4–1804	9–11–1805	25–10–1809	31–7–1810 [2]	—	1826
John Blankett		23–1–1780	—	14–2–1799	1–1–1801	—	—	—	—	—	—	1801
George Wilson (1)		1–2–1780	—	14–2–1799	1–1–1801	23–4–1804	—	9–11–1805	25–10–1809	31–7–1810 [2]	—	
Sir Charles Henry Knowles, Bart. (G.C.B. 1820)	24–8–1754	22–2–1780	—	14–2–1799	1–1–1801	23–4–1804	—	9–11–1805	31–7–1810	12–8–1812 [2]	—	28–11–1831
Hon. Thomas Pakenham (G.C.B. 1820)	1757	2–3–1780	—	14–2–1799	1–1–1801	23–4–1804	—	9–11–1805	31–7–1810	12–8–1812 [2]	—	2–2–1836
Robert Deans (1)		9–3–1780	—	14–2–1799	1–1–1801	23–4–1804	—	9–11–1805	31–7–1810	12–8–1812	—	1815
Cuthbert Collingwood (Lord Collingwood, 1805)	1750	22–3–1780	—	14–2–1799	1–1–1801	23–4–1804	—	9–11–1805	—	—	—	7–3–1810
James Hawkins Whitshed (*previously* Hawkins) (K.C.B. 1815; G.C.B. 1830; Bart. 1834)	1762	18–4–1780	—	14–2–1799	1–1–1801	23–4–1804	9–11–1805	28–4–1808	31–7–1810	12–8–1812 [2]	3–1–1844	1849
Arthur Kempe		10–5–1780	—	14–2–1799	1–1–1801	23–4–1804	9–11–1805	28–4–1808	31–7–1810	4–12–1813 [2]	—	
Smith Child	1729	15–5–1780	—	14–2–1799	1–1–1801	23–4–1804	9–11–1805	28–4–1808	31–7–1810	—	—	21–1–1813
Lord Chas. Fitzgerald (Baron Lecale, 1800)		23–5–1780	—	14–2–1799	1–1–1801	23–4–1804	9–11–1805	28–4–1808	—	—	—	17–2–1810
Thomas Taylor (2)		27–5–1780	—	14–2–1799	1–1–1801	23–4–1804	9–11–1805	28–4–1808	31–7–1810	—	—	
John Thomas Duckworth (K.B. 1801)	1748	6–6–1780	—	14–2–1799	1–1–1801	23–4–1804	9–11–1805	28–4–1808	31–7–1810	4–12–1813	—	31–8–1817
John Knowles		1–7–1780	14–2–1799	1–1–1801	—	—	—	—	—	—	—	14–3–1801
John Willett Payne	1752	8–7–1780	14–2–1799	1–1–1801	—	—	—	—	—	—	—	17–11–1803
Sir Robert Calder, Bart. (K.C.B. 1815)	2–7–1745	27–8–1780	14–2–1799	1–1–1801		23–4–1804	9–11–1805	28–4–1808	31–7–1810	4–12–1813	—	1–9–1818

James Richard Dacres (1)	2–1749	13–9–1780	14–2–1799	1–1–1801	23–4–1804	—	9–11–1805	28–4–1808	—	—	—	6–1–1810
Hon. George Cranfield Berkeley (G.C.B. 1815)	8–1753	15–9–1780	14–2–1799	1–1–1801	23–4–1804	—	9–11–1805	28–4–1808	31–7–1810	4–6–1814	—	28–2–1818
Thomas West		19–10–1780	14–2–1799	1–1–1801	23–4–1804	—	9–11–1805	28–4–1808	31–7–1810	4–6–1814	—	
James Douglas (2)	3–6–1755	20–10–1780	14–2–1799	1–1–1801	23–4–1804	—	9–11–1805	28–4–1808	31–7–1810	4–6–1814 [3]	—	8–6–1839
Peter Aplin	1753	23–11–1780	14–2–1799	1–1–1801	23–4–1804	—	9–11–1805	28–4–1808	31–7–1810	4–6–1814	—	17–4–1817
Henry Savage		31–1–1781	14–2–1799	1–1–1801	23–4–1804	—	9–11–1805	25–10–1809	31–7–1810	4–6–1814	—	
Bartholomew Samuel Rowley	1763	31–1–1781	14–2–1799	1–1–1801	23–4–1804	—	9–11–1805	25–10–1809	31–7–1810	—	—	7–10–1811
Sir Richard Hussey Bickerton, Bart. (K.C.B. 1815)	11–10–1759	8–2–1781	14–2–1799	1–1–1801	23–4–1804	—	9–11–1805	25–10–1809	31–7–1810	4–6–1814 [3]	—	9–2–1832
George Bowen (1)		14–2–1781	14–2–1799	1–1–1801	23–4–1804	9–11–1805	28–4–1808	25–10–1809	31–7–1810	4–6–1814	—	
Robert Montagu		3–3–1781	14–2–1799	1–1–1801	23–4–1804	9–11–1805	28–4–1808	—	31–7–1810	4–6–1814 [3]	—	
John Fergusson		21–3–1781	14–2–1799	1–1–1801	23–4–1804	9–11–1805	28–4–1808	—	31–7–1810	4–6–1814	—	
Edward Edwards	1742	25–4–1781	14–2–1799	1–1–1801	23–4–1804	9–11–1805	28–4–1808	—	31–7–1810	4–6–1814	—	1815
Sir John Borlase Warren, Bart., K.B.	1753	25–4–1781	14–2–1799	1–1–1801	33–4–1804	9–11–1805	28–4–1808	—	31–7–1810	4–6–1814	—	1822
Edward Tyrrel Smith		2–5–1781	—	1–1–1801	23–4–1804	9–11–1805	28–4–1808	31–7–1810	12–8–1812	12–8–1819	—	
Thomas Graves (3) (K.B. 1801)	1747	5–5–1781	—	1–1–1801	23–4–1804	9–11–1805	28–4–1808	31–7–1810	12–8–1812	—	—	29–3–1814
Thomas Macnamara Russell	1743	7–5–1781	—	1–1–1801	23–4–1804	9–11–1805	28–4–1808	31–7–1810	12–8–1812	12–8–1819	—	
Sylverius Moriarty		20–5–1781	—	1–1–1801	23–4–1804	9–11–1805	28–4–1808	—	—	—	—	
Sir Henry Trollope, Kt. (K.C.B. 1820; G.C.B. 1831)	20–4–1756	4–6–1781	—	1–1–1801	23–4–1804	9–11–1805	28–4–1808	31–7–1810	12–8–1812	12–8–1819 [3]	—	2–11–1839
Henry Edwyn Stanhope (Bart. 1807)	1754	16–6–1781	—		23–4–1804	9–11–1805	28–4–1808	31–7–1810	12–8–1812	—	—	20–12–1814
Robert M'Douall	1729	24–7–1781	1–1–1801	—	23–4–1804	9–11–1805	28–4–1808	31–7–1810	4–12–1813	—	—	16–2–1816
Billy Douglas	1750	15–8–1781	1–1–1801	23–4–1804	—	9–11–1805	28–4–1808	31–7–1810	4–12–1813	—	—	1817
John Wickey	1750	22–8–1781	1–1–1801	23–4–1804	—	9–11–1805	28–4–1808	31–7–1810	4–12–1813	12–8–1819 [4]	—	9–7–1833
John Inglis (2)		23–8–1781	1–1–1801	23–4–1804	—	9–11–1805	—	—	—	—	—	1807
John Fish	1758	23–8–1781	1–1–1801	23–4–1804	—	9–11–1805	28–4–1808	31–7–1810	4–12–1813	12–8–1819 [4]	—	1834
Jahleel Brenton (1)		3–9–1781	1–1–1801	—	—	—	—	—	—	—	—	1802
John Knight (2) (K.C.B. 1815)		21–9–1781	1–1–1801	23–4–1804	—	9–11–1805	28–4–1808	31–7–1810	4–12–1813	12–8–1819	—	
Edward Thornbrough (K.C.B. 1815; G.C.B. 1825)	27–7–1754	21–9–1781	1–1–1801	23–4–1804	—	9–11–1805	28–4–1808	31–7–1810	4–12–1813	18–8–1819 [4]	—	3–4–1834
James Kempthorne		25–9–1781	1–1–1801	23–4–1804	9–11–1805	—	—	—	—	—	—	
Sampson Edwards	1745	16–10–1781	1–1–1801	23–4–1804	9–11–1805		25–10–1809	31–7–1810	4–6–1814	12–8–1819 [4]	—	14–9–1840
George Campbell (K.C.B. 1815)		9–11–1781	1–1–1801	23–4–1804	9–11–1805		25–10–1809	31–7–1810	4–6–1814	12–8–1819	—	28–1–1821
Thomas Hicks	22–4–1731	10–11–1781	1–1–1801	—	—	—	—	—	—	—	—	9–5–1801
Henry Cromwell (*later* Frankland)		14–11–1781	1–1–1801	33–4–1804	9–11–1805		25–10–1809	31–7–1810	—	—	—	
Arthur Phillip	11–10–1738	30–11–1781	1–1–1801	23–4–1804	9–11–1805		25–10–1809	31–7–1810	4–6–1814	—	—	31–8–1814
Sir William George Fairfax, Kt.	1738	12–1–1782	1–1–1801	23–4–1804	9–11–1805		25–10–1809	31–7–1810	—	—	—	17–11–1813
Thomas Totty		31–1–1781	1–1–1801	—	—	—	—	—	—	—	—	2–6–1802
Sir James Saumarez, Kt. (Bart. 1801; K.B. 1801; Lord de Saumarez, 1831)	11–3–1757	7–2–1782	1–1–1801	23–4–1804	9–11–1805		31–7–1810		4–6–1814	12–8–1819 [4]	—	8–10–1836

[1] Promoted to be Admirals of the Red, 12–8–1819. [2] *Ib.*, 19–7–1821. [3] *Ib.*, 27–5–1825. [4] *Ib.*, 22–7–1830.

CHAPTER XXXV.

MAJOR OPERATIONS OF THE ROYAL NAVY, 1793–1802.

The fleet at the outbreak of the war of the French Revolution—British superiority—British allies—Sercey to the West Indies—Howe in the Channel—Mutiny in the French fleet—Howe and Vanstabel—Jervis to the West Indies—Hood in the Mediterranean—Toulon occupied—Evacuation of Toulon and destruction of French ships—Linzee to Corsica—Proceedings at Genoa and Spezzia—St. Pierre, Miquelon and Tobago taken—Miscarriage at Martinique—Commodore Ford at San Domingo—Successes in India—Reorganisation of the French Navy—Villaret-Joyeuse and Jean Bon St. André—Cruise of Howe—Manœuvres—Battle of the Glorious First of June—Montagu's cruise—Mutiny in the *Culloden*—Loss of the *Alexander*—Destruction of the *Ardent*—Operations in Corsica—Nelson at Bastia—Fall of Calvi—Chase of Martin—Hotham in the Mediterranean—Mutiny in the *Windsor Castle*—Capture of Martinique—Gallantry of Bowen and Faulknor—Capture of St. Lucia and Guadeloupe—Guadeloupe retaken—Ford at San Domingo—Raid upon Sierra Leone—The *Diamond* reconnoitres Brest—Disasters to the French fleet—Renaudin to Toulon—Cornwallis's retreat—Bridport's action off Groix—Warren's expedition to Quiberon—Loss of the *Berwick*—Hotham's action off Genoa—Loss of the *Illustrious*—Hotham off Hyères—Operations of Nelson—Chase of de Richery—Loss of the *Censeur*—Cruise of Ganteaume—Jervis in the Mediterranean—Holland allied with France—Duncan in the North Sea—Reinforcement and successes of Hugues—Capture of Cape Colony—Rainier off Ceylon—Malacca taken—Blockade of the Texel—Nelson on the Genoese coast—Evacuation of Leghorn—Spain joins France—Difficulties of Jervis—Man and de Langara—De Langara to Toulon—Man's desertion—French successes in the Mediterranean—Evacuation of Corsica—Sailing of Villeneuve—Loss of the *Courageux*—Jervis abandons the Mediterranean—De Richery in North America—Capture of Demerara, etc.—Christian takes St. Lucia, St. Vincent and Grenada—Repulse at Léogane—Colombo captured—Amboyna and Banda surrendered—Dutch squadron surrenders in Saldanha Bay—Expedition of Hoche to Ireland—The French evade Colpoys—Failure of the expedition—The *Indefatigable* and *Droits de l'Homme*—Jervis reinforced—Howe resigns command—Sailing of de Cordova—Battle of Cape St. Vincent—Intrepidity of Nelson, Troubridge and Collingwood—Berkeley and the *Santisima Trinidad*—Bowen and the same—Cadiz bombarded and blockaded—Nelson at Santa Cruz—Battle of Camperdown—Capture of Trinidad—Failure at Puerto Rico—Operations off San Domingo—Loss of the *Tribune*—The commands in 1798—The *Mars* and the *Hercule*—Dreams of an invasion of England—Napoleon's projects—The Invasion Flotilla—Operations at St. Marcou—Failure at Ostend—Burning of the *Confiante*—Humbert's expedition to Ireland—Warren's action—Fate of Bompart's squadron—Chase of Savary—Nelson to the Mediterranean—Napoleon's Egyptian schemes—Sailing of the Toulon fleet—Nelson in chase—The Battle of the Nile—Malta blockaded—Flight of King Ferdinand—Operations at Corfu—Blockade of Alexandria—Capitulation of Minorca—Events in San Domingo

—Defence of Belize—The commands in 1799—Bruix leaves Brest—Keith in chase —Massaredo leaves Cadiz—Capture of French frigates—Failure of Keith—Junction of Massaredo and Bruix—The allies enter Brest—Pole off the Isle of Aix—French progress in Italy—Blockade of Naples—Operations of Nelson—Suwaroff in Italy—Foote at Naples—Nelson and the Neapolitan rebels—Execution of Caracciolo—Naples, Gaeta, and Rome taken—Nelson "sicilified"—Napoleon in Syria—Bombardment of Alexandria—Sidney Smith on the coast of Syria—Raising of the siege of Acre—Napoleon returns to France—Operations in the Red Sea—French difficulties in Egypt—Combined expedition to Holland—Surrender of the Dutch squadron in Nieuwe Diep—Surrender of the Dutch squadron in the Vlieter—Evacuation of Holland—Surinam captured—The commands in 1800—Loss of the *Repulse*—Operations in Quiberon Bay—Loss of the *Marlborough*—Blockade of Malta—Burning of the *Queen Charlotte*—Operations near Genoa—French successes in Italy—Capture of the *Généreux*—Nelson returns to England—Capture of the *Guillaume Tell*—Capture of the *Diane*—Capitulation of Malta—The French in Egypt—Expedition to Ferrol—Surrender of Curaçoa—Union of Great Britain and Ireland—Confederation of the Northern Powers—Capture of the *Freja*—The Armed Neutrality—Parker to the Baltic—Battle of Copenhagen—The fleet in the Baltic—Murder of the Tsar Paul—Russia and Sweden make concessions—Nelson in the Downs—The Invasion Flotilla—Operations off Boulogne—Ganteaume to the Mediterranean—Search for the Brest fleet—Keith to Egypt—Operations near Elba—Ganteaume flees from the Egyptian coast—Loss of the *Swiftsure*—Keith at Alexandria—Expulsion of the French from Egypt—Operations in the Red Sea—Enforced hostility of Portugal—Linois leaves Toulon—Action off Algeciras—Saumarez in the Gut of Gibraltar—Swedish and Danish colonies captured—Madeira occupied—Losses of Holland—The Peace of Amiens—Gains and losses of the war.

Sam. J. Barrington

SIGNATURE OF THE HON. SAMUEL BARRINGTON, AS ADMIRAL.

AT the time of the outbreak of war with France in February, 1793, the British squadrons on foreign stations were very weak. In the Mediterranean there were one 50-gun ship and five small vessels;[1] on the Leeward Islands station there were two 50-gun ships and six small craft;[2] at Jamaica there was one 50-gun with nine small craft;[3] at Halifax and Newfoundland there were one 50-gun ship

[1] *Romney*, 50, Rear-Admiral Samuel Granston Goodall, Capt. William Domett; *Aquilon*, 32, Capt. the Hon. Robert Stopford; *Lapwing*, 28, Capt. the Hon. Henry Curzon; *Fury*, 16, Com. the Hon. William Paget; *Bulldog*, 14, Com. George Hope (1); and *Mutine*, cutter, 14, Lieut. Humphrey West.

[2] *Trusty*, 50, Vice-Admiral Sir John Laforey, Capt. John Drew (1); *Centurion*, 50, Capt. Samuel Osborn; *Blanche*, 32, Capt. Christopher Parker (2); *Hermione*, 32, Capt. John Hills; *Perseus*, 20, Capt. George Palmer; *Orestes*, 18, Com. Augustus Fitzroy; *Fairy*, 16, Com. Francis Laforey; and *Serpent*, 14, Com. Richard Lee.

[3] *Europa*, 50, Commod. John Ford, Capt. George Gregory; *Penelope*, 32, Capt. Bartholomew Samuel Rowley; *Proserpine*, 28, Capt. James Alms (2); *Triton*, 28,

and four small craft;[1] in the East Indies there were five frigates and small craft;[2] and on the coast of Africa there was one 44-gun ship.[3] But at home and in the Channel there was a large force in commission, including twenty-five ships of the line, three 50-gun ships, forty-six frigates of twenty-four guns and upwards, and above thirty smaller craft. There were, moreover, in serviceable condition in ordinary fifty-nine ships of the line, one 50-gun ship, and twenty-five frigates; and numbers of other ships of all classes were either undergoing repairs or awaiting them. In addition, twelve ships of the line and three 50-gun ships were building. It may be said that there were available for immediate service about seventy-five ships of the line, and that forty others were nearly ready. As against this total of one hundred and fifteen, or thereabouts, France could dispose of, at most, seventy-six, though she added to them with feverish rapidity. Great Britain, therefore, went into the conflict with a substantial numerical majority of ships in her favour. She had, it is true, wider interests than France to defend; for France had ceased in the previous contests to be an American and an Asiatic power; and, almost in proportion as she had lost, Great Britain had gained in both hemispheres. Great Britain had, moreover, to attend to the needs of a sea-borne commerce very considerably superior to that of France, and she was dependent upon the sea in a sense which France never had been, and never can be.

Yet, upon the whole, France was at an enormous disadvantage. The numerically superior fleet of King George was manned by people who were not tainted with the subversive opinions which had turned France into chaos; and in Howe, Peter Parker, Barrington, Edward Hughes, Thomas Graves, Sir Alexander Hood, Lord Hood, Sir Richard King, Sir John Jervis, Adam Duncan, Samuel Pitchford Cornish, Sir Hyde Parker, and Hon. Wm. Cornwallis, not to mention many more, it had flag officers who had

---

Capt. George Murray (3); *Hyæna*, 20, Capt. William Hargood (1); *Fly*, 16, Com. William Brown (1); *Falcon*, 14, Com. James Bissett; *Hound*, 14, Com. John Lawford; *Helena*, 14, Com. William Charleton; and *Advice*, cutter, Lieut. Edward Tyrrel.

[1] *Assistance*, 50, Vice-Admiral Sir Richard King, Capt. John Samuel Smith; *Winchelsea*, 32, Capt. Richard Fisher; *Hussar*, 28, Capt. Rupert George; *Placentia*, 12, Lieut. the Hon. Charles Herbert; and *Trepassy*, 12.

[2] *Minerva*, 38, Rear-Admiral Hon. William Cornwallis, Capt. John Whitby (after April); *Perseverance*, 36, Capt. Isaac Smith; *Phœnix*, 36, Capt. Sir Richard John Strachan, Bart.; *Atalanta*, 14; and *Swan*, 14.

[3] *Charon*, 44, Capt. Edmund Dod.

fought well, and for the most part with success, in the previous war; who were full of experience, and who possessed absolutely the confidence of the service and of the country. Above all, the British Navy had fresh, most splendid, and absolutely unbroken traditions at its immediate back. But the numerically inferior fleet of the Republic was in a very different condition. Discipline had become partially demoralised by the Revolution; many of

ADMIRAL JOHN MACBRIDE.

(From the engraving by James Fittler, after the portrait by J. Northcote, R.A., painted when Macbride was a Captain, 1765–93.)

the old aristocratic officers had been obliged to quit the service; most of the new officers were without either experience or authority; and monarchical opinions lingered in many a wardroom and captain's cabin, and rendered obscure the path of duty to conscientious officers.

In addition to all this Great Britain had, as her naval allies, soon after the conflict broke out, the Netherlands, which brought to the common cause about twelve serviceable ships of the line; Spain, which brought about thirty-five; Portugal, Sardinia, and, presently, the two Sicilies. It is probably within the mark to say that the confederacy could, in the early summer of 1793, dispose of one hundred and seventy-five ships of the line, or much more than twice as many as France. The broadside weight of metal of the French line is estimated by James at 73,957 lbs., thrown by 6002 guns; that of the British contingent alone at 88,957 lbs., thrown by 8718 guns. Prussia and Austria, which were almost entirely military powers, were also enemies of the Republic. Russia, Denmark, and Sweden were neutral. On the other hand, France had not a single ally.

The French fleet began to move within two or three weeks after the declaration of war. Towards the end of February Rear-Admiral Pierre César Charles Guillaume Sercey sailed from Brest with three 74-gun ships[1] and some frigates and small craft for the West Indies, whence he was to bring home a convoy. At about the same time, a fleet, drawn from Brest, Lorient, and Rochefort, began to assemble in Quiberon Bay. It would have been of the utmost importance to France could a formidable blow have been struck at the British West India Islands or at British commerce in the Atlantic. But the hands of the Republican government were bound by the consideration that there was a strong royalist feeling on many parts of the French littoral, and that there were signs that Great Britain meditated aiding the monarchists by making descents in their favour. Thus, although by August Vice-Admiral Morard de Galles had with him off Belleisle twenty-one ships of the line and four frigates, he remained in an attitude of expectancy, and did little or nothing.

Great Britain, also, was at first hampered by what may be called ulterior considerations. She had to reinforce her squadrons abroad; and not until she had done that was she able to send Lord Howe, with fifteen ships of the line and some frigates and sloops, to watch the then rapidly increasing force of Morard de Galles. Howe, with the Channel fleet, sailed from St. Helen's on July 14th. On the 18th, he had to send back to port the *Bellerophon*, 74, which had been damaged by collision with the *Monarch*, 74. For her the *London*, 98, was promptly substituted.

[1] *Eole*, *Jupiter*, and *America*. The *Phocion*, 74, had previously sailed to the West Indies.

On the 23rd, Howe anchored in Torbay. His strength was later brought up to seventeen ships of the line, nine frigates, and five small craft; and with this fleet he went to seek the French, who were supposed to be lying in wait to cover the convoy expected from the West Indies under Rear-Admiral Sercey. On the afternoon of July 31st, the French, then seventeen sail of the line, were sighted near Belleisle; but on that day, and again on August 1st, 2nd, and 3rd, Howe was baffled in his attempts to get near them; and, the weather then becoming stormy, the British had to stand off. On August 10th, they again anchored in Torbay.

Morard de Galles had, in the meantime, anchored once more in the Road of Belleisle. There, owing to administrative mismanagement, a mutiny broke out among the seamen, who, in September, desired Morard de Galles to carry them into Brest, which they represented as on the point of being surrendered by its inhabitants to the British. This idea was no doubt inspired by the knowledge of what, a few weeks earlier, had happened at Toulon. The Admiral had to yield; and on the 29th the fleet anchored in the Road of Brest.

On August 23rd, Howe had weighed from Torbay and sailed to the westward to escort to sea a convoy for Newfoundland, and to see home another coming from the West Indies. After a cruise, he returned to Torbay on September 4th. In October, he detached a squadron, under Commodore Thomas Pasley, to look for five French frigates which had chased a British vessel into Falmouth. On the 27th of that month, with the fleet increased to twenty-two sail of the line, he himself set out for a cruise in the Bay of Biscay. Pasley rejoined on November 7th off Scilly; and on the 17th two ships of the line parted company, leaving Howe with twenty-two sail of the line. On November 18th, in lat. 48° 32′ N., and long. 1° 48′ W., the *Latona*, 38, Captain Edward Thornbrough, signalled a strange squadron, which proved to be Commodore Vanstabel,[1] with six ships of the line, two frigates and two small craft from Brest,[2] under sail in Cancale Bay. The French at first approached, evidently taking the British fleet for the

[1] Pierre Jean Vanstabel. Born at Dunquerque, 1746; served the French East India Company; entered the navy, 1778; captain, 1793.

[2] *Tigre*, 74, *Aquilon*, 74, *Jean Bart*, 74, *Tourville*, 74, *Impétueux*, 74, *Révolution* 74, *Insurgente*, 36, *Sémillante*, 36, *Espiègle*, and *Ballon*.

expected convoy. But they were chased off by the *Russell*, 74, Captain John Willett Payne, *Audacious*, 74, Captain William Parker (1), *Defence*, 74, Captain James Gambier (2), *Bellerophon*, 74, Captain Thomas Pasley, and *Ganges*, 74, Captain Anthony James Pye Molloy. Howe pursued, endeavouring to keep touch with the enemy by means of his frigates. In the afternoon the *Latona* drew within shot of the two rearmost French frigates, but was driven off by two French seventy-fours, which went to their assistance. In their anxiety to get into action several British ships carried away their topmasts. The enemy was again sighted on the 19th; but bad and thick weather interfered with the operations, and, although Howe cruised until the middle of December, he failed to fall in with the foe.

M. Vanstabel had sailed from Brest on November 13th with the following object in view. What had occurred in the Mediterranean will be shown later. Suffice it now to say that Lord Hood had occupied Toulon in August. The French Government learnt of a supposed intention of the British Admiralty to despatch Vice-Admiral Sir John Jervis in November with four sail of the line, and a convoy conveying stores and troops to reinforce Hood; and, in order to intercept Jervis, Vanstabel had been sent to sea with a squadron of new ships chosen especially for their speed.

But Jervis was not destined for Toulon. He sailed from St. Helen's on November 26th with three ships of the line, two 44-gun ships, and several frigates, sloops, and transports to aid the French royalist cause, not in Toulon, but at Martinique. Vanstabel cruised for a time, but, not finding the expected convoy, returned to Brest on November 30th, having snapped up part of a homeward-bound Newfoundland fleet, which recompensed him for his disappointment. The French seem to have been further fortunate in that Rear-Admiral Sercey, who had been sent out to bring home a provision-laden convoy from the West Indies, saw it safely into Brest.[1]

At the time of the declaration of war France had a very powerful fleet in Toulon. To hold it in check, various detachments were successively sent out from England to the Mediterranean: one, early in April, under Rear-Admiral John Gell; a second, on April 15th, under Vice-Admiral Phillips Cosby; a third, early in May, under Vice-Admiral William Hotham; and a fourth, on

[1] Sercey, at least, returned thither with the *Eole*, *Jupiter*, and *America*.

May 22nd, under Vice-Admiral Lord Hood, who, upon reaching the station, superseded Rear-Admiral Samuel Granston Goodall as Commander-in-Chief. Hood arrived off Toulon in the middle of August, when his force consisted of the twenty-one or twenty-two sail of the line, and the other vessels mentioned in the note.[1]

The French had in the port, ready for sea, one 120, one 80, and fifteen 74's, besides one 120, one 80, and two 74's refitting, two 80's and seven 74's repairing, or needing repair, and one 74 building—a total of thirty-one ships of the line, in addition to twenty-seven frigates and corvettes.[2] The French naval com-

[1] Fleet under Vice-Admiral Lord Hood, employed at Toulon and on other services August to December, 1793:—

Ships.	Guns.	Commanders.	Ships.	Guns.	Commanders.
Victory	100	Vice-Admiral Samuel, Lord Hood (R). Rear-Admiral Sir Hyde Parker (2) (W). 1st Capt. Capt. John Knight (2).	*Agamemnon*	64	Capt. Horatio Nelson.
			St. Albans[2]	64	„ James Vashon.
			Romney	50	„ Hon William Paget.
			Aigle	36	„ John Nicholson Inglefield.
			Inconstant	36	„ Augustus Montgomery.
Britannia	100	Vice-Admiral William Hotham (W). Capt. John Holloway.	*Leda*	36	„ George Campbell.
			Romulus	36	„ John Sutton.
Windsor Castle	98	Vice-Admiral Phillips Cosby (B). Capt. Sir Thomas Byard, Kt.	*Isis*	32	„ George Lumsdaine.
			Juno	32	„ Samuel Hood (2).
			Aimable	32	„ Sir Harry Burrard, Bt.
Princess Royal	98	Rear-Admiral Samuel Granston Goodall (R). Capt. John Child Purvis.	*Lowestoft*	32	„ William Wolseley.
			Meleager	32	„ Charles Tyler.
			Mermaid	32	„ John Trigge.
St. George	98	Rear-Admiral John Gell (B). Capt. Thomas Foley.	*Aquilon*[2]	32	„ Hon. Robert Stopford.
			Castor[2]	32	„ Thomas Troubridge.
Alcide	74	Commod. Robert Linzee.[3] Capt. John Woodley.	*Dido*	28	„ Sir Charles Hamilton, Bt.
Terrible	74	„ Skeffington Lutwidge.	*Nemesis*	28	„ Lord Amelius Beauclerk.
Egmont	74	„ Archibald Dickson (1)	*Tartar*	28	„ Thomas Francis Fremantle.
Robust	74	„ Hon. George Keith Elphinstone.	*Amphitrite*	24	„ Anthony Hunt.
Courageux	74	„ Hon. William Waldegrave (1).[4]	*Bulldog*[2]	14	Com. George Hope (1).
			Dolphin, hosp. ship	44	„ James May.
Bedford	74	„ Robert Man (3).	*Gorgon*, st. ship	44	„ Charles William Paterson.
Berwick	74	„ Sir John Collins, Kt.			
Captain	74	„ Samuel Reeve.	*Camel*, st. ship	20	„ Benjamin Hallowell.[6]
Fortitude	74	„ William Young (1).	*Fury*[2]	14	„ Frank Sotheron.
Leviathan	74	„ Hon. Hugh Seymour Conway.[5]	*Weazel*[2]	12	„ William Taylor.
Colossus	74	„ Charles Morice Pole.	*Speedy*	14	„ Charles Cunningham.
Illustrious	74	„ Thomas Lenox Frederick.	*Scout*, brig	14	„ Joseph Hanwell.
			Eclair	20	„ George Henry Towry.
Ardent	64	„ Robert Manners Sutton.	*Tisiphone*	12	„ Thomas Byam Martin.
Diadem	64	„ Andrew Sutherland.	*Conflagration*, f.s.	14	„ Edward Browne.
Intrepid[1]	64	„ Hon. Charles Carpenter.	*Vulcan*, f.s.	14	„ John Matthews.[7]

1 Appears not to have joined until the end of August.
2 Employed on convoy service, etc.
3 Appointed in September.
4 When he went home with dispatches, Capt. John Matthews acted.
5 When he went home with dispatches, Capt. Benjamin Hallowell acted.
6 Later, Com. Joseph Short.
7 Later, Com. Charles Hare.

[2] French ships of the line at Toulon, distinguishing their fate:—Burnt or destroyed: *Triomphant*, 80; *Destin*, 74; *Centaure*, 74; *Duguay Trouin*, 74; *Héros*,

mander was Rear-Admiral the Comte de Trogoff, a warm royalist. Many of his officers were royalists also; and a large part of the population of the neighbourhood shared their opinions.

On August 22nd, two envoys came off from Marseilles to Hood's flagship, the *Victory*, to treat for the surrender of the port and shipping of Toulon to the British, with a view to aiding the re-establishment of a monarchical government in France. These

ADMIRAL JOHN HOLLOWAY.

(*From an engraved portrait by H. R. Cook, when Holloway was a Vice-Admiral,* 1804–9.)

74; *Liberté* (ex-*Dictateur*), 74; *Suffisant*, 74; *Thémistocle*, 74; *Tricolor* (ex-*Lys*), 74. Taken and fitted out by the British: *Commerce de Marseilles*, 120; *Pompée*, 74; *Puissant*, 74; *Scipion*, 74. Left to the French: *Dauphin Royal* (later *Sans Culotte*), 120; *Tonnant*, 80; *Languedoc* (later *Victoire*), 80; *Couronne* (later *Ça Ira*), 80; *Heureux*, 74; *Commerce de Bordeaux* (later *Timoléon*), 74; *Mercure*, 74; *Conquérant*, 74; *Barras*, 74; *Alcide*, 74; *Censeur*, 74; *Guerrier*, 74; *Souverain* (later *Souverain Peuple*), 74; *Généreux*, 74; *Entreprenant*, 74; *Apollon* (later *Gasparin*), 74; *Orion* (later *Trente et Un Mai*), 74; *Patriote*, 74. The frigates and small craft carried off by the British were: *Aréthuse* (later *Undaunted*), 40; *Topaze*, 40; *Perle* (later *Amethyst*), 36; *Aurore*, 36; *Lutine*, 36; *Poulette*, 28; *Belette*, 28; *Prosélyte*, 24; *Mozelle*, 20; *Mulet*, 18; *Sincère*, 18; and *Tarleton*, 14.

envoys represented that Toulon and its inhabitants agreed with their views and would also send off delegates to the *Victory*, though, as subsequently appeared, they had somewhat overstated the case. The delegates never arrived. In Toulon the state of parties was somewhat more evenly balanced than the people of Marseilles believed. Hood, however, at once publicly declared that, if Toulon were placed in his hands, the people of Provence should be assisted in securing their desire; and he also called upon the local population to rally to the monarchy. In the meantime, Rear-Admiral Saint-Julien, a republican, second-in-command of the fleet at Toulon, declared against Trogoff, and was instrumental in preventing the Toulon delegates from going on board the *Victory*. As the expected representatives did not arrive, Hood, on the 24th, sent Lieutenant

31st day of March 1791

Hood

SIGNATURE OF LORD HOOD, AS VICE-ADMIRAL.

Edward Cooke, of the *Victory*, to the town to ascertain the state of affairs there. This officer, by the exercise of great tact, managed to get into the dockyard at night, but was not permitted to land until the following morning. He was then taken before the royalist committee, which agreed to Hood's proposals. On his way back Cooke was arrested, but was rescued by the mob. He afterwards made a second trip, returning on the evening of the 26th with Captain Baron d'Imbert of the *Apollon*, 74, as Royalist Special Commissioner. D'Imbert assured Hood that Louis XVII. had been proclaimed in the town; whereupon Hood decided to land troops and to take possession of the various works commanding the ships in the road. It should, perhaps, be mentioned that, on the 25th, Marseilles had been compelled to open its gates to the French Republican general, Cartaux.

Saint Julien, in whose favour the republican seamen had superseded Trogoff,[1] had already occupied and manned the forts

[1] Trogoff had been seized with an attack of gout, which was probably of a diplomatic type.—'Mems. p. serv. à l'Hist. de Toulon en 1793.'

on the west side of the harbour. Hood on the 27th landed 1500 troops and about 200 seamen and Marines under Captain the Hon. George Keith Elphinstone, of the *Robust,* to take possession of Fort La Malgue,[1] on the east side; and Saint Julien was then informed that such ships as did not at once proceed to the inner harbour and land their powder, would be treated as enemies. Saint Julien, and about 5000 French seamen, promptly abandoned the fleet, and took refuge inland; and the French ships as a body then moved to the inner harbour, while the British, and a Spanish contingent of seventeen ships of the line which had just arrived under Admiral Don Juan de Langara, anchored in the outer road. On the same day Hood issued a fresh proclamation to the inhabitants; and on the 28th he received a satisfactory address from the civil and military authorities ashore. On that day Spanish reinforcements were landed at La Malgue; and Hood appointed Rear-Admiral Goodall to be governor of Toulon, and the Spanish Rear-Admiral Gravina to be military commandant.

During this time the French republican army had approached from the direction of Marseilles; and on August 31st, its advance guard was defeated and driven back from Ollioules by the British and Spanish under Captain Elphinstone.

In September, Cartaux's army from the west, and Lapoype's from the east, gathered round the town and perpetually annoyed the allies, whose difficulties were increased by the turbulent behaviour of the French seamen, lately belonging to the ships in harbour. Hood deported these on September 14th, sending them off under flags of truce in the French 74-gun ships *Orion*, *Apollon*, *Patriote,* and *Entreprenant,* the first going to Rochefort, the second to Lorient, and the third and fourth to Brest. He also sent the brig *Pluvier*, 16, to Bordeaux.

On the 18th the republicans opened two masked batteries at the head of the north-west arm of the inner road near La Petite Garenne, upon the prize frigate *Aurore*, 36, Captain Henry Inman, and a gunboat, which had been stationed near the Poudrière, to defend the head of the harbour and to cover Fort Malbousquet. On the 19th they opened another battery; and the *St. George*, 98, Rear-Admiral Gell, Captain Thomas Foley, and a second gunboat moved up to assist the *Aurore*. The gunboats, however, were presently obliged to slip their cables; but on the 20th they returned to

[1] Possession was not actually taken till the 28th.

the attack, and one of them was subsequently sunk by the enemy's fire. Rear-Admiral Gell was later detached to command the British, Spanish, and French Royalist squadron bound for Genoa; and the place of the *St. George* was taken on the 24th by the *Princess Royal*, 98, Captain John Child Purvis. A Spanish 74 also co-operated; and so the engagement went on day after day, at intervals, for several weeks. In the course of that time troops were brought from various quarters by ships which had been detached for the purpose; and the Neapolitan 74-gun ships, *Guiscardo* and *Tancredi*, arrived. On the night of the 30th the

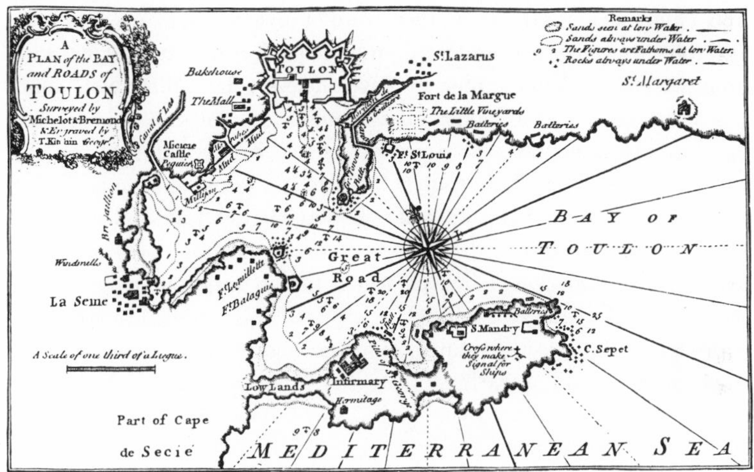

TOULON: FROM A PLAN IN THE "LONDON MAGAZINE."

(Many of the names are misspelt; but all should be recognisable.)

French seized the heights of Faron; but on the following day they were driven from them with great slaughter by Brigadier-General Lord Mulgrave, Rear-Admiral Gravina and Captain Elphinstone. Napoleon Bonaparte took a prominent part in this affair, and, it is also interesting to note, Nelson was present in the port in command of the *Agamemnon*. On October 5th the Neapolitan 74, *Samnita*, escorting more troops, came into the harbour; and on the 8th it was resolved to attempt the destruction of certain batteries which the French had recently erected to threaten the shipping. They were carried that night by a detachment of British, Spanish, Piedmontese and Neapolitans, with a British naval brigade, under

Lieutenant Walter Serocold; and the guns, which it was found impossible to remove, were destroyed.

But the circle of works to be held by the allies was large; there were only 2100 British troops in the place; and there was much friction, and even jealousy, between the Spanish and British. On one occasion de Langara even went so far as to covertly threaten Lord Hood. Reinforcements of men were obtained from the Grand Master of Malta; and other troops dribbled in from Naples and Sicily, till, at the beginning of November, the allies had a nominal force of little fewer than 17,000 men in the place. But only 12,000 were fit for duty, and three-fourths of them had to be actually on the line of defence. Moreover, they were of five different nationalities. On the other hand, there were, round Toulon, at least 30,000 men under General Dugommier. Nevertheless, the allies won some slight successes at Balaguier, on the night of November 15th; but on the 30th they received a severe check in an attempt upon a work opposite Fort Malbousquet. Early in December the besieging army had increased to at least 45,000 men, while the available strength of the besieged was less than 11,000 men, the majority being distributed over a line of works fifteen miles in length. On the night of December 14th, while a storm was raging, the French approached the works at three different points simultaneously, and began their final operations. By the afternoon of the 17th they had seized Fort Mulgrave on the height of Balaguier, and had made themselves masters of the works on Faron, so that the line of defence was broken in two essential places. Many of the ships had at once to unmoor and retire to safer points.

A council-of-war, composed of the allied naval and military commanders, was instantly held, and it was unanimously determined to evacuate Toulon as soon as the necessary arrangements could be made to carry off such ships, and with them such of the royalist insurgents, as could be taken away; and to destroy the remaining vessels, with the arsenal and magazine. So decided was the advantage gained by the besiegers that the council-of-war was anxious to begin these measures that very night. Admiral de Langara undertook personally to see to part of the destruction. The troops from the further posts were speedily yet quietly withdrawn; but the orderly evacuation of Forts Malbousquet and Miessiesy was prevented by a panic which seized on some Neapolitan soldiers, who retired to their ships in great confusion.

By the evening of the 18th, however, all the remaining troops were withdrawn into the town and Fort La Malgue, ready to be embarked as soon as the burning of the ships should announce that the right moment had arrived.

The important task of destroying the shipping and magazines was entrusted, at his own request, to Captain Sir William Sidney Smith, R.N., who had come as a volunteer in the *Swallow*, a little vessel purchased and manned by himself at Smyrna. On the afternoon of the 18th, with the *Swallow*, and three Spanish and three British gunboats, he entered the inner harbour, and in spite of falling shot and shell from the batteries of the besiegers, of the threatening attitude of a number of liberated galley slaves, and finally, of a heavy fire from the approaching French troops, he began his business at about 8 P.M. The *Vulcan*, fireship, Commander Charles Hare, was towed into the basin, and placed in the most advantageous position athwart the tier of French men-of-war

G: K: Elphinstone

SIGNATURE OF CAPT. THE HON. GEORGE KEITH ELPHINSTONE, LATER ADMIRAL VISCOUNT KEITH.

there. At 10 P.M. she, and all the trains laid to the magazines and storehouses, were simultaneously fired, upon signal being made. Instantly a gigantic blaze burst forth. By its light the British hurriedly sought to complete their mission of ruin, while the French from without, drawing ever nearer, sought to slay or drive off the destroyers. The excitement and danger of the situation seem to have proved too much for the Spaniards, who were co-operating with Smith. They have even, and with some show of reason, been accused of deliberate treachery. Instead of scuttling the *Iris*, 32,[1] which was laden with an immense quantity of powder, they fired her, and she blew up with a tremendous explosion, smashing to pieces the British gunboat *Union*, and another vessel, which lay near her. Providentially only three of the *Union's* people were killed, the rest being picked up. When Smith had finished his work in the dockyard to the westward, he

[1] Taken by the French from the British in 1779.

tried to enter the inner basin, which lies in front of the town quay and to the eastward of the arsenal; but its mouth had been boomed, and he could not get in. He destroyed, however, the *Héros* and *Thémistocle*, 74's, in the inner road; and then, having done all he could, he was about to retire, when a second powder vessel, the *Montréal*, 32,[1] blew up close to him, fortunately, however, causing no serious damage to the British. Half dead from the effects of heat and fatigue, Smith and his party went back to the fleet, Forts Balaguier and Aiguillette sending a few shots after them.

Among the number of officers who assisted Smith in this critical service were Commanders Charles Hare and William Edge (of the prize sloop *Albert*, which was destroyed), and Lieutenants Charles Tupper, Richard Holloway, Matthew Wrench, John Gore, Thomas Foord Richmond, John Melhuish, Ralph Willett Miller, Charles Dudley Pater, John Stiles, Robert Gambier Middleton, Joseph Priest, Francis Cox, James Morgan and Henry Hill. The loss was slight.

On the outburst of the conflagration in the dockyard the evacuation of the town had begun under the direction of Captains the Hon. J. K. Elphinstone, of the *Robust*, Benjamin Hollowell of the *Leviathan*, and John Matthews of the *Courageux*; and all the troops were on board the fleet by daylight on the 19th, having lost not a single man in the process of withdrawal. A British fireship, the *Conflagration*, being under repair, could not be moved, and was burnt to save her from falling into the hands of the enemy. The *Robust* was the rearmost ship as the fleet quitted the harbour. During the operations ashore, as well as afloat, the seamen behaved most admirably.

The fleet carried off 14,877 of the royalist population: it could not take on board more. The fate of those who were perforce left behind was terrible. Pursued by the victorious Republicans to the quay, men, women and children were shot down or bayoneted ruthlessly by hundreds, perhaps by thousands. Some rushed frantically into the water after the retreating boats of the allies, and were drowned. The French Government had deliberately decreed the death of all the inhabitants, and the demolition of the town. General Dugommier protested; but the Republican Deputies, not content with the slaughter by the troops, held daily executions,

[1] Captured from the Americans by the British, and, from them, by the French, in 1781.

until, so it was estimated, over 6000 of the Toulonnais had, in one way or another, paid the penalty.

The work of destruction was but badly done by the allies. Of thirty-one French ships of the line in port nine only were burnt or sunk, and four only carried off; so that no fewer than eighteen, including the four which had been despatched to Atlantic ports with the refractory seamen, remained to the Republicans.[1] Of the

ADMIRAL SIR SAMUEL HOOD (1), VISCOUNT HOOD, BART., G.C.B.

(From the portrait by Sir J. Reynolds.)

twenty-seven frigates and corvettes, five were destroyed, fifteen were carried off, and seven left to the Republicans. Still, looking to the suddenness of the events which compelled the hasty evacuation, to the jealousy and treachery of the Spaniards, and to the cowardice of the Neapolitans at the last moment, it is perhaps astonishing that so much was done as was done.[2]

[1] For the names, see note on pp. 203–4.

[2] 'Mém. p. serv. à l'Histoire de Toulon en 1793': 'Hist. de l'Armée des Bouches du Rhône,' etc. (J. E. Michel. Paris, 1797); Corresp. de Trogoff (Sect. Hist. de la

Hood detached from Toulon in September a small squadron[1] under Commodore Robert Linzee, who, after a vain endeavour to raise the Royalists at Ville Franche, stood across to Corsica, the garrisons of which he had been ordered to reduce if they should not declare in favour of the monarchy. A few peasants came down to the shore in the country districts and gladly accepted arms and ammunition from the squadron; but Calvi, San Fiorenzo, and Bastia, the strong places of the island, made no signs of amity. It was obviously impossible for Linzee, with but three ships of the line and two frigates, to attempt to blockade three separate parts. But the Commodore decided to do something, and began operations with an attack on the defences of Forneilli, a post about two miles from San Fiorenzo, which town lies at the head of a deep bay near the north end of the island. At the mouth of this bay, on the west shore, stood a remarkable tower, said to be the first of its kind, a Martello, or, more properly, a Mortella tower. It was a nearly cylindrical stone building, having one 24-pounder and two 18-pounder guns on its summit. The only means of entrance was by a door about twenty feet up the wall. After a couple of broadsides from the *Lowestoft*, the enemy abandoned the tower, which was taken possession of by boats under Lieutenants John Gibb and Francis Charles Annesley. The squadron then entered, and anchored in, the bay; but instead of at once attacking Forneilli, Linzee, for some unexplained reason, delayed until October 1st, when the garrison had perfected its preparations. Fire was opened on the main redoubt at 3.30 A.M. on that day by the *Ardent*, followed by the *Alcide* and *Courageux*; but no visible effect was produced on the work; and at 8.15 A.M. the Commodore signalled the ships to haul out of gunshot. The *Courageux* and *Ardent* had both suffered severely, and had lost, the former, Lieutenant Ludlow Sheils and 1 seaman killed, and 13 people wounded, and the latter 14 killed and 17 wounded. The guns opposed to the ships on this occasion were thirteen 24-pounders, two 8-pounders, and one 4-pounder, with six heavy mortars, mounted, some in the redoubt, and some near the town.

Marine); 'Révol. Royaliste de Toulon' (d'Imbert); 'Rapport sur la Trahison,' etc. (J. B. Saint-André); *Moniteur*, and other contemporary journals. In addition to the published British authorities.

[1] *Alcide*, 74, Commod. Robert Linzee, Capt. John Woodley; *Courageux*, 74, Capt. John Matthews; *Ardent*, 64, Capt. Robert Manners Sutton; *Lowestoft*, 32, Capt. William Wolseley; and *Nemesis*, 28, Capt. Lord Amelius Beauclerk.

Apart from the French fleet at Toulon there were, cruising in the Mediterranean, one 74-gun ship, twelve frigates, and four corvettes, belonging to the French Toulon fleet. Of these two were captured by a detachment which Hood, while at Toulon, had sent in search of them. The *Modeste*, 36, was discovered by the *Bedford*, 74, *Captain*, 74, and *Speedy*, 14, on October 5th, with two armed tartans, at anchor within the mole of Genoa. The French party being strong in the city, it was decided not to respect the nominal neutrality of the port; and in the afternoon, therefore, the British ships stood in, and the *Bedford*, Captain Robert Man (3), warping herself close to the *Modeste*, boarded and carried her, while the boats of the *Speedy*, Commander Charles Cunningham, took and brought off the tartans. The *Captain*, Captain Samuel Reeve, afterwards proceeded to Spezzia Bay, where the *Impérieuse*, 38, was known to be lying. On the morning of October 12th, Reeve towed in his ship and moored her close to the frigate, and to the battery of Santa Maria; and at 8 A.M. the *Captain's* boats took possession of the Frenchman, which was found to be abandoned and scuttled. The *Impérieuse*, however, was weighed and, under the name of the *Unité*, there being already an *Impérieuse* in the service, was added to the Royal Navy.

On more distant stations hostilities began very early in the year. On May 7th, in pursuance of instructions from home, a small military force was embarked at Halifax, and, convoyed by the *Alligator*, 28, Captain William Affleck, and the *Diligente*, an armed schooner, captured the French islands of St. Pierre and Miquelon without resistance on May 14th.

In pursuance of other instructions from home, a military force embarked on April 12th at Bridgetown, Barbados, on board the *Trusty*, 50, Vice-Admiral Sir John Laforey, Captain John Drew, *Nautilus*, 16, Commander Lord Henry Paulet, *Hind*, armed schooner, and *Hero*, merchantman, and, on the 14th, was landed on the French island of Tobago. The governor refused to surrender, and at 1 P.M. on the 15th the fort of Scarborough was carried by assault, the British losing only 3 killed and 25 wounded. The island then capitulated.

An attempt upon Martinique in co-operation with some French royalists was less successful. It was made by Rear-Admiral Alan Gardner's squadron, which included the *Queen*, 98, Captain John Hutt, *Duke*, 98, Captain the Hon. George Murray (2), *Hector*, 74,

Captain George Montagu, and *Monarch*, 74, Captain Sir James Wallace, troops from Barbados co-operating under Major-General Bruce. The attack miscarried owing to some misunderstanding, but many of the French Royalists were taken off. Those, however, who remained met, it is to be feared, with heavy punishment for having assisted the cause of the enemies of republican France.

On the Jamaica station Commodore John Ford was encouraged by Royalist overtures from San Domingo to attempt Jérémie and St. Nicolas Mole. Taking on board troops at Port Royal on September 9th, he proceeded, with his broad pennant in the *Europa*, 50, Captain George Gregory, to Jérémie, where he arrived on September 19th. Accompanying him were the *Goelan*,[1] 14, Commander Thomas Wolley and the *Flying Fish*, schooner. The British were welcomed with joy, and the place was taken possession of in the name of the French crown. On the 21st the Commodore was off St. Nicolas Mole, which was found to be in expectation of an assault from a body of blacks and mulattoes. He induced the place to capitulate; and, later in the year, he received the surrender of other towns in the island, including Léogane.

Information of the outbreak of war reached Fort George on June 1st, and Fort William on June 11th. The French were almost powerless in India; and Chandernagore, Carical, Mahé, and other ports were summoned, and yielded without resistance. But when Colonel Prosper de Clermont, governor of Pondicherry, was summoned on August 1st, he refused to capitulate. The town was, therefore, bombarded on and after August 20th, and on the 23rd it was induced to surrender. During the brief siege, the *Minerva*, 38, Rear-Admiral the Hon. William Cornwallis, Captain John Whitby, assisted by three East Indiamen, blockaded the port and on one occasion drove off the French frigate *Cybèle*, Captain Pierre Julien Tréhouart, which, with three smaller vessels, endeavoured to throw supplies and reinforcements into the town.

"During the year 1793," says James, "the British cruisers had effected the capture or destruction of 140 French armed vessels, including 52 belonging to the national navy. Of the national ships, but 35 were captured; and, out of these, 30 were added to the British Navy, exclusive of six of the 88 captured privateers. On the other hand, the loss sustained by the latter was comparatively slight, including but four vessels, and not one of these above a small 32-gun frigate."

The war had therefore begun well, although there had been no general engagement between the combatants.

[1] Such was the Navy List's rendering of the French *Goëland*, i.e., *Seagull.*

After the French Brest fleet had returned to that port from off Belleisle in September, 1793, the French republican Government remorselessly weeded out all officers and men who were believed to be disaffected to the new order of things. M. Louis Thomas Villaret-Joyeuse, previously a lieutenant,[1] was promoted to be rear-admiral, and was given command-in-chief in place of M. Morard de Galles. He hoisted his flag in the *Montagne*, a 120-gun three-decker, which had been previously known as the *Côte d'Or*, and still earlier as the *Etats de Bourgogne*. It was at about that time that the tricolour was adopted as the French national ensign. It was not believed in Paris that either the spirit of the officers and men or the ability of Villaret was sufficient to insure that the fine fleet assembled at Brest would do its duty. The deputy, Jean Bon Saint André, induced the National Convention to adopt a decree declaring that the captain and officers of any ship of the line belonging to the Republic who should haul down the national colours to the vessels, however numerous, of an enemy, unless the French ship should be shattered so as to be in danger of sinking before the crew could be saved, should be pronounced traitors to their country and suffer death; and that the captain and officers of any frigate, corvette, or smaller vessel, who should surrender to a force double their own, unless their ship was reduced to the before-mentioned extremity, should be punished in the same manner. Eventually Jean Bon Saint André himself accompanied the fleet to sea, in order to encourage or terrorise the officers and men into doing their best for the Republic.

The British Channel Fleet had lain at anchor during the winter; yet it had cruisers near the French coast, and it was always ready to put to sea on receipt of news that the Brest fleet had come out. But, as the spring drew on, additional duties claimed its services. Large convoys were preparing to sail for the East and West Indies, and for Newfoundland, and these had to be seen clear of the Channel; and a large French-American convoy, under Rear-Admiral Vanstabel, laden with stores, which were greatly needed

[1] Previous to the reorganisation of the French navy under the Republic, both Villaret-Joyeuse and Bouvet were merely lieutenants, and Nielly was only a sub-lieutenant. Of the twenty-six captains commanding French ships of the line on the glorious First of June, but one had been a captain under the monarchy. Of the rest, four had been lieutenants, ten sub-lieutenants, one a petty officer, and one a seaman in the navy; two had been merchant captains, and seven had been pilots, merchant mates, masters of coasting craft, etc.—Guérin, vi. 503, 504.

in France, was known to be on its way home, and this had to be, if possible, intercepted. The British outward-bound convoy assembled at St. Helen's by May 2nd. On that day it weighed, and on the 4th, being off the Lizard, it was ordered by Lord Howe, the Commander-in-Chief, to part company with him, Rear-Admiral George Montagu (B.) being directed, with six 74-gun ships and two frigates, to accompany it as far as the latitude of Cape Finisterre, and Captain Peter Rainier, with the *Suffolk*, 74, one 64, and four or five frigates, being directed to see it further on its voyage. These detachments reduced the fleet to twenty-six sail of the line, seven frigates, one hospital ship, two fireships, one sloop, and two cutters. Howe then made for, and early on the 5th arrived off, Ushant. He sent the *Phaeton* and *Latona*, covered by the *Orion*, round the island to ascertain if the French fleet were still in port, and they discovered the enemy to be at anchor in Brest Road. Howe realised that there was great probability of the French coming out to extend their protection to the expected convoy from America, and therefore he made for the latitude through which the latter would be likely to pass. From the 5th to the 18th he cruised in the Bay, but saw nothing of the French. On the 19th, having returned off Ushant, he again ordered the *Phaeton* and *Latona* to reconnoitre the anchorage, which was found to be empty; and the reconnoitring vessels came back with the information, derived from an American craft, that the French had sailed some days previously.

Rear-Admiral Vanstabel had left Brest on September 26th, 1793, with the *Jean Bart*, 74, *Tigre*, 74, two frigates and a brig, subsequently reinforced by two sail of the line, to bring home the American convoy. He had reached Virginia in February, 1794, and had sailed on his return on April 2nd, with a merchant fleet of 117 sail. On May 6th, Rear-Admiral Joseph Marie Nielly with the *Sans Pareil*, 80, the *Audacieux*, *Patriote*, *Téméraire*, and *Trajan*, 74's, and several frigates and corvettes, including the *Républicaine*, *Inconnue*, and *Maire Guiton*, had left Rochefort to meet Vanstabel and his convoy, and to see him into port. On May 16th, the main French fleet under Villaret, consisting of 25 ships of the line and a contingent of frigates and corvettes, had sailed from Brest with a fair north-east wind, its object being the same as that of Nielly's division, namely, the safety of the American convoy. It has since been established that on May 17th, during a fog, the French and British fleets were quite close to one another. On the 18th, however, when the fog lifted, they had passed out of sight.

On the 19th, Villaret was joined by the *Patriote*, of Nielly's squadron, with the information that Nielly had captured the *Castor*, 32, Captain Thomas Troubridge, and a large part of a British Newfoundland convoy; and on the same day Villaret himself took part of a Dutch Lisbon convoy.

On the 19th, also, the *Venus*, 32, Captain William Brown (1), from Rear-Admiral Montagu's squadron, joined Howe with the news that Montagu, having parted company with the East India convoy on the 11th, had afterwards cruised in search of the French American convoy, and had, on the 15th, captured the *Maire Guiton* of Nielly's squadron, and recaptured ten sail of the Newfoundland convoy. Montagu had learned from these captures that Nielly and Vanstabel were likely to unite, and that their strength would then be nine ships of the line, besides several frigates and corvettes; and he had, therefore, detached the *Venus* to request reinforcements, while he himself steered in a direction which, he believed, would enable him to intercept Vanstabel before Nielly could join him, or to receive the solicited reinforcement in time to give him power to strike at Nielly and Vanstabel united, should they join.

Howe, from information in his possession as to the course of Villaret, came to the conclusion that Montagu was in danger; and on the 20th, at 4 A.M., he made sail with the intention of joining his subordinate. Early in the morning of the 21st he sighted that part of the Dutch Lisbon convoy which had been taken by the French main fleet, and, in the course of the morning, he took and burnt more than half of it. The convoy had quitted Villaret on the 19th in lat. 47° 46′ N. and long. 11° 22′ W.

As, therefore, the French were probably quite close to him, Howe abandoned his intention of joining Montagu,[1] and went in pursuit of the enemy. He was, however, eventually driven too much to the south. At 8 A.M. on the 23rd he came upon some captured Dutch vessels, which had parted from the French fleet on

[1] Howe has been blamed for not having adopted measures to secure the junction with him of Montagu, when he had determined not himself to seek further for that officer. He might have sent frigates to look for him. Even then, however, he could not have ensured the presence of Montagu ere the meeting with the French fleet. On the other hand, any detachment of frigates would have weakened himself, and might have resulted in leading the enemy to Montagu.

the 21st. The wind then favoured him; and on the 24th, at noon, the British were within a few miles of where the French were estimated to have been on the 21st, namely in lat. 47° 34' N. and long. 13° 55' W. The British held a course about W.S.W. till 4 P.M. on the 25th, when a French 74, towing a merchant brig, was discovered far to windward, and two other strange ships were seen to the eastward. The brig was taken and proved to be an American. The 74, which cast off and escaped, was found to be the *Audacieux* on her way to join the Brest fleet from Nielly's squadron, which she had quitted only on the previous evening. She subsequently reached Villaret in safety. The two strange sail, the *Républicaine*, 20, and *Inconnue*, 16, which were also from Nielly's squadron, were taken; and as Howe did not desire to weaken his force by sending away prize crews, they were burnt.

The fleet tacked in chase, and, at noon on the 25th, again hauled on the starboard tack with the wind at N. by E. At dawn on the 26th it tacked once more, and at noon, when the wind had changed to W. by S., it steered to the north. On the 27th, at 9 A.M., Howe bore up, and ran to the eastward, with the wind then on his starboard quarter. On the 28th, at about 6.30 A.M., being, as the following noon observation showed, in lat. 47° 34' N. and long. 13° 39' W., with a fresh wind from S. by W. and a rough sea, the British look-out frigates signalled a fleet to windward. At 8.15 A.M. Rear-Admiral Pasley, with the weathermost division, consisting of his ship, the *Bellerophon*, and the *Russell*, *Marlborough*, and *Thunderer*, was ordered to reconnoitre; and at 9 A.M. the strangers, who had wore, were seen bearing down under topgallant sails. Upon that, Howe signalled to prepare for action, and, having recalled his frigates, directed Pasley, at 9.45, to shorten sail. At 10 A.M. the French fleet, of twenty-six sail of the line and five frigates, being then within nine or ten miles, hauled to the wind on the larboard tack, and lay to. A little later it formed a rather ragged line ahead. The British ships were ordered to wear in succession; and at 10.35 they came to on the larboard tack and pressed to windward in two divisions, with Pasley's division as a flying squadron. At 11.10 a signal was made to the effect that there would be time for the men to have dinner.

Soon after one o'clock the French filled, made sail, and began to tack. At 1.30 Howe ordered Pasley to annoy the enemy's rear, and at 1.45, as the French appeared to be inclined to make off, Howe ordered a general chase, signalling soon afterwards for the ships to engage the enemy as they came up with him.

At 2.40 the *Russell*, which was nearly a mile to windward of the rest of Pasley's division, fired a few rounds at the rearmost French ships as they hauled on the starboard tack, and was fired at by them. Just before 3 P.M., the enemy's rear ship being immediately abeam of her, the *Bellerophon* tacked; and soon afterwards th

ADMIRAL SIR THOMAS PASLEY, BART.

(*From an engraving by Roberts, after the painting by J. F. Abbot.*)

whole British fleet did the same by signal, except the *Russell*, *Marlborough*, *Thunderer*, and frigates, which, in order to get into the wake of the French fleet, then close hauled on the starboard tack in line ahead with a fresh and squally wind from the south, stood on for a short time longer. A little after 5 P.M. the French van and centre shortened sail to allow the *Révolutionnaire*, 110, which was rapidly falling astern, to regain her station. This, however, she did not do; and at 6 P.M. the *Bellerophon*, by excellent seamanship, got near enough to her to open fire. It would almost appear that the *Révolutionnaire*, in defiance of signals, assumed the rearmost position out of sheer devilry on the part of her captain, M. Vandangel. At 6.30 the *Marlborough*, which, with the *Russell* and *Thunderer*, was then on the *Bellerophon's* weather quarter, was signalled to engage the rear of the French, who, immediately before, had made sail. The *Bellerophon*, being damaged aloft, was obliged to take in her main topsail, and, after an hour and a half's unsupported action, informed the Commander-in-Chief that she was unable to continue the engagement, and bore up. By that time the *Russell*, *Thunderer*, and *Marlborough*, which had tacked their maintopsails, were firing at long range at the *Révolutionnaire*, and at the ships next ahead of her. The French three-decker had lost her mizen mast, and had suffered considerable damage; and she therefore wore round and put before the wind. No sooner had she done so than she was engaged by the *Leviathan*, which, with the *Audacious*, Captain William Parker, had passed to windward of the disabled *Bellerophon*. At 7.30 Howe signalled to assist the ships engaged, and, a little later, repeated the order and hoisted the pennants of the *Marlborough* and *Russell*. In the interval the *Leviathan* continued to engage the *Révolutionnaire* until the *Audacious* got up. The *Leviathan* then passed on, and fired a broadside at the next French ship; but at 8 P.M. she dropped down towards the body of the British fleet, signals having been made, to the *Bellerophon*, *Leviathan*, *Russell*, and *Marlborough*, to relinquish the chase, and, to the fleet, to form a line ahead and astern as most convenient.

The *Audacious*, on the *Révolutionnaire's* lee quarter, fired heavily. The *Russell*, until recalled, also annoyed the Frenchman very seriously. The *Révolutionnaire* had by that time become almost unmanageable, and the *Audacious* had great difficulty in avoiding being fouled by her. At a little before ten, the *Révolutionnaire*, which, besides her mizenmast, had lost her fore and mainyards and her main topsail yard, fell athwart the hawse of the *Audacious*. But Captain Parker extricated himself; and the French ship went to leeward. Some of the men of the *Audacious* reported that the *Révolutionnaire* struck while the ships were close to one another. The *Russell* also reported that the three-decker had no colours flying when she passed under the British ships astern. But possibly the colours had been merely shot away. The ship, however, had lost heavily; and she might, no doubt, have been taken, had the *Thunderer*, when hailed by the *Audacious* to take possession of her, attempted to do so. The *Audacious* herself was not under control, and was for some time unable to wear clear of the French line. Her injuries were chiefly aloft. She had, indeed, lost only 3 killed, and 3 mortally and 16 more slightly wounded, while the *Révolutionnaire* had lost nearly 400 men. As soon as Captain Parker had got clear, he did his best to repair damages with a view to regaining his station in the morning; but when, at dawn, he saw nine French sail to windward, he judged it best, looking to his crippled condition, to put before the wind. At that time he had his foresail and three topsails unbent, and his mainsail in the act of being bent. What the strange craft were has not been ascertained. They may have been the ships and prizes of Vanstabel, or the squadron of Nielly; but it is more likely that they belonged to one of two light squadrons which at that time were cruising out of Lorient and Rochefort.

The disabled *Audacious* was favoured by rain and mist; but, before she was again under anything like proper sail, the mist lifted, and she discovered two ships, which seem to have been the *Audacieux* and a brig, detached by Villaret to look after the *Révolutionnaire.* That ship, without a mast standing, lay then about a mile and a half away. Immediately afterwards the French frigate *Bellone*, 36, with a ship and a brig, appeared in the eastward. These vessels, discovering the state of the *Audacious*, and encouraged by the proximity of their friends, stood athwart Parker, and exchanged shots with him. The other craft soon fell astern, but the *Bellone* hung on the quarter of the *Audacious* until 12.30 P.M., when she hauled to the wind. During all this time the British ship, owing to the state of her masts, was powerless to alter course. She subsequently sailed into a fog; and, feeling that, all things considered, it was useless to attempt to rejoin the fleet, Parker proceeded for port, and on June 3rd anchored in Plymouth Sound. The *Révolutionnaire* was found by the French *Audacieux* and towed into Rochefort.

One of the chief lessons of this partial action on the 28th of May, seems to be the greater relative value of a vessel of large size as compared with several vessels of smaller size but, in the aggregate, of largely superior armament. The escape of the *Révolutionnaire*, after having had to deal with so many 74's, surely shows this.

The British and French fleets continued on parallel courses

during the night of the 28th, carrying a press of sail on the starboard tack. At dawn on the 29th the wind still blew freshly from south by west, and there was a heavy head sea. The fleets were then about six miles apart, the French being on the weather-bow of the British. By that time, Howe's signal of the previous evening for the fleet to form line ahead and astern of the *Queen Charlotte* as most convenient, had, of course, been carried out; and the order of the head of the British column was, *Cæsar*, *Queen*, *Russell*, *Valiant*, *Royal George*, *Invincible*, *Orion*, *Majestic*, *Leviathan*, *Queen Charlotte* and *Bellerophon*. With the object of making some impression on the enemy's rear, Howe, at 7 A.M., signalled his ships to tack in succession; and at 7.30, when the fleet was on the larboard tack, he ordered it to pass through the French line, in order to obtain the weather gage. But, in endeavouring to execute this manœuvre, the British fleet passed astern of the enemy's rear, the French firing when the ships were at a great distance, and the *Cæsar* and *Queen* returning the compliment when they were well within range. It is interesting to note that during this action all the ships in the fleet flew the Red Ensign, although there were present flag officers both of the Red and of the White squadrons. The Commander-in-Chief, who was at the time Vice-Admiral of England, flew the Union at the main.

At 8 A.M. the French van ships began to wear in succession to support their threatened rear, and, running to leeward of their line, edged down towards the British van and centre. When she was clear of the rear of her own fleet, the leading French ship, which was then about three miles distant from the British centre, hauled close to the wind; and her example was followed in succession by the ships astern of her. At a little after 9 A.M., when the whole French fleet was on the larboard tack, the van ships again bore away; and, at 10 A.M., opened an ineffectual fire upon the British van. But presently the distance between the two vans lessened; and the *Invincible* (which luffed out of the line in order to get nearer the foe), *Royal George*, *Valiant*, *Russell*, *Queen* and *Cæsar* exchanged broadsides with the French van. In this brush several of the British ships suffered aloft; and the leading French vessel, the *Montagnard*, received evident damage. At 11.30 Howe signalled to tack in succession in order to pass through the enemy's line; but when he found that his van was not still sufficiently advanced to cut off more than a few ships of the French rear, he annulled the signal and continued to stretch on as before. At 12.30 P.M. he again signalled to tack. There was then much smoke hanging about; and the signal was only partially obeyed; so that, in the result, when, at 1.15 P.M., signal was made to engage the enemy and pass through his line, the ships which had been ahead of the *Queen Charlotte* were, from various causes, not in a position to carry out in due order their share of the intended manœuvre.

This being so, some of his van ships being engaged at a considerable distance, and the French having begun to wear in succession, Howe, in the *Queen Charlotte*, at 1.30, set the example of breaking the line, which he passed through astern of the *Eole*, the sixth ship from the enemy's rear. The *Bellerophon* and *Leviathan* followed Howe's lead, the former passing across the bows, and the latter under the stern of the *Terrible*, the third ship from the enemy's rear. As soon as she was through, the *Queen Charlotte* put about on the larboard tack, hoisted the signal for a general chase, and devoted herself to the *Terrible*, which had lost her foretopmast and was struggling to regain her station. The two ships astern of her, the *Tyrannicide* and *Indomptable*, which had been previously engaged by the *Queen* and the *Royal George*, were both a good deal disabled. But the French van had, in the meantime, wore round on the starboard tack; and the *Terrible* managed to reach the centre of her own fleet ere the *Queen Charlotte* could get near her. The *Indomptable* was afterwards warmly engaged by the *Orion* and *Barfleur*, but she gallantly kept her colours flying till she and the *Terrible* were rescued by Admiral Villaret, who dexterously led his fleet on the starboard tack to their assistance. Howe, who had only the *Bellerophon* and *Leviathan*, both disabled, near him, could not prevent this, and was only able at about 4 P.M. to obtain sufficient support to cover the *Queen* and *Royal George*, which had suffered severely.

In the course of these operations the two vans once more approached one another within gunshot, and a partial action resulted, the *Glory* distinguishing herself by the accuracy and deadliness of her fire. But no general engagement followed, Villaret contenting himself with saving his disabled ships, and then wearing round, and standing away large on the larboard tack and rejoining his rear. The British wore in the same direction, keeping, however, the weather gage; and so the firing ceased. This was just after 5 P.M. Each fleet then formed line on the larboard tack, and set to work to repair damages. Among the officers killed in this encounter were Lieutenants George

Heigham, of the *Royal George*, and Roger R. Rawlance, of the *Queen Charlotte*, and Mr. William Mitchell, Master of the *Queen*. Captain Hutt, of the *Queen*, lost a leg, and subsequently died of his wound. The total British loss was 67 killed and 128 wounded. Several ships were much damaged, but they were quickly made again fit for action; and, at 10.30 A.M. on the 30th, the only vessel which reported herself as still unready was the *Cæsar*,[1] a ship which had been badly handled during the engagement, and which had probably, by her apparent hesitation, encouraged Villaret to attempt to cover his crippled ships.[2]

On the night of the 29th the weather was thick and foggy; but on the morning of the 30th it cleared for a time and the French were seen in the north-west on the starboard tack. After some preparations had been made on both sides to renew the action, the weather grew thicker than ever, and the ships in consequence became much dispersed. At 9 A.M. on the 31st the fog lifted, and the British ships at once took measures to regain their stations. At noon the French were seen to the northward, numbering twenty-six sail of the line and six others. At 2 P.M. Howe bore up, and the French, who had previously edged away a little, formed line on the larboard tack. Later in the day a general action might have been brought on; but Howe, mindful of the confusion which had occurred on the 29th, preferred fighting by daylight, when signals could be seen. At a little after 7 P.M., therefore, he hauled to the wind on the larboard tack, and so stationed a couple of his frigates as to ensure that he should be at once informed of any

[1] "On this occasion, we, the Lieutenants on the quarter-deck, were speaking our minds very freely respecting the conduct of the different Captains, and, upon some particular observation made by Larcom, first Lieutenant, on the conduct of the *Cæsar*, Lord Howe said: 'I desire you to hold your tongue, sir. I don't desire you to shut your eyes, but I desire you to hold your tongue till I call upon you, as I probably shall do hereafter, for your observations.'"—Bourchier, "Codrington," i. 20.

[2] Says Mahan: "The merit of Howe's conduct upon these two days does not . . . depend merely upon the issue, though fortunate. By persistent attacks, frequently renewed upon the same and most vulnerable part of the French order, he had in effect brought to bear a large part of his own fleet upon a relatively small number of the enemy, the result being a concentration of injury, which compelled the damaged ships to leave the field. At the same time the direction of the attack forced the French admiral either to abandon the endangered vessels, or, step by step, to yield the advantage of the wind, until it was finally wrested from him altogether. By sheer tactical skill, combined with a fine display of personal conduct, Howe had won a marked numerical preponderance for the decisive action. . . . Unfortunately, the tactical gain was soon neutralised by the strategic mistake which left Montagu's squadron unavailable on the day of battle."—'Fr. Revol. and Emp.' i. 135.

attempt on the part of Villaret to weather the British during the night.

After the action on the 29th, the *Montagnard* had deserted the French fleet, and the *Seine*, frigate, which had been sent after her, had also failed to rejoin. But on the evening of that day the *Trente-et-un Mai*, 74, Captain Honoré Ganteaume, had joined Villaret from Cancale Bay; and on the 30th the French admiral was further reinforced by the *Sans Pareil*, *Trajan* and *Téméraire*, of Rear-Admiral Nielly's squadron. This accession of force induced Villaret to send home the crippled *Indomptable*, convoyed by the *Mont Blanc*, 74, and left him still with twenty-six sail of the line.

During the night of the 31st the British stood to the westward; and at dawn on June 1st they were in lat. 47° 48′ N., and long. 18° 30′ W., with a moderate breeze from south by west and a fairly smooth sea. The French fleet, in line of battle on the larboard tack, was six miles on the starboard or lee bow of the British. At 5 A.M. the British, by signal, bore up together and steered north-west, and at 6.15 A.M. altered course to the north. At about 7.10 the fleet again hauled to the wind on the larboard tack. At 7.16 Howe signalled that he should attack the French centre, and, at 7.25, that he should pass through the enemy's line and engage from leeward. The two fleets were then about four miles apart. Howe himself had scarcely quitted the deck of his flagship for three days,[1] and the men were correspondingly fatigued. The fleet was, therefore, hove to, and the men breakfasted. At 8.12 A.M., Howe again filled and bore down. A little later, each ship was ordered to steer for, and to independently engage, the ship opposite her in the French line; and, with a view to making the combat as equal as possible, Howe effected some changes in his formation, after which, the order of the two lines was as follows:—

[1] Howe was then sixty-eight. Looking to his age, the manner in which he bore the fatigue and anxiety was marvellous. Codrington says: "When the report was brought to him" (on June 1st) "that the French fleet showed every symptom of determination to sustain a battle, I watched his face when he came to the quarter-deck to look at them. It expressed an animation of which, at his age, and after such fatigue of mind and body, I had not thought it capable." . . . "He went to bed completely done up after the action of the First. We all got round him; indeed, I saved him from a tumble. He was so weak that, from a roll of the ship, he was nearly falling into the waist. 'Why, you hold me up as if I were a child,' he said good-humouredly."—Bourchier, 'Codrington,' i. 27, 31. For nearly five days he had rested only in a chair. Yet the strain of naval warfare would press more hardly on a Commander-in-Chief to-day than it did in 1794.

British and French Lines of Battle on June 1st, 1794.

British.

Ships.	Guns.	Commanders.	Losses on May 28, 29, and June 1. Killed.	Wounded.
Cæsar . . .	80	Capt. Anthony James Pye Molloy.	18	71
Bellerophon .	74	Rear-Admiral Thomas Pasley (W).[1] Capt. William Johnstone Hope.[1]	4	27
Leviathan .	74	,, Lord Hugh Seymour.[1]	10	33
Russell . . .	74	,, John Willett Payne.[1]	8	26
Royal Sovereign	100	Vice-Admiral Thomas Graves (2) (R).[1] Capt. Henry Nicholls.[1]	14	44
Marlborough .	74	,, Hon. George Cranfield Berkeley.[1]	29	90
Defence. . .	74	,, James Gambier (2).[1]	18	39
Impregnable .	98	Rear-Admiral Benjamin Caldwell (W). Capt. George Blagden Westcott.	7	24
Tremendous .	74	,, James Pigott.	3	8
Barfleur . .	98	Rear-Admiral George Bowyer (W).[1] Capt. Cuthbert Collingwood.	9	25
Invincible . .	74	,, Hon. Thomas Pakenham.[1]	14	31
Culloden . .	74	,, Isaac Schomberg.	2	5
Gibraltar . .	80	,, Thomas Mackenzie.	2	12
Queen Charlotte	100	Admiral Earl Howe (Union).[1] Capt. Sir Roger Curtis, Kt. (1st)[1] ,, Sir Andrew Snape Douglas, Kt.[1]	14	29
Brunswick .	74	,, John Harvey.[2]	44	114
Valiant . .	74	,, Thomas Pringle.[1]	2	9
Orion . . .	74	,, John Thomas Duckworth.[1]	5	24
Queen . . .	98	Rear-Admiral Alan Gardner (W).[1] Capt. John Hutt.[2]	36	67
Ramillies . .	74	,, Henry Harvey.[1]	2	7
Alfred . . .	74	,, John Bazely (1).	..	8
Montagu . .	74	,, James Montagu.[2]	4	13
Royal George .	100	Vice-Admiral Sir Alexander Arthur Hood, K.B.(R).[1] Capt. William Domett.[1]	20	72
Majestic . .	74	,, Charles Cotton.	3	18
Glory . . .	98	,, John Elphinstone (2).[1]	13	39
Thunderer .	74	,, Albemarle Bertie.		
Phaeton, 38.	..	,, William Bentinck.	3	4
Latona, 38 .	..	,, Edward Thornbrough.		
Niger, 32 .	..	,, Hon. Arthur Kaye Legge.		
Southampton 32 . . .	..	,, Hon. Robert Forbes.		
Venus, 32 .	..	,, William Brown (1).		
Aquilon, 32 .	..	,, Hon. Robert Stopford.		
Pegasus, 28.	..	,, Robert Barlow.		
		Total . .	290	858

And the *Pharon*, 44, hosp. ship, Capt. George Countess; *Comet*, 14, fireship, Com. William Bradley; *Incendiary*, 14, fireship, Com. John Cooke; *Kingfisher*, 18, sloop, Com. Thomas Le Marchant Gosselin; *Rattler*, 16, cutter, Lieut. John Winne; and *Ranger*, 14, cutter, Lieut. Isaac Cotgrave.

French.

Ships.	Guns.	Commanders.
Trajan . . .	74	Capt. Dumoutier.
Eole. . . .	74	,, Bertrand Keranguen.[2]
America[3] . .	74	,, Louis L'Héritier.
Téméraire . .	74	,, Morel.
Terrible . .	110	Rear-Admiral François Joseph Bouvet. Capt. Julien Le Ray.
Impétueux[3] .	74	,, Douville.
Mucius . .	74	,, Larreguy.
Tourville . .	74	,, Langlois.
Gasparin . .	74	,, Tardy.
Convention .	74	,, Joseph Allary.
Trente-et-un Mai . . .	74	,, Honoré Ganteaume.
Tyrannicide .	74	,, d'Ordelin.
Juste[3] . . .	80	,, Blavet.
Montagne . .	120	Rear-Admiral Louis Thomas Villaret-Joyeuse. Capt. Bazire.[2]
Jacobin . .	80	,, Gassin.
Achille[3] . .	74	,, G. J. N. de La Villegris.
Vengeur du Peuple[4] . .	74	,, Jean François Renaudin.
Patriote . .	74	,, Lucadou.
Northumberland[3] . .	74	,, François Etienne.
Entreprenant .	74	,, Le Francq.
Jemmapes[5] .	74	,, Desmartis.
Neptune . .	74	,, Tiphaigne.
Pelletier . .	74	,, Berrade.
Républicain .	110	Rear-Admiral Joseph Marie Nielly. Capt. Pierre Jacques Longer.
Sans Pareil[3] .	80	,, Jean François Courand.
Scipion. . .	80	,, Huguet.
Précieuse, 36		
Naïade . .		
Proserpine, 40		
Tamise, 32 .	..	,, J. M. A. L'Hermite.
Papillon .		
Galatée, 36 .		
Gentille, 36 .		

And three or four small craft.

[1] Received medals, as having particularly signalised themselves. Capt. William Parker, of the *Audacious*, also received a medal for his conduct on May 28th, and Capt. Cuthbert Collingwood, of the *Barfleur*, after protest, received one at a later period.
[2] Killed, or mortally wounded.
[3] Struck and made prize of.
[4] Struck and foundered.
[5] Struck, but retaken by the French.

The French were in a close head and stern line,[1] heading west; and both fleets were under single-reefed topsails, some of the French lying to, and others backing and filling, to preserve station. The British headed about north-west with a fresh breeze from south by west; and they were moving at the rate of about five knots.

At 9.24 the French van opened a distant fire upon the British van, and especially upon the *Defence*, which was a little ahead of her line. At 9.50 the French fire became general, and the British fire opened, the flagship's bearing the signal for close action. It had been intended that each British ship should pass astern of her natural opponent, and engage her from leeward; but only a few vessels did this. The rest hauled up to windward and engaged, some at short, but many at longer, distance. At 10.10 A.M., Villaret in the *Montagne* made sail ahead, followed by the second astern, and afterwards by such other ships as had suffered little damage aloft. Howe ordered a general chase at 10.13. By 11.30 A.M. the action was practically over, though no ships had then been taken possession of. The British had eleven, and the French twelve, more or less dismasted vessels. The latter were doing their best to escape with such sail as they could make on their stumps; and they fired, from time to time, at such British ships as came within gunshot.

The *Montagne* and *Jacobin* stood on till nearly abreast of the French van, and then wore round, with several other French vessels making twelve sail in all, and steered for the *Queen*, which lay crippled on their starboard bow. Howe saw the *Queen's* danger, and, having signalled his ships to form line ahead and astern of him, managed to wear round on the starboard tack, and, followed by the *Barfleur*, *Thunderer*, *Royal Sovereign*, *Valiant*, *Leviathan* and others, stood away, with the wind abaft the beam, to assist Rear-Admiral Gardner. This induced Villaret to relinquish his design, and to stretch on to the support of five of his crippled ships, which were towing towards him in the eastward, two of them being wholly dismasted. He succeeded in covering and saving four of these, the *Républicain*, *Mucius*, *Scipion* and *Jemmapes*. The fifth, the *Terrible*, joined him by pluckily fighting her way through her opponents. There was no general firing after about 1.15 P.M.; but it was not

[1] The *Tyrannicide*, having lost her upper masts on May 29th, had to be towed until the opening of the battle of June 1st.

Q 2

until 2.30 that the six crippled ships, that lay nearest the body of the British, were secured. Several did not submit without firing upon the vessels which were about to take possession of them. A little after 6 P.M. the seventh French ship, the *Vengeur*, was taken; but she was so shattered that, ten minutes later, she went down, having still on board about 200 of her crew, chiefly wounded men.

The British loss in the three days' engagement was 290 killed and 858 wounded.[1] The French lost, in the six captured vessels alone, upwards of 1200 killed and wounded, and, in the whole fleet, about 7000 killed, wounded and prisoners. Among the British officers killed or mortally wounded, in addition to those already mentioned, were Captains James Montagu and John Harvey; Lieutenants Francis Ross, of the *Tremendous*, Richard Dawes, of the *Queen*, and Thomas Ireland of the *Royal George*; Masters William Webster, of the *Defence*, David Caird, of the *Impregnable*,

SIGNATURE OF ADMIRAL SIR THOMAS PASLEY, BART.

and George Metcalfe, of the *Glory*; and Captain of Marines Walter Smith, of the *Bellerophon*. Of the seven British flag-officers, three, Graves, Pasley and Bowyer, were wounded.

The general scheme of the action has now been made apparent. That scheme was of course not strictly carried out. No scheme of the kind ever is. It will, therefore, be well to say something about the experiences of individual ships; and, for the sake of convenience, these will be mentioned according to the order which they occupied in the line.

The *Cæsar*,[2] in bearing down to engage, dropped somewhat astern, and brought to about 500 yards to windward of the enemy, Captain Molloy, choosing to exercise a discretion,[3] which, as he

[1] Details will be found in the table on p. 226.

[2] Howe, owing to Molloy's previous behaviour, had been unwilling to put him at the head of the line. The unwillingness, justified when the action opened, had been waived at the personal request of Sir Roger Curtis, to whom Howe said significantly, after Molloy had brought to: "Look, Curtis, there goes your friend! Who is mistaken now?"

[3] The signal concluded as follows: "The different Captains and Commanders, not being able to effect the specified intention . . . are at liberty to act as circumstances require." This qualifying clause was wisely omitted when the signal code was next revised.

contended, was allowed him by Lord Howe's signal to pass through the line and engage from leeward. His reason, as suggested during the court-martial which was subsequently held upon him, was that, had he passed astern of the *Trajan*, his proper opponent, he must afterwards have shot so far ahead of her as to be beyond effective range. When he realised that he had made a mistake, and when he endeavoured to wear and make sail, his tiller became jammed;

ADMIRAL THOMAS GRAVES (2), LORD GRAVES.

(From a lithograph by Ridley, after the portrait by Northcote.)

and for half-an-hour the ship dropped astern. At length she did bear up; but it was then too late to be of much use.

The *Bellerophon* bore down upon the weather quarter of the *Eole*, and, at 8.45, opened fire with good effect. She continued this until the *Eole* wore round astern of her leader, and stood on the starboard tack, having had enough of it. As the *Bellerophon* had received the fire of both the *Trajan* and the *Eole*, especially towards the end, the British ship was so damaged aloft that she had to signal to the *Latona* to come to her assistance. The *Latona*, to make a diversion, gallantly fired on the two French 74's as she approached.

The *Leviathan* seems to have engaged the *America* without passing through the line, and, at length, to have dismasted her. The *Russell* did not pass through the line, but hove to windward of the *Téméraire*, which, at 11 A.M., made sail to leeward, and was followed through the line by the *Russell*, which, unable, owing to damage aloft, to trim her sails in more than one direction, found herself to leeward of the *Trajan* and *Eole*, and was by them badly mauled ere she could be assisted by the *Leviathan*. Later in the day she took possession of the *America*.

The *Royal Sovereign* engaged the *Terrible* at too great a distance; and a signal was consequently made for her to engage more closely. Eventually she forced the *Terrible* to bear up; and, while the French ship was doing so and yawing, the three-decker repeatedly raked her. She then chased her, until the French ship was aided by the *Montagne* and *Jacobin*. The *Valiant* assisted the *Royal Sovereign* a little; and, at length, the *Montagne* bore away followed, for a short distance, by Graves's flagship. In the afternoon, not knowing that the *Russell* had already taken possession of the *America*, the *Royal Sovereign* boarded that ship and sent back the *Russell's* men to their own vessel.

The *Marlborough* passed through the line astern of the *Impétueux*, and ranged up alongside of her to leeward. The two vessels presently fell on board one another, and a very fierce action ensued. At 10.15 the *Mucius*, which was next astern of the *Impétueux*, made sail ahead in order to free herself from her own opponent, the *Defence*, and fell on board the bow of the *Marlborough*; so that the *Marlborough*, *Impétueux* and *Mucius* formed a triangle. Soon afterwards, the *Marlborough* lost all her masts; but she nevertheless dismasted both her opponents. She was, a little later, raked by the *Montagne*, which passed by her stern; and, being at length obliged to signal for help, she was taken in tow by the *Aquilon*.[1] The

[1] After the *Marlborough* had been entirely dismasted and otherwise very seriously disabled, owing to her successive encounters with the *Sans Pareil*, *Mucius*, and *Montagne*, and the Captain and Lieutenant Michael Seymour (1) had been severely wounded, some whispers of surrender seem to have been heard on board; whereupon Lieutenant John Monckton resolutely exclaimed: "I'll be damned if she shall ever surrender: I'll nail her colours to the stump of the mast." This attitude, and the sudden crowing of a cock that had found its way out of a smashed coop, and perched itself on the stump of the mainmast, reanimated the crew, who at once gave three

Mucius escaped; but the *Impétueux* was ultimately taken possession of by the *Russell.*

The *Defence* got through the French line between the *Mucius* and the *Tourville*, and was presently in the thick of the action. She was so badly treated that, being threatened by the *Républicain*, she signalled for help, and was taken in tow by the *Phaeton*. Before the latter did this, she very pluckily engaged the *Impétueux* for ten minutes. The *Impregnable*, *Tremendous* and *Barfleur* kept much too much to windward to produce any great effect. The *Invincible*, instead of engaging her proper opponent, engaged the *Juste*,[1] and forced her to bear up until, meeting with the fire of the *Queen Charlotte*, she struck. The *Culloden* and *Gibraltar* also engaged somewhat too far to windward, and therefore did little damage. The *Queen Charlotte*, steering to cut the line astern of the *Montagne*, received, as she approached, a heavy fire from the *Vengeur* and *Achille*. As she was about to pass astern of the *Montagne*,[2] the *Jacobin* stretched ahead under that ship's lee, nearly taking the place which the *Queen Charlotte* was to have taken. Thanks, however, to the promptitude of Mr. James Bowen, Master of the *Queen Charlotte*, the British flagship was neatly luffed up between the two French vessels, and warmly engaged both, until the *Jacobin*[3] dropped astern, and the *Montagne* made sail and ranged ahead. It was then that Howe signalled for a general chase. The *Queen Charlotte* next engaged the *Juste*, which she dismasted, and ultimately forced to strike. But, in the interim, Howe was threatened by the *Républicain*; and he only escaped receiving severe damage from her owing to the opportune fall of the French

cheers, and thought no more of aught save victory. Lieutenant Michael Seymour received a ball between the elbow and the wrist, and the limb mortifying, the left arm had in a few days to be amputated well above the elbow.—Barrow, 'Howe'; 'Life of Seymour.'

[1] The *Juste*, according to Codrington, was a red-sided ship, yet, for a time she was mistaken by Lord Howe, and others in the *Queen Charlotte*, for the *Invincible*.

[2] The *Montagne* would appear to have been quite unprepared for Howe's mode of attack, and to have had her starboard or lee ports closed, and her guns on that side unloaded and unmanned until about the time when, having suffered very heavily, she ranged ahead.

[3] The French were placed at a disadvantage by the close proximity of the two ships. They could not use their sponges and rammers, which had rigid wooden shafts. The British, however, had sponges and rammers with flexible rope shafts, specially prepared for such an eventuality. The French, therefore, could only use with freedom a few forward and after guns on the starboard side of the lower deck while the ships remained in contact.

three-decker's main and mizen masts, thanks to the distant fire of the *Gibraltar*. This fire was, however, so carelessly directed that some of it struck the *Queen Charlotte*.[1]

The *Brunswick* was well forward at the commencement of the attack, and received much of the fire intended for the *Queen Charlotte*. This did her great damage before she returned a single shot. The French line closed up so much that Captain Harvey

CAPTAIN JOHN HARVEY (1), OF THE "BRUNSWICK."

(From an engraving by Ridley, after the portrait by Stuart.)

could not pass through astern of the *Jacobin*. He tried, as an alternative, to pass between the *Achille* and the *Vengeur*; but the latter stretched ahead and blocked the opening. The *Brunswick*, therefore, put her helm to port, and ran foul of the *Vengeur*, the starboard anchors of the British ship hooking into the French ship's larboard fore-shrouds and channels. The master, Mr. George Stewart, asked Harvey: "Shall I cut the ship clear, sir?" "No," said Harvey; "we have got her and we will keep her." The two

[1] Bourchier, 'Codrington,' i. 27.

ships at once swung close together, and, paying off before the wind, dropped out of the line. The seamen on the British ship's lower deck, finding that they could not open some of their lower ports owing to the pressure of the French ship's hull against them, blew them off; and so, with their heads to the north, the two vessels began a most sanguinary engagement. Harvey was soon wounded in the hand by a musket-shot, but remained on deck. At 11 A.M. the *Achille* bore down through the smoke upon the British ship's larboard quarter, and threatened to board. But the *Brunswick* shot away her last remaining mast as she came up, and, since the wreckage fell over the starboard or engaged side of the *Achille*, that ship was unable to continue the action; and, in a few minutes, struck. The *Brunswick* could not, however, take possession; and the *Achille* subsequently rehoisted her colours, and attempted to escape by setting her spritsail. She had got some distance away when another ship was seen bearing down on the *Brunswick*. This was at first taken for a foe; but she proved to be the *Ramillies*, commanded by Henry Harvey, brother to the Captain of the *Brunswick*. By that time the fire from the *Brunswick's* quarter-deck, forecastle, and poop had almost ceased;[1] but she fought her principal batteries as vigorously as ever.

"On the lower-deck," says James, "the seamen, profiting by the rolling of the *Vengeur*, frequently drove home the coins, and depressed the muzzles of the guns, each of which was loaded with two round shot, and then again withdrew the coins, and pointed the muzzles upwards; thus alternately firing into their opponent's bottom, and ripping up her decks. During this deliberate and destructive operation, Captain Harvey was knocked down by a splinter; but, although seriously hurt, he was presently on his legs again. Soon afterwards, however, the crown of a double-headed shot, which had split, struck his right arm, and this gallant officer was compelled to go below."

On this occasion Captain Harvey is reported to have said to his men: "Persevere, my brave lads, in your duty. Continue the action with spirit, for the honour of our King and country; and remember my last words: The colours of the *Brunswick* shall never be struck." After Captain Harvey's disablement, the command of the ship devolved upon Lieutenant William Edward Cracraft.

At about 12.45 P.M., the action having lasted some three hours,

[1] Some French accounts go so far as to say that, attracted by the deserted state of the *Brunswick's* upper deck, a few French seamen, seeing that fire had broken out on it, and considering the ship as good as taken, clambered over the British ship's bulwarks, and were not opposed; but that these people were withdrawn upon the approach of the *Ramillies*. Cf. Guérin, vi. 40.

the *Brunswick* and *Vengeur* swung apart, the *Brunswick's* three anchors being torn away. The *Ramillies* then attacked the *Vengeur*, the rudder of which was split by the last shots from the *Brunswick*, and which also received a large hole in her counter from the same discharges. The *Ramillies*, at not more than forty yards' distance, concentrated her fire on this hole, and soon reduced the *Vengeur* to a sinking state. The *Ramillies* only desisted when she saw the *Achille* making off, and felt it her duty to pursue her. The *Vengeur* then hung out a Union Jack in token of surrender. The *Brunswick*, which had no boats left, could do nothing to relieve her late foe; and she put her own head to the north, intending to make the best of her way to port. At 3 P.M. she fell in with the *Jemmapes*, which was dismasted and rolling her lower ports under. The *Brunswick* luffed up under her lee, whereupon the *Jemmapes* signified that she had already struck. The

SIGNATURE OF CAPT. WILLIAM EDWARD CRACRAFT, R.N.

Brunswick had lost her mizen. Her bowsprit, and her main and foremasts were badly wounded, and her running and standing rigging was shot away, all her yards being shattered, and all her sails in pieces. She had also twenty-three guns dismounted, had been on fire three times, had lost her starboard quarter-gallery, and had her best bower anchor, with the starboard cathead, towing under her keel.

The *Valiant* hove to to windward of the *Patriote*, which she soon drove to leeward. She next engaged the *Achille*. The *Orion* engaged the *Northumberland* and the *Patriote* until they bore up. She then hauled up to support the *Queen Charlotte*. The *Queen* suffered heavily while bearing down to engage, and failed to get abreast of the *Northumberland*. She therefore closed with the *Jemmapes*, keeping on her starboard quarter when the French ship made sail ahead, and bringing down her mizenmast. The *Queen* herself had lost her main and sprung her mizen; but she managed, in another quarter of an hour, to shoot away the main and foremasts of the *Jemmapes*, which struck, though the *Queen* was far too disabled to take possession. The latter had by that time lost her mizen-topmast, and was otherwise unmanageable for the moment; but, in an hour, she got her head towards the British fleet, and was steering to leeward of it, when she saw, at 12.30 P.M., twelve French ships standing towards her. She was fired at by ten of them, and by two frigates, which were towing the *Terrible*; but she pluckily returned the fire, and was presently relieved by the *Queen Charlotte* and the newly-formed

ADMIRAL SIR ROGER CURTIS, BART.

(From an engraving by Ridley, after the picture by Rivers.)

British line. The escaping French, however, rehoisted the colours of the *Jemmapes* and towed her away.

Of the British ships towards the rear of the line little need be said. The *Ramillies*, after succouring the *Brunswick*, secured the *Achille*. The *Alfred*, assisted by the *Culloden* and *Rattler*, cutter, took off great part of the crew of the gallant *Vengeur* ere the ship foundered. As she went down a few of her people cried, "*Vive la Nation!*" and "*Vive la République!*" and some one is said to have waved a tricolour flag from her deck. Her brave captain, Renaudin,[1] was happily saved.[2] The *Montagu* engaged the *Neptune*. The *Royal George*, after engaging the *Sans Pareil* and *Républicain*, passed through the French line between those ships, subsequently rendering very valuable service. The *Glory*, sailing badly, was slow in getting into action, but at last cut the French line astern of the *Scipion*, which she engaged from leeward, losing her own foretop-mast and mizen topgallant-mast, but entirely dismasting her opponent. Then, ranging ahead, she engaged the *Sans Pareil*, and, with the *Royal George*, attacked the *Républicain*, which was driven off greatly injured aloft. The *Scipion* and *Sans Pareil*, completely silenced, had dropped astern, but could not be taken possession of, the *Royal George* having lost her foremast, and main as well as mizen topmast, and having had her wheel rendered useless, and the *Glory* also being seriously disabled.

Having, as has been seen, saved what he could from the wreck of his fleet, Villaret went off to the northward, and, by 6.15 P.M., was almost out of sight.[3] Not until 5 A.M. on June 3rd had Howe

[1] Renaudin, exchanged soon afterwards, was made a rear-admiral on November 16th, 1794, and died on May 1st, 1809.

[2] Jean Bon Saint-André, in his report, makes no mention of the affair of the *Vengeur*. Not until July 10th, 1794, was the exaggerated story, much of which is still accepted in France, put forward by Barère in the Convention. Barère then announced, not only that three British vessels had been sunk, but also that the *Vengeur* had gone down firing at the enemy and with all her colours flying, while her people, preferring death to captivity in the hands of tyrants, cheered for the Republic, for Liberty, and for France. All this implied, of course, that the *Vengeur* never struck. Barère further suggested, if he did not actually declare, that Renaudin and the entire ship's company had shared the fate of the vessel. Thiers, by the way, also makes Renaudin to have perished. Upon the strength of Barère's declamations, the Convention decided that a small ivory model of the *Vengeur* should be suspended from the ceiling of the Salon de la Liberté. But when Renaudin reappeared, and when scores of other survivors of the gallant ship returned to France, the truth began to be realised by those in authority, and the project was not pursued. Not only Barère and Thiers, however, but also Lebrun and Lamartine, have allowed themselves to be carried away by the story of what never happened. The truth will be found in a *procès-verbal*, dated Tavistock, 1er Messidor, an II., and signed by Renaudin and other officers, which was first printed by M. Jal.—(' Rev. Brit.' vol. xxiii. 4th ser.)

[3] French authorities for the action of the 9th, 10th, and 13th Prairial: "Journal de J. B. Saint-André' (untrustworthy at all points, yet suggestive): "Précis des princ. Evénements,' by Admiral Kerguelen: *procès-verbal* signed by Renaudin, etc.; account by M. E. Dupaty, later of the Académie Française, who was in the *Patriote*; orders of Villaret-Joyeuse (Arch. de la Marine); reports of various captains (Sect. Hist. de la Marine); Report of Villaret-Joyeuse (published by M. Chasseriau), etc. The chief published English authorities, in addition to the official ones, are: Barrow, 'Life of Howe'; 'Mems. of Collingwood'; 'Life of Codrington'; 'The Naval Chronicle,' *passim*; 'A Narr. of the Procs. of H.M. Fleet,' etc. (4to, London, 1796); Marshall,

sufficiently refitted his fleet to be able to make sail. He then steered north-east, and at 11 A.M. on the 13th anchored, without further adventure, at Spithead, with his six prizes and all his fleet, except nine vessels of the line, which he had sent into Plymouth.

Rear-Admiral George Montagu had been ordered to cruise on the lookout for Vanstabel until May 20th, and then, if unsuccessful, to rejoin Howe. But in consequence of information which reached him, he took upon himself to cruise a little longer. In the interval, he recaptured some vessels of the Lisbon convoy, and from them he learnt that Villaret was at sea, looking, as he himself was, for Vanstabel. Montagu also learnt that Howe was no longer at the rendezvous off Ushant, but far to the westward. He, therefore, in compliance with the spirit of his orders, turned his head homewards, and on May 30th anchored in Plymouth Sound. The Admiralty, however, anxious to have the French-American convoy intercepted, at once ordered him to sea again, with a reinforcement, which brought his strength up to that set forth in the note.[1] He was directed to proceed off Ushant, and there await news from Howe, and, in the event of an action between the French and British fleets, to be ready to afford assistance in protecting damaged friends or in capturing damaged foes; but, above all things, to look out for the American convoy.

The *Audacious* reached Plymouth on June 3rd, with intelligence of the partial action between the fleets; but, no further orders reaching Montagu, he sailed on the 4th, and on the 8th arrived on his station. At 3.30 that afternoon he sighted and chased twelve sail in the E.S.E., there being a moderate breeze from the N.N.E.; and, half-an-hour later, he discovered eight of the strangers to be French line-of-battle ships; whereupon he formed a line of battle, and stood on to meet them. But, crowding sail, they stood into Bertheaume Bay, and Montagu at night tacked and stood off

---

'Roy. Nav. Biog.'; Steel, 'Navy List,' and 'Naval Chronologist'; Ralph, 'Nav. Chron.'; Charnock, 'Biog. Nav.,' and Brenton's and James's histories. The logs of the ships engaged have also been consulted.

[1] *Hector*, 74, Rear-Admiral George Montagu (B), Capt. Lawrence William Halsted; *Alexander*, 74, Capt. Richard Rodney Bligh; *Ganges*, 74, Capt. William Truscott; *Colossus*, 74, Capt. Charles Morice Pole; *Bellona*, 74, Capt. George Wilson; *Theseus*, 74, Capt. Robert Calder; *Arrogant*, 74, Capt. Richard Lucas; *Minotaur*, 74, Capt. Thomas Louis; *Ruby*, 64, Capt. Sir Richard Hussey Bickerton; *Pallas*, 32, Capt. Hon. Henry Curzon, and *Concorde*, 36, Capt. Sir Richard John Strachan.

under easy sail. This French squadron, under Rear-Admiral Cornic,[1] seems to have been sent from Cancale Bay to look out for Villaret.

On the 9th at 7 A.M., when the wind blew light from the north, Montagu sighted a fleet bearing west. It was soon made out to be a French fleet of nineteen ships of the line, three frigates, and two smaller vessels. As a matter of fact, it was the remains of Villaret's force returning to port. Five of the French ships, being wholly or

ADMIRAL ALAN, LORD GARDNER.

(*From a drawing by Geo. Dance, after a portrait by W. Daniell, painted in* 1794, *soon after Gardner had become a Vice-Admiral.*)

partially dismasted, were in tow of others. Yet, even deducting these, Villaret had a great superiority. Moreover, inshore of Montagu was Cornic's squadron of eight sail of the line. In these circumstances, the British Rear-Admiral deemed it advisable to avoid an action, and stood away to the southward. Villaret chased; but at 5 P.M., when his headmost ships were within four miles of

[1] An inexperienced man who had been lately raised to flag-rank, and who appears not to have been in the French Navy at all in 1791.

the British rear, he hauled upon a wind to the eastward, on the larboard tack, fearing lest, with his crippled vessels, he should be drawn to leeward of his port. Montagu then for a short time sought in vain for Howe; and, at 4 P.M. on the 10th, bore away for the Channel. On the 12th he anchored in Cawsand Bay. Villaret, in company with Rear-Admiral Cornic, had anchored in Bertheaume Bay on the 11th; and on the 12th, Rear-Admiral Vanstabel, with the long-expected American convoy, also arrived there. He had been previously joined by the *Montagnard*, and apparently, also, by the *Mont Blanc*.

For their services in these engagements, Howe received a diamond-hilted sword and a gold chain, and was visited on board

COMMEMORATIVE MEDAL OF LORD HOWE'S VICTORY OF JUNE 1ST, 1794.

(From an original lent by H.S.H. Captain Prince Louis of Battenberg, R.N.)

the *Queen Charlotte* at Spithead by the King and the royal family; Vice-Admiral Thomas Graves (2) was made Baron Graves in the Irish peerage; Vice-Admiral Sir Alexander Arthur Hood was made Viscount Bridport; Rear-Admirals Bowyer, Gardner, Pasley, and Curtis were created Baronets; and Bowyer and Pasley also received a pension of £1000 a year each, on account of their wounds. Certain Captains and Flag-officers, who are indicated in the table on page 226, were given medals; and the surviving first Lieutenants of every ship which had been in the line on June 1st, as well as he of the *Audacious*, were made Commanders. Several Lieutenants of the various flagships were also promoted. The officers, seamen, Marines, and soldiers who had been present received, of course, the thanks of both Houses. For Mr. James Bowen, who, both on

May 29th and on June 1st, had specially distinguished himself, as Master of the *Queen Charlotte,* special provision was made. In the navigating line he could not obtain further promotion. He was therefore reduced from the rank of Master, and was appointed a Lieutenant. He was rapidly promoted in his new career, being made a Commander in 1795 for his conduct in Lord Bridport's action, and a Post-Captain on September 2nd of the same year. He died a retired Rear-Admiral in 1835.

Several British ships had notoriously behaved themselves somewhat ill, both on May 29th and on June 1st. It would, therefore, have been but natural if courts-martial had followed; but the Government, anxious not to do anything to detract from the effect of the victory, did not take the initiative. Thus, only one court-martial was held. This was applied for by Captain Molloy, of the *Cæsar*. The court sat on board the *Glory,* at Portsmouth, from April 25th to May 15th, 1795; and, in the result, while admitting Captain Molloy's personal courage, it decided that he had not done his best to pass through the enemy's line on May 29th, nor to take up his proper station on June 1st. He was therefore sentenced to be dismissed his ship, and he was never again employed.

The *Culloden*, one of the other ships which had least distinguished themselves on June 1st, rendered herself further notorious towards the end of the year. She had been commanded, during the action, by Captain Isaac Schomberg, and that officer had been followed by Captain Richard Rundle Burges, and he again by Captain Thomas Troubridge. When, on December 3rd, the vessel lay at Spithead, the greater part of her crew suddenly burst into a state of mutiny, and barricaded themselves below. News of what had occurred was sent to the Admiral commanding in the Channel, and to Captain Troubridge, who was on shore; and the Marines were got under arms. On the morning of the 4th it was found that about two hundred and fifty of her people remained mutinous, and that the rest, including all the Marines but six, were well disposed. That afternoon, Admirals Lord Bridport, the Hon. William Cornwallis, and Colpoys went on board, and in vain endeavoured to persuade the men to return to their duty. Matters continued unsettled until the 11th, when Captain the Hon. Thomas Pakenham, going on board, succeeded in restoring discipline. The men were then mustered, and ten of the ringleaders seized and sent away for trial. They were court-martialled on December 15th. Two were acquitted and eight sentenced to be hanged. On January 13th, five of the eight were executed on board the *Culloden*. The other three were pardoned.

On June 22nd, Rear-Admiral the Hon. William Cornwallis, in the *Excellent*, 74, Captain John Whitby, with eleven other sail of the line, one 50-gun ship, and three frigates, sailed from Plymouth to escort an East India convoy clear of the Soundings, and to cruise in the Bay of Biscay. On September 7th, Lord Howe, in the *Queen Charlotte*, 100, with thirty-four sail of the line, including five Portuguese under Admiral de Valle, and with a number of frigates, left Torbay to cruise on the coast of France. After having made an ineffectual attempt to look into Brest Road, he steered down the Channel to protect the British, Spanish, and Dutch outgoing and incoming convoys. Bad weather supervened; and, on the 21st, Howe returned to Torbay. He again sailed in November; but he had no opportunity of again meeting the French fleet.

The main body of that fleet did not, in fact, put to sea until the last week of the year; but Rear-Admiral Nielly, with five 74's, three frigates, and a corvette, sailed from Brest early in November, in order to endeavour to intercept the homeward-bound British convoy from Portugal. On November 6th, at 2.30 A.M., in lat. 48° 25′ N. and long. 7° 53′ W., he fell in with the British 74's *Alexander*, Captain Richard Rodney Bligh, and *Canada*, Captain Charles Powell Hamilton, which had been engaged in escorting merchantmen out of Soundings. The British ships stood to the north-west and were chased. At daybreak, in order to confuse the enemy, they separated somewhat, the *Alexander* continuing her course, and the *Canada* steering more to the north. Of the enemy, two ships of the line and two frigates followed the *Canada*, and three ships of the line and one frigate pursued the *Alexander*. Between 8 and 9 A.M., both vessels had been gained upon sufficiently to allow of a running fight to begin. The British ships then endeavoured to rejoin for mutual support, but were prevented from doing so by the French admiral. At about 11 A.M. the *Alexander* was brought to close action by a vessel supposed to be the *Jean Bart*, which, in half-an-hour, was obliged to sheer off. The *Tigre* took her place; but in another half hour she lost her maintopmast, main yard, and mizen topmast. A third ship then took up the contest, until, at a little after 1 P.M., the *Alexander* had lost her main yard, spanker boom, and all three topgallant yards. She had all her other masts and yards wounded; her rigging and sails cut to pieces; her hull badly damaged and set on fire; and her hold nearly full of water. As the other French vessels were rapidly coming up, she struck. The *Canada* got safely into port.

The *Alexander* appears to have lost only forty killed and

ADMIRAL SIR RICHARD RODNEY BLIGH, G.C.B.

(*From a lithograph by Ridley, after the portrait by Opie.*)

wounded, and to have caused her opponent a loss, according to French accounts, of no fewer than four hundred and fifty men. She was carried into Brest. Her Captain, who, in the meantime, had been promoted to be Rear-Admiral, was very kindly treated by Captain Renaudin, the late commander of the gallant *Vengeur*; but there is ground for fearing that his people fared much less well. Bligh, after his exchange, was tried by court-martial on May 27th, 1795, and was most honourably acquitted.

After the evacuation of Toulon, Lord Hood, with the Mediterranean fleet, proceeded to Hyères Bay, and thence, hearing that the republicans in Corsica were in difficulties owing to lack of provisions and stores, detached several cruisers to prevent supplies from being thrown into the island. It was while engaged upon this duty that a sudden and terrible fate overtook the *Ardent*, 64, Captain Robert Manners Sutton. She was stationed off Villa Franca to watch two French frigates and a convoy, and, it is supposed, caught fire and blew up; but not a single soul survived to tell the tale.

Hood, however, meditated more active measures than a mere blockade; and, having opened communication with General Paoli, he got under sail on January 24th, and made for the Bay of San Fiorenzo. On the 25th the fleet was dispersed by a gale; and on the 29th, not without difficulty, it made Porto Ferrajo, in Elba. From that place Hood detached the 74's, *Alcide*, Commodore Robert Linzee, Captain John Woodley; *Egmont*, Captain Archibald Dickson, and *Fortitude*, Captain William Young (1); and the frigates *Lowestoft*, 32, Captain William Wolseley, and *Juno*, 32, Captain Samuel Hood (2), with transports, containing troops commanded by Major-General Dundas, to Mortella Bay, where they arrived on the 7th. The troops were landed that evening; and on the 8th a combined attack by land and sea was made on Mortella Tower, the *Fortitude* and *Juno* battering it for two hours and a half. The attempt miscarried, and the ships had to draw off, the *Fortitude* having lost 6 killed and 56 wounded, and having been set on fire. The fire from the artillery on shore, however, obliged the tower to surrender, after its little garrison had made a really magnificent defence. The next post attacked was the Convention Redoubt, which mounted twenty-one heavy guns, and was considered the key of San Fiorenzo. The seamen from the squadron, by incredible exertions, dragged some 18-pounders into a commanding position which had been supposed to be inaccessible, and, after a bombardment on the 16th and 17th, the redoubt was successfully stormed. The French retired to San Fiorenzo, where, on the 19th, they burnt the *Fortunée*, one of the two frigates which they had with them, and allowed the other, the *Minerve*, 38, to sink from the effects of the damage, which she had sustained from the fire of the British. They then retreated to Bastia. San Fiorenzo was occupied the same evening; and, within a few days, the *Minerve* was weighed and carried off. There being already a *Minerve* in the service, the prize was added to the Navy as the *San Fiorenzo*, 36. In this affair the British loss was small. General Paoli had been at hand to co-operate in case his assistance should be required.

Hood desired next to reduce Bastia; but Major-General Dundas considered the scheme impracticable with so small a force. Hood, therefore, who had, in the meantime, moved with the body of the fleet to San Fiorenzo, left his anchorage on the 23rd and made a demonstration off Bastia, cruising there for a fortnight, and gathering intelligence. He returned to San Fiorenzo Bay on March 5th; and, as Dundas still declined to act pending the arrival of 2000 troops from Gibraltar, the Commander-in-Chief merely embarked such soldiers as would supply the deficiency of Marines in his ships, together with a handful of artillerymen, and sailed on April 2nd, leaving, however, part of his fleet to watch Toulon. He anchored off Bastia on April 4th, and disembarked the troops, under the command of Lieut.-Colonel Vilettes, and some seamen, under the command of Captain Horatio Nelson, of the *Agamemnon*, at a spot a little to the north of the town. Exclusive of the Corsican patriots who co-operated, only 1248 officers and men were employed; while the garrison numbered fully 3000. Hood moored his fleet in crescent formation round the harbour, just out of reach of the batteries, and entrusted the inshore blockade of the harbour's mouth to Captain Benjamin Hallowell, with a flotilla of gunboats and armed launches. The *Impérieuse*, Captain William Wolseley, was detached, as a precautionary measure, to watch the island of Capraja, where the republicans had a depôt of stores.

On April 11th, when several British batteries had been erected in the heights and were ready to be opened, Hood summoned the town. But the French governor, General Lacombe Saint-Michel, refused even to read the communication. The batteries were, therefore, opened on the enemy's works, and were promptly and hotly replied to. The *Prosélyte*, a 12-pounder bomb, brought from Toulon, and under the orders of Commander Walter Serocold, was directed to act against one part of the defences, but, owing to a heavy swell, became for a time unmanageable under the guns of the batteries, and was set in flames by red-hot shot. Serocold, however, fought her gallantly, until he and his people were taken off by the boats of the squadron. The *Prosélyte* was ultimately burnt to the water's edge.

The siege continued with varying fortunes. Among the naval

officers who assisted Nelson on shore were Captain Antony Hunt (2), Commanders Joseph Bullen and Walter Serocold, and Lieutenants John Gore, Henry Hotham, John Stiles, George Andrews, and Charles Brisbane. On May 21st, after a siege lasting for thirty-seven, and negotiations lasting for four, days, the town and citadel surrendered. The capture cost the British army only 7 killed or mortally wounded, and 27 wounded or missing. The naval loss was Lieutenant Cary Tupper, of the *Victory*, and 6 seamen killed, and 1 lieutenant and 12 seamen wounded. As a result of this success, the island was induced by General Paoli to formally transfer its allegiance from France to Great Britain. The transfer was made to Sir Gilbert Elliot,[1] as viceroy, on June 19th; and the members of the Assembly took the oath of allegiance to King George.

Ere that time, the expected reinforcements of troops from Gibraltar had arrived; and preparations had been made to attack Calvi, which was still held by the republicans. Hood had gone away to watch Toulon, leaving Nelson as senior naval officer; and the latter transported troops to Port Agra, three miles from Calvi, and there landed them on June 19th. Hood sent a detachment of the *Victory's* seamen, with guns, etc., under the orders of Captain Hallowell and Commander Serocold, to assist; and on the 27th he himself arrived before the beleaguered town, and landed some guns. The siege lasted for 51 days, but, at length, on August 10th, the place capitulated. The British loss on the part of the army was 23 killed and 53 wounded, and on the part of the Navy, Commander Walter Serocold, 1 Midshipman, and 5 seamen killed, and 6 seamen wounded. Nelson was not reported as having been wounded; but, nevertheless, he was badly hurt by some particles of sand or gravel which had been driven up by a round shot; and eventually he lost the sight of one eye, though the injury does not appear to have kept him from duty even for a day. With Calvi were captured the French frigates *Mignonne*, 28, and *Melpomène*, 40. The former, being in bad condition, was never commissioned by her new owners; but the latter was added to the Navy as a 38-gun frigate.

Lord Hood's anxious watch on Toulon had been instigated by the knowledge that the French there were rapidly refitting such ships as had been left to them after the evacuation. The French,

[1] Sir Gilbert Elliot was the 4th Bart. of the creation of 1700. Born in 1751, he was created Baron Minto, of Minto, in 1797, and, having served as Governor-General of Bengal, was made Viscount Melgund and Earl of Minto in 1813. He died in 1814.

indeed, had actually put to sea on June 5th, with seven sail of the line and four or five frigates under Rear-Admiral Pierre Martin; and Hood had at once proceeded in search of them, with a fleet which, although it numbered thirteen sail of the line and four frigates only, had in it, owing to recent promotions, no fewer than eight flag-officers. Hood sighted the enemy on the 10th, and chased; and on the 11th he drove the French into Gourjean Bay, the only British ship fortunate enough to get within gunshot being the *Dido*, 28, Captain George Henry Towry. The Commander-in-Chief intended to follow the French, and to destroy them at their anchors; but he was prevented by unfavourable weather from making the attempt. A scheme for attacking the enemy with fire-ships had also to be abandoned; and Hood, with part of the fleet, proceeded, as has been seen, to Calvi, leaving Vice-Admiral Hotham, with eight ships of the line and four frigates, to watch Rear-Admiral Martin, who, however, during a spell of bad weather, managed to get out and re-enter Toulon.

At the beginning of November Hood went home in the *Victory*, leaving the command to Vice-Admiral William Hotham (1), who had his flag in the *Britannia*, Captain John Holloway. A few days later, on the 11th, a most serious mutiny showed itself in the *Windsor Castle*, 98, Rear-Admiral Robert Linzee, Captain William Shield. The crew expressed a dislike for the Rear-Admiral, Captain, first Lieutenant and Boatswain, and demanded that all should be changed. Vice-Admiral Hotham and Rear-Admiral Sir Hyde Parker (2) tried to settle the difficulty, and Shield asked for a court-martial, which honourably acquitted him. Nevertheless, Hotham, who seems to have behaved with regrettable weakness in this matter, sent to the *Windsor Castle* a new Captain, John Gore, and a new first Lieutenant and Boatswain, and even went the length of pardoning the mutineers. This incident throws some light on the condition of the Mediterranean fleet, save so far as particular ships were concerned, up to the time when the command passed into the firmer hands of Sir John Jervis.

Nothing of great importance happened during the year on the North American station, but in the West Indies events were many and rapid. Vice-Admiral Sir John Jervis, K.B., arrived at Barbados in the *Boyne*, 98, at the end of January, 1794, to take command. He was accompanied by Lieut.-General Sir Charles Grey, K.B., who was to command the troops to be employed against the French colonies. On February 2nd, an expedition composed of the ships mentioned in the note,[1] with about 6100 troops on board, sailed from Bridgetown, and on the 5th arrived off Martinique, of which island General Rochambeau was governor, and in which there were about 600 soldiers, including militia. But, although the island was ill-manned, its forts were well-armed, mounting as they did about ninety guns. The only French ships of war there were the *Bienvenue*, 32, at Fort Royal, and an 18-gun corvette at St. Pierre. The troops were disembarked at three several points, and, by March 16th, all the island except Fort Royal and Fort Bourbon, was in the possession of the British, who, however, by that time had lost 71 killed and 196 wounded or missing. The seamen co-operated with the troops on shore, and were most useful in dragging up guns and mortars. A division of 200 of them, under Lieutenants Thomas Rogers and William Gordon Rutherford, also greatly distinguished themselves in actual fight; and another, of 300 seamen with a few Marines, under Captains Eliab Harvey, William Hancock Kelly and Lord Garlies, materially aided in the reduction of Fort Bourbon. Lieutenant Richard Bowen of the *Boyne*, under the fire of Fort Louis and in broad daylight, boarded and attacked the *Bienvenue* on March 17th, but subsequently had to abandon her, as men could not be sent aloft to bend the sails on her yards. The success of

[1] Ships.	Guns.	Commanders.	Ships.	Guns.	Commanders.
Boyne	98	Vice-Admiral Sir John Jervis, K.B. Capt. George Grey.	*The following also shared in the operations at Guadeloupe, St. Lucia, etc.*		
Vengeance	74	Commodore Charles Thompson. Capt. Lord Henry Paulet.	*Assurance*	44	Capt. Velters Cornwall Berkeley.
Irresistible	74	,, John Henry.	*Experiment*, st.s.	44	Com. Simon Miller.
Asia	64	,, John Brown.	*Roebuck*	44	Capt. Alexander Christie.
Veteran	64	,, Charles Edmund Nugent.	*Ulysses*, st.s.	44	Com. Richard Morice.
Beaulieu	40	,, John Salisbury.[1]	*Terpsichore*	32	Capt Sampson Edwards.
Santa Margaritta	36	,, Eliab Harvey.	*Blanche*	32	,, Christopher Parker (2).[5]
Blonde	32	,, John Markham.	*Resource*	28	Com. Hon. Charles Herbert (1), act.
Solebay	32	,, William Hancock Kelly.	*Undaunted*	28	Capt. Robert Faulknor.[6]
Quebec	32	,, Josias Rogers.	*Inspector*	16	Com. Wyndham Bryer.
Ceres	32	,, Richard Incledon.	*Bulldog*	14	,, Edward Browne.
Winchelsea	32	,, Viscount Garlies.	*Seaflower*, cut.	14	Lieut. William Pierrepoint.
Rose	28	,, Edward Riou.[2]	*Tickler*, g.b.	..	,, Henry Wray.
Nautilus	16	Com. James Carpenter.	*Vernon*, g.b.	..	,, Thomas Henry Wilson.
Rattlesnake	16	,, Matthew Henry Scott.	*Teazer*, g.b.	..	,, J—— Hope.
Zebra	16	,, Robert Faulknor.[3]	*Vexer*, g.b.	..	,, R—— Smith.
Avenger	16	,, James Milne (1).[4]	*Spiteful*, g.b.	..	,, John Hindes Sparkes.
Vesuvius, bomb	8	,, Charles Sawyer.	*Tormentor*, g.b.	..	,, William Wells (2)
Dromedary, st.s.	24	,, Sandford Tatham.			
Woolwich, st.s.	44	,, John Parker.			

[1] Succeeded by Capt. Edward Riou.
[2] ,, ,, Matthew Henry Scott.
[3] ,, Com. Richard Bowen.
[4] Succeeded by Com. Henry William Bayntun.
[5] ,, Capt. Robert Faulknor.
[6] ,, ,, James Carpenter.

this daring venture of Bowen's led to an attack on the town of Fort Royal and its chief work, Fort Louis, under cover of the *Asia*, 64, and *Zebra*, sloop, the boats of the fleet being led in by Captains Nugent of the *Veteran*, and Riou, of the *Rose*, under the direction of Commodore Charles Thompson. On the 20th this attack was made, though the *Asia* was unfortunately unable to get into her assigned position. Commander Robert Faulknor, however, more than made up for the *Asia's* inability to co-operate; and running the *Zebra* close under the walls of Fort Louis, he jumped overboard with his ship's company and stormed and carried the work, greatly facilitating the success of the day's operations. The boats, meanwhile, attacked and took Fort Royal, the result being that, on the 22nd, General Rochambeau at Fort Bourbon surrendered, and the island passed into British hands. The British naval loss between the 16th and the 22nd was Commander James Milne (1), of the *Avenger*, and 13 seamen killed, and Commander Sandford Tatham, of the *Dromedary*, Lieutenants Thomas Henry Wilson and Thomas Clarke, and 25 others wounded. The *Bienvenue* was added to the Navy as a 28-gun frigate, under the name *Undaunted*, and the gallant Robert Faulknor was posted to the command of her, Lieutenant Richard Bowen being made, in his stead, Commander into the *Zebra*.

A garrison and a small squadron, under Commodore Charles Thompson, were left at Martinique; and on March 31st troops were embarked at Fort Royal for an attack on St. Lucia. The fleet arrived there on April 1st, and, in the course of the evening, the troops were landed at three different places. On the 4th, General Ricard surrendered. On the 5th, the greater part of the troops returned to Martinique; and on the 8th, Jervis sailed thence to attack Guadeloupe. On the 10th, he anchored in Gosier Bay in that island; but all his transports did not arrive till the 12th. On the 11th, however, some troops were landed under cover of the *Winchelsea*, 32, which silenced the enemy's batteries. Her captain, Lord Garlies, was the only person wounded on that occasion. On the 12th, Fleur d'Epée was taken by Major-General Dundas and Captain Robert Faulknor, and soon afterwards Fort St. Louis, Point à Pitre and a battery on Islot à Cochon were abandoned, thus handing over Grande Terre to the British. The conquest cost the Navy only 13 wounded. In the meantime a detached squadron, consisting of the *Quebec*, 32, Captain Josias Rogers, *Ceres*, 32,

Captain Richard Incledon, *Rose*, 28, Captain Matthew Henry Scott, and a sloop, had carried the works on the Saintes, on the 10th, without loss. Leaving small garrisons at Fleur d'Epée, Point à Pitre and other places, the rest of the troops quitted Grande Terre in transports on the 14th, and went round to Petit Bourg, on Basse Terre, where they landed without opposition. On the 20th, after some batteries had been carried, General Collot surrendered the entire

SIR CHARLES EDMUND NUGENT, G.C.H., ADMIRAL OF THE FLEET.

(From a lithograph by Ridley, after the portrait by R. Cosway, R.A.)

island but its dependencies. Major-General Dundas was placed in command, and the Vice-Admiral, with Sir Charles Grey, left the island.

But the British occupation of Guadeloupe was not for long accepted by the French. On June 4th, a squadron of nine vessels bearing the French flag appeared off Cape François, and, in the afternoon, anchored in Gosier Bay, there disembarking troops under Victor Hugues. The Royalist inhabitants behaved badly, and deserted the British; and Lieut.-Colonel Drummond, commanding in Basse Terre, had to retreat in boats to Grande Terre. The situation was reported, early on the 5th, to the Vice-Admiral, who was at St. Christopher; and he at once despatched reinforcements, following on the same day, with Sir Charles Grey, in the *Boyne*, with the *Veteran* in company, having sent the *Winchelsea* to Antigua, and the *Nautilus* to Martinique, for troops.

On June 7th, the Vice-Admiral and General arrived off Guadeloupe, and were there joined by Commodore Charles Thompson in the *Vanguard*, 74, Captain Charles Sawyer, with the *Vengeance*, 74. Sir Charles landed on Basse Terre, and Sir John Jervis, with the *Boyne*, *Vanguard*, *Vengeance* and *Veteran*, proceeded off Point à Pitre. A landing on Grande Terre was effected on June 19th, under cover of the *Solebay* and *Winchelsea*, at Anse à Canot without loss, two battalions of seamen co-operating under Captain Lewis Robertson, of the *Veteran*, and Captain Sawyer. Several skirmishes occurred, but without definite result; and, after a failure at Point à Pitre, the British forces were re-embarked on July 3rd. The Navy lost in the operations Captain Robertson, of the *Veteran*, and 6 men killed, and Lieutenant Isaac Wolley, Lieutenant of Marines John Mercer, and 27 men wounded, besides 16 men missing. The French remained at Grande Terre till September 27th, when, having received reinforcements from France, they landed at Goyanne and Lamentin in Basse Terre, whence they attacked the British camp at Berville. The British defended their position until October 6th, when they surrendered to Victor Hugues. The only post then remaining to them on the island was Fort Mathilde, the garrison of which, after a two months' siege, was cleverly taken off on the night of December 10th, by Captain Richard Bowen, of the *Terpsichore*. Bowen had the misfortune to be badly wounded while leaving the shore in the last of the boats. Vice-Admiral Sir John Jervis, who had gone home in November, had by that time been relieved by Vice-Admiral Benjamin Caldwell.

It has been seen that at the end of 1793, Commodore Ford was in possession of Jérémie, and other places in the French part of San Domingo. Meanwhile the Spaniards had taken possession of many posts on their side. On January 2nd, 1794, Ford detached the *Penelope*, 32, Captain Bartholomew Samuel Rowley offering terms of capitulation to Port au Prince. These were refused; and, in consequence, the Commodore blockaded the harbour. On February 3rd, Cape Tiburon was taken, after slight resistance; and on the 11th Aoul was carried. On May 31st, the *Europa*, 50, Commodore Ford, Captain George Gregory; *Irresistible*, 74, Captain John Henry; *Belliqueux* 64, Captain James Brine; *Sceptre*, 64, Captain James Richard Dacres (1), and three frigates and three sloops, with 1465 effective troops on board under Brigadier-General White, arrived in the Bay of Port au Prince from Cape Nicolas Mole. On June 1st, the *Belliqueux*, *Sceptre* and *Penelope* opened fire on Fort Brissoton, the *Europa* and *Irresistible*, under sail, lending occasional assistance; and, in the course of the day, troops were disembarked under the direction of Commander Thomas Affleck, of the *Fly*, sloop. The operations were interrupted at 6 P.M. by a most tremendous storm; but, in the consequent confusion and obscurity, the fort was rushed and carried. On the 3rd, the *Hermione*, 32, Captain John Hills, and the *Iphigenia*, 32, Captain Patrick Sinclair, bombarded a work at Bernadou to make a diversion during the advance of the troops; and, on the 4th, Port au Prince was taken possession of. There was little loss, the *Hermione* having 5 killed and 6 wounded, and the *Belliqueux* 10 wounded.

Tiburon, after its capture, was garrisoned by a small force under Lieutenant George Bradford of the 23rd Foot. Its main defences were a battery of three inefficient 18-pounders, and an armed transport, the *King George*. On December 25th, at dawn, a body of French from Aux Cayes made a descent, and sank the *King George* after she had made a plucky fight. They then drove out the garrison, who retired to Cape Donna Maria.

On the coast of Africa the French won a small and not particularly creditable success. On September 28th, a small squadron, under Captain Z. J. T. Allemande, approached Sierra Leone under British colours, and, suddenly changing them for French, began a bombardment of the town, which was entirely unprotected, and which quickly hauled down the British flag. In spite of this, firing was continued for nearly two hours; after which the French landed and began to plunder. The French commander studiously protected the mulattoes and half castes, but burnt the church, warehouses and residences of all British inhabitants. He later captured Banca; the garrison of which escaped. The French remained at Sierra Leone until October 23rd, and then, being very sickly, withdrew, destroying the Guineamen and other craft along the coast, and then returning home. They claim to have burnt or sunk during this raid 210 sail of British, Spanish and Portuguese vessels.

In spite of the numerous French losses, there were still in Brest, at the end of 1794, thirty-five sail of the line more or less ready for sea, besides five others that were being built or repaired.[1] But there was a great scarcity of stores, and there was immense difficulty in feeding the seventy-two thousand people in the town, who were more or less dependent on the government. It was, therefore, considered to be desirable to send some of these elsewhere, in order to relieve the pressure; and, at the same time, it was thought expedient to strengthen the French fleet at Toulon. In pursuance of these designs, six sail of the line, under Rear-Admiral Renaudin, who had been captain of the *Vengeur*, were filled up with six months' provisions, and sent out of Brest under convoy of the remainder of the Brest fleet, which was instructed to see them beyond the usual cruising-grounds of the British Channel fleet. This last had been joined by a weak Portuguese contingent. Owing to the scarcity at Brest, that part of the force which was merely to go out and return had but a fortnight's stores on board, and was, upon the whole, hardly fit to put to sea. The fleet, under the command of Vice-Admiral Villaret-Joyeuse, and consisting of thirty-five sail of the line, thirteen frigates, and sixteen small craft, sailed in the last week of December during a gale of wind, but, in going out, lost the *Républicain*, 110, and sustained so much other damage that it had to put back, and was not able to make an offing until December 31st.

Vague news of this reached England on January 2nd, 1795; and the British frigates *Flora*, Captain Sir John Borlase Warren, *Arethusa*, Captain Sir Edward Pellew, and *Diamond*, Captain Sir William Sidney Smith, were on that day despatched from Falmouth for Brest to ascertain what had really occurred. On the 3rd, being off the French port, Warren ordered the *Diamond* to look into the harbour, and, with an east wind, that ship began to beat up towards the entrance. At 2 P.M., Smith observed that three men-of-war, evidently French, were also working in. At 5 P.M. he anchored, so as to take advantage of the next flood tide, but he discovered that he was barely two miles from a ship of the line, apparently one of those vessels which he had seen beating to windward. At 11 P.M. the *Diamond* again began to work in, and, when the ebb tide made,

[1] In addition, there were building at Lorient one 80 and two 74's, and at Rochefort, one 110, one 80, and one 74. These, with all the ships at Brest, brought up the total of ships of the line in the French Atlantic ports to forty-six.

tacked between Bertheaume and Camaret Roads, so as to create as little suspicion as possible. She had previously passed close to a French frigate at anchor in Basse Buzée. At dawn on the 4th, Smith saw two vessels coming out, and fifteen small craft at anchor in Camaret Road, but he discovered nothing in Brest itself, and therefore bore up towards St. Mathieu. A little later, signals were made to him from the shore at Bertheaume, and, in consequence,

ADMIRAL SIR JOHN BORLASE WARREN, BART., K.B.

(From a lithograph by Ridley, after the portrait by Opie.)

the *Diamond* hoisted the French national colours. She stood on, and passed within hail of the line-of-battle ship, which was anchored off St. Mathieu, and which had jury yards and topmasts, and appeared to be very leaky. Sir Sidney was bold enough to ask the French captain if he needed help, and received a reply in the negative, and the information that the ship was the *Nestor*, 74, which, having suffered in a gale of wind, had left the Brest fleet three days earlier. Upon this the *Diamond* crowded sail, and rejoined her consorts, and, although the French frigate *Virginie*, 40, and the *Fougueux*, 74, which had lately been launched at Rochefort, and which had been escorted up the coast by the frigate, were quite close at hand, she safely rejoined Warren.

This exploit deserves attention because it indicates very pointedly the immense value to naval officers of a first-rate colloquial knowledge of a foreign language. Smith happened to speak French with admirable facility and purity. No one who did less could have accomplished what he effected. Seeing how exceedingly rare a thing it is to-day to encounter a British naval officer who can speak any language but his own, without at once betraying his lack of familiarity with it, it is unhappily doubtful whether, even if she were disguised as carefully as the *Diamond* was, and if she knew the private signals, a British cruiser could now, in war time, repeat the *Diamond's* audacious and successful reconnaissance.[1]

The gale, which had sent the *Nestor* back to port, damaged several other ships of the Brest fleet, and so much delayed the rest that the vessels destined for Toulon had to share their six months' stores among their consorts, and to surrender all idea of prosecuting the voyage at that time. A little later, during a fog, a division of eight sail of the line and some frigates parted company, and returned to port, but the other divisions still cruised together, chiefly perhaps for exercise, until January 28th, when they encountered a very violent storm, in which the *Neuf Thermidor* (ex *Jacobin*), 80, the *Scipion*, 80, and the *Superbe*, 74, foundered, with considerable loss of life, and the *Neptune*, 74, was wrecked on the rocks of Péros. The *Téméraire* made St. Malo; the *Convention* made Lorient, and the other part of the fleet, very crippled, made Brest on February 2nd. During its absence from port it had captured or destroyed about one hundred sail of merchantmen, besides the *Daphne*, 20, Captain William Edward Cracraft.

In the meantime, Howe, with the Channel fleet, had been lying at anchor, waiting for definite news of the French. On February 14th he sailed from Torbay, and, on the 15th, was joined

[1] In 1892, when the author was a passenger in H.M.S. *Northampton*, the Brazilian training ship, *Almirante Barroso*, entered Queenstown Harbour, where the cruiser lay at anchor. Upon the Brazilian captain putting off in his boat to visit his British colleague, inquiry was made for an interpreter; but no one among the officers of the British ship was found who could speak even French—much less Portuguese. The author, therefore, had to act as interpreter to the two captains.

off Plymouth by a British 74, and five Portuguese ships,[1] which brought up his strength to forty-two sail of the line, and about an equal number of frigates and small craft. He saw some foreign-bound convoys safely out of the Channel, and then, learning that the French were again in Brest, proceeded to Spithead.

As soon as Villaret had returned to port, every effort was made to again complete for sea the six French sail of the line intended for Toulon. By great exertions, this was done in time to enable Rear-Admiral Renaudin to sail on February 22nd. He reached his destination without serious misadventure on April 4th, with the *Formidable*, 80, *Jupiter*, 74, *Mont Blanc*, 74, *Jemmapes*, 74, *Révolution*, 74, *Tyrannicide*, 74, three frigates, and two or three small craft. This opportune reinforcement made the French fleet in the Mediterranean superior to the British.

Supplies were still short at Brest, and there was continued difficulty in refitting the ships there. Yet, early in May, it was found possible to send out Rear-Admiral Jean Gaspar Vence, with three seventy-fours, and six or seven frigates, to bring in a convoy of coasters, which had been collected at Bordeaux, in order to proceed up the coast.

It does not appear whether the sailing of this force was known in England; but, on May 30th, 1795, Vice-Admiral the Hon. William Cornwallis, with a squadron which is described in the note,[2] was

[1] *Vasco da Gama*, *Maria Primeira*, *Rainha de Portugal*, *Conde de Henrique* and *Princessa de Beira*, all 74's.

[2] Ships.	Guns.	Commanders.
Royal Sovereign	100	Vice-Admiral Hon. William Cornwallis. Capt. John Whitby.
Mars	74	„ Sir Charles Cotton, Bt.
Triumph	74	„ Sir Erasmus Gower, Kt.
Brunswick	74	„ Lord Charles Fitzgerald.
Bellerophon	74	„ James, Lord Cranstoun.
Phaeton	38	„ Hon. Robert Stopford.
Pallas	32	„ Hon. Henry Curzon.
Kingfisher [1]	18	Com. Thomas Le Marchant Gosselin.

[1] Detached on June 11th, with prizes.

The united French squadrons, after the junction of MM. Villaret-Joyeuse and Vence on June 15th, were composed as follows:—*Peuple*, 120; *Alexandre*, 74; *Droits de l'Homme*, 74; *Formidable*, 74; *Fougueux*, 74; *Jean Bart*, 74; *Mucius*, 74; *Nestor*, 74; *Redoutable*, 74; *Tigre*, 74; *Wattignies*, 74; *Zélé*, 74; *Brave* (rasé), 50; *Scévola* (rasé), 50; *Virginie*, 40; *Proserpine*, 40; *Insurgente*, 36; *Dryade*, 36; *Fraternité*, 40; *Fidèle*, 36; *Cocarde*, 36; *Régénérée*, 40; with another frigate, three armed ships, two brigs and two cutters.

detached from the fleet at Spithead to cruise off Ushant. On June 8th, being off Point Penmarck, Cornwallis sighted a number of sail E. by N. These ships were Vence's squadron returning with its convoy, which was a very large one. As soon as Vence had assured himself that the vessels in sight, and now in chase of him, were British, he stood for Belle Isle under a press of sail. The British sailed very unequally, and when, at 2 P.M., the *Kingfisher, Phaeton* and *Triumph* began to fire on the rear of the enemy, one at least of their consorts was hull down. As the leading French ships were already well under the island, Cornwallis signalled his vessels to close. At 4 P.M. he chased two French frigates, one with a ship in tow, in the S.W., and took the ship, which was cast off and abandoned as he approached. A little later, the leading British vessels exchanged shots with the batteries of Belle Isle. In the meantime, a few other vessels of the French convoy had been taken, and, having recalled his chasing ships, the Vice-Admiral stood off, leaving the enemy plying to windward for the anchorage in Palais Road. On the 11th, Cornwallis sent the *Kingfisher* into port with the prizes, and stood back to the S.E. to watch M. Vence.

By that time, news of what had occurred had reached Brest, and, as it was supposed by some French officers, and by the deputies there, that Vence was blockaded, all the available ships were ordered to proceed to his rescue, although, in fact, he could have reached Lorient in perfect safety without any assistance. On June 12th, therefore, Vice-Admiral Villaret-Joyeuse, in the *Peuple* (ex *Montagne*), 120, with Rear-Admirals Y. J. Kerguelen and Eustache Bruix, got under way, with nine sail of the line, two fifty-gun rasés, seven frigates, and four corvettes, and on the 15th, off Isle Groix, fell in with M. Vence, who was then on his way to Brest. The combined French fleet was then as given in the note above. On the 16th, at 10.30 A.M., while working off the land near Penmarck, with the wind W.N.W., the French sighted Cornwallis direct to windward, making for Belle Isle.

The *Phaeton*, after signalling that the enemy was of superior force, did not haul her wind, but stood on. Cornwallis, who probably had in his mind that he was in the presence merely of Vence and his convoy, did the same, and thus drew much nearer than he would have approached had he known how strong, as well as how numerous, were the French. But at 11 A.M., being obviously too weak to offer battle, he hauled to the wind on the starboard tack, under all sail, and formed a line ahead, the order being: *Brunswick, Royal Sovereign, Bellerophon, Triumph, Mars.* At 2 P.M., the French, then on the same tack as the British, separated into two divisions, one tacking and standing to the north, and the other continuing its course to the south. A little later the wind shifted to the north, and thus enabled the northern division to weather, and the southern division to lie well up for, the British squadron. At that time one French division bore, E. by N. from the *Bellerophon,* about eight miles, and the other, S.E., about ten miles, the one being on her starboard, and the other on her port quarter. In the night, however, during which the *Bellerophon* and the *Brunswick* had to cut away their anchors, and to throw overboard a quantity of gear and provisions in order to improve their sailing, the French formed in three divisions, and, at daylight on the 17th, were seen coming up fast, the weather division consisting of three sail of the line and five frigates; the centre division of five sail of the line and four frigates, and the lee division of four sail of the line and five frigates, two brigs, and two cutters; and the weather division being already abreast of the British rear.

At about 9 A.M., the French van ship, a seventy-four, opened on the *Mars,* and the frigate *Virginie,* 40, ran up on the lee quarter of the *Mars,* and repeatedly yawed to fire at her, the British ship, of course, replying. At 9.30 A.M., as the *Bellerophon,* of all the ships of the squadron, could least afford to lose a spar or a sail, Cornwallis ordered her ahead. She passed to leeward of the *Royal Sovereign,* which shortened sail for her, and the order of the line then stood: *Brunswick, Bellerophon, Royal Sovereign, Triumph, Mars.* Just before noon, all the British ships were engaged, each firing her stern and quarter guns as they could be brought to bear. At 1 P.M., the second ship of the French van took up the action, and at 1.30, the leading ship, having lost her main topgallant mast, sheered off, and dropped astern. For the following three or four hours the French van harassed the British rear, and, at length, the *Mars,* considerably damaged aloft, began to fall to leeward. Observing this, Cornwallis signalled her to alter course to starboard, or away from the French lee division, which was most troublesome to her; and then, in the *Royal Sovereign,* the Vice-Admiral himself bore round towards her, followed by the *Triumph,* and delivered raking broadsides into the bows of those French ships which were closest up with the chase. This manœuvre saved the *Mars,* and presently enabled Cornwallis to form anew a close order of battle. Four French van ships, which had bore up, hoping to secure the *Mars*, considered it wise to haul to the wind, and, although distant and desultory firing continued for a time, it entirely ceased at 6.10 P.M. Half-an-hour later the French shortened sail, and relinquished the pursuit.[1]

In the course of this admirably managed and celebrated retreat of Cornwallis, the *Mars* and *Triumph* were the only British ships

ADMIRAL SIR CHARLES COTTON, BART.

(*From an engraving by Page, after a family miniature.*)

that suffered from the enemy's fire. The *Mars* had her mainmast and her fore and main topsail yards damaged, and much standing and running rigging destroyed; but she had only twelve people wounded. The *Triumph* also was somewhat injured aloft; but she had no one hurt. All five ships, however, sacrificed their stern frames and galleries more or less in order to keep up the heaviest possible stern fire; and the *Triumph* cut away a large part of her stern, except the timbers, so as to improvise the necessary ports.

[1] 'Précis des Evénements,' by Kerguelen.

The failure to capture Cornwallis's little squadron is explained in French accounts by the statement that some of the French leading ships disobeyed signals and were badly handled, and that Bridport's fleet was sighted at the critical moment. The truth is that Bridport's force was never sighted at all. James points out that it is probable that the real cause of the failure was the moral effect produced by a ruse which was practised by the *Phaeton* on the morning of the 17th. Detached some miles ahead of her squadron, she made the signals for a fleet in the W.N.W., and, later, began pretended communications with this imaginary force to windward, indicating at the same time to Cornwallis that the supposed ships were of the line. This comedy was pursued until 6 P.M., when, by a strange chance, several small sail appeared in the quarter towards which all French eyes were by that time directed. The *Phaeton* then wore to rejoin her friends. That was enough. A short time afterwards Villaret tacked to the eastward. Thus, thanks to excellent discipline and faultless behaviour, combined with sound tactics, did five ships of the line make a triumphant escape from twelve, and from more than as many frigates.[1] Cornwallis in his modest dispatch said:—

> "I shall ever feel the impression which the good conduct of the Captains, officers, seamen, Marines, and soldiers in the squadron has made on my mind; and it was the greatest pleasure I ever received to see the spirit manifested by the men, who, instead of being cast down at seeing thirty sail of the enemy's ships attacking our little squadron, were in the highest spirits imaginable. I do not mean the *Royal Sovereign* alone: the same spirit was shown in all the ships as they came near me; and although, circumstanced as we were, we had no great reason to complain of the conduct of the enemy, yet our men could not help repeatedly expressing their contempt of them. Could common prudence have allowed me to let loose their valour, I hardly know what might not have been accomplished by such men."

It is characteristic of Cornwallis that his only allusion to the most gallant episode in the whole affair is the following:—

> "In the evening they made show of a more serious attack upon the *Mars*, and obliged me to bear up for her support."

---

[1] Cornwallis's thanks to his squadron were thus handsomely conveyed: "*Royal Sovereign*, June 18th, 1795. Vice-Admiral Cornwallis returns his sincere thanks to the Captains, officers, seamen, and Marines of the fleet under his orders, for their steady and gallant conduct in the presence of the French fleet yesterday; which firmness, he has no doubt, deterred the enemy from making a more serious attack. It would give the Vice-Admiral pleasure to put the whole of their exertions in effect by meeting a more equal force, when the country would receive advantage, as it now does honour, from the spirit so truly manifested by its brave men."

The thanks of both Houses were unanimously given to the participators in this action.

Cornwallis proceeded to Plymouth with his intelligence, and Villaret made for Brest; but, before he reached it, a gale from the north, lasting for twenty-seven hours, dispersed his fleet and drove him to take shelter under Belle Isle. There he collected his vessels, and, weighing, made sail; but scarcely had he done so ere, on June 22nd, the British Channel fleet appeared. Howe being ill, it was commanded by Admiral Lord Bridport. It had sailed from Spithead on June 12th and consisted of the ships set forth below.[1]

The Channel fleet had put to sea to protect an expedition bound, under Commodore Sir John Borlase Warren, in the *Pomone,* 40, for Quiberon Bay. This expedition, the proceedings of which will be narrated presently, had parted company on the 19th, near Belle Isle; and Bridport had then stood out from the coast with a view to preventing any interference from the direction of Brest, the absence from which of Villaret's fleet was then unknown. Warren's advanced frigate soon afterwards saw the French coming out from under Belle Isle; and the Commodore, altering course, sent a vessel with the information to Bridport. On the 20th Warren himself sighted the Commander-in-Chief; but he had already received an order from him to detach to the main fleet the three line-of-battle ships *Robust,* 74, Captain Edward Thornbrough, *Thunderer,* 74, Captain Albemarle Bertie, and *Standard,* 64, Captain Joseph Ellison, as a reinforcement.

Bridport, with his own fourteen sail of the line, kept between

[1] Lord Bridport's fleet in the action off Groix, June 23rd, 1795 :—

Ships.	Guns.	Commanders.
Royal George . .	100	Admiral Lord Bridport (W). Capt. William Domett.
Queen Charlotte .	100	,, Sir Andrew Snape Douglas, Kt.
Queen	98	Vice-Admiral Sir Alan Gardner. Capt. William Bedford.
London	98	Vice-Admiral John Colpoys (B). Capt. Edward Griffith.
Prince of Wales .	98	Rear - Admiral Henry Harvey (R). Capt. John Bazely (2).
Prince	98	,, Charles Powell Hamilton.
Barfleur . . .	98	,, James Richard Dacres (1).
Prince George . .	98	,, William Edge.
Sans Pareil . .	80	Rear - Admiral Lord Hugh Seymour (R). Capt. William Browell.
Valiant	74	Capt. Christopher Parker (2).
Orion	74	,, Sir James Saumarez, Kt.
Irresistible . . .	74	,, Richard Grindall.
Russell	74	,, Thomas Larcom.
Colossus	74	,, John Monkton.
Révolutionnaire .	44	,, Francis Cole.
Thalia	36	,, Lord Henry Paulet.
Nymphe	36	,, George Murray (3).
Aquilon	32	,, Robert Barlow.
Astræa	32	,, Richard Lane.
Babet	20	,, Edward Codrington.
Megæra, f.s. . .	14	,, Hon. Henry Blackwood.
Incendiary, f.s. .	14	,, John Draper.
Charon, hosp. s. .	44	Com. Walter Locke.
Argus, lugger . .	14	
Dolly, lugger.		

Warren and the French fleet, while Warren's three ships of the line were endeavouring to join from the N.W.; but, owing to a shift of wind, the Commander-in-Chief did not sight the enemy until 3.30 A.M. on June 22nd. The British were then in lat. 47° 4′ N., and long. 4° 16′ W. with Belle Isle bearing E. by N.½N., distant forty-two miles; and they were standing upon the starboard tack with a light wind from the S. by E.

Villaret appearing to have no desire for battle, Bridport at

ADMIRAL SIR ERASMUS GOWER, KT.

(From a lithograph by Ridley, after the portrait by Livesay.)

6.30 A.M. signalled the *Sans Pareil*, *Orion*, *Colossus*, *Irresistible*, *Valiant*, and *Russell*, his best sailing ships, to chase, and, at 6.45 A.M., ordered the entire fleet to do the same. Each ship thereupon set all possible sail that could be carried on a wind; and by 12 noon the centre of the French fleet, which was then standing in for the land, bore E.S.E., distant about twelve miles. It was then nearly calm; but such wind as there was had southed somewhat. At 7 P.M. the Commander-in-Chief signalled to harass the enemy's rear, and, at 7.25, to engage as the ships got up and to take stations for mutual support. By sundown the British fleet had gained considerably; but, at about 10.30 P.M., the ships were all taken aback, and it afterwards fell nearly calm. At 3 A.M. on the 23rd, however, a light breeze rose from the S.W. by S., and at daylight the French fleet was visible directly ahead, all the ships being in a crowd except three or four which tailed out. The rearmost of these was not more than three miles from the British van. The British were then much scattered, the *Irresistible* leading, the *Queen Charlotte*, which had been most excellently handled, being on her starboard quarter, and all the rest being astern. Behind the *Queen Charlotte* the next ships were the *Orion*, *Sans Pareil*, *Colossus*, and *Russell*.

At 4 A.M. Isle Groix bore on the *Queen Charlotte's* lee bow, that is nearly east, distant eight miles. The rearmost ship of the French fleet was then the *Alexandre*, which, as the *Alexander*, had been captured in the previous year from the British. She was a wretched sailer; and, at 5 A.M., she was taken in tow by a French frigate. Just before 6 A.M. she and a few of the ships next ahead of her began to fire their aft guns at the *Irresistible*, and at 6 the latter opened on the *Alexandre*, the example being soon followed by the *Orion*. Upon this, the *Alexandre* was abandoned by the frigate which had been towing her.

At about 6.15 A.M. the *Queen Charlotte* began to fire her starboard guns into the *Formidable*,[1] the next ahead of the *Alexandre*, the *Formidable* replying; but, at 6.30, after receiving in addition some shot from the *Sans Pareil*, the French ship caught fire on the poop. From that moment she suffered very severely, and began to drop astern; and when, at length, she lost her mizen mast, she bore up and struck. By that time, besides the *Irresistible*, *Queen Charlotte*, *Sans Pareil*, and *Orion*, the *Colossus*, *Russell*, *London*, and *Queen*, on the British side, and the *Peuple*, *Mucius*, *Wattignies*, *Nestor*, *Tigre*, and *Redoutable*, in addition to the *Alexandre*, on the French side, were, or had been, all more or less engaged. The other French ships, *Zélé*, *Fougueux*, *Jean Bart*, and *Droits de l'Homme*, were too far ahead, and the remaining British ships too far astern, to participate. The *Queen Charlotte*, which had already done so much, was so injured aloft as to have become almost unmanageable; but at 7.14 she was still able, by opening her broadside on the crippled

[1] Commanded by the celebrated C. A. L. Durand, Comte de Linois.

Alexandre, to compel that ship to surrender. At about the same time the *Tigre*, which had been already engaged by the *Queen Charlotte* and *Sans Pareil*, struck, after receiving the fire of the *Queen* and *London*.

It was not until a few minutes before 8 A.M. that Lord Bridport's flagship, the *Royal George*, passed ahead on the starboard side of the *Queen Charlotte*, which then lay repairing her damages aloft, but which almost immediately afterwards hauled her fore and main tacks on board to assist the Commander-in-Chief. At 8.15, although Rear-Admiral Kerguelen wrote of the British at that time that "s'ils avait bien manœuvré, ils auraient pu, ou prendre tous nos vaisseaux,

COMMEMORATIVE MEDAL OF LORD BRIDPORT'S ACTION, JUNE 23RD, 1795.

(From an original lent by H.S.H. Capt. Prince Louis of Battenberg, R.N.)

ou les faire périr à la côte," Bridport signalled the *Colossus*, then a mile and a half on the *Queen Charlotte's* starboard or weather bow. to discontinue the action; and, at 8.20, he made a similar signal to the *Sans Pareil*, which was about a mile and a half on her port bow, lying under the quarter of the *Peuple*. Directly afterwards the *Royal George*, being about half a mile from the west point of Isle Groix, bore up, and fired her starboard broadside into the stern and port quarter of the *Peuple*, and her other broadside into the *Tigre*, which she did not then know had struck. She thereupon wore round from the land, and from the French fleet, and was followed by the other British ships. The Admiral ordered the *Prince*, *Barfleur*, and *Prince George* to take the prizes in tow; and the fleet stood away with them to the S.W. The French, thus unexpectedly relieved, kept their wind, and, after making several tacks, took refuge between Isle Groix and the entrance to Lorient.

None of the British ships lost any spars; and the only ones which had any seriously damaged seem to have been the *Queen Charlotte*, *Sans Pareil*, and *Irresistible*. Among the officers killed were Lieutenant Charles Maurice Stocker, and Second Lieutenant of Marines William Jephcott, both of the *Sans Pareil*, and Captain Bacon of the 118th Regiment of Foot, who was in the *Russell*. Among the wounded were Captain Grindall, of the *Irresistible*, and Lieutenant Robert Mends, of the *Colossus*. The total loss in the British ships engaged was: *Irresistible*, 3 killed, 11 wounded; *Orion*, 6 killed, 18 wounded; *Queen Charlotte*, 4 killed, 32 wounded; *Sans Pareil*, 10 killed, 2 wounded; *Colossus*, 5 killed, 30 wounded; *Russell*, 3 killed, 10 wounded; *London*, none killed, 3 wounded; and *Royal George*, none killed, 7 wounded: total, 31 killed, and 113 wounded.

The total French loss cannot be stated; but the losses in the prizes were heavy, the *Tigre* losing 130, the *Alexandre* 220, and the *Formidable* 320; total, 670 killed and wounded in those three ships alone. The *Tigre* and *Alexandre* were added to the Navy by their old names. As there was already a *Formidable*, the prize of that name was adopted as the *Belleisle*, under the mistaken impression that the action had been fought off Belle Isle, instead of, as was actually the case, off Isle Groix.

As soon as Villaret was in comparative safety, he called a council of his flag-officers, who assured him that, if he anchored on the coast, he would imperil the rest of his fleet, which the British would certainly attack from windward. Under their advice, therefore, he anchored in the port of Lorient before 8 P.M.[1]

Bridport's strange and almost unaccountable forbearance provokes from Mahan the following remarks:—

"Such was the extreme circumspection characterising the early naval operations of the British, until Jervis and Nelson enkindled their service with the relentless energy and spirit inspired by Bonaparte on land. Those to whom St. Vincent and the Nile, Algeciras and Copenhagen, have become history, see with astonishment nine ships of capital importance permitted to escape thus easily from fourteen, forgetting the hold

[1] 'Précis des Evénements,' by Kerguelen, who was present with his flag in the *Fraternité*; Disp. of Villaret-Joyeuse; MS. notes of Adm. Linois: Report of M. Vence.

tradition has on the minds of men, and that it belongs to genius to open the way into which others then eagerly press. How the Admiralty viewed Bridport's action may be inferred from his retaining command of the fleet until April, 1800. The ships that reached Lorient had to remain till the winter, when they slipped back two or three at a time to Brest."[1]

Of the five British flag-officers present, three, viz., Bridport, Alan Gardner and Lord Hugh Seymour, received the thanks of Parliament. As James hints, it is difficult to understand the reason

ADMIRAL SIR WILLIAM DOMETT, G.C.B.

(From a lithograph by Ridley and Holl, after the portrait by Bowyer.)

for the selection, and why, while Gardner, whose flagship, the *Queen*, was not in action, was included, Colpoys, whose flagship, the *London*, was in action, was omitted. The anomaly was probably due chiefly to the meagre and almost grudging terms of Bridport's dispatch, wherein, for example, the *Queen Charlotte*, which had distinguished herself above all other ships that day,

[1] Some, however, went elsewhere.

was passed over unmentioned. That the action was a victory was true, but it left much to be desired. We may be pretty sure that had a Nelson, a Hawke, or even a Boscawen, commanded on the occasion, the fleet of Villaret would have been annihilated.

But, though the victory was thus unsatisfactory, it eventually cleared the way for the expedition to Quiberon. Consisting of the ships mentioned below,[1] and of many small craft and fifty sail of transports, having on board about 2500 French emigrants, commanded by the Comte de Puisaye, it entered the Bay of Quiberon on June 25th. On June 27th the troops were landed without loss, and drove back the few Republicans who opposed them. A vast quantity of arms for the disaffected population was also put ashore. Fort Penthièvre, on the northern extremity of the peninsula of Quiberon, soon fell; but on July 16th an attack, shared in by 200 British Marines, upon the French Republican army, under General Hoche, was repulsed; and the Royalists owed their safe retreat to the covering fire of some British small craft.[2] This misfortune led to desertion and encouraged treachery; and on the 20th the fort was surreptitiously handed over to the Republicans, and a terrible massacre ensued. Only about 1100 of the troops, and about 2400 inhabitants of the district, escaped to the fleet, leaving behind them about 10,000 stand of arms, and an enormous quantity of stores. Six newly-arrived transports also fell into the hands of the enemy. Warren took possession of the islands of Hoat and Hoëdic, and disembarked near Lorient, at their own request, 2000 of the people who had been brought from Quiberon. He also, but in vain, summoned Belle Isle. An attempt upon the Isle of Noirmoutier, at the mouth of

[1] Ships.	Guns.	Commanders.
Robust	74	Capt. Edward Thornbrough.
Thunderer	74	„ Albemarle Bertie.
Standard	64	„ Joseph Ellison.
Pomona	44	Commodore Sir John Borlase Warren.
Anson	44	Capt. Philip Calderwood Durham.
Artois	38	„ Sir Edward Nagle, Kt.
Arethusa	38	„ Mark Robinson (2).
Concorde	36	„ Anthony Hunt (2).
Galatea	32	„ Richard Goodwin Keats.

with several cutters, gunboats, etc.

[2] The *Pelter* and *Lark*.

the Loire, was unsuccessful; but later, the little Isle of Yeu was occupied.

In October, Warren was reinforced by the *Jason*, 32,[1] Captain Charles Stirling, with transports containing 4000 British troops under Major-General Doyle. Troops and stores were landed on Yeu, but the Royalist cause looked so black that, towards the end of the year, Yeu was evacuated, and the troops and stores were sent back to England.[2]

Lord Bridport cruised to protect the ill-fated expedition until September 20th, when he went to Spithead with some of his ships, leaving Rear-Admiral Henry Harvey to watch the French at Brest and Lorient. On the 17th and 18th of November, the British Channel experienced a most terrible westerly gale. Rear-Admiral Hugh Cloberry Christian, who had sailed for the West Indies with transports, troops, and a convoy, had to return in confusion to Spithead, having lost several merchantmen; and when he sailed again on December 5th, it was only to encounter another storm, which lasted for over a fortnight.

The events in the Mediterranean must now be described. Vice-Admiral Hotham, who was still in command there, loosely watched Toulon during the winter, using as his chief base the Bay of San Fiorenzo. While he was anchored there on January 16th, in a heavy cross swell, the *Berwick*, 74, Captain William Smith (2), which was refitting, rolled all three of her masts out of her. This led to a court-martial, and to the dismissal from their ship of the Captain, first Lieutenant and Master. Captain Adam Littlejohn was appointed in Captain Smith's place; and, directing him to follow the fleet as soon as the ship could be rigged with jury masts, Hotham sailed for Leghorn Road. It would have been, as the sequel will show, more prudent on his part to tow the disabled ship, supposing it to have been necessary for him to leave port immediately.

The observation of Toulon during Hotham's period of command was never very close or effective. Just previous to the accident, Commodore Perrée had safely returned thither, after a most successful cruise in the Mediterranean, with a squadron of six frigates.

[1] On board her was the Comte d'Artois.

[2] There is a very curious account of these Quiberon operations by Moreau de Jonnès in his 'Avent. de Guerre.' See also, 'Vie et Corr. de Hoche'; 'Relat. du Baron Antrechaus'; 'Méms. de Puisaye'; 'Méms. de Vaublanc'; 'Méms. sur la Guerre Civile' (1823).

The impunity which had attended his sally, and the removal of the British fleet from San Fiorenzo to Leghorn, encouraged the French to issue forth in greater strength, and to attempt the recovery of Corsica. The latter scheme was a mad one, in view of the "potential" fleet which still lay, comparatively speaking, close at hand. The proper way to recover Corsica would have been to begin by defeating Hotham. But the attempt was fatal to the *Berwick.* On March 3rd, Rear-Admiral Martin, with fifteen sail of the line and six frigates, carrying about 5000 troops, put to sea, and on the 7th sighted Cape Corse. As the advanced French frigates were about to look into San Fiorenzo Bay, they sighted the jury-rigged *Berwick* coming out. She was chased and engaged by the *Alceste,* 36,[1]

Princess Royal at Spithead
the 29th April 1791 —

W Hotham

SIGNATURE OF SIR WILLIAM HOTHAM (1), AFTERWARDS LORD HOTHAM, AS VICE-ADMIRAL.

Minerve, 38, and *Vestale,* 36, and, possibly,[2] by one or two ships of the line as well; and in less than an hour, after losing Captain Littlejohn, the only person on board who was killed, she was surrendered by Lieutenant Nesbit Palmer. Her jury-rig may be held to have excused her easy capture. Upon her officers being exchanged and tried by court-martial, they were honourably acquitted.

On March 8th, Hotham, who still lay at Leghorn, learnt that the French had been seen two days earlier off Isle Ste. Marguerite. He despatched the *Tarleton,* brig, to San Fiorenzo, with orders for the *Berwick* to join him off Cape Corse; and, on the 9th, he

[1] Lieut. Lejoille, commanding this frigate, was made a post-captain for his share in the affair.—Biog. by Hennequin.

[2] That any ships of the line were concerned is strenuously denied by all French historians.

weighed with the fleet, a list of which is given in the note.[1] After receiving certain intelligence from the *Moselle*, and apparently also from some other source, he altered course during the night from S.W. to N.W., and, on the 10th, his look-out vessels sighted the French standing towards Cape Noli, or, in other words, back towards Toulon against a S.W. wind. They had, no doubt, learnt from the *Berwick's* people that they were close to the British. On the afternoon of the 11th, the enemy's fleet of fifteen sail of the line, six frigates and two brigs, was seen in the south by some British ships of the line, which were five or six miles to windward of their main body. At dawn on the 12th they were again seen; and soon afterwards they bore up as if to reconnoitre. When she was within about three miles of the *Princess Royal*, the French van ship hauled to the wind on the larboard tack, and was followed in succession by the vessels astern. The wind was then very light, and there was a nasty swell from the west; but, towards evening, a fresh breeze sprang up from the S.W., and the British closed and formed in order of battle heading to the westward. During the night the

	[1] Ships.	Guns.	Commanders.
Van.	*Captain*	74	Capt. Samuel Reeve.
	Bedford	74	„ Davidge Gould.
	Tancredi (Neap.)	74	„ Chev. Caraccioli.
	Princess Royal	98	Vice-Admiral Samuel Granston Goodall (W). Capt. John Child Purvis.
	Agamemnon	64	„ Horatio Nelson.
	Minerva (Neap.), 32	..	
	Pilade (Neap.)	..	
	Lowestoft, 32	..	„ Benjamin Hallowell (actg.).
	Poulette, 26	..	Com. Ralph Willett Miller.
	Tarleton, brig,[1] 14	..	„ Charles Brisbane.
Centre.	*Illustrious*	74	Capt. Thomas Lenox Frederick.
	Courageux	74	„ Augustus Montgomery.
	Britannia	100	Vice-Admiral William Hotham (1) (R). Capt. John Holloway.
	Egmont	74	„ John Sutton.
	Windsor Castle	98	Rear-Admiral Robert Linzee (R). Capt. John Gore (1).
	Inconstant, 36	..	„ Thomas Francis Fremantle.
	Meleager, 32	..	„ George Cockburn.
Rear.	*Diadem*	64	„ Charles Tyler.
	St. George	98	Vice-Admiral Sir Hyde Parker (2), Kt. (B). Capt. Thomas Foley.
	Terrible	74	„ George Campbell.
	Fortitude	74	„ William Young (1).
	Romulus, 36	..	„ George Hope (1).
	Moselle, 18	..	Com. Charles Dudley Pater.
	Fox, cutter	..	Lieut. John Gibson.

[1] Detached, but rejoined on night of March 9th.

weather became squally, and the *Mercure*, 74, losing her main topmast, was allowed by Rear-Admiral Martin to part company and to proceed, attended by a frigate. She and her escort ultimately anchored in Gourjean Bay, where the *Berwick* also lay with a frigate in attendance.

On the 13th, soon after daylight, as the French showed no signs of any intention to engage, Hotham signalled for a general chase, and, the wind being fresh and squally, good progress was at once made. At 8 A.M. the *Ça Ira*, 80, the third ship from the French rear, fouled her second ahead, the *Victoire*, 80,[1] and carried away her own fore and main topmasts. This misfortune was at once taken advantage of by the *Inconstant*, 36, Captain Thomas Francis Fremantle, which had advanced far ahead. At about 9 A.M. she ranged close up on the port quarter of the *Ça Ira*, gave her a broadside, and stood on. The *Vestale*, 36, thereupon bore down, firing distantly at the *Inconstant*, and took the disabled 80 in tow; but the *Inconstant*, having tacked, again passed under the *Ça Ira's* lee, and repeated the broadside. In the meantime the *Ça Ira* had cleared away the wreck of her topmasts, and, opening fire, so punished the gallant *Inconstant* as to oblige her to bear up.

At 10.45 the *Agamemnon* placed herself upon the *Ça Ira's* quarter, and, aided for a time by the *Captain*, annoyed the French 80 till about 2.15 P.M., when, several French ships bearing down to protect their consort, Captain Nelson dropped into his station in the line. During this time there had also been a partial action between the *Bedford* and *Egmont* and the three French rear ships; but all firing ceased when the *Agamemnon* bore up. The French then put about on the port tack, and kept close to the wind under all sail, the wind being moderate from the S.S.E. The British fleet followed on a port line of bearing with all possible despatch. In the course of the night, by accident or mismanagement, the *Sans Culotte*, 120, separated from her consorts, so that the French were left with thirteen two-deckers against the British four three- and eleven two-deckers. During the night, also, the *Censeur*, 74, instead of the *Vestale*, 36, took the *Ça Ira* in tow, and, with her, fell astern and to leeward of the French line.

At sunrise on the 14th, Genoa bore N.E., distant about twenty miles. The French were seen to windward, standing as before on the port tack with a moderate south wind. At 5.30 A.M., the breeze

[1] Ex-*Languedoc*.

changed to the N.W., thus bringing the British fleet to windward. At 6.30 the *Captain* and *Bedford*, by signal, stood for, and engaged, the *Censeur* and *Ça Ira*. The *Captain*, being well ahead of her consort, had to sustain alone the broadsides of both French ships for fifteen minutes, ere she could make effectual return; and, when she had been engaged for an hour and a half, she was very badly injured aloft, and had received serious damage to her hull and boats as well. Captain Reeve, therefore, signalled for assistance, and was presently towed clear. The *Bedford*, also, was eventually obliged to discontinue the engagement, and to be towed out of the line. But, in the interval, the *Illustrious* and *Courageux* had made sail to support the *Captain* and *Bedford*, and had got well ahead, and somewhat to leeward, of the British line. To cover the *Ça Ira* and *Censeur* from these, Rear-Admiral Martin ordered his fleet to wear in succession and to form line upon his van ship, the *Duquesne*, 74. His design was to pass on the starboard tack to leeward of the British line, which was then on the port tack, and to windward of his threatened ships. The *Duquesne*, in the light wind, came round slowly: in fact, just then, nearly every ship in both fleets was more or less out of control, owing to the lack of breeze; and in the consequent confusion the *Lowestoft's* stern was exposed to a distant fire from the *Duquesne's* port batteries. But Captain Hallowell saved his people by ordering all, except the officers and the man at the wheel, to go below; and he suffered only a little aloft ere the attention of the French 74 was taken off by the Neapolitan frigate *Minerva*. When, at length, the *Duquesne* got round on the starboard tack, she failed to obey the signal and, instead of leading her line to leeward of the British van, led it to windward of it.

At 8 A.M., the *Illustrious* began, at a distance of a little more than a quarter of a mile, to engage in succession the *Duquesne* and the *Victoire*. She and the *Courageux* subsequently kept up a hot fire with these ships and with the *Tonnant*. At 9 A.M. the *Illustrious* lost her fore-topmast, and, at 9.15, her main mast, which also brought down her mizen. Her other spars were by that time badly wounded, and her hull was mauled in every direction; and the *Courageux*, which had lost her main and mizen masts, was in little better condition. Owing to the calm, the remainder of the French line could not get up to them, nor, on the other hand, could assistance reach them. But, happily, the three French ships at length drifted ahead, and so relieved them from a situation which was at one time extremely perilous. After very little more firing, the French abandoned the crippled *Ça Ira* and *Censeur*, and, as the breeze freshened, stood away under all sail to the westward. The action, which had begun at 6.20 A.M., entirely ceased at about 2 P.M., when Hotham, influenced by the condition of his van ships, thought it desirable not to tack in pursuit. The two fleets in consequence soon lost sight of one another. The *Ça Ira*[1] and *Censeur*, which had made a most gallant defence, and had lost together about 400 killed and wounded, had, in the meantime, been taken possession of. The loss in the other French ships is not known.[2]

The allied loss in personnel was as follows: *Captain*, 3 killed, 19 wounded; *Bedford*, 7 killed, 18 wounded; *Tancredi*, 1 killed, 5 wounded; *Princess Royal*, 3 killed, 8 wounded; *Agamemnon*, 0 killed, 13 wounded; *Illustrious*, 20 killed, 70 wounded; *Courageux*, 15 killed, 33 wounded; *Britannia*, 1 killed, 18 wounded; *Egmont*, 7 killed, 21 wounded; *Windsor Castle*, 6 killed, 31 wounded; *Diadem*, 3 killed, 7 wounded; *St. George*, 4 killed, 13 wounded; *Terrible*, 0 killed, 6 wounded; *Fortitude*, 1 killed, 4 wounded; *Inconstant*, 3 killed, 14 wounded; and *Minerva*, 0 killed, 4 wounded; total, 74 killed, and 284 wounded. No commissioned officers were killed, but among the wounded were Lieutenants Wilson Rathbone, of the *Captain*, Thomas Miles, of the *Bedford*, Thomas Hawker, of the *Windsor Castle*, and Robert Honeyman, of the *St. George*.

James estimates that, on March 14th, the relative strength of the two fleets, as regards ships of the line, was, British, 14 sail; 557 guns, throwing broadsides weighing 12,711 lbs.; and 8810 men; and French, 13 sail; 490 guns, throwing broadsides weighing 12,307 lbs.; and 9520 men. On the earlier days, of course, the French had a slight superiority in every respect.

Again, as in the case of the action off Isle Groix, it was an unsatisfactory victory. Hotham took two ships of the line, but gained little credit, seeing that he might have, and should have, done much more.

[1] It is stated in French accounts that Capt. Coudé, of the *Ça Ira*, surrendered his sword to Vice-Admiral Goodall, and that the latter said: "Sir, I will keep this glorious sword for myself, but I beg you to accept mine in recognition of your noble courage."

[2] French authorities for this action: 'Précis des Evénements,' etc., by Kerguelen; Reports of Marec, in the *Moniteur*; Letter of Capt. Coudé (of the *Ça Ira*); and papers of Martin, Coudé, Savary, etc., in the Arch. de la Marine. The published account of the Republican deputy, Le Tourneur, who was present, is recognised, even by the French, to be mendacious.

Taking in tow his dismasted ships and the prizes, he bore away for Spezzia Bay. On the night of the 17th, in a S.E. gale, the *Meleager*, with the *Illustrious* in tow, separated from the fleet; and, when the hawser parted and a new one could not be passed from the frigate, the *Illustrious* hove to, labouring heavily, shipping much water, and losing her jury masts by the board. At dawn on the 18th, as land was seen ahead, both ships headed to the eastward. At noon the *Meleager* parted company. At 2 P.M., after having experienced various additional trials, Captain Frederick, upon making the land eastward of the Gulf of Spezzia, delivered up charge of his ship to a self-professed pilot; but the man, at 7.30 P.M., managed to run the vessel ashore in Valence Bay, between Spezzia and Leghorn; and the ship became a wreck. The arrival of the *Tarleton*, on the evening of the 19th, of the *Lowestoft*, on the evening of the 20th, and, eventually, of other craft from the fleet, enabled the men and part of the stores to be taken off; but the *Illustrious* had to be set on fire and destroyed. On the 25th, after the damaged ships had been partially repaired, the fleet weighed from Spezzia Bay, and on the 26th anchored off San Fiorenzo, where it lay refitting until April 18th, when Hotham, by that time promoted to be Admiral of the Blue, left his prizes behind, and proceeded to Leghorn, where he anchored on the 27th.

It has already been noted that, on April 4th, Rear-Admiral Renaudin, with six sail of the line, three frigates and two or three corvettes, safely reached Toulon from Brest, and gave Martin, who on March 22nd had been made a Vice-Admiral, seventeen serviceable sail of the line. Martin, after having lain for a time in Hyères Bay, moved into the Road of Toulon, where he had much trouble with the crews of some of the Toulon ships, who became mutinous, until, thanks to the influence of the Republican deputy, Niou, who worked upon their patriotism, the men, repentant, pledged themselves "to purge their offence in the blood of the enemies of the state." Hoping to profit by the sentiments thus aroused, Martin put to sea on June 7th with his seventeen sail of the line, six frigates, and two or three smaller craft.

On May 8th, anticipating, perhaps, for the moment that the French Toulon fleet might have some idea of proceeding to the Atlantic, Hotham sailed from Leghorn to cruise off Cape Mola, the S.W. point of Minorca; and he was there joined on June 14th by nine sail of the line from Gibraltar and England, under Rear-

Admiral Robert Man (3). These ships were the *Victory*, *Barfleur*, *Gibraltar*, *Bombay Castle*, *Saturn*, *Cumberland*, *Defence*, *Culloden* and *Audacious*. Hotham cruised till the 24th, when he bore up for the eastward, and on the 29th anchored in San Fiorenzo Bay. On July 4th, he detached Commodore Nelson in the *Agamemnon*, 64, with the *Meleager*, *Ariadne*, *Moselle* and *Mutine*, to proceed to Genoa, and then to cruise along the coast to the westward; and, on the 7th, being off Cape del Melle, Nelson discovered the Toulon fleet about fifteen miles to the N.W. In the evening, the French chased him, and in the night they nearly came up with the *Moselle*. At 7.20 A.M., on the 8th, Nelson, being off Cape Corse, began to fire guns as signals to the fleet at San Fiorenzo; and, by 9.30 A.M., the French could see the British fleet of twenty-two sail of the line at anchor in the bay. They therefore relinquished the chase.

The fleet was, however, neither fit nor able to sail at once. Many ships were refitting or watering, and the wind blew right into the bay; but at 9 P.M. Hotham's fleet succeeded in getting under way, and in taking advantage of the land wind. The fleet, when rejoined by Nelson's squadron, was composed of the ships named in the note.[1]

On the 9th, having cleared the land, Hotham steered to the west under all sail, with a S.S.W. wind. On the 12th, being off Isle du Levant, he learnt that the French had been seen a few hours earlier to the south of *Hyères*, and consequently he prepared for action, and made sail to the S.W. In the night a heavy gale from the W.N.W. split the main-topsails of several British ships, and on

[1] Ships.	Guns.	Commanders.	Ships.	Guns.	Commanders.
Britannia	100	Admiral William Hotham (B). Capt. John Holloway.	*Terrible*	74	Capt. George Campbell.
			Defence	74	„ Thomas Wells (1).
			Egmont	74	„ John Sutton.
Victory	100	Rear-Admiral Robert Man (3) (B). Capt. John Knight (2).	*Culloden*	74	„ Thomas Troubridge.
			Bedford	74	„ Davidge Gould.
Princess Royal	98	Vice-Admiral Samuel Granston Goodall (R). Capt. John Child Purvis.	*Courageux*	74	„ Benjamin Hallowell.
			Audacious	74	„ William Shield.
St. George	98	Vice-Admiral Sir Hyde Parker (2), Kt. (R). Capt. Thomas Foley.	*Guiscardo* (Neap.)	74	
			Samnita (Neap.)	74	
			Agamemnon	64	Commod. Horatio Nelson.
Windsor Castle	98	Vice-Admiral Robert Linzee (W). Capt. John Gore (1).	*Diadem*	64	Capt. Charles Tyler.
			Meleager	32	„ George Cockburn.
Blenheim	90	„ John Bazely (1).	*Cyclops*	28	„ William Hotham (2).
Gibraltar	80	„ John Pakenham (1).	*Ariadne*	24	Capt. Robert Plampin.
			Comet	14	
Captain	74	„ Samuel Reeve.	*Eclair*	20	
Fortitude	74	„ William Young (1).	*Flèche*	20	Com. Thomas Boys (1).
Bombay Castle	74	„ Charles Chamberlayne.	*Resolution*, cutter		
			Moselle	18	Com. Charles Brisbane.
Saturn	74	„ James Douglas (2).	*Mutine*	12	
Cumberland	74	„ Bartholomew Samuel Rowley.			

the 13th, at dawn, when the wind was still fresh and there was a heavy swell, and while these ships were bending new sails, the French were seen about five miles off on the lee beam, standing in very scattered order on the starboard tack. The British were then standing on the port tack to the southward. At 3.45 A.M. Hotham signalled his fleet to form on a starboard, and, an hour later, on a larboard line of bearing, and preserving that order, to make all possible sail. The professed object of this was to keep the wind and to cut off the enemy from the shore.

At 8 A.M. the French fleet, formed in a close line on the port tack about two points off the wind, which was from the west, was

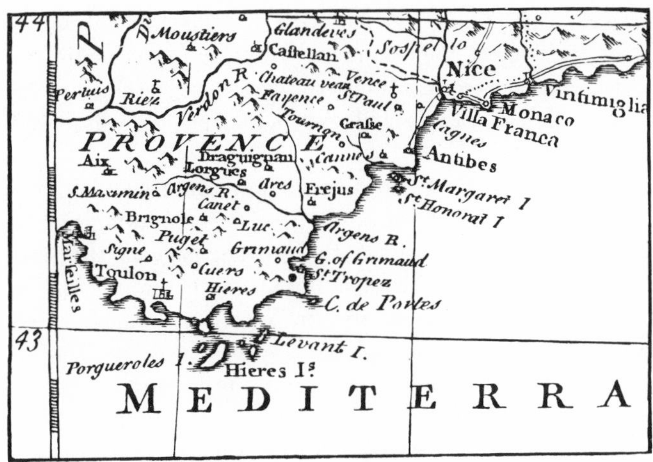

SCENE OF HOTHAM'S ACTION, JULY 13TH, 1795.

doing its best to get away without fighting. Hotham, therefore, made the signal for a general chase, directing his ships to take suitable stations for mutual support and to engage the enemy as they came up with him. In the course of the morning the wind moderated, and southed somewhat; and at noon, in consequence of the eagerness of the chase and of the unequal sailing of the ships, although the French rear, bearing N.N.E., was only three-quarters of a mile from the British van, the British rear ship was nearly eight miles to the W.S.W. At 12.30 a shift of wind from S.W. by N. to N., brought the starboard broadsides of the three rear French ships to bear upon the British van, and especially upon the *Victory*, *Culloden* and *Cumberland*, which led it. This brought on a partial action, in which the French ship *Alcide*, 74, soon suffered very severely. By 1.30 the *Culloden* also had her main topmast shot away; but she continued to use every effort to close with the enemy. Just before 2 P.M. the *Alcide* struck[1] to the *Cumberland*, which, not stopping to take possession, passed on to the second ship from the French rear. As she did so, the French frigate *Alceste*, 36, Captain Hubert, which, with the *Justice*, had approached to take the *Alcide* in tow, lowered a boat for the purpose. This was cut in two by a shot from one of the British ships; and the French frigates, very ably handled, made off. At that time the *Agamemnon*, *Blenheim*, *Captain* and *Defence*, were just getting into action; but at 2.42 P.M., when the *Cumberland*, having assisted in driving off the *Justice*, had almost got up with another French ship of the line near the rear of the column, a signal, to the general astonishment, was made to discontinue the action. The *Victory* had to repeat it, with the *Cumberland's* pennants, ere that ship paid any attention.

At that moment Cape Roux[2] bore from the *Victory* N.W. ½ W. distant twelve miles. It is true that the French, owing to a change of wind to the east, had gained the weather gage on the starboard tack, and were standing with a light breeze towards the bay of Fréjus, while the British centre and rear were almost becalmed; but it turned out that, as the breeze again shifted at about 7 P.M. to the south-west, Vice-Admiral Martin's progress to his anchorage was very slow. "Had the British fleet," says an officer,[3] who was present in the *Victory*, "only put their heads the same way as the enemy's and stood inshore at four o'clock, the whole of the French line might have been cut off from the land, taken, or destroyed; and, even afterwards, they might have been followed into Fréjus Bay, and wholly destroyed."

Of the few British ships engaged in what James calls "this miserable action," the *Culloden* alone lost a mast. The *Victory* and *Cumberland*, however, suffered considerably aloft. The losses in personnel were, *Culloden*, 2 killed, 5 wounded; *Victory*, 5 killed, 15 wounded; *Blenheim*, 2 killed, 2 wounded; *Captain*, 1 killed; and *Defence*, 1 killed, 6 wounded: total, 11 killed and 28 wounded. The *Cumberland*, strange to say, had no one hurt. No commissioned officers were killed. Among those wounded were Lieu-

[1] This is not admitted by the French. [2] The French call the action by this name.
[3] Admiral Sir Edward Hamilton, Bart.

tenants Tristram Whitter, of the *Culloden*, and John Hinton, of the *Victory*. Soon after having struck, the *Alcide* caught fire in the foretop. The conflagration could not be stayed, and, spreading till about 3.45 P.M., then caused an explosion, which blew up the vessel with more than half her crew.

The French fleet returned to Toulon. The British went, first to San Fiorenzo, and then to Leghorn. Hotham sailed again on August 6th, and on the 8th looked into Toulon Road, where he saw the French fleet. He then detached Commodore Nelson, in the *Agamemnon*, with the *Inconstant*, *Meleager*, *Tartar*, *Southampton*, *Ariadne*, and *Speedy*, to co-operate with the Austrian and Sardinian armies in Genoese territory, and himself stood to the eastward. On August 26th, Nelson's squadron, under Nelson's personal direction, cut out of the bays of Alassio and Langueglia, near Vado, two French gun brigs, two five-gun galleys, and five vessels laden with stores, and destroyed two other vessels, without losing a man.

The French Government was at that time anxious to make some kind of demonstration in the neighbourhood of Newfoundland, but was unwilling to detach from the Brest fleet any force for such a purpose. On the contrary, it was anxious rather to strengthen that fleet. It therefore directed Rear-Admiral Joseph de Richery,[1] with the *Victoire*, 80, *Barras*, 74, *Jupiter*, 74, *Berwick*, 74, *Résolution*, 74, *Duquesne*, 74, and the frigates *Embuscade*, *Félicité*, and *Friponne*, to seize an opportunity to slip out of Toulon, and then proceed to Newfoundland, finally returning to Brest. De Richery, therefore, put to sea on September 14th.

News of the evasion did not reach Hotham at San Fiorenzo until September 22nd; and not until October 5th was Rear-Admiral Robert Man (3), with the *Windsor Castle*, 98, *Cumberland*, 74, *Defence*, 74, *Terrible*, 74, *Audacious*, 74, and *Saturn*, 74, and the frigates *Blonde* and *Castor*, detached in pursuit. The French had thus a start of three weeks, and, as will be seen later, Man naturally failed to be of any service. Indeed, the method in which he carried out his mission led later to the imperilling of the whole British fleet in the Mediterranean. The laxity displayed by Hotham on that occasion, both in regard to the observation of the French movements at Toulon, and with regard to the pursuit of the escaped force, offers additional proof of that officer's unfitness for the very important com-

[1] Born at Allons, Provence. He had been expelled from the Navy during the Terror, but afterwards reinstated.

mand with which he had been entrusted. Moreover, de Richery's escape led to immediate bad results, even in European waters.

Hotham had detached for England in the early autumn the *Fortitude*, 74, Captain Thomas Taylor (2), *Bedford*, 74, Captain Augustus Montgomery, and the French prize 74, *Censeur*, which was jury-rigged and armed *en flûte*, and which was commanded by Captain John Gore (1). This squadron left Gibraltar for the Channel on September 25th, reinforced by the *Argo*, 44, Captain Richard Rundle Burges, *Juno*, 32, Captain Lord Amelius Beauclerk, *Lutine*, 32, Commander William Haggitt (acting), and *Tisiphone*, fireship, Commander Joseph Turner, with a valuable convoy of sixty-three sail from the Levant. That same night the *Argo*, *Juno*, and thirty-two of the convoy parted company, the remainder keeping with the senior officer until October 7th, when, being off Cape St. Vincent, they fell in with de Richery's squadron. Signal was at once made for the convoy to disperse, and the *Fortitude*, *Censeur*, and *Bedford* formed line so as to show as good a face as possible to the enemy. But hardly had the line been formed, ere the *Censeur* rolled away her foremast, and was forced to drop astern; and as the French were rapidly approaching, Captain Taylor deemed it proper to bear up. This was soon after 1 P.M. At 1.50 the leading French ship opened fire on the *Censeur*, which made a spirited return to the best of her ability, and was assisted by the after guns of the *Fortitude* and *Bedford*. In the meantime the French frigates were picking up the merchantmen. At 2.30 the *Censeur*, having expended nearly all her powder, and having lost her two remaining masts, struck. The other British men-of-war escaped; but, of the convoy, thirty out of thirty-one sail were taken. The thirty-two merchantmen with the *Argo* and *Juno* safely reached their destination. De Richery, with his prizes, put into Cadiz, where he may be left for the present.

This squadron of de Richery's was not the only one which, in the autumn of 1795, escaped from Toulon, owing, to some extent, to the bad management or incompetence of Hotham. Towards the end of September, Commodore Honoré Ganteaume, with the *Mont Blanc*, 74, *Junon*, 40, *Justice*, 40, *Artémise*, 36, *Sérieuse*, 36, *Badine*, 28, and *Hasard*, 16, left Toulon expressly to intercept the convoy, part of which subsequently fell into the hands of de Richery. That convoy was supposed by the French to be then to the eastward of Malta; and Ganteaume steered for the Levant, where he not only made many prizes but also raised the blockade of Smyrna, in which port two French frigates and a corvette had been shut up by the *Aigle*, 38, Captain Samuel Hood (2), and the *Cyclops*, 28, Captain William Hotham (2). Ganteaume cruised in the Archipelago until the *Justice* was dismasted in a storm. He then made for the Dardanelles, but, learning that two British ships of the line and three or four frigates were in search of him, and conscious that, as the French had not respected the neutrality of the Turkish ports, the British would attack him no matter where he might anchor, he left the *Justice*, and made for the westward. On December 27th, the British squadron under Captain Thomas Troubridge, consisting of the *Culloden*, 74, *Diadem*, 64, *Inconstant*, 36, *Flora*, 36, and *Lowestoft*, 32, being off Cape Matapan, chased the *Badine*, which had been detached by Ganteaume expressly to mislead his enemy. The *Badine* could not rejoin, and took refuge in the Gulf of Coron; but Ganteaume, escaping pursuit, re-entered Toulon on February 5th, 1796.

On November 1st, 1795, Hotham struck his flag, and was temporarily succeeded by Vice-Admiral Sir Hyde Parker (2). On November 11th the fleet left Leghorn, and, on the 20th, put into San Fiorenzo Bay. On the 30th, there arrived from Portsmouth the *Lively*, 32, Captain Lord Garlies, having on board Admiral Sir John Jervis, who had been appointed Commander-in-Chief. On December 3rd, Jervis shifted his flag from the *Lively* to the *Victory*, and, on the 13th, he sailed with the fleet to cruise off Toulon.

Since the commencement of hostilities in 1793, the political situation had altered considerably to the disadvantage of Great Britain. France had conquered Holland,[1] and had ranged that country on her side. In consequence of this, orders were issued early in 1795 for the seizure of all Dutch vessels in British ports.

On February 9th, further orders were issued for the detention of neutrals bound for Dutch ports; measures were taken to attack the Dutch settlements over sea; and a small squadron, under Vice-Admiral Adam Duncan, in the *Venerable*, 74, was sent to watch the Dutch ships in the Texel. In August, Duncan was joined on his station by an ill-found fleet of twelve Russian[2] ships of the line, and

[1] It was in the course of this campaign that, on January 20th, 1795, some French hussars and horse artillery captured a Dutch squadron, which was ice-bound at the time.

[2] In this fleet there were several officers of British nationality or birth, including Rear-Admiral Tate, and Captains Frederick Thesiger and Brown.

seven frigates; but, during the autumn and winter, the combined fleets saw nothing of the enemy, and had nothing before it save the honourable, yet far from exciting, work of observation and blockade in the North Sea. Letters of marque and reprisals were issued against Holland on September 15th. In the interim, Great Britain had also lost the countenance of Prussia, which had made her peace with France on April 30th.

The French no sooner learnt of the success of Victor Hugues at Guadeloupe, than they sent to him from Brest a number of transports, with supplies, and about three thousand troops, convoyed by the *Hercule*, 50, *Astrée*, 36, two corvettes, and some armed ships. This convoy was fallen in with off Désirade on January 5th, 1795, by the *Bellona*, 74, Captain George Wilson, and *Alarm*, 32, Captain Charles Carpenter; but, owing apparently to mismanagement on the part of Wilson, only one French vessel, the *Duras*, 20, was taken. The rest of the convoy reached Pointe à Pitre, Guadeloupe, on January 6th. The reinforcement thus brought to him enabled Hugues to prosecute his designs against St. Lucia, St. Vincent, Grenada, and Dominica. At St. Lucia he was quickly successful, that island being evacuated on June 19th by the British troops, which were taken off by the *Experiment*, armed storeship, Lieutenant John Barrett,[1] and a transport. At Dominica he was unsuccessful. In Grenada and St. Vincent his schemes were still in progress at the end of the year. In these operations, the British naval officers who, in addition to Lieutenant Barrett, most conspicuously distinguished themselves, were Captains Josias Rogers, of the *Quebec*, Charles Sawyer, of the *Blanche*, and Frederick Watkins, of the *Resource*.

The hostility of Holland led to the despatch from England of an expedition against the Dutch colony at the Cape of Good Hope. This expedition consisted of the ships mentioned in the note,[2] under

[1] Drowned, Captain of the *Minotaur*, in 1810.

[2] Ships.	Guns.	Commanders.
Monarch	74	Vice-Admiral Sir George Keith Elphinstone, K.B. (B). Capt. John Elphinstone (2).
Victorious	74	„ William Clark.
Arrogant	74	„ Richard Lucas.
America	64	„ John Blankett.
Stately	64	„ Billy Douglas.
Echo	16	Com. Temple Hardy.
Rattlesnake	16	„ John William Spranger.

Vice-Admiral Sir George Keith Elphinstone, K.B., with a detachment of the 78th Regiment, under Major-General Craig. The squadron anchored in Simon's Bay early in July, and proposals were made to the Dutch governor to place the colony under British protection. The governor refused, and was making preparations to burn Simon's Town, when, on July 14th, the 78th Regiment and 350 marines landed and seized it. The Dutch withdrew to Muijzenburg, six miles from Cape Town. Elphinstone reinforced the army ashore by landing 1000 seamen under Commanders Hardy and Spranger, by improvising a gunboat, and by arming the launches of the squadron. On August 7th, when the troops began their advance, the *America*, *Stately*, *Echo*, and *Rattlesnake*, also cooperated, the result being that the Dutch were easily driven from post to post with very slight loss to the British. On the 8th, the enemy attempted to regain some of his lost positions, but was again compelled to retire, largely in consequence of the admirable behaviour of Commander Hardy's battalion of seamen and Marines. Elphinstone detained such Dutch vessels as he found, and subsequently commissioned one of them, the *Willemstadt*, as the *Princess*, 20. On September 3rd, the Dutch were about to make a general attack on the British positions, when they were deterred by the sudden appearance in the offing of fourteen sail of British East Indiamen, which brought a large reinforcement of stores and troops under General Alured Clarke. These were all disembarked by the 14th, and an advance on Cape Town was begun, while the *America*, *Echo*, *Rattlesnake*, and an Indiaman, made a demonstration in Table Bay. This induced the Dutch governor, on the following night, to send a flag of truce, with a request for a cessation of hostilities, pending negotiations of a capitulation, the result being that, on the morning of the 16th, the town and colony, together with about 1000 regular troops, the East Indiamen, *Castor*, and the armed brig *Star*, 14, were surrendered. The *Star* was added to the British Navy as the *Hope*.

The British Commander-in-Chief in the East Indies was Commodore Peter Rainier, who, it may be remembered, had taken a convoy thither in the early summer of 1794, with his broad pennant in the *Suffolk*, 74. Rainier, in June, 1795, obtained his flag. On July 21st, in pursuance of orders, he sailed from Madras in the *Suffolk*, Captain Robert Lambert, with the *Centurion*, 50, Captain Samuel Osborn, and some transports with troops under Colonel

James Stuart, to make an attempt against the Dutch possessions in Ceylon. At the same time he detached the *Resistance*, 44, Captain Edward Pakenham, with a tender and a transport, to reinforce a little expedition which, under Captain Henry Newcome, of the *Orpheus*, 32, had previously sailed against Malacca.

On July 23rd, off Negapatam, Rainier was joined by the *Diomede*, 44, Captain Matthew Smith (1), and one or two more transports, with additional troops, and on August 1st, after having been joined on the previous day by the *Heroine*, 32, Captain Alan Hyde Gardner, he anchored in Back Bay. Two days were expended in negotiations, and on the third day, while the *Diomede* was working into the bay with a transport in tow, she unfortunately struck on an uncharted rock, and went down with all her stores. But the troops were landed on August 3rd, four miles from Trincomale, without opposition. By the 23rd, it was found possible to open the British batteries, and by the 26th, a practicable breach was effected. A summons was then sent in, and, after some discussion and misunderstanding, the place surrendered, with 679 officers and men, and nearly 100 serviceable guns. This conquest cost a loss to the British and East India Company's troops of 15 killed and 54 wounded, and to the Navy of 1 killed and 6 wounded. On the 31st, the fort of Oostenburg also surrendered, and, on September 18th, Baticalo followed suit. Jaffnapatam, near Point Pedro, was quietly taken possession of on September 28th by a subsidiary expedition under Captain Samuel Osborn, of the *Centurion*, and Colonel Stuart. Muletivu was similarly occupied on October 1st by Lieutenant Benjamin William Page, commanding the *Hobart*, 18, and by a detachment of the 52nd Regiment under Captain the Hon. Charles Monson; and the island of Manar surrendered on October 5th to a detachment from Jaffnapatam. The expedition to Malacca was not less successful. Malacca itself capitulated on August 17th to Captain Henry Newcome and Major Brown, and, before the end of the year, Cochin, and all the other Dutch settlements on the Indian mainland, were under the British flag.

Until quite the end of the year 1796 the Brest fleet did not quit port; but, during the whole summer and autumn, it was known to be preparing assiduously for some great stroke. According to one view, Ireland was to be attacked; according to a second, Gibraltar; and according to a third, Portugal; and, as the French carefully and successfully kept their intentions secret, the British Admiralty had to be ready for any development. In consequence of this necessity, it divided the Channel fleet into three divisions. One, under Rear-Admiral Sir Roger Curtis, in the *Formidable*, 98, cruised to the westward; another, under Vice-Admiral Charles Thompson, in the *London*, 98, was stationed off Brest; and another, under Lord Bridport, Commander-in-Chief, in the *Royal George*, 100, remained at Spithead. On October 29th, Vice-Admiral Sir John Colpoys relieved Vice-Admiral Thompson off Brest, and, for a short time after November 7th, Curtis, with seven sail of the line, joined Colpoys, who had twelve. But Curtis anchored at St. Helen's on November 17th. The proceedings of the Brest fleet, after it had put to sea, belong rather to the events of 1797 than to those of 1796.

It has already been said that Vice-Admiral Adam Duncan's squadron blockaded or watched the Dutch force in the Texel. On February 23rd, during the temporary absence of the blockading squadron, a Dutch division of two 64's, one 54, one 44, and several frigates and sloops, escaped to sea, but was observed by the *Espiègle*, 16, Commander Benjamin Roberts, and a cutter, which had been sent by Duncan to reconnoitre the port. The Dutch headed to the northward, with a fresh N.E. wind, and were followed for some hours by the *Espiègle*, while the cutter went home with the news. On the 24th, when the enemy was 120 miles north-east of Yarmouth, Commander Roberts left him. Two or three days afterwards, the Dutch fell in with a part of Rear-Admiral Pringle's division of Duncan's squadron, consisting of the *Glatton*, 54, Captain Henry Trollope, and a few smaller vessels, but made no effort to force an action.[1] Not long afterwards, Duncan resumed his station, and effectually shut up the Texel for the rest of the year.

Jervis, who, at the end of 1795, had succeeded Hotham as Commander-in-Chief in the Mediterranean, had under him, at the beginning of 1796, eighteen sail of the line, and a large number of frigates and small craft. At Toulon were fifteen French sail of the line, besides three building; and at Cadiz was the division of Rear-Admiral de Richery. In addition to all these, there were at Cartagena seven Spanish sail of the line, which, owing to the condition of politics in the peninsula, needed to be carefully watched; and there was a very large Spanish fleet at Cadiz. The position of Jervis was, therefore, difficult and perplexing. It called for the exercise

[1] Its object being, as will be seen, the recapture of the Cape of Good Hope.

of great ability and firm determination if a catastrophe were to be avoided, and it demanded, as it providentially found, the services of a man of more than common qualities. Jervis, from the first, adopted a line of policy such as had not been properly illustrated in the Mediterranean since the days of Dilkes and Walton, and which had not, perhaps, been illustrated with equal thoroughness since the days of Blake. He realised that, above all things, he was sent to look after British interests, and that, in comparison with them, all other interests were perfectly subsidiary. One of his first acts was a characteristically high-handed one. The captured British frigate *Nemesis*, 28, lay, with two French vessels, in the neutral port of Tunis. Jervis despatched Vice-Admiral the Hon. William Waldegrave, in the *Barfleur*, 98, with four 74's, to bring out the *Nemesis* at all hazards, and, on March 9th, the service was executed with little opposition, thanks, no doubt, to the overwhelming strength of the force employed. Jervis, indeed, never made the mistake of failing to employ even an excessive force for the execution of an object when such a force happened to be available. Said Nelson: "Where I would take a penknife, Lord St. Vincent takes a hatchet."

The most active of the numerous exceptionally able officers who served with Jervis was, of course, Nelson. On April 23rd, Jervis, then cruising off Vado, detached Nelson, in the *Agamemnon*, 64, with the *Diadem*, 64, Captain George Henry Towry, *Meleager*, 32, Captain George Cockburn, and *Petrel*, 16, Commander John Temple,[1] to blockade Genoa, and to annoy the French along the coast. Nelson learnt that a convoy laden with stores for the French army lay at Finalmarina, in Loano Bay, and on April 25th he made for that place. Four vessels were found anchored under the batteries, which opened on the *Petrel* as she approached, leading in the boats which were to attack; but the fire from the ships covered the little expedition, and, in a very short time, the British brought off the transports, losing only three wounded, including Lieutenant James Noble. Among the other officers who distinguished themselves on the occasion were Lieutenants Maurice W. Suckling, Henry Compton, Charles Ryder, and John Culverhouse. Nelson was subsequently joined by the *Blanche*, 32, Captain d'Arcy Preston, and *Speedy*, 16, Commander Thomas Elphinstone. On May 31st, cruising off Oneglia, he chased six French vessels under a battery.

[1] Drowned, Captain of the *Crescent*, in 1808.

The *Meleager*, *Agamemnon*, *Petrel* and *Speedy*, anchored close in, with only a few inches of water under them, and silenced the battery; and then the boats, in spite of the fire from three 18-pounders in the French ketch *Génie*, and one 18-pounder in a gunboat,[1] carried both. The other four vessels, which were transports, had, in the meantime, run themselves ashore, yet they were not only taken, but also brought off, in the face of a heavy musketry fire from the beach. The British loss was but one killed and three wounded. The transports were full of guns and stores destined for employment at the siege of Mantua, operations against which city, it is believed, failed mainly in consequence of the non-arrival of these supplies.

Another very active officer under Jervis was Captain Thomas Francis Fremantle, of the *Inconstant*, 36, who, when Leghorn was seriously threatened by the French, was employed, with some storeships in company, to remove thence the British residents, and public and private property. Fremantle embarked everybody, and nearly everything having a claim upon his care, on the morning of June 27th, and also brought away thirty-seven merchant vessels, large and small, and two hundred and forty oxen, which had been purchased for the use of the fleet. At noon on the same day, the French entered the town, and at 1 P.M. their batteries opened on the *Inconstant*, which, however, got away without damage or loss. Commodore Nelson, now transferred from the *Agamemnon* to the *Captain*, 74, anchored off the Malora to warn unsuspecting ships of the change in the ownership of the town, and the rest of the British fleet on the coast rejoined Jervis, who was then in the Bay of San Fiorenzo.

The French occupation of Leghorn was palpably a step towards the recovery of the possession of Corsica. Leghorn then belonged to the Grand Duke of Tuscany. There was little doubt but that the French would also attempt to occupy Elba, another possession of the Grand Duke, and another useful base for operations against Corsica. With the object of frustrating anything of the kind, Sir Gilbert Elliot, Viceroy of Corsica, and Sir John Jervis, entered into negotiations, in pursuance of which, Commodore Nelson, on July 10th, quietly occupied Porto Ferrajo.

At that time, Great Britain's difficulties were increasing rapidly. On August 19th, an offensive and defensive treaty of alliance was

[1] Called No. 12.

signed at Madrid between France and Spain, and it was therein stipulated that either of the parties should be entitled to call upon the other to place at its disposal fifteen sail of the line, and ten large frigates or corvettes. France hastened to exercise her new right, even before the treaty was actually signed, by asking for a Spanish fleet to escort the squadron under Rear-Admiral de Richery clear of the squadron of Rear-Admiral Man, who was supposed to be still watching it at Cadiz. De Richery, with the *Victoire*, 80, *Barras*, 74, *Berwick*, 74, *Censeur*, 74, *Duquesne*, 74, *Jupiter*, 74, and *Révolution*, 74, and his three frigates, left the port on August 4th, escorted by a Spanish fleet of twenty sail of the line, and fourteen frigates and corvettes, commanded by Admiral Don Juan de Langara, Hood's old colleague at Toulon. The collection of this huge force was, in reality, quite unnecessary, for Rear-Admiral Man, with his modest seven sail of the line, had left the neighbourhood on July 29th, having been ordered by Jervis to rejoin him off the coast of Corsica. Soon after making an offing, de Langara detached Rear-Admiral Solano, with ten sail of the line and six frigates, to see M. de Richery 300 miles to the westward. Solano did this, and de Richery then proceeded to North America, his original destination.

The Franco-Spanish treaty was ratified in Paris on September 12th; and, immediately afterwards, Great Britain laid an embargo on all Spanish ships still in her ports. On October 8th, Spain formally declared war against Great Britain. But, before this, de Langara, who had returned to Cadiz, left that port again, with nineteen sail of the line, and ten smaller craft, and headed to the eastward. On October 1st, when off Cape de Gata, he was sighted by Rear-Admiral Man, who was then on his way from San Fiorenzo to Gibraltar, with three transports and a brig under his convoy. He had been sent back by Jervis for the reason that he had imprudently gone eastward with scarcely any stores on board. Jervis was naturally unable to supply the deficiencies of his subordinate, and, therefore, ordered him again to Gibraltar to fill up with what he lacked. The Spaniards chased Man, and, on the morning of the 3rd, captured the brig and one of the transports. But Man's squadron and the other transports got safely into Rosia Bay, close to Gibraltar Mole. De Langara then returned to the eastward, and, calling off Cartagena, was joined by seven ships from that port, bringing up his total force to twenty-six sail of the line, besides frigates. With this formidable fleet he cruised as far as Cape Corse, near which he was sighted, on October 15th, by some of the cruisers belonging to the fleet of Sir John Jervis, who then, with only fourteen sail of the line, lay in Mortella Bay. The only other British ships of the line east of Gibraltar were the *Captain* and *Egmont*, which were at Bastia. De Langara might theoretically have overwhelmed Jervis; but, instead, he made for Toulon, where he anchored in the last week of the month, and found twelve French ships of the line; so that the allies then had a combined fleet of thirty-eight sail of the line, and eighteen or twenty frigates.

Man, as has been said, had been sent back by Jervis to Gibraltar to supply himself with stores, which he ought to have taken on board previous to sailing for San Fiorenzo. His business was to take them on board, and to return. He had been given no discretion. Upon anchoring at Gibraltar, however, instead of following out the orders both of the Commander-in-Chief and of the Admiralty, he called a council of his Captains, and he and they, influenced apparently by the knowledge of the immense Franco-Spanish force to the eastward, decided to proceed to England. This extraordinary decision deprived the Mediterranean fleet, at one of the most critical moments in its history, of just one-third of its force. When the squadron reached home, Man's action was severely disapproved, and he was ordered to strike his flag, nor was he again employed afloat.[1] "When," says Mahan, "it is remembered that only forty years had elapsed since Byng was shot for an error in judgment, it must be owned men had become more merciful."

Bonaparte's successes in Italy had dealt a heavy blow at British prestige in the Mediterranean. Sardinia had already yielded Savoy and Nice to France; the Two Sicilies had solicited, and obtained, a cessation of hostilities; and, with Sardinia and the Sicilies neutral, and Spain as an active ally, France seemed to be upon the point of attaining all her ambitions in the Mediterranean. The situation naturally led to renewed trouble in Corsica, where the partisans of France were greatly inspirited. The Viceroy soon perceived that he was threatened with a rising of formidable proportions; and, in consequence of his representations to the home Government, it was ordered that Corsica should be evacuated, and that the troops and stores should be removed to Porto Ferrajo, in Elba. Before this order could be fully carried out, the island was invaded by a small

[1] He died, a full Admiral, in 1813.

force from Leghorn under General Casalta, who landed in Corsica on October 19th. Casalta, who was a popular Corsican, marched against Bastia, before which he arrived on October 21st. He summoned the place to surrender. In the town was a respectable British garrison, and in the port were the *Captain*, 74, and *Egmont*, 74. Under the superintendence of Nelson, who, by his determined attitude, deterred any interference, nearly the whole of the British garrison, besides a vast amount of public and private property, was taken off. Immediately afterwards, the French party occupied not only Bastia, but also San Fiorenzo and Bonifacio. Casalta, having been joined from Leghorn by General Gentili, a brother Corsican, with a large reinforcement, Ajaccio was also presently captured. By November 2nd, the British evacuation, so far as it could be carried out, had been completed, and Jervis, who had learnt of the arrival of de Langara at Toulon, and who did not know what had become of Man, sailed from Mortella Bay with fifteen sail of the line and several frigates, besides a convoy of merchant vessels from the Levant. On December 1st, he anchored in Rosia Bay, Gibraltar, and, for the first time for generations, not a single British ship of the line lay or cruised on the waters of the Mediterranean.

Jervis[1] had been forced to proceed westwards owing to scarcity of provisions and stores. His relative weakness must also have had some effect on his proceedings. On his way to Gibraltar, while his crews were on half rations, or even less, he received instructions countermanding the evacuation of Corsica, if it had not already been carried out, and, in the other event, ordering the retention of Elba. Man had then put it out of the power of the Commander-in-Chief to go back. Had Man obeyed orders, and promptly rejoined Jervis, it is possible that, as Mahan says, the battle of Cape St. Vincent would have been fought in the Mediterranean.[2] It is probable also, that that sea would never have been abandoned, even for an hour. Napoleon was elated.

"The expulsion of the English," he wrote, "has a great effect upon the success of our military operations in Italy. We must exact more severe conditions of Naples.

---

[1] The limits of his command had been extended from the Mediterranean to embrace the Atlantic coasts of Spain and Portugal.

[2] Such, too, was Jervis's opinion.—'Life of St. Vincent' (Tucker), i. 240 'Nelson's Disps.,' ii. 294.

It has the greatest moral influence upon the minds of the Italians; assures our communications; and will make Naples tremble even in Sicily."[1]

Sir Gilbert Elliot, a far-seeing statesman, must have been correspondingly depressed.

"I have always thought," he wrote, "that it is a great and important object in the contest between the French Republic and the rest of Europe, that Italy, in whole or in part, should neither be annexed to France as dominion, nor affiliated in the shape of dependent republics; and I have considered a superior British fleet in the Mediterranean as an essential means for securing Italy and Europe from such a misfortune."

Just previous to Sir John Jervis's arrival at Gibraltar, the Spanish fleet, accompanied by Rear-Admiral Villeneuve, with one French 80, four French 74's, and three French frigates, put to sea from Toulon. De Langara, with his twenty-four sail of the line, and twelve or thirteen frigates, put into Cartagena, leaving Villeneuve to prosecute his voyage to Brest alone. For the moment, it looked as if the allies were destined to lose a great part of the advantage which they had so recently gained, thanks to the withdrawal of Rear-Admiral Man; for it is inconceivable that Villeneuve can have supposed that Jervis lay ahead of him when the French squadron parted from the Spanish fleet; and it is certain that, owing solely to accidental circumstances, Villeneuve was not annihilated as he traversed the Gut. On the afternoon of December 10th, Villeneuve, as he passed the Rock, was sighted by some of the British ships at anchor in the Bay, and he would have been chased, had not a heavy gale from the E.S.E prevented the British from getting out in time to have any chance of coming up with him. Jervis, who imagined that the enemy was bound for the West Indies, despatched a sloop, on the 11th, with warnings to the Commanders-in-Chief at Jamaica and Barbados.

The gale of December 10th, which was so favourable to Villeneuve, was fatal to the British 74-gun ship *Courageux*, temporarily commanded by Lieutenant John Burrows, acting for Captain Benjamin Hallowell, who was on duty ashore. She drove from her anchors, brought up almost under the guns of a Spanish battery on the N.W. side of the Bay, and, when she weighed again and stood towards the African coast, ran on some rocks below Ape's Hill, where, in a few minutes, she became a wreck. Of 593 persons who were apparently on board at the time, only 129 escaped. The *Gibraltar*, 80, Captain John Pakenham (1), and the *Culloden*, 74,

[1] 'Napol.'s Corr.,' ii. 76.

Captain Thomas Troubridge, also drove from their anchors, and were only saved from destruction by good seamanship and strength of hull.

Jervis entrusted the naval command at Porto Ferrajo to Commodore Nelson, who, for the purpose, transferred his broad pennant from the *Captain* to the *Minerva*.[1] With the remainder of the fleet, the Commander-in-Chief sailed, on December 16th, for the Tagus, where he hoped to be speedily joined by a reinforcement from home. He arrived there on the 21st. During these movements his fleet was further unfortunate, for the *Zealous*, 74, greatly injured herself by fouling a rock off Tangier, and the *Bombay Castle*, 74, Captain Thomas Sotheby, while endeavouring to avoid a collision with the storeship *Camel*, ran on a sandbank at the mouth of the Tagus, and could not be got off again. The loss of the *Bombay Castle* was, however, in some measure made up by the fact that, at Lisbon, the Commander-in-Chief found the *St. Albans*, 64, flagship of Vice-Admiral George Vandeput. He had, therefore, still fourteen sail of the line, though he had presently to send home the damaged *Gibraltar* to be docked at Plymouth.

Had the French and Spanish, in November and December, 1796, strained every effort to assume the offensive with their thirty-eight sail of the line, they could scarcely have failed to change the whole course of European history. Jervis, it is of course possible, might have evaded them; but it is also quite possible that he would not have refused them had they seriously challenged him, and it is still more likely that he might not have been able to refuse them.[2] The opportunities then lost did not recur during the remainder of the war of the French Revolution. After following the movements of de Langara and his Toulon friends, the student is inclined to ask himself whether the Spaniards and French of that day had even the vaguest suspicion of the simple truth that the first objective in naval warfare should be the enemy's fleet.

Rear-Admiral de Richery, after his release from Cadiz, made for North America, and, on August 28th, 1796, arrived on the Banks of Newfoundland. The British Commander-in-Chief on the station was Vice-Admiral Sir James Wallace, Kt., who had under his orders

[1] For the further proceedings of Nelson in the Mediterranean in 1796, see next Chap.

[2] "The Admiral is as firm as a rock. He has at present fourteen sail of the line against thirty-six, or perhaps forty. If Man joins him, they will certainly attack, and they are all confident of victory."—'Life of Minto,' ii. 358.

only the *Romney*, 50, and three or four frigates; and, of his whole force, only the *Venus*, 32, Captain Thomas Graves (3), happened to be at St. John's. Graves, and most of his crew, went ashore to assist in manning the batteries; and de Richery, looking into the port, liked the appearance of the defences so little that he bore away to the southward. On September 4th, he entered the Bay of Bulls, where he plundered or destroyed the huts, boats and stages, of the fishermen. On the 5th, he detached Commodore Zacharie Jacques Théodore Allemand, with the *Duquesne*, *Censeur*, and *Friponne*, to the Bay of Castles, in Labrador, and, with the rest of his squadron, proceeded to St. Pierre and Miquelon, where he did the same kind of damage as in the Bay of Bulls. Allemand, delayed by adverse winds and fogs, did not make the Bay of Castles till September 22nd, and, ere that time, most of the fishing vessels had left for Europe. He demanded the surrender of the settlement, which was refused; but, as his ships approached, the people themselves burnt their fishing-stages. Both the French divisions went home independently, de Richery reaching Rochefort on November 5th, and Allemand entering Lorient on November 15th. This expedition destroyed about one hundred fishing and merchant vessels, and took a great many prisoners, most of whom were, however, sent in a cartel to Halifax.

Vice-Admiral Sir John Laforey, Bart., who had succeeded Vice-Admiral Benjamin Caldwell, in June, 1795, as Commander-in-Chief on the Leeward Islands' station, detached the *Malabar*, 54, Captain Thomas Parr, with one 64, and a few frigates[1] and transports, and some troops under Major-General John Whyte, on April 15th, 1796. On April 23rd, this expedition quietly took possession of the Dutch settlements of Demerara and Essequibo, and, on May 2nd, of Berbice. At Demerara, the *Thetis*, 24, *Zeemeeuw*, 12,[2] and several richly laden merchantmen were made prizes of.

Rear-Admiral Hugh Cloberry Christian, who was made a K.B. on February 20th, 1796, had left England, on December 9th, 1795, for the West Indies,[3] with two ships of the line, five other men-of-war,

[1] *Scipio*, 64, Captain Francis Laforey; *Undaunted*, 40, Captain Henry Roberts; *Pique*, 40, Captain David Milne; and *Babet*, Captain William Granville Lobb.

[2] The *Thetis* was afterwards sunk at Demerara, and the *Zeemeeuw* was lost.

[3] Vice-Admiral the Hon. William Cornwallis, with his flag in the *Royal Sovereign*, sailed with reinforcements for the West Indies on February 29th, 1796, but, his flagship being disabled in a gale, he put back to Spithead on March 14th. Cornwallis was at the time in ill-health. He was tried by court-martial on April 17th, and following

and a large fleet of transports, but had been driven back by bad weather in January. He did not finally leave Spithead till March 20th, 1796, reaching Carlisle Bay, Barbados, on April 21st. On the following day Laforey and Christian proceeded with their whole force to Marin Bay, Martinique, where they anchored on the 23rd; and, on the 24th, Laforey resigned his command to Christian, and returned to England in the *Majestic*, 74.

Christian's first object was the reinforcement of St. Lucia. On

REAR-ADMIRAL SIR HUGH CLOBERRY CHRISTIAN, K.B.

(From an engraving by H. R. Cook, after the portrait by J. Northcote, R.A.)

April 26th, with a squadron, in which was a large body of troops under Lieutenant-General Sir Ralph Abercromby, he made for that island, off which he arrived on the following morning. A landing

days, for having returned in defiance of orders, for having omitted to shift his flag when the *Royal Sovereign* was disabled, and for having disobeyed an Admiralty order to hoist his flag in the *Astræa* and proceed. He was, however, acquitted. Soon afterwards he struck his flag at his own request, and did not again hoist it until February, 1801.

was at once effected in Longueville Bay, under the guns of the *Ganges*, 74, Captain Robert M'Douall, and the *Pelican*, 18, Commander John Clarke Searle. On the 28th another landing was made in Choc Bay, and, on the 29th, a third, in Anse La Raye. Eight hundred seamen, under Captain Richard Lane, of the *Astræa*, 32, and Commander George Frederick Ryves (1), of the *Bulldog*, bomb, were then set ashore to co-operate in the projected military operations. Morne Chabot was carried on April 28th; but, on May 3rd, an attack on some batteries, and, on May 17th, an assault on Vigie, were repulsed with heavy loss. The French, however, finally retired to Morne Fortunée; and, on May 24th, the whole island capitulated, 2000 men surrendering. From St. Lucia the expedition went to St. Vincent, which capitulated, after an obstinate resistance, on June 11th, and to Grenada, which surrendered a few days later. In June, Christian was relieved in the command of the Leeward Islands' station by Rear-Admiral Henry Harvey, and returned to England in the *Beaulieu*.

On the Jamaica station, where Rear-Admiral William Parker (1) commanded, the Navy co-operated in an attack, made by the troops under Major-General Forbes from Port au Prince, San Domingo, upon Léogane, in the same island. The forces were landed on March 21st, under the fire of the *Ceres*, 32, Captain James Newman Newman, *Lark*, 16, Commander William Ogilvy, *Iphigenia*, 32, Captain Francis Farrington Gardner, *Cormorant*, 18, Commander Francis Collingwood, and *Sirène*, 16, Commander Daniel Guerin; and the town and works were simultaneously cannonaded by the *Leviathan*, 74, Captain John Thomas Duckworth, *Africa*, 64, Captain Roddam Home, and *Swiftsure*, 74, Captain Robert Parker. But the place proved stronger than had been anticipated, and, the *Leviathan* and *Africa* having been considerably damaged aloft by the guns on shore, the attempt was abandoned. It is noteworthy that in spite of the large British force on the station and of the undoubted activity and vigilance of the British officers, in spite too of the close watch kept upon the French Atlantic ports, the enemy, early in the year, was able to send from Rochefort and Brest large reinforcements to Cape François. Still more remarkable is it that the two squadrons, one under Commodore Henri Alexandre Thévenard, and the other under Captain Guilleaume Thomas, which convoyed these reinforcements, both returned in safety to France.

In the East Indies the operations against the Dutch were

continued. On February 5th an expedition, composed of the *Heroine*, 32, Captain Alan Hyde Gardner, *Rattlesnake*, 16, Commander Edward Ramage, and *Echo*, 16, Commander Andrew Todd, with five Indiamen and troops under Colonel Stuart, arrived off Negombo, near Colombo, from the Cape of Good Hope, and proceeded to occupy the port and disembark the forces. The troops marched to Colombo, before which the squadron had in the meantime stationed itself; and on February 15th that valuable possession surrendered.

On February 16th, Rear-Admiral Peter Rainier, Commander-in-Chief in the East Indies, arrived, with the force set forth in the

SIGNATURE OF CAPT. EDWARD PAKENHAM, R.N., WHO PERISHED IN H.M.S. 'RESISTANCE,' 1798.

note,[1] off Amboyna, in the Moluccas, and took possession of the island and its dependencies without resistance. On March 5th the Rear-Admiral weighed and made for the Banda Islands; and on the 8th he disembarked a force on Banda Neira, under cover of the *Orpheus* and an Indiaman. Though some resistance was met with, it was speedily overcome, and the islands were surrendered on the same evening. At each of these places large stores of valuable spices and considerable amounts of public money were taken. A Captain's share of the prize money for Amboyna and Banda is said to have been £15,000.

It has been already mentioned that in February, 1796, a small Dutch squadron escaped from the Texel and subsequently was seen by the *Glatton*, and other British ships, in the North Sea. The

[1] Ships.	Guns.	Commanders.
Suffolk	74	Rear-Admiral Peter Rainier (B). Capt. Robert Lambert.
Centurion . . .	50	„ Samuel Osborn.
Resistance . . .	44	„ Edward Pakenham.
Orpheus . . .	32	„ Henry Newcome.
Swift	16	Com. John Sprat Rainier.
Amboyna,[1] brig .	10	Lieut. William Hugh Dobbie (1).

[1] Ex *Harlingen*, taken from the Dutch, and added to the squadron at Amboyna.

object of this squadron, the constitution of which will be found below,[1] was the recapture of the Cape of Good Hope. The force was in fact entirely inadequate for the purpose; but James considers that the Dutch had been misled, either as to the strength of the British squadron at the Cape, or as to the probability of French co-operation being offered to them.

On August 3rd, when Vice-Admiral Sir George Keith Elphinstone, with his squadron,[1] was lying in Simon's Bay, it was reported in Cape Town that this Dutch squadron had arrived off Saldanha Bay, fifty or sixty miles to the northward. Owing to the weather and other causes, Elphinstone could not put to sea until August 6th, and then, learning that some suspicious sail had been seen off False Bay, he steered to the south and west. The weather became worse, and, several of the ships being damaged, he had to return to Simon's Bay on August 12th, and there received the intelligence that nine sail of vessels had been in Saldanha Bay since the 6th. He could not sail again until the 15th; and, on the evening of the 16th, when off the port, he sent in the *Crescent*, which saw the Dutch squadron at anchor. The British ships then formed in line, and anchored within gunshot of the Dutch, who were invited to surrender quietly to the vastly superior force of which they were in presence. On the 17th a capitulation was agreed to. No reflection attaches to Rear-Admiral Lucas for having thus given up his squadron, seeing

[1] British and Dutch Squadrons at the Cape of Good Hope, August, 1796.

British.			Dutch.		
Ships.	Guns.	Commanders.	Ships.	Guns.	Commanders.
Monarch	74	Vice-Admiral G. K. Elphinstone, K.B. (B). Capt. John Elphinstone (1).	*Dordrecht*	64	Rear-Admiral Engelbertus Lucas.
Tremendous	74	Rear-Admiral Thomas Pringle (R). Capt. John Aylmer (1).	*Revolutie*[1]	64	Capt. Jan Rijnbende.
America	64	„ John Blankett.	*M. H. Tromp*	54	Com. Jan Valkenburg (actg.).
Ruby	64	„ Hon. Henry Edwyn Stanhope.	*Castor*[2]	44	Capt. Jacob Claris.
Stately	64	„ Billy Douglas.	*Brave*[3]	42	Com. Jacob Zoetemans (actg.).
Sceptre	64	„ William Essington.	*Sirene*[4]	26	„ C. De Cerf (actg.)
Trident	64	„ Edward Oliver Osborn.	*Bellona*[5]	24	„ G. A. De Falck (actg.).
Jupiter	50	„ George Losack.	*Havik*	18	Lieut. Pieter Besemer.
Crescent	36	„ Edward Buller.	*Vrouw Maria*	16	„ Hermanus Barbier.
Sphinx	24	Com. Andrew Todd.			
Moselle	16	„ Charles Brisbane.			
Rattlesnake	16	„ Edward Ramage.			
Echo	16	„ John Turnor.			
Hope	14	Lieut. John Alexander (1).			

[1] Ex *Prins Frederik*; renamed *Prince Frederick*.
[2] Later *Saldanha*, 38.
[3] Ex *Princes Fr. Louisa Wilhelmina*.
[4] Later *Laurel*.
[5] Later *Vindictive*.

that it mounted little more than half as many guns, and that it had on board less than half as many men, as the British squadron. In October, Elphinstone relinquished his command to Rear-Admiral Thomas Pringle, who had previously been his second, and returned to England in the *Monarch*. The only other transaction on the station during the year that calls for notice here was the capture and destruction, on December 2nd, of the French settlement at Foul Point, Madagascar, by the *Crescent*, 36, Captain John William Spranger, *Brave*, 36, Captain Andrew Todd, and *Sphinx*, 24, Commander Francis Holmes Coffin; which also captured five merchantmen there.

By the middle of 1796, the young French Republic had rid itself of its gravest internal difficulties. The disaffection in the south had been quelled, and the royalists of La Vendée had been subdued. Nor did France any longer stand alone. She had with her the resources of Holland, and she was about to command the active co-operation of Spain. It seemed, therefore, to those who had the direction of her naval and military forces, that the moment had arrived for her to concentrate her energies in the dealing of as serious a blow as possible at Great Britain, her most formidable enemy. At first it was intended to attempt upon a grand scale an invasion of England; but it was soon realised that to do this with a reasonable prospect of success would necessitate an expenditure greater than could be incurred with convenience at that time. Ireland, however, was disaffected; and it was imagined that a force much smaller than any with which it could be hoped to make a direct impression upon England might, if despatched to Ireland, enable the rebels there to gain their object. An Ireland freed by French help from its connection with Great Britain could, it was felt, scarcely fail to become a useful ally of the Republic, and a grave menace to the United Kingdom. The French government, accordingly, offered to send 25,000 men under General Hoche, to the support of the rebellion. The Irish delegates in Paris considered that 15,000 men would be sufficient; and, when France had made some progress with her preparations for the despatch of that number of troops, and of supplies of arms and ammunition for the insurgents, Lord Edward Fitzgerald and Mr. Arthur O'Connor met General Hoche at Bâle, and settled with him the details of the coming campaign.

The broad outlines of this had been already arranged by Hoche in conjunction with Vice-Admiral Truguet, French minister of marine. Vice-Admiral Villaret-Joyeuse, with fifteen sail of the line which lay at Brest, was to carry to Ireland a first division of the invading force. In the meantime seven sail of the line under Rear-Admiral de Richery, from Lorient, and five sail of the line under Rear-Admiral Villeneuve, from Toulon, were to proceed to Brest, and, taking on board the rest of the expedition, were to follow Villaret-Joyeuse, who, after landing his part of the army, was to detach himself with his eight fastest two-deckers, and make the best of his way to the Indian seas, where he was to assist Tippoo Sahib and the Dutch, and to act with energy against the British possessions, in co-operation with Rear-Admiral Sercey, who was already on the station. But the plan was presently altered. Hoche, believing that Villaret-Joyeuse attached too much importance to the Indian, and too little to the Irish part of the scheme, induced his government to supersede Villaret-Joyeuse in favour of Vice-Admiral Morard de Galles as commander-in-chief, and to consent to the whole expedition being transported at once, instead of in two divisions. This change in the plans involved delay. According to the original intention, the first division should have left Brest at about the end of October, 1796; but de Richery, while on his way from Lorient, was induced, by the proximity of a British squadron under Rear-Admiral Sir Roger Curtis, to put into Rochefort on November 5th; and he did not again get under way until December 8th. On the 11th, having evaded the squadron which lay off the port under Vice-Admiral Sir John Colpoys, he entered Brest. It was then found that only two of his ships of the line were in a condition to go to sea again immediately. Moreover, Villeneuve, from Toulon, had not arrived.[1] Nevertheless, it was decided to wait no longer. On December 15th, part of the fleet weighed and anchored outside the port; and, by midday on the 16th, having been joined by the remaining vessels, it began to make sail with a fair easterly wind. The naval force which thus set out had on board about 18,000 troops of all arms, numerous field-guns, much ammunition, and stores of all sorts in profusion; and it appears to have been unusually well-equipped, though it was provisioned for too short a period. Under Hoche

[1] On December 23rd, Villeneuve was driven by Colpoys to take refuge in Lorient.

were Generals Humbert and Grouchy, besides others of less note. The constitution of the fleet is set forth in the note.[1]

M. Morard de Galles at first intended to make an offing by way of the Passage du Raz, in order to evade the observation of the British Admiral who was cruising off Ushant; but, when darkness came on and the wind grew variable, he altered his design, and signalled from the frigate *Fraternité*, where he temporarily flew his flag, for the fleet to proceed through the Passage d'Iroise, which presents a wider and easier channel. As the signal was seen by only a few ships, part of the fleet pursued the original, and part the

[1] Fleet of M. Morard de Galles, for the Convoy to Ireland of the Army under General Hoche, 1796–97.

	Ships.	Guns.	Commanders.	Remarks.
Van.	*Séduisant*[1]	74	Capt. Dufossey.	Wrecked on night of Dec. 16th.
	Pluton	74	„ J. M. Lebrun.	
	Trajan	74	Commod. J. Le Ray.	
	Constitution	74	„ L. L'Heritier.	Proper flagship of Rear-Adm. J. M. Nielly.
	Wattignies	74	Capt. H. A. Thévenard.	
	Rasé, *Scévola*,[1] 44; Frigates, *Impatiente*,[1] 44, *Résolue*, 40 (flag of Rear-Adm. Nielly), *Surveillante*,[1] 36, *Charente*, 36; Brigs, *Affronteur*, 16, *Vautour*, 16.			
Centre.	*Indomptable*	80	Commod. J. Bedout.	Proper flagship of Vice-Adm. Morard de Galles.
	Fougueux	74	„ E. T. Maistral.	
	Mucius	74	„ P. M. J. Querangal.	
	Redoutable	74	Capt. Moncousu.	
	Patriote	74	„ La Fargue.	
	Révolution	74	Commod. P. R. M. E. Dumanoir Le Pelley.	
	Frigates, *Fraternité*, 40 (flag of Vice-Adm. Morard de Galles), *Romaine*, 40, *Sirène*, 36, *Tortue*,[1] 40; Powder vessel, *Fidèle*, 40; Brigs, *Atalante*,[1] 20, *Voltigeur*, 16.			
	Nestor	74	C. A. L. Durand-Linois.	
Rear.	*Cassard*	74	Capt. Dufay.	
	Droits de l'Homme[1]	74	Commod. J. R. La Crosse.	Proper flagship of Rear-Adm. F. J. Bouvet.
	Tourville	74	Capt. J. B. Henry.	
	Eole	74	Capt. J. P. A. Malin.	
	Pégase	74	Rear-Admiral de Richery. Capt. C. Laronier.	
	Frigates, *Cocarde*, 40, *Bravoure*, 40, *Immortalité*, 40 (flag of Rear-Adm. Bouvet), *Bellone*, 40; Brigs, *Mutine*,[1] 14, *Renard*, 16.			

Transports: *Nicodème*, *Justine*,[1] *Fille Unique*,[1] *Ville de Lorient*,[1] *Suffren*,[1] *Allègre*,[1] *Expériment*.

[1] Taken or lost before their return to port.

new course; and thus, at the very commencement of the voyage, the expedition fell into confusion. This confusion was increased by the guns which were fired and the lights which were shown by the *Fraternité* to call attention to her movements; by the firing of more guns by the *Atalante*, which was detached by the commander-in-chief after that part of the fleet which had not followed him; by the firing of still more guns by the British frigate *Indefatigable*, 44,

ADMIRAL SIR JOHN COLPOYS, K.B.

(From an engraving by Ridley, after the picture by Mather Brown.)

which had been watching the port; and by the signals of distress which proceeded from the *Séduisant*, 74. In her efforts to make the Passage du Raz she had struck on the Grand Stevenet, where, ere morning, she became a total loss, about 680 of her people perishing with her.

The *Indefatigable* was then commanded by Captain Sir Edward Pellew, who, with the *Révolutionnaire*, 38, Captain Francis Cole, *Amazon*, 36, Captain Robert Carthew Reynolds, *Phœbe*, 36, Captain

Robert Barlow, and hired armed lugger, *Duke of York*, Mr. Benjamin Sparrow, had been stationed to get early information of any movement at Brest, and to communicate it to Vice-Admiral Sir John Colpoys at a rendezvous about twenty miles west of Ushant. On December 11th, Pellew had sent the *Amazon* to England and the *Phœbe* to Colpoys with news of the arrival of de Richery at Brest, and on the 15th he had again sent the *Phœbe* to Colpoys[1] to report that the French fleet was coming out. In the afternoon of the 16th he had also sent the *Révolutionnaire* to further inform the Vice-Admiral of what was going forward. Pellew remained to watch the enemy, which he even allowed to get within gunshot of him ere he made off. Early on the 17th, he sent the *Duke of York* to Falmouth with dispatches; and soon afterwards, having lost sight of the French in the night, he followed her.[2]

At dawn on December 17th, part of the French fleet had cleared the Passage du Raz. Rear-Admiral Bouvet was the senior officer with this part, and, seeing nothing of the rest of the expedition, he opened his instructions, in accordance with the directions which he was to follow in case of separation, and learnt from them that he was to make Mizen Head, in county Cork, and to cruise off it for five days to await orders. He steered nearly due west until the morning of the 19th, when he altered course to the north. Soon afterwards he fell in with some of his missing consorts, the result being that by noon he had with him the whole of the expedition except the *Nestor*, 74, *Fraternité*, 40, *Cocarde*, 40, *Romaine*, 40, three of the brigs, and two of the transports. The command, in the absence of M. Morard de Galles, who was still in the *Fraternité*, thus devolved upon M. Bouvet, who, on the morning of December 21st, sighted Mizen Head, and, soon afterwards, made the signal to prepare to anchor in Bantry Bay.

[1] The *Phœbe* on this occasion did not reach Colpoys until the 19th, when he, with thirteen sail, was in latitude 48° 51′ N., and longitude 5° 43′ W., whither he had cruised. On the following day he sighted, and sent some of his ships in chase of, Villeneuve's squadron, which was on its way from Toulon, and which escaped into Lorient. Then, having suffered in a gale, he had to bear away for Spithead. Thus he failed to sight Bouvet.

[2] Pellew reached Falmouth late on December 20th. On the 25th, Bridport weighed from Spithead to go in chase of the Brest fleet, but he was delayed by a series of accidents, and was unable to leave St. Helen's until January 3rd, 1797. Proceeding first off Ushant and then off Bantry, he saw nothing of the enemy until, on the 10th, as will be seen, he vainly chased the *Révolution* and *Fraternité*.

From pilots who, mistaking the fleet for a British one, went out unsuspiciously to it, and were detained, the French learnt that no vessels had appeared off the coast during the previous three days; and that the only force lying in the Cove of Cork[1] consisted of six frigates. There was a fresh wind from the eastward; and, as the fleet made little way in beating up against it, M. Bouvet, at 4 P.M. on the 22nd, anchored the *Immortalité* to windward of the eastern end of Bere Island, another frigate, eight ships of the line, four brigs, and one transport anchoring near her. The other ships remained under way, and, on the morning of the 23rd, were not visible from the anchorage. During the following twenty-four hours there was a heavy gale from the eastward. On the 24th, at the instance of Grouchy, who was the senior military officer present, preparations were made to land troops, either at Waterfall or in the mouth of the little river Ardrigole, higher up the Bay. To facilitate the landing, the ships weighed in order to move nearer in; but, the weather again becoming dirty, the squadron re-anchored. On the 25th, the weather was so bad that such vessels as did not voluntarily put to sea drove from their anchors;[2] and, for the next three days, there was no possibility of again entering the Bay. When, on the 29th, the weather moderated and the wind became fair, Bouvet, who did not know what had become of his consorts, and who had only a few days' provisions remaining on board the *Immortalité*, headed his frigate for Brest, which he reached on January 1st, 1797. On the same day the *Indomptable*, *Mucius*, *Fougueux*, *Patriote*, and *Redoutable* also entered the road.

The *Nestor*, *Fraternité*, *Cocarde*, *Romaine*, and small craft, which, on December 19th, had become separated from the rest of the French fleet, lost sight of one another during the 20th. On the 21st, the *Fraternité*, still bearing the flag of M. Morard de Galles, was chased by a British frigate and driven far to the westward of her destination; and not until the morning of the 29th was she able to stand for Bantry Bay. On her course thither she fell in with the *Révolution*, which was occupied in taking out the people from the *Scévola*, the latter having become quite unseaworthy owing to the bad weather which she had encountered. No French ships were

[1] Now Queenstown Harbour.

[2] On this occasion the *Indomptable*, 80, fouled the *Résolue*, 40, and carried away all her masts.

found off Bere Island; and, as both the *Révolution* and the *Fraternité* were now overcrowded and getting short of provisions, Morard de Galles and Hoche decided to return to France. On their way, the two French ships, on January 8th, sighted, and tacked away from, the British frigates *Unicorn*, 32, Captain Sir Thomas Williams, and *Doris*, 36, Captain the Hon. Charles Jones,[1] which were themselves at the same time being chased by a considerable part of the returning expeditionary squadron, and which might have been easily taken, if the French commander-in-chief had only known how near his friends were to him. On the 10th, again, the *Révolution* and *Fraternité* were chased by Lord Bridport's fleet;[2] but, thanks to the thick weather, they got away, and, on the 14th, entered Rochefort.

Some of the ships which had failed to make Bantry proceeded eventually to the mouth of the Shannon; but they attempted nothing there; and, after a short stay, headed again for France. One of them was the *Droits de l'Homme*, 74, on board of which was General Humbert. After quitting the Shannon, off which she captured a rich letter of marque, and looking a second time into Bantry Bay, she left the coast of Ireland on January 9th, and made for Brest. On the 13th the weather was thick, and, although Captain La Crosse believed himself to be near his destination, he stood to the southward under easy sail with the wind on his starboard beam. Early in the afternoon he imagined himself to be chased by two vessels, and, in his endeavours to escape from them,[3] he ran up against two more, which were sighted at 3.30 P.M., and which turned out to be the *Indefatigable*, 44, Captain Sir Edward Pellew, and the *Amazon*, 36, Captain Robert Carthew Reynolds. These frigates were still engaged in watching Brest, and were then in latitude 47° 30′ N., Ushant bearing N.E. 50 leagues. When they first saw the French 74, she bore N.W. from them. At 4.15 P.M. the *Droits de l'Homme* was so unfortunate as to carry away in a squall her main topsail braces and, soon afterwards, her fore and main topmasts; but long before 5.30 P.M., when the *Indefatigable*, then seven miles ahead of her consort, got within hail, the Frenchman had cleared away the wreck. A hot action then began, the

[1] These frigates belonged to a squadron stationed off the coast of Ireland under Vice-Admiral Robert Kingsmill. The Hon. C. Jones was afterwards Viscount Ranelagh. He died, still a Captain, in December, 1800.

[2] The Channel Fleet.

[3] They seem, after all, to have been French ships.

natural superiority of the two-decker being to some extent neutralised by her crippled condition, and by her inability to keep open her lower ports when she was rolling in a heavy sea with but little sail to steady her. At about 6.45 P.M. the *Amazon* came up, and poured a broadside into the Frenchman's quarter; but Captain La Crosse handled his ship so as to avoid being raked, and so as to bring both of his opponents on one side of him, and at 7.30 P.M. he was temporarily relieved by both the British ships shooting ahead, the *Amazon*, on account of the quantity of sail which she carried, and the *Indefatigable*, to repair damages aloft. The *Droits de l'Homme* utilised the respite as best she could, and continued running to the east-south-east. At 8.30 the action was renewed, the frigates stationing themselves one on each bow of the 74, and yawing to rake her, and she, from time to time, also yawing to rake them, though without much effect. At 10.30 P.M., she was obliged to cut away her mizen; whereupon the frigates took up positions on her quarters. With a brief intermission, the fight continued until about 4.20 A.M. on January 14th, when land was suddenly sighted close ahead. The *Indefatigable* promptly hauled off, and made sail to the southward. The *Amazon* wore to the northward; but, being unable, owing to her crippled state, to work off, she ran aground in about half an hour and became a wreck. Except six men, all her people saved themselves, though they were, of course, made prisoners.[1]

In this action the *Indefatigable* had all her masts wounded; and, at its conclusion, she had four feet of water in her hold; but she had only Lieutenant John Thompson[2] and 18 men wounded, and nobody killed. The *Atalante* suffered almost as severely aloft and in hull, and had 3 men killed and 15 badly wounded.

As for the gallant *Droits de l'Homme*, which, in the engagement, had lost no fewer than 103 killed and about 150 wounded, she also altered course, hoping to avoid the danger, but immediately afterwards lost her foremast and bowsprit. In vain did she try to bring up. In a few minutes she struck on a sandbank in the Bay of Audierne. As she pounded there her mainmast went by the board. During the whole of the following day and night, and also on the

[1] Captain Reynolds and his officers were "most honourably and fully acquitted," with the court's highest approbation. C.M., September 29th, 1797.

[2] First Lieutenant. He was promoted to be Commander, but died in that rank in 1804. The first Lieutenant of the *Amazon*, Bendall Robert Littlehales, who was also promoted, died a Vice-Admiral in 1847.

15th and 16th of January, she lay, her people being washed out of her by the heavy sea, or being drowned in their endeavours to make the shore. Few managed to reach it. On the 17th, when the weather had cleared, the *Arrogante*, brig, and *Aiguille*, cutter, reached the spot; and on that day and the following the survivors were taken off from the wreck. The disaster is supposed to have cost the loss of upwards of 1000 lives.[1] This was the most terrible episode of an adventure which, from beginning to end, was singularly unfortunate.[2]

Lord Bridport, though on the look-out for the returning remnants of the Brest fleet, failed to intercept any part of it; and, on January 19th, having satisfied himself that nothing of importance remained for him to intercept, he detached five ships of the line and a frigate[3] to Gibraltar under Rear-Admiral William Parker (1) to reinforce Sir John Jervis. For a few days longer he cruised with the rest of his fleet off Ushant, and then went, by way of Torbay, to Spithead, where he dropped anchor on February 3rd. He sailed again on March 3rd for a cruise off Brest, and returned to his anchorage on the 30th. On April 6th, it being held that it would be sufficient merely to watch the enemy, Rear-Admiral Sir Roger Curtis, with nine sail of the line, sailed to take up a position off the enemy's port. Up to about that time Lord Bridport had been only the *locum tenens* for Lord Howe in chief command of the Channel Fleet; but Howe's continued ill-health then obliged him to resign. It was on April 15th, when Bridport signalled to prepare for sea with a view to making his first cruise as real Commander-in-Chief, that the great mutiny,

[1] 'Nav. Chron.,' vii. 465; Marshall, 'Nav. Biog.,' ii., under "Littlehales"; 'Vict. et Conquêtes,' vii. 296.

[2] Those of the expeditionary ships which never returned to port are to be thus accounted for: *Séduisant*, 74, wrecked, December 16th, 1796, going out of Brest; *Droits de l'Homme*, 74, wrecked, January 13th, 1797, while in action off the Penmarcks; *Scévola*, 44, foundered, December 30th, off Ireland; *Impatiente*, 44, wrecked, December 30th, near Crookhaven; *Surveillante*, 36, wrecked in January in Bantry Bay; *Tortue*, 40, taken, January 5th, off Ireland, by the *Polyphemus*, 64; *Atalante*, 20, taken, January 10th, by the *Phœbe*, 36; *Mutine*, 14, taken May 29th, at Santa Cruz; *Justine*, taken, December 30th, by the *Polyphemus*, 64; *Fille Unique*, foundered January 6th, in the Bay of Biscay; *Ville de Lorient*, taken, January 7th, by the *Unicorn*, 32; *Suffren*, taken by the *Jason*; retaken by the *Tortue*; again taken by the *Dædalus*, 32, and sunk; *Allègre*, taken January 12th, by the *Spitfire*, 16.

[3] *Prince George*, *Namur*, *Orion*, *Irresistible*, *Colossus*, and *Thalia*. These were given a rendezvous with Admiral Sir John Jervis off Cape St. Vincent, where, as will be seen, they joined him on February 6th.

some account of which is given in the previous chapter, broke out at Spithead. That regrettable event had the effect of postponing the weighing of the fleet until May 16th, and, even then, it was not able to make an offing until the 17th. Thenceforward, during the rest of the summer, Bridport remained almost continuously cruising in the Channel, while frigate squadrons under Sir Edward Pellew and Sir John Borlase Warren more closely observed the enemy's harbours; but, chiefly owing to political convulsions in Paris, the French did not venture out, and a meditated second attempt upon Ireland had to be, for that year, abandoned. Elsewhere the foes of Great Britain were much more active.

Admiral Sir John Jervis, with the fleet which had temporarily abandoned the Mediterranean in the previous year, remained in the Tagus until January 18th, 1797, when, with eleven sail of the line, he left Lisbon in order to escort to a safe latitude a Brazil convoy, and to make rendezvous off Cape St. Vincent with the reinforcement which Rear-Admiral William Parker (1) was bringing out from the Channel. In attempting to leave the river the *St. George*, 98, Captain Shuldham Peard, after colliding with a Portuguese frigate, grounded on the Cachopo Shoal, and suffered so much damage that she had to return for repairs. The Admiral's force was thus reduced to ten ships of the line; but, after he had seen his convoy on its way and was making for St. Vincent, he fell in, on February 6th, with the reinforcements which had been detached from the Channel Fleet. This brought up his immediately available strength to fifteen ships of the line, besides frigates. In addition the *St. George*, 98, and *Zealous*, 74, were repairing at Lisbon, and the *Gibraltar*, 80, at Plymouth.

In the meantime the grand fleet of Spain, under Admiral Don José de Cordova, who had superseded Admiral de Langara, lay at Cartagena. It consisted of 27 sail of the line, 12 frigates, a brig-corvette, and some smaller craft. According to the plans of the allies this fleet was eventually to make its way to Brest, and there to join the French and Dutch fleets in order to clear the way for an invasion of England. But it was not to attempt to make the voyage to Brest directly. It was to halt on its way at Cadiz for refreshment and supplies.

Sir John Jervis, upon whom devolved the task of preventing Don José de Cordova from joining hands with M. Morard de

Galles, had with him a numerically inferior force. Moreover he did not know that the Spaniards intended to put into Cadiz. And, seeing that he expected his enemy off Cape St. Vincent, which is far to the westward of Cadiz, he could have neither fought nor sighted Don José when he did, had the Spanish admiral been able to carry out his design. But for an accidental circumstance Don José would have got safely into Cadiz; and, instead of the glories

ADMIRAL WILLIAM, LORD RADSTOCK, G.C.B.

(From an engraving by Ridley, after the portrait by J. Northcote, R.A.)

of St. Vincent, the British fleet would probably have tasted the monotonous weariness of a long period of blockading duty. That accidental circumstance was the continuance, for a comparatively long period, of strong easterly and south-easterly winds in the neighbourhood of the Strait.

After his reinforcement had joined him Jervis worked slowly up against these winds for his station off Cape St. Vincent. Don José de Cordova had already left Cartagena on February 1st. On the 5th, as he passed Gibraltar, he sent into Algeciras a number of gunboats and transports, escorted by the *Neptuno*, 80, *Bahama*, 74, *Terrible*, 74, and *Nuestra Señora del Guadalupe*, 34. One of the two-deckers rejoined the fleet at once. The other two[1] ships of the line did not leave port until the 10th, and, on the 11th, sighted and chased the *Minerve*, 38, Commodore Horatio Nelson, Captain George Cockburn, which was returning from Porto Ferrajo with Sir Gilbert Elliot, late Viceroy of Corsica, Lieut.-Colonel Drinkwater, and other officials on board. The *Minerve* escaped without much difficulty, and, early on the 13th, joined Jervis, to whom she brought the first news[2] of the Spaniards being at sea.

Ere that time Don José de Cordova would have been in Cadiz, had not the easterly gale driven him much to westward of his port, and into the neighbourhood of the British fleet. Not until the night of the 13th did the wind change to west-by-south. The Spaniards[3] then began to crowd in towards the land without much regard to order. Their signal guns had been already heard by the British; and at 2.30 A.M. on the 14th Jervis learnt from a Portuguese frigate that the enemy was but about five leagues from him, to windward.

The early morning of the 14th of February, 1797, was misty and dark. The British fleet was then standing in two columns on the starboard tack, with the wind west by south, Cape St. Vincent bearing east by north, distant twenty-five miles. At about 6.30 A.M. the *Culloden* signalled five sail in the south-west by south; and a little later the news was confirmed by the *Niger* and *Lively*, which were able to add that the strangers were by the wind on the starboard tack. Thereupon the *Bonne Citoyenne* was directed to reconnoitre; and at 8.15 A.M. the Admiral ordered his fleet to form in close order. He had already, over night, ordered it to prepare for action. He now repeated that signal, and, at 9.30, detached ahead the *Culloden*, *Blenheim*, and *Prince George*, reinforced twenty minutes later by the *Irresistible*, *Colossus*, and *Orion*, to chase to the south-west. Still, neither side knew the numerical strength of its foe. The Spaniards, unintentionally misled by an

[1] They did not rejoin the flag until the afternoon of the 14th, during the action.

[2] The *Niger*, 32, Captain Edward James Foote, had kept company with and observed the Spaniards for several days, but did not join the fleet until 5 A.M. on the 14th.

[3] They had previously sighted some of the British ships, but, mistaking them for merchantmen, paid little attention to them.

American skipper who had sighted the British on the 4th, believed that Jervis had but nine sail of the line with him. The British at 9 A.M. could count but twenty sail of the line. Not until about 11 A.M. did the Spaniards realise that fifteen sail of the line were opposed to them, nor did Jervis know that he had to deal with twenty-six.[1] Up to that time the two parallel British lines had been heading for a gap which separated the Spanish fleet into two divisions, one, the larger, of twenty-one ships, being to windward,

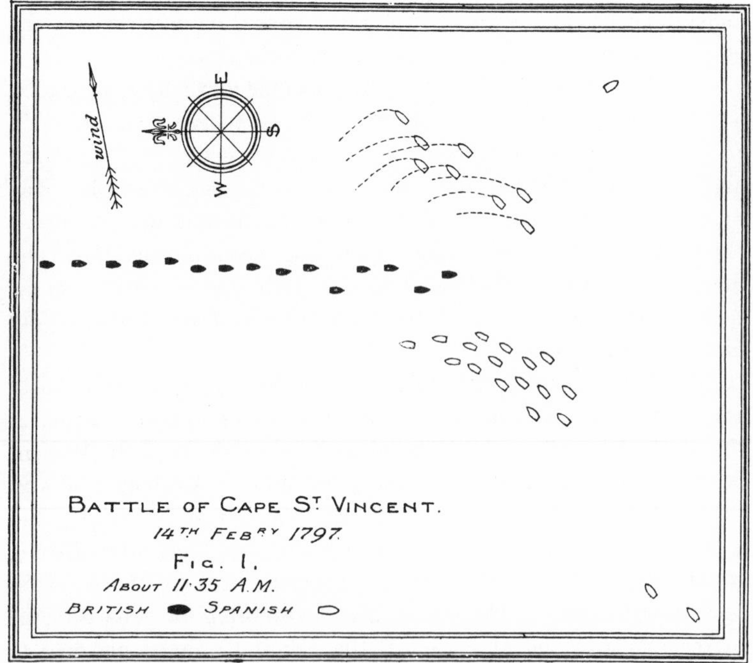

running (with the exception of two, which were far to the south-west) in a mass under all sail with the wind on the starboard quarter, and the other, the smaller, of six ships, being to leeward, close-hauled on the port tack, and endeavouring to join the larger ere Jervis could cut in between the two.

At a few minutes before 11 A.M. some of the headmost ships of

[1] The logs of the *Victory* and *Bonne Citoyenne*, as well as Jervis's dispatch, as published in the 'Gazette,' put the number at only twenty-five, but the two line-of-battle ships which had put into Algeciras, and which had not already rejoined, joined during the battle.

the Spanish weather division began to wear and trim on the port tack, as if with the intention of ultimately forming line and passing along the British weather column, so exposing that column, consisting of eight ships only, to the fire of twenty or twenty-one vessels, and, at the same time, preventing the British lee column from using its guns for fear of injuring its friends. Jervis's reply was, at 11 A.M., to order his own ships to form in single column ahead and astern of the *Victory*, as most convenient, and to steer S.S.W., or close-hauled on the starboard tack, a course which kept the Spanish lee division upon the British lee or port bow. When this signal had been obeyed the order of the column was as given in the note below.[1] A little later Jervis made the signal to pass through the enemy's line; and, at about the same time, five of the six ships of the Spanish lee division, perceiving

[1] FLEET OF ADMIRAL SIR JOHN JERVIS IN THE BATTLE OFF CAPE ST. VINCENT, FEBRUARY 14TH, 1797, with the Names of the Captains and First Lieutenants, and the numbers Killed and seriously Wounded in each ship.

Ships.	Guns.	Commanders.	Killed.	Wounded.	First Lieutenants.[1]
Culloden	74	Capt. Thomas Troubridge	10	47	Anselm John Griffiths.
Blenheim	98	,, Thomas Lenox Frederick	12	49	Robert Campbell (1).
Prince George	98	Rear-Adm. William Parker (1) (R.) Capt. John Irwin	8	7	Robert Williams (1).
Orion	74	,, Sir James Saumarez	..	9	James Barker.
Colossus	74	,, George Murray (3)	..	5	Richard Prater.
Irresistible	74	,, George Martin	5	14	William Bevians.
Victory	100	Admiral Sir John Jervis, K.B. (B.) Capt. (1st) Robert Calder ,, (2nd) George Grey (1)	1	5	William Selby.
Egmont	74	,, John Sutton	..	..	George Burdett.
Goliath	74	,, Sir Charles Henry Knowles, Bart.	..	8	William Collis.
Barfleur	98	Vice-Adm. Hon. William Waldegrave (B.) Capt. James Richard Dacres (1)	..	7	John Bligh (2).
Britannia	100	Vice-Adm. Charles Thompson (B.) Capt. Thomas Foley (3)	..	1	Valentine Collard.
Namur	90	,, James Hawkins Whitshed	2	5	James Nash.
Captain	74	Commod. Horatio Nelson Capt. Ralph Willett Miller	24	56	Edward Berry (Com.) actg.
Diadem	64	,, George Henry Towry	..	2	Henry Edward Reginald Baker.
Excellent	74	,, Cuthbert Collingwood	11	12	John Mortimer.
Minerve . . . 38	..	,, George Cockburn	..	..	
Southampton . 32	..	,, James Macnamara (2)	..	..	
Lively . . . 32	..	,, Lord Garlies	..	..	
Niger . . . 32	..	,, Edward James Foote	..	..	
Bonne Citoyenne 20	..	Com. Charles Lindsay	..	..	
Raven, brig. . 18	..	,, William Prowse (1)	..	..	
Fox, cutter . . 10	..	Lieut. John Gibson	..	..	
			73	227	

[1] Promoted to be Commanders, chiefly on March 8th, 1797. Commander Berry was posted on March 6th.

SPANISH SHIPS OF THE LINE PRESENT IN THE ACTION: 130 guns, *Santisima Trinidad*; 112 guns, *Concepción, Conde de Regla, Mexicano, Principe de Asturias, Salvador del Mundo* (taken), *San Josef* (taken); 80 guns, *Neptuno, San Nicolas* (taken); 74 guns, *Atlante, Bahama, Conquistador, Firme, Glorioso, Oriente, Pelayo. San Antonio, San Domingo, San Firmin, San Francisco de Paula, San Genaro, San Ildefonso, San Juan Nepomuceno, San Pablo, San Ysidro* (taken), *Soberano, Terrible.*

that the British were for the moment neglecting them, and that they could not in any case cross Jervis's bows, hauled up on the starboard tack as if in indecision, but finally settled upon a north-east course. The sixth ship, a 74, made off at once and alone under a crowd of sail to the south-east, and was soon out of sight; but the five were almost simultaneously reinforced by two three-deckers and one two-decker,[1] which, standing across the head of the British column, joined them. These evolutions reduced the

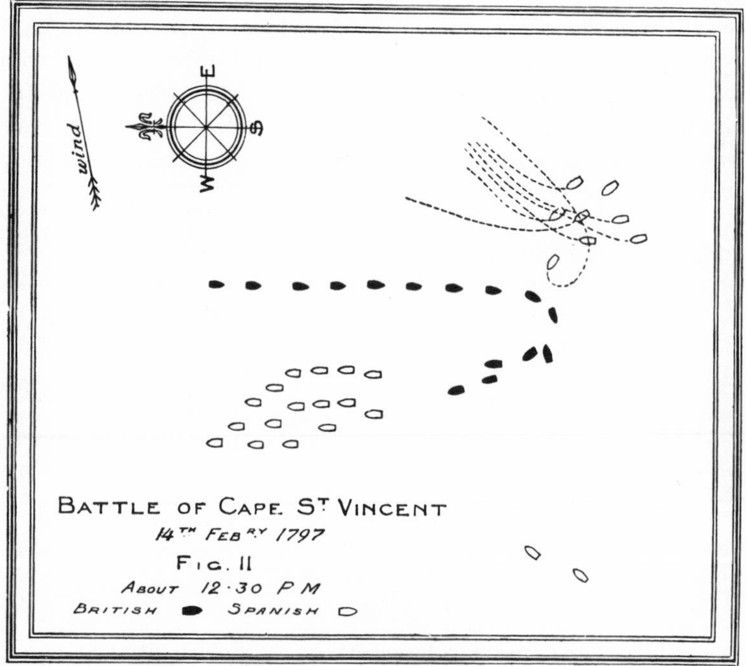

Spanish weather division to eighteen sail of the line, inclusive of the two vessels which were about to rejoin from Algeciras. At 11.31 A.M., when the *Culloden* was abreast of the leading ships of the enemy's weather division, she opened fire upon them by signal, and was replied to, though the range was distant. The ships in her wake followed her example as they approached within gunshot; and at 12.8 P.M., just as Troubridge had passed the last ship of the Spanish weather division, he was signalled to tack. The *Blenheim* did the same a little later, and then the *Prince George*, which was

[1] Probably *Conde de Regla*, 112, *Principe de Asturias*, 112, and *Oriente*, 74.

a good deal out of station to leeward. At about that time the Spanish lee division put about on the port tack as if with the intention of cutting the British column at the point at which the vessels composing it were tacking in succession. The *Orion* got round; the *Colossus*, her next astern, was in the act of going about, when her foreyard and fore-topsail yard were shot away in the slings, and her fore-topmast went a little above the cap. She had, in consequence, to wear instead of tack; and while her head still pointed to leeward, the headmost Spaniard of the lee division drew so near as to threaten her with a raking broadside. Seeing Murray's danger and exposed position, Saumarez most gallantly backed his main topsail, and lay by to cover his friend; but the danger passed. Jervis signalled to his van to alter course one point to starboard, and to pass through the enemy. As he got up to the tacking point the *Irresistible*, his next ahead, became hotly engaged with the Spanish lee division. When she had tacked after the van the advancing Spaniards made an effort to break the line ahead of the *Victory*; but the British flagship was too quick for the enemy, and the leading Spaniard, a three-decker, had to tack close under the *Victory's* lee, receiving a raking broadside as she did so, and then bearing up in confusion. Her seven consorts, with more or less determination, tried to pass ahead or astern of the *Egmont* and *Goliath*, but were driven off, and, with the exception of the *Oriente*, obliged to bear up. The *Oriente* continued on the port tack, and, passing to leeward of the British rear under cover of the smoke, succeeded in joining the Spanish weather division.

It was about 1 P.M. when the *Excellent*, the rearmost ship of the British line, had advanced so far ahead on her course on the starboard tack as to leave, as James puts it, an open sea to leeward of the Spanish weather division, and when the leading ships of the latter bore up together by way of making an effort to join their friends to leeward. This was the critical moment of the action, which, up to that time, had been of a very partial character, and which, had the Spaniards been allowed unchecked to accomplish their purpose, would, no doubt, either have ended indecisively almost at once, or have become a long and tedious running fight, the quicker Spaniards crowding sail for Cadiz, and the better-handled British hanging upon their rear and doing such damage as they might. Nelson, in the *Captain*, quickly perceived this, and realised that the head of the doubled up British column, pursuing the main body of the Spaniards, was too far astern of it to be able to interfere unaided with success. Giving, therefore, a very wide interpretation to a signal[1] which had been hoisted by the *Victory* at 0.51 P.M., the Commodore ordered Captain Miller to wear the *Captain*. As soon as the two-decker was round, he took her between the *Diadem* and the *Excellent*, and ran her athwart the bows of the Spanish ships forming the central mass of the

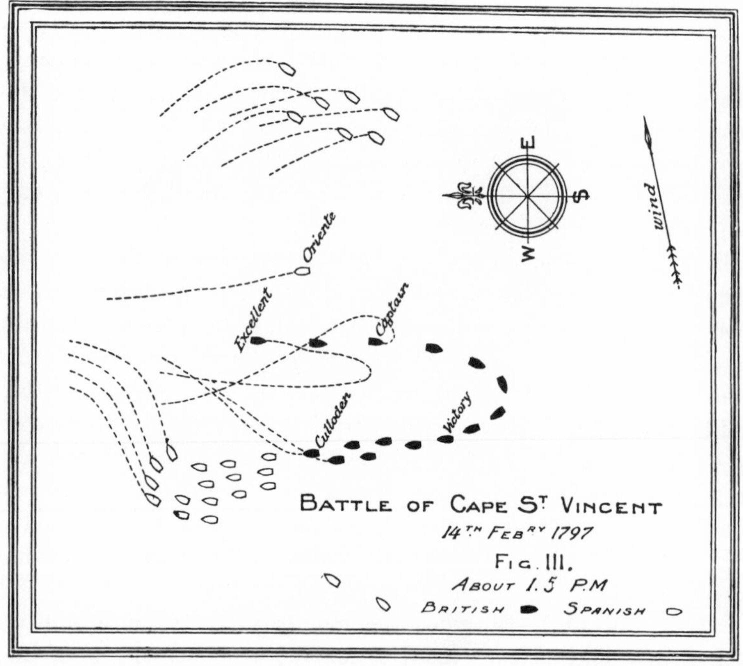

weather division. This mass included the *Santisima Trinidad,* 130, *San Josef,* 112, *Salvador del Mundo,* 112, *San Nicolas,* 80, *San Ysidro,* 74, and another three-decker which is supposed to have been the *Mexicano,* 112. At about 1.30 P.M., when the *Culloden,* which had gradually overhauled the Spanish rear, had for ten minutes sustained a renewed, but as yet not very close, engagement with this same group of ships, the *Captain* opened fire upon her gigantic opponents. Yet ere that Jervis, at 1.19 P.M., had signalled

[1] "To take suitable stations for mutual support, and engage the enemy, as coming up in succession."

to his rearmost ship, the *Excellent*, to come to the wind on the larboard tack, and, in compliance, Collingwood had hauled sharp up, so that, by 2.15 P.M., he had reached a station ahead of the leading or weather portion of the British line. The *Blenheim* and *Prince George* being then well up behind the *Culloden*, and there being thus five British ships in a position to bar the way, the Spanish plan was effectively frustrated. Indeed, the enemy had

SIR JAMES HAWKINS WHITSHED, BART., G.C.B., ADMIRAL OF THE FLEET.

(*From a lithograph by H. R. Cook, after the portrait by J. Northcote, painted when Sir James was Rear-Admiral,* 1799–1804.)

already relinquished the design of running to leeward of the British, and had hauled upon the starboard tack.

"At about 2 P.M.," says James, "the *Culloden* had stretched so far ahead as to cover the *Captain* from the heavy fire poured upon her by the Spanish four-decker and her companions, as they hauled up and brought their broadsides to bear. Of the respite thus afforded to her, the *Captain* took immediate advantage, replenishing her lockers with shot, and splicing and repairing her running rigging. Shortly afterwards the *Blenheim*, passing also to windward of the *Captain*, afforded her a second respite, which was taken advantage of as before. The two more immediate opponents of the

Captain and *Culloden* had been the *San Ysidro* and *Salvador del Mundo*: these, having already lost some of their topmasts, and being otherwise in a crippled state, the *Blenheim*, by a few of her heavy broadsides, sent staggering astern, to be cannonaded afresh by the *Prince George*, *Orion*, and other advancing ships .... At 2.26 P.M. the *Excellent*, having been directed by signal to bear up, edged away, and at 2.35, arriving abreast of the disabled Spanish three-decker, *Salvador del Mundo*, engaged the latter upon her weather bow for a few minutes; then passing on to the next Spanish ship in succession, the *San Ysidro*, whose three topmasts had already been shot away. This ship Captain Collingwood engaged closely on the lee beam until 2.53 P.M.; when, after a gallant defence in her crippled state from the fire of her former opponent, the *San Ysidro* hauled down the Spanish, and hoisted the English flag [1] .... Very soon after the *Excellent* had quitted the *Salvador del Mundo* for the *San Ysidro*, the *Irresistible* and *Diadem* commenced an attack upon the former, the 74 stationing herself upon the weather bow, and the 64 upon the lee quarter, of the Spanish three-decker, then, with her fore and main topmasts gone, and otherwise much disabled .... Observing the *Victory* about to pass under her stern, and that the *Barfleur* was following close, the *Salvador del Mundo*, whose mizen topmast had since shared the fate of the fore and main, very judiciously hauled down her flag as soon as some of the *Victory's* bow guns [2] began to bear upon her .... At about 3.15 P.M. the *Excellent* .... came to close action with the 80-gun ship *San Nicolas*, then with her fore topmast gone, and who, until the *Excellent* arrived abreast of her to leeward, had been in hot action with the *Captain*. Passing within ten feet of the *San Nicolas's* starboard side, the *Excellent* poured in a destructive fire, and, in compliance with the signal then flying, to fill and stand on, made sail ahead. In luffing up to avoid Captain Collingwood's salute, the *San Nicolas* ran foul of the *San Josef*, whose mizen mast had already been shot away, and who had received considerable other damage .... As soon as the *Excellent* was sufficiently advanced to be clear of her, the *Captain* luffed up as close to the wind as her shattered condition would admit; when her fore topmast, which had already been severely shot through, fell over the side. In this unmanageable state, with her wheel shot away, and all her sails, shrouds, and running rigging more or less cut; with the *Blenheim* ahead, and the *Culloden* crippled astern, no alternative remained but to board the Spanish two-decker. As a well-judged preparative, the *Captain* reopened, within less than twenty yards, her larboard broadside, the heavy fire from which the *San Nicolas* returned with spirit for several minutes, when the *Captain* suddenly put her helm a-starboard, and, on coming to, hooked with her larboard cat-head the starboard quarter-gallery of the *San Nicolas*, and, with her spritsail yard, the latter's main [3] rigging." [4]

The account of the extraordinary feat which followed may be given in Nelson's own words. He called for the boarders, and ordered them to board the *San Nicolas*, on the port side of which lay the *San Josef*, still foul of her consort.

"The soldiers of the 69th," wrote Nelson in a paper [5] which was published some time afterwards, "with an alacrity which will ever do them credit, and Lieutenant Pearson

---

[1] "But Captain Collingwood, disdaining the parade of taking possession of a vanquished enemy, most gallantly pushed up, with every sail set, to save his old friend and messmate, who was to appearance in a critical state." Nelson: 'A Few Remarks relative to Myself,' etc.

[2] It is doubtful whether she fired any of them at the three-decker.

[3] Nelson says "the mizen rigging"; and such it obviously was.

[4] James (ed. 1837), ii. 38–40.

[5] 'Nav. Chron.,' ii. 500.

of the same regiment, were almost the foremost on this service:—the first man who jumped into the enemy's mizen chains was Captain Berry, late my first lieutenant (Captain Miller was in the very act of going also, but I directed him to remain); he was supported from our sprit-sail yard, which hooked in the mizen rigging. A soldier of the 69th regiment having broken the upper quarter-gallery window, I jumped in myself, and was followed by others as fast as possible. I found the cabin doors fastened, and some Spanish officers fired their pistols: but having broke open the doors, the soldiers fired, and the Spanish Brigadier (Commodore with a distinguishing pendant) fell, as retreating to the quarter-deck. I pushed immediately onwards for the

REAR-ADMIRAL SIR THOMAS TROUBRIDGE, BART.

(*From a drawing by W. Evans, after a picture by Sir Wm. Beechey, R.A.*)

quarter-deck, where I found Captain Berry in possession of the poop, and the Spanish ensign hauling down. I passed with my people, and Lieutenant Pearson, on the larboard gangway, to the forecastle, where I met two or three Spanish officers, prisoners to my seamen:—they delivered me their swords. A fire of pistols, or muskets, opening from the admiral's stern-gallery of the *San Josef*, I directed the soldiers to fire into her stern; and calling to Captain Miller, ordered him to send more men into the *San Nicolas*; and directed my people to board the first-rate, which was done in an instant, Captain Berry assisting me into the main chains. At this moment a Spanish officer looked over the quarter-deck rail, and said they surrendered. From this most welcome intelligence, it was not long before I was on the quarter-deck, where the Spanish captain, with a bow, presented me his sword, and said the admiral was dying of his wounds. I asked him on his honour, if the ship was surrendered. He declared she was: on which I gave him my hand, and desired him to call on his officers and ship's company, and tell them of it: which he did:—and on the quarter-deck of a Spanish first-rate, extravagant as the story may seem, did I receive the swords of vanquished Spaniards: which, as I received, I gave to William Fearney, one of my bargemen, who put them, with the greatest *sang-froid*, under his arm."

There is no doubt that Nelson believed that the surrender of the *San Josef* was brought about chiefly if not entirely by the fact that he boarded her from the *San Nicolas*; but it is practically certain that the immediate cause of the surrender, both of the *San Nicolas* and of the *San Josef*, was the heavy fire to which, at the time, they were being treated by the *Prince George*, and which was not, indeed, suspended until the *Captain* hailed Parker's flagship to say that the Spaniards had struck. Yet, even if such be the truth, it detracts nothing from Nelson's dash and gallantry. He boarded, supposing on each occasion that he was boarding a still unbeaten foe.

After having left the *San Nicolas*, the *Excellent* added her fire to that which, by that time, the *Blenheim*, *Orion*, and *Irresistible* were pouring into the *Santisima Trinidad*. The four-decker is said not only to have struck, but to have actually hoisted British colours: yet, be this as it may, she became no prize, for, relieved by two of her van ships, which wore to her support, by the two vessels which all day had been coming up from the west-south-west, and by the approaching junction of the Spanish lee division, she at length got clear of her foes. At 3.52 P.M., perceiving how many fresh ships were coming up, Jervis signalled to his fleet to prepare to bring to, in order to be ready to cover the four prizes and the disabled vessels. At 4.15 P.M. the frigates were directed to take the prizes in tow; and at 4.39 the fleet was ordered to form close line ahead in wake of the *Victory*. The action had then practically ceased, although as late as 4.50 the *Britannia* and *Orion* exchanged some shot with the ships which were covering the *Santisima Trinidad*.[1]

The numbers killed and wounded in each of the British ships have already been given in a note. It should be explained that the numbers returned as wounded included only the very severely injured, and that, though the practice of omitting them was not usual in the service, the less seriously hurt were not counted. With these latter, the total of the wounded probably amounted to 400

[1] Nelson, at 5 P.M., shifted his broad pennant from the disabled *Captain* to the *Irresistible*.

officers and men. The only officers killed were Major of Marines William Norris (*Captain*), Lieut. of Marines George A. Livingstone (*Culloden*), Midshipman James Goodench (*Captain*), and Boatswain Peter Peffers (*Excellent*). The officers wounded were: Commodore Nelson (bruised only), Lieutenants Andrew Thompson (*Irresistible*) and Edward Libby (*Blenheim*); Master's Mates Hugh M'Kinnon (*Irresistible*), Edward Augustus Down (*Excellent*), and Joseph Wixon (*Blenheim*, mortally); Midshipmen Thomas Mansel (*Orion*), William Balfour (*Irresistible*), and Thomas Lund (*Captain*); and Boatswains James Peacock (*Blenheim*), and —— Carrington (*Captain*). The *Captain* was the only British ship that lost any mast; but the *Colossus*, *Culloden*, *Egmont*, and *Blenheim* all had masts and spars badly wounded, and were severely cut up. Only about ten of the Spanish vessels, exclusive of the prizes, appear to have been seriously handled, the greatest sufferer being the *Santisima Trinidad*, which, moreover, lost upwards of 200 people killed and wounded. All the prizes lost masts; and the casualties on board them were: *Salvador del Mundo*, 42 killed, 124 wounded; *San Ysidro*, 29 killed, 63 wounded; *San Josef*, 46 killed, 96 wounded; and *San Nicolas*, 144 killed, 59 wounded.

It was a great victory, but not, in the circumstances, a surprising one. True, twenty-seven Spanish ships were opposed to the British fifteen, and the numerical advantage of the Spaniards was even greater in guns and men than it was in ships. But, while Jervis commanded a highly disciplined and splendidly trained force, Don José de Cordova had under his orders little better than a raw and presently a panic-stricken mob of men. Some of his ships, with complements ranging from 530 to 950 people, had on board but 60 or 80 seamen apiece, all the rest being soldiers and fresh landsmen. The poor wretches fought courageously enough, but, naturally, many of them lost their heads; and no better testimony of the general disorganisation can be cited than the fact that, after the *San Josef* had been taken possession of, it was found that some of the guns on the side on which she had been most hotly engaged had still their tompions in them. The inexperience of the crews was in no wise compensated for by any skill on the part of the officers. From first to last the Spanish fleet was so much in confusion that half the ships composing it could not use their guns without inflicting more damage on their friends than on their foes. The officers were as brave as gentlemen of their nationality commonly are; but, from highest to lowest, they were excelled by Jervis's officers in knowledge, seamanship, coolness, and prescience. Jervis himself, in boldly attacking what seemed to be so alarmingly superior a force; Troubridge, in leading with an undaunted front; and Nelson and Collingwood, in resourcefully doing the right thing at the right moment, all contributed equally to the general result; yet so weak were the Spaniards that they must have given way before almost any opponents bold enough to be blind to mere numerical superiority and to lay on with dash, skill, and decision. Indeed, the deed was done when it was shown that the Spaniards were not feared.

Why then was the victory not more complete? Why were only

COMMEMORATIVE MEDAL OF THE BATTLE OF CAPE ST. VINCENT, 1797.

(From an original lent by H.S.H. Captain Prince Louis of Battenberg, R.N.)

four ships taken? Why did Jervis allow his opponent to carry off his disabled vessels, three or four of which were almost entirely crippled? It is difficult to reply. Night, it is true, was coming on when Jervis at 5 P.M. stopped the pursuit, but, as James says, "it was that very night which would have brought the two fleets nearer to an equality. The greater the difficulties of manœuvring, the greater were the chances in favour of the British; and, with 12 ships formed as British ships usually are formed, it is a question whether, when the darkness of a February night added its horrors to the destructive broadsides of a gallant and well-disciplined, though numerically inferior enemy, the Spanish admiral would not have abandoned the whole of his crippled ships to the conquerors."

During the night of February 14th, both fleets lay to in order to repair damages, and at dawn on the 15th, the two were within sight of one another in line of battle ahead on opposite tacks. The Spaniards had the wind, and could have provoked a renewal of the action; but they contented themselves with bearing down at 2.30 P.M., and hauling their wind as soon as Jervis hauled his. They then disappeared, and, on the afternoon of the 16th, the British fleet and its prizes anchored in Lagos Bay. When last the enemy was seen, his disabled four-decker, the *Santisima Trinidad*, was distant from the main body, and in tow of a frigate. Jervis, therefore, with a view to the possibility of picking her up, detached from Lagos the *Emerald*, 36, Captain Velters Cornwall Berkeley; *Minerve*, 38, Captain George Cockburn; *Niger*, 32, Captain Edward James Foote; *Bonne Citoyenne*, 20, Commander Charles Lindsay; and *Raven*, 18, Commander James Prowse (1), to look for her. The little squadron sighted the *Santisima Trinidad* at 3 P.M. on February 20th, about eighty miles south-south-east of Cape St. Vincent; and Berkeley, who was senior officer, signalled for a chase. The *Emerald*, *Minerve*, and *Niger*[1] were overhauling the enemy, when, at about 6 P.M., Berkeley made a signal "to keep sight of the enemy, or make known their motions by day or night," and then, as the *Emerald's* log puts it, "only being answered by the *Minerve*, wore ship to the northward." Why Berkeley behaved in this extraordinary manner has never been satisfactorily explained. It has been suggested that he had reason to believe that he could not count upon the co-operation of the *Bonne Citoyenne*. But against this theory are to be set the two facts that he never brought the Commander of that ship to a court-martial, and that, although soon after 6 P.M. he was joined by the *Terpsichore*, 32, Captain Richard Bowen, he still kept his ships headed to the northward, and so presently lost sight of the disabled Spaniard. Bowen parted company almost immediately, and, whether by accident or design, found the *Santisima Trinidad* at 7 P.M. on February 28th. On March 1st, although he was then alone, he pluckily engaged her. He was naturally unable to effect much against his huge antagonist, but he nevertheless kept company with her until, off Cape Spartel, she fell in with part of the Spanish fleet. It is perhaps unfair to draw comparisons between the conduct of Berkeley[2] and that of Bowen; but it is difficult to avoid regretting that the motives of the former for his mysterious action have never been made public, and that

[1] The *Raven* had previously parted company.

[2] Berkeley soon afterwards, as James says, "judiciously," resigned his command.

they are not by any means so obviously creditable as is Bowen's gallantry.

On February 23rd, Sir John Jervis sailed from Lagos, where he had landed his prisoners, for Lisbon. For his services, he was created[1] Baron Jervis of Meaford and Earl St. Vincent, in the peerage of Great Britain, and was granted a pension of £3000 a year; Vice-Admiral Thompson[2] and Rear-Admiral Parker[3] were made Baronets; Vice-Admiral Waldegrave[4] was rewarded with the governorship of Newfoundland; Nelson[5] was rewarded with a K.B., and the freedom of the city of London; and Captain Calder was knighted. The thanks of both Houses were voted to the fleet, and a gold medal was conferred upon each of the Flag-officers and Captains. Collingwood sturdily refused to receive his, unless he should first be given one for the Glorious First of June, on which occasion, he said, he had equally done his duty. His country honoured itself by sending him both medals, together with an apology.

The unfortunate Spanish admirals and captains had to pay heavily for the folly of their government in sending to sea a fleet that was not fit to fight. Many of them were deprived of their rank; others were suspended; and yet others were publicly reprimanded. The defeated fleet took refuge in Cadiz, where Admiral Massaredo assumed command of the twenty-six or twenty-eight sail of the line that lay in the port.

Jervis, who had been reinforced, lost no time in blockading the enemy. He left Lisbon on March 31st, and appeared off Cadiz on April 4th. But he could not induce the Spaniards to risk another general action, although, with a view to provoking them into coming out and doing so, he bombarded the town on the night of July 3rd, sending in the *Thunder*, bomb, 8, Lieutenant John Gourly, to throw her 13·5 in. shells into the place. The *Thunder* was covered by gunboats, launches, and boats of the fleet, under the orders of Nelson, who commanded the inshore squadron; but, it being presently discovered that her largest mortar was unserviceable, she had to be withdrawn, protected by the fire of the *Goliath*, 74, Captain Thomas Foley (3), *Terpsichore*, 32, Captain Richard

[1] On May 27th, 1797. [2] On June 23rd, 1797. [3] On June 24th, 1797.

[4] Subsequently created Lord Radstock in the peerage of Ireland, December 29th, 1800.

[5] Promoted to be Rear-Admiral on February 20th, six days after the battle.

Bowen, and *Fox*, cutter, 10, Lieutenant John Gibson. As she retired, she was chased by gunboats and launches from the harbour, and these were met by similar craft under the personal leadership of Nelson, who, in a boat containing but sixteen hands all told, came into close and fierce conflict with the barge of Don Miguel Tyrason, manned with a crew of twenty-eight men. Eighteen of the Spaniards were killed; all the rest, including Tyrason, were wounded and taken prisoners; and, after the enemy had been driven under the forts, the British retired with two mortar boats and the barge, and with a loss of but one killed and twenty wounded. Among the latter were Captain Thomas Francis Fremantle (*Seahorse*), Lieutenants William Selby (*Ville de Paris*), Henry Nathaniel Rowe (*Diadem*), and Gregory Grant (*Prince George*), Master's Mate Hugh Pearson (*Barfleur*), and Midshipman Robert Tooley (*Prince George*). Nelson's cockswain, John Sykes, who had stood with him on the quarter-deck of the *San Josef*, was severely wounded while defending the Rear-Admiral.

Another bombardment was effected on the night of July 5th, Nelson again commanding. Three bombs, the *Thunder*, 8, *Terror*, 8, and *Stromboli*, 8, were employed, and were covered by the *Theseus*, 74, Captain Ralph Willett Miller, the *Terpsichore*, 32, Captain Richard Bowen, and the *Emerald*, 36, Captain Thomas Moutray Waller. Much damage was done, and part of the Spanish fleet, apprehending a renewal of the firing, warped out of range on the following day. As before, the small craft encountered one another during the darkness; but the British lost, in the desultory fighting, only three killed and sixteen wounded, the latter including Captain of Marines, Thomas Oldfield (*Theseus*), Lieutenants John Collins (*Victory*), and John Hornsey (*Seahorse*), and Midshipmen John Collier (*Theseus*), and John Stephenson (*Audacious*). A third bombardment, planned for the night of the 8th, had to be relinquished owing to the state of the weather.

While the blockade still went on, Lord St. Vincent determined to make an effort for the capture of a rich galleon which, it was rumoured, had arrived at Santa Cruz,[1] Tenerife, from Manilla. The

[1] Here, on May 29th, the boats of the *Lively*, 32, Captain Benjamin Hallowell, and *Minerve*, 38, Captain George Cockburn, under the orders of Lieutenant Thomas Masterman Hardy, first of the *Minerve*, had cut out in broad daylight, under a heavy fire, the French corvette *Mutine*, 14. Hardy, and Midshipman John Edgar, with thirteen men, were wounded in the affair, but no one was killed, and Hardy, for his gallantry was made a Commander into the prize.

Commander-in-Chief, who perhaps for once underrated the difficulties of an enterprise, entrusted the expedition to the orders of Rear-Admiral Sir Horatio Nelson, who, when his force was complete, had under him the following vessels :—

Ships.	Guns.	Commanders.
Theseus	74	Rear-Adm. Sir H. Nelson, K.B. (B.). Capt. Ralph Willett Miller.
Culloden	74	„ Thomas Troubridge.
Zealous	74	„ Samuel Hood (2).
Leander[1]. . . .	50	„ Thomas Boulden Thompson.
Seahorse	38	„ Thomas Francis Fremantle.
Emerald	36	„ Thomas Moutray Waller.
Terpsichore[2]. . .	32	„ Richard Bowen.
Fox, cutter . . .	10	Lieut. John Gibson.
and a mortar boat.		

1 *Leander* joined on July 24th. 2 *Terpsichore* joined on July 16th.

Nelson parted company on July 15th, and on the 20th arrived off Tenerife, and on that night the *Seahorse*, *Emerald*, *Terpsichore*, and *Fox*, with some of the boats of the squadron, endeavoured to land men to seize a fort on the north-east side of the bay, but failed, owing to adverse winds and currents. On the 22nd, the squadron drew closer in, and, at night, succeeded in landing some men; but, as the heights were found to be strongly held, the people were re-embarked. On the evening of the 24th, Nelson anchored his squadron to the north-east of the town, and made a feint as if to disembark a force in that direction; but at 11 P.M. he put 700 seamen and Marines into his boats, 180 more into the Fox, and yet another 75 into a captured provision boat, and, himself assuming the command, pushed off in rough weather and thick darkness for the mole head. At 1.30 A.M. on the 25th, the *Fox* and the boats containing Nelson, Fremantle, Thompson, and, Bowen, as well as a few other craft, got undiscovered within half gunshot of their destination; when suddenly an alarm was sounded and a heavy fire was opened on them. The *Fox* was sunk, and with her went down 97 men, including Lieutenant Gibson. Nelson was struck on the right elbow, just as he was drawing his sword and jumping ashore from his barge, and he had to be conveyed back to his ship.[1] Another shot sank Bowen's boat, drowning seven or eight people. Yet, in spite of these disasters, that part of the British force landed and carried the mole head, driving off in confusion the three or four

1 His right arm was immediately amputated.

hundred men who had held it, and capturing and spiking six 24-pounders mounted upon it. But a heavy fire of musketry and grape was immediately afterwards directed upon the mole from the citadel and houses near it, and the British were mowed down by scores, the brave Bowen and his first lieutenant, George Thorpe, being among the killed.

During this time the boats under Captain Troubridge, Captain Waller, and others, unable, owing to the darkness and the surf, to make the mole, had landed under a battery to the southward of the citadel; and Captains Hood and Miller subsequently landed further to the south-west. Several boats, however, had to put back. Troubridge and Waller, having collected a few men, advanced to the great square of the town, where they expected to meet the Rear-Admiral and the remaining Captains. They sent a summons to the citadel, but, receiving no answer, they joined Captains Hood and Miller, and resolved to make an attempt upon the citadel, although they had lost all their scaling ladders. No sooner did they begin to move than they discovered that the place was crowded with troops, and that every street was commanded by field-pieces. To add to their difficulties, most of their ammunition was wet, and nearly all their boats were stove in. Unable, thus, either to advance or to retire, Troubridge, with magnificent effrontery, sent Hood with a flag of truce to the governor, to say that, if the Spaniards advanced, the British would burn the town. At the same time, he offered to capitulate on the following terms: the British to be allowed to embark with their arms in their own boats, or, if these were destroyed, in others to be furnished to them; and the ships before the town to molest it no further, and not to attack any of the Canary Islands.

The Spanish governor[1] seems to have been taken captive by the very audacity of these proposals, coming as they did from people who were already practically at his mercy. Not only did he provide the British with boats, and allow them to depart, but he also supplied them with wine and biscuit, ordered that the wounded should be received into his own hospital, and sent a message to Nelson to the effect that the squadron was at liberty, during its stay, to send on shore and purchase whatsoever refreshments it might need.

This lamentable but not inglorious affair, was very costly to the squadron. In addition to Captain Bowen, and Lieutenants George

[1] Don Juan Antonio Gutteri.

Thorpe and John Gibson (*Fox*), Lieutenants John Weatherhead (*Theseus*) and William Earnshaw (*Leander*), Lieutenants of Marines, Raby Robinson (*Leander*) and William Basham (*Emerald*), and twenty-three seamen and fourteen Marines were killed. Rear-Admiral Nelson, Captain T. F. Fremantle, and T. B. Thompson, Lieutenant John Douglas (2) (*Seahorse*), Midshipman Robert Watts, and eighty-five seamen and fifteen Marines were wounded. In addition, ninety-seven seamen and Marines were drowned, and five were reported missing.

The Mediterranean, which had been abandoned by the British in the previous year, was not again effectively occupied by them during 1797. Nelson, as has been seen, having effected the evacuation of Elba, passed the Strait in the middle of February; and from that moment, until November, scarcely a British frigate went east of Gibraltar. Even in November, nothing approaching to a re-occupation was attempted. Lord St. Vincent merely detached from his fleet in the Tagus the *Leander*, 50, Captain Thomas Boulden Thompson, the *Hamadryad*, 36, Captain Thomas Elphinstone, and a sloop, to Algier, to settle some disputes with the Dey; and, when the service had been executed, the little force withdrew. This long abandonment was contemporary with a great and natural increase of the French power on the Mediterranean coasts. Austria and the Pope relinquished, for the time, the struggle with the Republic; which, by the Treaty of Campo Formio,[1] acquired, besides the Austrian Netherlands, Corfu, Zante, Cephalonia, and the other Venetian islands south of the Gulf of Drin. The republic of Genoa, moreover, had ceased to exist on June 6th, and, under the name of Liguria, had become French. And, with the Ionian islands, France had seized, and added to her navy, six Venetian 64-gun ships and six frigates, beside other men-of-war which she had seized at the capture of Venice in May. The islands, and the ships there, were taken over without resistance, and garrisoned or manned by a squadron from Toulon, under Rear-Admiral Brueys, reinforced by a flotilla of transports under Captain G. F. J. Bourdé. Brueys returned to Toulon in November.

In the North Sea, the observation of the Dutch ports was, for a time, almost put a stop to by the mutinies and disaffection in the fleet. Towards the end of May, Admiral Duncan's effective force was, in fact, reduced to two ships, the *Venerable*, 74, and the

[1] October 17th, 1797.

Adamant, 50. Yet the gallant old officer did not hesitate to proceed to, and maintain, his station off the Texel, where lay a Netherlands fleet of fifteen sail of the line and 50-gun ships. By repeatedly signalling, as if to ships in the offing, he conveyed to the Dutch the impression that he was amply supported, and so induced them to remain in harbour while he was anxiously awaiting reinforcements. These began to join him in the shape of single ships and small

VICE-ADMIRAL SIR WILLIAM GEORGE FAIRFAX.

(*From an engraving by Ridley*, 1801.)

groups in the second week of June; and at length Duncan was again in a position to deal with the enemy. But, at the beginning of October, being short of stores and having received a certain amount of damage in boisterous weather, Duncan put into Yarmouth road to revictual and refit, leaving Captain Henry Trollope, of the *Russell*, 74, with the *Adamant*, 50, *Beaulieu*, 40, *Circe*, 20, and *Martin*, 16, to observe the motions of the Dutch.

Early in the morning of October 9th, the hired armed lugger, *Black Joke*, appeared at the back of Yarmouth sands with the signal flying for an enemy. Duncan succeeded in weighing before noon with the eleven ships of the line then with him, and at once steered across, with a fair wind, for his old station. Later in the day he was joined by the *Powerful*, 74, *Agincourt*, 64, and *Isis*, 50; and on the afternoon of the 10th, he was off the Texel, within which his scouts counted twenty-two square-rigged vessels, chiefly merchantmen. Trollope had informed him of the course which the Dutch fleet had taken, and, in consequence, the British headed to the southward, parallel with the shore. At 7 A.M. on the 11th, the *Russell*, *Adamant*, *Beaulieu*, which were in the south-west, signalled that the enemy was in sight to leeward; and at 8.30 A.M. the Dutch fleet was visible in the indicated quarter. The two forces thus in presence of one another are set forth below.

THE FLEETS IN THE ACTION OFF CAMPERDOWN, OCTOBER 11, 1797; indicating their order, or intended order in line of battle, and showing the numbers killed and wounded in each British ship, and the fate of each Dutch ship. (NOTE.—The British starboard division led; but several ships of both British divisions were out of station. The Dutch line was as given.)

BRITISH.

	Ships.	Guns.	Commanders. [* Killed or mortally wounded.]	Killed.	Wounded.
Port, or Lee.	*Russell* . . .	74	Capt. Henry Trollope.	..	7
	Director . . .	64	,, William Bligh.	..	7
	Montagu . .	74	,, John Knight (2).	3	5
	Veteran . . .	64	,, George Gregory.	4	21
	Monarch. . .	74	Vice-Adm. Richard Onslow (R). Capt. Edward O'Brien.	36	100
	Powerful . .	74	,, William O'Brien Drury.	10	78
	Monmouth . .	64	Com. James Walker (2) actg.	5	22
	Agincourt . .	64	Capt. John Williamson (1).	..	..
Starboard, or Weather.	*Triumph* . .	74	,, William Essington.	29	55
	Venerable . .	74	Admiral Adam Duncan (B). Capt. William George Fairfax	15	62
	Ardent . . .	64	,, Richard Rundle Burges.*	41	107
	Bedford . . .	74	,, Sir Thomas Byard.	30	41
	Lancaster . .	64	,, John Wells.	3	18
	Belliqueux . .	64	,, John Inglis (2).	25	78
	Adamant . .	50	,, William Hotham (2)	..	..
	Isis	50	,, William Mitchell.	2	21
	Beaulieu . .	40	,, Francis Fayerman.		
	Circe	28	,, Peter Halkett.		
	Martin . . .	16	Com. Hon. Charles Paget.		
	Rose, hir. cutter	10	Lieut. Joseph Brodie.		
	King George, do.	12	,, James Rains.		
	Active, do. . .	12	,, J— Hamilton.		
	Diligent, do. .	6	,, T— Dawson.		
	Speculator, hir. lugger. . .	8	,, H— Hales.		

DUTCH.

Ships.	Guns.	Commanders. [* Killed or mortally wounded.]	T. Taken. E. Escaped.
Gelijkheid . .	68	Com. H. A. Ruijsch.	T.
Beschermer .	56	Capt. Hinxt.*	E.
Hercules . .	64	Com. Ruijsoort.	T.
Admiraal T. H. De Vries .	68	Capt. J. B. Zegers.	T.
Vrijheid . .	74	Vice-Adm. J. W. De Winter. Com. L. W. van Rossum.*	T.
Staten Generaal	74	Rear-Adm. Samuel Storij. ..	E.
Wassenaar .	64	Com. A. Holland.	T.
Batavier . .	56	,, Souter.	E.
Brutus . . .	74	Rear-Adm. J. A. Bloijs van Treslong. Com. Polders.	E.
Leijden . .	68	,, J. D. Musquetier.	E.
Mars, rasé . .	44	,, D. H. Kolff.	E.
Cerberus . .	68	,, Jacobson.	E.
Jupiter . .	72	V.-Adm. H. Reijntjes.	T.
Haarlem . .	68	Capt. O. Wiggerts.	T.
Alkmaar . .	56	Com. J. W. Krafft.	T.
Delft . . .	54	Capt. G. Verdooren.	T.
Atalante, brig	18	Com. B. Pletsz.	E.
Heldin . . .	32	,, Dumenil de Lestrille.	E.
Galathée, brig	18	,, Riverij.	E.
Minerva . .	24	,, Eijlbracht.	E.
Ajax, brig . .	18	Lieut. Arkenbout.	E.
Waakzaamheid	24	Com. M. van. Nierop.	E.
Embuscade .	36	,, J. Huijs.	T.
Daphné, brig .	18	Lieut. Frederiks.	E.
Monnikendam	44	Com. Th. Lancester.	T.
Haasje, adv. boat . . .	6	Lieut. Hartingveld.	E.

The Dutch had left the Texel at 10 A.M. on October 8th, with a light breeze from east by north. According to French writers, Admiral De Winter quitted port expressly to meet and fight Duncan; but it is upon the whole more probable that his immediate object was to join hands with the French at Brest. Be this as it may, Trollope discovered the Dutch that night, the wind being then south-west, and the enemy to windward. De Winter made for the mouth of the Maas, where he had expected to be joined by a 64-gun ship; but, not finding her, he stood to the westward, still observed by Trollope. He made some efforts to drive off or capture the little British force; but on the night of the 10th, he was obliged to recall his chasers upon learning that Duncan was within about thirty miles of him; and, getting his ships together, he made, with a north-west wind, for a point off Kamperduin his place of rendezvous.

At daylight on the 11th, the Dutch were about eighteen miles off Scheveningen in loose order. Soon afterwards, seeing Trollope's signals to windward, and knowing from them that his enemy was close at hand, De Winter ordered his captains to their stations, and, to facilitate the junction of his rearmost ships, stood towards the land. When the nearest coast bore east, about twelve miles, he directed his fleet to haul to the wind on the starboard tack; and, as soon as he sighted Duncan in the north-west, he put about on the port tack, formed a close line from south-west to north-east, and, with main yards square, awaited the attack.

The British fleet, when first it had sight of the Dutch, was in very straggling order, chiefly owing to the unequal sailing of the ships. Duncan made his van ships shorten sail, and, at about 11.10 A.M., brought to on the port tack; but, observing a little later that the Dutch, who kept their main topsails now shivering and now full, were drawing in with the shore, he signalled in quick succession; for each ship to engage her opponent in the enemy's line; to bear up and sail large; and for the van to attack the enemy's rear. At 11.30, when the centre of the Dutch line bore south-east, distant between four and five miles, the British bore down, still, however, in straggling, and, indeed, in somewhat confused order. At 11.53 A.M., Duncan signalled that he should pass through the enemy's line and engage from leeward; but, as the weather was thick, this signal was not generally taken in. At about 12.5 P.M. there was substituted for it the signal for close action.

It was about 12.30, when the *Monarch*, leading the larboard division of the British fleet, cut through the Dutch line between the *Jupiter* and the *Haarlem*, firing, as she did so, a broadside into each, and then luffing up alongside the *Jupiter*, while the *Powerful*, coming up, tackled the *Haarlem*. To leeward of his line of battle, De Winter had stationed a subsidiary line of frigates and brigs; and two of these, the *Monikendam* and the *Daphné*,[1] each seized the

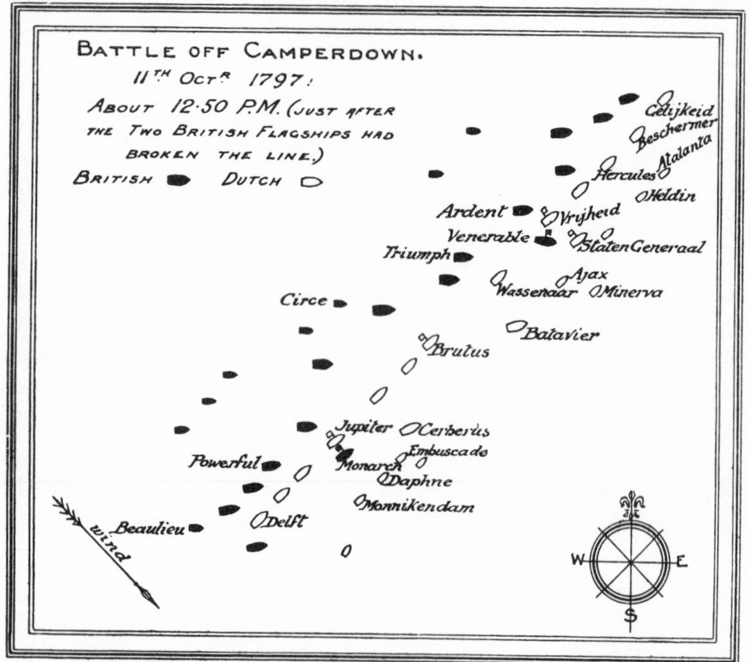

opportunity of pouring a raking fire into Vice-Admiral Onslow's flagship as she rounded to. Both the small craft suffered severely for their temerity in thus deliberately inviting attention from a ship of the line. Most of the other vessels of the British larboard division were close behind the leaders; and, in a very few minutes, the Dutch rear, with the exception of the three headmost ships[2] of it, was very closely engaged. Those three ships were exposed only to a more distant fire; and it was to some extent owing to this that

[1] James says that the brig was the *Atalanta*, not the *Daphné*; but he is mistaken. The *Atalanta* was the headmost ship in the Dutch second line.

[2] *Brutus*, *Leijden*, and *Mars*.

they were subsequently able to attempt to succour De Winter, and that they ultimately escaped capture.

About eighteen minutes after the *Monarch* had broken the rear of the Dutch line, the *Venerable*, first endeavouring to pass astern of the *Vrijheid*, but being frustrated by the promptitude of the *Staten Generaal* in closing the interval, put her helm to larboard, and delivered such a broadside into the port quarter of Storij's flagship as obliged her to bear up. The *Venerable* then ranged along the lee side of the *Vrijheid*, while the *Ardent* engaged the same vessel from windward. A little later, the *Triumph* got into close action with the *Wassenaar*, and the *Bedford* with the *Admiraal Tjerk Hiddes De Vries* and the *Hercules*. The last named presently took fire; and, although the flames were promptly extinguished, the danger was at one moment so great that she had to throw all her powder overboard. In the meantime she had lost her mizen mast; and, having no means of defence, she struck. In her encounter with the *Wassenaar* the *Triumph* experienced no interruption; and she shortly compelled that vessel to surrender.[1] She then passed ahead towards the *Vrijheid*, which, though terribly mauled, was still firing, and which, indeed, distantly assisted by ships from the rear, had compelled the *Venerable* to haul off and wear round on the starboard tack. Nor, until De Winter's flagship had defended herself long and bravely, and, losing all her masts, had had her starboard battery put out of action by their fall, did she haul down her colours. She seems to have struck at about the same moment as the *Jupiter*; and, with the surrender of these two flagships, the action ceased. The British were then masters of seven ships of the line, two 50's, and two frigates,[2] or more than half the strength of the Dutch fleet. To attempt to pursue the rest was out of the question, for Duncan was already in but nine fathoms, and the low land, between Kamperduin and Egmond, was only five miles off.

It had been a most determined and sanguinary fight. On the side of the Dutch, Rear-Admiral Johan Arnold Bloijs van Treslong,[3] and Commander Souter,[4] and, on that of the British, Captain John

[1] The *Wassenaar*, after striking, was fired at by a Dutch brig, which induced her to rehoist her colours; but she struck again later to the *Russell*.

[2] *Vrijheid, Jupiter, Gelijkheid, Admiraal De Vries, Haarlem, Hercules, Wassenaar, Alkmaar, Delft, Monnikendam,* and *Embuscade.*

[3] Condemned, but subsequently reinstated.

[4] Broken and imprisoned.

Williamson (1),[1] were, it is true, afterwards charged with dereliction of duty. But, upon the whole, and equally on both sides, the combatants fought with a thoroughness and pertinacity which recalled the hot work of the old Dutch wars. A full list of the Dutch losses is not obtainable; but it is known that, of killed alone, there were 40 in the *Gelijkheid*, 43 in the *Delft*, 61 in the *Jupiter*, 50 in the frigate *Monnikendam*, and 58, besides 98 wounded, in the *Vrijheid*. These figures suffice to indicate the gallantry of the defence, and to prove that the victory was no easy one. As for the captured ships, they were all, says James, "either dismasted outright, or so injured in their masts that most of the latter fell, as soon as the wind and sea, in the passage home, began to act powerfully upon them. As to their hulls, the ships were like sieves, and

COMMEMORATIVE MEDAL OF THE BATTLE OF CAMPERDOWN, 1797.

(*From an original lent by H.S.H. Captain Prince Louis of Battenberg, R.N.*)

only worth bringing into port to be exhibited as trophies." The *Embuscade*, driven upon the Dutch coast, was re-captured[2] by her original owners; the *Monnikendam* was wrecked off West Capelle; and the *Delft*, with many hands still in her, foundered in a storm[3] on the 14th. The other prizes reached British ports, and were all added to the service, the *Jupiter* as the *Camperdown*, the *Hercules*

[1] Convicted of disobedience to signals, and of not going into action, and sentenced to be placed at the bottom of the post-list of 1797, and to be rendered incapable of further service C.M. December 4th to January 1st. Captain Williamson, who was acquitted of cowardice or disaffection, died in 1799.

[2] Only to become again a British prize in August, 1799.

[3] In striving to save the people from this disaster, Lieutenant Heiberg, late first of the ship, and Lieutenant Charles Bullen, in charge of the prize, vied with one another in gallantry. Heiberg perished; Bullen, who only saved himself by swimming, died Admiral Sir Charles Bullen in 1853.

as the *Delft*, and the rest under their own names, but none of them were ever again fit for sea. Their old masters had effectively used them up in that hard tussle.

The British ships also suffered very severely, but almost exclusively in the hulls. The Dutch had not wasted time in efforts to destroy rigging. They had fired low, and had generally reserved their fire until it could hardly fail to tell. The *Ardent* had 98 round shot in or through her timbers. The *Venerable*, *Bedford*, *Belliqueux*, *Triumph*, and *Monarch*, too, had been badly mauled; but no ship lost any more important spar than a foreyard. The casualties, therefore, as will be seen on reference to the note above, were relatively heavy, almost exactly ten per cent. of the whole number of officers and men engaged in the British line being killed or wounded. The officers killed were: Captain R. R. Burges (*Ardent*); Lieutenants Francis Ferrett (*Veteran*), and Robert Webster (*Belliqueux*); Master Michael Dun (*Ardent*); Master's Mate James Milne (*Belliqueux*), and four midshipmen, of whom two, J. P. Tindall and Moyle Finlay, belonged to the *Monarch*. Among the wounded officers were Captain Essington (*Triumph*), and Lieutenants Edward Sneyd Clay and William Henry Douglas (*Venerable*), James Retalick (*Monarch*), George Keenor (*Bedford*), Ulick Jennings (*Powerful*), James Rose and John Sobriel (*Ardent*), Robert England (*Belliqueux*), Benjamin Morgan (*Lancaster*), Patrick Chapman and George Trollope (*Triumph*), Ralph Sneyd (*Montagu*), and David Johnson (*Russell*). The Dutch loss in officers, both by immediate death and by mortal wounds, was equally heavy; but it is not true that, as Mr. James says, Admiral De Winter died in London during his captivity.[1] On the contrary, that gallant officer enjoyed many years of useful activity after his exchange, receiving from King Louis the rank of Marshal and the title of Graaf van Huessen, and, in 1810, taking the oath of allegiance to Bonaparte, when the kingdom of Holland was incorporated with the Empire.[2]

Admiral Duncan reached the Nore on October 16th. On the

[1] James, ii. 72 (ed. 1837).

[2] Authorities for the battle of Camperdown: Duncan's dispatch of October 13th; Journal of an Officer in 'Nav. Chron.,' iv.; 'Biography of Sir H. Trollope' in *U.S. Journal*, 1840; 'Sententie' of Admiral De Winter; 'Volledige Verslag,' etc., (1797); Rear-Admiral C. Richardson in *U.S. Magazine*, 1844; 'Anecs. of Camperdown' in *U.S. Journal* of 1841; Decree of Nat. Ass. of November 9th; 'Aanmerk. van een Zee-Officier' (1805); 'Leven van V.-Ad. Ruijsch'; 'Life of Duncan'; 'Voorloopig Bericht,' etc.; Mins. of C.Ms., British and Dutch.

20th of the same month he was created Baron Duncan of Lundie, and Viscount Duncan of Camperdown in the peerage of Great Britain; and, on the 30th, Vice-Admiral Onslow was made a baronet, while, a little later, Captains Henry Trollope and William George Fairfax were knighted. Duncan was further granted a pension of £3000 a year for three lives. The city of London presented its freedom to Duncan and Onslow, and to the former a

ADMIRAL SIR RICHARD ONSLOW, BART.

(*From a lithograph by D. Orme*, 1805.)

sword costing 200 and to the latter one costing 100 guineas. The thanks of both Houses were unanimously voted to the fleet; gold medals were granted to the Flag-officers, and to all the Captains, except Captain Williamson, who had fought in the line; most of the first Lieutenants engaged were promoted; and the King was only prevented[1] by adverse winds from visiting the fleet and the prizes. On December 19th, his Majesty went in state to St. Paul's to return

[1] He embarked for the purpose in the *Royal Charlotte* on October 30th.

thanks for the three great naval victories which thus far had blessed his arms since the beginning of the war.

The most important colonial expedition of the year 1797 was the one which led to the capture of Trinidad. On the Leeward Islands' station Rear-Admiral Henry Harvey (1) commanded, and, in pursuance of instructions, he quitted Port Royal, Martinique, on February 12th, with a squadron, on board of which was a body of troops under Lieut.-General Sir Ralph Abercromby. At a rendezvous off Carriacou, on the 14th, he picked up reinforcements, and, on the 16th, made Trinidad, and steered for the Gulf of Paria by way of Boca Grande. At 3.30 P.M., just as the British had cleared the channel, they discovered at anchor, in a bay[1] within, a Spanish squadron of four sail of the line and a frigate.[2] As the entrance to the enemy's anchorage appeared to be well protected by a battery of twenty guns and two mortars posted upon the island of Gaspargrande, and as the day was already far advanced, Harvey sent his transports, protected by the *Arethusa*, *Thorn*, and *Zebra*, to find a berth about five miles from Port of Spain, and ordered the *Alarm*, *Favourite*, and *Victorieuse* to keep under sail between the enemy and Port of Spain, while, with his ships of the line, he anchored within long gunshot of the Spanish ships and batteries, with the intention of preventing the foe from escaping during the night, and of taking measures in the morning for his destruction. But, to the surprise of the British, the Spaniards,

[1] Called Shaggaramus Bay in the dispatches.

[2] SQUADRON OF REAR-ADMIRAL HENRY HARVEY AT THE CAPTURE OF TRINIDAD, FEBRUARY, 1797, AND LIST OF THE SPANISH SQUADRON BURNT OR TAKEN IN SHAGGARAMUS BAY ON FEBRUARY 17TH.

British.			Spanish.		
Ships.	Guns.	Commanders.	Ships.	Guns.	Commanders.
Prince of Wales	98	Rear-Adm. Henry Harvey (1) (R.). Capt. John Harvey (2).	*San Vincente*[1]	80	Rear-Adm. Don S. R. de Apodaca. Capt. Don G. Mendoza.
Bellona	74	„ George Wilson.	*Gallardo*[1]	74	„ Don. G. Sorondo.
Vengeance	74	„ Thomas Macnamara Russell.	*Arrogante*[1]	74	„ Don R. Bonasa.
Invincible	74	„ George William Cayley.	*San Damaso*[2]	74	„ Don J. Jordan.
Scipio	64	„ Charles Sydney Davers.	*Santa Cecilia*[1]	34	„ Don M. Urtesebal.
Arethusa	38	„ Thomas Wolley.			
Alarm	32	„ Edward Fellowes.			
Favourite	16	Com. James Athol Wood.			
Zebra	16	„			
Thorn	16	„ John Hamstead.			
Victorieuse	12	„ Edward Stirling Dickson.			
Terror, bomb	8	„ Joseph Westbeach.			

[1] Burnt. [2] Added to the Navy.

at about 2 A.M. on the 17th, began to set fire to their ships, and, ere daylight, four out of the five were practically destroyed. The fifth, the *San Damaso*, 74,[1] escaped the flames, and was brought off without resistance by the boats of the squadron, the Spaniards having evacuated Gaspargrande island. This was occupied in the early morning by part of the Queen's Regiment, and, in the course of the day, other troops were landed, without interruption, three miles from Port of Spain, which was quietly entered that evening. On the following day the island of Trinidad peacefully capitulated. The Spaniards, it afterwards appeared, had burnt their ships because they had barely half enough officers and men wherewith to man them.

From Trinidad Harvey proceeded to the attack of Puerto Rico,[2] for which island he sailed on April 8th, having been joined by the *Alfred*, 74, Captain Thomas Totty, *Tamer*, 38, Captain Thomas Byam Martin, and a few smaller craft. He anchored off Congrejos point on the 17th, and, on the following day, disembarked some troops with but slight opposition; but San Juan, upon being reconnoitred, was found to be strongly fortified, and to be well provided with floating defences; and, after it had been bombarded without effect, Abercromby, on the 30th, abandoned the enterprise and re-embarked the troops, of whom he had lost during the operations 31 killed, 70 wounded, and 124 prisoners or missing. During the rest of the year, the squadron on the Leeward Islands' station confined its efforts to capturing the enemy's cruisers and protecting British trade.

Vice-Admiral Sir Hyde Parker (2), who commanded at Jamaica, drove ashore[3] and obliged the destruction, near Jean Rabel, in San Domingo, of the French frigate *Harmonie*, 44, on April 16th. It was discovered that she had been sent to sea from Cape François to convoy thither a number of captured provision-laden American vessels, which had been collected at Port au Paix and Jean Rabel by French privateers. The *Hermione*, 32, Captain Hugh Pigot (2), was accordingly despatched, with the *Quebec*, 32, Captain John Cooke (2), *Mermaid*, 32, Captain Robert Waller Otway, *Drake*, 16,

[1] Brenton mistakenly calls her the *San Domingo* (i. 425.)

[2] In the meantime, on March 22nd, the *Hermione*, 32, Captain Hugh Pigot (2), had most pluckily sent in her boats, under Lieutenants Samuel Reid and Archibald Douglas, and had cut out or burnt from a bay under a small battery at the west end of Puerto Rico, three French privateers and their twelve prizes. On the day following, Lieutenant Reid again landed and dismantled the battery, all without the loss of a man. This was six months before the mutiny which is described in the previous chapter.

[3] By means of the *Thunderer*, 74, Captain William Ogilvy, and *Valiant*, 74, Captain Edmund Crawley.

Commander John Perkins, and *Penelope*, cutter, Lieutenant Daniel Burdwood, to capture or destroy the craft in the last-named port. Towards midnight on April 20th, the boats of the squadron were sent in, and by 4 A.M. on the 21st, in spite of a heavy musketry fire, a ship, three brigs, three schooners, and two sloops, had been taken possession of, and were standing out with a land breeze. On the night of April 6th, another resort of privateers, at Cape Roxo, San Domingo, was raided by the boats of the *Magicienne*, 32, Captain William Henry Ricketts, and *Regulus*, 44, Captain William Carthew, under the orders of Lieutenants John Maples, and Alexander M'Beath, assisted by Lieutenants of Marines Philip Luscombe Perry and George Frazer, and by other officers. The harbour was entered, thirteen sail of square rigged vessels and schooners lying in it were taken, sunk, or burnt, and two batteries were destroyed. Both at Jean Rabel and at Cape Roxo the work was done without the loss of any British life. On his way back to Jamaica after his visit to Cape Roxo, Captain Ricketts[1] was able, on the 22nd, to frustrate a French attack upon the port of Les Irois, near Cape Tiburon, and to capture a privateer sloop and four schooners, besides a number of field-pieces, and a quantity of ammunition and supplies. In this service the Navy lost 4 killed and 11 wounded.

On other foreign stations no actions of much importance happened in the course of 1797. In North America the *Tribune*, 44, Captain Scory Barker, was unhappily lost, with nearly all hands, in particularly sad circumstances, off Herring Cove, near Halifax, November 16th; and, at the Cape, as elsewhere, the mutinous spirit then rife in the Navy manifested itself and had to be violently repressed. But allusion to this will be found in the previous chapter; and such other occurrences as deserve mention may be looked for in the following one.

In 1798, Admiral Lord Bridport, with several flag officers under him, continued to command in the Channel; Admiral Lord Duncan, in the North Sea; and Admiral Lord St. Vincent, on the Mediterranean and Lisbon station. Vice-Admiral Robert Kingsmill commanded at Cork; Vice-Admiral George Vandeput, in North America; Vice-Admiral the Hon. William Waldegrave, at Newfoundland; Rear-Admiral Henry Harvey (1), at the Leeward Islands; Vice-Admiral Sir Hyde Parker (2) at Jamaica; Rear-Admiral Thomas Pringle, and later Rear-Admiral Sir Hugh Cloberry

[1] Who then had also in company the *Fortune* schooner.

Christian, at the Cape of Good Hope; and Rear-Admiral Peter Rainier, in the East Indies. At Portsmouth, Admiral Sir Peter Parker, Bart.; at Plymouth, Admiral Sir Richard King (1), Bart.; in the Downs, Admiral Joseph Peyton (1); and at the Nore, Vice-Admiral Skeffington Lutwidge commanded.

On January 25th, Lord Bridport detached a division of the Channel fleet, under Vice-Admiral Sir Charles Thompson, Bart., to watch the French in the Bay of Biscay; on April 9th, he detached a smaller division, under Rear-Admiral Sir Roger Curtis, Bart., to cruise off the coast of Ireland; and, on April 12th, the Commander-in-Chief, with the main body of the fleet, left St. Helen's for Brest. On the 21st, at 11 A.M., as the fleet was standing across the Iroise[1] on the port tack, with the wind N.E. by E., the look-out ships to windward sighted and gave chase to two sail, distant about 12 miles to the eastward. At 2 P.M., when the advanced British ships were getting abreast of the strangers, a third and much larger vessel was seen in the E.S.E. distant about 15 miles, working up under the shore towards Brest. This was chased by the *Mars*, 74, Captain Alexander Hood, *Ramillies*, 74, Captain Henry Inman, and *Jason*, 38, Captain Charles Stirling, the only ships of the fleet near enough to see her. At 6.20 P.M., the *Ramillies* carried away her fore topmast and dropped astern; but the *Mars* continued to overhaul the French ship of the line—for such she was seen to be—and also to outsail the *Jason*.

At 7.30 P.M., when the Penmarcks bore S.E.½E., distant about 7 miles, the enemy betrayed a design to make his escape through the Passage du Raz. A little later the *Mars* went about on the starboard tack; and at 8.30 P.M., when Bec du Raz bore N. by E. two or three miles, the Frenchman abandoned the effort to work up against the current, and, dropping anchor, furled his sails, and carried out a spring abaft, so as to be able to bring as heavy a fire as possible to bear upon the *Mars*, then fast coming up. The enemy was the *Hercule*, 74, Captain Louis L'Heritier, and was on her way from Lorient, where she had been built, to join the Brest fleet.

At 8.45 P.M., the *Mars*, which had run the *Jason*[2] nearly out of sight, hauled up her courses, and, at 9.15, received and returned the fire of the starboard broadside of the *Hercule*; but, prevented

[1] The Iroise may be called the wide outer bay of Brest. It lies outside the fifty fathom line, between Ushant and the peninsula of Douarnenez which ends in Point du Raz.

[2] The *Jason* was still two miles away when the *Hercule* surrendered.

by the current from fighting to the best advantage under sail, Hood, at 9.25, ranged a little ahead of his opponent, let go an anchor, and dropped astern, the anchor on the port bow of the *Mars* hooking the anchor on the starboard bow of the *Hercule*, so that the two ships lay close, broadside to broadside. From that time until 10.30, the well-matched 74's fought with equal desperation; and then, the *Hercule* having twice failed in efforts to board, and having suffered terribly, hailed to announce her surrender.[1] The damages of both vessels were chiefly confined to their hulls, and the French ship, by the estimate of her own officers, had lost 290 killed and wounded. The *Mars* also had lost heavily, but far less so than her gallant foe. She had 30 killed or missing,[2] including among the former, Captain Alexander Hood, Captain of Marines Joseph White, and Midshipman James Blythe; and 60 wounded, including Lieutenants George Argles and George Arnold Ford, and Midshipman Thomas Southey. Hood[3] was wounded twenty minutes after the beginning of the action, by a ball in the femoral artery, and died just after the enemy had submitted. The force of the two ships is thus given by James:—

—		*Mars.*	*Hercule.*
Broadside guns . . .	No.	41	39
	Lbs.	984	985
Crew on board		634	6[illegible]0
Tons		1,853	1,876

There was, therefore, little on paper to choose between the opponents; but, whereas the *Mars*, to quote Lord St. Vincent, was "an old-commissioned, well-practised ship," the *Hercule* was brand-new, and had only been twenty-four hours out of port. The command of the *Mars*, after Hood's death, devolved on Lieutenant William Butterfield, who was at once promoted to be a Commander.

The French Brest fleet, as a body, gave little trouble during 1798 to the British commanders in the Channel. It was kept in port, perhaps as an object upon which the attention of Great Britain might be expected to concentrate itself while the Egyptian aspira-

[1] She was added to the Navy under her old name.

[2] These had probably been knocked overboard during the French efforts to board.

[3] Alexander Hood was a nephew of Lords Hood and Bridport; born 1758; Commander and Captain, 1781.

tions of France were developing themselves, perhaps as the nucleus of a force with which a serious invasion of England was to be attempted. Bonaparte himself apparently favoured the latter plan, for, in a letter[1] of April 13th, 1798, he thus explained his views on the subject:—

"In our position we ought to fight England with success, and we can do so. Whether we have peace or war, we ought to spend forty or fifty millions in reorganising our navy. Our land army will be neither more nor less powerful in consequence; but, on the other hand, war will force England to make immense preparations which will ruin her finances, destroy her commercial spirit, and completely change the constitution and manners of her people. We ought to spend the whole summer in getting ready our Brest fleet, in exercising our seamen in the roadstead, and in finishing the vessels which are under construction at Rochefort, Lorient, and Brest. If we put some energy into this business, we may hope to have, in September, thirty-five ships[2] at Brest, including the four or five which can be built at Lorient and Rochefort.

"Towards the end of this month we shall have in the various ports of the Channel nearly two hundred gunboats. These should be stationed at Cherbourg, Le Hâvre, Boulogne, Dunquerque, and Ostend, and should be utilised throughout the summer for training our soldiers. If we continue to grant to the Commission des Côtes de La Manche 300,000 francs every ten days, we can effect the construction of two hundred other boats, larger in size, and fit for the transport of horses. Thus we should have in September four hundred gunboats at Boulogne and thirty-five ships of war at Brest. By that time the Dutch should also have twelve ships of war in the Texel.

"In the Mediterranean we have ships of two kinds: twelve ships of French build which, between now and September, can be supplemented by two new ones; and nine of Venetian construction. It would be possible, after (the accomplishment of the objects of) the expedition which the government is projecting in the Mediterranean, to send round the fourteen to Brest, and to retain in the Mediterranean only the nine Venetian ships; and thus, in the course of October or November, we should have at Brest fifty men of war and nearly as many frigates.

"It would then be possible to transport to any desired spot in England 40,000 men, without even fighting a naval action if the enemy should be in stronger force; for, while 40,000 men would threaten to cross in the four hundred gunboats and in as many Boulogne fishing-boats, the Dutch squadron, with 10,000 men on board, would threaten to land in Scotland. An invasion of England, carried out in that way, and in the month of November or December, would be almost certainly successful. England would exhaust herself by an effort which, though immense, would not protect her against our invasion.

"The truth is that the expedition to the East will oblige the enemy to send six additional ships of war to India, and perhaps twice as many frigates to the mouth of the Red Sea. She would be forced to have from twenty-two to twenty-five ships at the entrance to the Mediterranean; sixty before Brest; and twelve off the Texel: and these would make a total of a hundred and three ships of war, besides those already in America and India, and besides the ten or twelve 50-gun ships and the score of frigates which she would have to keep ready to oppose the invasion from Boulogne. In the meantime we should always be masters of the Mediterranean, seeing that we should have there nine ships of Venetian build.

---

[1] 'Victoires et Conquêtes,' x. 375.

[2] Bonaparte speaks of "vaisseaux de guerre," or simply "vaisseaux," when he means "ships of the line."

"There would be yet another way of augmenting our forces in that sea; that is, by making Spain cede three vessels of war and three frigates to the Ligurian Republic. That republic can no longer be anything more than a French department; it possesses more than 20,000 excellent seamen. It is excellent policy on the part of France to favour the Ligurian Republic, and even to see to it that she shall possess a few ships of war. Should difficulties be foreseen in inducing Spain to hand over to us or to the Ligurian Republic three vessels of war, I think that we ourselves might usefully sell to the Ligurian Republic three of the nine ships which we have taken from the Venetians, insisting that the Republic shall construct three more for itself. We should find that we had thus gained a good squadron manned by good seamen. With the money which we should have from the Ligurians we might cause three good vessels of our own construction to be built at Toulon; for the ships of Venetian build require as many sailors as a fine 74[1]; and sailors are our weak point. In future events which may occur, it will be much to our advantage that the three Italian republics, which should balance the forces of the King of Naples and the Grand Duke of Tuscany, shall have a stronger navy than that of the King of Naples."

But, although the Brest fleet lay beyond reach of attack, there was plenty to occupy the attention of the British force in the Channel during 1798. Since the autumn of 1797, all the harbours along the coast, from Antwerp to Cherbourg, had been rapidly filling with gun-vessels and flat-bottomed boats for the much advertised invasion of England. The creation and maintenance of this flotilla was the business of that Commission des Côtes de La Manche of which Bonaparte spoke in the above letter. The Commission consisted of General Andréossi, director-general, M. Forfait,[2] director, and Rear-Admiral La Crosse, inspector-general; and as local inspectors, under La Crosse, were Captains Ganteaume, Decrès, Dumanoir Le Pelley, and de Casa Bianca. The flat-bottomed boats, which were built by hundreds by order of the commission, were popularly known as "bateaux à la Muskein," after an Antwerper named Muskein who had introduced the plans of them to France; but the plans themselves seem to have been the work of the Swedish naval architect Chapman. As these boats, and the seamen and soldiers who were intended to man them, accumulated in the ports, it occurred to the French authorities that, pending the sailing of the flotilla, parts of it might be usefully employed for local purposes. It was, moreover, desirable to familiarise the men with the vessels, and to prevent them from stagnating in idleness.

In the road of St. Vaast, within sight of La Hougue, lie the two small islands of St. Marcou. They are three or four miles

[1] Bonaparte apparently, therefore, contemplated the building at Toulon of only 60 or 64 gun ships. Otherwise it is hard to grasp his meaning.

[2] Pierre A. L. Forfait, one of the most distinguished naval architects and marine engineers of his time. Born, 1752; died, 1807.

distant from the shore, and near the route of coasters plying between Le Hâvre and Cherbourg. As he considered they would form a good base for harassing the traffic between those two ports, Captain Sir William Sidney Smith, of the *Diamond*, 38, took possession of them in July, 1795, without opposition; and they were subsequently held by a force of about 500 seamen and Marines, and placed under the orders of Lieutenant Charles Papps Price, of the *Badger*, 4, a Dutch hoy which had been purchased and armed for the service. It was determined by the French to attempt the recapture of these islands. On April 8th, the *Diamond*, 38, Captain Sir Richard John Strachan, and *Hydra*, 38, Captain Sir Francis Laforey, discovered in the Road of Caen thirty-three flat-bottomed boats, which, accompanied by a few gun-brigs and commanded by Muskein[1] in person, were on their way from Le Hâvre to St. Marcou to oust the little garrison. The British frigates worked up to the enemy and opened fire, but, owing to the grounding of the *Diamond*, were unable to effect much that night. On the following morning the flotilla proceeded to the westward; but, upon the appearance in the offing of the *Adamant*, 50, Captain William Hotham (2), it ran back to the eastward, pursued by the frigates, and finally took refuge in the Orne. There it was in time joined by about 40 additional flats and armed fishing-boats, and seven gun-brigs from Cherbourg; and at length, quitting his shelter, Captain Muskein, with his largely increased force, made his way unobserved along the coast as far as the road of La Hougue, where he lay, awaiting neap tides and calm weather, in order to attack Lieutenant Price.

His opportunity came on the night of May 6th. The British had warning of his approach; but, owing to the utter absence of wind, the *Adamant*, 50, *Eurydice*, 24, Captain John Talbot, and *Orestes*, 18, Commander William Haggitt, the only cruisers in the neighbourhood, could not get near the islands to co-operate in their defence. In the darkness, the French, who brought up no fewer than 52 craft, having on board five or six thousand men, stationed themselves in the most advantageous positions; and at daybreak on the 7th the enemy's brigs were seen to be ranged at a distance of about 350 yards from the British works, which instantly opened fire upon them from the only 17[2] guns which would at first bear. The French replied vigorously, and their flats advanced

[1] Made capitaine de vaisseau in the French navy.

[2] Six 24-pounders, two 6-pounders, four 4-pounders, two 32-pounder carronades, and three 24-pounder carronades. These had been borrowed from ships on the station,

with great determination in order to land their men; but, when six or seven flats had been sunk, the rest were glad to retire. The loss of the attacking force was never officially announced; but one French authority has put it at upwards of 1200 killed, drowned and wounded. On the British side, but one man was killed, and only four were wounded, in spite of the fact that the defence had been exposed to the fire of upwards of 80 guns. As the enemy drew off, the three British cruisers managed to get within range, but the calm prevented them from cutting off the retreat of the flotilla. Lieutenant Charles Papps Price, who commanded the whole position, and Lieutenant Richard Bourne (1), of the *Sandfly*, 5, who commanded the eastern island, were promoted for this service to be Commanders.

But all the encounters which resulted from the threatened invasion of England were not equally successful. In the spring of the year it became known to the British government that very many small craft were fitting at Flushing for the transport of troops, and were about to be conveyed, by way of the Bruges Canal, to Ostend and thence to Dunquerque. It was determined,[1] if possible, to frustrate this plan by destroying the lock gates and sluices at Ostend, and so rendering the canal useless; and, for the purpose, the naval force mentioned in the note[2] was entrusted to Captain Home Riggs Popham; and a body of troops under Major General Sir Eyre Coote was embarked in the vessels composing it.

---

and were on the western island. The work on the eastern island, where Lieutenant Richard Bourne (1) commanded, mounted, among other guns, two 68-pounder carronades; but it could not do much until towards the close of the action.

[1] Popham Papers, in Author's Coll.

[2] Expedition to Ostend, under Captain Popham and Major-General Sir Eyre Coote, May, 1798:—

Ships.	Guns.	Commanders.	Ships.	Guns.	Commanders.
Expedition, flûte (44)	26	Capt. Home Riggs Popham.	*Hecla*, bomb	8	Com. James Oughton.
			Wolverine	2	Lieut. Lewis Mortlock.
Circe	28	„ Robert Winthrop.	*Blazer*[1]	2	„ D—— Burgess.
Vestal	28	„ Charles White.	*Harrier*	..	„ Thomas Lowen.
Ariadne	20	„ James Bradby (2).	*Vesuve*	4	„ William Elliott.
Champion	24	„ Henry Raper.	*Crash*[1]	2	„ Bulkley Mackworth.
Hébe, flûte (38)	14	Com. William Birchall.			
Minerve, flûte (42)	14	„ John Mackellar.	*Boxer*[1]	2	„ Thomas Gilbert.
Druid, flûte (32)	12	„ Charles Apthorp.	*Acute*[1]	2	„ Jeremiah Seavers.
Harpy, brig	18	„ Henry Bazely.	*Asp*[1]	2	„ Joseph Edmonds.
Savage	16	„ Norborne Thompson.	*Furnace*[1]	2	„ Maurice William Suckling.
Dart	18	„ Richard Raggett.	*Vigilant*		
Kite, brig	16	„ William Brown.	*Biter*[1]	2	„ John Denis de Vitré.
Tartarus, bomb	8	„ Thomas Hand.			

[1] Carrying ten 18-pr. carronades, besides two long 24-prs.

The expedition assembled off Margate, sailed for the opposite coast on May 14th, and anchored off Ostend at 1 A.M. on May 19th. Although the weather was most unfavourable, all the troops,[1] with the exception of those on board the *Minerve*, which had parted company and had not yet rejoined, were at once landed to the north-east of the town without opposition. At about 4.15 A.M., the Ostend batteries, having been alarmed, opened fire upon the nearest British vessels, the *Wolverine*, *Asp*, and *Biter*, and, by about 8.30, had so severely damaged the two former, that Popham signalled to them to weigh and move further out. The *Hecla* and *Tartarus* had already begun to shell the town and harbour; and, upon the withdrawal of the *Wolverine* and *Asp*, the *Dart*, *Kite*, and *Harpy* took their places as nearly as the fact of its then being low tide would admit.

At 9.30 A.M. the *Minerve* rejoined; and her Commander went ashore by Popham's order to report her arrival to the general. Lieut.-Colonel Ward, with part of the First Regiment of Guards, would also have hastened on shore from the *Minerve*, had he not been stopped and dissuaded while on his way by the prudent counsels of Captain James Bradby (2), of the *Ariadne*.

The lock gates and sluices, together with several gunboats, are said to have been destroyed by the troops at 10.20 A.M.; but at noon, when it was sought to re-embark, the weather was found to render the attempt perfectly hopeless. The British had, in consequence, to remain; and, being attacked on the 20th by the French in force, they were obliged, after they had lost 65 killed and wounded, to capitulate. Among those who surrendered was Commander Mackellar, of the *Minerve*. It is doubtful whether the objects to be attained justified the risks involved in this unfortunate expedition; it is still more doubtful whether those objects were attained, for the French deny the fact; and it is certain that, whether the objects were attained or not, the troops ought never to have been landed at a time when every indication went to show that it would be difficult, if not impossible, to re-embark them until after the lapse of some days.

Another action in which the invasion flotilla was concerned took place on May 30th. Early in the morning of that day, the *Hydra*, 38, Captain Sir Francis Laforey, the *Vesuvius*, bomb, 8, Commander Robert Lewis Fitzgerald, and the *Trial*, cutter, 12, Lieutenant Henry Garrett, while standing in towards

[1] About 1140 officers and men, with six guns.

Le Hâvre to observe the preparations there, discovered the French frigate *Confiante*, 36, Captain E. Pevrieux, which, accompanied by the *Vésuve*, 20, and a cutter, was bound from Le Hâvre to Cherbourg. The British ships chased the Frenchmen back towards Le Hâvre, the *Hydra* warmly engaging the *Confiante* for about 50 minutes, at the expiration of which time the latter ran herself ashore opposite Beuzeval, and the *Vésuve*, harassed by the *Vesuvius* and *Trial*, beached herself under a battery near the mouth of the Dives. On the following morning the boats of the *Hydra*, under Lieutenants George Acklom, and William Joseph Symons, burnt the *Confiante*, which had been abandoned by her people; but the *Vésuve*, being refloated, escaped, and joined Muskein's gunboats and flats. These lay at Sallenelle, so well protected by batteries that it was judged useless to attempt to attack them. The destruction of the *Confiante* was effected without any loss on the British side.

The disaffection in Ireland, which, at the end of 1796, had encouraged the Directory to attempt to send French troops to the island, developed, in 1798, into open rebellion. Apart from the fact that the Republicans in Paris were, to a large extent, morally responsible for the outbreak, and were, therefore, morally bound to support it in every way, it was obviously to the advantage of France to lose no opportunity of feeding and fanning a conflagration that could not but gravely preoccupy Great Britain, and add immensely to her numerous anxieties. It cannot be said that the Republic manifested great promptitude in proceeding to the assistance of its unfortunate and over confiding pupils; yet, after much delay, it organised two independent expeditions, which were to have sailed simultaneously, one from Rochefort and one from Brest. Owing to lack of money at the latter port for the payment of the forces, the plan for the simultaneous departure of the two squadrons was not carried out; and the Rochefort division, which had on board 1150 troops and 4 field-guns, under General Humbert, with a quantity of ammunition, arms, and accoutrements, was the first to leave. This division consisted of the following ships:—

Concorde . . .	40	{Commodore Daniel Savary. {Capt. André Papin.
Franchise . . .	36	„ J. L. Guillotin.
Médée	36	„ J. D. Coudin.
Vénus	28	„ A. Senez.

Savary weighed from Aix road on August 6th, 1798, and, on the 22nd of the same month, anchored off Kilcummin Head, at the mouth of Killala Bay, in Mayo. That evening he disembarked his troops, in face of a very feeble resistance; and, on September 7th, having returned to France without sighting an enemy, anchored in the mouth of the Gironde. On the following day, Humbert, after having won some successes and marched halfway across Ireland, was obliged to surrender to the British forces at Ballinamuck. That Savary escaped the attention, both going and returning, of the very numerous British line-of-battle ships and cruisers in the Bay and at the mouth of the Channel, and of the considerable squadron of frigates on the Irish station, is, upon the whole, surprising; but it must be borne in mind that the expedition was one which, in itself, was almost entirely impotent either for good or for evil. The squadron was not strong enough to defend itself against any but the smallest naval flotilla; the corps of Humbert was not strong enough by itself to meet a couple of British regiments. The raid could have produced effect only by evasion in the first place, and by powerful Irish co-operation in the second. A serious invasion is a different affair altogether. It cannot be organised in holes and corners; it cannot move with the secrecy and speed of a little frigate squadron; and it cannot afford to neglect a "potential fleet." Therefore, although Savary went and returned unobserved, and although Humbert was, as it were, flung ashore to shift for himself, it by no means follows that, had Savary had a more formidable squadron, and Humbert a force of more independent character, the expedition would have enjoyed even that very qualified degree of success which actually attended it. That such is the case is shown by the history of the second French expedition of 1798 to Ireland.

This was a much more serious expedition, consisting, as it did, of about 3000 troops under Generals Ménage and Hardy, a number of field and siege guns, and a vast quantity of stores, embarked in the ships named below:—

Hoche[1]	74	Commodore J. B. F. Bompart. Capt. D. M. Maistral.
Romaine . . .	40	„ M. C. Bergevin.
Loire	40	„ A. J. Ségond.
Immortalité . .	40	„ J. F. Legrand.
Coquille . . .	36	„ L. de Péronne.
Bellone. . . .	36	„ L. L. Jacob.
Résolue . . .	36	„ J. P. Bergeau.
Embuscade . .	36	„ N. Clément de La Roncière.
Sémillante. . .	36	„ M. A. Lacouture.
Biche	36	„ Lieut. J. M. P. La Bastard.

[1] Ex *Pégase*. Renamed in honour of General Hoche, who had died at Wetzlar on September 18th, 1797.

Bompart sailed from Brest on the evening of September 16th, hoping to get out unobserved during the night by way of the Passage du Raz. But, at daylight on the 17th, he was seen by the *Boadicea*, 38, Captain Richard Goodwin Keats, *Ethalion*, 38, Captain George Countess, and *Sylph*, 18, Commander John Chambers White, cruisers belonging to the Channel fleet. Keats at once went northward to communicate with Lord Bridport, and Countess and White kept company with the French and watched their motions. On the 18th, at 2 A.M., the *Ethalion* and *Sylph* were joined by another cruiser, the *Amelia*, 44, Captain the Hon. Charles Herbert. That morning the French, after working up as if they intended to make Lorient, chased the British frigates, but without success. They then steered as if they might be bound for the West Indies. On the 20th, the *Anson*, 44, Captain Philip Charles Durham, joined Countess. At noon that day the British were in latitude 46° 27′ N., and longitude 5° 3′ W., and the French were nearly hull down to the S.W. by S. At noon on the 22nd, Bompart was seen to be steering W.N.W., and, in the afternoon of the 23rd, Countess, having no longer much doubt as to the real destination of the foe, sent the *Sylph* to warn the Commander-in-Chief on the Irish station.

The three British frigates kept the enemy in sight until the evening of October 4th, and then, the weather being dirty and there springing up a gale from the S.S.E., they hauled up. On the 7th, the *Amelia* parted company; on the 9th, the *Anson* rolled away her main topmast and mizen top-gallant-mast; and on the 11th Countess and Durham joined the squadron of Commodore Sir John Borlase Warren off the coast of Donegal.

Warren had been despatched from Cawsand Bay on September 23rd, when it became known that Bompart had sailed, and had made direct for Achill Head, it being supposed that the French, if bound for Ireland, would steer for some point not very far distant from that at which Humbert had landed. He had been joined on the 10th by two frigates, which had left Lough Swilly in consequence of the intelligence brought by the *Sylph*, and one of which, the *Doris*, 36, Captain Lord Ranelagh, he immediately detached to warn the coast. On the following day, reinforced by Countess and Durham, his squadron consisted of:—

Canada . . .	74	Commodore Sir John Borlase Warren.
Foudroyant . .	80	Capt. Sir Thomas Byard.
Robust	74	„ Edward Thornbrough.
Magnanime . .	44	„ Hon. Michael de Courcy (1).
Anson	44	„ Philip Charles Durham.
Amelia . . .	44	„ Hon. Charles Herbert.
Ethalion . . .	38	„ George Countess.
Melampus . . .	36	„ Graham Moore.

It had, in fact, been intended by the French to disembark in Killala Bay; but, it not being known what had become of Humbert, and it being imagined that he would be found somewhat more to the northward, it was determined to attempt to land in Lough Swilly. On the 11th, at noon, however, Bompart was on his way thither, and was bearing up for Tory Island, when his leading ship, the *Immortalité*, signalled the appearance of the British to leeward. Bompart, in consequence, eventually bore away to the south-west, intending to land his troops at any point where occasion should offer. Warren, on learning of the presence of the enemy, instantly ordered a general chase, and directed his ships "to form in succession as they arrived up with the enemy." That night it blew very hard from N.N.W.; and, while the *Anson* carried away her mizen-mast, main-yard, and main-topsail yard, the *Hoche*, still more unfortunate, lost her main-topmast and her fore and mizen top-gallantmasts, and the *Résolue* sprang a bad leak. Soon after 5.30 A.M. on the 12th, when the two squadrons were again able to see one another, the following were, according to James, their relative positions:—

"The French squadron, loosely formed in two rather distant lines, with the *Hoche*, who had bent herself a new mainsail, in the centre of the second line, was standing to the south-west, the wind, as before, from the north-north-west, but now very moderate. Right astern, at the distance of about four miles, were the *Robust* and *Magnanime*; about a point on the lee quarter, at a somewhat greater distance, the *Amelia*; a little further forward in that direction, and at about the same distance, the *Melampus*; a little before the lee beam, at the distance of seven or eight miles, the *Foudroyant*; and on the lee bow, about a mile nearer, the *Canada*.[1] The *Anson*, at this time, was not in sight of either squadron. Consequently, M. Bompart, in his crippled state, the wind being in the north-west, found every avenue of escape shut against him, except the south-west, the direction in which he was steering."

By 7 A.M., M. Bompart had formed his ships in a single straggling line ahead, the order being: *Sémillante*, *Romaine*, *Bellone*, *Immortalité*, *Loire*, *Hoche*, *Coquille*, *Embuscade*. The *Résolue* had previously gone in shore as a precautionary measure,

[1] The position of the *Ethalion* is not here given. She seems to have been near the *Amelia*.

on account of her leakiness; and the *Biche* had been sent after her with orders. Warren was thus in every way superior to his enemy, and could have easily afforded to keep flying the signal for a general chase; but, instead, he formed line of battle, directing the *Robust* to lead, "and the rest of the ships to form in succession in the rear of the van." This order brought the *Robust*, which was followed by the *Magnanime*, within long-range stern fire of the *Embuscade* and *Coquille* at about 7.10 A.M. About fifteen minutes later,[1] the *Robust*, having returned the fire of the two Frenchmen, hauled up her mainsail, and, taking in her spanker, bore down to leeward of them. By 8.50 A.M., she closed in this manner with the *Hoche*, and began a hot action with her, broadside to broadside, checking

COMMEMORATIVE MEDAL OF WARREN'S ACTION, OCT. 12TH, 1798.

(*From an original lent by H.S.H. Capt. Prince Louis of Battenberg, R.N.*)

her way to keep alongside of the enemy. The *Magnanime* engaged the *Embuscade* and *Coquille*, and, passing on to leeward of the *Robust*, had to starboard her helm to clear the latter. The *Loire*, *Immortalité*, and *Bellone* bore out of line to rake her as she did so; but they were soon driven to resume their south-west course, the *Foudroyant*, *Amelia*, and *Ethalion* then coming up. These ships, as well as the *Melampus*[2] and *Canada*, all helped more or less to distress the *Hoche*, which at 10.50 A.M., after a brilliant defence, struck.[3] The *Embuscade*, badly treated first by the *Magnanime*

[1] *I.e.*, at 7.23 A.M., when the Rosses bore from the *Canada*, S.S.W., distant fifteen miles.

[2] Captain Moore either did not see, or neglected, Warren's signal to form line, and so got into action much sooner than he could otherwise have done.

[3] In the *Hoche* was Wolfe Tone, one of the chiefs of the Irish insurgents.

and afterwards by the *Foudroyant,* surrendered at 11.30 to the *Magnanime,* which, having herself suffered severely, remained by her prize. The other British ships, with the exception of the *Robust,* which was disabled, and the *Anson,* which was still struggling up from the south-east, chased vigorously; the results being that the *Coquille* struck in about an hour and a half, and that the *Bellone,* after having made a desperate resistance to the *Foudroyant* and *Melampus* in succession, hauled down to the *Ethalion,* but not until she had fought her for very nearly two hours. The other French vessels escaped for the moment, and, as they got away, engaged the *Anson,* and inflicted considerable damage upon her.

The British losses were as follows: *Canada,* 1 wounded (mortally); *Foudroyant,* 9 wounded; *Robust,* 10 killed, 40 wounded; *Magnanime,* 7 wounded; *Anson,* 2 killed, 13 wounded; *Ethalion,* 1 killed, 4 wounded; and *Melampus,* 1 wounded; total, 13 killed, and 75 wounded. No one in the *Amelia* was hurt, and the only British officers injured were Lieutenant David Colby, and Lieutenant of Marines William Cottle, both of the *Robust.* This was, all things considered, a very slight loss; for the French had fought well. Of the prizes, the *Hoche* had 270 killed and wounded; the *Embuscade,* 15 killed and 26 wounded; the *Coquille,* 18 killed and 31 wounded; and the *Bellone,* 35[1] killed and wounded. The *Hoche* (renamed *Donegal*), *Bellone* (renamed *Proserpine*), and *Embuscade,* were added to the Royal Navy. The *Coquille* probably would have been, had she not been accidentally burnt at Plymouth on December 14th, 1798.

It can hardly be said that Warren's conduct of this little action was particularly brilliant, or that his subsequent dispositions were particularly wise; for, in consequence of his having ordered the *Robust,* which was seriously crippled aloft, to tow the still more disabled *Hoche* into Lough Swilly, he narrowly escaped losing the largest of his prizes. Indeed, had not the *Doris,* 36, Captain Lord Ranelagh, come to the *Robust's* assistance, and had not the crew of the *Hoche* most loyally worked to save their ship for her captors, the 74 must in all probability have been abandoned, or retaken. Yet the service rendered was, after all, no small one; and Sir John, his officers, and men richly deserved the thanks which were voted to

[1] This is the number given in the French reports. Some British reports put it at 65.

them by both Houses. The action seems also to have won promotion for Lieutenants David Colby (*Robust*), George Sayer (2) (*Ethalion*), and William James Turquand[1] (*Canada*).

The five French frigates which made off to leeward were chased by the *Canada*, *Foudroyant*, and *Melampus*. At about midnight on the 13th, the *Melampus* sighted the *Immortalité* and *Résolue*, running out of St. John's Bay before a fresh wind; and at 1 A.M. on the 14th she succeeded in bringing to action the latter frigate, which, after attempting a feeble reply to a few broadsides, surrendered, having lost ten killed and several wounded. She was making four feet of water an hour,[2] and she appears to have had some of her maindeck guns housed, and to have been unable to fight them. The *Melampus*, which, it should be remembered, was of about twice the *Résolue's* force,[3] and which had no one hurt, was in a condition to at once engage the *Immortalité*, had that ship been still at hand. But unable to near her consort, she had prudently made off.

Two other frigates of M. Bompart's squadron, the *Sémillante* and *Loire*, were sighted on the morning of October 15th by the *Révolutionnaire*, 38, Captain Thomas Twysden, *Mermaid*, 32, Captain James Newman Newman, and *Kangaroo*, 18, Commander Edward Brace, off the mouth of Blacksod Bay, and, after having been chased before the wind, separated. The *Révolutionnaire*, which followed one, lost her in the evening, and saw her no more. The *Mermaid* and *Kangaroo* pursued the other, and also lost her, but found her again at dawn on the 16th, and renewed the chase. This one was the *Loire*. At 3 P.M. the *Kangaroo*[4] got up with her, and most pluckily engaged, until she lost her fore-topmast and had her foremast badly wounded. She then had to drop astern. At daybreak on the 17th, the *Loire* shortened sail to allow the *Mermaid*, which was then alone, to come up; and at 6.45 A.M., the two frigates went off together in hot action nearly before the wind. After an engagement of two hours and a half, the *Loire* sensibly slackened her fire, and Captain Newman had given orders to run athwart the hawse of his sorely crippled opponent, when the *Mermaid* lost her mizen-mast by the board, the falling wreckage disabling several of her after guns. Soon afterwards she also lost her main-topmast, and, being in many

1 Drowned in command of the *Hound*, 18, in September, 1800.
2 Chiefly in consequence of the leak already mentioned.
3 The *Melampus* carried 24's, and the *Résolue* only 12-prs.
4 She carried sixteen 32-pr. carronades and two long 6-prs.

other ways terribly mauled, she had to discontinue the action; whereupon the enemy put before the wind and made off. The gallant *Mermaid*[1] lost 4 killed and 13 wounded. We know from French sources that she inflicted very severe damage upon her opponent; and, indeed, she must have done so in order to induce an officer like Captain Ségond[2] to quit so small and so crippled a foe as the British frigate. But the *Loire* was not to escape. At daybreak on the 18th, being by that time without a main as well as without a fore-topmast, she found herself to leeward of the *Anson*, 44, Captain Philip Charles Durham, and the *Kangaroo*. The *Anson* was as crippled as the *Loire*. The *Kangaroo*, since the 16th, had got up a new fore-topmast and made good her other damages. An action between the two larger vessels began at 10.30 A.M.; and at 11.45 A.M., when they had almost completely disabled one another, the brig was able to throw the weight of her broadside into the scale and to decide the issue. When the *Loire* struck, she had six feet of water in her hold, and, according to French returns, had 46 killed and 71 wounded. The *Anson* lost but 2 killed and 13 wounded, and the *Kangaroo* had no one hurt. Both the *Loire*[3] and the *Résolue* were added to the Navy.

Yet another of M. Bompart's vessels never returned to a French port. The *Immortalité*, while making for Brest, and, in fact, while nearing it, was fallen in with, on October 20th, by the *Fishguard*, 38, Captain Thomas Byam Martin, a frigate of fairly matched force.[4] An action began at 12.30 P.M., and, although the *Fishguard* had at one time to drop astern, and was, towards the conclusion, half full of water, she obliged her opponent to strike at about 3 P.M., after having reduced her to a sinking state and killed or wounded 115 of her people, including Captain Legrand, who fell fighting his ship most gallantly. The *Fishguard's* loss was 10 killed and 26 wounded.

[1] She was only a 12-pr. 32-gun frigate. The *Loire*, a 40, carried 18-prs. The weight of broadside was: *Mermaid*, 252 lbs; *Loire*, 442 lbs.; and the tonnage was: *Mermaid*, 693; *Loire*, 1100.

[2] Born 1769; died 1813. Upon his return to France, after his captivity, he was not received with favour, on account of his intolerance of discipline; and in 1803 he resigned his commission in disgust. At one time he proposed to the Minister of Marine a romantic scheme for kidnapping George III. from Weymouth.

[3] Guérin, in his anxiety to magnify Ségond's defence, says: "Quant à *La Loire*, elle ne tarda pas à couler bas." On the contrary, she was of much service to her new masters.

[4] *Fishguard*: broadside guns, 23; weight of broadside, 425 lbs.; crew, 284; tons, 1182. *Immortalité*: broadside guns, 21; weight of broadside, 450 lbs.; crew, 330; tons, 1010.

The prize was purchased for the British service, and refitted as an 18-pr.[1] 36-gun frigate. The *Fishguard's* first lieutenant, John Surman Carden,[2] was promoted.

Of M. Bompart's remaining ships, the *Romaine*, after having communicated with the Irish coast, surrendered all idea of landing troops, and returned to Brest. On her way thither she picked up the *Biche*; and the two vessels anchored in their port of destination on October 23rd. The *Sémillante* reached Lorient.

In the meanwhile much anxiety had arisen in France as to the fate of Humbert and Bompart; and, on October 12th, Commodore Savary had been despatched from Rochefort, with his old squadron, consisting of the *Concorde*, *Médée*, *Franchise*, and *Vénus*, to discover what had happened to his compatriots. He was so fortunate as to make Sligo Bay, on the 27th, without adventure; and, learning of the fate of his friends, he at once headed again for home. On the 28th, 29th, and 30th he was chased by the *Cæsar*, 80, Captain Roddam Home, *Terrible*, 70, Captain Sir Richard Hussey Bickerton, Bart., and *Melpomène*, 38, Captain Sir Charles Hamilton; but he succeeded in escaping from them and in getting back safely to Rochefort.

After his misfortune at Santa Cruz in July, 1797, Nelson returned to England to allow his wound to heal, and to recover his health; and he did not rejoin the fleet off Cadiz until April 29th, 1798. During his absence, the Mediterranean remained practically abandoned by the British. But, at about the time of his return, the Admiralty became very anxious concerning the object of the preparations which were being made by the French at Toulon; and orders were accordingly sent to Lord St. Vincent to detach Nelson[3] with a few ships to endeavour to discover what was going forward. In pursuance of these orders, Nelson, with his flag in the *Vanguard*, 74, Captain Edward Berry, parted company on May 2nd, and, on the 4th, reached Gibraltar. There he found, and took under his command the *Alexander*, 74, Captain Alexander John Ball, *Orion*, 74, Captain Sir James Saumarez, Kt., *Emerald*, 36, Captain Thomas Moutray Waller, *Terpsichore*, 32, Captain William Hall Gage, and *Bonne Citoyenne*, 20, Commander Richard Retalick. With these he

[1] Her 24-prs. were deemed too heavy for her.

[2] He died, an Admiral on the retired list, in 1858, aged 87.

[3] Unless, indeed, St. Vincent saw fit to go himself. The selection of Nelson gave great umbrage to Rear-Admirals Sir William Parker (1), Bart., and Sir John Orde, Bart., both of whom were with the fleet, and both of whom were Nelson's seniors.

proceeded on May 9th. On the 17th, when off Cape Sicié, he obtained news that there were in Toulon nineteen sail of the line, of which fifteen were ready for sea, and that an immense body of troops, under Bonaparte, lay ready to embark for an unknown destination. Very early in the morning of the 21st the squadron suffered severely in a gale, south of Hyères, and, in consequence, the *Emerald*, *Terpsichore* and *Bonne Citoyenne* lost company.[1] The *Vanguard*, much crippled, towed by the *Alexander* and accompanied by the *Orion*, made for the coast of Sardinia, and, on the 22nd, anchored in the road of San Pietro, where she refitted.

The genesis of the plan of Bonaparte's Egyptian campaign is thus summarised by James:—

> "During the negotiations at Campo-Formio, in the summer of 1797, General Bonaparte took away from the Ambrosian Library at Milan all the books he could find on subjects connected with the East; and, on their being brought to Paris, marginal notes were discovered in every page that treated specially on Egypt. Hence, it has been inferred that Bonaparte was, even at this time, ruminating upon the plan in the attempted execution of which his military fame subsequently received so serious a check. . . . At all events, in the early months of the year 1798, he submitted the plan of a campaign in Egypt to the Directory, and, on the 5th of March, was appointed its commander-in-chief. 'Les ministres de la Guerre, de la Marine, et des Finances,' proceeds the letter of appointment, 'sont prévenus de se conformer aux instructions que vous leur transmettrez sur ce point important dont votre patriotisme a le secret, et dont le Directoire ne pouvait pas mieux confier le succès qu'à votre génie et à votre amour pour la vraie gloire.'"

Bonaparte's original view seems to have been that the Ottoman Empire was likely to crumble to pieces in his day, and that France ought either to sustain it, or to take a share in it.[2] He next acquired the belief that if, at the peace, the Cape of Good Hope should be confirmed to Great Britain, Egypt would form a satisfactory compensation for France,[3] and that any attempt to sustain the Ottoman Empire was vain.[4] Later still he undoubtedly fancied that he saw in Egypt the door to a career of world-wide conquest similar to that of Alexander, and, above all, the way to India and to Great Britain's position there. Yet, although he could say, "Let us concentrate all our activity upon the navy, and destroy England,"[5] he was capable of embarking upon his Egyptian expedition without having first reflected upon the elementary principles of sea power, and of landing his army without paying the slightest attention to the risks

[1] Owing, apparently, to the assumption of their Captains that the *Vanguard* was so seriously damaged that she must return to Gibraltar.

[2] 'Corr. de Nap.' Aug. 16, 1797.

[3] *Ibid.*, iii. 392.

[4] *Ibid.*, iii. 313.

[5] *Ibid.*, iii. 520.

to which he was exposed by doing so while a "potential" fleet remained to threaten his communications. Had not Napoleon been thus blind upon a single point, he might perhaps have attained all his ambitions.

In pursuance of his directions, immense preparations were made in most of the Mediterranean ports then under French control; and, on May 8th, Bonaparte reached Toulon from Paris to assume the command. The expeditionary force was made up of fifteen sail of the line (including two armed *en flûte*), fourteen frigates (including six armed *en flûte*), and other vessels of war bringing the total to seventy-two, besides about four hundred sail of transports,[1] under the orders of Vice-Admiral Brueys, and Rear-Admirals Villeneuve, Blanquet du Chayla, and Decrès; together with an army of 36,000 men, commanded, under Napoleon, by the Generals of Division, Kleber, Desaix, Bon, Regnier, Vaubois, Menou, Duqua, Dumas and Dumuy.

On May 19th, the Toulon division of this fleet got under way, and, running towards Genoa, was joined by the transports from the ports along the coast. Then, standing southward, it made Cape Corse on the 23rd; and from that day until the first week in June it remained in sight of Corsica awaiting further transports from Civita Vecchia. On June 3rd, having learnt that some British ships had been seen off Cagliari, Napoleon sent a division of vessels to look for them; but the detachment rejoined, having discovered nothing; and, as the expected convoy from Civita Vecchia had not arrived, the French proceeded without it, and passed Mazzaro del Vallo, on the south-west coast of Sicily, on the 7th. On the following day Bonaparte received news, which was, in fact, erroneous, that he was closely pursued by Nelson. On the 9th, the French, being off Malta, were joined by the transports from Civita Vecchia, numbering seventy sail; on the 10th, landings were effected at seven points on the island; and on the 12th, after slight resistance, Malta, Gozo and Comino capitulated, with two 64-gun ships, one frigate, and three galleys which were in port.

By almost incredible exertions the *Vanguard* was refitted in four

[1] The figures here given are those from the 'Hist. Scient. et Milit. de l'Expedition,' etc. (Paris, 1830–36). But it is right to say that, according to the 'Camp. d'Egypte et de Syrie,' as dictated by Napoleon to Bertrand, and published in 1847, there were but 33 men-of-war, 8 flûtes, and 224 transports, having on board 24,300 infantry, 4000 cavalry, and 3000 artillery. M. Thiers, on the other hand, exaggerates even the figures given in the text. 'Hist. du Cons. et de l'Emp.'

days, and on May 27th, she and her two consorts put to sea again, and made for Toulon, off which port they found themselves on the 31st. Nelson had by that time learnt of the sailing of the French, but he had nothing to guide him on the subject of their destination. On June 5th, the *Mutine*, 16, Commander Thomas Masterman Hardy, joined him from Lisbon at the rendezvous with news that reinforcements were on their way to him from the Commander-in-Chief, and with orders that, after their junction, he should go in search of the fleet from Toulon. The reinforcement fell in with the Rear-Admiral on June 7th.

This reinforcement, consisting of ten sail of the line and a 50-gun ship, had been detached by St. Vincent on the night of May 24th. It would have been detached earlier, but it could not be spared from the work of blockading Cadiz until after a reinforcement from England, under Rear-Admiral Sir Roger Curtis, had reached the Commander-in-Chief; and Sir Roger did not join the Commander-in-Chief until May 24th. Unhappily, St. Vincent, who supposed that the *Emerald*, *Terpsichore*, and *Bonne Citoyenne* were still with Nelson, omitted to send to his subordinate any more frigates; so that the Rear-Admiral, although at length in command of thirteen sail of the line and a 50-gun ship, had, to scout for him on a service the success of which essentially depended upon his ability to secure intelligence, nothing but a single brig-rigged sloop.

Nelson's orders from St. Vincent were:—

> "To proceed in quest of the armament preparing by the enemy at Toulon and Genoa, the object whereof appears to be either an attack upon Naples or Sicily, the conveyance of an army to some part of the coast of Spain for the purpose of marching towards Portugal, or to pass through the Straits, with a view to proceeding to Ireland."[1]

Nelson was further told that he might follow the enemy to any part of the Mediterranean or even into the Black Sea. There is, however, nothing in the instructions to indicate that St. Vincent, or the Admiralty, whose views he translated, ever dreamt that Napoleon was bound for Egypt; and all that the Rear-Admiral had to guide him was the single fact that the Toulon fleet had quitted Toulon with a north-west wind. As soon, therefore, as he could move, he steered for Corsica; and, on June 12th, he was off Cape Corse. That night he detached the *Mutine* to Civita Vecchia to seek intelligence, while he pursued a course down the Tuscan

[1] Dated May 21st.

coast. The *Mutine* rejoined without having secured any news. The *Leander* spoke a Moorish craft which falsely reported the French to be at Syracuse. On the 17th, the fleet stood into the Bay of Naples. Sir William Hamilton, the British Ambassador, suspected that the enemy had gone to Malta; and, following his indication, Nelson entered the Strait of Messina on the 20th, and learnt from the British Consul at Messina that Malta and Gozo had fallen, and that the French were believed to be off the latter island. A north-west breeze carried the Rear-Admiral through the strait; but on the 22nd, when the fleet was about thirty-five miles south-east of Cape Passaro, intelligence was obtained to the effect that the enemy had quitted Malta on the 18th with a north-west wind. This news suggested Alexandria as the probable aim of the French; and, in consequence, Nelson bore up, and steered south-east under all sail. During the next five days, nothing was heard of the foe, and when, on the 28th, Alexandria was sighted, and the *Mutine* was sent in, it appeared that no enemy either was, or had been, on the coast.

Nelson, accordingly, on the 29th, steered north-east with a fresh north-north-east breeze, and made the coast of Anatolia on July 4th. For several days afterwards the weather was unfavourable, but on the 19th, the British were able to put into Syracuse for provisions and water. Supplies were obtained, thanks mainly to the determination of the Rear-Admiral to secure them at all costs, and to suffer no difficulties to stand in the way of his Majesty's service. Nelson himself believed, however, that he would not have obtained them as he did, but for the influence of Lady Hamilton, the wife of the British Ambassador at the Court of Naples. By July 24th, the fleet was again able to sail. Nelson was practically certain that the French were not at Corfu nor to the westward of that island; and once more, therefore, he determined to make for Alexandria. He steered first, however, for the Morea, and on the 28th, being off Cape Gallo, sent the *Culloden* into Coron, the governor of which informed Troubridge that the French had been seen about four weeks earlier off the coast of Candia, heading south-east. South-east, thereupon, went Nelson with a fresh wind astern. At 10 A.M. on August 1st he sighted for the second time the minarets of Alexandria. The French flag flew over the city; the harbours were crowded with shipping; and for an instant it appeared as if the British had found the object of their long and indefatigable search. But when the *Alexander* and

Swiftsure stood in to reconnoitre, they reported, to the general disappointment, that the flotilla in port was almost entirely composed of transports and merchantmen, and that there were with it but eight ships of war,[1] none of which were large.

After quitting Malta, where a garrison of four thousand men was left under General Vaubois, the French had headed eastward with a favourable breeze, and on June 30th had made Cape Durazzo, in Candia. They had then steered for a point on the African coast about seventy miles westward of Alexandria, and, having made the land, had proceeded along the shore and anchored before the city on July 1st. A landing had been immediately begun. On the 2nd, after a slight action, Alexandria had been seized; and on the 8th, the Old Harbour being supposed to be inconvenient for the men-of-war, Vice-Admiral Brueys, with his ships of the line and such of his frigates as were not armed *en flûte,* had anchored in Aboukir Bay,[2] twelve or fifteen miles to the eastward.

Thus it was that the *Alexander* and *Swiftsure,* upon looking into Alexandria, failed to find the ships which they desired. But the disappointment caused by their signal lasted but for a short time. A few minutes before 1 P.M. the *Zealous,* from which the Pharos then bore S.S.W., distant about fourteen miles, signalled that seventeen ships of war, thirteen or fourteen of which were formed in line of battle, lay at anchor in a bay upon her larboard bow. Nelson instantly hauled up, and headed eastward under topgallant sails, with a brisk breeze varying from N. by W. to N.N.W.[3]

[1] The *Dubois, Causse,* and six ex-Venetian vessels.

[2] Napoleon, on hearing of this, sent a message ordering Brueys to remove to the Old Harbour; but the message never reached him. Brueys, however, upon his own initiative, was thinking of removing thither when Nelson caught him. (Brueys to Nap., July 30th.)

[3] It may be convenient to give in the following form some tabulated particulars of Nelson's celebrated search for Brueys:—

Date.	Nelson.	Brueys.	Date.	Nelson.	Brueys.
May 2	Cadiz, dep.		June 14	Off Civita Vecchia.	
,, 4–9	Gibraltar.		,, 17	Off Naples.	
,, 17	Off Cape Sicié.		,, 20	Off Messina.	
,, 19	..	Toulon, dep.	,, 22[1]	Off Cape Passaro.	
,, 21	80 miles S. of Hyères.		,, 28–29	Off Alexandria.	
,, 22	San Pietro, arr.		,, 30	..	Off Cape Durazzo.
,, 23	..	Off Cape Carbonara.	July 1	..	Off Alexandria.
,, 27	San Pietro, dep.		,, 4	Off Anatolia.	
,, 31	Off Toulon.		,, 8	..	Aboukir Bay, arr.
June 8	Off Toulon, dep.	Off Mazzara.	,, 18	Off Cape Passaro.	
,, 10–19	..	Malta.	,, 19–24	Syracuse.	
,, 12	Off Cape Corse.		Aug. 1	Off Alexandria.	

[1] On the 22nd and the two following days the fleets were comparatively near one another.

The fleets which had for so long played hide and seek with one another, and which were at length about to meet, were thus composed:—

British.

Ships.	Guns.	Commanders. * Lost their lives.	Killed.	Wounded.
Goliath	74	Capt. Thomas Foley (3).	21	41
Zealous	74	,, Samuel Hood (2).	1	7
Orion	74	,, Sir James Saumarez.	13	29
Audacious	74	,, Davidge Gould.	1	35
Theseus	74	,, Ralph Willett Miller.	5	30
Vanguard	74	Rear-Adm. Sir H. Nelson, K.B. (B). Capt. Edward Berry.	30	76
Minotaur	74	,, Thomas Louis.	23	64
Defence	74	,, John Peyton.	4	11
Bellerophon	74	,, Henry d'Esterre Darby.	49	148
Majestic	74	,, George Blagden Westcott.*	50	143
Leander	50	,, Thomas Boulden Thompson.	0	14
Alexander	74	,, Alexander John Ball.	14	58
Swiftsure	74	,, Benjamin Hallowell.	7	22
Culloden[1]	74	,, Thomas Troubridge.	0	0
Mutine	16	Com. Thomas Masterman Hardy.		

[1] Grounded, and failed to get into action.

French.

Ships.	Guns.	Commanders. * Lost their lives.	Fate.
Guerrier	74	Capt. J. F. T. Trullet (1).	T *
Conquérant	74	,, S. Dalbarade (2).	T
Spartiate	74	,, M. J. Emeriau.	T
Aquilon	74	,, H. A. Thévenard (2).*	T
Peuple Souverain	74	,, P. P. Raccord.	T
Franklin	80	Rear-Adm. A. S. M. Blanquet du Chayla. Capt. M. Gilet.	T
Orient	120	Vice-Adm. F. P. Brueys.* Capt. H. Ganteaume, 1st. ,, L. de Casa Bianca, 2nd.*	Burnt
Tonnant	80	,, A. A. Dupetit Thouars.*	T
Heureux	74	,, J. P. Etienne.	T †
Mercure	74	,, Cambon.	T *
Guillaume Tell	80	Rear-Adm. P. C. J. B. S. Villeneuve. Capt. Saulnier.	Escpd
Généreux	74	,, Le Joille.	Escpd.
Timoléon	74	,, J. F. T. Trullet (2).	Burnt
Sérieuse	36	,, C. J. Martin.	Sunk
Artémise	40	,, P. J. Standelet.	Burnt
Diane	40	Rear-Adm. D. Decrès. Capt. E. J. N. Solen.	Escpd.
Justice	40	,, Villeneuve (2).	Escpd.
Railleur, brig			
Alerte, brig			

and three bombs, besides several gunboats.

* Burnt, as useless, August 18th.
† Burnt, as useless, August 16th.

The Bay of Aboukir lies along the coast, a few miles to the north-east of Alexandria, and is a nearly semi-circular indentation opening to the northward, between Aboukir Point, on the west, and the Rosetta mouth of the Nile, on the east, a distance of about sixteen miles. This opening is not, however, an uninterrupted one, for, from Aboukir Point, in a nearly northerly direction there extends a chain of shoals and rocks. Of the rocks, the largest, Aboukir Island, is about two miles from Aboukir Point, and in 1798 both it and the town of Aboukir, on Aboukir Point, were fortified and held by the French. There is no passage, save for very small craft, between the shoals and rocks composing the chain above-mentioned, and a continuation of the shoal extended in 1798 north-eastward beyond Aboukir Island for nearly a mile; so that the mouth of the bay, so far as large vessels were concerned, practically narrowed itself to little more than thirteen miles.

The French ships, in line, at single anchor with springs on their cables,[1] extended from a point about 2400 yards south-east of Aboukir Island, towards the south-east, in the direction of the shore. The line was not quite straight, but was slightly bowed to seawards. The *Guerrier*, at the north-western end, lay about 1000 yards from the edge of the shoal that surrounds the island, and, as the ships were anchored with intervals of about 160 yards, the length of the

REAR-ADMIRAL SIR EDWARD BERRY, BART.

(From the engraving by D. Orme, after the portrait by himself, painted about 1805, *when Berry was a Captain.)*

whole line was about 2850 yards. Within it, with its edge curving in the direction away from the convexity of the line, was a shoal; yet this shoal was not so close but that there was room for ships to work in between it and the French fleet. Nearly midway between the line and the shoal, and parallel with the former, Brueys anchored

[1] When Brueys perceived that Nelson was about to attack, he ordered each ship to lay out an anchor to S.S.E., and to send a stream cable to the ship next astern of her, making a hawser fast to it. 'Vict. et Conq.,' ix. 89.

his four frigates. His bombs and gunboats were still closer inshore, under Aboukir; and all these vessels, as well as a battery of two brass and two iron 12-pounders, two 13-inch brass mortars, and some lighter pieces, on Aboukir Island, were so disposed as to lend more or less support to the whole position, the general nature of which is made clear by the accompanying plans.

It was 2 P.M. when the *Heureux* signalled the presence of a fleet of twelve sail of the line[1] in the N.N.W. The French commander-

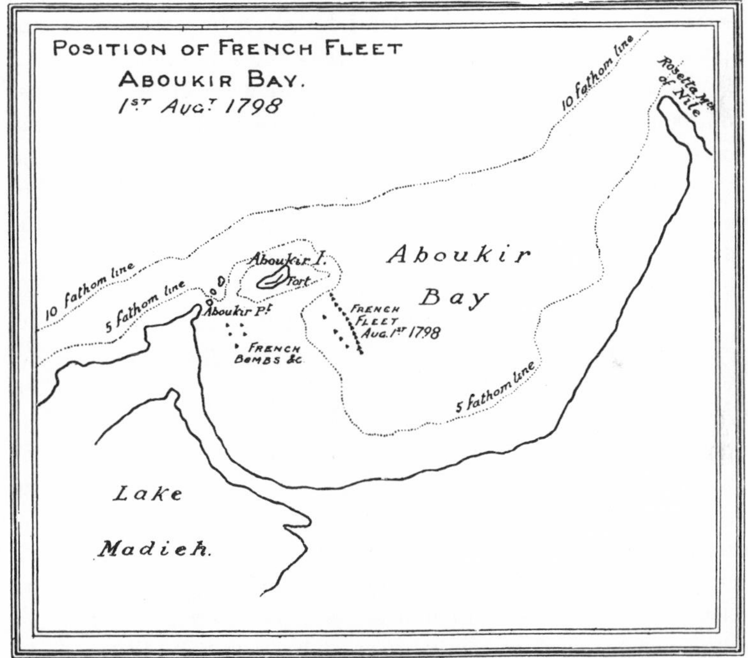

in-chief at once recalled to the ships a number of men who were on shore with water-casks, and ordered part of the crews of the frigates to go on board the vessels of the line. At 3 P.M. he further signalled to prepare for battle, and, at the same time, detached the brigs *Railleur* and *Alerte* to endeavour to tempt the advancing British on to the Aboukir shoals. At 4 P.M., when he learnt that not twelve, but fourteen ships were about to fall upon him, he betrayed symptoms of an intention to get under way, and ordered top-gallant yards to be crossed; but he seems to have subsequently

[1] The *Alexander* and *Swiftsure* being not then in sight.

concluded that his enemy would not attack him until the following morning, and to have, in consequence, decided to remain at anchor.

At 2.15 P.M., when the *Alexander* and *Swiftsure*, which had reconnoitred the harbours of Alexandria, and had been recalled by signal, were standing under all sail to rejoin the Rear-Admiral, they were about twelve miles from the main body which was making the best of its way to the eastward. At 3 P.M., Nelson signalled to prepare for battle, and at 4 P.M., when the *Orient* bore S.E. by S., distant about nine miles, he ordered his ships to prepare to anchor by the stern. Each ship, in pursuance of this direction, made fast a stream cable to her mizenmast, and, passing it out of one of her gun-room ports, carried it along her side, just below the lower deck ports (from several of which it was slung by spun yarn lashings), and then bent it to an anchor at her bow, so that, upon that anchor being let go, the ship would run over the cable leading from the hawse-hole, and would bring up by the cable out of the gunroom port. This arrangement had a double object; namely, to prevent the ships, upon anchoring, from swinging head to wind, and from, perhaps, being seriously raked while doing so; and to enable them, by hauling upon one cable and slackening the other, to bring their broadsides to bear in any desired direction. Having signalled to prepare to anchor, Nelson next intimated that he intended to attack the enemy's van and centre.[1] As he had previously explained to his captains the general plan upon which he purposed to proceed in case he should discover the French in such a position as that which they were actually found to occupy, he was then able, with confidence, to leave the execution of the details to his subordinates.[2]

The manœuvres of the *Railleur* and *Alerte* failed to divert the attention of the British van. "The bait," admits Guérin, "was a clumsy one to put before a man like Nelson," and the fleet paid absolutely no attention to it. At 5.30 P.M., when he was nearly abreast of the Aboukir Island shoal, the Rear-Admiral signalled to form line of battle ahead and astern of the flagship, as most convenient, and, soon afterwards, he hailed Hood, of the *Zealous*, inquiring whether the latter thought that the ships were far

[1] Brueys, strange to say, had anticipated a concentration upon his rear. Brueys to Nap., July 13th. But it may be that, when he wrote, his rear lay to windward, and could not, consequently, be readily succoured by his van.

[2] Sir E. Berry in 'Nav. Chron.,' i. 52.

enough to the eastward to be able to clear the shoal if they bore up.[1] There was no trustworthy chart of the bay, and the ground was strange to every Captain present. Hood answered that he was then in 11 fathoms, and that, if permitted, he would bear up, sounding carefully, and so serve as guide to the fleet. Nelson assented; and, while the *Zealous* cautiously rounded the head of the shoal, with the *Goliath* on her port or outer bow, the *Vanguard* hove to and allowed several vessels to pass her. As the *Theseus* approached, Miller was hailed by Berry and told that he was to be Nelson's next ahead. The *Theseus* accordingly ran past, the *Vanguard* filled, and at 6 P.M., by signal, the column stood on, the order then being: *Goliath, Zealous, Orion, Audacious, Theseus, Vanguard, Minotaur, Defence, Bellerophon, Majestic, Leander*, with, considerably to the northward, *Culloden*, and, still far to westward, *Alexander* and *Swiftsure* under a press of sail.

At 6.20 P.M. the *Conquérant*, followed by the *Guerrier*, opened

Thos. Foley

SIGNATURE OF ADMIRAL SIR THOMAS FOLEY (3).

fire upon the *Goliath* and *Zealous*, and the battery on the island began to throw shells, but without effect. Ten minutes afterwards the *Goliath*, which had with difficulty kept ahead of the *Zealous*, passed under the forefoot of the *Guerrier*, fired a raking broadside into that vessel, and endeavoured to anchor on her port bow. As, however, the anchor was let go rather late, the *Goliath* ran down somewhat further than Foley had intended, and only brought up abreast of the port quarter of the *Conquérant*, with which ship, and with the *Sérieuse*,[2] on her starboard bow, she began a warm action. The *Zealous*, also rounding the head of the French line, brought up, in only five fathoms, abreast of the port bow of the *Guerrier*. It was sunset; and, as the *Zealous* brought down the *Guerrier's* fore-

[1] Williams, who was present, tells a slightly different story. "Nelson hailed Hood, and asked him *if he thought there was sufficient depth of water for our ships between the enemy and the shore.* 'I don't know, sir,' replied Hood; 'but, with your permission, I will stand in and try.'" According to this, Nelson inquired not about getting round the shoal, but about getting round the head of the French line.

[2] The *Sérieuse* had, of course, already fired at her. So, also, had the *Hercule*, bomb, to which the *Goliath* distantly replied.

mast ere she had been five minutes in action, the advancing British ships gave three cheers. (Fig. on opposite page.)

The *Orion*, which was next in order, rounded the starboard quarter of the *Zealous*, and running along outside her and the *Goliath*, poured her starboard broadside into the presumptuous *Sérieuse*, dismasted her, cut her cable, reduced her to a sinking condition, and then, dropping anchor, veered away so as to bring up head to wind a little abaft the port beam of the *Peuple Souverain*, but at a rather greater distance from her than Saumarez had intended.[1] In the meantime the *Audacious*, cutting between the *Guerrier* and the *Conquérant*, dropped her small bower anchor so as to bring up close athwart the latter ship's hawse, and, presently swinging round head to wind, came to again less than fifty yards from the *Conquérant's* port bow. The *Theseus*, taking a shorter course than the *Orion*, passed round the head of the French line, and between it and the already anchored *Zealous* and *Goliath*, and herself anchored by the stern, abreast of, and about three hundred yards from the *Spartiate*.

Nelson, in the *Vanguard*, followed; but, instead of cutting through the line, he anchored at 6.40 P.M. on the starboard beam of the *Spartiate*, at a distance of about eighty yards. The *Minotaur* passed along the *Vanguard's* disengaged side, and at 6.45 P.M., anchored abreast of the *Aquilon*; and the *Defence*, passing in a similar manner along the disengaged side of the *Minotaur*, brought up at 7 P.M. on the beam of the *Peuple Souverain*. At that moment, therefore, the five leading French ships found themselves in conflict with eight British, five of which were on their port, and three on their starboard hand. It was at about that time that the fleet, which had gone into action with the White Ensign flying,[2] began to hoist the lights which Nelson had prescribed in order that his vessels might easily recognise one another—four disposed horizontally at the mizen peak. At about the same time, also, the *Bellerophon* anchored by the stern abreast, and on the starboard side, of the *Orient*. A few minutes later the *Majestic*[3] brought up in a similar

[1] Saumarez had to deviate from his course, in the first place, in order to deal with the *Sérieuse*, and, in the second, in order to avoid fouling the *Theseus*, which had anchored before him.

[2] Nelson, although he was then of the Blue Squadron, had a peculiar affection for the White Ensign, under which he eventually fell.

[3] At about 8.30, finding that she was drifting athwart the hawse of the *Heureux*, the *Majestic* slipped her stern cable, and, letting go her best bower, brought up again head to wind on the port bow of the *Heureux*.

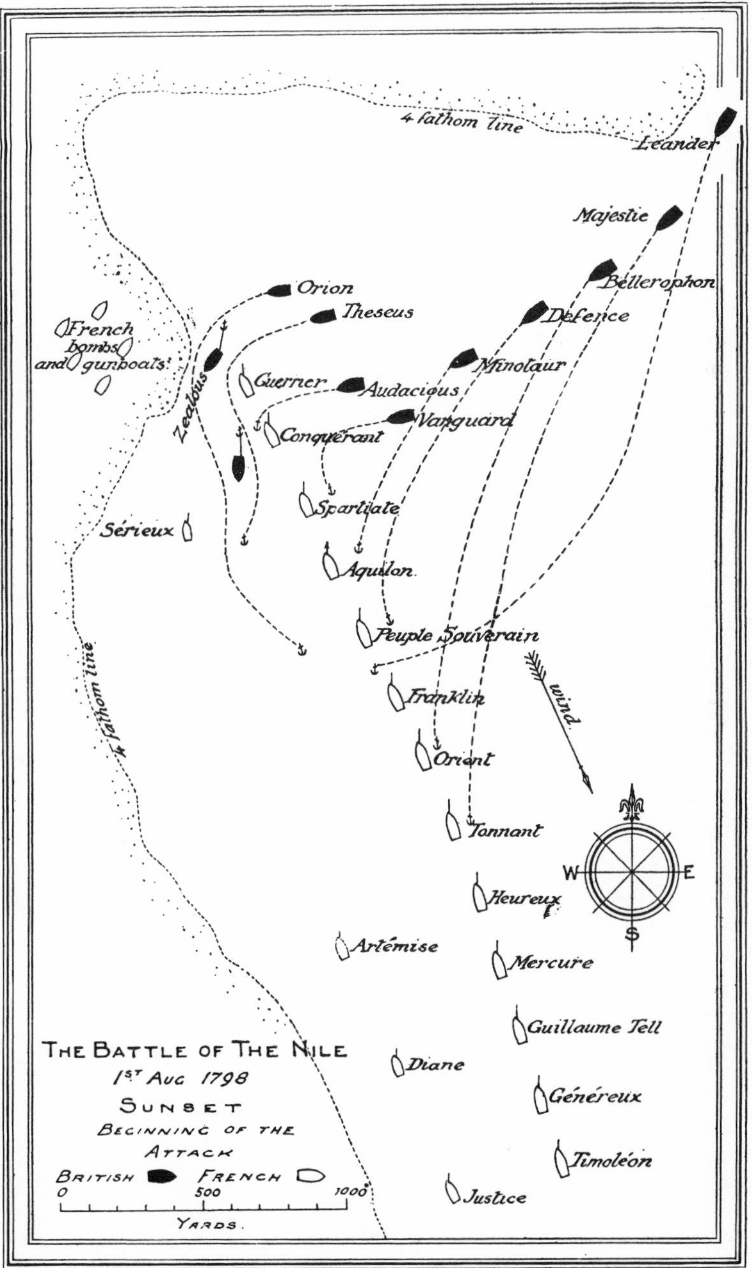

4 fathom line
Leander
Majestic
Bellerophon
Orion
Theseus
Defence
French bombs and gunboats
Minotaur
Guerrier
Audacious
Zealous
Vanguard
Conquérant
Spartiate
Sérieux
Aquilon
Peuple Souverain
wind
Franklin
4 fathom line
Orient
Tonnant
W
E
S
Heureux
Artémise
Mercure
Guillaume Tell
THE BATTLE OF THE NILE
1ST AUG 1798
SUNSET
BEGINNING OF THE ATTACK
Diane
Généreux
BRITISH
FRENCH
Timoléon
0
500
1000
Justice
YARDS.

[*To face p.* 362.

position with regard to the *Tonnant*. Such was the situation in the immediate neighbourhood of the French line at about 7.15 P.M.

At about 6.40 P.M. the *Culloden*,[1] while rounding the point of shoal eastward of Aboukir Island, had, unfortunately, grounded and stuck fast, to the immense mortification of the gallant Troubridge and his ship's company, who soon realised that the accident must debar them from having any share in the furious action that was going on under their eyes. The accident for a time detained the *Leander*, which was the *Culloden's* next ahead; but, quickly perceiving where he could be of most use, Captain Thompson proceeded on his course towards the enemy. All that was possible was done to get the *Culloden* off; and the *Mutine*, after a time, anchored hard by and lent her assistance; but not until 2 A.M. on August 2nd could the ship haul herself clear; and by that hour she had bumped her rudder off and was making seven feet of water an hour. As soon, however, as she had grounded, she had signalled

SIGNATURE OF REAR-ADMIRAL SIR THOMAS TROUBRIDGE, BART.

her mishap; and her signals warned the *Alexander* and *Swiftsure*, as they came up, of the danger in their way; so that although, just as they were rounding the shoal, the wind shifted from N.N.W. to N., they cleared it. To do so, however, the *Alexander* had to tack, and so surrendered her lead to the *Swiftsure*, which, as she neared the centre of the French line at a few minutes after 8 P.M., fell in with a dismasted hull, drifting without lights or colours. Hallowell providentially hailed her instead of at once firing into her, and learnt that she was the *Bellerophon*, going out of action disabled. Hallowell, in the darkness, smoke, and general confusion, could not tell exactly where he was, but, realising that he was quite close to some part of the French line, he at once let go and brought up by the stern opposite the interval between the *Franklin* and the *Orient*, at a distance of a cable from the latter's starboard bow. A little earlier the *Peuple Souverain* had parted her cable

[1] Ekins makes the extraordinary mistake of saying that the *Culloden* grounded while leading the fleet in. 'Nav. Battles,' 237.

and dropped out of the French line, and the *Leander*, arriving on the scene of action, and observing the gap thus occasioned in it, had kept for a time under way in the vacant space, and had then anchored with great judgment athwart the bows of the *Franklin*, in such a manner that with her port broadside she raked the *Franklin* and the ships astern of her, while, with her starboard broadside, she could also rake the *Aquilon*, receiving comparatively little harm herself. The *Alexander* had, ere that, cut the line astern of the *Orient*,[1] and, coming round to the wind, had anchored by the bow on the three-decker's port quarter.

It is now time to look at the fortunes of the French ships which were thus attacked.

The *Guerrier*, raked not only by the *Zealous*, which was anchored on her port bow, but also by the *Orion*, *Theseus*, *Audacious*, and *Goliath* as they proceeded to their stations, speedily lost all her masts. She nevertheless fought on with great heroism until after 9 P.M., when she surrendered to the *Zealous*. The *Conquérant*, first engaged by the *Goliath*, then raked by the *Audacious*,[2] and finally assailed with steady persistency by both ships, resisted only for about twelve minutes; yet, when she struck, she had lost her fore and mizen masts and was completely disabled. The *Spartiate*, engaged first by the *Theseus*, and then by that ship and the *Vanguard*, received also some more distant fire from the *Minotaur*, and ultimately from the *Audacious* as well. The *Aquilon*, her next astern, assisted her for a time by using her springs to bring her port broadside to bear upon the *Vanguard's* bows; but at length the *Spartiate* was completely dismasted, and soon after 9 P.M. she struck. The *Aquilon* had as her nearest opponent the *Minotaur*, which alone of all the ships in the two fleets carried, as an upper battery, a tier of 32-pounder carronades. The *Theseus*, though much more distant, also devoted some attention to the *Aquilon*, which, having lost all her masts and suffered heavily, hauled down her flag at 9.25 P.M. The *Peuple Souverain*, hotly assailed by the *Defence* and *Orion*, both of which occupied advantageous positions with respect to her, soon lost her fore and main masts, and either parted her cable, or had it shot away. She consequently dropped down abreast of the *Orient*, where she

[1] The manœuvre being facilitated by the fact that the *Tonnant* had driven a little to leeward.

[2] The *Conquérant* also received a passing fire from the *Orion* and *Theseus*.

reanchored, having ceased firing. The *Franklin* had for a time no near opponent, but received a distant fire from the starboard quarter guns of the *Orion*. The *Leander* then, as has been seen, placed herself athwart the hawse of the French 80, and began systematically to rake her; the *Swiftsure* gave her the fire from her starboard quarter and stern guns; and the *Defence*, together with the *Minotaur*, when the latter had settled matters with the *Aquilon*,

VICE-ADMIRAL SIR THOMAS BOULDEN THOMPSON, KT. AND BART.

(From Ridley's lithograph after the miniature by G. Engleheart, painted when Thompson was a Captain.)

annoyed the *Franklin* on her starboard bow and beam. But before the *Franklin* was silenced there happened an event of so awful a character as for a time to paralyse, as it were, both fleets.

The French flagship *Orient*[1] was first sought out by the *Bellerophon*, which anchored close alongside of the great three-decker, but which soon found the position untenable. By 7.50 P.M.

[1] She had previously been known as the *Sans Culotte*, and had been renamed in honour of the object of the expedition.

the British 74 had lost her mizen mast; a little later her main mast went over the starboard bow, and she caught fire in several places; and at 8.20 P.M., being absolutely disabled, she set her sprit-sail, cut her stern cable, and got clear. An attempt to set her fore-topsail brought down her shattered foremast. In that condition she was fired into by the *Tonnant*,[1] and, as has been shown, narrowly escaped being fired into by the *Swiftsure*. The attack upon the *Orient* was almost instantly taken up by the *Swiftsure* and the *Alexander*; and at 9 P.M. the former vessel perceived the French flagship to be on fire. The *Swiftsure* concentrated as much of her broadside as possible upon the burning spot, and thus probably interfered with the attempts to extinguish the flames. Early in the action Vice-Admiral Brueys had received two wounds, and at about 8 P.M., while descending from the poop to the quarter-deck, he had been almost cut in two by a round shot; but, when asked to allow himself to be taken below, had proudly answered, "Un amiral français doit mourir sur son banc de quart." He had not survived to witness the outbreak of the fire. Soon after his death his flag-captain, de Casa Bianca, had fallen dangerously wounded; and it would appear, from the accounts of survivors, that, ere the conflagration began, the ship had already become a shambles. Yet worse was in store. The flames increased and spread along the deck and leapt up the rigging. Foreseeing the inevitable catastrophe, all the vessels near the doomed three-decker either shifted their berths, or, closing their ports and hatchways, and removing all ammunition from their upper decks, held in readiness large bodies of men with filled buckets. At about 10 P.M. the *Orient* was blown into the air by the explosion of her magazine.[2] The concussion alone was so violent as to seriously injure ships which lay even at some distance; and the hurtling fragments of spars and wreckage presently fell a burning shower all around. Some fell in the *Swiftsure*, some in the *Alexander*, but most in the *Franklin*. The latter two vessels were set on fire; yet in both cases the flames were quickly extinguished.

[1] Many French accounts have it that the *Bellerophon's* people, while near the *Tonnant*, "et principalement les officiers, jetèrent de grands cris, pour faire connaître qu'il était rendu." 'Vict. et Conq.,' ix. 101; Guérin, vi. 168, etc. There is not a shadow of evidence that any soul in the ship ever dreamt of surrender; but there is evidence that her crew was a noisy one.

[2] About 70 of her people were saved by British boats, and Capt. Ganteaume and a few more made their way to the French brig *Salamine*; but, with these exceptions, all perished.

It is clear that the physical and moral effects of the shock stupefied almost everyone in both fleets. All accounts of eye-witnesses agree in declaring that not for several minutes after this frightful catastrophe was another gun fired on either side. The *Franklin*, though nearly disabled, was the first ship to renew the struggle; but she did not much longer maintain it. The *Defence* and *Swiftsure* brought down her main and mizen masts; and, being scarcely able to make any reply, she hauled down her flag. By midnight, therefore, all the ships of the French line ahead of the *Tonnant* had struck or had been destroyed. The *Tonnant* continued her most gallant resistance. She had thus far been engaged chiefly with the *Majestic*, whose main and mizen masts she had shot away, but, more distantly, with the *Swiftsure* and *Alexander*. At length, when all her own masts had been cut off close to the deck and had encumbered her batteries with their wreckage, she had to cease firing, but, instead of immediately surrendering, she managed, by letting out cable, to drop into a station in which, for the time, she suffered but little further annoyance. She had indeed offered a magnificent defence; and the end of her captain, the brave Dupetit Thouars, deserves to be remembered as one of the brightest episodes in an action which was full of splendid deeds. Round shots deprived him successively of his right arm, his left arm, and one of his legs; whereupon the heroic officer, instead of letting himself be taken below, caused himself to be placed in a tub of bran, whence he continued to give his orders until from loss of blood he became insensible. One of these was for nailing the French flag to the ship's masts.[1] Almost his last words were to implore his people to sink rather than surrender.[2]

In her new position the *Tonnant* practically constituted the head of a fresh but very irregular line, which had been formed inside and to leeward of the tail of the old one, by the ships of the French rear, all of which, with the exception of the *Tonnant*, were still undamaged. At about 4 A.M. on the 2nd, as day was breaking, some of these ships became distantly engaged with the *Alexander*

[1] As these afterwards fell, the precaution was useless.

[2] Aristide Aubert Dupetit Thouars: born, 1760; fought at Ushant and in North American waters; captain, 1783; led the expedition in search of La Pérouse. His son Abel, another brilliant naval officer, established the French protectorate over Tahiti, and died a vice-admiral, 1864. His son Abel (2), also a naval officer, served in the Crimea, at Simonosaki, and at Strasburg (1870), and died a rear-admiral in 1890.

and *Majestic*. The firing attracted to the spot the *Theseus* and *Goliath*, which anchored near the French frigate *Artémise*. Her captain fired a broadside into the *Theseus*, and then struck; but, when taken possession of, she was found to be on fire; and she afterwards blew up. In the meantime the vessels of the French rear, and the two remaining frigates, had dropped so much further to leeward as to be almost out of gunshot. The *Heureux* and *Mercure*, in fact, had gone to the length of running themselves on shore in the bight of the bay.

At 6 A.M. the *Zealous*, *Goliath*, and *Theseus* were signalled to weigh, and the first-named was presently directed to chase the frigate *Justice*, which was making for the disabled *Bellerophon* with a view to summoning her to surrender. The other two British 74's, accompanied by the *Alexander* and *Leander*, followed up the *Heureux* and *Mercure*, and, after exchanging a few shots with them, forced them to strike. The *Zealous* easily induced the *Justice* to abandon her absurd design against the *Bellerophon*, and then, by Nelson's direction, joined Captain Darby's ship in order to protect her from molestation by any more serious foe.

While the *Zealous*, *Goliath*, *Theseus*, *Alexander*, and *Leander* were thus employed, the *Guillaume Tell*, *Généreux*, *Timoléon*, *Tonnant*, and *Diane*, which had been rejoined by the *Justice*, found themselves with no British vessels very near them. The *Tonnant*, of course, could not move; the *Timoléon*, which had got herself fairly embayed among the shoals to leeward, endeavoured to make sail upon the port tack, and, in the effort, ran herself ashore. But the other French ships had room to manœuvre and were perfectly able to do so; and, seizing their opportunity, they hauled close on the port tack, and made a bold bid for safety. The *Zealous*, observing them, chased and was, a few minutes afterwards, actually engaging single-handed the four uninjured ships, and endeavouring to cut off the rearmost frigate, when Nelson recalled her. Thus did Rear-Admiral Villeneuve, with the *Guillaume Tell*, *Généreux*, *Diane*, and *Justice*, escape from the fatal Bay of Aboukir.[1] The whole of the rest of the fleet of Brueys either fell into the hands of the victors or was destroyed; for, on the morning of August 3rd, the *Tonnant*, being

[1] These escaped only for a time. The *Généreux* was taken on Feb. 18th, the *Guillaume Tell* on March 30th, and the *Diane* on Aug. 24th, 1800. The *Justice* was captured at Alexandria on Sept. 2nd, 1801.

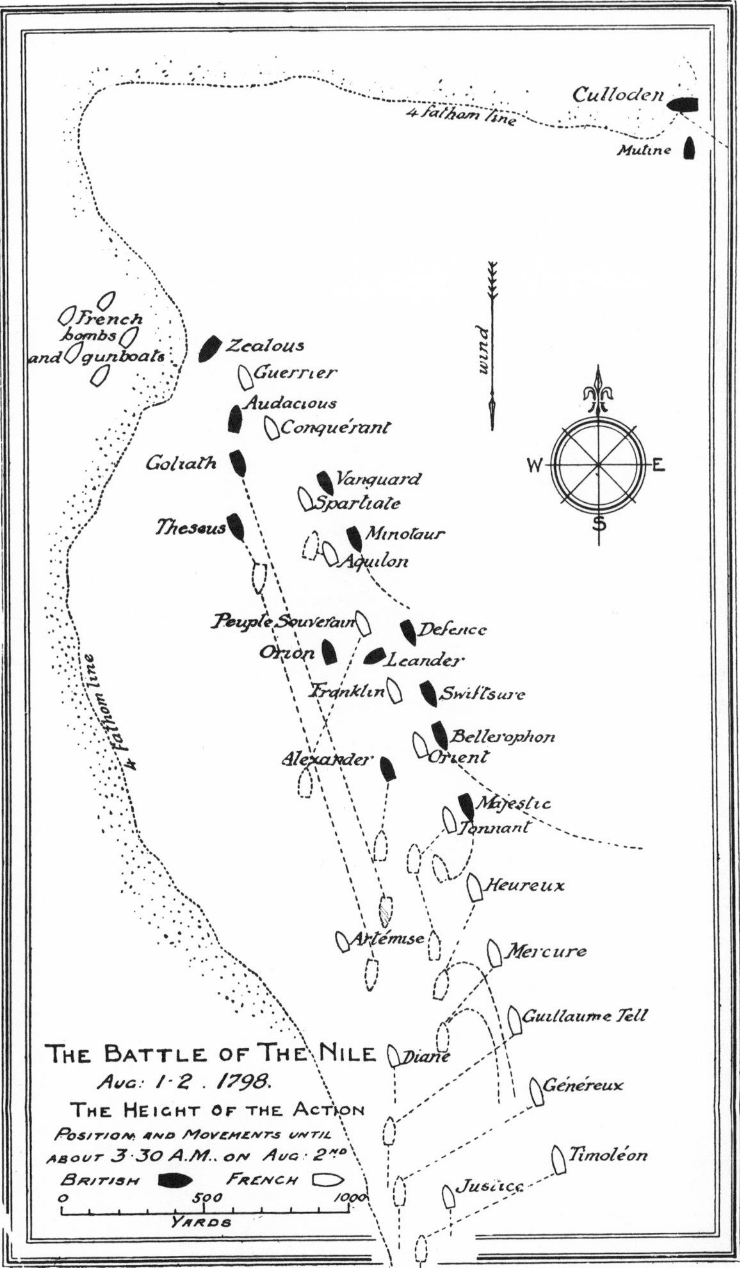
Culloden
4 fathom line
Mutine
French
bombs
and gunboats
Zealous
Guerrier
Audacious
Conquérant
Goliath
Vanguard
Spartiate
Theseus
Minotaur
Aquilon
wind
W
E
S
Peuple Souverain
Defence
Orion
Leander
Franklin
Swiftsure
Bellerophon
Orient
Alexander
4 fathom line
Majestic
Tonnant
Heureux
Artémise
Mercure
Guillaume Tell
THE BATTLE OF THE NILE
Aug: 1·2 . 1798.
THE HEIGHT OF THE ACTION
POSITION AND MOVEMENTS UNTIL
ABOUT 3·30 A.M.. ON AUG: 2ND
Diane
Généreux
Timoléon
BRITISH
FRENCH
Justice
0
500
1000
YARDS

[To face p. 368.

threatened by the *Theseus* and *Leander*, struck, and, during the afternoon of the same day, the grounded *Timoléon* was set on fire by her crew, and eventually blew up.

Nearly all the British ships had suffered in their rigging. The *Bellerophon* lost all three masts, the *Majestic* lost her main and mizen. But these were the only vessels which had lost any lower masts, and the damages of the others aloft were, with few exceptions, not very serious. The chief sufferers in their hulls were the *Bellerophon*, the *Majestic*, and the *Vanguard*. The total loss of each British ship in killed and wounded will be found set forth in the table on page 357. The officers killed were: Captain George Blagden Westcott (*Majestic*); Lieutenants Robert Savage Daniel (1783), Philip William Launder (1790), and George Jolliffe (1797), (*Bellerophon*), John G. Kirchner (*Minotaur*), and John Collins (*Alexander*); Captain of Marines William Faddy (*Vanguard*), Master's Mates William Davies (*Goliath*), Peter Walter (*Minotaur*), and Thomas Ellison (*Bellerophon*); Midshipmen Andrew Brown (*Goliath*), Thomas Seymour and John George Taylor (*Vanguard*), and Zebedee Ford (*Majestic*); Captain's Clerk —— Baird (*Orion*); and Boatswain Andrew Gilmore (*Majestic*). Among the officers wounded were Rear-Admiral Sir H. Nelson; Captains A. J. Ball, Sir J. Saumarez, and H. d'E. Darby; Lieutenants Nathaniel Vassall and John Miller Adye (*Vanguard*), Richard Hawkins (*Theseus*), John Jeans (*Audacious*), William Wilkinson (*Goliath*), and Thomas Irwin (*Minotaur*); Mr. John Campbell, Nelson's secretary, and Captains of Marines John Creswell (*Alexander*), and John Hopkins (*Bellerophon*).

Nelson was wounded early in the action by a splinter, which struck him above his blind right eye, and which left pendent a strip of flesh. For a short time he believed the wound to be a mortal one, but, when it had been sewn up, the Rear-Admiral was able to return to his duties on deck. Captain Westcott,[1] of the *Majestic*, lost his life by a musket ball fired from the *Tonnant*. After his death, the ship continued to be most effectively fought by her first lieutenant, Robert Cuthbert.[2]

[1] George Blagden Westcott was made Commander in 1787, and was posted on Oct. 1st, 1790.

[2] The first Lieutenants of the ships engaged were, it would appear: *Goliath*, George Jardine; *Zealous*, William Henry Webley; *Orion*, James Barker; *Audacious*, Thomas White (2); *Theseus*, Richard Hawkins; *Vanguard*, Edward Galwey; *Minotaur*, Charles Marsh Schomberg; *Defence*, Richard Jones (1); *Bellerophon*,

From what has been already written, it will be understood that the French ships which were closely engaged were all very badly damaged. Five of them were left without a stick standing, and were so shattered in hull as to be, for the time, quite unseaworthy. Two others remained with but one mast each, and with riddled hulls. Estimates of the French loss in killed, drowned, burnt, wounded, taken and missing, vary between 2000 and 5000, but no official returns exist. It is probable, all things considered, that about 3500 was the true number. Among the French officers who perished were, in addition to Vice-Admiral Brueys,[1] and Captain Dupetit Thouars, Captains Thévenard (2), and de Casa Bianca.[2] Captain Dalbarade (2) never recovered from his wounds.

The *Culloden*, it will have been seen, was able to take no part whatsoever in the action; yet, even if she be counted as part of Nelson's effective force, the British in this great battle were in tonnage and gun power inferior to their opponents. Brueys, leaving aside his frigates, had thirteen ships, mounting nominally[3] 1026 guns. Nelson had fourteen ships, mounting nominally 1012 guns. But the French ships threw, upon the whole, much heavier broadsides than the British, and were also, upon the whole, much larger vessels. The biggest British ship in the battle was the *Minotaur*, of 1718 tons. Of the prizes, the *Spartiate* measured 1949, the *Franklin*, 2257, and the *Tonnant*, 2281 tons. The *Orient*, the *Guillaume Tell*, and several more were also larger than anything in the British line on that glorious occasion. And when

---

Robert Savage Daniel, killed; Robert Cathcart, senior surviving; *Majestic*, Robert Cuthbert; *Swiftsure*, John Lawes Waters; *Alexander*, John Yule; *Leander*, William Richardson (1). These seem to have been all promoted, though one, Lieutenant Schomberg, did not receive that reward until 1802, and another, Lieut. Yule, until 1805. Lieut. Cathcart was posted. Owing to the fact that two Lieutenants of the name of Thomas White were made Commanders in 1798, and that both these officers were posted in 1810, it is exceedingly difficult to separate all their services; but the first Lieutenant of the *Audacious* was the officer who was born in 1755, made a Commander on Oct. 8th, 1798, and posted on Oct. 21st, 1810, and who died in 1833, being still a Captain. (*Naut. Mag.*, ii. 624.) I have not succeeded in ascertaining the name of the *Culloden's* first Lieutenant; but he also was ordered to be promoted.

[1] François Paul, Comte de Brueys d'Aigailliers; born 1753 at Uzès; lieutenant 1780; captain before the Revolution; made a rear-admiral by Truguet and a vice-admiral by Bonaparte. He was brave, but quite incapable as a flag-officer.

[2] Lucien, Comte de Casa Bianca; born, 1755. His son, aged ten, perished with him.

[3] I say "nominally," in order to avoid having to enter here into elaborate explanations of the real number of guns carried by each ship. As a matter of fact, the ships on both sides carried more than their nominal number of guns: but in real, as in nominal number, the French were superior.

it is remembered that the *Culloden* had no share in the fight, and that Nelson had no frigates, while Brueys had four frigates, nominally mounting 152 guns, besides a battery on shore to support the head of his line, the disadvantages under which the British laboured become even more noteworthy. Looking, therefore, to the unflinching determination with which the French fought, to the completeness of the victory gained, and to the effects produced, the Battle of the Nile may justly be deemed the most splendid and glorious success which the British Navy gained up to the end of the eighteenth century. Nelson not only defeated an enemy of superior force, but practically annihilated his fleet. In addition, he inflicted the first serious blow upon the

COMMEMORATIVE MEDAL OF THE BATTLE OF THE NILE, 1798.

(From an original lent by H.S.H. Capt. Prince Louis of Battenberg, R.N.)

colossal schemes of Napoleon, and saved, certainly great part of the Ottoman Empire, and possibly also India, from becoming, temporarily at least, a prey to France.

To what causes, then, was the victory owing? They were both positive and negative. The chief causes were Nelson's prescience and unrivalled boldness, and the complete military efficiency of his ships, his officers, and his men. The plan of attacking the head and centre of the enemy's line and of doubling upon it was, of course, at the root of all. Yet the negative causes were, it must be admitted, scarcely less instrumental than the positive in securing the result. Brueys, in spite of his personal bravery, was both sluggish and incompetent. He stationed his fleet so that the two sides of it which formed the angle, the apex of which was the

Orient, could not, without moving, support one another. He deliberately, in spite of the advice of his most experienced officers, elected to fight at anchor. He underrated his enemy. Till the very hour of the onset he exclaimed, "They dare not attack me." In spite of the number of small craft at his disposal, both at Aboukir and at Alexandria, he had no scouts out, and secured no warning of the approach or the force of his foe. He had no assurance, for he did not take the trouble to sound the passage, that the British, by entering between Aboukir and the island, could not get inside his line; and he must have known, had he reflected, that they could get round the head of it; yet he caused his fleet to clear for action only on the starboard or seaward side; and so imperfectly did his own ship clear that numerous special cabins which had been fitted in her for military and civilian passengers were never removed at all. Nor were the junior flag-officers, Villeneuve and Decrès, less remiss than their chief. If, as James says, the six French rear ships—and I would add, the frigates—as soon as they saw the manœuvre that was about to be practised on their friends in the van,—had

"got under way and stood out, they would have found full employment for the five or six British ships that had not yet got into action. They would undoubtedly have captured the *Culloden*, and prevented the *Alexander* and *Swiftsure* from entering the bay. Had those six French ships weighed at any time before 7 P.M., they might, with the wind as it then was, have made a good stretch out of the bay, and, by tacking, when the wind, as it afterwards did, shifted to north, might have stood for the van of their line with their yards nearly square."

Of the nine prizes, the *Guerrier*, *Heureux*, and *Mercure*, as being useless, were ultimately burnt by the victors. The *Peuple Souverain*, having been brought as far on the way to England as Gibraltar, was renamed *Guerrier*, and was left there as a guardship. The five remaining ships, which arrived in safety at Plymouth, were added to the Navy, the *Franklin* as the *Canopus*, the *Aquilon* as the *Aboukir*, and the others under their old names.

On August 5th, Nelson sent off dispatches for his Commander-in-Chief, Lord St. Vincent, by Captain Berry, late of the *Vanguard*, who sailed in the *Leander*. Berry's place as flag-captain was taken by Thomas Masterman Hardy, previously of the *Mutine*; and Hardy's place as Commander of the *Mutine* was given to the Hon. Thomas Bladen Capell,[1] who, on the 13th, sailed in his sloop for Naples with

[1] He had been junior and signal Lieutenant of the *Vanguard*.

duplicate dispatches. Berry, as will be seen in the next chapter, had the misfortune to be captured, while on his way to Cadiz, by the *Généreux*, 74; but Capell safely reached his destination. With a view to reassure the officials of the East India Company, Nelson also sent overland to Bombay Lieutenant Thomas Duval, of the *Zealous*, who arrived there, after many adventures, on October 21st. On August 14th, the main part of the fleet, under Sir James Saumarez, and such of the prizes[1] as were to be removed, stood out of the road, and on the following day proceeded westward; and on the 19th Nelson himself, in the *Vanguard*, with the *Culloden* and *Alexander*, sailed for Naples, leaving Captain Samuel Hood (2), as senior officer, before Alexandria, with the *Zealous*, *Goliath*, *Swiftsure*, *Seahorse*, 28,[2] *Emerald*, 36,[3] *Alcmène*, 32,[4] and *Bonne Citoyenne*, 20.[5] Napoleon learnt on the 14th of what had happened in Aboukir Bay.

News of the victory, travelling by way of Naples, reached the Admiralty on October 2nd. For three months prior to that day, Nelson's popularity had been under a cloud, and had not saved the Rear-Admiral from the most baseless accusations of remissness and incompetence. The Government hastened to make amends for the popular unreasonableness. On October 6th, the victor was created Baron Nelson of the Nile, and of Burnham Thorpe; on November 20th, at the opening of Parliament, the King's speech contained a most handsome reference to the triumph which had been won; and this was presently followed by the granting of a pension of £2000 a year to Nelson and his two next heirs male by the Parliament of England, and of one of £1000 a year by the Parliament of Ireland. Both Parliaments also voted thanks to the officers and men who had been concerned; gold medals were presented to the Rear-Admiral and his Captains, including Troubridge; the first Lieutenants of all ships present were ordered to be promoted; the East India Company gave Nelson £10,000; the Porte created a new order in honour of the occasion and made the Rear-Admiral the first member of it; and rewards or presents were showered upon the conqueror by the

[1] Ultimately commissioned as follows: *Canopus*, Capt. Bartholomew James; *Tonnant*, Capt. Loftus Otway Bland; *Conquérant*, Capt. George Clarke; *Guerrier* (ex *Peuple Souverain*), Capt. Thomas Stephenson; *Spartiate*, Capt. Hon. Charles Herbert Pierrepont; and *Aboukir*, Capt. Thomas Bowen.

[2] Capt. Edward James Foote, joined on the 17th.

[3] Capt. Thomas Moutray Waller, joined on the 13th.

[4] Capt. George Hope (1), joined on the 13th.

[5] Com. Richard Retalick, joined on the 13th.

corporations of London and of Liverpool, by the Sultan, and by several other foreign sovereigns.

While on his way to Gibraltar with the prizes, Sir James Saumarez fell in, near Malta, with a small Portuguese squadron, which, under Rear-Admiral the Marques de Niza, had been sent into the Mediterranean by St. Vincent to reinforce Nelson. On September 25th, Saumarez and de Niza summoned the French garrison of Valetta, which, however, declined to submit; and, being precluded by the nature of his orders from unnecessarily delaying his voyage, Sir James contented himself, ere he proceeded, with putting ashore, for the use of the numerous islanders who were well disposed to the British, 1200 muskets and a quantity of ammunition. De Niza remained for a time in the vicinity, and was presently joined by the *Alexander*, 74, Captain Alexander John Ball, *Culloden*, 74, Captain Thomas Troubridge, and *Colossus*, 74, Captain George Murray (3), which had been detached by Nelson from Naples for the blockade of Malta. That blockade became effective from about October 12th;[1] and on the 24th, Nelson himself, in the *Vanguard*, with the *Minotaur*, 74, Captain Thomas Louis, assumed immediate command of the blockading force. The French position in the island was already a precarious one. The garrison, of about 3000 soldiers and seamen, had been driven by the inhabitants, who occupied Old Valetta under Neapolitan colours, into New Valetta; and the invaders were very short of supplies. General Vaubois commanded the troops, Rear-Admiral Decrès commanded the seamen who had been put ashore, and Rear-Admiral Villeneuve had under him in the harbour the *Guillaume Tell*, 80, *Diane*, 40, *Justice*, 40, *Athénien*, 64,[2] *Dégo*, 64,[2] and *Carthagénaise*, 36;[2] but, on the other hand, 10,000 Maltese were in arms, and the patriots possessed not only cannon but also armed galleys and gunboats. It was expected, therefore, that Malta would not hold out for very long, and this expectation seemed to receive some degree of justification when, on October 28th, the French garrison of the neighbouring and dependent island of Gozo capitulated. Captain John Cresswell, of the *Alexander's* Marines, hoisted British colours on the castle and took temporary possession; and on the day following the place was handed over to the islanders, the Neapolitan flag was sub-

[1] It nominally commenced on September 26th, and lasted till the surrender of Malta on September 4th, 1800.

[2] Formerly of the Maltese navy.

stituted, and the sovereignty of Ferdinand IV. was acknowledged. From that time forward, however, little progress was made; and, for very many months afterwards, the observation of Malta remained one of the most anxious duties of the British fleet in the Mediterranean.

In the meantime, the check inflicted on the French arms by the Battle of the Nile encouraged the tottering Italian kingdoms to make new struggles for life. As soon, however, as Sardinia made a movement, the French drove King Charles Emmanuel from the mainland and occupied Piedmont. The efforts of Naples were not quite so quickly stifled. The French, indeed, were actually driven from Rome; but, in little more than a fortnight, they repossessed themselves of it, and then marched upon Naples. Despairing of his ability to resist, and distrusting his own people, Ferdinand IV., on December 21st, took refuge on board Nelson's flagship, the *Vanguard*, and, five days later, landed at Palermo, the capital of his Sicilian dominions. Russia and Turkey were similarly stimulated to activity, and, by October 10th, their fleets, under Vice-Admiral Ushakoff[1] and Cadir Bey, had deprived the French of all their new acquisitions at the mouth of the Adriatic, except Corfu, where General Chabot held command, and where there lay in harbour the *Généreux*, 74, her prize, the *Leander*, 50, the *Brune*, 28, a bomb, a brig, and four armed galleys. Ushakoff and Cadir appeared before that island on October 20th, and presently disembarked troops and began siege operations; but, although they gradually reduced the defenders to great straits, they could not, or at least did not, prevent the *Généreux* from getting away to Ancona; and, at the end of the year the French flag still flew over Corfu.[2] A reinforcement from Ancona intended for the island was, however, deterred by the obvious hopelessness of the French position from attempting a landing.

The French naval force blockaded in Alexandria by the division under Captain Samuel Hood (2) consisted of the *Causse*, 64,[3] *Dubois*, 64,[3] *Junon*, 38, *Carrère*, 38,[3] *Muiron*, 38,[3] *Alceste*, 36, *Courageuse*, 36, *Leoben*, 32,[3] *Mantoue*, 32,[3] *Montenotte*, 32,[3] four brig-corvettes, and nine gunboats, etc.[4] These vessels had left Toulon armed *en flûte*; but, after having disembarked their troops

[1] Feodor Feodorovitch Ushakoff; entered the Russian navy, 1766; fought against Turkey, 1768–74; retired, 1807; died, 1817.

[2] Chabot did not capitulate until March 3rd, 1799.

[3] Previously of the Venetian navy.

[4] Ganteaume's return of 14 Fructidor (August 31st).

in Egypt, they had all got up such guns as they had stowed below, and were once more fully armed. Moreover, as appears from an official return which was intercepted by the British, they were fully manned. They were commanded, first by Rear-Admiral Ganteaume,[1] and subsequently by Commodore Dumanoir Le Pelley. Besides the squadron at Alexandria, there were, co-operating with the army up the Nile, fifteen large gun-vessels under Commodore Perrée. Several gallant deeds were done during the early part of the blockade; and some of them must be recorded here.

The *Alcmène*, on August 22nd, was in the act of capturing the French gunboat *Légère*, 6, carrying dispatches for Bonaparte, when a French officer on board the prize was observed to throw some papers overboard. Although the *Alcmène* was travelling at the rate of nearly six knots, the seamen John Taylor and James Harding instantly jumped into the water and saved the whole of the papers at the risk of their lives. Three days later, the boats of the *Goliath*, under Lieutenant William Debusk, most bravely cut out in the small hours of the morning from under the guns of the castle of Aboukir the armed ketch *Torride*, 7. And on September 2nd, after the French cutter *Anémone*, 4,[2] had been driven ashore, and had gone to pieces, near Marabou, when it was seen that the crew, which had got safely ashore, was about to be attacked by a party of Arabs, boats from the British squadron generously attempted to rescue the unfortunate Frenchmen. A landing was found to be impossible, owing to the breakers; but Midshipman Francis William Fane,[3] of the *Emerald*, voluntarily swam through the heavy surf with an empty keg to which a line had been fastened, and so brought off enseigne de vaisseau Blaise Gaudran and four men, in spite of the fact that some of the fugitives had actually fired on the boats which were trying to save them. Many of the rest were massacred by the natives before the eyes of the British, who were powerless to interfere.

In October, the Portuguese squadron, under the Marques de Niza appeared for a short time off Alexandria, but soon returned to Malta. The *Lion*, 64, Captain Manley Dixon, which had been serving with the Portuguese, was left with Hood; and later in the month the blockading force was further strengthened by the arrival

[1] Commodore until November 7th, 1798, when he was promoted.

[2] Six days from Malta, with dispatches, and a few officers and soldiers.

[3] Died a Rear-Admiral in 1844.

of two Russian frigates, two Turkish corvettes, and sixteen other Turkish craft, chiefly gunboats. On October 21st, Captain Benjamin Hallowell, with the *Swiftsure* and three gunboats, was detached to attack the castle of Aboukir and a French camp lying on the shores of Lake Madieh. The Turks being found to be too careful of their skins, Hallowell sent fifteen of his own men on board each gunboat; and from the 25th to the 28th the enemy was daily annoyed, though no great damage was done on either side. It is worth noting that the most effective missiles thrown by the gunboats were certain fireballs and shells which had been taken in the *Spartiate* at the battle of the Nile, and that, little suspecting the origin of these missiles, some French officers went off under a flag of truce to protest against the employment of such incendiary projectiles. In December the Turkish and Russian contingents departed, and the *Lion* rejoined Nelson; yet, though Hood was ultimately left with but two ships of the line[1] and one or two frigates, no attempt was made to drive him from his station.

After the departure eastward of Nelson and the reinforcements which followed him, Lord St. Vincent continued to blockade Cadiz with, upon the whole, much success, although, on April 12th, the *Monarca*, 74, with two frigates and a small convoy of merchantmen, managed to get to sea. The blockade continued throughout the summer with but little excitement or variety; and it is probable that it was his growing familiarity with the lukewarmness of the Spanish attitude towards France, and with the unenterprising character of Admiral Massaredo, that induced the Commander-in-Chief, at the end of October, to weaken his numerically inferior fleet by detaching a squadron against Minorca. This squadron, commanded by Commodore John Thomas Duckworth, and constituted as shown below,[2] carried a body of troops under General the Hon. Charles Stuart, and appeared off Fornello, on the north of the island, on November 7th. After but slight resistance had been offered, a landing was effected in the neighbouring creek of Addaya. Fornello was abandoned by the Spaniards, and the troops quickly took possession of Mercadal,

[1] *Zealous* and *Swiftsure*.

[2] *Leviathan*, 74, Commodore J. T. Duckworth, Capt. Henry Digby; *Centaur*, 74, Capt. Thomas Markham; *Argo*, 44, Capt. James Bowen (1); *Dolphin*, 44, Capt. Josiah Nisbet (actg.); *Aurora*, 28, Capt. Thomas Gordon Caulfeild; *Cormorant*, 20, Capt. Lord Mark Robert Kerr; *Petrel*, 16, Com. Charles Long; *Ulysses*, 44, storeship, Com. Thomas Pressland; *Calcutta*, 24, armed transport, Com. Richard Poulden; *Coromandel*, 24, armed transport, Lieut. Robert Simmonds; *Constitution*, hired armed cutter, Lieut. John Whiston, and several merchant transports.

thence following up the enemy to Ciudadella and to Mahon. On November 9th, Fort Carlos, an outpost of the latter town, surrendered; on the 13th, Duckworth chased off a small Spanish squadron, and retook from it the late British sloop, *Petrel*;[1] and on the 15th, the whole island capitulated, together with its garrison of about 3500 men, an unfinished brig, which was afterwards completed and named *Port Mahon*, and several small craft.[2] In these excellently managed operations, the British suffered no loss whatsoever. For the service, General Stuart was made a K.B.; but Commodore Duckworth, apparently in consequence of the rather ungenerous manner in which St. Vincent officially wrote of him, received no reward whatsoever.

In the North Sea, no great events happened during the year. The Dutch, taught by the lesson received off Camperdown, and threatened by largely superior forces, remained in their ports, and were observed, or blockaded, by a British fleet[3] under Lord Duncan, and a Russian one[4] under Vice-Admiral Makaroff. Both in the Portuguese and in the Russian contingents, which were co-operating with the Navy of Great Britain, many British officers served,[5] and it may be said without exaggeration that each contingent owed much of such efficiency as it possessed to its British Captains.

In distant waters, also, the year 1798 witnessed no very important transactions. Early in May, the British troops, under Brigadier-General the Hon. Thomas Maitland, still holding outlying ports in the western part of San Domingo, evacuated Port au Prince, Saint Marc, and Aux Cayes, in pursuance of an agreement arrived at with the republican general Toussaint Louverture, and, together with those of the inhabitants who desired to leave, were embarked in British ships of war, and conveyed to Cape Nicolas Mole. A little later, the position of the French was further strengthened by the arrival at Cape François, with supplies from Europe, of three French frigates, which, eluding the blockade, safely re-entered Lorient on December 4th. In September, the Spaniards made repeated attacks upon the British settlements in the Gulf of Honduras, and especially upon the approaches to Belize, which was garrisoned by small

[1] Belonging to the squadron. She had been captured on the 12th, and owed her recapture to the *Argo*, 44.

[2] Including fourteen gun-vessels.

[3] Of sixteen sail of the line, and many 50-gun ships and frigates.

[4] Of ten sail of the line.

[5] See lists in James, ii. 181; Schomberg, iv. 595.

detachments of the 63rd regiment, and of the 6th West India regiment, under Lieut.-Colonel Thomas Barrow. The only ship of the Royal Navy in the port was the *Merlin*, 16, Commander John Ralph Moss, but the colony had fitted out and armed the gunboats *Tickler*, *Towzer*, and *Mermaid*, and the schooners *Teazer* and *Swinger*, besides eight gun launches; and with this force, under the direction of Captain Moss, the vastly superior Spanish flotilla was beaten back on September 3rd, 4th, and 5th, off Montego Key; on the 6th, off St. George's Key; and on the 10th, in the same neighbourhood. On the British side no one was hurt. The Spaniards, whose loss is unknown, remained off Key Chapel until the 15th, when they retired, some going to Bacalar and some to Campeche. They appear to have employed in these futile operations about twenty schooners and sloops and about ten transports and victuallers, having on board five hundred seamen and nearly two thousand troops.

In the year 1799, the chief naval commands at home and abroad were held as follows:—

Portsmouth		Admiral Sir Peter Parker, Bt. (W).
„	Sept. 14th	Admiral Mark Milbanke (W).
Plymouth		Admiral Sir Richard King (1), Bt. (B).
„	Mar. 29th	Vice-Adm. Sir Thomas Pasley, Bt. (R).
The Downs		Admiral Joseph Peyton (1), (B).
„	Ap.	Vice-Adm. Skeffington Lutwidge (R).
The Nore		Vice-Adm. Skeffington Lutwidge (R).
„	Ap.	Vice-Adm. Andrew Mitchell (B).
„	Aug.	Vice-Adm. Alexander Græme (W).
Cork		Admiral Robert Kingsmill (B).
The Channel		Admiral Lord Bridport (W).
The North Sea		Admiral Lord Duncan (W).
Lisbon and Mediterranean		Admiral Lord St. Vincent (W).
„	June	Vice-Adm. Lord Keith (R).
North America		Admiral George Vandeput (B).
Newfoundland		Vice-Adm. Hon. William Waldegrave (R).
Leeward Islands		Vice-Adm. Henry Harvey (1), (W).
„	later	Vice-Adm. Lord Hugh Seymour (B).
Jamaica		Admiral Sir Hyde Parker (2), (B).
Cape of Good Hope		Vice-Adm. Sir Roger Curtis, Bt. (W).
East Indies		Vice-Adm. Peter Rainier (1), (B).

It has been seen that the external preoccupations of France had been much added to by reason of her sudden attack upon Egypt in the previous year; that Sardinia and Naples, though with no great success, had recommenced active hostilities against her; and that Turkish and Russian fleets had been provoked into aiding her other foes in the Mediterranean. In 1799, Austria joined the coalition against the Republic. But the exertions of France grew greater as the number of her enemies increased. She laid down many new ships; she stinted herself to pay the arrears of wages due to her seamen; and Vice-Admiral Bruix,[1] her Minister of Marine, himself went to Brest to accelerate the preparations, and to take command of the rapidly increasing fleet in that port.

The British squadron off Brest during the earlier part of the year consisted of but eight or nine sail of the line detached from the Channel Fleet and successively commanded by Vice-Admiral Sir Charles Thompson, Bart., Vice-Admiral Lord Hugh Seymour, and Rear-Admiral the Hon. George Cranfield Berkeley. On April 16th, though chased by this squadron, a large and valuable French convoy succeeded in getting into the harbour; and on the following day Lord Bridport, arriving in the *Royal George*, 110, with five or six other ships, himself assumed the command of the watching force. In the forenoon of the 25th, Bridport, who had with him or near him sixteen sail of the line and three or four frigates, looked into Brest, and saw thirteen French ships of the line at anchor, and five more under way in Bertheaume road, as if preparing to put to sea with the fresh north-east wind which was then blowing. It is difficult to guess what were the conclusions of the British Commander-in-Chief; but it is probable that he believed that if the French really put to sea, Ireland would be their destination. Be that as it may, he made sail at 2 P.M. to the W.N.W.; and at 4 P.M. he was about twelve miles W.S.W. of Ushant. That evening, while Bridport had thus for a time lost touch of his foe, Bruix left port with a fleet which, after it had been joined on the following day by one or two vessels that were late in weighing, consisted of twenty-five ships of the line, five frigates, and several small craft,—one of the best manned and best found fleets that ever issued from a French harbour.

At 9 A.M. on the 26th, when part of this fleet was rounding the Saintes, it was discovered by Captain Percy Fraser, of the *Nymphe*, 36, who at once made all sail to rejoin Lord Bridport, but who, in doing so, lost sight of the enemy. At 1 P.M. Fraser signalled

[1] Eustache Bruix; born 1759; obliged to quit the Navy at the Revolution; rejoined it and served under Villaret-Joyeuse; as Minister of Marine took the Brest fleet to the assistance of Masséna at Genoa; returned with it in safety; commanded the Invasion Flotilla; resigned because of ill-health; died 1805.

his intelligence to the *Dragon*, 74, Captain George Campbell, and the *Dragon* instantly repeated it to the Commander-in-Chief, who immediately steered again for Brest, to find, at noon on the 27th, that Bruix had vanished. Bridport instantly sent off dispatches to England, directing reinforcements to join him off Cape Clear; to Lord Keith,[1] off Cadiz; and to Lord St. Vincent, off Gibraltar; and then made the best of his way towards the coast of Cork, which he sighted on the 30th, and where he found ships which augmented his fleet to twenty-six sail of the line. Unhappily, the conviction, which he had by that time certainly formed, that Bruix was bound for Ireland, was fortified by the perusal of some dispatches which had been taken on the 27th in the French chasse-marée *Rebecca*, 16, by the hired armed lugger *Black Joke*, 10, Lieut. James Nicolson, and which had been deliberately prepared for the purpose of being captured. While, therefore, Bridport remained off the Irish coast, Bruix was able, unhampered, to steer across the Bay of Biscay before a fine north wind.

St. Vincent, who was in bad health, had delegated the active work of the blockade of Cadiz, where Admiral Massaredo still lay, to a force varying from eleven to fifteen sail of the line under Vice-Admiral Lord Keith. Keith made occasional trips to Tetuan to water his ships, but, upon his return, invariably found the Spaniards where he had left them. On May 3rd he was off the port when he was joined by the *Childers*, 14, Commander James Coutts Crawford, with news that five Spanish sail of the line had left Ferrol;[2] and by the *Success*, 32, Captain Shuldham Peard, with the still more important intelligence that the Brest fleet had been seen at noon on May 1st about one hundred miles west of Oporto steering S.W. by S. Keith, who then had with him fifteen ships of the line and no frigate save the *Success*, instantly weighed and prepared for action, at the same time sending the *Childers*, with three transports under her convoy, to Lord St. Vincent at Gibraltar. The fleet stood off and on with a fresh N.W. breeze until 8.30 A.M. on May 4th, when the French were sighted about fifteen miles to the W.N.W. At 10 A.M. the *Majestic*, 74, Captain Robert Cuthbert, signalled that they numbered thirty-three sail. At about that time they wore from the rear, and formed on the port tack with their heads to the N.E., the British soon afterwards forming on the same tack; but a little

[1] Second in command of the Lisbon and Mediterranean station.

[2] These ships, failing to fall in with Bruix, ultimately put in to Rochefort.

later, when the wind had very much increased, the enemy wore again, and stood S.W. By 5 P.M., owing to the mist and spray, the French were almost invisible from the flagship *Barfleur*. As the gale blew right into Cadiz, it was impossible for Massaredo to come out; but, on the other hand, nothing could be more favourable for the French, who obviously desired to pass the Strait. On the 5th, at break of day, four more French ships, stragglers from the main fleet, were sighted by the British, to windward of whom they passed at a distance of about seven miles; and, in the afternoon of the same day, twenty-six sail of the enemy, of which at least nineteen were of the line, were observed from Gibraltar,[1] bound eastward through the Strait.[2]

The immediate object of the French Government, and of Bruix, was to effect in the Mediterranean as large a concentration of men-of-war as possible, and then, by employing overwhelming force, to again oust the British, who, since the battle of the Nile, had resumed their activity and influence in that sea, and to re-open communications with Egypt. There is no evidence that Bruix, in the prosecution of this plan, ever thought of entering[3] Cadiz. The idea seems rather to have been that when the French fleet should show itself off those Spanish ports in which lay men-of-war ready for sea, the Spanish vessels should go out, and join the great armament which was bound for Toulon. Five sail of the line had quitted Ferrol in accordance with this scheme, but had missed Bruix and had found their way to Rochefort. The ships in Cadiz, as has been seen, had been prevented by the state of the weather from leaving port. The French, in consequence, having failed to pick up any reinforcements[4] on their way, did not acquire that overwhelming superiority of force which was necessary for the complete fulfilment of their ambitions. Yet the appearance of Bruix within the Strait once more rendered the British position in the Mediterranean most precarious; for, though St. Vincent's command was formidable, it was scattered; and several of the detached

[1] There was at the time no effective British force at the Rock. St. Vincent had his flag in the guardship *Guerrier*; and Rear-Adm. Thomas Lenox Frederick was living on shore.

[2] It entered Toulon on May 13th, without serious adventure.

[3] Brenton says that he "wished to enter" it, but produces no evidence to that effect. i. 478.

[4] Instead of gaining, they actually lost strength, on their voyage; for certainly the *Censeur*, 74, and possibly two other French ships as well, suffered so much in the bad weather of the 4th as to be obliged to run for Cadiz.

divisions of it were liable to be surprised and cut off ere they could be warned of what had happened. So soon, therefore, as the Commander-in-Chief learnt, by the arrival of the *Childers* at Gibraltar, of the movements of the French, he took steps to concentrate his forces. Keith was still off Cadiz with his fifteen sail of the line; the *Edgar*, 74, Captain John M'Dougall, was at Tetuan; Duckworth, with four sail of the line, was at Minorca; other vessels were at

GEORGE KEITH ELPHINSTONE, VISCOUNT KEITH, K.B., F.R.S., ADMIRAL OF THE RED.

(From a drawing by J. Jackson, after a portrait by G. Saunders, painted when his Lordship was an Admiral of the White.)

Palermo with Nelson; yet others were with Ball blockading Malta; and yet others were at Alexandria. Keith's squadron, and the *Edgar*, were ordered to join the Admiral at Gibraltar; and the other detached commands were communicated with, and directed as to the course which was to be pursued in certain contingencies; but Keith, and the *Edgar*, did not reach Gibraltar until May 10th; and not until the morning of the 12th was St. Vincent able to weigh and bear up for the Mediterranean with the sixteen sail of the line named in the note.[1] On the 17th and 18th he encountered bad weather; but on the 20th he was off Minorca, and was joined by Rear-Admiral John Thomas Duckworth, with the four 74's *Leviathan*, *Centaur*, *Bellerophon*, and *Powerful*. That night he anchored in Port Mahon.

In the meantime, encouraged by the knowledge that a strong French fleet was to the eastward of him, and by the disappearance of the blockading force under Keith, Admiral Massaredo had, on May 14th, put to sea from Cadiz with seventeen sail of the line. The bad weather of the 17th and 18th did him more harm than it did to St. Vincent; and when, on the 20th, he struggled into Cartagena, nine of his seventeen ships of the line were more or less dismasted, three of them, besides a frigate, having lost every stick.

St. Vincent, who by that time knew that Bruix had reached his port, weighed from Mahon on May 22nd, and made sail for Toulon; but, on the 26th, in consequence, so James believes, of information that the Spaniards were at Cartagena, he altered course to the westward, so as to place himself between Massaredo and Bruix, and, from the 27th to the 30th, cruised off Cape de Creus. On the 30th he received news that the French had left Toulon on the 27th, and, fearing for Nelson at Palermo, he at once detached Rear-Admiral Duckworth, with the *Leviathan*, 74, *Foudroyant*, 80, *Northumberland*, 74, and *Majestic*, 74, to reinforce him there. Later on the same day the Commander-in-Chief was joined by Rear-Admiral James Hawkins Whitshed, with the *Queen Charlotte*, 100, *Captain*, 74, *Defiance*, 74, *Bellona*, 74, and *Repulse*, 64; and, with the twenty-one sail of the line thus at his disposal, he cruised down the Spanish coast until he was off Barcelona, and then returned to the north-east, having seen nothing of the enemy. By that time St. Vincent's health was in such a bad state that, on June 2nd, his lordship, in the *Ville de Paris*,[2] quitted the fleet, the charge of which

[1] *Ville de Paris*, 110 (flag of Adm. Lord St. Vincent); *Barfleur*, 98 (flag of Vice-Adm. Lord Keith); *Prince George*, 98 (flag of Vice-Adm. Sir William Parker (1) Bt.); *Princess Royal*, 98 (flag of Rear-Adm. Thomas Lenox Frederick); *London*, 98; *Namur*, 90; *Foudroyant*, 80; *Gibraltar*, 80; *Edgar*, 74; *Montagu*, 74; *Northumberland*, 74; *Marlborough*, 74; *Warrior*, 74; *Hector*, 74; *Defence*, 74; and *Majestic*, 74.

[2] James reproaches St. Vincent for having thus withdrawn a 110-gun ship from the fleet, when a frigate would have answered. But St. Vincent was very feeble, and could ill bear transfer from ship to ship, while, in addition, frigates were scarce.

he handed over to Lord Keith, and proceeded to Port Mahon, whence he determined to go home.

Keith continued towards Toulon, and, on the 3rd, when he was close off the port, his advanced ships, the *Centaur*, 74, Captain John Markham, and *Montagu*, 74, Captain John Knight, captured four settees, from the people in which it was learnt that the French fleet had gone to the eastward. Eastward, therefore, Keith also went; and on the 15th he was informed by the hired armed brig *Telegraph*, Commander James Andrew Worth,[1] that on the previous evening the enemy had been seen at anchor in Vado Bay, near Savona.[2] The British headed in that direction, and on the 6th were fired at in passing by some small island forts off Antibes. On the 8th, however, ere he could enter the Gulf of Genoa, Keith received three separate dispatches from St. Vincent at Port Mahon, ordering him to send off two additional 74's to Nelson, and then, with the rest of the fleet, to proceed to Rosas Bay, on the north-east coast of Spain, so as to be ready to intercept the French who, he had reason to believe, were on their way to join the Spaniards in Cartagena.[3] The Vice-Admiral, therefore, detached the *Bellerophon* and *Powerful* to Palermo, and crowded sail to the south-west. But instead of making direct for Rosas Bay, he steered for Cape de la Mola in Minorca, off which he was joined on June 15th by the *Ville de Paris*.[4] He then went to the northward, and on the 19th, when he was about sixty miles south of Cape Sicié, his advanced division, consisting of the *Centaur*, 74, Captain John Markham, *Bellona*, 74, Captain Sir Thomas Boulden Thompson, *Captain*, 74, Captain Sir Richard John Strachan, *Emerald*, 36, Captain Thomas Moutray Waller, and *Santa Teresa*, 42, Captain George Barker, were so fortunate as to capture a French squadron, bound from Jaffa to Toulon, and made up of the *Junon*, 40 (bearing

[1] He had been so promoted on March 29th, but still held what was only a Lieutenant's command.

[2] This news, so far as the French fleet itself was concerned, was incorrect. There were probably transports at Vado; but the fleet had left the bay on the 1st or 2nd.

[3] Keith's lack of success during this cruise is attributed by Dundonald to the manner in which St. Vincent hampered him, and to the Commander-in-Chief's professional jealousy. 'Autobiog. of a Seaman' (Ed. 1861), i. 84, 85. Dundonald was in Keith's flagship at the time; but he wrongly states that St. Vincent ordered Keith to return to Port Mahon, instead of to Rosas Bay, and so somewhat vitiates the value of his testimony.

[4] St. Vincent remained at Port Mahon, preparing to go home. On the 14th Keith had shifted his flag to the *Queen Charlotte*, and Whitshed his to the *Barfleur*.

the flag of Rear-Admiral Perrée), *Alceste*, 36, *Courageuse*, 32, *Salamine*, 18, and *Alerte*, 14.[1] Lord Keith cruised off Toulon until June 23rd, and, seeing no more of the enemy, looked into Vado Bay on the 24th, and into Genoa on the 26th: but, still learning nothing fresh concerning his foe, he next headed for Minorca.

The French fleet, then including twenty-two sail of the line, had indeed quitted Toulon on May 27th, and had gone to the eastward. On the 31st it had anchored in Vado Bay, there landing troops and stores for the relief of Savona, which was besieged by the Russians and Austrians. On June 3rd it had appeared off Genoa; and it had remained there until the 6th, when it had made sail to the westward. On the 9th it had passed in sight of Toulon; and on the 22nd it had arrived off Cartagena. If, therefore, Keith, upon receiving St. Vincent's orders on June 8th, had proceeded with the greatest possible despatch direct for Rosas Bay, it is more than possible that he would have fallen in with the French, and would have been able either to bring them to action or to prevent them from uniting with the Spaniards. The Vice-Admiral's reasons for not implicitly obeying the instructions of the Commander-in-Chief have never received adequate explanation. But, so far as British interests in the Mediterranean were concerned, Keith's conduct, though it may have deprived him of a victory, led to no immediately baneful results. The allies, no doubt, knew that Keith had with him nineteen sail of the line; that Nelson, Ball, and Troubridge had fifteen (besides two or three Portuguese 74's); and that sixteen sail of the line had been detached from the Channel Fleet for Lisbon and the Mediterranean. Although, therefore, the French and Spaniards in Cartagena numbered 40[2] sail of the line ready for sea, their leaders appear to have arrived at the conclusion that that huge fleet would find a more untrammelled field for action in the Atlantic than in the Mediterranean; and, after they had transferred to a flotilla of transports a body of about five thousand troops destined for Majorca, they quitted Cartagena in company on June 24th, when Keith was off Vado, and headed for the Strait of Gibraltar.

Keith reached Minorca from Genoa on July 6th; but he was

[1] These were all added to the Navy, the *Junon* as the *Princess Charlotte* (later the *Andromache*), the *Alerte* as the *Minorca*, and the rest under their old names.

[2] In addition, two 74's, which had been left under repair at Toulon, eventually joined the allies.

still in ignorance of the movements of the enemy. On the 7th, he was joined by twelve[1] out of sixteen[2] ships of the line which had been detached to him from the Channel Fleet.[3] A day later, news reached him that the junction, of which St. Vincent had forewarned him, had been effected between Bruix and Massaredo; and on the 10th, he weighed and went in pursuit, after having sent orders to Nelson to detach ships for the protection of Minorca.[4] On July 26th, the British put into Tetuan for water; and on the 29th they made Gibraltar, to find that the allies had passed the Strait three weeks ahead of them.

The allies had, in fact, passed on July 7th, capturing on their way the British hired cutter *Penelope*, 18, Lieut. Frederick Lewis Maitland, which had been sent out of harbour to reconnoitre, and which, unfortunately, had on board a considerable sum of money. On the 10th and two following days the enemy entered Cadiz, and on the 21st they sailed once more, bound for Brest. As they were leaving port, the *Santa Ana*, 112, grounded, and was with difficulty floated again. Being leaky, she was sent back under convoy of the *Mexicano*, 112; and Admiral Massaredo proceeded with fifteen sail of the line, Bruix having twenty-five.[5] In the afternoon of July 30th, an easterly wind sprang up, and Keith, with his thirty-one sail of the line, continued the pursuit. On August 8th, when off Cape Finisterre, he fell in with a Danish vessel which had passed through the allied fleets two days earlier. On the 9th, he was met by the *Stag*, 36, Captain Joseph Sydney Yorke, with news that the allies had been seen off Cape Ortegal, steering north-east. On the 14th, when he detached Sir Edward Pellew to look into Brest, that officer saw the French and Spaniards moored in the road. They had arrived only on the previous day, so that Lord Keith, in the chase, had almost overtaken them.

[1] *Prince*, 98 (flag of Rear-Adm. Sir Charles Cotton); *Triumph*, 74 (flag of Rear-Adm. Cuthbert Collingwood); *Formidable*, 98; *St. George*, 98; *Neptune*, 98; *Glory*, 98; *Dragon*, 74; *Impétueux*, 74; *Terrible*, 74; *Superb*, 74; *Pompée*, 74; and *Canada*, 74.

[2] The other four ships had put into the Tagus, to escort thence a convoy and the Nile prizes. They were the *Royal Sovereign*, 110 (flag of Admiral Sir Alan Gardner); *Cæsar*, 80; *Magnificent*, 74; and *Russell*, 74.

[3] It is remarkable that these ships did not sight the allies. They must, at one time, have been very near them.

[4] Nelson deliberately disobeyed this order, although it was more than once repeated.

[5] This number included the *Alliance*, 74 (ex *San Sebastian*), which had been presented by Spain to the Republic to take the place of the unseaworthy *Censeur*.

This cruise of Bruix was, in many respects, a very remarkable one; but, owing rather to the vacillating plans of the French and Spanish leaders than to any strategy on the part of the British Admirals, it was practically futile. It has been suggested that Bruix, after he had joined the Spaniards, would have sought and fought Keith, had he not seen signs which convinced him that Massaredo's ships were not to be depended upon. This explanation may be correct. There was no reason to believe that the fighting quality of the Spanish navy had improved since the day of the battle of St. Vincent; and, although Keith had showed himself but a poor strategist, it was notorious that his fleet was in a most efficient state. If, therefore, he, with his thirty-one sail of the line, had been offered an opportunity of trying conclusions with the forty or forty-two sail of the allied line, he would almost certainly have defeated them. But, though he was the man to have won a victory, he was, unhappily, not the man to find the enemy and to force him, against his will, to fight.

It should be added that the arrival at Rochefort of the five Spanish ships of the line[1] from Ferrol, and the southward course of the Brest fleet,[2] had been promptly reported to Admiral Lord Bridport, who then lay in Berehaven, waiting for the anticipated French invasion of Ireland; and that, in pursuance of orders from the Admiralty, he had, on June 1st, detached Admiral Sir Alan Gardner, with the sixteen sail of the line named in the notes on page 387 to reinforce Lord St. Vincent.

This detachment left Lord Bridport with but ten sail of the line under his immediate orders. He sailed, also on June 1st, for Basque road, and, on June 4th, sighted the Spanish squadron, which, as soon as it perceived him, moved to the road of Aix. The Admiral remained off Rochefort until the 8th, when he returned to England with the *Royal George*, 100, *Atlas*, 98, *Achilles*, 74, and *Agincourt*, 64, leaving, as a blockading force, the six 74-gun ships *Mars* (flag of Rear-Admiral the Hon. George Cranfield Berkeley), *Venerable*, *Renown*, *Ajax*, *Ramillies*, and *Robust*. Within the next few weeks, this squadron was joined by the *Sans Pareil*, 80, the

[1] These had been watched by the *Indefatigable*, 44, Captain the Hon. Henry Curzon, from April 28th, when they left port, till April 30th. The news of their having entered Rochefort was brought by another cruiser.

[2] Reported by the *Childers*, which had been sent home from Gibraltar by Lord St. Vincent.

Royal George, 100 (then bearing the flag of Rear-Admiral Charles Morice Pole), and several bombs and small craft; and, on the other hand, the *Mars* and *Ramillies* parted company. On July 2nd, Pole made an attack upon the Spanish ships, which were moored in line ahead between the Isle of Aix and the Boyart shoal, and which were protected by a floating mortar battery; but it was soon found that the French mortars were of so much greater range than the British that, while the latter could not reach their target at all, the former threw shells well over not only the British bombs but also the covering frigates. When, therefore, the enemy, finding that he could not be injured, began to assume the offensive, and to send gunboats to inflict additional annoyance upon the attacking party, both frigates and bombs were ordered to weigh and stand out. They were followed, for a time, by the hostile gunboats; and, in consequence, the French claimed the affair as a British defeat; but the fact is that on neither side was there any loss or damage.[1] For some time afterwards, the Spaniards were blockaded, but in the middle of September they managed to put to sea. They first endeavoured to enter Brest, but, finding it too well watched, returned at last to Ferrol. During the absence of Bruix, five additional French sail of the line had been commissioned at Brest, so that, after his return with Massaredo, no fewer than forty-seven ships of the line[2] lay in the port, ready for service; yet, strange to say, this immense fleet made no further movement during 1799.

In the meantime great events were in progress in that part of the Mediterranean which had fallen to Nelson's command. In January the French had captured Capua and Naples; in March they had seized Florence and Leghorn, and, while Ferdinand of Naples had retired to Palermo, Charles Emmanuel of Sardinia had fled to Cagliari; the Grand Duke of Tuscany had sought refuge in Austria; and the Pope had been taken prisoner.[3] On the other hand, the Russians and Turks had completed the reduction of the

[1] The British ships present at this harmless affair were: *Royal George*, 100, Rear-Adm. Charles Morice Pole, Captain William Domett; *Sans Pareil*, 80, Captain William Browell; *Venerable*, 74, Captain Sir William George Fairfax; *Renown*, 74, Captain Albemarle Bertie; *Ajax*, 74, Captain Hon. Alexander Inglis Cochrane; *Robust*, 74, Captain Herbert Sawyer; *Boadicea*, 38, Captain Richard Goodwin Keats; *Uranie*, 38, Captain George Henry Towry; *San Fiorenzo*, 36, Captain Sir Harry Burrard Neale; *Unicorn*, 32, Captain Philip Wilkinson; *Sylph*, 18, Commander John Chambers White; and the bombs *Sulphur*, *Explosion*, and *Volcano*.

[2] Besides nearly forty frigates and corvettes.

[3] He died soon afterwards at Valence.

Ionian Islands, capturing at Corfu, which capitulated on March 3rd, the *Leander*, 50, and the *Brune*, 28. The former, which had been taken by the French from the British, was restored by the Tsar to her original owners. Later in the year, an Austrian army, assisted by Russian and Turkish squadrons, retook Ancona.

Before he was reinforced, Nelson occupied himself at Palermo in inducing the authorities to mount in the batteries guns which had been brought from Naples, and to fit out a number of gunboats. Troubridge joined him from Alexandria on March 18th, with his own ship, the *Culloden*, 74; the *Zealous*, 74, Captain Samuel Hood (2); the *Swiftsure*, 74, Captain Benjamin Hallowell; the *Seahorse*, 38, Captain Edward James Foote; the *Perseus*, bomb, Commander James Oswald, and the *Bulldog*, bomb, Commander Adam Drummond. The *Minotaur*, 74, Captain Thomas Louis, also joined on the 24th; whereupon Nelson, on the 31st, despatched Troubridge with the *Culloden*, *Zealous*, *Swiftsure*, *Minotaur*, *Seahorse*, *Perseus*, *Bulldog*, and the Portuguese *São Sebastião*. 74, to blockade Naples. The squadron anchored in the bay on April 2nd, and, on the part of King Ferdinand, quietly took possession of Procida, Ischia, Capri, and the Ponza Islands. But on May 13th Nelson hurriedly recalled Troubridge to Palermo, in consequence of having received intelligence [1] that the fleet of Bruix had passed the Strait of Gibraltar and was in the Mediterranean. Nelson also sent on the disquieting news to Captain Ball, who was off Malta with the *Alexander*, 74, *Goliath*, 74, and, perhaps, a Portuguese ship of the line; and to the Russian Admiral. Troubridge, who, by direction, left his small craft to take care of the newly surrendered islands, joined the Rear-Admiral on the 17th with the *Culloden*, *Swiftsure*, and *São Sebastião*, the *Minotaur* following on the 20th, and another Portuguese 74, the *São Affonso*, arriving. Nelson previously had with him his flagship the *Vanguard*, 74, Captain Thomas Masterman Hardy, a Portuguese, 74 (*Principe Real*), and a frigate, and the *Haarlem*, 64 (*en flûte*), Captain George Burlton; and with these ships he cruised for several days off the western end of Sicily, being joined in the meantime by the *Zealous*, 74, and the *Lion*, 64, Captain Manley Dixon. On the 30th he returned and re-anchored off Palermo. The *Audacious*, 74, Captain Davidge Gould, arrived on June 1st;

[1] The *Espoir*, 14, Com. James Sanders, reached Palermo on the 12th, with news that the French had been seen off Oporto; and an officer who had travelled through Sicily reported on the 13th that they had passed Gibraltar.

and on June 7th the squadron was further reinforced by Rear-Admiral John Thomas Duckworth,[1] with the *Foudroyant*, 80, Captain William Brown (1), *Leviathan*, 74 (flag), Captain Henry Digby, *Northumberland*, 74, Captain George Martin (2), and *Majestic*, 74, Captain George Hope (1). On the 8th, Nelson shifted his flag to the *Foudroyant*, taking Captain Hardy with him. Captain Brown exchanged to the *Vanguard*. The whole squadron put to sea on the 13th, and met on the 14th with the *Bellerophon*, 74, Captain Henry d'Esterre Darby, and *Powerful*, 74, Captain William O'Brien Drury,[2] its total strength being thus brought up to sixteen sail of the line, of which thirteen were British. Unfortunately Nelson had with him no frigates; and although he cruised off Sicily and did his best to learn something of the whereabouts of the enemy, he was able to discover little or nothing. His small craft, the *Seahorse*, 38, Captain Edward James Foote (senior officer), *Perseus*, bomb, Commander James Oswald, *Mutine*, 14, Commander William Hoste, and *San Leon*, 16, Commander John Harward, were in the Bay of Naples; and the *Espoir*, 14, and *Bulldog*, bomb, appear to have been detached elsewhere.

On shore the French were by that time hard pressed. Count Alexander Suwaroff, with a very large Austro-Russian army, had entered Italy in April, and was triumphantly moving southward: Cardinal Ruffo defeated the Republicans on June 5th near Naples; and on June 14th and 15th Rivigliano and Castellamare surrendered to Captain Foote, it being agreed that the garrisons should march out with the honours of war, and that any part of them might claim and receive the protection of the British flag.[3] This arrangement left the forts of Castel del' Uovo, Castel Nuovo, and Castel St. Elmo as the sole points still in the possession of the French at Naples.[4] On June 17th, the *Seahorse* and *Perseus* proceeded off Castel

[1] Detached by St. Vincent on May 30th.

[2] Detached by Keith on June 8th.

[3] Curiously enough, my researches into what really happened at Naples on this occasion led me, in the summer of 1897, to consult certain new evidence, which, I since find, has also been consulted by Mr. F. P. Badham ('Eng. Hist. Rev.', Ap. 1898). I was directed to most of these authorities by a paper in the *Rivista Marittima*—a valuable storehouse of facts and suggestions bearing upon the naval history of the Italian States. The results arrived at do not materially touch the conclusions of James and the contentions of Capt. Foote; but, as they throw so unfavourable a light upon Nelson's action, and as much of the evidence seems to have escaped the attention of Mahan, I give fuller references than usual. For a few points, which might otherwise have escaped me, I am indebted to Mr. Badham's paper.

[4] *See* chart on following page.

del' Uovo; and on the following day Captain Foote, who had been directed to co-operate with Ruffo, the Sicilian commander-in-chief on shore, sent in Commander Oswald to offer British protection to the commandant and garrison. The commandant declined the honour; and Foote thereupon informed Ruffo, who was the king's vicar-general, of his intention at once to attack the fort. Ruffo appearing to concur, the attack was begun on the 19th; but scarcely had it commenced ere Foote, to his astonishment, received from the Cardinal a letter begging him to desist, and not to resume hostilities so long as a flag of truce remained flying, for that negotiations were

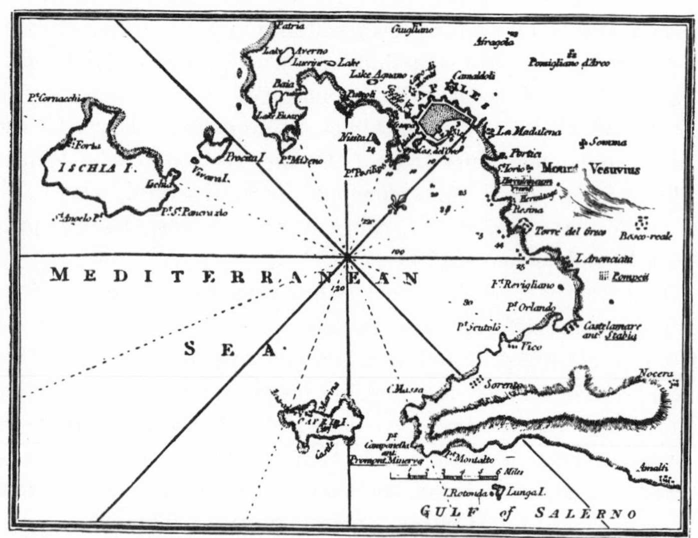

in progress. Foote acquiesced; but that night he sent an officer to the Cardinal, protesting against so long a suspension of hostilities, and asserting his right to be kept informed of Ruffo's proceedings. The Cardinal answered that the negotiations were being conducted by Micheroux, a Russian officer serving with the Neapolitans on shore, and that Micheroux would furnish the particulars; and upon Foote refusing to act with Micheroux, of whom he knew nothing, Ruffo declared that he was ignorant of what was going on. This, of course, was very unsatisfactory; but on the 20th, when the Cardinal sent to Foote terms of capitulation which already had been signed by himself and Micheroux, and begged the British officer to affix his signature, the latter, anxious to further what seemed to be the interests of King Ferdinand, complied, declaring, however, that he considered the terms to be unduly easy.

The document, which stipulated for the capitulation both of Uovo and of Nuovo, was ultimately signed also by the Turkish representative on the spot, and approved by Colonel Méjan, the French officer commanding at St. Elmo. It specified, among other things, that the garrisons, chiefly Neapolitan rebels, and about one thousand five hundred in number, should march out with military honours; that their private property should be respected; that they might either remain in Naples or embark in cartels for Toulon; that, until the cartels should be ready, the garrisons should retain possession of the forts; and that, pending the receipt from Toulon of a report that the persons to be despatched thither had arrived, four hostages should be detained at St. Elmo.

Preparations were accordingly made for sending away the garrisons; transports were assembled; and on both sides flags of truce remained hoisted; but the arrangement had not been entirely carried into effect, when, on June 24th, Lord Nelson,[1] with his whole squadron entered the bay, the *Foudroyant* flying a signal annulling the flag of truce. In the course of the afternoon, at a conference[2] at which not only Nelson and Ruffo, but also Sir William Hamilton, British ambassador to the court of Naples, and his wife, were present, the Cardinal warmly held that the treaty ought to be most scrupulously observed, the Rear-Admiral as warmly maintaining that a settlement entered into with rebels ought not to have any validity so long as it was not expressly approved by King Ferdinand. Ruffo thereupon retired. When, in the evening, Foote went on board the flagship, Nelson gave him all credit for his zeal and good intentions, but said that he had been imposed upon by the Cardinal, and that Ruffo was not loyal to his sovereign.[3] Foote excused himself for having signed the capitulation by pointing out that

[1] He had left Palermo on June 21st.

[2] For accounts of this: *see* Sacchinelli, 'Mem. s. vita del Card. Ruffo'; 'Nel. Disps.,' iii. 390; Sic. Papers, P.R.O., xlv.; and Harrison, 'Life of Nelson' (Lady Hamilton's version).

[3] Nelson wrote to this effect to the king at Palermo, and on June 30th received authority to arrest the Cardinal if necessary; but Ruffo eventually gave way to the Rear-Admiral. It is certain that until the 30th Nelson had no power to arrest, supersede, or override the Cardinal. 'Nel. Disps.,' vii. addenda, p. 186; 'Morrison Coll.,' 405; Sic. Papers, P.R.O., xlv.; 'Borboni di Napoli,' iv. 92; 'Rose's Diaries,' i. 230. The dispatches giving Nelson power over Ruffo and enjoining the latter to obey were dated June 27th.

when he had signed it he had thought it far more probable that a French than that a British fleet was in the neighbourhood; and he excused himself for having been guided by Ruffo by pointing out that, since the Cardinal was in high authority, it was but natural to assume that he had his sovereign's confidence and was acting in his sovereign's interests.

On the 26th, in spite of what had occurred, the garrisons, in conformity with the treaty, having liberated their prisoners, marched out with the honours of war, grounded their arms, and, with but few exceptions, went on board the small transports,[1] fourteen in number, which had been prepared to carry them to Toulon. They believed, of course, that they were to go thither. Instead, by Nelson's orders, they were detained, pending King Ferdinand's decision as to what should be done with them.

Nelson's conduct in all this unfortunate business was not, it must be admitted, quite that of a man of scrupulous honour. When he arrived before Naples, the treaty was already signed, and had already been so far executed that the gate (Porta Reale) leading to Castel Nuovo had been surrendered; the garrisons had released their British prisoners; some of the non-emigrating part of the garrisons had left the forts; and the stipulated hostages had been lodged in St. Elmo.[2] It had been represented to Nelson by Ruffo that if the treaty had to be annulled, the only just way of annulling it, and the only way which would insure the safety of the hostages, was by restoring the *status quo ante*.[3] Achmet, the Turkish, and Baillie, the Russian military commander, had both protested that to violate the treaty would be to outrage public faith.[4] Moreover, Nelson had no legal power, even though he knew that the arrangement was contrary to the wishes of the king, to go behind Ruffo's action. Yet, impelled by his zeal in the cause, stimulated by his dislike and suspicions of the Cardinal, and not restrained by Hamilton, the man who ought to have been a guardian of British honour, Nelson, misusing his might, took back the pledges which Ruffo and Foote had given. Nay, he did

[1] There is some slight evidence that part embarked as early as the 23rd. Foote, 'Vind.,' 193; Hamilton to Grenville, July 14th; Pepe, 'Mems.,' i. 105 (1847).

[2] Foote, 'Vindic.,' 48; Hamilton to Grenville, July 14th; memorial of Ricciardi in Williams's 'Sketch of Manners,' ii. 325; 'Arch. stor. per le Prov. Napol.' (1888), 72; Add. MSS., B.M., 34,912. The evidence is overwhelming.

[3] 'Mem. del Card. Ruffo,' 254, 264.

[4] *Ibid.*, 251.

worse; for it can, unhappily, be shown that he permitted the garrisons to go on carrying out the provisions of the treaty in all good faith, after he had decided that he, on his part, would not be bound by them. Nelson, it is admitted, signalled to Foote on June 24th annulling the flag of truce, and declared that, instead of observing the treaty, he would attack the forts: but we know that Ruffo refused to be a party to anything of the kind, and that the refusal induced the Rear-Admiral to abandon the project. It is admitted, too, that on the 25th, Nelson wrote a message which was to be sent to the forts by Ruffo, and in which it was stated that the garrisons would not be allowed to embark; but we know that Ruffo declined to transmit this message; and, although Nelson, after his conduct had been publicly called in question, asserted[1] that he had thereupon forwarded the message direct, his *ex parte* assertion not only stands without corroboration, but is distinctly contradicted by a large mass of circumstantial evidence.[2] Conceding, however, that Nelson, up to the evening of the 25th, had no thought of leaving the garrisons under any misapprehension, how is it possible that there can be two opinions concerning his attitude on and after the 26th? On that day Hamilton wrote to Ruffo:—

> "Lord Nelson begs me to assure your Eminence that he is resolved to do nothing which can break the armistice which your Eminence has accorded to the châteaux of Naples." [3]

And, in reply to some comment or question from Ruffo, Nelson himself wrote on the same day:—

> "I am just honoured with your Eminence's letter; and as Sir W. Hamilton wrote this morning that I will not on any consideration break the armistice entered into by you, I hope your Eminence will be satisfied that I am supporting your ideas. I send once more Captains Troubridge and Ball." [4]

Again, on the 27th, replying to a letter of thanks from Ruffo, Hamilton wrote:—

> "I can assure your Eminence that Lord Nelson congratulates himself on the decision which he has taken, not to interrupt your Eminence's operations, but to assist you with all his power to terminate the affair which your Eminence has so well conducted up to the present." [5]

---

[1] 'Nel. Disps.,' iv. 232.

[2] Espec. by Albanese's letter of June 29th in 'Mem. del Card. Ruffo,' 262.

[3] 'Mem. del Card. Ruffo,' 255.

[4] Printed in 'Nel. Disps.,' iii. 184; but there misdated. Ruffo's letter is not to be found.

[5] 'Mem. del Card. Ruffo,' 259.

It is noteworthy and significant that when Troubridge and Ball saw Ruffo on the 26th, they verbally confirmed the assurance conveyed in Nelson's letter of that date above quoted, but they declined to sign a formal document to the same effect.[1] Yet Ruffo was satisfied,[2] and he at once directed Micheroux to desire the garrisons to embark immediately. Micheroux went with Ball and Troubridge to deliver this intimation; and at about 5 P.M. the emigrating part of the garrisons embarked. At Castel dell' Uovo, a specific pledge was given, when the place was handed over, that thirty-four non-emigrants, who were there, should be sent home at 11 o'clock.[3] There can be no doubt at all that the embarking garrisons fully believed, and were entitled to fully believe, that the stipulations of the treaty would be religiously observed. Even after the fourteen transports (polaccas) had been detained for three days, the emigrants did not altogether realise that they were prisoners, for, on the 29th, they complained that there had been delay although the wind was fair.[4] Yet ere that, although the garrisons did not know it, Hamilton had practically admitted that, as Foote words it, they had been enticed from the castles "under pretence of putting the capitulation I had signed into execution."[5] Hamilton cynically wrote to Acton on June 28th :—

> "Lord Nelson kept the promise which he had given to the Cardinal. He did not oppose the embarkation of the garrisons ; but, when the garrisons were once embarked, it became clear what the situation was."[6]

Prince Francesco Caracciolo,[7] a Neapolitan naval officer of some distinction, who had served side by side with the British, and, indeed, with Nelson, in the action off Genoa on March 14th, 1795, had been faithful to his sovereign during the earlier part of the revolutionary disturbances in Italy; but, influenced to some extent by Ferdinand's abandonment of Naples, and to a greater degree by a decree of the Parthenopæan Republic ordering the confiscation of the property of absent Neapolitans, he at length joined the Republican navy. He was in Castel Nuovo when it was about to

[1] 'Mem. del Card. Ruffo,' 256, and app.

[2] Up to the evening of the 25th he had suspected Nelson. Ruffo to Massa: 'Mem. del Card. Ruffo,' 252.

[3] 'Mem. del Card. Ruffo,' 257.

[4] *Ibid.*, 262–64.

[5] 'Vind.,' 39.

[6] 'Borboni di Nap.,' iv. 94. The letter is in Italian.

[7] He was in 1799 about 47 years of age; yet English writers have usually referred to him as an old man.

capitulate; and, doubtful of what fate was in store for him, he fled, probably on June 17th, and secreted himself. His whereabouts became known to Ruffo; and Nelson requested the Cardinal to hand over the Prince;[1] but the Cardinal turned a deaf ear to the Rear-Admiral, and expressly forbade the making of any arrests without his personal authority.[2] It has been seen that, until June 30th, Nelson had no legal authority to supersede or override Ruffo, the king's vicar-general; yet Nelson caused Caracciolo to be privily arrested on shore during the night of the 28th, to be abducted in such a manner as to evade the notice of Ruffo's officers, to be embarked at Granatello, and to be brought[3] on board the *Foudroyant*.[4] Within an hour of his delivery on board, he was, by Nelson's directions, put on trial before a court-martial which met in the *Foudroyant*, but which was composed of Neapolitan officers, whose president was Count Thurn, an old enemy of the prince.[5] Caracciolo pleaded,—and it can be proved,—that he had served the Republicans unwillingly and under a threat of death;[6] but he was not allowed any opportunity of producing evidence. He had asked to be tried by British officers.[7] After his condemnation by a majority,—not all,—of his judges, he demanded a second trial.[8] But all in vain. His death had been predetermined;[9] and at 5 P.M., on June 29th, five hours after his sentence had been pronounced, he was removed from the *Foudroyant*, and hanged at the fore-yard arm of Count Thurn's ship, the *Minerva*. The arrest had been ordered by Nelson; the trial had been ordered by Nelson; the request for a second trial had been refused by Nelson; a plea for shooting instead of hanging, as the punishment, had been rejected by Nelson; even Thurn's and Hamilton's desires that twenty-four hours should be allowed to intervene between the sentence and its execution had been denied by Nelson.[10] The

[1] Rose, 'Diaries,' i. 238.

[2] 'Borboni di Nap.,' iv. 92.

[3] Caracciolo was bound, until Hardy ordered him to be released.

[4] 'Mem. del Card. Ruffo,' 267.

[5] One of the charges was that Caracciolo had fired on these officers. They were therefore prejudiced. 'Vind.,' 101; 'Saggio Storico' (1865), 427.

[6] 'Nel. Disps.,' iii. 341; 'Pettigrew,' i. 251; Thurn's report in 'Mem. del Card. Ruffo,' 265.

[7] 'Borb. di Nap.,' iv. 101.

[8] Clarke and M'Arthur, quoting Lieut. William Standway Parkinson, who had charge of the prisoner.

[9] 'Borb. di Nap.,' iv. 75, 76, 87-89.

[10] Hamilton to Acton, in 'Borb. di Nap.,' iv. 111.

responsibility for all, therefore, is Nelson's; and one cannot escape the disagreeable conclusion that Nelson was, in effect, guilty of hanging a foreign officer because he had fought against the British. For Nelson had no Sicilian authority or mandate; it was not for him to look upon Caracciolo as a rebel; and, in fact, the main point upon which the Prince was condemned was that he had fired upon a vessel which, though Sicilian, was at the time under the orders of the British Captain Foote. Whether, and if so to what extent, Nelson's conduct in these proceedings was influenced by Lady Hamilton, are questions which need not be touched upon here. Lady Hamilton was not a responsible person: Nelson was: and Nelson must bear the blame, if any blame be deserved. Caracciolo's guilt towards his sovereign is not in dispute, although, be it remembered, there were mitigating circumstances connected with it. The points for consideration are: what right had the Rear-Admiral, on June 28th and 29th, to override Ruffo's order and to effect any arrest whatsoever on shore? what right had he to deal with Caracciolo as a rebel? what right had he to order a man to be tried by his personal enemies? what right had he to hang a foreign officer for firing, in the course of war,[1] upon a vessel under the orders of a British captain? what right had he, while insisting that the fate of the would-be emigrants should be decided only after reference to King Ferdinand, to reject Caracciolo's appeal for a reconsideration of his case? what right had he to insist, in defiance of custom, upon an almost instant execution of the sentence?

It is an unpleasant business; and further discussion of it is unnecessary. But it must be added that, in consequence of Nelson's attitude towards the would-be emigrants, those poor wretches were kept, half starving and ravaged by disease, on board the polaccas, until after the arrival of King Ferdinand off Naples on July 8th; and that there then began a series of most vindictive and barbarous executions, not even women,—for there were women among those who had capitulated,—being spared.[2]

The surrender of Castel Nuovo and Castel dell' Uovo had deprived the French party of all their positions at Naples except

[1] It is true that the Republicans were not recognised by Great Britain as belligerents; but, by implication, at least, Ruffo had so recognised them when he granted what Nelson called "the armistice"; and Nelson, on the 26th, had committed himself by promising, in writing, to support Ruffo.

[2] Williams: 'Sketches,' 399; 'Borb. di Nap.,' iv. etc., etc.

Castel St. Elmo, which was held by Major-General Méjan and about eight hundred men. Troubridge,[1] having landed a body of British and Portuguese Marines, began a formal siege of this work on June 29th. Batteries were opened against it on July 3rd; and on the 11th the place capitulated, it being arranged that the garrison should be conveyed to Toulon, and the arrangement being, in this case, carried out. The reduction of St. Elmo cost the allies thirty-seven killed and eighty-four wounded. On July 22nd, Troubridge, with one thousand British seamen and Marines and some Portuguese troops, appeared before Capua, about fifteen miles northward and inland from Naples; and on the 29th the French garrison capitulated and marched out, and was subsequently sent to Toulon. Gaeta, which had been blockaded by the fleet, but not besieged, surrendered on the 31st;[2] and on September 29th and 30th, after negotiations, Civita Vecchia, Corneto, Tolfa, and Rome were handed over. Captain Louis, of the *Minotaur*, was rowed up the Tiber in his barge, and hoisted British colours over the Capitol. Thus, thanks largely to the Navy, was a large part of Italy freed from French dominion.

But although the Navy thus brilliantly distinguished itself in the Mediterranean, Nelson, who, during great part of 1799, was the senior officer there, not only suffered himself, in those regrettable months spent in Sicily and off Naples, to be led from the path of private honour, but also allowed himself to be induced to pay,—as he himself afterwards expressed it,—" more attention to another sovereign than my own." His conscience,—to again use his own word,—was " Sicilified." While his followers were winning glory, he, enslaved by a beautiful woman, and giving way to the enervating influences of a court which, in saner moments, he recognised as a centre of vice, folly, and corruption, injured his health, grieved his truest friends, and narrowly escaped sacrificing for ever his professional prospects. So obvious was his infatuation, and so serious were likely to be its results, that even his Captains dared to remonstrate pointedly yet guardedly with the Rear-Admiral on his conduct.[3] His thrice-repeated disobedience to

[1] For these services Troubridge was created a Baronet on Nov. 30th, 1799.

[2] Both at Capua and at Gaeta, Sicilian subjects were delivered up to the allies; and many of them were afterwards executed after trial by their compatriots.

[3] These conclusions are denied by the commentator of the 'New Nelson Manuscripts,' published in *Literature*, Feb.–May, 1898; but the denial appears quite inconclusive to one who has carefully gone through all the published evidence, though

Keith's reiterated orders to despatch ships to Minorca would have ruined him infallibly, if either Minorca had been attacked by the enemy, or Keith had chosen to deal sternly with his insubordinate lieutenant. Happily for Great Britain, Nelson, when at length he turned his back upon Sicily, soon re-acquired all his old strength, energy, and single-minded devotion to duty: happily the enemy did not attack Malta: and happily Keith, with a tenderness which does him the more honour, seeing that Nelson had no love for him, did not press matters against a man to whose greatest and noblest qualities he gave the most generous recognition. Nelson escaped with only a mild rebuke from the Admiralty.[1] It was during this period that King Ferdinand conferred upon him the Duchy of Bronte, in Sicily, with estates estimated to be worth about £3000 a year.

Bonaparte, at the beginning of 1799, was still in Egypt, watched only by a small squadron of British, Russian and Turkish ships. To improve his position there, he had added to the fortifications of Alexandria, Rosetta, and Damietta, attempted to come to a friendly arrangement with the Porte, and endeavoured to induce the Pasha of Acre, on the coast of Syria, to assist his projects. The Pasha, although on bad terms with his master, the Sultan, had declined to aid the French, and had at once replied to the French overtures by seizing the frontier fortress of El Arich. This led Bonaparte to set out from Cairo early in January, 1799, to invade Syria, with an army of about thirteen thousand men. At the same time he sent orders to Rear-Admiral Perrée, who was at Alexandria, to put to sea with the frigates *Junon*, *Alceste*, and *Courageuse*, and the corvettes *Alerte* and *Salamine*, and to convey heavy guns and stores along the coast for the use of the expedition; but, as the port was then closely blockaded, Perrée did not sail until some weeks later; and the only vessels which, early in the advance, co-operated with the French were some small craft from Damietta. The whole invading force was assembled before El Arich by February 18th.

In the meantime, on February 2nd, Captain Thomas Troubridge, in the *Culloden*, 74, with the *Theseus*, 74, Captain Ralph Willett Miller, *Bulldog*, bomb, Commander Adam Drummond, *Perseus*,

---

it is true that certain expressions of Troubridge have been misread owing to the carelessness of Clarke and M'Arthur.

[1] For a discussion of Nelson's conduct on these and similar occasions, see a very plain-spoken article in *Edinburgh Review*, 1814, p. 405.

bomb, Commander James Oswald, and *Alliance*, storeship, 22, Captain David Wilmot, arrived off Alexandria to relieve the *Zealous*, 74, Captain Samuel Hood (2), and the *Swiftsure*, 74, Captain Benjamin Hallowell, on the station. On the 3rd, and again on the 4th, 5th, 7th, 8th, 13th, and 22nd of February, the *Bulldog* and *Perseus* stood in and shelled the town, but did little damage,

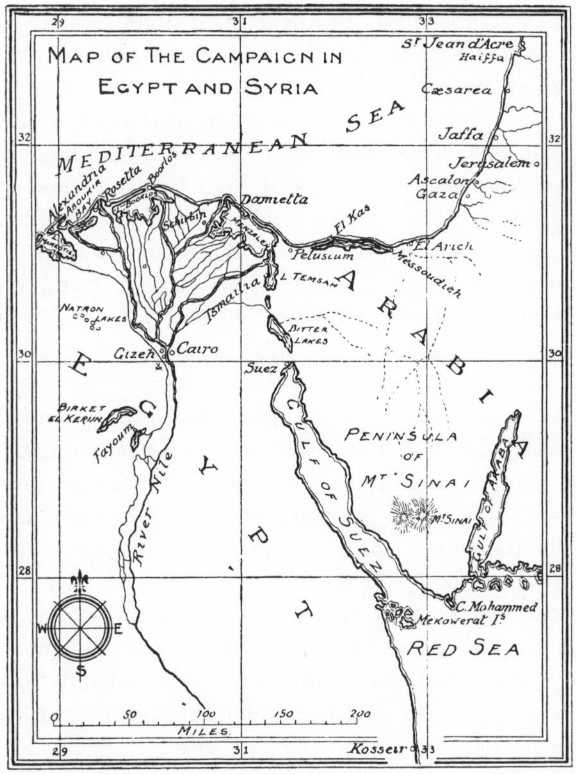

though the bursting of the *Perseus's* 13-in. mortar killed and wounded four men. On March 3rd, Troubridge was superseded in command of the blockading squadron by Commodore Sir William Sidney Smith,[1] who arrived in the *Tigre*, 80, with the *Marianne*, 4, a French gun-vessel captured on March 1st, and who, with Troubridge's concurrence, at once despatched Lieut. John Westley Wright and an interpreter to settle a scheme of co-operation with

[1] Who had also the rank of Joint Minister Plenipotentiary to the Porte, and who had been at Constantinople and Rhodes to arrange a plan of campaign.

the Pasha of Acre. On the 7th, the *Culloden*, *Perseus*, and *Bulldog*[1] sailed to join Lord Nelson; and Smith was left with the *Tigre*, 80, *Theseus*, 74, *Alliance*, 22, *Torride*, 2, and *Marianne*, 4, Midshipman James Boxer, to conduct the further operations. On the same day the Commodore learnt that Bonaparte had advanced and had carried Jaffa by storm. On the 8th, the *Theseus* was despatched to Acre, the *Tigre* remaining for a time to watch Alexandria, but presently following, and anchoring in the bay on March 15th. Measures were at once taken, in conjunction with Achmet Djezzar, the Pasha, to strengthen the very inadequate defences of the town. On the 17th the *Theseus* was sent to reconnoitre to the southward. That morning the French advanced guard was seen marching along the sea-side; and its passage over the little river Kerdanneh was effectively checked by the *Tigre's* launch under the orders of Lieut. John Bushby, the result being that the French had to make a detour. Owing to the fire from the ships, they were also prevented from investing those defences of the town which lay nearest to the coast, and which happened to be the weakest, and were obliged to concentrate their forces to the north-east. On the 18th Sir Sidney had the good fortune, after a three hours' chase, to capture the little flotilla[2] which had left Damietta with the guns, ammunition and siege equipage of the French army, and to recapture the *Torride*, which, on her passage from Alexandria, had been taken that morning by the enemy. Both the prizes and the guns proved most useful for the defence of Acre.

The siege lasted until May 20th. In the course of it, a British attempt upon some French lighters in the port of Haifa was repulsed on March 21st; a French mine was most gallantly seized and destroyed on April 7th by Lieut. John Westley Wright, R.N., and Major John Douglas, of the Marines; Perrée's squadron, leaving Alexandria, landed guns at Jaffa, and these, forwarded by land, reached the besiegers on April 27th; many attempts to storm the town were repulsed; the defenders, on May 7th, received reinforcements of troops from Rhodes; in a new assault many of the enemy were deliberately allowed to enter the place in order that they might more surely be destroyed; the Syrian chiefs were persuaded to harass Bonaparte's communications; a successful sortie was

[1] The *Swiftsure* had already departed.

[2] *Foudre*, 8, *Dangereuse*, 6, *Negresse*, 6, *Marie Rose*, 4, *Deux Frères*, 4, and *Dame de Grâce*, 4.

made on May 19th; twice assassins attempted Sir Sidney's life; and at last a treacherous assault, delivered while a flag of truce was flying, was victoriously repulsed. In consequence, the siege was raised on the night of May 20th, the enemy leaving behind him 23 siege guns, minus their carriages, and regaining El Arich on June 2nd, having suffered enormous loss. The British, apart from the Turkish, loss in the fighting was not very serious, as it amounted

ADMIRAL SIR WILLIAM SIDNEY SMITH, G.C.B.

(From Ridley's engraving, executed in 1800, *when Sir William was a Captain.)*

to but 22 killed, 66 wounded, 4 drowned, and 82 taken prisoners; but a lamentable catastrophe, caused on May 14th by a mishap to some shells in the *Theseus*, added 40 killed and drowned and 47 wounded to the total. By this accident the gallant Captain Ralph Willett Miller,[1] and Midshipmen Charles James Webb and James Morrison Bigges Forbes, perished. The ship herself narrowly escaped destruction. Among the officers killed by the enemy were

[1] Born Jan. 24th, 1762: Commander, 1794; Captain, 1796. He commanded a ship both at St. Vincent, where he was Nelson's Captain, and at the Nile.

Captain David Wilmot,[1] of the *Alliance*, and Major of Marines Thomas Oldfield. At the time of the accident to the *Theseus*, she had just begun to chase Rear-Admiral Perrée's squadron off Cæsarea. In consequence of it, the enemy escaped.[2]

The Commodore left Acre on June 12th, and, calling at Beirut and Larnaca, proceeded to Constantinople to concert further measures with the Porte. As for Bonaparte, injured in reputation by the course of events at Acre, and advised by the Directory [3] that his presence was needed at home, he was most anxious to return to France. He therefore ordered Rear-Admiral Ganteaume, who had quitted the headquarters for Alexandria, to prepare for sea the *Carrère* and *Muiron*, the fastest of the ex-Venetian frigates in that port. But ere Bonaparte could sail, a very large fleet of Turkish men-of-war and transports under Hassan Bey, conveying about eighteen thousand troops under Seyd Mustapha Pasha, entered Aboukir Bay on July 11th. General Marmont hurried from Alexandria to oppose a landing; but, upon hearing that some of the Turks had already disembarked, he re-entered the town to await reinforcements. By the 17th, Aboukir and its defences had fallen, and the whole expeditionary force was on shore. Moreover, Sir W. S. Smith, with the *Tigre* and *Theseus*,[4] was once more off the coast. On July 23rd, Bonaparte in person took command at Alexandria; on the 25th he won a most sanguinary battle close to Aboukir; and on August 2nd Aboukir Castle surrendered to him. He then went for a few days to Cairo, returned to Alexandria on August 21st, committed the command in Egypt to General Kléber, and, learning that the British and Turkish men-of-war had temporarily withdrawn from off the port,[5] embarked on the 22nd, in the *Muiron*, bearing the flag of Rear-Admiral Ganteaume, and, with the *Carrère, Revanche, Indépendant*, and *Foudre*,[6] sailed on the 23rd.

[1] A Captain of 1798. He was killed by a rifle-shot, on May 1st, while defending the breach.

[2] Sir William Sidney Smith was voted a pension of £1000 a year for his conduct at Acre, and thanked by both Houses. By the Sultan he was given a diamond aigrette, a sable coat, and the order of the Crescent.—Life by Barrow.

[3] Disp. of May 26th.

[4] Commander Edward Jekyll Canes had acted as her Captain after the death of Captain Miller, until the appointment of Captain John Stiles.

[5] They had sailed on the 9th, and had anchored on the 16th off Cyprus.

[6] The *Foudre*, not sailing as well as the other vessels, was presently ordered back to Alexandria. She seems to have been the same vessel which, on March 18th, had been taken by Sir W. S. Smith, and to have been retaken, together with the *Marianne*, by the French. But no record of the recapture can be found.

By keeping close in with the African coast until it had passed Cape Bon, the little squadron evaded the British cruisers and reached Ajaccio on October 1st. On the 9th Bonaparte, whose fortunes seemed, for the moment, to be almost hopeless,—for Mantua had been lost, Italy had been reconquered, and Holland had been invaded,—disembarked at Fréjus.

The Mediterranean fleet was not the only one which had a part in harassing the operations of the French in Egypt; and, before going on to review what happened at the mouth of the Nile after Bonaparte's flight, it is right to say a word concerning the movements, though they were of little importance, of certain British

COMMEMORATIVE MEDAL OF CAPT. SIR W. S. SMITH'S DEFENCE OF ACRE, 1799.

(From an original lent by H.S.H. Capt. Prince Louis of Battenberg, R.N.)

vessels in the Red Sea, on the coasts of which, and especially at Suez and Kosseir, the French had established small garrisons.

The invasion of Egypt by the French had caused Vice-Admiral Peter Rainier (1), Commander-in-Chief in the East Indies, to detach to the western limits of his station a number of vessels, which were reinforced from the squadron at the Cape. Two of these, the *Centurion*, 50, Captain John Sprat Rainier, and the *Albatross*, 18, Commander Charles Adam, appeared before Suez on April 27th, chased two French gunboats into the harbour, and created great alarm during the two months for which they remained in the neighbourhood. But, having no troops on board, they did not endeavour to take the town. In the meantime, Rear-Admiral John Blankett, in the *Leopard*, 50, Captain Thomas Surridge, with the *Dædalus*, 32, Captain Henry Lidgbird Ball, *Fox*, 32, Commander Henry

Stuart (acting Captain), and some smaller vessels, with troops under Major-General Craig, had arrived from Bombay at Mocha. There Captain Rainier joined him, reporting what he had been able to learn or to observe on his passage. On August 14th, the *Dædalus* and *Fox*, detached by Blankett, stood into Kosseir Bay, and, finding the Republicans in possession of the town, opened a cannonade, which was continued at intervals, and resumed very hotly on the early morning of the 15th. During the firing, several dhows were cut out from under the walls of the place, and an attempt, which had to be abandoned, was made to land and destroy the wells. On the 16th, a landing, under Commander Stuart, was again essayed, but was repulsed, the British losing one man killed, and having to leave a 6-pdr. on the beach. Apart, therefore, from the capture of the dhows, the only services effected were the partial disablement of the fort, and the ruining of the town. Troops were subsequently landed on the shores of Upper Egypt; but, with the withdrawal on August 16th of the *Dædalus* and *Fox* from before Kosseir, the participation of the Navy in the operations on the Red Sea littoral ended for the year.

Commodore Sir William Sidney Smith returned to the mouth of the Nile towards the end of October with a fleet of Turkish men-of-war and a large body of troops from Constantinople, and, on the 29th, 30th, and 31st, and November 1st, with his boats, assisted in preparing the way for, and in covering a landing near Damietta. The French were at first driven back, but the Turks, getting out of hand, were finally compelled to retreat to their boats in great confusion and with terrible slaughter. In spite, however, of their successes at Aboukir and Damietta, the situation of the French in Egypt, where guns, money, and medical comforts were lacking and where the invaders were threatened from all directions, became towards the end of the year so desperate that Kléber opened negotiations with the British Commodore, and sent General Desaix and M. Poussielgue on board the *Tigre* to treat. That some such step was advisable is indicated by the fact that on December 29th the French garrison of El Arich revolted, and delivered up the place to the British and Turks, the latter of whom, it is to be regretted, could not be prevented from massacring about three hundred of the traitors. But, no sooner were the commissioners on board the *Tigre* than a heavy gale of wind drove the ship out to sea; so that at the close of the year no settlement had been arrived at. As will be seen later, the French were not destined to quit Egypt so quickly or so easily as Kléber no doubt expected.

The operations in the North Sea during 1799 were of great importance. Believing that public opinion in the Netherlands had become somewhat less republican, and more favourable to the cause

ADMIRAL SIR ANDREW MITCHELL (1), K.B.

(From an engraving by H. R. Cook, after the painting by Bowyer.)

of the dispossessed Stadtholder, the British Government, early in the summer, quietly and secretly prepared an expedition on a very large scale with the object of contributing towards the restoration of the Prince of Orange. In the meantime, Admiral Lord Duncan's fleet, and a Russian division, continued to blockade the Dutch squadron, which, under Vice-Admiral Samuel Storij,[1] still lay within the Texel. Other Dutch ships lay in Nieuwe Diep,

[1] He was a Schout-bij-Nacht, with temporary rank as vice-admiral.

at Amsterdam, and in the Maas, but made no attempt to put to sea.

Troops for the expedition were assembled at Southampton, Barham Downs, Ramsgate, Margate, and Yarmouth, to the number of about 27,000 men.[1] Russia engaged, in return for pay and subsidy, to provide 17,593 more, together with transports and convoy for them; and the military command was entrusted to H.R.H. Frederick Augustus, Duke of York, under whom, with other officers of distinction, went Lieut.-General Sir Ralph Abercromby, commanding the first division. This division, consisting of about 17,000 men, sailed from Margate Road and the Downs on August 13th, 1799. The entire fleet transporting it was made up of upwards of 250 craft of all sizes, under the orders of Vice-Admiral Andrew Mitchell (1) (B.); but the effective fighting portion of it was confined to the vessels named in the note.[2] On the 15th, Lord Duncan, in the *Kent*, 74, Captain William Johnstone Hope, met the fleet and assumed command; but, bad weather coming on, the expedition did not get near the Texel until the evening of the 21st, when it anchored off Kuikduin. On the following morning the transports weighed and re-anchored within half a mile of the shore; and the *Coburg*, cutter, conveying Captain

[1] Less than 20,000 British, and about 17,000 Russians seem to have actually landed in Holland.

[2] Ships.	Guns.	Commanders.
Ratzivan	74	Capt. Greig } Russian.
Mistisloff	66	„ A. Moller } Russian.
Monmouth	64	„ George Hart.
Ardent	64	„ Thomas Bertie (2).
Belliqueux	64	„ Rowley Bulteel.
America	64	„ John Smith (3).
Overyssel	64	„ John Bazely (2).
Veteran	64	„ Archibald Collingwood Dickson.
Glatton	54	„ Charles Cobb.
Isis	50	Vice-Adm. Andrew Mitchell (1). Capt. James Oughton.
Romney	50	„ John Lawford.
Melpomene	44	„ Sir Charles Hamilton, Bart.
Latona	38	„ Frank Sotheron.
Shannon	32	„ Charles Dudley Pater.
Juno	32	„ George Dundas.
Lutine	32	„ Lancelot Skynner.
[1] *Circe*	28	„ Robert Winthrop.
[1] *Victor*	18	Com. John Rennie.
[1] *Coburg*, cutter, hired	16	Lieut. Terence O'Neill.

[1] Did not sail with Vice-Adm. Mitchell, but joined, and were present on August 28th and 30th.

Robert Winthrop, of the *Circe*, 28, and Colonel Frederick Maitland, went in under a flag of truce with a message to Vice-Admiral Storij. Almost immediately afterwards the wind shifted from east to south-west, and the weather began to look so threatening that all the ships had to stand off from the land; nor did they again anchor in their assigned stations until the 26th.

Storij, in reply to Admiral Lord Duncan's summons, declined to deliver up his ships for the use of the Prince of Orange, and declared that he would defend them if attacked, but promised to forward the summons to his government, which, on receiving it, answered on the 23rd, approving of Storij's attitude. Covered by a hot fire from the squadron, a landing was therefore effected on the mainland, near the Helder, in the early morning of the 27th. As soon as the troops began to move from the beach they were attacked by a Franco-Dutch force under Lieut.-General Daendels; but after a long action the latter retired, and the British, who had suffered much less seriously than the enemy, prepared to attack the Helder, which contained a garrison of two thousand men. These, however, evacuated the town in the night, and retreated towards Medemblik. The Helder, in consequence, was occupied at dawn on the 28th by a detachment under Major-General Moore; and the following Dutch vessels, chiefly old, which were anchored in ordinary in Nieuwe Diep, were simultaneously taken possession of, without resistance, by Captain Robert Winthrop, of the *Circe*:—

Ships.	Guns.	Ships.	Guns.
Verwachting	64	*Heldin* [2]	32
Broederschap	54	*Minerva* [3]	24
Belle Antoinette	44	*Alarm*	24
Constitutie	44	*Valk* [2]	24
Duif	44	*Venus* [4]	24
Expeditie	44	3 Indiamen	
Hector [1]	44	1 sheerhulk	
Unie	44		

1 Added to the Navy as *Pandour*.
2 Added to the Navy.
3 Added to the Navy as *Braak*.
4 Added to the Navy as *Amaranthe*.

Captain Winthrop also seized the naval depôt at Nieuwe Werk, with ninety-seven guns and a quantity of ordnance stores.

Early on August 30th, Vice-Admiral Mitchell's squadron weighed, and stood in towards the entrance to the Vlieter, where lay the ships of Storij's command. In going in, the *Ratzivan*, *America*, and *Latona* grounded, the channel being narrow, and the buoys having been removed by the Dutch, and replaced, possibly with no great accuracy, by the British. The other vessels, joined by the *Latona* as soon as she got off, stood on, and at length anchored in line ahead, a little outside the Dutch, in the following order: *Glatton, Romney, Isis, Veteran, Ardent, Belliqueux, Monmouth, Overyssel, Mistisloff*, and frigates. While still on his way in, Mitchell sent the *Victor*, 18, Commander John Rennie, to summon Storij. She met two Dutch captains, under a flag of truce, coming from that officer, and at once took them, ere the allies had anchored, on board the *Isis*, where it was arranged that Storij should be allowed one hour wherein to make up his mind as to surrendering. In less than an hour the captains returned to say that it was decided to give up the ships of his squadron. These, particulars of which are given below, were, accordingly, taken possession of forthwith, a British officer being appointed to take charge of each :—

Ships.	Guns.	Men.	Commanders.
Washington[1] . .	70	550	Vice-Adm. Samuel Storij. Capt. T. F. van Capellen.
Cerberus[2] . . .	68	450	„ C. De Jong.
De Ruijter . . .	64	450	„ J. Huis.
Gelderland . . .	64	450	Com. J. H. Waldeck.
Leijden	68	450	Capt. Æ. van Braam.
Utrecht	68	450	„ D. H. Kolff.
Batavier	56	350	„ W. H. van Senden.
Beschermer . . .	56	350	„ H. J. F. Eilbracht.
Amphitrite . . .	44	280	Com. J. D. Schutter.
Mars, rasé[3] . . .	44	280	„ D. Bock.
Embuscade . . .	34	230	„ J. Riverij.
Galathée	16	90	Lieut. J. J. Droop.

[1] Renamed *Princess of Orange*. [2] Renamed *Texel*.
[3] Renamed *Vlieter*. All the twelve prizes except the *Utrecht* were added to the Royal Navy, by purchase.

For this capitulation Storij was afterwards declared infamous, banished, and forbidden, on pain of death, to re-enter the territories of the Batavian Republic. Captains van Capellen, van Braam, Kolff, De Jong, and Bock were also punished.[1] James, endeavouring to explain why those who had fought so valiantly at Camperdown surrendered without a blow in the Texel, says :—

"The fact is, the sailors had become politicians; and, differing in opinion from their officers, had adopted a course which, if not the most honourable, was, under present

[1] Several of these were ultimately restored to their rank; and van Capellen lived to command the Dutch contingent at the bombardment of Algier in 1816.

circumstances, undoubtedly the most safe. They mutinied, and refused to fight; and, as if fearful that the guns would go off by themselves, they in many instances drew the charges, and threw the shot overboard. Under such, we must add, discreditable circumstances, Admiral Storij and his officers had no alternative but to surrender; and surely no one will think that in so doing they compromised in the slightest degree their professional character."[1]

There is some truth in all this; but, on the other hand, Storij, previous to the surrender, was guilty of so much carelessness and indecision that he cannot escape from blame. Upon the first appearance of the British, he quitted a fairly defensible anchorage in the Texel, and carried his squadron into the Vlieter and the fairway leading to it. There he stationed his ships in such a confused and straggling manner that they could not support one another; and, when at length he realised the danger of the position, and attempted to return to the Texel, first accidental circumstances and finally the direction of the wind, prevented him from doing so, the consequence being that Mitchell caught him in a narrow *cul de sac*, where he could neither defend himself nor manœuvre. It is not surprising therefore that, leaving their Orange tendencies out of the question, the seamen declined to fight at such a disadvantage. But Storij, though blameworthy, was not more so than the Dutch admiralty, which sent him contradictory orders, and which must be held responsible for his having ever withdrawn from the Texel.[2]

The army under Abercromby, having entrenched itself, repulsed with heavy loss an attack which was made upon it on September 10th by the Franco-Dutch under General Brune; and three days later H.R.H. the Duke of York disembarked at the Helder from the *Amethyst*, 38, Captain John Cooke (1), and the stipulated Russian contingent arrived. The next action was disastrous, the Anglo-Russians, who attacked, being compelled to fall back upon their entrenchments, with a loss, in killed, wounded, and prisoners, of about two thousand five hundred and fifty officers and men.[3] During the day, three little gunboats, on the Alkmaar canal, under Captain Sir Home Riggs Popham and Lieutenant William Godfrey, R.N., rendered good service, but lost four killed and

[1] James, ii. 309.

[2] Van der Aa, 'Geschied. v.d. Oorlog'; Vonk, 'Geschied. der Landing'; Storij's 'Verantwoording,' and 'Sententie'; Jong's 'Verantwoording'; Walsh, 'Narr. of the Exped. to Holland'; Maccarthy, 'Hist. de la Campagne en 1799'; papers in Archief v. het Hoog. Mil. Geregtshof, and Rijks Archief, etc.

[3] This loss, according to the British dispatches, was, nevertheless, not so great as that suffered by the enemy.

eight wounded. On October 6th, the Duke of York drove back the enemy; but, on the day following, he was himself crushingly defeated and induced to negotiate with General Brune, the result being the evacuation of Holland by the British and Russian military forces.[1] The retirement of the army obliged Vice-Admiral Mitchell to withdraw from the Zuider Zee, which, after having shifted his flag to the *Babet*, 20, he had entered with a small flotilla. Before he withdrew, a detachment of seamen and Marines which, under Commander James Boorder, of the *Espiègle*, 16, held the town of Lemmer, signalised itself on October 11th by repelling without loss a prolonged attack by a vastly superior force of the enemy.

The expedition was, upon the whole, a most unfortunate and costly one. None of the Dutch vessels captured were of great value. On the other hand, four British ships of war, the *Nassau*, 64 (*en flûte*), *Blanche*, 32, *Lutine*, 32, and *Contest*, 12, were wrecked on the difficult and dangerous coast during the operations, forty-two men perishing in the *Nassau*, and the entire crew, except two, in the *Lutine*, which also carried down with her a sum of £140,000 intended for the payment of the troops.[2] In addition, about four thousand eight hundred British soldiers, besides Russians, were killed, wounded, or taken prisoners. But the failure was in nowise due to the Navy, which deservedly received the thanks of Parliament.[3] Vice-Admiral Mitchell was afterwards rewarded with a K.B.[4]

The only other event of the year to be noticed here is the surrender of the Dutch colony of Surinam to a naval force under Vice-Admiral Lord Hugh Seymour, consisting of the *Prince of Wales*, 98 (flag), Captain Adrian Renou; *Invincible*, 74, Captain George William Cayley; *Tamer*, 38, Captain Thomas Western; *Unité*, 38, Captain John Poo Beresford; *Syren*, 32, Captain Thomas Le Marchant Gosselin; *Lapwing*, 28, Captain Thomas Harvey; *Amphitrite*, 28, Captain Charles Ekins; *Daphne*, 20, Captain Richard Matson; and *Requin*, 12, Lieutenant William Wood

[1] The convention to this effect was signed on Oct. 20th, and the whole army was embarked by Nov. 19th.

[2] Many years later many of the ship's guns and much of the treasure were recovered. One of the guns, little the worse for its long immersion, was shown at the Roy. Nav. Exhib., 1891.

[3] The services of Sir Ralph Abercromby and of the army were similarly recognised. The prime cause of insuccess seems to have been the military incapacity of the Duke of York.

[4] Jan. 9th, 1800.

Senhouse, conveying troops under Lieut.-General T. Trigge. The expedition sailed from Port Royal, Martinique, on July 31st, and made the coast of Surinam on August 11th. After negotiations extending over several days, a capitulation was ratified by the Dutch governor on August 20th, and on the following day the garrison of Fort Amsterdam marched out with the honours of war, and the place was taken possession of. On the 22nd other important ports, including Paramaribo, were occupied, and the whole colony, now known as Dutch Guiana, became, for the time, British. In the river Surinam were found the Dutch brig-sloop *Camphaan*, 16, and the French *Hussard*, 20 (later *Surinam*, 18), both of which were added to the Royal Navy, the former being provisionally commissioned by Lieutenant Richard Thwaits, and the latter by Lieutenant Christopher Cole.

In spite of the checks which had been inflicted on French ambition, and of the ignominious flight of Bonaparte from Egypt, the popularity and influence of the great Corsican suffered little in France; and on November 10th Napoleon was able to dissolve the Executive Directory and to substitute for it a Consulate composed of Roger Ducos, himself, and Emanuel Joseph Sieyès. In December, he went further, and, getting rid of his colleagues, secured his own appointment as First Consul, with Jean Jacques Régis de Cambacérès and Charles François Lebrun as his associates. The reorganisation of the government was immediately followed by a reorganisation of the French navy,[1] and by the putting forward by Bonaparte of vague proposals, addressed to King George, for a general peace.[2] France, however, offered no concessions; and it was felt in Great Britain that she was at the moment more anxious for a temporary suspension of hostilities than for a permanent settlement. Nothing, therefore, came of the negotiations.

The chief British naval commands at home and abroad were held as follows in the year 1800:—

Portsmouth		Admiral Mark Milbanke (W).
Plymouth		Vice-Adm. Sir Thomas Pasley, Bt. (R).
The Downs		Vice-Adm. Skeffington Lutwidge (R).
The Nore		Vice-Adm. Alexander Græme (W).
Cork		Admiral Robert Kingsmill (B).
„	Aug.	Admiral Alan, Lord Gardner (B).

[1] See especially the report of Com., 6th Frimaire (29th Nov., 1799).

[2] Disp. of 5th Nivôse (25th Dec., 1799).

The Channel	Admiral Lord Bridport (W).
„ Ap.	Admiral Earl St. Vincent (W).
The North Sea	Admiral Viscount Duncan (W).
Mediterranean.	Vice-Adm. Lord Keith (R).
North America	Admiral George Vandeput (B).
„ Mar.	Vice-Adm. Sir William Parker (1), Bt. (W).
Newfoundland	Vice-Adm. Hon. William Waldegrave (R).
„ later	Rear-Adm. Charles Morice Pole (R).
Leeward Islands	Vice-Adm. Lord Hugh Seymour (B).
„ later	Rear-Adm. John Thomas Duckworth (W).
Jamaica	Admiral Sir Hyde Parker (2), (B).
„ later	Vice-Adm. Lord Hugh Seymour (B).
Cape of Good Hope	Vice-Adm. Sir Roger Curtis, Bt. (W).
East Indies	Vice-Adm. Peter Rainier (1), (B).

As in the previous year, the French at Brest were watched by a detachment of the Channel Fleet. Of this detachment, then under the orders of Vice-Admiral Sir Alan Gardner, Bart., the *Repulse*, 64, Captain James Alms (2), formed part, when, on March 10th, she struck on a rock about seventy-five miles S.W. of Ushant, and was so damaged that she had to be run ashore near Quimper, where she ultimately became a total loss. Her people, except twelve who reached Guernsey in a boat, landed on one of the Glénan Islands and were made prisoners. When Captain Alms returned home and was tried,[1] he and all his officers and men were honourably acquitted, save the first Lieutenant, John Carpenter Rothery, and the Master, George Finn, who had left in the boat, and who, for disobedience to orders, were dismissed the service. As Captain Alms, previous to the wreck, had been incapacitated for duty by an accident, the desertion of the ship by the officer next in command was the more disgraceful.

Later in the same month, Lord Bridport, in person, assumed the command off Brest, with his flag in the *Royal George*, 100, and with a fleet which numbered thirty-eight sail of the line; but he presently returned to England, and on April 24th hauled down his flag. Two days later Earl St. Vincent succeeded him, hoisting his flag in the *Namur*, 100,[2] and proceeding off Brest; and on June 1st he detached Captain Sir Edward Pellew, in the *Impétueux*, 78, with the *Ramillies*, 74, Captain Richard Grindall; *Ajax*, 80, Captain the Hon. Alexander Inglis Cochrane; *Canada*, 74, Captain the Hon. Michael de Courcy (1); *Terrible*, 74, Captain William Wolseley; *Captain*, 74, Captain Sir Richard John Strachan; *Fishguard*, 74, Captain Thomas Byam Martin; *Amelia*, 44, Captain the Hon. Charles Herbert (1); *Amethyst*,

[1] C.M., 26th June, 1800.

[2] And later in the *Ville de Paris*, 100.

38, Captain John Cooke (1); *Diamond*, 38, Captain Edward Griffith; *Doris*, 36, Captain Viscount Ranelagh; *Thames*, 32, Captain William Lukin; and *Cynthia*, 16, Commander Micajah Malbon; together with the *Diadem*, 64, Captain Sir Thomas Livingstone, Bart.; *Europa*, 50, Captain James Stevenson (1); *Inconstant*, 36, Commander John Ayscough; *Thisbe*, 28, Commander John Morrison; and *Cyclops*, 28, Commander John Fyffe, armed *en flûte*, and having on board the 2nd, 20th, 36th, 82nd, and 92nd regiments, and two hundred artillerymen under Major-General Maitland. This squadron was directed to co-operate with the insurgent French Royalists in the Morbihan; and with that object it anchored in Quiberon Bay cn June 2nd. On the 4th, the *Thames* and *Cynthia* attacked and silenced some forts, which were afterwards destroyed by a landing party, the *Cynthia* losing two killed and one wounded; and early on the 6th, a body of troops, acting with a division of boats under Lieutenant John Pilfold, of the *Impétueux*, burnt the *Insolente*, 18, carried off several small craft and about one hundred prisoners, destroyed some guns, and blew up a magazine, only one seaman being killed. It was intended to attack Belle Isle; but the garrison of that island was found to be very strong, and the idea was therefore abandoned. The troops from the squadron were eventually landed on the island of Houat, whence they were re-embarked later and conveyed to the Mediterranean. A few months later, while the *Captain*, one of the ships of the above expedition, was cruising with the *Marlborough*, 74, Captain Thomas Sotheby, to the westward of the peninsula of Quiberon, the latter struck on a ledge of rocks near Groix, and although, by great exertion, she was got off, she had received so much damage that she ultimately sank. All her people were saved; and her Captain, officers, and ship's company were subsequently acquitted of all blame, it being held that the accident had been due to the "uncertain situation" of the rocks.[1]

In the Mediterranean, there was no considerable French force at Toulon, and no considerable Spanish one at Cartagena or Cadiz. Lord Keith was, therefore, chiefly occupied in the blockade of Malta, in preventing the passage of supplies along the coast of the Riviera, and in assisting the Austrians in their endeavours to drive the French out of Tuscany and Piedmont. On March 16th the Commander-in-Chief, who contemplated an attack upon Capraia, landed at Leghorn, with part of his staff, and ordered Captain Andrew Todd, of the flag-

[1] C.M., Jan. 2nd, 1801.

ship *Queen Charlotte*, 100, to proceed off that island and reconnoitre it. On the following morning, at a little before 6 A.M., while making for Capraia, the *Queen Charlotte* was found to be on fire; and, although assistance was at once despatched from the shore, and all was done that could be done,[1] the vessel was completely burnt by about 11 o'clock, the misfortune being, unhappily, accompanied by the most dreadful loss of life. Eleven persons belonging to the ship were on shore at the time. Of the 829 on board, only 156 were saved; and among the 673 who perished were Captain Andrew Todd,[2] Lieutenants William Bainbridge and James Erskine, Captain of Marines Joseph Breedon, the Master, Purser, Surgeon, and Boatswain, four Master's Mates, and no fewer than eighteen Midshipmen.[3] The accident seems to have been due to the fact that some hay had been left lying under the half-deck, and that a live match, kept in a tub close by for firing signal guns, had, by some means, communicated with it. Two or three American vessels lying near the scene of the catastrophe rendered valuable aid, and sacrificed several men in their efforts to save life. Lord Keith subsequently hoisted his flag, first in the *Audacious*, 74, Captain Davidge Gould, and later in the *Minotaur*, 74, Captain Thomas Louis.

Pressed on the land side by the Austrians, and prevented by the British from obtaining supplies by sea, the main body of French, towards the end of April, concentrated in Genoa, under General Masséna, and were at once besieged there by General Baron von Melas, and afterwards by Baron von Ott; while a smaller detachment, under General Buget, was shut up in Savona. Savona, actively blockaded by the *Santa Dorothea*, 36, Captain Hugh Downman, *Chameleon*, 18, Lieutenant Samuel Jackson (actg.), and a Neapolitan brig,[4] surrendered on May 15th. Genoa was blockaded by Lord Keith in person; and, under his direction, great assistance was rendered to the Austrians by the *Phaeton*, 38, Captain James Nicoll Morris, and by the gun and mortar vessels and armed boats of the fleet under Captain Philip Beaver, R.N.[5] To repel the attacks of

[1] Owing to the guns going off as they became heated, many boats were deterred from approaching the ship to take off the people.

[2] A Captain of 1796. His first commission dated from 1783.

[3] Among these Midshipmen, it is curious to note, were a son (Charles Dickson) of the ship's Gunner, and a son (Thomas Bridgman) of the ship's Boatswain. 'Nav. Chron.,' iii. 299–302, 323.

[4] *Gazette*, 1800, 620. Keith to Nepean, May 16th.

[5] Then of the *Aurora*. Keith to Nepean, May 21st.

the latter force, the French organised a small flotilla, consisting of a galley named the *Prima*, an armed cutter, three settees, and several gunboats; and on May 21st at about 1 A.M., when Captain Beaver was bombarding the town for the fourth time, the French succeeded in causing him considerable annoyance, particularly by means of two long brass 36-prs., which were mounted in the galley. Beaver therefore determined to endeavour to cut out the *Prima*, although she lay chain-moored under heavy batteries. Ten boats, containing about one hundred officers and men, were told off for the purpose, and were led in as silently as possible; but, a gunboat opening fire upon them, they had at last to make a quick dash for their prey. When they got near her they found that her oars, fifty-two in number, had been lashed to their benches in such a manner as to form a kind of projecting defence all round her; that her bulwarks had been built up and mounted with swivel guns, and that she was full of men,[1] who, having been alarmed by the gunboat, were on the alert. Nevertheless, some people from a boat belonging to the *Haarlem*, managed, under the leadership of Midshipman John Caldwell, to enter her amidships on the starboard side; and other parties, under Captain Beaver, and Lieutenant William Gibson, of the *Vestal*, almost instantly afterwards boarded her by the stern, the result being that the galley was soon carried. By dint of great exertions, her moorings were cleared away, and, in spite of a tremendous fire, she was safely towed out, the galley-slaves helping at the sweeps. The capture was effected with a loss of only five men wounded on the British side. As soon as the craft was out of danger, the slaves were allowed to free themselves from their chains; but, to the disgrace of the British arms, they were not given their liberty. The garrison of Genoa was known to be in a state bordering upon famine; and, with a view to increasing the difficulties of the French, Keith restored not only such of the fighting crew of the *Prima* as he had taken, but also all the slaves, except about fifty, who, having been provisionally berthed in the *Expedition*, 44, had been blown to sea in her: and Masséna, learning how the miserable wretches had contributed to the carrying out of the galley, and not anxious, we may fairly suppose, to feed mouths upon which he could not depend, ordered the whole of them to be shot.

Reduced by starvation, Masséna, on June 4th, agreed to evacuate

[1] The number of men on board was 257, besides upwards of 300 galley slaves.

Genoa, and to retire with such troops as were able to follow him, to Nice. On June 5th, the *Minotaur*, 74 (flag), Captain Thomas Louis, *Audacious*, 74, Captain Davidge Gould, *Généreux*, 74, Captain Manley Dixon, *Charon*, storeship, 44, Commander Richard Bridges, *Pigmy*, cutter, and several Neapolitan vessels, anchored within the mole. But the success of the Allies was of little use. Bonaparte had in the meantime crossed the Alps. On June 4th he entered Milan, and re-erected the Cisalpine Republic. Von Melas abandoned Piedmont, and concentrated his forces at Alessandria. The French, on the 9th and 10th, defeated von Ott at Casteggio and Montebello; on the 14th, crushed von Melas at Marengo; and, on the 15th, by the convention of Alessandria, were put in possession of Alessandria, Tortona, Milan, Turin, Arona, Piacenza, Savona, Genoa, Pozzighettone, Corio, and other strongholds. The reverse of fortune was so sudden and unexpected that on June 22nd, when Suchet reoccupied Genoa, the *Minotaur* had difficulty in warping out in time to avoid finding herself under batteries fully manned by the enemy.

General Vaubois still held Malta, although, at the beginning of 1800, he had received no supplies from without since the early part of February, 1799, and although his army, shut up in Valetta, and closely pressed by Maltese, Neapolitans, and British, was already suffering to some extent from disease as well as from incipient famine. In February, 1800, Lord Keith's blockading force off the island consisted of the *Queen Charlotte*, 100 (flag), Captain Andrew Todd; *Foudroyant*, 80, Rear-Admiral Lord Nelson, Captain Sir Edward Berry; *Audacious*, 74, Captain Davidge Gould; *Northumberland*, 74, Captain George Martin (2); *Alexander*, 74, Lieut. William Harrington (actg.[1]); *Lion*, 64, Captain Manley Dixon; the Neapolitan frigate *Sirena*, and two or three small craft. On February 15th the Commander-in-Chief learnt from the *Success*, 32, Captain Shuldham Peard, which had been cruising off the south-west of Sicily, that a small French squadron was about to attempt to throw troops and stores into Malta. This squadron, which had quitted Toulon on February 7th,[2] consisted, as it afterwards appeared, of the *Généreux*, 74, flagship of Rear-Admiral Perrée, *Badine*, 28, *Fauvette*, 20, *Sans Pareille*, 20, and two or three transports, among which was the *Ville de Marseilles*. To prevent

[1] For Captain Alexander John Ball, who was serving ashore at Malta.

[2] Some French authorities say the 10th.

this little force from carrying out its mission, Keith, in the *Queen Charlotte*, kept close off the entrance to Valetta harbour, and ordered the *Foudroyant*, *Audacious*, and *Northumberland* to chase to windward, the wind being south-east, and the *Lion* to watch the channel between Malta and Gozo. The *Alexander* was at the time on the south-east side of the island.

At dawn on February 18th, the *Alexander* sighted and chased M. Perrée, and was observed by Nelson's division. At 8 A.M., Harrington forced the *Ville de Marseilles* to bring to. At 1.30 P.M., the *Badine* and the two corvettes tacked, but the *Généreux*, not having it in her power to do so without getting to close quarters with the *Alexander*, bore up. At that time, the *Success*, 32, which was to leeward, greatly annoyed the Frenchman by lying athwart his hawse and raking him repeatedly; but she could not avoid presently receiving a broadside, which killed one, and wounded nine of her people. By 4.30 P.M., the *Foudroyant* and *Northumberland* coming up, the *Généreux*, after a couple of guns had been discharged at her, fired a broadside and struck her colours. That the enemy did not make a more determined defence is probably due to the fact that, early in the action, Perrée was badly injured in the left eye, and that a little later he was mortally wounded by a shot which carried away his right thigh. He was a gallant and capable man, whose loss was much regretted by the many British officers who had met him either as friend or as foe.

The non-arrival of the *Généreux* and convoy was a bitter blow to Vaubois, although, as Perrée's squadron had on board three thousand troops, the supplies, had they been thrown into the place, would have been quickly consumed. In Valetta an egg was already worth tenpence; a rat, one and eightpence; and a rabbit, ten shillings; and typhus was raging. The French general, therefore, determined to send Rear-Admiral Denis Decrès, in the *Guillaume Tell*, 80, to Toulon to apprise the government of his condition, and to explain that, unless relieved, he could not hold out beyond June.

In the meantime, Lord Keith, by proclamation, announced a blockade of Toulon, Marseilles, Nice, and the Riviera, and proceeded in the *Queen Charlotte* to Leghorn, off which port, as has been seen, the three-decker so miserably perished. Lord Nelson, also, quitted the neighbourhood of Malta, going first to Palermo, and thence, with the Hamiltons, to Leghorn, and so overland to England.[1] It

[1] Landing at Yarmouth on Nov. 6th, having spent nearly five months on the journey.

is clear, both from his correspondence and from the testimony of all who met him on the way, that he was still very much "Sicilified," and that, indeed, he did not possess the mental balance which was ordinarily his most striking characteristic; and it is well, perhaps, for his country, if not for his private reputation, that, instead of remaining any longer in the Mediterranean, where the exigencies of the service and the remonstrances of his best friends prevented him from freely enjoying the society of the woman whom he loved, and so kept him in a state of fever and unrest,[1] he flung aside, for a season, his public ties, and devoted himself entirely to the passion which, for the time, monopolised his thoughts. The absence of the flag-officers left Troubridge, in the *Culloden,* in charge of the blockade of Malta; and, when Troubridge was

COMMEMORATIVE MEDAL OF NELSON'S RETURN TO ENGLAND IN 1800.

(From an original lent by H.S.H. Capt. Prince Louis of Battenberg, R.N.)

temporarily called elsewhere, towards the end of March, the British force off the island consisted of the *Lion,* 64, Captain Manley Dixon; *Foudroyant,* 80, Captain Sir Edward Berry; *Alexander,* 74, Lieut. William Harrington (actg.); *Penelope,* 36, Captain the Hon. Henry Blackwood, and a few small craft.

It was on March 30th that at 11 P.M. on a dark night and with a strong southerly gale, the *Guillaume Tell,* Captain Saulnier, with Rear-Admiral Decrès on board, weighed in pursuance of the determination of Vaubois, and put to sea. Within the hour, the *Penelope* sighted her, and at once despatched the *Minorca,* 16,

[1] "I have been left here" (off Malta) "very unwell, and am this day going to Palermo for the benefit of my health." Nelson to Lady Nelson, March 10th, 1800 (*Literature,* 1898, p. 359). The Hamiltons were then at Palermo. Spencer, on May 9th, wrote to Nelson that he had better come home than remain at Palermo inactive in a foreign court. Nicolas, iv. 242.

Commander George Miller, to warn Captain Dixon, who lay at anchor at some little distance off the harbour's mouth. Blackwood then stood after the Frenchman, who was on the starboard tack under a press of sail, and, at 12.30 A.M. on March 31st, luffed up under the 80's stern, and delivered into it her port broadside of 18-prs.; next bearing up under the enemy's port quarter and delivering into that her starboard broadside. Decrès replied only with his stern guns, realising as he did that, if he brought to to engage, his little opponent would soon receive assistance; for ships were visible on the horizon. He therefore continued on a north-east course; and Blackwood, manœuvring the *Penelope* with consummate skill, and again and again raking his enemy, at length brought down the Frenchman's main and mizen topmasts and main yard. By that time day was about to break. Soon after 5 A.M. the *Lion*, which had slipped her cable, interposed herself between the *Penelope* and the *Guillaume Tell*, gave the latter at the closest possible range a passing broadside of treble-shotted guns, and, luffing up across her bows and carrying away the enemy's jibboom, raked her steadily until about 5.30 A.M. By that time the *Lion* was so damaged that she was unmanageable, and dropped astern; but neither she nor the *Penelope* ceased firing occasionally. At 6 A.M., the *Foudroyant*, which, upon the alarm being given, had been at anchor three miles north-east of Valetta lighthouse, and which had slipped and crowded sail, arrived upon the scene, and, running along the *Guillaume Tell's* starboard side, summoned her to strike, at the same moment pouring in a treble-shotted broadside. The French 80 gallantly replied, and with good effect; and the *Foudroyant*, carrying too much sail, shot ahead, and could not at once regain a position yardarm to yardarm. When she did so, she quickly suffered badly, losing in a few minutes her foretopmast, maintopsail yard, jibboom, and spritsail yard, and being reduced to quit her brave foe, which, however, was still engaged on the port side by the *Lion*, and on the port quarter by the *Penelope*. At 6.30 A.M. the *Guillaume Tell* lost her main and mizen masts, and the *Foudroyant*, having freed herself from the wreck of her spars, was again in action. At 8 A.M. the Frenchman's foremast went; and at 8.20, with the *Foudroyant*, 80, on her starboard quarter, the *Lion*, 64, on her port quarter, and the *Penelope*, 36, close ahead of her, the *Guillaume Tell*, after a most splendid defence of nearly eight hours, hauled down her colours.

The two British line-of-battle ships were too damaged to take possession of her: the honour, therefore, became the *Penelope's*.[1]

In this memorable action the *Foudroyant* lost 8 killed and 69 wounded (out of a complement of 719); the *Lion*, 8 killed, and 38 wounded (out of a complement on board of only about 300); and the *Penelope*, 1 killed and 3 wounded; the total British loss being, therefore, 17 killed and 110 wounded.[2] The *Guillaume Tell's* loss does not appear to be accurately known. One French account puts it at "upwards of 200 killed and wounded"; another, at "half her people." She certainly lost heavily. Both Decrès and Saulnier were badly wounded. The former was rewarded with a grant of the "Arms of Honour," which Napoleon instituted as a decoration ere he founded the Legion of Honour; and, on his exchange, he was at once made maritime prefect at Lorient.

The *Penelope* towed the prize to Syracuse. She was a vessel of 2265 tons measurement, or 203 tons larger than her chief opponent, the *Foudroyant*; and, renamed *Malta*, she became, next to the *Tonnant*, the greatest two-decker in the British Navy.

In spite of the non-arrival of succour, General Vaubois held Valetta through April, May, July, and August. Food, water, fuel were gradually exhausted; and towards the end of the blockade his men died at the rate of upwards of a hundred a day. When he realised that capitulation was inevitable, he made an effort to save the frigates *Diane*, 40, and *Justice*, 40, by sending them to sea on the night of August 24th; but they were quickly seen and chased by the *Northumberland*, 74, Captain George Martin (2), *Généreux*, 74, Captain Manley Dixon, and *Success*, 32, Captain Shuldham Peard; and, although the *Justice*, Captain Jean Villeneuve, escaped and reached Toulon, the *Diane*, Captain Solen, which had but one hundred and fourteen men on board, was engaged and taken, thanks mainly to the *Success*. As there was already a *Diana* in the service, the prize was ultimately added to the Navy as the *Niobe*.[3]

On September 4th, the wretched remains of the Valetta garrison sent out a flag of truce to the commander of the allied forces on shore; and on the following day the terms of capitulation were

[1] Dixon to Keith, Mar. 31st.

[2] The British officers killed were Mr. Henry Damerell, Master (*Penelope*), and Mr. Hugh Roberts, Midshipman (*Lion*).

[3] She measured 1142 tons, and was one of the best vessels of her class.

settled, on the one hand by Major-General Pigot, and Captain George Martin (2), and, on the other, by General Vaubois and Rear-Admiral Villeneuve. There were surrendered with the port the two Maltese 64's *Athénien* (which was added to the Navy) and *Dégo* (which was not seaworthy), the Maltese frigate *Cartagénaise* (which also was not seaworthy), and two merchantmen, one brig, a xebec, and several gunboats and small craft. Soon afterwards, Captain Alexander John Ball, to whom the fall of Valetta was very largely owing, was, to the great joy of the inhabitants, appointed governor of Malta.

It has already been mentioned that at the end of 1799, General Kléber sent commissioners on board the *Tigre* to treat with Commodore Sir William Sidney Smith for the evacuation of Egypt, and that, immediately afterwards, the *Tigre* was blown off the coast by a gale of wind. During her absence at sea conferences were carried on, and, in consequence of them, after her return to Alexandria on January 17th, the representatives of the countries concerned landed and went to El Arich, where, on January 24th, a convention was agreed to and signed by the French and Turkish commissioners. On January 28th, it was ratified at Salahieh by General Kléber himself; but it was not signed by the Commodore,[1] who contented himself with sending home a copy of it. On March 25th, the *Gazette* announced that, in virtue of it, it had been agreed "that the French troops now in Egypt shall evacuate the country and shall be allowed to return to France." In the meantime, however, Lord Keith, who had been apprised of the terms of the convention, declined, in pursuance, it would appear, rather of general than of particular instructions from home, to consent to any capitulation which did not involve the surrender of the French as prisoners of war. Information to this effect was conveyed to Kléber in March; and the general, who was naturally much surprised, at once determined to retaliate by wreaking what vengeance he could upon the Turks, the only body of his enemies that lay within his reach.[2]

Kléber, therefore, attacked the Turks on March 20th at Heliopolis, and, after five days' fighting, defeated them with enormous

[1] Smith had, however, signed on December 29th a preliminary agreement, which, he considered, fully bound his country. Nelson strongly urged him not to treat.

[2] Keith's refusal to agree to the convention was the more mortifying to Kléber, seeing that, confident that it would be ratified, the French had already, in pursuance of it, evacuated certain positions with a view to embarking.

slaughter, and presently repossessed himself of most of his old positions.[1] In June, the British Government, having in the interval thought better of the convention of El Arich, authorised Lord Keith to renew negotiations and to accede to the arrangements as originally determined by Sir William Sidney Smith; but Kléber, perhaps distrustful of those who, he imagined, had already deceived him, and certainly more firmly established than he had been in December, 1799, was no longer in a compliant mood; nor, after his assassination on June 14th, was his successor, General Menou, any more inclined to treat.[2]

After the visit of Sir Edward Pellew's squadron to the coasts of the Morbihan, in June, part of that squadron, together with other ships, was put under the orders of Rear-Admiral Sir John Borlase Warren, and detached from the Channel upon an expedition against six Spanish ships of the line[3] which lay ready for sea in the port of Ferrol. On August 25th, Sir John reached the bay of Playa de Dominos with the following vessels:—[4]

Ships.	Guns.	Commanders.
Renown	74	Rear-Adm. Sir J. B. Warren, Bart., K.B. (B). Capt. Thomas Eyles.
London	98	„ John Child Purvis.
Impétueux . . .	78	„ Sir Edward Pellew, Bart.
Courageux . . .	74	„ Samuel Hood (2).
Captain	74	„ Sir Richard John Strachan, Bart.
Indefatigable . .	44	„ Hon. Henry Curzon.
Amelia	44	„ Hon. Charles Herbert (1).
Amethyst	38	„ John Cooke (1).
Stag	32	„ Robert Winthrop.
Brilliant	28	„ Hon. Charles Paget.
Cynthia	18	„ Micajah Malbon.[1]

[1] Posted Aug. 11th.

and some small craft and transports, conveying troops under Lieut.-General Sir James Pulteney. That evening, after a fort had been silenced by the fire of the *Impétueux*, *Brilliant*, *Cynthia*, and *St. Vincent*, gunboat, the troops, with sixteen field-guns, were

[1] In particular, he drove out a small British detachment which had been landed from the *Centurion*, 50, at Suez.

[2] This eccentric man had been a colonial deputy in the Constituent Assembly, and had since embraced Mahometanism, and assumed the name of Abdallah.

[3] Part of Massaredo's fleet. They were the *San Hermenegildo*, 112; *Real Carlos*, 112; *San Fernando*, 96; *Argonauta*, 80; *San Antonio*, 74; and *San Augustin*, 74.

[4] The *Gibraltar*, 80, Captain William Hancock Kelly, and *Ajax*, 80, Captain Hon. Alexander Inglis Cochrane, which were detached with Warren, proceeded directly to Gibraltar.

disembarked without loss, and, aided by a detachment of seamen, drove back a body of the enemy. This skirmish was followed by a somewhat more serious one at daybreak on the 26th, the upshot being that the British made themselves masters of the heights overlooking the town and harbour. But the General, deterred, as his dispatch suggests, by the strength of the enemy and of the defences, made no further effort, and later in the day re-embarked his men. It seems likely that he allowed himself to be misled by the reports of prisoners, and that, in fact, he could have easily taken Ferrol had he seriously attempted the task. The failure did not, however, reflect in the slightest degree upon the Navy.

Proceeding, Warren joined the Commander-in-Chief at Gibraltar; whence, on October 2nd, Lord Keith sailed with twenty-two ships of the line, thirty-seven frigates and sloops, and eighty transports, carrying about eighteen thousand men under General Sir Ralph Abercromby. His object was an attack upon Cadiz and the capture of the Spanish squadron which lay at anchor there; but, upon the town being summoned, it appeared that the plague was raging in the place. From motives, therefore, of prudence as well as of humanity, the project was abandoned, and the expedition returned to the Rock. When it sailed again, its destination was the coast of Egypt; but its operations against the enemy in that quarter did not begin until the following year.

In extra-European waters the Navy did little that calls for mention in this chapter, although it did some brilliant deeds which will claim attention in the next. On September 11th, the *Néréide*, 36, Captain Frederick Watkins, being off Amsterdam, in the island of Curaçoa, received on board a deputation from the inhabitants, who, tired of republican domination, claimed British protection. On the 13th, a capitulation was signed in form; and Captain Watkins, by landing his men and occupying the forts, induced such French troops as were in the island to evacuate it on the 22nd. There were in the harbour forty-four craft of various sorts, but no ships of war, and, apparently, only one privateer. Some other privateers had made their escape, after having been much annoyed by Acting Lieut. Michael Fitton, who, commanding the *Active*, a little eighty-four ton schooner, which was tender to the flagship on the station, and which mounted eight 12-pr. carronades, more than once won the warm approval of Captain Watkins.[1]

[1] *Gazette*, 1800..1330, 1331.

The year 1801 witnessed great changes both in the internal and in the external relations of the British islands. On the first day of the year the parliamentary union of Great Britain and Ireland took effect, and the present Union Flag was adopted as expressive of that union;[1] and, a few months later, a confederation of the northern Powers, entered into with the object of obliging Great Britain to forego the long-established right of searching neutrals for contraband of war, threatened to add materially to the difficulties of King George's government, and forced it to employ swift and strong measures in order to protect its interests.

Questions connected with the enforcement of the right of search had already led to difficulties with the northern Powers, and had been responsible for the formation in 1780 of the coalition known as the First Armed Neutrality; but Sweden had abandoned that coalition in 1787; and Russia in 1793 had by treaty expressly recognised Great Britain's right to search neutral vessels.[2] The formation of the Second Armed Neutrality arose generally out of the conviction on the part of the northern Powers that, with the right of search abolished, they could carry on a profitable trade with France; and this conviction was, it need hardly be said, carefully encouraged by Bonaparte. But the immediate causes of the Northern Coalition of 1801 were as follows.

On July 25th, 1800, a small British squadron[3] under Captain Thomas Baker, being off Ostend, fell in with the Danish frigate *Freja*, 40, having under her convoy two ships, two brigs and two galliots. Captain Baker hailed her to say that he would send his boat on board the convoy. The Danish captain, Krabbe, replied that, if such an attempt were made, he would fire into the boat. Baker lowered a boat and put a Midshipman and four men into her; whereupon the *Freja* fired several shot,[4] striking the *Nemesis* and killing a man. Baker at once returned a broadside, and, after a spirited action of twenty minutes, the *Freja* struck, and was carried, with her convoy, into the Downs. She had lost two killed and five

[1] *See* description and sketches in the previous chapter, p. 188.

[2] Koch and Schöll, iv. 34; vi. 92; and judgments of Sir W. Scott in Robinson's 'Reports.'

[3] *Nemesis*, 28, Captain Thomas Baker; *Prévoyante*, 40, Captain John Seater; *Terpsichore*, 32, Captain William Hall Gage; *Arrow*, 18, Com. William Bolton (1); and *Nile*, lugger, 10, Lieut. Richard Whitehead.

[4] Krabbe's report distinctly charges the British with having fired first, and declares that the *Freja's* first shot did not take effect.

wounded. The *Nemesis* and *Arrow* each had two killed and several wounded. Vice-Admiral Skeffington Lutwidge, commanding in the Downs, ordered the *Freja's* colours and pennant to be kept flying, and maintained only an unarmed party of British officers and seamen in her. Seeing that a somewhat similar affair [1] had occurred in the Mediterranean during the previous December, the British government despatched Lord Whitworth to Copenhagen with instructions to come to an understanding on the subject; and, to support the negotiator, it also sent to the Sound a squadron [2] of men-of-war under Vice-Admiral Archibald Dickson. On August 29th, it was agreed between Lord Whitworth and Count Bernstorff that the *Freja* and her convoy should be repaired at British expense and then released; that the asserted right of search should be further discussed at a further conference to be held in London; and that, in the meantime, Danish vessels in the Mediterranean should have convoy only to protect them from the Algerines, and should be liable to be searched as before. It was also agreed that the convention to this effect should be ratified within three weeks.

The difficulty with Denmark, therefore, was in a fair way of adjustment. Russia, however, chose to enter into the quarrel, and, having sequestered [3] all British property in the Empire, mobilised her army and navy. When, in November, 1800, she learnt of the capture of Malta, to which the Tsar had pretentions, she took the additional step of laying an embargo on all British shipping in Russian ports; and in December, in conjunction with Sweden, she revived the Armed Neutrality of 1780. To this Denmark was induced by Russia and Prussia to adhere.

Great Britain could not abandon the right of search; and measures were at once taken to prove to the coalition that she had no idea of giving way.

On March 12th, 1801, a large fleet [4] under Admiral Sir Hyde Parker (2), Vice-Admiral Lord Nelson, and Rear-Admiral Thomas Graves (3), [5] and having on board the 49th Regiment, under Colonel

[1] In that case the *Emerald* and *Flora* were the British vessels concerned.

[2] In this squadron the first trial at sea was made of the improved system of signals invented by Sir H. R. Popham.

[3] This sequestration was annulled in about three weeks.

[4] The bulk of the fleet sailed on the 12th, but a few vessels departed later.

[5] Rear-Adm. Totty did not sail with the fleet, but, following it in the *Invincible*, 74, Captain John Rennie, was wrecked on Hammond's Knowl, off the coast of Norfolk, on March 16th. Captain Rennie and about 400 people perished. Rear-Adm. Totty afterwards proceeded in the *Zealous*, 74, and joined after the action.

Isaac Brock, two companies of rifles (the 95th Regiment), and some artillery commanded by Captain Peter Fyers,[1] the whole under Colonel Stewart, sailed from Yarmouth road for the Baltic. James comes to the conclusion that in that sea Denmark then had ready for service ten, Sweden eleven, and Russia about twenty effective ships of the line; and, as the British fleet consisted only of eighteen, besides frigates and small craft, the force despatched, even though it had Nelson with it, and although the possible enemy included three different nationalities, was not excessive.

Ahead of the fleet went the *Blanche*, 32, Captain Graham Eden Hamond, carrying the Hon. Nicholas Vansittart, who had full power to treat, and whom, it was hoped, the Danes would listen to; but on March 23rd, when the *Blanche* rejoined, bringing away the British *chargé d'affaires*, Mr. Drummond, she reported that the Danes were openly defiant, and that they were doing all that lay in their power to add to their means of defence.

In the interim the progress of the fleet had been delayed by bad weather. It did not make the Naze[2] until March 18th, and during the two following days it experienced such heavy gales that, on the 21st, Parker anchored at the entrance of the Sound to collect his scattered command. In the course of the gale, the *Tickler*, gun-brig, 12, and *Russell*, 74, narrowly escaped being lost; and the *Blazer*, gun-brig, 12, Lieut. Jonah Tiller,[3] being driven under the Swedish batteries at Varberg, was there captured.[4] Even when the weather had improved, Parker delayed. He listened to pilots who magnified the dangers of the passage which he was about to attempt, and he sent a flag of truce to Helsingör,[5] to ask if the governor of that fortress purposed to oppose the passage of the fleet through the Sound. But at 6 A.M. on March 30th, the British weighed, and, with a fine N.N.W. breeze, entered the Sound in line ahead, the van being commanded by Lord Nelson who, on the 29th, had shifted his flag from the *St. George*, 98, to the *Elephant*, 74, as being of less draught, and the rear being commanded by Graves, in the *Defiance*. An hour later the Helsingör batteries opened on the leading ship, the *Monarch*, 74; and they fired successively

[1] Fyers was appointed by Parker engineer to the expedition, he having had previous opportunities of examining the defences. White, 'Mems. of Nelson,' 198, etc.

[2] Lindesnes.

[3] Lieutenant, 1783.

[4] She was subsequently restored.

[5] The Elsinore of Shakespeare.

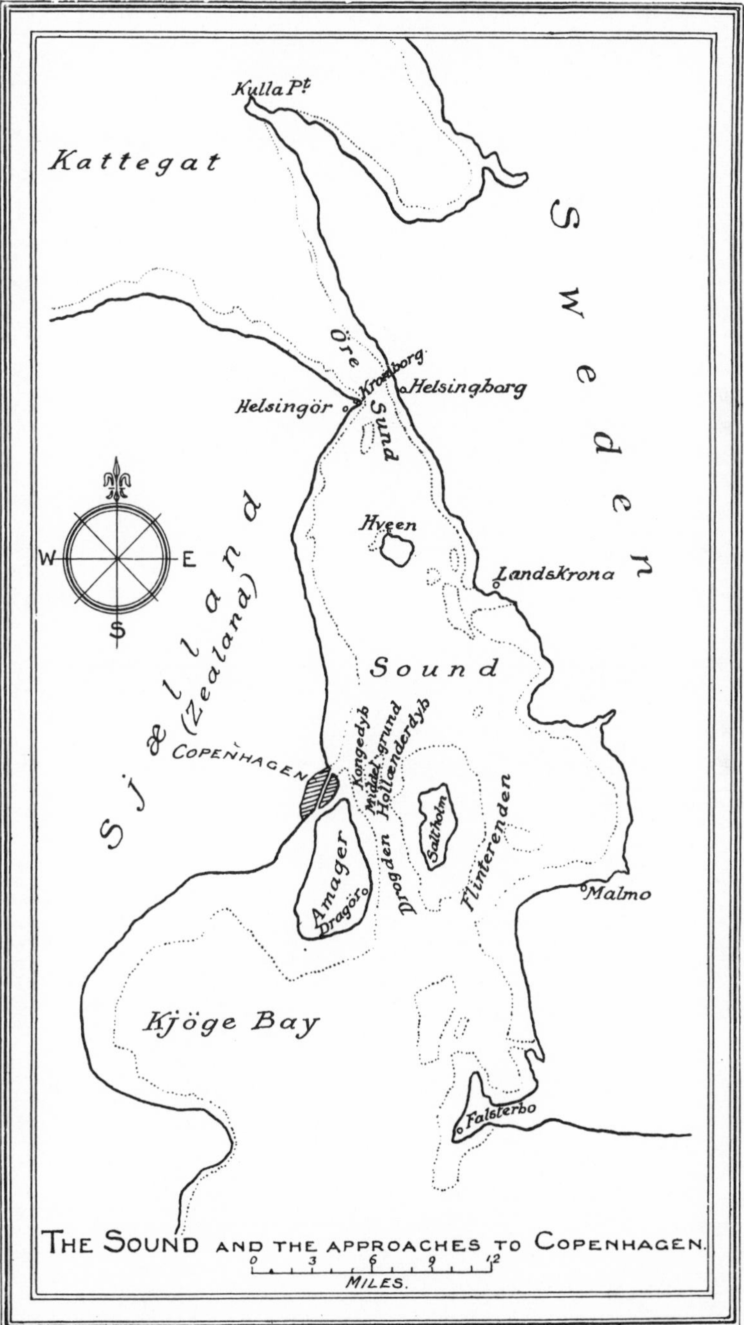

The Sound and the approaches to Copenhagen.

[To face p. 428.

at the other ships as they passed; but the range was too great for any damage to be done. Only the van ships replied, and these contented themselves with discharging two or three broadsides. The bomb-vessels, however, threw numerous shells into Kronborg and Helsingör, and caused some casualties. The sole loss on the British side was occasioned by the bursting of a 24-pr. in the *Isis*, where seven men were killed or wounded. The guns of Helsingborg, on the Swedish side of the strait, remained silent; and, as soon as it was observed that they were not firing, the British line crossed over so as to pass near them and avoid all danger from the Danish batteries.

Soon after midday the fleet dropped anchor above the Swedish island of Hveen, which is about fifteen miles from Copenhagen; and the Commander-in-Chief, accompanied by Lord Nelson, Rear-Admiral Graves, and Captain William Domett, Captain of the Fleet, proceeded, in the *Lark*, lugger, 14, Lieut. Thomas Henry Wilson, to reconnoitre. They came to the conclusion that the defences of Copenhagen were of an exceedingly formidable nature; yet, at a council of war held in the evening, Nelson, after warmly opposing a policy of delay, which was urged by some officers, offered to undertake the attack with ten sail of the line, and the small craft attached to the fleet. The offer was willingly accepted by Parker, who gave Nelson not only the ten sail of the line asked for, but also a 54 and a 50-gun ship. The Vice-Admiral's detachment, as ultimately constituted, was composed, therefore, of the ships mentioned in the note on the following page.

Apart from the works defending the city, there were many obstacles in the way of the success of Nelson's undertaking. The channel of approach was intricate and little known; the buoys had been removed from it, or had been intentionally displaced; and a considerable number of hulks, which, though old, were well armed and manned, were moored in such a position as to support and co-operate with the forts on the sea-front. No sooner, then, was the council of war over than Nelson, accompanied by several officers, went away in a boat to sound and re-buoy what is known as the Outer Channel,[1] a narrow passage lying between the Island of Saltholm and the Middelgrund shoal. It was at one time purposed to attack the Danish defences from the north; but, the Vice-Admiral having made a further examination of the position on March 31st,

[1] Otherwise called Hollænderdyb.

and the wind having changed, it was determined to approach from the south.

The nature of the Danish position will be best grasped by reference to the accompanying plan.[1] It consisted, as will be seen, of a line of eighteen men-of-war, armed hulks and floating batteries, moored nearly north and south over a distance of about a mile and a half along the edge of the shoal bordering Amager Island and facing the deep-water channel called Kongedyb. The order of these vessels, proceeding from south to north, is indicated in note[2] on page 431. On shore, behind this line of vessels, were several covering batteries. At the north end of the line were the two Trekroner Forts,[3] built on piles, and mounting, one, thirty 24-prs., and the other, thirty-eight 36-prs.; and moored near them were the two-deckers *Elephanten* and *Mars*, without their masts. Beyond the Trekroner Forts, and in the fairway leading south westwards to the

Squadron under Lord Nelson in the action with the defences of Copenhagen, April 2nd, 1801, with the loss suffered by each ship, as officially returned. (The slightly wounded are not included.)

Ships.	Guns.	Commanders. * Killed. † Wounded.	Loss. Killed.	Loss. Wounded.	First Lieutenants. * Killed. † Wounded.
Elephant	74	Vice-Adm. Lord Nelson, K.B. (B). Capt. Thomas Foley (3).	10	13	William Wilkinson.
Defiance	74	Rear-Adm. Thomas Graves (3), (W). Capt. Richard Retalick.	24	51	David Mudie.
Edgar	74	„ George Murray (3).	31	111	Edmund Johnson.*
Monarch	74	„ James Robert Mosse.*	56	164	John Yelland.
Bellona	74	„ Sir Thomas Boulden Thompson.†	11	72	John Delafons.
Ganges	74	„ Thomas Francis Fremantle.	7	1	William Morce.
Russell	74	„ William Cuming	..	6	Samuel Bateman.
Agamemnon	64	„ Robert Devereux Fancourt.			
Ardent	64	„ Thomas Bertie (2).	30	64	Andrew Mott (1).
Polyphemus	64	„ John Lawford	6	25	Edward Hodder.
Glatton	54	„ William Bligh.	18	37	Robert Brown Tom.
Isis	50	„ James Walker (2).	33	88	Robert Tinkler.
Amazon	38	„ Edward Riou.*	14	23	Joseph Ore Masefield.
Désirée	40	„ Henry Inman.	..	4	Andrew King.†
Blanche	36	„ Graham Eden Hamond.	7	9	Thomas M'Culloch.
Alcmène	32	„ Samuel Sutton.	5	19	Robert Wallace Dunlop.
Jamaica	26	„ Jonas Rose.			
Arrow	30	„ William Bolton (1)			
Dart	30	„ John Ferris Devonshire.	3	1	Richard Edward Sandys.*
Cruiser	18	Com. James Brisbane			
Harpy	18	„ William Birchall.			
Discovery, bomb	16	„ John Conn.			
Explosion, bomb	8	„ John Henry Martin.			
Hecla, bomb	10	„ Richard Hatherill.			
Sulphur, bomb.	10	„ Hender Whitter.			
Terror, bomb	8	„ Samuel Campbell Rowley.			
Volcano, bomb	8	„ James Watson (1).			
Zebra, bomb	16	„ Edward Sneyd Clay.			
Otter, fireship	14	„ George M'Kinley.			
Zephyr, fireship	14	„ Clotworthy Upton.			

and six gun-brigs, which, however, were unable to get into action, owing to the current. They were in charge of Captain Rose of the *Jamaica*.

[1] *See* opposite.

[3] These and the xebecs had furnaces for heating shot.

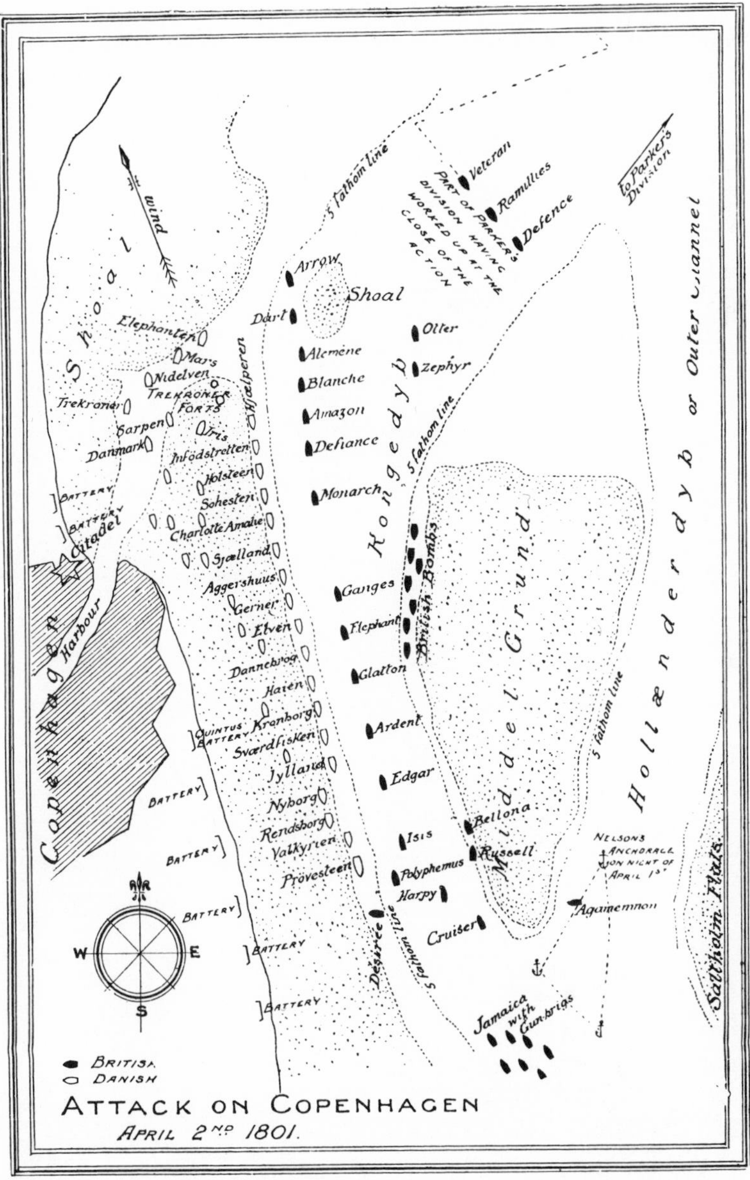
ATTACK ON COPENHAGEN
APRIL 2ND 1801.
Wind
Shoal
Copenhagen
Harbour
Citadel
Trekroner
Elephanten
Mars
Nidelven
TREKRONER FORTS
Hjælperen
Sarpen
Danmark
Iris
Infødstretten
Holsteen
Sohesten
Charlotte Amalie
Sjælland
Aggershuus
Gerner
Elven
Dannebrog
Haien
Kronborg
QUINTUS BATTERY
Sværdfisken
Jylland
Nyborg
Rendsborg
Valkyrien
Provesteen
BATTERY
5 fathom line
Arrow
Dart
Shoal
Alcmene
Blanche
Amazon
Defiance
Monarch
Ganges
Elephant
Glatton
Ardent
Edgar
Isis
Polyphemus
Harpy
Cruiser
Desiree
Bellona
Russell
Otter
Zephyr
British Bombs
Kongedyb
Middel Grund
Veteran
Ramillies
Defence
PART OF PARKER'S DIVISION HAVING WORKED UP AT THE CLOSE OF ACTION
to Parker's Division
Hollænderdyb or Outer Channel
NELSONS ANCHORAGE ON NIGHT OF APRIL 1ST
Agamemnon
Jamaica with Gunbrigs
Saltholm Flats
BRITISH
DANISH
W
E
S

[To face p. 430.

harbour of Copenhagen, lay two other ships of the line, a 40-gun frigate, and two 18-gun brigs; while on the north-west shore of this fairway were other batteries, and, on the shoal to the south-east of it, a number of armed xebecs, other xebecs being distributed to cover some of the intervals in the line of hulks.

On the morning of April 1st the whole British fleet weighed from its anchorage off Hveen, and presently reanchored, about six miles from Copenhagen, off the north-west point of the Middelgrund, the shoal which lies in front of the city, and which divides the Hollænderdyb from the Kongedyb. Nelson went on board the *Amazon*, and again reconnoitred; and at 1 P.M., after his return to the *Elephant*, he signalled to his squadron to weigh, the signal being received with cheers. There remained with the Commander-in-Chief:—

Ships.	Guns.	Commanders.
London	98	Admiral Sir Hyde Parker (2), (B). Capt. William Domett, 1st. " Robert Waller Otway, 2nd.
St. George . . .	98	" Thomas Masterman Hardy.[1]
Warrior	74	" Charles Tyler (1).
Defence	74	" Lord Henry Paulet.
Saturn	74	" Robert Stuart Lambert.
Ramillies . . .	74	" James William Taylor Dixon.
Raisonnable . . .	64	" John Dilkes.
Veteran	64	" Archibald Collingwood Dickson.

[1] Captain Hardy, however, accompanied Nelson in the *Elephant*

[2] Floating defences of Copenhagen, April 2nd, 1801:—

Vessels.	Guns.	Description.	Fate.
1. *Prövesteen* . . .	56	Three-decker, rasé, without masts.	Abandoned, taken, burnt.
2. *Valkyrien* . . .	48	Two-decker, without masts.	" " " "
3. *Rendsborg* . . .	20	Masted cavalry transport.	Driven ashore, taken, burnt.
4. *Nyborg*	20	" " "	Escaped, but sank.
5. *Jylland*	48	Two-decker, without masts.	Taken and burnt.
6. *Sværdfisken* . .	20	Masted floating battery.	" " "
7. *Kronborg* . . .	22	Frigate, without masts.	" " "
8. *Haien*	20	Masted floating battery.	" " "
9. *Dannebrog* . . .	62	Dismantled two-decker.	Took fire, and blew up after action.
10. *Elven*.	6	Sloop, rigged.	Escaped.
11. *Gerner*	24	Battery, without masts.	"
12. *Aggershuus* . . .	20	Cavalry transport, without masts.	Escaped, but sank.
13. *Sjælland*. . . .	74	Two-decker, unrigged.	Driven ashore, taken, burnt.
14. *Charlotte Amalie* .	26	Old Indiaman.	Taken and burnt.
15. *Söhesten*	18	Masted floating battery.	" " "
16. *Holsteen*	60	Rigged line of battleship.	Taken and added to the Navy.
17. *Infödstretten* . .	64	Two-decker, without masts.	Taken and burnt.
18. *Hjælperen* . . .	20	Rigged frigate.	Escaped.
Elephanten . . .	70	Line of battleship, without masts.	
Mars	74	" " " "	
Harbour mouth. *Danmark* . . .	74	Rigged line of battleship.	
Harbour mouth. *Trekroner* . . .	74	" " "	
Harbour mouth. *Iris*	40	Rigged frigate.	
Harbour mouth. *Sarpen*	18	Rigged brig.	
Harbour mouth. *Nidelven* . . .	18	" "	
12 xebecs, each. .	4		

Lord Nelson's squadron, piloted by the *Amazon*, entered the Outer Channel, or Hollænderdyb, and, with a N.W. wind, proceeded along the exterior edge of the Middelgrund, and anchored near the southern point of that shoal at about 8 P.M. In order to draw closer to the town, the ships would have had to beat up against the wind along a narrow and difficult channel; and the Vice-Admiral had, of course, no intention of allowing them to attempt such a perilous adventure in the dark. Indeed, he would have scarcely permitted them to do so had it been day; for not until 11 P.M. that night did he know for certain that the channel was practicable. At that hour he was informed of the fact by Captain Hardy, who, having put off in a small boat, had cautiously and silently ascertained the bearing of the south point of the Middelgrund, and had even satisfied himself, using a pole to avoid the splash accompanying the use of the lead, of the depth of water within a few yards of the *Prövesteen*.[1] Nelson was too preoccupied to sleep, but sat up, arranging the order of battle, and preparing instructions, assisted by Foley and Riou.

At 7 A.M. on April 2nd, the wind then blowing from the S.E. and being therefore favourable for the attack, Nelson signalled for his Captains, each of whom, an hour later, was in possession of all necessary directions.[2] Riou, to whom, besides his own ship, the *Amazon*, were entrusted the *Blanche*, *Alcmène*, *Arrow*, *Dart*, *Otter*, and *Zephyr*, was ordered,[3] in the first place, to co-operate against the northern end of the Danish line and against the vessels lying off the harbour's mouth, and, in the second, to act as circumstances might indicate. Rose, of the *Jamaica*, with the six gun-brigs, was to endeavour to take up a position from which to rake the Danish

[1] Hardy discovered that the water was deeper near the Danish line than on the Middelgrund side; and, had his discovery been acted upon, the *Russell* and *Bellona* would not have grounded when going into action.

[2] Nelson's plans, as disclosed in the orders given out on the morning of April 2nd, indicate that he had an incorrect idea of the number and force of the ships forming the Danish line off Amager Island and south of the Trekroner Forts. He put the number at twenty, instead of at eighteen; and he included in it nine, instead of only six ships of the line. To show how completely these plans were upset by the accidents which occurred, it may be mentioned that the *Polyphemus*, which, in the action, was the most southward ship of the British line, was to have been the most northward; and that the three northern ships of the Danish line, which were to have been engaged by the *Russell* and *Polyphemus*, would have been left entirely without opponents, had not the *Defiance* and *Monarch* proceeded beyond the stations originally assigned to them.

[3] The written order was "to perform such service as he is directed by Lord Nelson."

line from the south. The *Désirée* was to rake the *Valkyrien* and the two ships north of her. The seven bombs were to take station outside the British line, and to throw their shells over it. And it was intended that, upon the fire of the larger of the Trekroner Forts being silenced, the battery should be seized and occupied by the 49th Regiment, and by a party of five hundred seamen under Captain Fremantle. As for the larger vessels, which had already prepared themselves, as before the battle of the Nile, by leading cables out of their stern ports, they were to anchor by the stern abreast of the ships in the enemy's line; and, in proceeding to their stations, ships were to pass their leaders on the starboard hand,[1] it being still supposed, in spite of Hardy's discovery to the contrary, that there was less risk of grounding on that side than on the other. These arrangements, as will be seen, could not all be carried out.

At 9 A.M. Nelson caused the pilots and some of the Masters to visit him; and half an hour later he signalled for his squadron to weigh in succession. The *Edgar* led; and, entering the channel, was fired at as soon as she was within range of the *Prövesteen.* The *Agamemnon* was to have followed, but, having anchored to eastward of the shoal, was unable to weather its southern point, and had, in consequence, to bring up. In the meantime the *Polyphemus* had been signalled to take the *Agamemnon's* place; and, with as much despatch as possible, she followed, although, owing to the *Agamemnon's* misfortune, the *Edgar* remained unsupported for a considerable period. The *Isis* followed the *Polyphemus.* The *Bellona,* next in order, passing the *Isis* on the starboard hand, grounded on the Middelgrund, "owing to the unskilfulness or unsteadiness of her Master, Mr. Alexander Briarly, who had undertaken the office of pilot."[2] The *Russell,* her next astern, took a similar course, and grounded close behind her leader. The *Elephant,* when Nelson perceived what had happened, put her helm a-starboard, and, passing the grounded ships on their port hand, proceeded safely to her station.[3] The remaining heavy vessels, *Defiance, Ganges, Monarch, Ardent,* and *Glatton,* pursuing the same course, also

1 This direction was given in deference to the wishes of the pilots, who were chiefly mates of vessels trading from British northern ports to the Baltic, and who seem to have been very incompetent.—Marshall, ii. 155.

2 James, iii. 71.

3 Abreast of the *Dannebrog,* bearing the broad pennant of Commodore Fischer, who afterwards shifted to the *Holsteen,* and, at about 2 P.M., to one of the Trekroner Forts.

reached without accident points more or less close to the positions assigned to them; but, in consequence of the absence from their posts of the *Agamemnon*, *Bellona*, and *Russell*,[1] some ships found themselves confronted with much more work than it had been intended to burden them with; and, especially at the northern end, where Riou and his little squadron most gallantly opposed the Trekroner Forts, the line was unduly weak. The action began

VICE-ADMIRAL SIR THOMAS BERTIE (FORMERLY HOAR), KT.

(*From an engraving by Page, after the portrait by Lea.*)

at 10.5 A.M.; by 10.30 about half the British squadron was engaged; and before 11.30 the battle became general. The *Désirée* took up a most excellent position athwart the hawse of the *Prövesteen*; but the *Jamaica* and gun-brigs, except one of the latter, were prevented by a strong current from reaching their stations; and the bombs were not able to be of much use.

When Nelson weighed, Parker did likewise, with a view to

[1] The two latter, though aground, were within gunshot, and fired at the defences abreast of them as opportunity offered.

threatening the ships and defences off the harbour's mouth; but, with wind and current against him, his progress was very slow. Not until towards the close of the fight were any of his ships[1] able to approach sufficiently near to become more than a general menace to the enemy.

For three hours the cannonade was furious. At 1 P.M. very few of the Danish guns had been silenced; and, on the other hand, the *Bellona* and *Russell* were flying signals of distress, and the *Agamemnon* was flying a signal of inability. Parker, who was at some distance from the scene of the fighting, could not know all the circumstances of the situation. He had at his elbow a Captain of the Fleet who was exceedingly apprehensive that disaster was very possible, if not imminent and inevitable; and, at that officer's pressing suggestion, he hoisted the signal to discontinue the action—intending it not, however, as a positive order so much as an authority to Nelson to withdraw in case such a measure should appear to him to be advisable. This signal was made at about 1 P.M., and was read by Nelson[2] as Parker intended it to be read, though Nelson did not at the time know that he had acted in accordance with his chief's desires. The Vice-Admiral acknowledged but did not repeat it, and, in the meantime, continued flying his own signal for close action. Graves, in the *Defiance*, repeated it, but hoisted it only at his lee maintopsail yardarm, and kept the signal for close action flying at the maintruck. Riou's division, which had been sorely mauled by the Trekroner batteries, and which was too feeble to make head against them, alone took

[1] The *Defence*, *Ramillies*, and *Veteran* were detached with directions to make special efforts to succour the Vice-Admiral.

[2] "About this time the signal-lieutenant" (of the *Elephant*) "called out that No. 39 (the signal for discontinuing the action) was thrown out by the Commander-in-Chief. He" (Nelson) "continued to walk the deck, and appeared to take no notice of it. The signal-officer met him at the next turn, and asked if he should repeat it. 'No,' he replied; 'acknowledge it.' Presently he called after him to know if the signal for close action was still hoisted; and, being answered in the affirmative, said, 'Mind you keep it so.' He now paced the deck, moving the stump of his lost arm in a manner which always indicated great emotion. 'Do you know,' said he to Mr. Ferguson, 'what is shown on board the Commander-in-Chief? Number 39!' Mr. Ferguson asked him what that meant. 'Why, to leave off action.' Then, shrugging up his shoulders, he repeated the words, 'Leave off action? Now damn me if I do! You know, Foley,' turning to the Captain, 'I have only one eye: I have a right to be blind sometimes;' and then, putting the glass to his blind eye, in that mood of mind which sports with bitterness, he exclaimed, 'I really do not see the signal.' Presently he exclaimed, 'Damn the signal! Keep mine for closer battle flying! That's the way I answer such signals. Nail mine to the mast.'"—Southey, ii. 124.

advantage of the permission thus accorded by the Commander-in-Chief. Had these gallant little ships not done so, they would probably have been destroyed. Unhappily, as the *Amazon* was hauling off, her brave and admirable Captain was cut in two by a round shot.[1] Parker's motive in making the signal was excellent; and the result, in so far as the frigates were concerned, was good; yet it is difficult to avoid the reflection that the signal was even more dangerous than the situation which it was designed to relieve. If, for example, Graves, with his division, had taken advantage of it, and had withdrawn, unconscious, as he well might have been, owing to the smoke, that Nelson, with his division, was merely acknowledging it, the consequences might well have been terrible, and Nelson might have been annihilated. There are few things more risky in naval warfare than for a Commander-in-Chief to issue directions, which are likely to be read as inflexible orders, when he is not on the spot, or when he is not fully cognizant of the situation on the spot.

Half an hour later the Danish fire sensibly diminished, and before 2 P.M. it ceased along the greater part of the southern end of the line, although it was still very warm near the Trekroner Forts, and, especially abreast of the *Monarch* and *Defiance*, it was perhaps hotter than ever. Nelson was undoubtedly uneasy as to the position of those vessels. He was also annoyed by the behaviour of the Danes, who continued to fire even from those craft which had struck,[2] and who would not allow his boats to take possession.[3] He felt that he might destroy some, at least, of the prizes by sending his two fireships against them; but he was anxious to avoid useless expenditure of life; and the destruction of the prizes would not, he knew, relieve the ships at the north end

[1] Edward Riou was a Lieutenant of 1780, a Commander of 1790, and a Captain of 1791. He seems to have been about forty-three years of age at the time of his death. He had won a golden reputation for courage and resource on account of his conduct when in command of the leaky convict transport *Guardian* in 1789–90. *See* p. 106.

[2] The *Dannebrog*, which both had struck and was on fire, behaved in this way to the *Elephant's* boat. Thereupon, the *Elephant* and *Ganges* re-opened their batteries upon her until she drifted off in flames before the wind. At about 3.30 P.M. she blew up.

[3] "This arose from the nature of the action. The crews were continually reinforced from the shore; and fresh men, coming on board, did not inquire whether the flag had been struck, or, perhaps, did not heed it; many, or most of them, never having been engaged in war before, knowing nothing, therefore, of its laws, and thinking only of defending their country to the last extremity."—Southey.

of his line, or enable them and the others to extricate themselves from the narrow channel of the Kongedyb. It was then that, resting on the casing of the rudder-head, he wrote to the Crown Prince of Denmark the following letter:—

"To the Brothers of Englishmen, the brave Danes.

"Vice-Admiral Lord Nelson has been commanded to spare Denmark, when she no longer resists. The line of defence which covered her shores has struck to the British flag. Let the firing cease, then, that he may take possession of his prizes, or he will blow them into the air along with their crews who have so nobly defended them. The brave Danes are the brothers, and should never be the enemies, of the English."[1]

Refusing to fasten up the letter with a wafer, Nelson sent to the cockpit for a candle; and, having obtained wax and one of his own desk seals which was larger than that which he ordinarily used, he sealed the letter, remarking: "This is no time to appear hurried and informal."

The letter was carried in, under a flag of truce, by Commander Sir Frederick Thesiger, who was acting as an aide-de-camp to Lord Nelson, and who found the Crown Prince near the sally-port. In Thesiger's absence, the fire of the *Holsteen*, *Infödstretten*, and *Hjælperen* ceased, partly owing to the effect of the broadsides of the *Monarch* and *Defiance*, and partly, perhaps, owing to the approach to the scene of action of the *Defence* and *Ramillies*, which had for some time been working up against the wind from Parker's division. But the Trekroner Forts, and particularly the larger of them, which had been reinforced, and which were still almost uninjured, fought nearly as freshly as ever, and were, moreover, considered to be too strong to be stormed. Nelson believed that it was his duty to take advantage of the continuation of a favourable wind to concentrate his ships upon the Trekroner batteries, and reduce them; but Fremantle and Foley dissuaded him from attempting this, and suggested that it would be wiser to endeavour to extricate the squadron from its critical situation while the breeze still served. Preparations to this end had been begun when Thesiger returned, bringing with him Lindholm, the Danish adjutant-general. Upon seeing his flag of truce, the Trekroner Forts ceased firing; and the action was not again renewed. It was then after 3 P.M.

The Crown Prince, through Lindholm, desired to know the

[1] Several versions of this letter exist. The one here given is taken from a copy which was, in 1820, in the possession of Sir Thomas Foley. All the versions, however, though differing verbally, are much to the same effect. The original letter appears to have been translated into Danish by Thesiger.

immediate object of the Vice-Admiral's letter. Nelson sent back Thesiger with a reply in writing to the effect that his object was humanity, and that he proposed to put an end to hostilities upon conditions that the wounded Danes should be removed to the shore, and that he should remove his unwounded prisoners from the prizes, and burn or carry away the captured vessels as he might deem best. He ended his second letter with the expression of a hope that his victory would lead to a reconciliation. And while he despatched Thesiger with the letter to the Crown Prince, he referred General Lindholm to Sir Hyde Parker, who was four miles away, and who alone could make any definite arrangement. Nelson thus gained time.

He at once signalled for his ships to weigh or slip, and proceed. They did so; but the *Monarch* almost immediately grounded. She was, however, shoved off again by the *Ganges*. The *Glatton* passed out in safety. The *Defiance* and *Elephant*, ships of deeper draught, piled up on the shoal about a mile from the Trekroner Forts, and, but for the armistice, would have been in a most dangerous position. The *Elephant* could not be moved until 8; the *Defiance* remained hard and fast until 10 P.M. At the other end of the line, the *Désirée*, having gone to the assistance of the *Bellona*, grounded near her. The *Bellona*, in the meantime, got free by sending a boat, picking up the cable of the *Isis* when that ship slipped, and hauling off by it.

Nelson had intended to rejoin the Commander-in-Chief in the *Elephant*; but when that ship grounded, and it seemed likely that she would not immediately float again, he followed Lindholm in a boat to the *London*. Soon after he had reached the flagship, a twenty-four hours' truce was concluded, in order to allow of further negotiations; and it was arranged that the British should take possession of the prizes. Lindholm then returned to Copenhagen, and Nelson went on board his permanent flagship, the *St. George*.

The losses in the British ships engaged are set forth in the note on page 430. The figures there given are taken from the official returns, which, however, did not include a certain number of slightly wounded. James considers that, had these been taken into account, the number of killed and wounded in the fleet would have had to be put at upwards of one thousand two hundred instead of at less than nine hundred and fifty. The killed and mortally wounded, he believes, numbered three hundred and fifty, many of the seriously wounded having eventually succumbed.[1] The British naval officers

[1] James, iii. 76.

killed were: Captains James Robert Mosse (*Monarch*), and Edward Riou (*Amazon*); Lieuts. Edmund Johnson (*Edgar*), George Gray (*Defiance*), and Richard Edward Sandys (*Dart*); Masters Daniel Lamond (*Isis*), and Robert Stewart (*Ganges*); Master's Mate Henry Yaulden (*Elephant*); Midshipmen James Bell (*Polyphemus*), George M'Kinley and Thomas Ram (*Isis*), the Hon. George Tucket (*Amazon*), and George Hoare (*Ardent*); and Captain's Clerk Joseph Rose (*Amazon*). In addition, there fell Lieutenants of Marines Benjamin Spencer (*Edgar*), and Henry Long (*Isis*), besides a captain and a lieutenant of foot, and two pilots. Among the officers wounded were Captain Sir Thomas Boulden Thompson (*Bellona*); and Lieuts. Andrew King (*Désirée*), Thomas Southey and Thomas Wilks (*Bellona*), Richard Cormack (*Isis*), Joshua Johnson and William Goldfinch (*Edgar*), William Tindall (*Glatton*), William Minchin (*Monarch*), and Henry Baker (*Alcmène*).

Most of the British ships were badly hit about the hull, and lower rigging, the Danes having fired low. The *Glatton* was the only vessel that lost a topmast. Numerous guns were disabled, some by the enemy's shot, some by their own recoil, and, in the *Bellona* and *Isis*, some by bursting. There is no doubt that the cast-iron guns of the period, after long use, became very dangerous, owing to changes which occur in the structure of masses of metal subjected to frequent violent shocks; and it is probable that the guns which burst, burst solely on account of their age, both the *Bellona* and *Isis* being old ships.

More than half of the Danish craft which had formed the line along the shore of Amager Island were practically destroyed by the British fire. They were reduced, that is, to a condition of absolute uselessness. According to British accounts, the gallant enemy lost in killed, wounded, and prisoners, about 6000 men. Commodore Fischer estimated the number of killed and wounded, including 270 lost in the *Dannebrog* when she blew up, at not fewer than between 1600 and 1800. The fate of the Danish vessels is shown in the table on page 431. The defence had been most spirited and desperate; and the extraordinary bravery of two officers is to this day commemorated in the Danish navy, where there are still craft bearing the names *Hauch*[1] and *Willemoes*.[2]

[1] Hauch commanded the *Kronborg* and fell during the action.

[2] Willemoes was a boy of seventeen, who had pushed off from the shore on a kind of raft carrying six small guns, and manned by twenty-four men, and had placed

In comparing the strength of the forces engaged, James,[1] curiously enough, omits from his computation the Trekroner Forts, and Riou's flotilla, which was opposed to them. It does not seem to be fair to do this, seeing, especially, that the forts, though hotly engaged, were never reduced, and that, towards the end of the action, they greatly annoyed the *Defiance*. He also leaves out the *Bellona* and *Russell*, though he admits that their fire was not wholly ineffective. Including, on the one hand, Riou's flotilla and the *Bellona*[2] and *Russell*, and, on the other, the Trekroner Forts, we get a total of about 1014 guns and carronades on the British, and 696 guns,—there do not seem to have been any carronades,—on the Danish side. James, by his deductions, makes the totals much more nearly equal, viz., British, 700; Danish, 628.

During the night following the battle, the British got off all their grounded ships, except the *Désirée*, and brought out such of the prizes as could be moved. In the succeeding six days, while negotiations were going on, all the prizes, except the *Holsteen*, were destroyed. On the 9th, an armistice for fourteen weeks was agreed upon, it being arranged that in the meanwhile Denmark would take no action under the treaty of armed neutrality, and that the British might obtain from the shore water, food, and supplies. The prisoners were returned upon the understanding that they would still be held good for exchange in case hostilities should be renewed. Sir Hyde sent home the *Monarch* and *Isis*, with the *Holsteen* and most of his wounded; and on April 12th he left the roadstead with all the rest of his command except the *St. George* and one or two small craft, his next object being to intimidate the Swedes and Russians.[3]

He entered the Baltic by the difficult passage of the Hollænderdyb and Drogden, between the islands of Amager and Saltholm, although, ere he could do so, his heavier ships had to hoist out many of their guns, put them into merchantmen, and, after getting

---

himself close under the stern of the *Elephant*. The ship's guns could not reach him; but her Marines killed or wounded twenty of his people. Willemoes died fighting in the *Prinds Christian Frederik*, on the occasion of her capture by the *Stately* and *Nassau*, Mar. 22nd, 1808.

[1] James, iii. 79 (ed. 1837).

[2] She was near enough to lose eighty-three killed and wounded.

[3] Nelson was very annoyed that so much time had been spent in negotiation, after the power of Denmark had been crippled. Had he been in command, he would have hurried at once to Reval, as he wrote to Lord St. Vincent.

over the shallows, hoist them in again; and although, in spite of these precautions, several vessels were unable to avoid grounding. The Russian fleet lay at Reval, still frost-bound;[1] the Swedish squadron was at or near Karlskrona; and Parker was anxious to attack the former, ere it could join the latter. On his way to Reval, however, he learnt that the Swedes were at sea; and, sending on the news to Nelson, who was still detained off Amager in the *St. George*, he made for the northern point of Bornholm.

On April 19th, in the evening, Nelson received the news; but the wind and current were contrary, and the *St. George*, though at length she had crossed the shoals, could have made but little progress against them. The Vice-Admiral, therefore, scenting a possibility of battle, instantly embarked in a six-oared cutter, and, without

MEDAL COMMEMORATIVE OF THE BATTLE OF COPENHAGEN, 1801.

(From an original lent by H.S.H. Capt. Prince Louis of Battenberg, R.N.)

waiting even for a boat-cloak, set off to join the Commander-in-Chief, who was twenty-four miles away. Mr. Alexander Briarly,[2] Master of the *Bellona*, who had been assisting the *St. George* in her passage over the grounds, and who, by order, accompanied Nelson, has left an interesting account of the long night row, and of Nelson's extraordinary keenness on the occasion:—

"All I had ever seen or heard of him could not half so clearly prove to me the singular and unbounded zeal of this truly great man. His anxiety in the boat for nearly six hours lest the fleet should have sailed before he got on board one of them, and lest we should not catch the Swedish squadron, is beyond all conception. I will quote some expressions in his own words. It was extremely cold, and I wished him to put on a great-coat of mine which was in the boat. 'No, I am not cold; my anxiety for my country will keep me warm. Do you think the fleet has sailed?' 'I should suppose not, my Lord.' 'If they have, we will follow them to Karlskrona in the boat, by God!'"

[1] It was not, in fact, free from field-ice that year until April 29th.

[2] A Master of 1795.

Karlskrona was one hundred and fifty miles away. Happily the fleet had not left Bornholm; and at midnight Nelson was safely on board the *Elephant*. But already the Swedes[1] had retired to Karlskrona. Thither Parker followed them; and, after negotiation, it was agreed, on April 22nd, that the differences between Great Britain and Sweden should be settled amicably.

The Tsar Paul, of Russia, had been murdered on March 23rd, and had been succeeded by Alexander I. The British fleet was on its way from Karlskrona to Reval, when, on April 23rd, Parker received from the Russian ambassador at Copenhagen dispatches indicating that the policy of the new monarch was more pacific than that of the old had been. The Commander-in-Chief returned, therefore, to Kjöge Bay, where he found the *St. George*, and where, on May 5th, he was apprised of his recall to England.[2] When he sailed for home in the *Blanche*, the command of the fleet devolved upon Nelson.

Nelson does not appear to have had such implicit confidence as Parker in the amiable intentions of Russia. He thought, at least, that the presence of a British force could do no harm in the Gulf of Finland; and on the 7th he weighed. On the 8th, he left Captain George Murray (3) to watch Karlskrona with the *Edgar*, *Saturn*, *Russell*, *Raisonnable*, *Agamemnon*, *Glatton*, and a frigate, and sent in word to the Swedish vice-admiral that, though Swedish trade would not be annoyed, the Swedish squadron, if it put to sea, would be treated as the fleet of an enemy. With the remaining eleven sail of the line, a frigate and two sloops, Nelson proceeded for Reval, off which place he anchored on May 14th, only to find that the Russians had departed on the 3rd for Cronstadt. The authorities were alarmed at his arrival, and he was officially informed that, if his intentions were friendly, he would best demonstrate the fact by withdrawing. Lest, therefore, he should prejudice the negotiations which were going on elsewhere, he left the road on the 17th; and, two days later, Russia and Sweden removed the embargo which had been laid on British vessels in their ports. Friendly relations were thus restored.

Nelson was back at Kjöge Bay on June 6th; and on June 13th,

[1] Their fleet included only six ships of the line; and it was, therefore, obliged to retire before Parker's.

[2] Nelson had already petitioned for his own recall. The First Lord, St. Vincent, probably influenced by the wish to keep Nelson away from Lady Hamilton, recalled Parker chiefly in order to induce Nelson to remain for a time.

in reply to his repeated requests to be relieved on the score of his indifferent health, he received permission to return to England. Four days afterwards Vice-Admiral Sir Charles Morice Pole,[1] in the *Æolus*, 32, appeared to take over the command; and on the 19th Nelson left for home in the *Kite*, 18.

The rewards for the victory of Copenhagen were grudgingly bestowed. The Admirals, Captains, officers, and men of Parker's

VICE-ADMIRAL VISCOUNT NELSON, DUKE OF BRONTE, K.B.

(*From a lithograph by P. Roberts, after the portrait painted by J. F. Abbot, when Nelson was a Rear-Admiral, soon after the Battle of the Nile.*)

fleet received, indeed, the thanks of both Houses; Nelson was given the title of Viscount; and Graves was made a K.B. Some promotions, also, were made among the officers of subordinate rank. But the gold Flag-officers' and Captains' medals, which had, by that time, come to be looked upon as the most honourable pay-

[1] Pole remained on the station till the end of July, when, there being no longer need of a large fleet in the Baltic, he was ordered home. He distinguished himself during his command by taking the fleet through the difficult passage of the Great Belt against a nearly head wind.

ment for great services, were not granted; and the City of London did not formally recognise the value of the work which had been done for British commerce. The prize-money, moreover, was of small account, so many of the prizes having been destroyed, and no special allowance being made in respect of them.

Nelson's health had suffered in consequence of his exposure in the *St. George's* boat; but he was not allowed a month for its re-establishment. He landed at Yarmouth on July 1st; he was reappointed to a command on July 24th; and he rehoisted his flag on July 30th, on a service which, perhaps, was unworthy of his exceptional powers, and might have been as well performed by an officer of more ordinary abilities, yet which, nevertheless, demanded at its head a man in whom the country placed unquestioning confidence. For the people of the United Kingdom, half starved, and overburdened with the taxes and the trials of the long war, believed that at length a serious and mighty attempt was about to be made to invade them, and so to end the exhausting struggle. Nelson's acceptance, in such circumstances, of the command in the Downs would, it was felt, put an immediate check upon the rising panic. That, no doubt, was the main motive for his appointment. There was, however, another motive. At the Admiralty were two of his truest friends, St. Vincent and Troubridge. They knew that, in spite of the changes and chances of life at sea, Nelson's glorious reputation was safer there than at home.

The conclusion of the Treaty of Lunéville, by putting a period to the active hostility of Germany, gave Bonaparte an opportunity of turning more of his attention than ever towards Great Britain. It has been seen that France had long since made extensive preparations for an invasion. During the year 1800, however, the preparations had been suspended. Great Britain, indeed, had for some time ceased to be pressingly anxious on the subject, when, on July 12th, 1801, the First Consul ordered a concentration at Boulogne of nine divisions of gun-vessels, of a large mass of troops, and of several detachments of artillerymen. Rear-Admiral La Touche Tréville,[1] one of the best naval officers of France, was

[1] René Madeleine Le Vassor de La Touche Tréville: born 1745; entered the navy; left it for the cavalry, 1768; returned to the navy; commanded a frigate during the American war; imprisoned and degraded as a Royalist, 1793; restored as a rear-admiral by Bonaparte, and given command first at Brest and then at Boulogne; vice-admiral, 1801; died in command of the Toulon fleet, 1804. But for his death, he would have commanded at Trafalgar.

given the command of the flotilla; and he at once began to train his men in embarking and disembarking, in weighing and anchoring, in working the vessels, and in using the guns.

It was then that, among other measures designed to calm the public mind, Nelson was appointed to command the defences of the coast from Orford Ness to Beachy Head. He hoisted his flag in the *Medusa*, 32, Captain John Gore (2), at anchor in the Downs; and on August 3rd, in consequence of directions from the Admiralty, crossed to Boulogne to endeavour to destroy the flotilla which was assembled under the guns of the lately strengthened fortifications of the place. He had with him thirty craft, chiefly gun-vessels and bombs. The latter on the 4th shelled part of the French flotilla, consisting of twenty-four armed vessels, and, according to an order which was issued by Nelson on the 5th, entirely disabled ten of them. The British dispatches, however, leave it to be inferred that only three flats and a brig were permanently disabled; and the French official account, while it does not expressly state that no other material harm was done, says that two gunboats which had been damaged were at once refitted for service, and that no Frenchman was either killed or wounded. On the British side three persons were wounded. It was evident—for the bombs had expended more than nine hundred shells—that, if effective damage was to be done, other means must be employed. Nelson, therefore, determined to try the effect of a cutting-out expedition on a large scale.

He organised the armed boats of the squadron into four divisions, commanded respectively by Commander Philip Somerville (1), Commander Edward Thornbrough Parker, Commander Isaac Cotgrave, and Commander Richard Jones (1), and, on the night of August 15th, sent them in accompanied by a division of howitzer boats under Commander John Conn. The boats, having assembled round the *Medusa*, put off from her at about 11.30 P.M.; but, owing to the darkness, the tide, and the currents, the divisions soon became separated, and could not, in consequence, co-operate according to the pre-arranged plans. The boats of Somerville's division, driven far to the eastward, had to quit one another and proceed independently. Just before dawn on the 16th, some of these succeeded in reaching and attacking a brig which lay close to the pier-head; but, though they carried her, they were forced to abandon her, as she was secured by a chain which they could not sever, and was swept by the fire of four craft moored quite close to her. As daylight broke, Somerville's division retreated, with a loss of 18 killed and 55 wounded.[1]

Parker's division, the second, was less impeded by the current, and, at about 12.30, part of it ran alongside the brig *Etna*. But boarding nettings and a heavy fire forced the men back. Another part carried a lugger, but was repulsed by the brig *Volcan*; and the two sub-divisions retired with a loss of 21 killed and 42 wounded.[2]

Cotgrave's division, the third, was also driven back after it had fought most gallantly and had lost 5 killed and 29 wounded.[3] The fourth division, unable to get near the enemy before day broke, put back without loss. Commander Edward Thornbrough Parker, a promising officer of only twenty-two, who had greatly endeared himself to Nelson, and who had been acting as his aide-de-camp, died of his wounds at Deal on September 27th.

The French, who had been reinforced since August 4th, claimed to have run down eight British boats and to have taken four, and to have lost only 10 killed and 30 wounded.[4] Whether they did so much damage may be doubted; but it is certain that the affair must be counted as a British defeat, and, having regard to the total loss, 44 killed and 126 wounded, as a sanguinary one. Both Nelson, however, and St. Vincent, handsomely recognised that officers and men had behaved most gallantly.

No other attack on a large scale was attempted against the invasion flotilla; but on the night of August 20th, the boats of a small squadron detached under Captain Jonas Rose, of the *Jamaica*, 24, attacked six French flats, which lay covered by five field-pieces and a party of infantry between St. Valery and Etaples. Three were taken and brought off, and the other three were scuttled by their crews. Each mounted an 8-inch brass howitzer. The British loss was only 1 killed and 4 wounded.

Towards the end of 1800 Bonaparte had satisfied himself that the large British force which, in October, had appeared under

[1] Officer killed: Master's Mate Alexander Rutherford (*Jamaica*). Among the wounded were Lieuts. Thomas Oliver and Francis Dickinson (*Leyden*), Jeremiah Skelton (*Jamaica*), and William Basset (actg.) (*Eugénie*), and Captain of Marines, George Young (*Leyden*).

[2] Officers killed: Midshipmen William Gore and William Bristow (*Medusa*). Among the wounded were Com. E. T. Parker (mortally); and Lieuts. Charles Pelly and Frederick Langford (*Medusa*).

[3] Officer killed: Midshipman —— Berry

[4] Tréville to Min. of Mar., Aug. 16th.

Lord Keith before Cadiz, was to be despatched to Egypt, and that strong measures were at length to be adopted to expel the French from that country. During 1800 he had been unsuccessful in several attempts, all made on a small scale, to send stores and reinforcements to his army in the delta of the Nile; but, as the situation of the expeditionary force became more and more perilous, he decided that a serious effort must be made to succour it. At Toulon he had no squadron equal to the task. The flower of the French navy was concentrated at Brest. He therefore ordered Rear-Admiral Ganteaume to leave Brest with the ships set forth in the note,[1] and with 5000 troops under General Sahuguet, and to endeavour to reach the Levant; and he announced at the same time that the reinforcement was intended for San Domingo.

Ganteaume quitted Brest and anchored in Bertheaume road on January 7th, 1801. At about the same time, in order to distract and confuse the attention of the officers in charge of the blockade along the coast, such French vessels as lay in the other ports of the Channel and the Bay of Biscay either put to sea or made obtrusive preparations for doing so. On the 8th Ganteaume weighed and stood out by the Passage du Raz; but he was at once observed and chased by Vice-Admiral Sir Henry Harvey (1), K.B., and a division of the Channel Fleet; and he found it prudent, soon afterwards, to anchor off the mouth of the Vilaine, whence he presently returned to Brest, where he lay to await a gale which would drive the British from their station.

On January 23rd it blew heavily from the northward; and, at night, Ganteaume again put to sea, going out by the Iroise Channel. The weather was so bad that no British cruisers were there to

[1] Ships.	Guns.	Commanders.
Indivisible . . .	80	Rear-Adm. Honoré Ganteaume. Capt. A. L. Gourdon.
Indomptable . . .	80	Commod. Moncousu.
Formidable . . .	80	Rear-Adm. Comte de Linois. Capt. J. Allary.
Desaix	74	Commod. J. A. C. Christi-Paillière.
Dix Août[1] . . .	74	Capt. J. Bergeret.
Constitution . . .	74	" G. A. Faure.
Jean Bart . . .	74	" F. J. Meynne.
Créole	40	" P. P. Gourrège.
Bravoure. . . .	40	" L. A. Dordelin, junr.
Vautour, lugger . .	12	Lieut. Vimel.

[1] Ex *Tyrannicide*.

sight him. It was also so bad that, besides depriving two or three of his ships of their topmasts, it separated the *Indivisible* and *Créole* from their consorts, though not until a rendezvous for the squadron had been ordered first off Cape Spartel, and next off Cape de Gata. The remaining ships were sighted at 9 P.M. on January 27th, off Cape Finisterre, by the *Concorde*, 36, Captain Robert Barton. The *Bravoure* proceeded in chase of the British frigate, which, when about six miles from the French squadron, hove to, and awaited the enemy. The action which resulted was indecisive, but would probably have been otherwise but for the proximity of the French ships to windward. The *Concorde* lost 4 killed and 19 (one mortally) wounded, and the *Bravoure*, 10 killed and 24 wounded. The latter rejoined her friends, and, proceeding with them, found Ganteaume, off Cape Spartel, on January 30th. Ganteaume, on the previous day, had taken and scuttled the fireship *Incendiary*, 16, Commander Richard Dalling Dunn. The French passed through the Strait of Gibraltar under a press of sail on February 9th. Keith, as will be shown later, had already departed thence for the eastward, and the only vessel in port ready for sea was the *Success*, 32, Captain Shuldham Peard. Peard weighed very promptly, and made after the enemy, confident that he was bound for Egypt, and hoping to pass him, and to warn Keith. On the 10th Ganteaume took and scuttled the cutter *Sprightly*, 12, Lieutenant Robert Jump. During the following night the *Success* passed the French; but in the morning she was in full sight of them; nor could she, owing to the light and variable winds, get away from them on the 11th and 12th. On the night of the 12th, a fresh southerly breeze seemed to promise attainment to Peard's wishes; yet, on the morning of the 13th, the enemy was so close that escape from him was clearly impossible. The *Success*, therefore, to delay her pursuers, put back to the westward; and at 3 P.M., after some of the two-deckers had opened fire upon her, she struck her flag.[1]

His prisoners informed Ganteaume that Keith was already on the coast of Egypt,[2] and that a squadron under Sir John Borlase Warren[3] was probably close at his heels. This news induced him to make for Toulon, where he anchored on February 19th, and where the first part of his adventurous cruise ended.

[1] She was retaken by the *Pomone* and consorts on Sept. 2nd following.

[2] This, as will be seen, was incorrect. Keith was still on the coast of Asia Minor.

[3] Which had been stationed off Cadiz.

In the meantime, the *Concorde*, 36, Captain Robert Barton, had made the best of her way to England with the intelligence of Ganteaume's escape, and had reached Plymouth on February 3rd. The view there and at the Admiralty was that the French were bound to the West Indies; and to the West Indies, in consequence, Rear-Admiral Sir Robert Calder was detached from the Channel Fleet in pursuit, with the *Prince of Wales*, 98 (flag), *Juste*, 80, *Pompée*, 80, *Courageux*, 74, *Cumberland*, 74, *Montagu*,[1] 74, *Spencer*, 74, *Magicienne*, 32, *Thames*, 32, and a brig. It was scarcely a force suited for the occasion; for the flagship was notoriously slow.

> "Nothing," says James, "can afford a stronger proof of the national confidence, as well as fairness, in naval warfare, than the sending in pursuit of an enemy's squadron a British squadron of the same numerical force; but we cannot help asking, what was the use of selecting six of the fastest two-deckers from the Channel Fleet, when the flag-officer in command of them was to take his passage in a three-decker?"

But, since Calder was sent in chase of a phantom, he had the more comfortable cruise out and home again.

If, instead of making for Toulon, Ganteaume had waited for Warren, the French might have won a victory; for Warren was of inferior force. He was cruising off Cadiz on February 8th, when he learnt that Ganteaume was in the neighbourhood; and he at once headed for Gibraltar with his whole division, which consisted of the *Renown*, 74 (flag), Captain John Chambers White; *Gibraltar*, 80, Captain William Hancock Kelly; *Dragon*, 74, Captain John Aylmer (1); *Généreux*, 74, Captain Manley Dixon; *Hector*, 74, Captain John Elphinstone (2); *Haarlem*, 64 (but with only part of her lower battery on board), Captain George Burlton; *Mercury*, 28, Captain Thomas Rogers; *Champion*, 20, Captain Lord William Stuart; and *Salamine*, 18, Commander Thomas Briggs. Reaching the Rock early on the 10th, he heard that the French were ahead of him. He was not able to leave Gibraltar till the 13th, when he steered for Minorca, having detached frigates to reconnoitre Cartagena and Toulon. From the 20th to the 24th he lay refitting at Port Mahon; from the 24th to the 27th he cruised in the vicinity; and on the 27th, having suffered in a gale of wind, he put back. On March 4th, he sailed again, leaving at Mahon the *Généreux* and *Salamine*, as some protection against a Franco-Spanish attack. On the 7th, he learnt that King Ferdinand

[1] Put into Lisbon disabled.

of Naples had concluded an armistice with General Murat; and, in order to look to British interests in Sicily, he laid his course for Palermo; but, having been joined, on the 18th, by the *Athénien*, 64, Captain Sir Thomas Livingstone, and on the 22nd, by the *Alexander*, 74, Captain Alexander John Ball, both from Malta, he stood back in the direction of Toulon. On the 25th, however, the *Salamine*, detached by Captain Manley Dixon, brought news to the Rear-Admiral that Ganteaume,[1] with seven sail of the line, three frigates, and three merchantmen, had again left Toulon on March 15th, making apparently for Egypt. The French, as afterwards appeared, experienced a heavy gale on the night of their departure from port, and had to send back one of their line-of-battle ships. They also lost company with one of their merchantmen, which was afterwards taken by the *Minerve*, 42, Captain George Cockburn. At daybreak on the 25th, they were sighted by Warren's squadron off the eastern coast of Sardinia, and were chased; but the bad sailing of the *Gibraltar* and *Athénien* delayed the pursuit, and caused the British to lose sight of the enemy; and, while Sir John hurried off to the south-east, Ganteaume once more made for Toulon, where he anchored on April 5th.

Bonaparte was not satisfied that the rear-admiral had done all that was possible to reach Egypt, and ordered him to make yet another attempt. Ganteaume accordingly sailed once more on April 27th, having, in addition to his original squadron, another frigate, the *Muiron*, 40, a corvette, and two storeships. He had directions to take measures, while on his way, for the reduction of Porto Ferrajo, in Elba. In pursuance of that part of his mission, he put into Leghorn, whence he ultimately sent back to Toulon the *Formidable*, *Indomptable*, *Desaix*, and *Muiron*, which he considered to be too short-handed to proceed on the voyage. Before following Ganteaume, it will be well to relate what happened in Elba.

Porto Ferrajo was invested from the first week in May by about 1500 French troops who had been carried across from Piombino on the 2nd of the month; and it was subsequently blockaded by the French frigates *Carrère*, 40, *Bravoure*, 40, and *Succès* (late British *Success*), 32. The garrison, chiefly Tuscan, but assisted

[1] His orders were, in case he should find the coast of Egypt blockaded by superior forces, to land his troops anywhere between Tripoli and Cape "Razat" (Qy. Ras el Mella), that they might reach their destination by way of the desert. The carrying out of this plan "would have condemned five thousand Frenchmen to death by famine."—Mathieu Dumas, vii.

by a small British contingent,[1] held the place with determination, in spite of the fact that, late in July, General Watrin brought over 5000 additional troops from the mainland, and assumed command of the siege. On August 1st, two of the French frigates were chased from off the island,[2] and the blockade was raised by the squadron of Sir John Borlase Warren; and on the 3rd, the *Phœnix*, 36, Captain Lawrence William Halsted, *Pomone*, 40, Captain Edward Leveson Gower, and *Pearl*, 32, Captain Samuel James Ballard, while cruising on the west side of Elba, fell in with the remaining frigate, the *Carrère*, which was on her passage from Porto Ercole to Porto Longone with three hundred barrels of powder; and the *Pomone*, after an action of ten minutes, took her. The *Pomone's* loss was only two killed and four wounded. The *Carrère* is said to have lost much more heavily. Unfortunately, the whole of a small convoy which she had with her escaped.

At the end of the month, learning that the *Phœnix* was at anchor alone off Piombino, General Watrin sent orders to the *Succès* and *Bravoure* to endeavour to capture her. Those frigates put to sea on August 31st, but, early on September 2nd, as they were nearing the *Phœnix*, which, in the meantime, had been rejoined by the *Pomone*, they were chased by the *Minerve*, 42, Captain George Cockburn. Cockburn made the signal for an enemy to Halsted and Gower, who at once weighed, and bore up in chase under all sail. At 10.30 A.M., perceiving that she was dropping astern, the *Succès*, Captain J. F. I. Bretel, ran herself ashore, and, being fired at in passing by the *Minerve*, struck without returning a shot. The *Pomone* took possession of her, while the *Minerve* stood on after the *Bravoure*, which finally, baffled by a shift of wind, missed stays and grounded under a battery about four miles south of Leghorn. There her masts presently went by the board and she became a total loss. Lieutenant William Kelly (2),[3] of the *Minerve*, boarded her, but was able to bring away only very few prisoners. Lieutenant Charles Thompson (2), of the *Phœnix*, succeeded in floating the *Succès*, and she was restored to the Royal Navy. These affairs cost no loss of British life.

In September, the little garrison of Porto Ferrajo was tem-

[1] Commanded at one time by Capt. Gordon, and later by Lieut.-Col. George Airey.

[2] The *Bravoure* and *Succès* took refuge in Leghorn.

[3] *Gazette*, 1801, 1355.

porarily reinforced by a detachment of seamen and Marines from the squadron[1] of Sir John Borlase Warren, who reappeared off the port on the 12th. Before dawn on the 14th, after the *Dragon* and *Généreux* had on the previous day made a diversion, these seamen and Marines, 689 in number, disembarked under Commander George Long, of the *Vincejo*, and, with about 1000 Tuscans, the whole under the direction of Captain John Chambers White, of the *Renown*, carried and destroyed several French batteries, and took a number of prisoners, but were at last compelled to retire with a loss of 32 killed, 61 wounded, and 105 missing. The naval casualties alone amounted to 15 killed, 38 wounded, and 77 missing; and among the killed was Commander Long. In spite of this partial success, and although Warren had to quit the island with his squadron on September 22nd, General Watrin failed to reduce the place; and Lieut.-Colonel Airey contrived to hold it, until its fate was determined by Art. XI. of the Treaty of Amiens.

Ganteaume left Leghorn in the middle of May with the *Indivisible*, 80, *Dix Août*, 74, *Constitution*, 74, *Jean Bart*, 74, *Créole*, 40, *Héliopolis* (corvette), and four storeships, and passed the Strait of Messina on the 25th. Having waited for a time off Brindisi, where he expected to be joined by some Neapolitan frigates, he proceeded for Egypt, and, on June 5th, chased, but failed to get up with, the *Pique*, 36, Captain James Young (2). On the 7th, when he was about two hundred miles westward of Alexandria, he detached the *Héliopolis* to ascertain the whereabouts of the blockading fleet; and on the 9th, the corvette, after having been chased by the *Kent*, 74, *Hector*, 74, and *Cruelle*, cutter, had to take refuge in Alexandria, instead of rejoining. Keith had been opportunely warned, on the evening of the 7th, by the *Pique*, of the approach of the French, and had made sail to the westward in search of them.

As the *Héliopolis* did not return to him, Ganteaume concluded that she had been captured, and that, a hostile fleet being off Alexandria, he would not be able to land his troops in that neighbourhood. He therefore made up his mind to attempt a disembarkation at Bengasi, a small town on the coast of Barca. But scarcely had he anchored off the place ere some British ships were sighted to the eastward; and, as the inhabitants were hostile, he relinquished his design, cut his cables, and made all sail to escape, abandoning,

[1] *Renown*, *Gibraltar*, *Dragon*, *Alexander*, *Généreux*, *Stately*, *Pomone*, *Pearl*, and *Vincejo*.

however, two of his storeships, which were taken by the *Vestal*, 28 (*en flûte*), Commander Valentine Collard, and consorts.

Ganteaume fled to the westward, and at 3.30 A.M. on June 24th, being off the coast of Barbary, and the wind being N.W., he was sighted by the *Swiftsure*, 74, Captain Benjamin Hallowell, which was on her way to join Sir John Borlase Warren off Malta.[1] Hallowell, having heard that Ganteaume was on the coast, felt sure that the strangers were enemies, and did his best to get away from them; but the French outsailed him,[2] and by 2 P.M. the *Indivisible*, *Dix Août*, and *Créole* were almost within gunshot. Noticing that the other ships, though fast coming up, were separated from their consorts, Hallowell decided to bear down upon the three nearest, try to disable them before the rest could interfere, and then endeavour to escape to leeward. At 3 P.M., therefore, he bore down under all sail, and, the French tacking and standing towards him, the *Indivisible* and *Dix Août* opened their fire at about 3.30. So superior were the sailing and handiness of the enemy's ships, that the *Swiftsure* was foiled in all her efforts to get to leeward of them. She fought them, nevertheless, until 4.37 P.M., when, the *Jean Bart* and *Constitution* having also arrived within gunshot, and continued resistance signifying merely useless expenditure of life, she surrendered.[3] The chief aim of her opponents had been to disable her aloft. Although, therefore, her masts, yards, and rigging had suffered severely, she had lost only two killed, and eight (two mortally) wounded. The French, on the other hand, lost, according to Ganteaume's return, in killed and wounded thirty-nine. On July 22nd the captors, without further adventure, carried their prize into Toulon.[4] Hallowell was tried on board the *Généreux* at Port Mahon for having quitted his convoy and lost his ship; and he and his officers and men were, of course, honourably acquitted, it being decided that in leaving the convoy he had acted with judgment and zeal, and that he had defended the *Swiftsure* with equal gallantry and ability.[5]

Ganteaume certainly displayed, during these three sorties from port, a certain kind of cleverness in evading his numerous foes. His

[1] She had been despatched from Aboukir to Malta with a convoy, but, learning of Ganteaume's proximity, had left the convoy, and hurried on to join Warren, who, Hallowell feared, might be surprised.

[2] The *Swiftsure* at the time was both foul and leaky.—Marshall, i. 479.

[3] She was retaken at Trafalgar.

[4] In this cruise Ganteaume had with him Jérôme Bonaparte, the youngest brother of the First Consul.

[5] C.M., Aug. 18th, 1801.

lack of boldness, and his anxiety to hide himself rather than fight have, however, excited the unfavourable comments even of French historians. It should be remembered on his behalf that the tactics which he employed were only half his. For example, Bonaparte, not Ganteaume, was responsible for the mad idea of disembarking the expeditionary troops at or near Bengasi, and for risking there a repetition of the disaster of Aboukir Bay. Ganteaume was responsible for cutting his cables when Keith's scouts appeared, and for thus saving his ships from capture or destruction. His caution was, after all, less dangerous to his country than the rash and infatuated naval strategy of his master.

The proceedings of Lord Keith and General Sir Ralph Abercromby have now to be followed. It has been seen that, after the appearance of those officers off Cadiz in October, 1800, they returned to Gibraltar.[1]

Keith, bound at length for Egypt, had quitted Gibraltar again several weeks before Ganteaume entered the Mediterranean. After calling first at Minorca and then at Malta, he reached Memorije Bay, on the coast of Asia Minor, on January 31st, 1801. His fleet, to which was attached a Turkish contingent, was a very large one, including, as it did, the vessels mentioned hereunder,[2] besides

[1] *See* p 425.

[2] Ships.	Guns.	Commanders.
Foudroyant	80	Adm. Lord Keith, K.B. (B) Capt. Philip Beaver, 1st. Com. William Young (actg.), 2nd.
Swiftsure	74	Rear-Adm. Sir Richard Hussey Bickerton, Bt. (W). Capt. Benjamin Hallowell.
Ajax	80	,, Hon. Alexander Inglis Cochrane.
Tigre	80	Capt. Sir William Sidney Smith.
Kent	74	Capt. William Johnstone Hope.
Minotaur	74	Capt. Thomas Louis.
Northumberland	74	,, George Martin (2).
Flora	36	,, Robert Gambier Middleton.
Bonne Citoyenne	20	Com. Robert Jackson.
Cameleon	18	,, Edward O'Bryen (2).
Cynthia	18	,, John Dick.
Minorca	16	,, George Miller.
Port Mahon	18	,, William Buchanan.
Petrel	16	,, Charles Inglis (2).
Victorieuse	12	
Malta, sch.		
Cruelle, cut.	..	Lieut. David M'Gie.
Mondovi	16	Com. John Stewart.
Entreprenante, cut.	14	Lieut. William Swiney (2).
Tartarus, bomb	8	Com. Thomas Hand.
Fury, bomb	16	,, Richard Curry.
Dangéreuse, g.v.		
Janissary, g.v.		
Negresse, g.v.		

Ships.	Guns.	Commanders.
SHIPS ARMED *en flûte.*		
Diadem	64	Capt. John Larmour.
Dictator	64	,, John Okes Hardy.
Stately	64	,, George Scott (1).
Trusty	50	,, Alexander Wilson.
Europa	50	,, James Stevenson (1).
Experiment	44	Com. John Griffin Saville.
Expedition	44	,, Thomas Wilson (1).
Charon	44	,, Richard Bridges.
Dolphin	44	,, James Dalrymple.
Regulus	44	,, Thomas Pressland.
Renommée	44	,, Peter M'Kellar.
Thetis	38	,, Henry Edward Reginald Baker.
Hebe	38	Com. George Reynolds.
Inconstant	36	,, John Ayscough.
Romulus	36	,, John Culverhouse.
Druid	32	,, Charles Apthorp.
Blonde	32	,, John Burn (1).
Niger	32	,, James Hillyar.
Iphigenia	32	,, Hassard Stackpoole.
Astræa	32	,, Peter Ribouleau.
Eurus	32	,, Daniel Oliver Guion.
Heroine	32	,, John Hill (2).
Dido	28	,, David Colby.
Alligator	28	,, George Bowen (3).
Cyclops	28	,, John Fyffe.
Resource	28	,, John Crispo.
Thisbe	28	,, John Morrison.
Vestal	28	,, Valentine Collard.

NOTE.—In June Sir R. H. Bickerton shifted his flag to the *Kent.* Captain John Elphinstone (2) succeeded Captain Beaver as Captain of the Fleet, and Captain John Clarke Searle became Lord Keith's flag-captain.

numerous small craft. On board were 16,150 troops, under General Sir Ralph Abercromby, K.B., and Major-Generals Sir John Hely Hutchinson, Eyre Coote, Cradock, Hon. G. J. Ludlow, John Moore, and the Earl of Cavan.

While this force was moving eastward, Bonaparte, in addition to the squadron under Ganteaume, sent from France several frigates and other craft with men, stores, and dispatches for his army in Egypt. Many of these were successful in entering Alexandria. The *Egyptienne*, 48, and *Justice*, 46, got in from Toulon on February 23rd; the *Régénérée*, 32, from Rochefort, found her way past Keith's fleet on March 1st; and, on the same day or in the course of the following night, the brig *Lodi*,[1] from Toulon, also ran the blockade. But other ships were less fortunate, and the supplies brought by the vessels above named were, of course, too small in quantity to afford much relief to the necessities of General Menou and his army, which amounted to upwards of 23,000 men.

Delayed by the non-arrival of part of the Turkish contingent and by bad weather, Keith did not leave Memorije until February 22nd, and did not sight Alexandria until March 1st. Even then, his whole force was not with him, for some of the Turkish vessels had been driven by a moderate gale to take refuge in the ports of Cyprus and elsewhere. On the 2nd the fleet anchored in Aboukir Bay. Northerly winds and a heavy swell prevented a disembarkation until the 8th; but at 2 A.M. on that day the boats began to fill with troops, and at 9 A.M. the landing was begun under the direction of Captains the Hon. A. I. Cochrane, George Scott (1), John Larmour, and James Stevenson (1), and Commanders Charles Apthorp and John Morrison, and under the protection of the *Tartarus*, *Fury*, *Petrel*, *Cameleon*, *Minorca*, *Cruelle*, *Dangéreuse*, *Janissary*, *Entreprenante*, *Malta*, *Negresse*, and two armed launches. Sir William Sidney Smith, with Commanders Peter Ribouleau, John Griffin Saville, Daniel Oliver Guion, James Hillyar and John Burn (1), had charge of a battalion of 1000 seamen who were put ashore to co-operate with the army. The whole force disembarked on the morning of that day amounted to 7000 men. The landing was vigorously opposed by about 2500 French under General Louis Friant, and by the guns in the castle of Aboukir; but the beach was quickly reached and seized; the enemy was driven back; and before nightfall on the 9th, the entire British army was on shore. In these

[1] The *Lodi* escaped from Alexandria in May, and reached Nice on June 28th.

preliminary operations the naval brigade lost 22 killed, 70 wounded, and three missing. Among the wounded were Lieutenants Josias Bray, George Thomas (1), and Francis Collins (1).[1]

The army advanced on March 12th, by which time the French in front numbered about 7000 men. On the 13th the latter attacked, but were driven back with an admitted loss of 750 killed and wounded. The gunboats of the fleet, manœuvring in Lake Aboukir under Commanders Frederick Lewis Maitland (2) and James Hillyar, and the Marines, under Lieut.-Colonel Walter Smith, as well as the seamen, rendered most valuable service in the action, at the close of which the British occupied a position about three miles from Alexandria, between the canal of Alexandria and Lake Mareotis. This engagement cost the Navy and Marines 33 killed and 54 wounded; but the total loss on the side of the victors was not less than 186 killed, 1135 wounded, and one missing.

On the 18th the castle of Aboukir surrendered; an indecisive cavalry skirmish occurred; and a Turkish squadron arrived. On the same day, also, it would appear, a French vessel managed to slip out of Alexandria harbour with dispatches for France; and, in the evening, the French at Alexandria were cheered by the arrival from Cairo of General Menou with troops which, according to the *Moniteur*, brought up the strength of the garrison to upwards of 14,000 men.[2]

On March 21st, before daybreak, the French made a general attack, and, after a bloody contest, were defeated with a loss of at least 1500 men, and probably many more.[3] The British army also suffered very heavily, having 234 killed, 1190 wounded, and 34 missing. The military commander-in-chief, the gallant Sir Ralph Abercromby, received a musket-ball in the upper part of the thigh; and, being, at his own desire, removed to the *Foudroyant*, he lingered until March 28th, when he died, as much regretted by the Navy as by his own service. The Marines were not present at the action, which is known by the French as that of Canopus; but the naval brigade under Sir William Sidney Smith, who was himself slightly hurt, lost 4 killed and 50 wounded.

[1] The army on the same occasion lost 102 killed, 515 wounded, and 35 missing; and the French admitted a loss of 400 killed and wounded.

[2] The number was almost certainly exaggerated. It was in reality, it would seem, about 11,500. The British may have had 16,000 men on shore, but probably not more than 10,000 effectives at the front.

[3] The French loss is, in fact, set down, even by some French authorities, at about 3000.

In the subsequent military operations along the banks of the Nile, the British and Turkish gunboats, under Captain James Stevenson (1), and Commanders John Morrison, James Hillyar and Richard Curry, rendered most useful co-operation, until the capitulation of General Belliard's division of the French army at Cairo on June 27th. The Navy also contributed to the expulsion of the French from Egypt by landing on the coast of the Red Sea two detachments of troops, which, marching into the interior, ultimately joined hands with the force on the Nile. One[1] of these detachments, both of which had been sent from India, was disembarked on May 14th from a small squadron under Rear-Admiral John Blankett, whose flag was in the *Leopard*, 50, Captain Thomas Surridge, and, proceeding across the desert from Suez, which had been occupied on April 22nd, reached the neighbourhood of Cairo on June 11th or 12th. The other detachment[2] was put on shore at Kosseir from a division of the same squadron under Captain Sir Home Riggs Popham, of the *Romney*, 50, and started across the desert in the middle of June, but did not reach Cairo until after the place had surrendered.

After the prisoners taken at Cairo and elsewhere had, in accordance with the terms of the capitulation, been despatched in cartels from France, the attention of the British Navy and army was concentrated upon the reduction of Alexandria, the last stronghold of the French in Egypt. On the night of August 16th about 5000 troops under Major-General Eyre Coote were embarked on Lake Mareotis, and escorted by a flotilla of gunboats under the orders of Captain James Stevenson (1) to a position westward of the town, while another flotilla, under Captain Sir W. S. Smith, made a diversion against the sea-front of Alexandria. Owing to these movements the French set fire to and blew up nearly all their own gunboats, which they saw no prospect of saving. On the night of the 18th a combined naval and military attack[3] was made on Marabou Island, which capitulated on the 21st; and that same evening Captain the Hon. A. I. Cochrane, with the *Cynthia*, *Bonne Citoyenne*, *Port Mahon*, *Victorieuse*, and three Turkish corvettes, entered the great harbour, the eastern end of which the French thereupon essayed to block by sinking merchant vessels across it. Thus pressed on all sides, General Menou, on August 27th, requested a three days'

[1] Part of the 86th Regiment under Lieut.-Col. Lloyd.

[2] Under Major-General Baird.

[3] Upon this occasion the Navy lost two killed and two wounded.

armistice, and, on September 2nd, surrendered, it being agreed that the garrison, of about 8000 troops and 1300 seamen, should, like that of Cairo, be conveyed to France at the expense of Great Britain.

In the old harbour were found, and taken, the *Causse*, 64, *Justice*, 48, and an ex-Venetian 26-gun frigate, which were handed over as prizes to the Turks, and the *Egyptienne*, 48, *Régénérée*, 32, and a second Venetian 26-gun frigate, which were retained by the British. The *Egyptienne* and the *Régénérée* were added to the Navy, the latter being renamed *Alexandria*.[1]

For the services of the Navy in Egypt Lord Keith received promotion from the peerage of Ireland to that of Great Britain; and Sir John Hely Hutchinson, for his exertions, was given a K.B. Both Commanders-in-Chief were also voted the thanks of Parliament. Navy and army had alike behaved magnificently during the campaign; but it is sad to reflect that although the business involved a loss, in killed, wounded, and missing, of upwards of 2200 British officers and men, and was otherwise exceedingly expensive, it secured, in September, 1801, no better results than might have been secured, without the bloodshed or the cost, in February, 1800, if only Keith had considered himself justified in ratifying the convention of El Arich.

Portugal had been loyal to her ancient ally, Great Britain, since the beginning of the war; and she would, no doubt, have remained as loyal as ever, had not Spain, after the Treaty of Lunéville, been induced by France to declare war against her, and had she not lost the province of Alemtejo. Her disasters obliged her, by the terms of the Treaty of Badajos, signed on June 6th, 1801, to consent to expel the British from her ports. France had assisted Spain in this attack on Portugal, and had, perhaps as some compensation, received from her six Spanish sail of the line, which, at the time, lay in Cadiz. These, officered and manned by Frenchmen, were, it was at first arranged, to be employed, in conjunction with some French and some Spanish vessels, for a descent upon Lisbon; but, after the submission of Portugal, it was decided to utilise, for the purpose of carrying reinforcements to Egypt, the squadron which was to have been sent to the Tagus. As a preliminary measure, the ships which, as has been seen, had been left by Ganteaume at Leghorn in April,

[1] The *Egyptienne* had been laid down as a 74, but was altered, and launched in 1799 as a frigate of 1430 tons. She was re-armed by the British as a 24-pr. 48-gun frigate. The *Régénérée* became a 12-pr. 36-gun frigate; she was a very fine sailer of 902 tons.

and had later returned to Toulon, were instructed to proceed to Cadiz under Rear-Admiral Linois, and to there pick up the six newly acquired French ships, under Rear-Admiral Dumanoir Le Pelley, as well as six Spanish ships under Vice-Admiral Don Juan J. de Moreno.

Linois sailed from Toulon on June 13th, with the :—

Ships.	Guns.	Commanders.
Formidable . . .	80	Rear-Adm. Linois. Capt. Laindet Lalonde.
Indomptable . . .	80	„ Moncousu.
Desaix	74	„ Christi-Paillière.
Muiron	40	„ Martinencq.

having on board 1560 soldiers under Brigadier-General Devaux. Proceeding westward, he drove from off Marseilles one or two British frigates which had been left cruising there by Sir John Borlase Warren,[1] and allowed a convoy from that port to enter Toulon. Then he steered south, but, owing to contrary winds, did not sight Gibraltar until July 1st. The only British vessel at the Rock was the *Calpe*, 14, Commander the Hon. George Heneage Lawrence Dundas. She could not venture out in face of such a force; but Captain Dundas sent Lieut. Richard Gaire Janvrin, in a small boat, to apprise Rear-Admiral Sir James Saumarez, who was observing Cadiz, of the appearance of the French squadron bound west; and Lieut. Janvrin safely reached Sir James in the early morning of July 5th.

In the meantime, Linois, working up against a strong W.N.W. wind, had, while still in the strait, captured, on the 2nd, a British brig which was employed on packet duty to Minorca, and, on the 3rd, the *Speedy*, 14, Commander Lord Cochrane.[2] He then learnt that Saumarez, with a superior force, was off Cadiz, and, temporarily abandoning the idea of making his port, he bore up for Algeciras. At 10 A.M. on the 4th, he rounded Cabareta Point; and at 5 P.M., in full view of Gibraltar, he anchored.

[1] Warren was then at Malta, about to go in pursuit of Ganteaume.

[2] Cochrane's behaviour was so admirable that when he presented his sword to Capt. Paillière of the *Desaix*, that officer returned it with a request that he would continue to wear what he had so nobly used. Cochrane remained in the French squadron until after the battle of Algeciras.

Saumarez had with him off Cadiz six ships of the line only, a seventh, the *Superb*, 74, Captain Richard Goodwin Keats, being at the time to the northward, watching the mouth of the Guadalquivir. As soon as he had seen Lieut. Janvrin, the Rear-Admiral tacked off shore; and presently, learning by means of another dispatch from Commander Dundas that the French had put into Algeciras, he ordered off the *Thames*, 32, Captain Aiskew Paffard Hollis to recall the *Superb* and direct her to follow the squadron, which then (excluding the brig *Pasley*, Lieut. William Wooldridge, in company with the *Superb*) consisted of:—

Ships.	Guns.	Commanders.
Cæsar	80	Rear-Adm. Sir James Saumarez (B). Capt. Jahleel Brenton.
Pompée	74	„ Charles Stirling (1).
Spencer	74	„ Henry d'Esterre Darby.
Venerable. . . .	74	„ Samuel Hood (2).
Hannibal. . . .	74	„ Solomon Ferris.
Audacious . . .	74	„ Shuldham Peard.

At 8 A.M. the *Cæsar* signalled to prepare for battle, and to be ready to anchor by the stern, and bore away for the strait with a good breeze from N.W., although the *Superb* and *Pasley*, which were just visible in the N.W., were at that time becalmed. The breeze soon also failed the main body, which, however, was carried to the eastward by the current, and was soon out of sight not only of the *Superb* and *Pasley* but also of the *Thames*. These three vessels, having been subsequently informed by an American ship that Linois had left Algeciras with but three sail of the line, concluded that they would not regain Saumarez in time to be of use, and that in any case their services would be superfluous. They therefore returned to their station off Cadiz. Light airs from the W.N.W. and more calms succeeded one another until about 3 A.M. on July 6th, when, there being again some breeze, the rest of the squadron, which had been joined by the *Plymouth*, 10, lugger, from Gibraltar, crowded sail. Saumarez had already issued a memorandum prescribing the course to be pursued by his command.

"If the Rear-Admiral," he directed, "finds the enemy's ships in a situation to be attacked, the following is to be the order in which it is to be executed:—

Venerable To lead into the bay, and pass the enemy's ships without coming to anchor.

Pompée	To anchor abreast of the inner ship.
Audacious *Cœsar* *Spencer* *Hannibal*	To anchor abreast of the enemy's ships and batteries.

"The boats of the different ships to be lowered down and armed in readiness to act where required."

The *Venerable* had been chosen to lead because of the local knowledge of her Captain. At 7 A.M. she opened Cabareta Point,

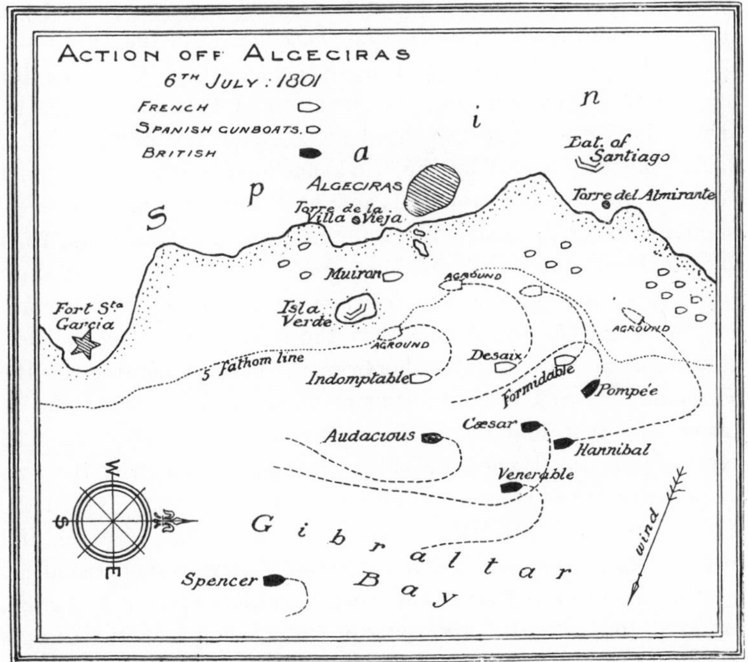

and reported that she saw the French, who were then occupied in warping towards the batteries. The *Cæsar* at once signalled to engage the enemy in succession upon arriving up with him.

Linois moored his ships in from nine to twelve fathoms, and with intervals of about five hundred yards, in the positions shown in the plan. The southern end of his line was covered by a battery of seven long 18 and 24-prs. on Isla Verde: its northern end, by five long 18-prs. in the battery of Santiago. There were also guns on shore in Fort Santa Garcia, about a mile and a half south of the anchorage, and in the towers of La Villa Vieja and Almirante. Further protection was afforded by the presence in the shallow of fourteen heavy Spanish gunboats, of which three lay S.W. of Isla Verde, four off Santiago, and seven to the northward of Almirante. But the French had not warped as far in as they desired when the British attacked.

The partial and failing nature of the breeze prevented the ships from getting into action in the order which had been assigned to them. The *Pompée,* having been distantly fired at while rounding Cabareta Point at 7.50 A.M., passed close to Santa Garcia and Isla Verde, and, receiving in succession the broadsides of the *Muiron, Indomptable, Desaix,* and *Formidable,* to the two latter of which she replied, dropped her anchor at 8.45 A.M. near the *Formidable's* starboard bow,—so near, indeed, that she brought up inside the French ship's anchor-buoy. About five minutes later, the *Audacious,* baffled by the wind, anchored abreast of, but not so close to, the *Indomptable*; and at 8.55 A.M., the *Venerable,* similarly hindered, anchored still further from the *Desaix* and from the starboard quarter of the *Formidable.* As soon as these ships had clewed up their sails, they began a furious action, in the course of which the *Formidable,* if not the other French ships also, continued to warp slowly shorewards. This withdrawal of the *Formidable* proved to be a fortunate thing for the *Pompée*; for at about 9.15 that ship was so swung by the current that her head lay towards the French flagship's broadside; and, had the two vessels then been as close to one another as they were when the *Pompée* anchored, the latter might have been raked with frightful results. It was at that time that the *Cæsar,* having anchored ahead of the *Audacious,* sprang her port broadside upon the *Desaix.* At 9.20, the *Hannibal* also got up, and anchored on the *Cæsar's* starboard bow; but the *Spencer,* having fallen too far to leeward, and being, in addition, as much baffled as her consorts, failed to approach near enough to exert much effect upon the French ships, though she was still near enough to suffer from the fire of the Spanish batteries.

Until after 10 A.M. the cannonade on both sides was extremely heavy, and very little intermittent, although at one time the *Formidable* had been for a short space nearly silent, and although, owing to the manner in which she had swung, the *Pompée* was able to use only her foremost guns. It was, probably, with a view to relieving the *Pompée* that Saumarez, at about 10.12 A.M., ordered the *Hannibal* to "go and rake the French admiral."

Captain Ferris instantly cut his cable and made sail to the northward with such light wind as there was. When he dared proceed no further for fear of the shoals, he tacked so as to place himself between the *Formidable* and the shore; but at 11 P.M., when she was nearly abreast of the Almirante Tower, the *Hannibal* grounded. Some of her foremost larboard guns bore upon the French flagship, some of her starboard foremost ones upon the Almirante Tower and the battery of Santiago, and yet others upon the Spanish gunboats; and she opened as brisk a fire as possible upon every enemy whom she could reach, while she tried by every conceivable means to get herself off. As soon as she had made known her unfortunate situation, boats were sent to her by the *Cæsar* and the *Venerable*. The *Cæsar's* boat was sunk alongside by a round shot; and, as the men were of no use to him, Captain Ferris sent them all back.

Apprehensive lest other British ships might endeavour, with better success, to get between his line and the shore, and encouraged by the fact that, soon after the *Hannibal* had grounded, a light and puffy breeze sprang up from the north-east,[1] Linois, at about 11.15 A.M., signalled to his vessels to cut their cables and to allow themselves to run ashore. He was obeyed, but, owing to the nature of the wind, his ships were long getting round. In the meantime Linois seems to have repented of his decision so far as his own ship was concerned, for, instead of running ashore, the *Formidable* brought up again, when she had but a few inches of water under her bottom. The *Desaix* and *Indomptable*, however, grounded, the one in front of Algeciras, and the other north-east of Isla Verde.

The movements of the French left the British ships at too great a distance to use their guns with full effect. Saumarez, therefore, ordered the cables to be cut, and set the example of endeavouring to stand into a position more favourable for continuing the action; but the untrustworthiness of the breeze, the unfavourable current, and the rocks and shoals to leeward, finally confounded the effort; and, in the meantime, it was found necessary to direct the boats of the squadron to tow out the *Pompée*, the situation of which had become precarious.[2] Nearly all such boats as were

[1] "Ce fut précisément cet heureux changement dont je profitai, qui me rendit possible cette manœuvre qui sauva ma division en m'évitant d'être doublé."—Linois: priv. letter to M. Guérin.

[2] Linois stated positively in his dispatch that the *Pompée* struck "to the fire of Isla Verde and of the *Indomptable*." She was never near enough, after the action had

not thus employed had been destroyed. In consequence, the Rear-Admiral was also forced to forego an intention of sending his Marines to storm the island battery, which had been reinforced by the French; and at 1.35 P.M.[1] he signalled to cease action, and withdrew his five uncompromised ships, leaving the *Hannibal*, partially dismasted, shattered, silent, and aground, but still with her flag flying.

Captain Ferris, when he saw that to prolong an active resistance would be only to needlessly sacrifice his people, ordered firing to cease and directed his officers and men to shelter themselves from the enemy's shot. At about 2 P.M., realising that he could hope no more to save his ship, he hauled down his colours. A little while afterwards these colours were rehoisted upside down, and, in consequence, the *Calpe*, which had approached from the direction of Gibraltar, sent a boat to the *Hannibal's* assistance. The French had by that time taken possession; and the boat's crew was therefore made prisoners.[2]

The losses on both sides were very heavy. The *Cæsar* had 9 killed and 33 wounded or missing; the *Pompée*, 15 killed and 69 wounded; the *Spencer*, 6 killed and 27 wounded; the *Venerable*, 8 killed and 25 wounded; the *Audacious*, 8 killed and 32 wounded; and the *Hannibal*, 75 killed and 66 wounded or missing: total 373 killed, wounded, and missing, besides the prisoners taken with the *Hannibal*. The officers killed were: Masters William Grave (*Cæsar*), and Robert Roxburgh (*Pompée*); Midshipmen —— Steward (*Pompée*), and William Gibbons (*Venerable*); Captain's Clerk David Lindsey (*Hannibal*); and Lieutenant of Marines James D. Williams (*Hannibal*). Among the officers wounded were Lieuts. Richard Cheeseman, Arthur Stapledon, and Thomas Innes (*Pompée*), and John Turner (*Hannibal*). The *Hannibal* had her fore and main-masts shot away and many of her guns disabled; the *Pompée* had not a mast, yard, shroud, rope, or sail uninjured; the *Cæsar* had all her masts and yards more or less wounded, and several shot in her hull; but the remaining British vessels had received no very serious injuries. Captain Ferris, after his return to England, was

begun, to be seriously inconvenienced by the fire from the island. The ship's log mentions that the colours were shot away and quickly rehoisted. Hence, probably, the error of Linois.

[1] *Cæsar's* Log. Log of *Audacious* says 1.20.

[2] Ferris: 'Narrative,' 'Vict. et Conq.,' xiv. 161. *Venerable's* Log. *Calpe's* Log, probably in error, puts time of *Hannibal's* striking as late as 4 P.M.

tried, with his officers and ship's company, for the loss of the *Hannibal*, and was most honourably acquitted.[1] The French lost, according to their own reports, 306 killed, and 280 wounded, among the former being Captains Moncousu and Laindet Lalonde. Their ships were much damaged as well aloft as in their hulls; and of the Spanish gunboats five had been driven ashore or sunk. But Saumarez's first impression that the whole French squadron had been rendered "entirely unserviceable," was, as will be seen, soon proved to be incorrect.

The British Rear-Admiral, having taken his ships to Gibraltar, set to work, with almost unexampled energy, to fit them again for service. It was judged hopeless to attempt to repair the *Pompée* in time to make her ready for further work against Linois; and her people were turned over to help in bringing forward the rest of the squadron. Saumarez himself was inclined also to despair of the *Cæsar*; and he shifted his flag from her to the *Audacious*; but Captain Jahleel Brenton was more sanguine, and, appealing to his men not to allow the Rear-Admiral to go to sea in another ship, ordered them to work all day, and by watch and watch at night; the result being that the *Cæsar* was ready when she was again wanted, and that Saumarez, on the 12th, rehoisted his flag in her. The business was done with an energy and rapidity that have never been exceeded.

It has already been said that Rear-Admiral Dumanoir Le Pelley was at Cadiz in charge of the six ships of the line which had been transferred by Spain to France. He had arrived there from Brest on June 13th, with the frigates *Liberté*, 40, and *Indienne*, 40, after a smart chase by the *Venerable* and *Superb*; but he still lacked many of the officers and men to enable him to take over the squadron. As soon as Linois had floated his grounded ships and his prize at Algeciras, he sent a message to Dumanoir Le Pelley and Massaredo, at Cadiz, begging them to come or send to his assistance, ere the British should be in a position to again attack him. Both flag officers were willing enough to aid him. Indeed, succour would probably have been despatched so soon as the danger of Linois

[1] C. M., Sept. 1, 1801. French historians assert that after Capt. Ferris had surrendered his ship, he quitted his people, and fled in a boat to Gibraltar, being fired upon by the French as he went, but escaping. That there is no truth in this is proved by the fact that after the action Capt. Jahleel Brenton was sent to Algeciras to negotiate the exchange of, among others, Ferris and Lord Cochrane (Brenton, iii. 36; James, iii. 122), and that Ferris was eventually liberated on parole.

became known, but for the non-arrival of the French officers and seamen, and for the impossibility of getting the Spanish authorities to move with promptitude. On July 8th, however, Vice-Admiral Don Juan Joaquin de Moreno anchored in the outer road of Cadiz with five Spanish and one Franco-Spanish sail of the line, three frigates and a lugger, in readiness to sail for Algeciras on the following morning. His proceedings were observed by the *Superb*, *Thames*, and *Pasley*, which were by that time again off the port.

At daylight on the 9th Moreno put to sea with all his squadron except the *Saint Antoine* (ex-*San Antonio*), which was delayed, but which rejoined on the following morning; and made sail towards the Gut of Gibraltar, while the *Superb*, *Thames*, and *Pasley* kept ahead of him. That forenoon the *Pasley* pressed on and entered Gibraltar signalling the approach of an enemy; at 3 P.M. the *Superb* and *Thames* joined Saumarez; and a little later the squadron from Cadiz joined Linois off Algeciras. On the two following days the British worked harder than ever to make ready for sea; and when, at dawn on July 12th, the Franco-Spaniards loosed sails, the squadron of Saumarez, except the *Pompée*, was prepared to meet them. The enemy began to get under way at noon; by 1 P.M. their headmost ships were off Cabareta Point,[1] and the *Cæsar* was warping out of Gibraltar mole, her band playing "Come, cheer up, my lads," and the garrison band answering with "Britons, strike home." At 3 P.M. Saumarez signalled for the rest of his squadron to weigh and prepare for battle. The forces about to be opposed one to another are set forth in the note.[2]

[1] The *Hannibal*, towed by the *Indienne*, left with the fleet; but, being unable to keep up with it, the two vessels eventually returned to Algeciras.

[2] BRITISH.			FRANCO-SPANISH.		
SHIPS.	Guns.	COMMANDERS.	SHIPS.	Guns.	COMMANDERS.
Cæsar	80	Rear-Adm. Sir James Saumarez. Capt. Jahleel Brenton.	*Real Carlos* (S) .	112	Don J. Esquerra.
Venerable . . .	74	,, Samuel Hood (2).	*San Hermenegildo* (S) . .	112	,, J. Emparran.
Superb . . .	74	,, Richard Goodwin Keats.	*San Fernando* (S)	94	,, J. Malina.
Spencer . . .	74	,, Henry d'Esterre Darby.	*Formidable* (F) .	80	Com. A. G. Troude.
Audacious . .	74	,, Shuldham Peard.	*Indomptable* (F)	80	,, — Lucas.
—			*Argonauta* (S) .	80	Don J. Herrera.
Thames . . .	32	,, Aiskew Paffard Hollis.	*San Augustin* (S)	74	,, R. Topete.
Carlotta (Portug.)	..	,, Craufurd Duncan.	*St. Antoine* (F) .	74	Commod. Julien Le Roy.
Calpe, polacre .	14	Com. Hon. George Heneage Lawrence Dundas.	*Desaix* (F) . .	74	Capt. J. A. Christi-Paillière.
Louisa, armed brig. . . .	8	Lieut. Francis Truscott.	—		
			Sabina (S)[1] . .	44	
			Liberté (F) . .	40	,, Proteau.
			Muiron (F) . .	40	,, Martinencq.
			Vautour (F) . .	14	,, Kémel.

[1] Flags of Vice-Adm. Moreno and Rear-Adm. Linois.

The wind was from the east; and, as soon as they were clear of the shelter of the Rock, the British ships formed in line ahead on the port tack. At 7 P.M. they wore together, and stood on the starboard tack, until a little after 8 P.M., when, the enemy having all cleared Cabareta Point, Saumarez bore away in chase. A little previously, Don Juan Moreno, in accordance with the Spanish custom of the time, had shifted his flag from a line-of-battle ship to the frigate *Sabina*, and had, with considerable difficulty, persuaded M. Linois to leave the *Formidable* for the same vessel.

At 8.40 P.M. the Rear-Admiral hailed the *Superb*, and ordered her to make sail ahead, and attack the rearmost of the enemy's ships, none of which were at that time visible. Captain Keats, in response, quickly passed the flagship; and by 10 P.M., when the wind had freshened, only the *Cæsar* and *Venerable*, of her own squadron, remained visible from her deck. By 11 P.M. her next astern, the *Cæsar*, was fully three miles away, and the *Venerable* could not be seen at all. Twenty minutes later, Keats distinguished the *Real Carlos*, 112, about a point before his port beam, and the *San Hermenegildo*, 112, and *St. Antoine* on the three-decker's port side. He therefore shortened sail, and, quite regardless of the fact that he was alone, opened his port guns on the *Real Carlos* when he was at a distance of about a cable and a half from her. He had given the Spaniard three broadsides and had brought down her foretop-mast, when, perceiving her to be on fire, he again made sail. In the meantime the *Real Carlos*, after having for a short time continued her course, came suddenly to the wind, dropped astern, and began, with her two nearest consorts, firing wildly. Each, in the darkness, mistook the others, it would appear, for an enemy.

Having passed on, the *Superb*, at 11.50 P.M., brought the *St. Antoine* to action, and, after half an hour's engagement, some of which was fought at close quarters upon a wind, the Frenchman hailed that she surrendered.[1] She was afterwards, owing to her broad pennant having been accidentally left flying, fired into by the *Cæsar*, *Venerable*, *Spencer*, and *Thames* as they got up; but it was not long ere it was made known that she had already struck. Just before she surrendered, the *Real Carlos*, which had never succeeded in extinguishing her fire, blew up; but, ere she did so, she had

[1] In this contest the *Superb* had 15 (including Lieut. Edmund Waller) wounded. The *St. Antoine* was added to the Navy, but after reaching Portsmouth she never again went to sea.

fouled, and also set fire to, her unfortunate consort the *San Hermenegildo*, which, in turn, at about 12.30 A.M. on the 13th, exploded. From these two three-deckers, 38 persons reached the *Superb*, and 262 more were taken up by other ships; but the rest of the complements, amounting to about 1700 officers and men, perished. The *Superb*, *Carlotta*, *Calpe*, and *Louisa* remained by the prize, and the rest of the squadron pressed on after the enemy.

After midnight the wind temporarily increased to a gale, and at 4 A.M., when the *Venerable* and *Thames* led the squadron and were getting up with the *Formidable*, the *Cæsar* was some distance astern of them, the *Spencer* was far astern of her, and the *Audacious* and *Superb* were out of sight. At about that time the wind began to drop, and even to fail; and, in spite of all that could be done, only the *Venerable* and *Thames* were able to gain materially upon the chase. At 5.15 A.M. the *Formidable* opened with her stern guns upon the *Venerable*; and, a little later, the light and baffling airs threw the two ships broadside to, within musket shot of one another. A hot action then ensued. By 5.30 the *Venerable* had lost her mizen topmast; at 5.45, by order, the *Thames* hauled up and raked the *Formidable* from astern; at 6.45 the *Venerable's* mainmast went by the board, and the British 74 fell alongside her opponent, who, profiting by the confusion, stood on, though slowly, and, as she went, plied the *Venerable* for some time from her stern-chasers. Neither the *Cæsar* nor the *Spencer* was able to get within gunshot of her. Captain Hood's ship was left unmanageable. At 7.50, to add to her difficulties, she lost her foremast; and almost simultaneously she struck upon the shoals in front of San Pedro, about twelve miles south of Cadiz. At about 8 A.M. her mizenmast went over the side, and Saumarez, by boat, sent to her Captain permissive directions to abandon and destroy the vessel in case the enemy should show any disposition to attack her again, while he also ordered the *Thames* to be ready to take on board her people. But Hood did not despair of saving his ship; and, when the *Audacious* and *Superb* at length showed in the southward, the enemy, who had previously betrayed some slight inclination to renew the engagement, hauled up for, and presently entered Cadiz. The *Venerable* had lost eighteen killed and eighty-seven wounded, among the former being her Master, John Williams, and among the latter Lieutenant Thomas Church. The *Thames* had escaped scot free.

The total casualties suffered by the enemy[1] cannot be ascertained; but they had lost three ships, two by fire and one by capture; and this they have never attempted to deny. The action is, nevertheless, always chronicled in French histories as a victory, and, indeed, as a most glorious victory, for France. That this is so is, no doubt, due almost entirely to the extraordinary report which, after reaching Cadiz, Commander Troude,[2] of the *Formidable*, sent to Rear-Admiral Linois. At about midnight, so he declared, he had sustained the fire of five British ships; and at daybreak he had been attacked by three ships and a frigate, and had driven them all off, completely dismasting one of them.[3] This exaggerated story was accepted by the French government, and has been credited by the French people; and Troude, not so much on the strength of his other performances, some of which were far more worthy of applause, as on the strength of this imaginative dispatch, has ever since ranked among the most brilliant naval heroes of his country. That he made a good defence is true. That he disabled the *Venerable*, a ship of force inferior to his own, is true also. But that he drove off the British squadron, or that the action was, in any sense of the words, a French or a Franco-Spanish victory, is, of course, utter nonsense. Dumanoir Le Pelley, in his report[4] to the Minister of Marine, ingenuously adopted and gave currency, nevertheless, to all Troude's self-glorification.

After the disappearance of the allies, the British, thanks mainly to the *Thames* and to the boats of the *Cæsar* and *Spencer*, succeeded in hauling off the *Venerable*, which, by 8 A.M. on the 14th, owing to the energy of her own people, had got up three spars to serve as masts and had made some sail on them, though she still had to be towed. Saumarez returned to Gibraltar with her and the prize, and left the *Spencer*, *Audacious*, and *Thames* to watch the enemy in Cadiz. He sent home his dispatches[5] by Lieutenant Philip Dumaresq, first of the *Cæsar*, who, upon delivering them, was made a Commander. The first Lieutenants of the *Superb* and *Venerable*,

[1] Troude speaks of having had 3 killed and 2 wounded in the night action, and 20 killed or severely wounded in the morning one.—Report to Linois.

[2] Aimable Gilles Troude; born 1762; entered the Navy at the beginning of the American War; posted for this action on July 14th, 1801; subsequently served in the West Indies; rear-admiral, 1811; convoyed Louis XVIII. to France, 1814; retired, 1816; died, 1824.

[3] Troude to Linois, July 15th, in *Moniteur*.

[4] Cadiz, July 16th.

[5] In the *Louisa*.

Samuel Jackson and James Lillicrap, were also deservedly promoted; and Saumarez himself, for his promptitude in striking at two parts of a force largely in excess of his own, for the quickness with which he had refitted his squadron, and for the gallantry which he had displayed in pursuing and in beating a numerically superior squadron, was made a K.B., and given a pension of £1200 a year. In common, too, with his officers and men he received the thanks of Parliament. In itself the success was not of first-rate importance, though it was brilliant. But it was important as part of the system which was then in process of enforcement by Great Britain in all the waters of Europe. The application of sea-power had begun to hamper Napoleon by confounding his plans and preventing his combinations. His enemy had begun to seize and hold the interior positions, and to beat his detachments in detail whenever they ventured far from port. And it is the merit of Saumarez that, when the time came for him to do his share of work in the general scheme, he did it, in spite of a preliminary check, and in face of superior numbers.

It has been seen that, either upon their own initiative or at the instigation of others, Russia, Sweden, Denmark, and Portugal had added themselves, in this last year of the war, to the ranks of the enemies of Great Britain. Such of these countries as possessed outlying possessions were promptly made to realise how dangerous for them was the new policy. Sweden was promptly deprived by Rear-Admiral John Thomas Duckworth and Lieut.-General Thomas Trigge [1] of her small colonies in the West Indies. St. Bartholomew surrendered on March 20th, and St. Martin on March 24th. Denmark suffered in a similar way. St. Thomas and St. John capitulated on March 29th, and St. Croix on March 31st to the same force. Nor did Portugal [2] fare any better. On July 23rd a British squadron anchored in Funchal Bay and landed a detachment which, under the orders of Colonel Clinton, took possession of the forts and occupied Madeira. British garrisons were also placed in all the East Indian colonies of Portugal except Macao. Holland, too, was made to suffer for her subservience to France. The French were obliged on April 16th to evacuate St. Eustatia, which, with

[1] Both Duckworth and Trigge were made Knights of the Bath for these services, June 6th.

[2] Portugal bought off France by a treaty which was signed at Madrid on Sept. 29th, 1801, and which ceded to France part of Portuguese Guiana.

Saba, was occupied by Captain John Perkins,[1] of the *Arab*, 20, and a few troops under Colonel Blunt, of the 3rd Buffs; and, in the East, Ternate, after a stubborn resistance of fifty-two days, capitulated on June 21st to the East India Company's forces under Colonel Barr and Captain Hayes, H.E.I.C.; but, save at the place last mentioned, and at St. Martin, where the enemy lost about fifty killed and wounded, the operations involved little or no fighting.

In the meantime the belligerents had become, for the moment, weary of the contest: and on October 1st, after some negotiations, preliminary articles of peace were signed in London. Ratifications were exchanged on October 10th, and King George, on the 12th, proclaimed a cessation of hostilities by sea and land; but the definitive treaty of peace was not signed at Amiens until March 27th, 1802;[2] and, more than once in the interval, it looked as if hostilities were on the point of being resumed. Indeed, few at any time regarded the settlement as likely to be of long duration.

The peace, such as it was, provides, however, a convenient halting place for the course of this history, the present chapter of which will be fitly concluded with some account of the gains and losses of the contracting parties[3] and of others concerned.

In Europe, France had restored to her the little islands of St. Marcou; the republic of the Seven (Ionian) Islands was acknowledged; Portugal returned to the *status quo ante*, save as regards Alemtejo, which, under the treaty of Badajos, she had ceded to Spain; the French were to evacuate Neapolitan and Roman territory; and the British were to evacuate all the ports,[4] save Gibraltar, which they held in the Mediterranean, restoring each to its previous owner. It was expressly stipulated, moreover, as to Malta, Gozo, and Comino, which were to revert to the Order of St. John of Jerusalem, that they were to be evacuated by British troops within

[1] This John Perkins was a gallant but very extraordinary character, a Lieutenant of 1782, a Commander of 1797, and a Captain of 1800. He is supposed, by a writer in the 'Nautical Magazine,' who knew him, to have been of illegitimate birth, and to have had negro blood in his veins. He could only write to the extent of signing his name mechanically; and he served almost exclusively in the West Indies, where, when on half-pay, he lived with little regard to the decencies of civilisation. He was known on the station as "Jack Punch," the *Punch*, schooner, having been one of his earliest commands. His name occurs more than once in this history. He died in 1812. 'Naut. Mag.,' 1842, 387–391, 461–465; 'Nav. Chron.,' xvii. 458, xxvii. 351.

[2] Peace was proclaimed in London on April 29th, 1802.

[3] Great Britain, France, Spain, and the Batavian Republic.

[4] Including Minorca, which reverted to Spain.

three months of the exchange of the ratification. Egypt and the territories of the Porte, were to be maintained in their integrity as before the war.

The numerous foreign conquests of Great Britain were thus disposed of under the treaty. To France were restored St. Pierre and Miquelon; Pondicherry, Chandernagore, and Foul Point, Madagascar; Gorée; and, in the West Indies, Tobago, Martinique, and St. Lucia. To the Batavian Republic were restored Malacca and its dependencies; Amboyna, Banda, and Ternate; the Cape of Good Hope; and Demerara, Essequibo, Berbice, Surinam and Curaçao. To Denmark and Sweden were restored their little islands in the West Indies; and Portugal received back Madeira. Only Trinidad, which had been won from Spain, and the settlements in Ceylon, which had been won from Holland, were retained by Great Britain as trophies of her victorious war. The reason why she held so little and surrendered so much was that, one after another, her continental allies had failed her; and that France, though beaten at sea, was not to be gainsaid on shore except by the indirect influences of sea-power. Yet, upon the whole, Great Britain had little cause for dissatisfaction. As Mahan justly points out, she had successfully traversed a long stage towards the final solution of a great difficulty. France, in 1793, had begun the war, posing as the champion of ideas which she desired to force upon the whole world. French republican quixotism and popular aggressiveness had, in the nine years, been bled and bled until their feverish energy had left them. There remained unaffected, it is true, the ambition and aggressiveness of a single man, France's master, Napoleon. But the vicious impulse of one man, no matter how able, is always a much easier force to deal with than the vicious impulse of an entire nation; and the Peace of Amiens, though it did not end the whole danger, did effectively tame the most threatening tendencies of the French revolution. Great Britain, or, to be exact, Great Britain's sea-power, had been the chief factor in the accomplishment of this result; and Great Britain, without having lost a yard of the territory that had belonged to her in 1793, had gained not only her moral object, but also two rich islands in distant seas. She gained, therefore, very substantial advantages.

Nor had her commerce, which is her wealth, suffered materially during the struggle. While the merchant ships of France had literally been swept from the seas, the British merchant navy had grown to greater proportions than ever. It suffered heavy losses,[1] of course; but the gains soon became even more considerable than the risks; and the general result of the war was to make British trade a hundred per cent. more flourishing than it had been in any previous time of peace.[2]

Between the conclusion of peace and the renewal of the war in 1803, the Royal Navy saw no active service that requires a chronicle. The government of the United States was engaged, during the interval, in hostilities with the piratical states of the Barbary coast; and France embarked upon an unfortunate and costly expedition for the reduction of San Domingo, which had fallen into the hands of the exceptionally able mulatto general and statesman, Toussaint Louverture;[3] but these operations called neither for the aid nor for the interference of Great Britain.

[1] According to Lloyd's returns, 3466 British ships were captured from 1793 to 1800 inclusive. The enemy lost less only because he had far less to lose. The percentage of British trade captured was but about $2\frac{1}{2}$ per cent. French trade, on the other hand, disappeared.

[2] Chalmers: 'Hist. View,' 351.

[3] Louverture capitulated and was allowed to return to his home, but he was afterwards arbitrarily arrested and deported to France, where he died in prison. This treacherous treatment of him served only to rekindle the hostility of the blacks.

SIGNATURE OF ADMIRAL SIR FRANCIS LAFOREY, BART.

CHAPTER XXXVI.

MINOR OPERATIONS OF THE ROYAL NAVY, 1793–1802.

H. W. Wilson.

Beginning of hostilities—Capture of privateers—The *Iris* and *Citoyenne Française*—Loss of the *Hyæna*—The *Venus* and the *Sémillante*—The *Nymphe* takes the *Cléopâtre*—The *Boston* and the *Embuscade*—The *Crescent* takes the *Réunion*—Nelson and a French squadron—The *Thames* and the *Uranie*—Loss of the *Thames*—Capture of the *Inconstant*—The *Antelope* takes the *Atalante*—Escape of the *Juno*—Defence of the *Pigot*—Capture of the *Pomone* and *Engageante*—The *Orpheus* takes the *Duguay Trouin*—The *Swiftsure* takes the *Atalante*—Loss of the *Castor*—Her recapture—Escape of the *Crescent*, *Druid*, and *Eurydice*—The *Romney* takes the *Sibylle*—Loss of the *Hound*—Destruction of the *Volontaire*—Saumarez frightens Weymouth—Capture of the *Révolutionnaire*—Captain Matthew Smith's action—Loss of the *Daphne*—Faulknor at Désirade—The *Blanche* takes the *Pique*—Loss of the *Espérance* and capture of the *Requin*—The *Lively* takes the *Espion* and the *Tourterelle*—The *Coureuse* and *Jean Bart* taken—The *Astræa* takes the *Gloire*—The *Hannibal* takes the *Gentille*—Blowing up of the *Boyne*—French convoy destroyed in Camaret Bay—Capture of French storeships—The *Courier National*, *Prompte*, and *Liberté* taken—Capture of the *Minerve*—The *Alliantie* taken—The *Southampton* and the *Vestale*—Capture of the *Superbe*, *Brutus*, *Républicaine*, *Bonne Citoyenne*, *Aspic*, and *Mutine*—Sidney Smith at Erqui—Warren's action with a convoy—The *Révolutionnaire* takes the *Unité*—Smith taken prisoner—Fremantle at Bona—Capture of the *Virginie*—The *Ecureuil* burnt—The *Spencer* takes the *Volcan*—The *Argo* taken—The *Santa Margarita* takes the *Tamise*, and the *Unicorn* the *Tribune*—Cutting out of the *Utile*—The *Dryad* captures the *Proserpine*—Capture of the *Légère* and *Renommée*—The *Glatton* and French frigates—Indecisive actions—The *Andromaque* destroyed—Escape of the *Raison*—The *Topaze* takes the *Elisabeth*—Frigate action off Sumatra—Blowing up of the *Amphion*—Defence of the *Pelican*—The *Terpsichore* captures the *Mahonesa*—The *Lapwing* at Anguilla—The *Terpsichore* and the *Vestale*—Capture and recapture of the *Sabina*—The *Blanche* and the *Ceres*—Capture of the *Tartu*—Escape of Indiamen—An Algerine pirate taken—Landing of French criminals at Fishguard—Capture of the *Résistance* and *Constance*—The *Ninfa* and *Santa Elena* taken—Destruction of the *Calliope*—Capture of the *Gaîté*—Action with the *Béolaise*, etc.—The *Ranger* and the *Hyène* taken—The *Phœbe* takes the *Néréide*—Capture of the *Daphné*—The *Sibylle* and *Fox* at Manilla—The *Speedy* and the *Papillon*—Action with the *Charente*—Escape of the *Pearl*—Taking of the *Corcyre* and *Mondovi*—The *Seahorse* takes the *Sensible*—Capture of the *Seine*—Capture of the *Santa Dorotea*—Blowing up of the *Resistance*—Escape of the *Brilliant*—Cutting out of the *Aventurier*—The *Espoir* takes the *Liguria*—Capture of the *Vaillante* and of the *Neptune*—Loss of the *Leander*—Capture of the *Décade*—Taking of the *Furie* and *Waakzaamheid*—Dickson at Margarita—Loss of the *Ambuscade*—Defence of the *Wolverine*—Wreck of the *Proserpine*—The *Argo* taken—The *Dædalus* takes the *Prudente*—The *Espoir* takes the *Africa*—The *Sibylle* captures the *Forte*—Frigate action off Hoëdic—Loss of the *Fortune*—Cutting out affair at La Selva—Recapture of the *Crash*—The *Clyde* takes the *Vestale*—The *Tamar* captures the *Républicaine*—Taking of the *Draak* and *Gier*—Action in Algoa Bay—Escape of the *Preneuse*—Taking of the *Aréthuse* and *Bordelaise*—Blowing up of the *Trincomale*—Capture of the *Thetis* and *Santa Brigida*—The *Cerberus* and Spanish frigates—Cutting out of the *Hermione*—The *Speedy* off Gibraltar—Capture of the *Galgo*—The *Solebay* off San Domingo—Burning of the *Preneuse*—Action off Madeira—Capture of the *Pallas*—The *Petrel* takes the *Ligurienne*—Capture of the *Carmen* and *Florentina*—Taking of the *Albanaise*—Affairs off St. Croix and Noirmoutier—Cutting out of the *Désirée*—Cutting out of the *Cerbère*—Capture of the *Concorde* and *Médée*—The *Seine* takes the *Vengeance*—Cutting out of the *Esmeralda* and *Paz*—Taking of the East Indiaman *Kent*—Capture of the *Vénus*—Cutting out of the *San Josef*—The *Milbrook* and the *Bellone*—Destruction of the *Réolaise*—Cutting out of the *Sénégal*—Capture of the *Eclair* and of the *Sanspareille*—Gallant action of the *N. S. de los Dolores*—Capture of the *Dédaigneuse*—Taking of the *Curieux*—Action of the *Penguin*—The *Phœbe* takes the *Africaine*—Lord Cochrane in the *Speedy*—The *Mercury* at Ancona—Affair off Oropeso—Cutting out of the *Chevrette*—Gallant action of the *Pasley*—Mysterious engagements of the *Sylph*—Capture of the *Chiffonne*—The *Victor* and the *Flèche*—Recapture of the *Bulldog*—Unsatisfactory nature of ships' logs—Criticism of French tactics—Influence of chance—Effects of weight of metal upon the results of actions—Value of the carronade—Various categories of actions—British promptitude in refitting—Successes of merchantmen—Distribution of British cruisers.

MESS KETTLE. XVIII. CENT.

ON January 2nd, 1793, the first act of hostility between France and England in Europe occurred, the *Childers*, sloop, being fired upon by the Brest forts whilst standing in towards the harbour.

On May 13th occurred the first naval action of the war,[1] though previously, on March 13th, the British sloop, *Scourge*, Commander George Brisac, had captured one French privateer, and on April 14th a British squadron had taken another. The *Iris*, 32, Captain George Lumsdaine, sighted a strange sail in the Bay of Biscay, early in the morning, and gave chase. The stranger was closed at about 6.30 A.M., and engaged, but after an hour and a half of sharp fighting made off; and the *Iris*, having lost her foremast, maintopmast, and mizenmast, was unable to overhaul her. The stranger was at the time supposed to be the French *Médée*, but has been proved by James to have been the *Citoyenne Française*, 32.

[1] James, i. 100 (Edit. 1886. London, 6 vols. 8 vo.). No notice in Troude.

—	Tons.	Guns.	Broadside.	Men.	Killed.	Wounded.[3]	Total.
			Lbs.				
Iris . . .	688	40[1]	246[2]	217 n.	4	32	36
Citoyenne F..	800?	36	270?	275 n.	16	37	53

90 minutes.

[1] Carronades, which are not counted in the rating, are always included in these comparisons.
[2] Allowance has been made for the greater weight of the French pound in these tables. *Vide* James, i. 45.
[3] Slightly wounded men were rarely included in the returns.

On May 27th, in the West Indies, the *Hyæna*, 24, Captain William Hargood (1), was seen and chased by the *Concorde*, 40, Captain Vandongen, and by several other French vessels.[1] She was quickly overhauled, and, after a few shots, struck her colours.

	Guns.	Broadside.
Concorde	44	410 lbs.
Hyæna	30	153 „

On the same day, to the west of Cape Finisterre,[2] the British *Venus*, 32, Captain Jonathan Faulknor (2), sighted the *Sémillante*, 32, Captain Gaillard. The two closed, the *Venus* being to windward, and began a warm fire at about 8 A.M. After two hours' fighting the *Sémillante's* guns seemed to be silenced; and the *Venus* was bearing down to take possession, when another ship under French colours hove in sight, and the *Venus* retired. The *Sémillante* lost her captain and first lieutenant killed, and had her masts, sails, and hull badly injured, and five feet of water in her hold. The *Venus* was much damaged in her masts, sails, and rigging. She was fortunate in escaping the strange ship, which was the *Cléopâtre*, 36, and in rejoining the British *Nymphe*, 36, from which she had parted two days before.

—	Tons.	Guns.	Broadside.	Men.	Killed.	Wounded.	Total.
			Lbs.				
Venus . .	722[1]	38	222	192	2	20	22
Sémillante .	940	36[2]	270	300?	12	20	32

[1] Charnock gives a *Venus*, 36, of this tonnage, built in 1758. She is the same ship.
[2] James credits the *Sémillante* with ten 6-prs.; Troude, with only four. *Vide* note in James, i. 103. I have followed Troude.

On June 18th, the British frigate, *Nymphe*, 36, Captain Edward

[1] James, 105; Troude, ii. 302.
[2] James, 103; Troude, 302; C. Williams, 'Liverpool Privateers,' 314.

Pellew, whilst cruising in the Channel, sighted the *Cléopâtre*, 36, Captain Mullon, and bore down upon her.[1] The French ship shortened sail and waited for the British attack. The two vessels were within hail before a shot had been fired. The *Nymphe's* men gave three cheers for the King; the French replied; and Captain Mullon, standing in the gangway, waved his hat and shouted, "Vive la nation!" At 6.15 A.M., Pellew, who had been standing with his hat in his hand, put it on his head, as the concerted signal for opening fire. About seven the *Cléopâtre's* mizenmast fell, masking some of her guns on the engaged side; and just at the same time Israel Pellew, the Captain's brother, who was on board as a volunteer, succeeded in shooting away the *Cléopâtre's* wheel, on which she fell on board the *Nymphe*, with her other broadside bearing, her jib-boom striking the *Nymphe's* mainmast. The jib-boom broke, but one of the *Cléopâtre's* studding sail boom-irons hooked the *Nymphe's* maintopsail leech-rope, and the latter had to be cut away to save the mast. The *Nymphe* anchored that the French ship might clear her, but before this could happen the *Cléopâtre* had fallen. Pellew noticed that the French were gathering to board, and ordered his men to prepare to repel them; on which the British seamen swept on board the enemy and carried the ship. The heroic Mullon was discovered in the agony of death, striving to bite to pieces a paper which, he thought, contained the French secret coast-signals.[2] His failing consciousness did not reveal to him that he was destroying the paper containing his commission. For this action Captain Pellew was knighted, and his brother, Israel, was promoted to post rank.

—	Tons.	Guns.	Broadside.	Men.	Killed.	Wounded.	Total.
			Lbs.				
Nymphe . .	938	40	322	240	23	27	50
Cléopâtre. .	913	40[1]	290[1]	320	—	—	63

55 minutes.

[1] Troude differs from James as to the armament, giving *Cléopâtre* thirty-six guns, with a broadside of 204 lbs.; but, as *Cléopâtre* was captured, it may be assumed that the English figures are the more correct. *Cf.* also Pellew, in Osler, 59, who gives her forty guns, some 18's.

---

[1] Troude, ii. 303; James, i. 106; Osler, 'Lord Exmouth,' 54 (2nd edition).

[2] As a trait of chivalrous generosity, it should be recorded that Pellew sent pecuniary aid to Capt. Mullon's widow.

The *Cléopâtre* was purchased for the British Navy, and re-named *Oiseau*.

In July, Captain George William Augustus Courtenay of the British frigate *Boston*, 32, cruising off New York, sent in a challenge to Captain Jean Baptiste François Bompard of the French frigate *Embuscade*, 34, having first captured by an adroit stratagem the *Embuscade's* first lieutenant with a boat's crew.[1] Courtenay offered to wait for three days off Sandy Hook, and had a written copy of the challenge posted up in one of the New York coffee-rooms. On July 30th, a considerable French fleet passed, but the *Boston* kept her station, and in the night of the 31st saw a large ship standing towards her. The *Embuscade* had come out to fight. Both ships hoisted their colours at about dawn, and, soon after five, closed and began action—the *Boston* with her larboard and the *Embuscade* with her starboard broadside. Their evolutions were watched by a great crowd on the New Jersey beach, twelve miles away. In less than an hour the *Boston's* rigging was so injured that she lost command of her sails, and a little later her maintopmast went overboard. By 6.20 Captain Courtenay and the Lieutenant of Marines were killed; the two Lieutenants borne on the ship's books were both severely wounded; and the mizenmast was tottering. The crew fell into confusion, but the wounded first Lieutenant, John Edwards, took command and fought the ship. With difficulty the *Boston* avoided an attempt of the *Embuscade* to rake her. Her condition was desperate, as the wreck of the maintopmast hampered the service of her guns, and all her chief officers were killed and wounded. She turned and fled before the wind, followed for some distance by the *Embuscade*, which had, however, been too much injured in masts, sails, and rigging to overtake her. After an hour's chase, the Frenchman put about and returned to New York. The *Boston* was much the weaker and smaller ship; and at that time indiscipline had not destroyed the *moral* of the French navy. On her return to New York the *Embuscade* had to remove her masts. Captain Bompard was presented with a gold medal, and Captain Courtenay's widow and children were pensioned by the King. Brenton accuses Lieutenant Edwards of cowardice, but, it would appear, on quite insufficient evidence.

[1] James, i. 110; Brenton [ed. 1837], i. 263; Troude, ii. 304.

—	Tons.	Guns.	Broadside.	Men.	Killed.	Wounded.	Total.
			Lbs.				
Embuscade .	906	34 [1]	230 [1]	327	—	—	50
Boston . .	676	38	210	204	10	24	34

About 1 hour 40 minutes.

1 So Troude. James differs, giving thirty-eight guns and 240-lb. broadsides. Brenton calls her an 18-pr. frigate.

The battery of the *Boston* included six very indifferent 12-pr. carronades, which, James states, were of the "useless monkey-tailed" type.

On October 20th, the *Crescent*, 36, Captain James Saumarez, sighted the French *Réunion*, 36, Captain François A. Déniau, and a cutter, at daylight, off Cherbourg.[1] Saumarez had been informed that there was a French frigate at Cherbourg, which left that port at nightfall, cruised during the night, and returned early in the morning. This was in fact the procedure of the *Réunion*. The *Crescent* was on her way with dispatches from Portsmouth to the Channel Islands. She had just been docked and sailed very fast. At 10.30 A.M., the *Crescent* was close enough to the enemy to open fire, both ships being on the larboard tack. The cutter had made off. In three-quarters of an hour the *Réunion* lost her foreyard and mizen-topmast, and was in consequence exposed to the raking fire of the *Crescent*, which ship, by a singularly adroit manœuvre of Saumarez, had wore round on her heel. Keeping under the enemy's stern, the *Crescent* was able to use her larboard broadside, receiving scarcely a shot from the *Réunion*. After a brave resistance which had lasted over two hours, the *Réunion* struck, as the British *Circe*, 28, was approaching in the distance. She had lost her main top-gallant mast, in addition to her mizen-topmast, and was a good deal damaged. The *Crescent's* only loss was one man wounded by the recoil of a gun.

—	Tons.	Guns.	Broadside.	Men.	Killed.	Wounded.	Total.
			Lbs.				
Crescent . .	888	36	315	257	0	0	0
Réunion . .	951	40	310 [1]	320	33	48	81

2 hours 10 minutes.

1 Saumarez makes her weight of metal 330 lbs., which is a slight exaggeration.

1 James, 114; Troude, 309; Ross, 'Saumarez,' i. 101.

Captain Saumarez was knighted for this action. The *Réunion* was purchased for the Navy, and retained her French name.

On October 22nd, the *Agamemnon*, 64, Captain Horatio Nelson, cruising off Sardinia, sighted a French squadron composed as follows:—[1]

Melpoméne, 40 . . .	Capt. Gay.	*Mignonne*, 28.
Minerve, 38	„ [Z. J. T. Allemand?]	*Hasard*, [?] 14.
Fortunée, 36	„ Maistral.	

and made sail in chase.[2] By 4 A.M. he was close enough to one of the hostile frigates to speak her, and, as she did not answer his hail but fired her stern-chasers at him, opened on her. She constantly yawed and fired at the *Agamemnon's* rigging, whilst the slower-sailing British ship could make but little reply. At first the *Agamemnon* and her enemy had far outdistanced the other French ships, but at about nine the *Agamemnon* ran into a calm, and her enemy, hauling up, joined her French consorts. The *Agamemnon* was too crippled to pursue, and the frigates were very satisfied to get away. The British loss was one killed and six wounded. The frigate engaged was apparently in a sinking state, but her loss is unknown.

On October 24th, the *Thames*, 32, Captain James Cotes, sighted the *Uranie*, 36, Captain Tartu, in the Bay of Biscay.[3] The two closed at once, and in thick weather began action at a little before 11 A.M., the *Thames* passing and repassing the *Uranie* on the opposite tack, the ships each time exchanging fire. At 2.20 the *Uranie* succeeded in raking the *Thames*, and tried to board, but was raked in turn and driven off. She dropped to the south, and the British crew hailed her retreat with cheers. She finally spread all sail and retired, the *Thames* being too badly damaged to pursue

[1] Nicolas, 'Nelson Dispatches,' i. 334; Troude, 313; James, 117.

[2] So James. Nelson speaks of four frigates—one looking like a ship of the line—and a brig; he omits the *Fléche*, and gives the *Fouchet*, 24, and an unknown brig. Troude gives the *Fléche*, 18, and omits *Mignonne* and *Hasard*. But as he makes Z. J. T. Allemand the captain of the *Minerve*, when his own and other accounts show Z. Allemand, at about this very time, to have been commanding the *Carmagnole* in the Bay, his authority cannot be accepted. It is much to be regretted that there is no really trustworthy French history of this war. The *Gazette de France* ceases to afford valuable information; and deliberate falsification of facts, which is not noticeable in 1778–1783, becomes too common. Chevalier omits minor actions with some rare exceptions. Troude misdates this action.

[3] Troude, 310; James, 118; Marshall, 'Nav. Biography,' III., ii. 252; C. M., 72, June 11th.

her. The *Thames* had suffered very severely in masts and rigging. Her hull was terribly shattered, three guns were dismounted, and almost all the gun-tackles and breechings had been carried away. The *Uranie's* rigging was very much cut up, and her captain wounded. Having on board many Spanish prisoners from the *Alcoudia*, 16, which she had captured some days before, she made for Rochefort.

—	Tons.	Guns.	Broadside.	Men.	Killed.	Wounded.	Total.
			Lbs.				
Uranie . .	1100	40[1]	280[1]	260[1]	?	?	?
Thames . .	656	32	174	187[2]	11	23	34

3 hours.

[1] Troude. James, forty-four guns, 403-lb. broadside. [2] Captain Cotes's letter, 134 men and boys.

Whilst the battered *Thames* was refitting, at about 4 P.M., four sail came in sight. Escape was out of the question for her, and one of the strangers drew up under her stern and fired a broadside, when she struck. Her captor was the *Carmagnole*, 40, Captain Zacharie Jacques Théodore Allemand. The British crew were treated with great severity and rigidly imprisoned. Captain Cotes's official letter did not reach the Admiralty till May 7th, 1795, as the French intercepted all correspondence. The *Uranie's* name was changed to *Tartu*,[1] after the battle, in memory of her captain.

On November 25th, the British frigates *Penelope*, 32, Captain Bartholomew Samuel Rowley, and *Iphigenia*, 32, Captain Patrick Sinclair, fell in, off San Domingo, with the French *Inconstante*, 36, Captain Riouffe.[2] The *Penelope* began the action at about 1.30 A.M.

—	Tons.	Guns.	Broadside.	Men.	Killed.	Wounded.	Total.
			Lbs.				
{ *Penelope* . .	720	40	246	217 n.	1	7	8
{ *Iphigenia* .	681	40	246	217 n.	0	0	0
Inconstante .	—	40	270	300 n.	7	21	28

30 minutes.

[1] English authorities say *Tortue*, and that the change was made to hide the discreditable "defeat" of the French. But *Tartu* seems to have been the name, *cf.* Troude. When in 1796 she entered the British service she was renamed *Urania*.

[2] James, 122; Troude, 313.

The hammock cloths on her engaged side soon took fire, but this did not compel her to haul off. At two the *Iphigenia* came up, and the *Inconstante* struck. The French captain was caught by a superior force, with his ship unprepared for action, and could do little. The *Inconstante* was purchased for the Navy.

On November 30th, the French brig *Espiègle*, 16, was captured off Ushant by the British frigates *Nymphe* and *Circe*.[1]

On December 2nd, the diminutive West India packet *Antelope*, 6 (3-prs.), with an effective crew of twenty-one, fought and captured a French privateer, the *Atalante*, 8, fitted out at Charleston, South Carolina, and manned with a crew of sixty-five men, many of whom were Americans. The *Antelope* lost three killed and four wounded. Of her crew a French royalist, named Nodin, distinguished himself most.

On January 8th, 1794, the *Hind*, 28, Captain Philip Charles Durham, was chased by five French frigates and a brig.[2] She escaped with the loss of twelve men killed or wounded. The British ships of the line, *Impregnable*, 90, and *Majestic*, 74, were close at hand, but at first would give no aid, because they were weakly manned, fresh from port, and took the *Hind* for a decoy.

On January 11th, 1794, after the evacuation of Toulon, the British frigate *Juno*, 32, Captain Samuel Hood (2), arrived from Malta at that place.[3] Hood was not aware that the British had abandoned it, and could exchange no signals, as it was night when he neared the port. He entered the inner harbour unchallenged, but took the ground slightly, in attempting to pass a brig. That vessel hailed him, and was answered by his informing her of his ship's name and nationality. The *Juno* anchored with her stern on the shoal and hoisted out a launch to warp off. Whilst she was thus engaged, a boat rowed alongside, and from it two officers came up the ship's side, and directed Hood to go to another part of the harbour. Something in their words attracted attention, and a Midshipman, looking carefully at them in the dim light, saw that they wore tri-coloured cockades. They were seized, the cable was cut, and the *Juno's* sails were set, whereupon the stern came off the ground and the ship stood down the harbour. All the forts fired at her, but she escaped without the loss of a man. Some damage to sail and rigging was the only result of the brush with the formidable works of Toulon. This

[1] Troude, 293; Log of *Nymphe*.
[2] A. Murray, 'Sir P. Durham,' 27.
[3] James, 216.

incident shows the ease with which the forts of those days could be passed at night, even by a sailing ship.

On January 17th, two large French privateers, the *Résolue*, 26, and *Vengeur*, 34, attacked the *Pigot*, East Indiaman, George Ballantyne, master, near Bencoolen, and were ignominiously beaten off. Though the action lasted for nearly two hours the *Pigot* only lost one man. Five days later the privateers were attacked by five British East Indiamen[1] and captured. Their loss was heavy: the British loss trifling.

On April 23rd, the British frigates *Flora*, 36, Commodore Sir John Borlase Warren; *Arethusa*, 38, Captain Sir Edward Pellew; *Melampus*, 36,[2] Captain Thomas Wells (1); *Concorde*, 36, Captain Sir Richard John Strachan; and *Nymphe*, 36, Captain George Murray (3), whilst cruising off the Channel Islands, sighted the French ships *Engageante*, 36, Commodore Desgarceaux; *Résolue*, 36, Captain P. Villéon; *Pomone*, 44, Captain Etienne Pévrieu; and *Babet*, 20, Lieutenant P. J. P. Belhomme.[3] The French formed in line of battle: the British came up one by one to windward of them. The *Flora* began the action at 6.30 A.M., but lost her maintopmast, had her rigging cut to pieces, and dropped behind. The *Arethusa*, after engaging the *Babet*, took the *Flora's* place, whilst both sides crowded all sail—the French to escape, the British to pursue. The *Arethusa* and *Melampus* captured the *Babet* at 8.30: the *Engageante* and *Résolue* had left the *Pomone* behind, and on that ship next fell the brunt of the British onset. Already the *Pomone* had been much damaged by the *Flora's* fire. The *Arethusa* completed her discomfiture by shooting away her main and mizen-masts, and setting her on fire. She struck at 9.30. The *Concorde* and *Melampus* then pushed on after the *Résolue* and *Engageante*, but could not separate the pair nor delay them both enough to enable the other ships to come up. The *Concorde* accordingly decided to secure one, and closed the *Engageante*. The two fought side by side almost uninterrupted, as the *Résolue* quickly retired and the other British ships were too far astern to give help. At 1.45 P.M. the *Engageante* struck. In comparative force the British had a great superiority—210 guns to

[1] *William Pitt*, *Britannia*, *Nonsuch*, *Houghton*, and brig *Nautilus*.

[2] In the 'Navy List Book,' a 38.

[3] James, 222; Troude, 323; Osler, 64; Brenton, i. 122. The British cruiser squadron was to protect trade. Its cruising ground extended from Cape Finisterre to Cherbourg. It was found so useful that other light squadrons of three or four frigates were sent out to scour the same waters.

144:[1] 40 of those in the *Résolue* were scarcely engaged, as against as many in the *Nymphe* which were not in action, owing to that ship being left behind. None of the British ships were very severely damaged. Their loss is stated as follows:—

British.	Men.	Killed.	Wounded.	Total.	French.	Men.	Loss.
Flora . . .	267	1	3	4	*Engageante* .	?	?
Arethusa . .	277	3	5	8	*Pomone* . .	341	80–100
Melampus .	267	5	5	10	*Babet* . . .	178	30–40
Concorde . .	257	1	12	13			

The *Pomone* was of 1239 tons, of unusual beam, and an excellent sailer.[2] She was purchased for the Navy.

On May 5th, in East Indian waters, the *Orpheus*, 32, Captain Henry Newcome; *Centurion*, 50, and *Resistance*, 44, chased the French *Duguay Trouin*, 34, and another ship.[3] The *Orpheus* closed the *Duguay Trouin*, and began action before noon. In little more than an hour the Frenchman struck. She had been an East Indiaman, and was probably weakly built.

—	Tons.	Guns.	Broadside.	Men.	Killed.	Wounded.	Total.
			Lbs.				
Orpheus . .	708	40	246	194	1	9	10
Duguay Trouin	—	34	194?	?	21	60	81

The *Centurion* and *Resistance* were coming up fast when the enemy surrendered.

On the same day the *Swiftsure*, 74, Captain Charles Boyles, and *St. Albans*, 64, with a convoy out from Cork, saw and chased the French frigate *Atalante*, 36, Captain Charles Alexandre Léon Durand Linois, and the corvette *Levrette*.[4] The *Swiftsure* chose the former as her quarry, and after a long chase, in which the two exchanged fire more than once, brought her to close action on the 7th at 2.30 A.M. The *Levrette* seems to have escaped. After fifty-five minutes' fighting the *Atalante* struck. Her masts and rigging were in bad order before

[1] Troude, 136.

[2] According to Osler and James she carried 24-prs. on her main-deck; according to Brenton, 18's.

[3] James, 226. Not in Troude. Possibly the *Duguay Trouin* was a privateer.

[4] James, 227; Troude, 376; Hennequin, 'Biographie Maritime,' i. 320.

the action, and were now disabled. Her crew was weak, and had been for two whole days and nights at quarters.

—	Tons.	Guns.	Broadside.	Men.	Killed.	Wounded.	Total.
			Lbs.				
Swiftsure .	1612	82	928?	644	1	0	1
Atalante . .	986	40?	280?	274	10	32	42

55 minutes.

The *Swiftsure* and her prize were seen and unsuccessfully chased by three 74's of M. Nielly's squadron. The *Atalante* was purchased for the Navy, and renamed *Espion*.

On May 10th, the *Castor*, 32, Captain Thomas Troubridge, was captured on her way to Newfoundland, without any resistance,[1] by the French *Patriote*, 74, one of Admiral Nielly's squadron. On the 29th she was sighted by the *Carysfort*, 28, Captain Francis Laforey, and, after seventy-five minutes' action, recaptured. On board were twenty of the *Castor's* British crew.

—	Tons.	Guns.	Broadside.	Men.	Killed.	Wounded.	Total.
			Lbs.				
Carysfort .	599	32	156	180	1	4	5
Castor . .	678	36	222	200	16	9?	25?

75 minutes.

On May 25th, Lord Howe's fleet captured and destroyed the French *Républicaine*, 20, and *Inconnue*, 12.[2]

On June 8th, the *Crescent*, 36, Captain Sir James Saumarez; *Druid*, 32, Captain Joseph Ellison; and *Eurydice*, 24, Captain Francis Cole, fell in with the French cut-down 74's, *Scévola*, 50, and *Brutus*, 50, two 36-gun frigates and a brig, but succeeded in making their escape. The *Crescent* drew off the French pursuit, from the slower ships, heading into Guernsey road by a channel till then unused by warships. Captain Saumarez was a Channel Islander, and his local knowledge stood him in good stead. This was an achievement as brilliant as it was gallant and skilful.

On June 17th, Captain the Hon. William Paget in the *Romney*, 50,

[1] James, 228; Troude, 379; C.M., 71, June 24th.

[2] Logs of *Audacious* and *Niger*.

with a convoy, discovered the French *Sibylle*, 40, Captain J. M. Rondeau, at anchor in the harbour of Mykonos.[1] Three other British vessels were in sight from the *Romney's* masthead, and, as her convoy would for that reason be safe, she went into the harbour, anchored close to the *Sibylle*, and summoned her to surrender. The *Sibylle's* captain refused, and the *Romney* opened fire. After seventy minutes' fighting most of the French crew fled ashore, and Captain Rondeau struck his colours. The *Sibylle* fought 14 instead of 13 guns on her main-deck engaged broadside.

—	Tons.	Guns.	Broadside.	Men.	Killed.	Wounded.	Total.
			Lbs.				
Romney . .	1046	54[1]	462	266	8	30	38
Sibylle . .	1091	44	380	380	44	112	156

70 minutes.

1 James gives her no carronades, but I have allowed her four Troude gives her ten, and reduces the *Sibylle's* battery to thirty-two guns.

The *Sibylle* was purchased into the British Navy.

On July 14th, the sloop *Hound*, 16, Commander Richard Piercy, on her way home from the West Indies, was captured, thirty miles to the west of the Scillies, by the French frigates *Seine*, 40, and *Galatée*, 36.[2] To a force so superior she offered no resistance.

On August 23rd, early in the morning, the British frigates *Flora*, Captain Sir John Warren; *Arethusa*, 38, Captain Sir Edward Pellew; *Diamond*, 38, Captain Sir William Sidney Smith; *Artois*, 38, Captain Edmund Nagle; *Diana*, 38, Captain Jonathan Faulknor (2); and *Santa Margarita*, 36, Captain Eliab Harvey, discovered the French frigate *Volontaire*, 36, Captain Papin, off Brest, and compelled her to anchor off the Penmarcks.[3] There she was vigorously attacked by four of the British ships, and, cutting her cables to take up a better position, was driven ashore. Her pumps could not keep the water down, and therefore Captain Papin abandoned her. At the same time the French corvettes *Alerte*, 12, and *Espion*, 18, were driven ashore in Audierne Bay, and boarded by British boats. Fifty-two French prisoners were brought off, but the vessels, as they had many wounded on board, could not be destroyed. The

1 James, 231; Troude, 381.
2 C.M., 72, June 29th.
3 James, 233; Troude, 383; Osler, 67.

Espion was got off by the French[1] in the night. The *Alerte* was lost.

On September 14th, an amusing incident happened. Captain Saumarez's squadron of four frigates was sighted off Weymouth, where at that time was the Royal family, and failed to answer the guardship *Trusty's* private signal. It was immediately supposed that the French were making an attempt to carry off the King, and the troops at Weymouth stood to arms, the batteries were manned, and carriages for the Royal household were got ready. The misunderstanding was, however, cleared up after dark, when Saumarez entered the road.

On October 21st, the *Arethusa*, *Artois*, *Diamond*,[2] and *Galatea*, 32, Captain Richard Goodwin Keats, off Ushant, saw and chased a French frigate, the *Révolutionnaire*, 44, Captain H. A. Thévenard. The French ship was with some difficulty cut off from the land and brought to action by the *Artois*, 38, Captain Edmund Nagle, which had outsailed the other British ships. A warm action of forty minutes' duration followed before the *Diamond* came up astern of the Frenchman, though Smith would not spoil the *Artois'* game by firing. Then, after a gallant and creditable defence in the face of a greatly superior force, Captain Thévenard struck his colours, as his men would no longer fight the ship. He was but just out from port with a raw crew.

—	Tons.	Guns.	Broadside.	Men.	Killed.	Wounded.	Total.
			Lbs.				
Artois . . .	996	44	370	281 n.	3	5	8
Révolutionnaire	1148	44	403	351	8	5	13

40 minutes.

Captain Nagle was knighted, and his capture purchased for the Navy.

On October 22nd, whilst cruising off Mauritius, the *Centurion*, 50, Captain Samuel Osborn, and *Diomede*, 44, Captain Matthew Smith (1),[3] saw and chased four French ships, the *Cybèle*, 40, Captain Tréhouart; *Prudente*, 36, Commodore[4] Jean Marie Renaud; *Jean Bart*, 20, and

[1] The *Espion* was finally taken, however, by the *Lively*, in 1795.

[2] For guns and Captains see above p. 486. James, 235; Troude, 384; Osler, 68.

[3] James, 236; Troude, 370.

[4] *Chef de division*.

Courier, 14, which had put to sea with the express purpose of fighting the British squadron. The *Centurion* and *Diomede* placed themselves opposite the French frigates and opened action at about 3.30 P.M. The *Centurion* was soon so much cut up in her rigging that she dropped behind, and the *Prudente*, leaving the French line, was able to get away from her. The *Cybèle*, passing the *Centurion*, brought down the latter's mizen and foretopgallant-mast, but, on the wind dropping, was engaged by the powerful British ship and roughly handled. The *Diomede* did little or nothing, except fire from a distance at the French. Soon after five the wind again freshened, and the *Cybèle* got away with her maintopgallant-mast gone. Though both British ships pursued her they could not prevent the *Prudente* from taking her in tow, and with her escaping.

—	Tons.	Guns.	Broadside.	Men.	Killed.	Wounded.	Total.
			Lbs.				
Centurion .	1044	54	462	345 n.	3	24	27
Diomede . .	891	54	408	297 n.	0	0	0
Prudente. .	897	40	280	300 n.	15	20	35
Cybèle . .	—	44	410	330 n.	22	62	84
Jean Bart .	—	20	?	?	1	5	6
Courier . .	—	14	?	?	0	0	0

Captain Smith for his behaviour was court-martialled and dismissed the service, but the sentence was quashed in 1798. He retired, however, in 1806.

On December 22nd, the *Daphne*, 20, Captain William Edward Cracraft, was captured by Admiral Villaret's fleet in the Bay. She made no resistance.

On December 30th, the boats of the *Blanche*, 32, Captain Robert Faulknor (3), cut out a French armed schooner at Désirade, Guadeloupe, with the loss of only six men.[1]

On January 5th, 1795, the *Blanche*, 32, whilst cruising off Guadeloupe, encountered the French *Pique*, 36, Captain Conseil.[2] The action began soon after midnight, when the *Blanche* passed the *Pique* on the opposite tack, exchanging broadsides with her. Then, as the *Blanche* tacked and came up in the wake of the *Pique*, the French ship, having the weather gage, wore to rake her; but Captain Robert Faulknor (3) was able to defeat the manœuvre by also

[1] James, 308.

[2] *Ib.* 309; Troude, 439; Brenton, i. 247; 'Nav. Chron.,' 16, 40.

wearing. The ships fought broadside to broadside till 2.30 A.M., when the *Blanche* shot ahead. At that moment, just as the *Blanche* was preparing to rake the *Pique*, the *Blanche's* mizen and mainmasts fell, and the *Pique* ran foul of her, receiving a terrible raking fire. An attempt on the part of the French to board was repulsed with heavy loss. At about 3 A.M. the heroic Captain Faulknor was shot dead as he was endeavouring to lash the *Pique's* bowsprit to the

CAPTAIN ROBERT FAULKNOR (3), R.N.

Killed in command of H.M.S. *Blanche*, Jan., 1795.

(From the portrait by Holl.)

Blanche. The lashing parted, and the two ships first drifted clear of each other, and then fouled again, the *Pique* falling on the *Blanche's* starboard quarter. The *Pique's* bowsprit was promptly lashed to the stump of the *Blanche's* mainmast. It was at that time that the top-fire of the *Pique's* sharpshooters began to trouble the *Blanche's* seamen, whilst the British frigate, having no stern ports on her main deck, could not bring her guns to bear astern on the Frenchman. In this difficulty it was decided to make ports in the ship's stern, by the simple expedient of firing two shotted 12-prs. through it, leaving firemen with buckets of water to put out the flames caused by such an heroic measure. The 12-prs. thereafter maintained a most effective fire, until the *Pique* was dismasted; but she did not strike for another two hours. At 5.15 A.M., she hauled down her flag. She had fought most gallantly, and had lost more than two-thirds of her crew.

—	Tons.	Guns.	Broadside.	Men.	Killed.	Wounded.	Total.
			Lbs.				
Blanche . .	710	38	228	198	8	21	29
Pique. . .	906	38	273	279	76	110	186

5 hours.

The *Pique* was purchased for the British Navy.

On January 8th, the French *Espérance*, 22, was captured off the Chesapeake by the British *Argonaut*, 64, and *Oiseau*, 36.[1] On February 20th, the *Requin*, 12, was taken off Dunkirk by the British *Thalia*.

On March 2nd, the British *Lively*, 32, Commander George Burlton (actg. Captain),[2] captured the French corvette *Espion*, 18, Captain Magendie, off Brest, after a two hours' action.[3]

On March 13th, the *Lively*, 32, Commander George Burlton (actg. Captain), sighted the French *Tourterelle*, 28, Captain G. S. A. Montalan, in the Channel.[4] The French vessel did not decline the unequal battle, but stood to meet the *Lively*. Both opened fire soon after 10 A.M., when Captain Montalan, discovering the great superiority of his opponent, turned and attempted to retreat. In this he was unsuccessful, and the *Lively* closing the *Tourterelle* fought her till she struck at 1.30 P.M., in a very shattered state. The *Tourterelle* carried a furnace for heating shot, and had made use of it against the *Lively*, burning the latter's sails badly. The furnace was thrown overboard just before the French flag was lowered. At that time the use of hot shot was, perhaps rather foolishly, considered a breach of the tacit conventions of war.

[1] Troude, 441.

[2] The *Lively's* Captain, Lord Garlies, was sick on shore at the time.

[3] Troude, 441.

[4] James, 313; Troude, 445, dates the action May 15th, an evident mistake.

—	Tons.	Guns.	Broadside.	Men.	Killed.	Wounded.	Total.
			Lbs.				
Lively . .	806	38	324	251	0	2	2
Tourterelle .	581	30	188	230	16	25	41

On March 25th, the French *Coureuse*, 18, was captured by a squadron of British frigates off Lorient,[1] and the *Jean Bart*, 18, on her way from the West Indies to France, was taken by the British ships *Santa Margarita* and *Cerberus*.

On April 10th, a British fleet under Rear-Admiral John Colpoys was cruising off Brest, when three sail were seen.[2] The fleet scattered in chase, and the *Astræa*, 32, Captain Lord Henry Paulet, outsailing the ships of the line, came up with one of the three, the French *Gloire*, 36, Captain Beens. The action between the two opened at 6 P.M. At 10.30 the *Astræa* closed her adversary, and after an hour's fight made her strike her flag. The *Astræa's* maintop-mast went overboard just after the close of the action, and her other topmasts were so wounded that they had to be removed.

—	Tons.	Guns.	Broadside.	Men	Killed.	Wounded.	Total.
			Lbs.				
Astræa . .	703	32[1]	174	212	0	8	8
Gloire . .	877	42	286	275	?	?	40

4½ hours.

[1] James gives her no carronades; but this must be doubtful. Possibly eight 18's should be added to her battery.

The *Gloire* was purchased for the Navy, but did not long remain in the service. Of the other French vessels, the *Gentille*, 36, Captain Canon, was taken on the 11th by the *Hannibal*, 74. The third escaped. The easy capture of the *Gloire* should probably be ascribed to the presence of one or two British ships of the line at no great distance.

On May 1st, the *Boyne*, 98, Captain the Hon. George Grey, took fire at Spithead, and blew up. All her crew, except eleven men, were saved, but her shotted guns, discharged by the heat, killed or wounded three men in the fleet.[3]

[1] Troude, 442–3. [2] James, 315; Troude, 443.
[3] C.M., vol. 72, May 19th.

On May 9th, Captain Sir Richard John Strachan, in the *Melampus*, 36, with the frigates *Diamond, Hebe, Niger,* and *Siren,* whilst at anchor off Jersey, saw a French convoy running along the enemy's coast.[1] Giving chase, he drove the convoy into Carteret Bay, where the boats of his squadron attacked it and captured or burnt every vessel but one, with the loss of two killed and seventeen wounded.

On May 15th, the French corvette *Hirondelle,* 18, was attacked in the Bay of Frénay, near St. Malo, by a British squadron, but, being supported by the fire of a small fort, repulsed the ships.[2]

On May 17th, the *Thetis,* 36, Captain the Hon. Alexander Forester Inglis Cochrane, and *Hussar,* 28, Captain John Poor Beresford, captured off Cape Henry two large French storeships of a squadron of five.[3] The names of the prizes were the *Prévoyante* and *Raison.* The British loss was eleven wounded. On the 28th, the *Thorn,* 16, Commander Robert Waller Otway, captured the French corvette, *Courier National,* 18, in the West Indies, with a loss of six wounded; the French ship having seven killed and twenty wounded.[4] On the 28th, the French corvette *Prompte,* 28, was captured; and, on the 30th, the French *Liberté,* 20, was attacked and sunk off San Domingo by the *Alarm,* 32, Captain David Milne[5] (actg.).

In June, almost at the same time, the Admirals commanding the French and British fleets in the Mediterranean despatched each two frigates to ascertain one another's movements.[6] The British pair were the *Dido,* 28, Captain George Henry Towry, and *Lowestoft,* 32, Captain Robert Gambier Middleton; the French, the *Minerve,* 40, Captain Delorme, and *Artémise,* 36, Captain Decasse. The enemies sighted each other to the north of Minorca on June 24th, early in the morning. The French retired, and meanwhile cleared for action. Having first drawn far ahead, they turned and stood to meet the *Dido* and *Lowestoft.* The *Minerve* was in advance, and engaged the *Dido* at 8.30 A.M. The *Minerve* attempted to run down her opponent, but, owing to the *Dido* porting her helm, only struck an oblique blow, and entangled her bowsprit in her enemy's rigging. The French endeavoured to board, but were beaten off, and in the heavy swell the *Minerve's* bowsprit snapped and went overboard carrying

[1] James, 318. [2] Troude, 445. [3] James, 319.

[4] Marshall, 'Naval Biography,' i. 693.

[5] Captain Milne was posted on Oct. 2nd following. Troude, 447; *Alarm's* log missing. According to the List Book, the British Captain was (the Hon.) Charles Carpenter; (but this is an error. 'Nav. Chron.' xxxix., App.—W. L. C.)

[6] James, 321; Troude, 448.

with it the *Dido's* mizen-mast. The *Minerve* passed along the *Dido's* larboard side, carrying away sails and rigging, but, as soon as she was clear, was attacked by the *Lowestoft*, and had her foremast, main and mizentop-mast shot away. The *Artémise*, instead of helping her consort, only fired a broadside at each of the British ships, and retreated, pursued by the *Lowestoft*. Left to themselves, the *Minerve* and *Dido* repaired damage and cleared their decks. At 10.30 the *Lowestoft* was recalled by signal. At 11.30 she placed herself on the *Minerve's* quarter and opened a heavy fire, whilst the *Dido* made sail to renew the attack. At 11.45 the *Minerve* hailed to say that she surrendered. The action reflects great credit upon the senior British officer, Captain Towry,[1] who had so boldly engaged a far superior force.

—	Tons.	Guns.	Broadside.	Men.	Drowned and Killed.	Wounded.	Total.
			Lbs.				
{ *Dido*	595	32	156	193	6	15	21
{ *Lowestoft*	717	36	210	212	0	3	3
{ *Minerve*	1102	42	370	318	?	?	28
{ *Artémise*	—	40	283	300 n.	?	?	?

3¼ hours.

The *Artémise's* captain was tried by jury for his conduct, but acquitted. The *Minerve* was purchased for the Navy.

On August 22nd, the British ships *Isis*, 50, Captain Robert Watson; *Réunion*, 36, Captain James Alms (2); *Stag*, 32, Captain Joseph Sydney Yorke; and *Vestal*, 28, Captain Charles White, captured the Dutch frigate *Alliantie*, 36, after an hour's fight.[2] The Dutch vessels *Argo*, 36, and *Vlugheid*, 16, which were with her, escaped into the Norwegian harbour of Egerö. The British loss was 5 killed and 17 wounded. The *Argo* lost 2 killed and 15 wounded. The *Alliantie's*[3] loss is unknown.

On August 31st, the two French corvettes, *Suffisante*, 14, and *Victorieuse*, 14, were captured off the Texel by Admiral Duncan's squadron.[4] They were on a cruise against the British whale fisheries.

On September 2nd, the *Diamond*, 38, Captain Sir William

[1] After serving as a Commissioner of the Navy, Captain George Henry Towry died in 1809.

[2] James, 324; Log of *Stag*.

[3] Added to the Navy as *Alliance*.

[4] Brenton, i. 92; Troude, ii. 453.

Sidney Smith, chased and drove on the rocks of the Breton coast the French *Assemblée Nationale,* 14.

On September 29th, the *Southampton,* 32, Captain James Macnamara (2), cruising off Genoa, chased the French vessels *Vestale,* 36, Captain Foucaud, *Brune,* 24, *Alceste,* 14, and *Scout,* 14.[1] Selecting the *Vestale* as his quarry, Captain Macnamara opened on her at 10 P.M., and maintained a running action with her whilst she crowded all sail to get away. At about 10.30 the *Southampton's* rigging was so damaged that she fell astern, but she effected repairs and came up again at about 11, only to lose her mizen-mast. Profiting by this incident, the *Vestale* escaped, but was chased in the course of the night by the British sloop *Moselle,* 18, Commander Charles Brisbane. The French ships had a convoy under their charge, a fact which explains their strange conduct in retiring with so superior force on their side.

—	Tons.	Guns.	Broadside.	Men.	Killed.	Wounded.	Total.
			Lbs.				
Southampton	671	40?	246	217 n.	?	?	?
Vestale . .	—	40	280	300 n.	8	9	17

½ hour.

On October 1st, the *Vanguard,* 74, Captain Charles Sawyer, captured the French *Superbe,* 24, Captain Doudoux, in the West Indies.[2]

On October 10th, the *Mermaid,* 32, Captain Henry Warre, captured off Grenada the French *Brutus,* 10, and, four days later, the French *Républicaine,* 18. The British loss was only 4; the French 20. One of the prizes had a French general and troops on board, destined for Grenada, where a savage war between the British, on the one hand, and the French and Caribs, on the other, was then raging.

On March 10th, 1796, the *Bonne Citoyenne,* 20, Captain La Bourdonnais, was chased by three British frigates, and captured in the Bay by the *Phaeton,* 38, after the exchange of a few shots.[3] The *Bonne Citoyenne* was one of Rear-Admiral Sercey's squadron on her way to Mauritius. On the same day the French cutter,

[1] James, 325; Marshall, i. 636; Troude, 454; Log of *Southampton.*

[2] James, 328; Troude, 455.

[3] James, 387; Troude, iii. 21.

Aspic, was captured in St. George's Channel by the *Quebec*, 32. The French brig, *Mutine*, fell to the British frigates in the Bay a few days later.

On March 18th, Captain Sir William Sidney Smith in the *Diamond*, 38, with the *Liberty*, 14, Lieutenant George M'Kinley, and *Aristocrat*, Lieutenant Abraham Gossett, made a dash at a French corvette and some smaller vessels lying in the Breton port of Erqui.[1] Three guns, mounted in commanding positions on the cliffs, were stormed by a party of seamen and Marines. The French corvette, *Etourdie*, 16, four brigs, two sloops, and a lugger were then set on fire and destroyed. In this dashing operation the British loss was only 2 killed and 7—amongst whom were two Lieutenants—wounded.

On March 20th, off Pointe du Raz, the British frigates, *Pomone*, 40, Captain Sir John Borlase Warren; *Anson*, 44, Captain Philip Charles Durham; *Artois*, 38, Captain Sir Edmund Nagle, and *Galatea*, 32, Captain Richard Goodwin Keats, saw and chased a large French convoy under the charge of the frigates *Proserpine*, 40, *Unité*, *Coquille*, and *Tamise*, all of 36, and the corvette *Cigogne*, 20.[2] After taking several prizes from the convoy, the British squadron passed the French on the opposite tack, exchanging fire. The *Galatea* was roughly handled. Tacking, the British stood after the French, who steered for Pointe du Raz and Brest, whither they succeeded in effecting their escape. A French armed storeship, the *Etoile*, 28, was, however, added to the list of British prizes. The force of the British was superior in this affair, and it is not obvious why the French escaped so easily. Warren, the British senior officer, absurdly exaggerated the strength of his enemy in his report of the business. Of the convoy six ships in all were taken. The British loss was 2 killed and 6 wounded.

On April 12th, Sir Edward Pellew's squadron of five frigates, whilst cruising off Brest, saw and chased the French *Unité*, 36, Captain C. A. L. Durand Linois.[3] The British *Révolutionnaire*, 38, Captain Francis Cole, closed her late in the evening at 11.30, and called upon Captain Linois to surrender to such a superior force.

[1] James, 355; Troude, 22.

[2] James, 356; Troude, 24.

[3] Osler, 'Lord Exmouth,' 80; James, 357. Troude, 23, calls the French ship the *Variante*, Capt. Durand, and gives the date as the 11th. Pellew in a letter to the Admiralty speaks of her as "*l'Unité* alias *la Variante*." The Log of the *Révolutionnaire* fixes the date as the 12th.

Linois refused, and a hot action began. The French crew, however, composed mostly of conscripts and not of seamen, fought badly. Thirty men fled below and pretended that they were wounded. Eighteen Vendéens refused to fight. Captain Linois, in these circumstances, struck at 11.50, just as the British *Concorde*, 36, came up. The *Révolutionnaire* by herself was far more than a match for the *Unité* in weight of metal, as she carried, besides her thirty-eight guns, eight 32-pr. carronades. Captain Linois had several passengers on board, who were transferred to a neutral ship by Sir E. Pellew.

——	Tons.	Guns.	Broadside.	Men.	Killed.	Wounded.	Total.
			Lbs.				
Révolutionnaire	1148	46	425	287	0	0	0
Unité . . .	893	38	240	255	9	11	20

20 minutes.

On April 17th, Captain Sir William Sidney Smith of the *Diamond*, 38, was captured.[1] He led a boat attack upon a privateer, the *Vengeur*, at Havre, and carried her. The privateersmen, however, had cut their cable, and, as the tide was rising, the *Vengeur* was swept up the river, two miles above Havre. Smith attempted to escape with the boats, but, as there were French ships on the move at the river's mouth, that was impossible. The intrepid officer and his men had not long to wait before they were attacked. They were surrounded by small craft and compelled to surrender with the loss of 4 killed and 7 wounded. Smith and Midshipman John Wesley Wright were considered state prisoners and shut up in the Temple. They escaped, however, in May, 1798.

On April 20th, the French corvette *Unité*, 24, was carried off from the neutral harbour of Bona by the British frigate *Inconstant*, 36, Captain Thomas Francis Fremantle.[2] The *Unité* offered no resistance. She was purchased for the Navy and renamed *Surprise*.

On the same day Sir Edward Pellew, in the *Indefatigable*, 44, with the *Amazon*, 36, Captain Robert Carthew Reynolds, and *Concorde*, 36, Captain Anthony Hunt (2), sighted the French *Virginie*, 40, Captain

[1] James, 359; Troude, 28.

[2] Troude, 28; Schomberg, ii. 431; James, ii. 405. Log of *Inconstant* gives the *Unité* 34 guns and 318 men.

Bergeret, off the Lizard.[1] The three British ships at once crowded all sail and stood after the enemy. The wind was south-east, and prevented the *Virginie* from retreating to Brest. After a fifteen hours' chase the *Indefatigable* got close enough to begin a running fight. At about midnight the action commenced. After an hour and three-quarters' firing the *Virginie* lost her mizen-mast and main-top-mast, and the *Indefatigable* her mizen-topmast and gaff. By reason of these injuries the British ship shot ahead and was all but raked. She was repairing damages when the *Concorde* came up astern of the *Virginie,* whereupon the latter struck in a very crippled condition, with four feet of water in her hold. The *Virginie* had been bravely fought against a very superior force.

—	Tons.	Guns.	Broadside.	Men.	Killed.	Wounded.	Total.
Indefatigable	1384	46	Lb. 702	327	0	0	0
Virginie . .	1066	44	342	339	15	27	42

1 hour 45 minutes.

The presence of the *Concorde* and *Amazon* at the close of the action must also be taken into account. The *Virginie* was purchased for the Navy.

On April 27th, the British frigate *Niger,* 32, Captain Edward James Foote, drove the French armed lugger, *Ecureuil,* ashore on the Penmarck rocks.[2] After cannonading her, Captain Foote sent in his boats, which, in spite of a desperate resistance on the part of the French, burnt her. The British loss was seven wounded.

On April 21st, the French corvette *Perçante,* 26, Captain Tourtelet, was chased ashore on the San Domingo coast by the British *Irresistible,* 74, a frigate, and two smaller vessels.[3]

On May 4th, the *Spencer,* 16, Commander Andrew Fitzherbert Evans, brought the French gun-brig *Volcan,* 12, to action, after a long chase, south of Bermuda.[4] The *Spencer* was armed almost entirely with carronades, having only two long guns. Her broadside threw 88 lbs., against the French vessel's 26 lbs. The *Volcan,* before she struck, had her topmasts shot away, and lost many men, some of whom were killed by the explosion of hand-grenades which had been prepared by her crew for use against the British

[1] James, 361; Troude, 29; Log of *Indefatigable.*
[2] James, 362.
[3] Troude, 32.
[4] James, 363; Troude, 33.

sloop. The *Spencer* sustained a loss of one killed and one wounded, and much injury to her rigging. Three of her carronades upset in the action, which lasted for seventy-five minutes.

On May 12th, Admiral Adam Duncan's squadron, cruising off the Texel, chased the Dutch frigate *Argo*, 36, three brigs and a cutter.[1] The *Argo* was quickly overhauled by the *Phœnix*, 36, Captain Lawrence William Halsted, and brought to action, when, after twenty minutes' fighting, seeing British ships on all sides of her, the Dutchman struck. Two of the Dutch brigs were chased on shore; the third was captured, and the cutter shared her fate on May 13th. The *Argo* was purchased for the Navy, and renamed *Juno*, there being already an *Argo* in the service.

On May 2nd,[2] the British *Dryad*, 36, Captain Lord Amelius Beauclerk, for whom Commander John King Pulling was acting, captured the French corvette *Abeille*.[3]

On June 8th, the British frigates *Santa Margarita*, 36, Captain Thomas Byam Martin, and *Unicorn*, 32, Captain Thomas Williams (4), sighted in the Channel the French *Tribune*, 36, Captain Jean Moultson, *Tamise*, 36, Captain J. B. A. Fradin, and *Légère*, 18, Lieutenant J. M. M. Carpentier.[4] As the British ships approached, the *Légère* drew away from her two consorts. A running fight began at 1 P.M., as the result of which the British vessels suffered much in their masts and rigging. At 4 P.M., however, the *Santa Margarita* closed the *Tamise*, and fought her broadside to broadside, whilst the *Unicorn* continued the pursuit of the *Tribune*. After twenty minutes' fighting the *Tamise* struck.

—	Tons.	Guns.	Broadside.	Men.	Killed.	Wounded.	Total.
			Lbs.				
Santa Margarita	993	40	250	237	2	3	5
Tamise	656	40	279	306	32	19	51

3 hours 20 minutes.

The *Tamise* was restored to the Navy under her original name, *Thames*.

The *Unicorn* after a long chase closed the *Tribune* at 10.30 P.M.,

[1] James, 363; Schomberg, ii. 421.

[2] Log of *Dryad*.

[3] James, 364, gives the capture by the *Suffisante*, 14, of the French *Revanche*, 12, on May 27th, without stating that the latter was a privateer. Troude, 34, omits this action.

[4] James, 365; Troude, 36.

and fought her for thirty-five minutes, when the Frenchman dropped astern. The *Unicorn*, backing her sails, followed her adroitly, placed herself on the *Tribune's* weather bow, brought down her foremast, mainmast and mizentop-mast, and compelled her to strike.

—	Tons.	Guns.	Broadside.	Men.	Killed.	Wounded.	Total.
			Lbs.				
Unicorn . .	791	44	348	240	0	0	0
Tribune . .	916	38	260	339	37	14	51

It is, as James comments, extraordinary that the *Unicorn* should have suffered no loss; and the only conclusion is that the French gunnery was exceedingly bad. This was the third frigate action within a few months in which the same phenomenon occurred.

On June 9th, the British Mediterranean fleet was cruising off Toulon when a French corvette was noticed in Hyères Roads.[1] Sir John Jervis, the British Admiral, summoned Captain James Macnamara (2) of the *Southampton*, 32, on board the flagship and pointed out "this eyesore." Macnamara accepted the hint: stood in under easy sail past the French batteries, which took his ship for a neutral, dashed at the corvette, *Utile*, 24, boarded and carried her, and then, taking her in tow, repassed the forts under a heavy fire. Lieutenant Charles Lydiard, who led the *Southampton's* boarders, was promoted by Jervis on the spot to the command of the *Utile*.[2] The British loss was one killed; the French, eight killed and seventeen wounded.

On June 11th, the French corvettes *Trois Couleurs*, 14, and *Betsy*,[3] 18, were taken off Brest by the *Amazon*, 38, and other British frigates.[4]

On June 13th, to the south of Cape Clear, the *Dryad*, 36, Captain Lord Amelius Beauclerk, brought the French frigate *Proserpine*, 40, Captain Pévrieu, to action at about 8 A.M.[5] For an hour the engagement was a running one. Then the *Dryad* came up on the Frenchman's larboard quarter and began a close action. After forty-five minutes of this the French ship struck. Neither

[1] Tucker, 'St. Vincent,' i. 185; James, 370; Troude, 38.

[2] Lydiard, who was further promoted on Jan. 1st, 1801, to the rank of Captain, was drowned in the *Anson* in 1807.—W. L. C.

[3] The *Betsy* appears in the prize lists as the *Blonde*.—W. L. C.

[4] Troude, 38; Log of *Amazon*.

[5] James, 369; Troude, 39; Log of *Dryad*.

vessel lost a spar, and neither was much damaged in sails or rigging.

—	Tons.	Guns.	Broadside.	Men.	Killed.	Wounded.	Total.
			Lbs.				
Dryad . .	924	44	407	254	2	7	9
Proserpine .	1059	42	366	346	30	45	75

1¾ hours.

ADMIRAL SIR HENRY TROLLOPE (1), KT.

(From H. R. Cook's engraving, after the portrait by Bowyer, painted when Sir Henry was a Vice-Admiral, 1805–1812.)

The *Proserpine* was purchased for the Navy and re-named *Amelia*.

On June 22nd, the French corvette *Légère*, 18, was captured off Brest by the British frigates *Apollo*, 38, and *Doris*, 36.[1]

On July 12th, the French frigate *Renommée*, 36, Captain Pitot, was overtaken by the British *Alfred*, 74, Captain Thomas Drury, off

[1] James, 370.

San Domingo.[1] Two broadsides from the *Alfred* disabled the French frigate, several shots striking the latter below the water-line, and flooding the magazines in a moment.

Late in the evening of July 15th, the *Glatton*, 56, with twenty-eight 68-pr. carronades on her lower deck, and as many 32-pr. carronades on her upper deck, under Captain Henry Trollope, met a French squadron of seven or eight ships in the North Sea. These were probably the *Brutus*,[2] 46 or 50, *Incorruptible*, 38, *Rassurante*, 36, *Républicaine*, 28, and four small corvettes. The French formed in line ahead. The *Glatton* stood past the small ships and attacked the largest of her enemies. Two of the other French frigates hung about her, but all three were very roughly handled and beaten off. The *Glatton*, however, was so wounded in her masts and rigging, at which the enemy fired, and was withal so slow a sailer, that she could not take possession of any of her opponents. It is astonishing to record that only two men were wounded in her. Her 68-pr. carronades were very effective at close quarters, but she had not enough men to fight both broadsides at once. It is said that one of the French ships foundered on the squadron taking refuge in Flushing, whither it was chased by the *Glatton*.

On July 22nd, off Guadeloupe, the British *Aimable*, 32, Captain Jemmett Mainwaring, chased the French *Pensée*, 36, Captain Valteau.[3] After exchanging fire in the evening, the *Pensée* fled and drew ahead during the night. At about 7 A.M., however, she shortened sail; the *Aimable* closed; and the two captains saluted one another. Then, as the *Pensée* was again retreating, the *Aimable* bore up at about 8.40 A.M. and fired into her, but, after a running engagement, dropped astern out of range.

—	Tons.	Guns.	Broadside.	Men.	Killed.	Wounded.	Total.
			Lbs.				
Aimable . .	782	40	246	217 n.	0	2	2
Pensée . .	—	40[1]	280[1]	300 n.	?	?	90?

[1] Troude, 43, forty-two guns, 320-lb. broadside.

On August 8th, in the same waters, the *Mermaid*, 32, Captain

[1] Troude, 41.

[2] James, 372. Troude, 41, does not mention the *Brutus*. The *Glatton*'s carronades appear to have been mounted on the non-recoil principle.

[3] James, 377.

Robert Waller Otway, engaged the French *Vengeance*, 40, at 11.50 A.M.[1] A prolonged but indecisive action followed, until, on the British *Beaulieu*, 40, Captain Francis Laforey, coming up, the *Vengeance* retired, under shelter of the Basseterre batteries. The French ship sustained most of her loss when twice missing stays.

—	Tons.	Guns.	Broadside.	Men.	Killed.	Wounded.	Total.
			Lbs.				
Mermaid . .	689	40	246	217 n.	0	0	0
Vengeance .	1180	44[1]	410	330 n.	12	26	38

[1] James says fifty-two.

On August 22nd, Commodore Sir John Borlase Warren's squadron of four frigates and a sloop, cruising off the mouth of the Gironde, chased the French frigate *Andromaque*, 36.[2] She was cut off from the Gironde by the *Galatea*, 32, Captain Richard Goodwin Keats, and *Sylph*, 18, Commander John Chambers White, and, after she had several times been lost sight of through the darkness of the night, was driven ashore on the morning of the 23rd. The *Sylph* proceeded to fire into her bottom, and in the afternoon sent in her boats and burnt her.

On August 25th, the *Raison*, 20, Captain John Poo Beresford, was chased by the French *Vengeance*, 40, to the west of the Gulf of Maine.[3] The British vessel, however, after a running action of two hours, escaped from her powerful antagonist with the loss of three killed and six wounded, whilst the French lost six killed and an unknown number of wounded. The *Raison* was helped in her escape by the very foggy weather.

On August 28th, the French *Elisabeth*, 36, was captured by the *Topaze*, 36, Captain Stephen George Church, off Cape Henry, after a broadside had been exchanged.[4] A large British squadron was coming up behind the *Topaze*.

On September 9th, off the coast of Sumatra, Rear-Admiral Sercey's squadron, composed of the *Forte* and *Régénérée*, 38, *Vertu* and *Cybèle*, 36, *Prudente*, 32, and the armed ship *Seine*, was attacked by the *Arrogant*, 74, Captain Richard Lucas, and *Victorious*, 74, Captain William Clark (1), which had been following since the

[1] James, 379; Ralfe, 'Naval Biography,' iv. 7.

[2] James, 383.

[3] James, 384.

[4] *Ib.*, 385; Troude, 43.

previous day.[1] The enemies passed on opposite tacks, exchanging fire, but the *Arrogant* was very soon so much damaged in her rigging that she fell behind and ceased firing, having, however, almost crippled the *Vertu*. Four of the British ship's guns were disabled or dismounted. The *Victorious* continued the action, but without great success. She was out-manœuvred by the French frigates, which kept as far as possible outside the field of fire commanded by her broadside, and attempted to rake her. Sercey retired at 10.55, and at 11.15 A.M. the *Victorious* ceased her fire.

—	Tons.	Guns.	Broadside.	Men.	Killed.	Wounded.	Total.
			Lbs.				
British . .	—	164	1676	1200?	24	84	108
French [1] . .	—	220?	1700?	1400?	42	104	146

[1] The *Seine's* armament being uncertain, a minimum of force has been allowed her.

Sercey appears to have had the undoubted advantage, and this though he was engaging ships of the line with stouter sides than his frigates. His orders to avoid fighting and attack commerce probably prevented him from obtaining a more significant success.

On September 22nd, the *Amphion*, 32, Captain Israel Pellew, blew up at Plymouth from some unexplained cause. Captain Pellew was saved, with ten out of 312 officers and men or visitors on board.

On September 23rd, the *Pelican*, 18,[2] Captain John Clarke Searle,[3] attacked the French *Médée*, 36, in the West Indies, and fought with her a close action of two hours' duration, when the Frenchman retired. The *Pelican* was so cut up that she could not pursue. After such an astounding action the value of the carronade, in certain cases, seems self-evident.

—	Tons.	Guns.	Broadside.	Men.	Killed.	Wounded.	Total.
			Lbs.				
Pelican . .	—	18	262	97	—	1	1
Médée . .	—	40	410	300 n.	?	?	33

2 hours.

[1] James, 391; Troude, 18; Chevalier, 'La Mar. Franç. sous la République,' 245.

[2] James, 396, sixteen 32-pr. carronades, two long 6's.

[3] Searle had been posted on the previous 13th of July, but still retained his Commander's command.

It appears that the *Médée's* captain imagined that the *Pelican* was a frigate "with her mizen-mast out."

On October 13th, off Cartagena, the *Terpsichore*, 32, Captain Richard Bowen, with a weak and sickly crew, engaged the Spanish *Mahonesa*, 34, Captain Don T. Ayaldi.[1] After a two hours' warm action the *Terpsichore* dropped astern with serious injuries to masts and rigging. Refitting in twenty minutes, she came up again, when the *Mahonesa* struck her colours.

—	Tons.	Guns.	Broadside.	Men.	Killed.	Wounded.	Total.
Terpsichore .	682	40	Lbs. 276	182	0	4	4
Mahonesa .	921	34?	180?	275	30	30	60

120 minutes.

The *Terpsichore* had her three masts wounded, and shots through her spars and boats: otherwise she was little the worse. The *Mahonesa* was added to the Navy.

On November 25th, the *Lapwing*, 28, Captain Robert Barton, was summoned from St. Kitts to the aid of Anguilla, in the West Indies, where a French force had disembarked.[2] She arrived on the 26th, and immediately the French re-embarked in the *Décius*, 20, and *Vaillante*, 10; but the *Décius* was captured after an hour's action, in which she lost 120 killed and wounded out of 336 on board. The *Lapwing* had one killed and six wounded. The *Vaillante*, to avoid capture, ran ashore, and was destroyed by the *Lapwing's* guns.

On December 12th, the *Terpsichore*, Captain Richard Bowen, chased the French *Vestale*, 36, Captain Fourcaud, off Cadiz.[3] On the 13th the Frenchman hove to, and waited for the *Terpsichore*, which came up at 11.30 P.M. and began a hot action in stormy weather. At 1.20 A.M. the *Vestale*, with all her masts and her bowsprit tottering, struck. Her mizenmast fell just after her surrender; and, before the British boats could reach her, her main-mast, foremast and bowsprit followed.

[1] James, 399; Log of *Terpsichore*.

[2] James, 401.

[3] James, 402; Troude, 45; Chevalier, 'Mar. Franç. sous la République,' 261; Log of *Terpsichore*.

—	Tons.	Guns.	Broadside.	Men.	Killed.	Wounded.	Total.
			Lbs.				
Terpsichore .	682	40	276	166	4	18	22
Vestale . .	—	40	286	300?	30	37	67

1 hour 40 minutes.

The high sea and strong wind prevented the *Terpsichore* from placing an adequate crew on board the prize, or transferring the prisoners, and, on the 14th, the *Vestale's* men rose on the British party, recaptured the ship, and reached Cadiz. For this action the gallant Bowen received no warm commendation from Sir John Jervis, and no reward from the country. The merchants of London gave him, however, a piece of plate.

On December 19th, Commodore Horatio Nelson in the *Minerve*, 38, Captain George Cockburn, with the *Blanche*, 32, Captain d'Arcy Preston, fell in with two Spanish frigates, *Sabina*, 40, Captain Don Jacob Steuart, and *Ceres*, 40, off Cartagena. At 10.40 the *Minerve* engaged the *Sabina*.[1] In fifty minutes the Spanish ship's mizen-mast went overboard, and at 1.20 A.M. she struck.

—	Tons.	Guns.	Broadside.	Men.	Killed.	Wounded.	Total.
			Lbs.				
Minerve . .	1102	42	370	286	7	34	41
Sabina . .	—	40	300	286	?	?	164

2 hours 40 minutes.

Lieutenants John Culverhouse and Thomas Masterman Hardy, with a prize crew, were placed on board the *Sabina*; but at 4 A.M. of the 20th the *Minerve* had to cast off the tow-rope and engage a second Spanish frigate, the *Matilda*, 34, which she drove off with the loss of ten wounded. As a Spanish 112-gun ship and two more frigates were coming up, the *Minerve* was then obliged to look to her own safety. She owed her escape to the fact that Hardy and Culverhouse hoisted the British colours above the Spanish in the *Sabina*, and thereby drew off the enemy's attention. The *Sabina* was recaptured.

The *Blanche* meanwhile engaged the *Ceres* and quickly brought her colours down, but could not take possession owing to the arrival

[1] Nicolas, 'Nelson,' ii. 312; James, 406.

of the other Spanish ships. The *Blanche* lost no one; the *Ceres*, seven killed and fifteen wounded.

On December 30th, the *Polyphemus*, 64, Captain George Lumsdaine, captured the French *Tartu*,[1] 40, after a running fight of four hours.[2] The *Tartu* had formed part of the ill-fated expedition to Ireland. She was purchased for the Navy, in which she figured under her old name, *Urania*.

On January 28th, 1797, five large East Indiamen, under Charles Lennox, master of the *Woodford*, met Rear-Admiral Sercey's squadron of six French frigates off Java.[3] Lennox, with remarkable judgment, hoisted a British admiral's flag and made signals, so that the French, convinced that they saw before them Rear-Admiral Peter Rainier's squadron, were only too pleased to retire.

On January 31st, an Algerine corsair of twenty-four guns, mistook the British *Andromache*, 32, Captain Charles John Moore Mansfield, cruising on the Mediterranean station, for a Portuguese frigate, and found that she had caught a tartar.[4] The Algerine lost sixty-six killed and fifty wounded, to the *Andromache's* two killed and four wounded, and struck her colours.

On February 22nd, the French vessels *Résistance* and *Vengeance*, 40, *Constance*, 22, and *Vautour*, lugger, landed in Fisgard[5] Bay, Pembroke, a nondescript force of 1500 criminals, armed and dressed as soldiers. The instructions to the French captains were to destroy Bristol and then attack Liverpool, but their hearts failed them. The criminals were captured with ridiculous ease by Welsh yeomanry, militia, and fencibles.

On March 9th, the British frigates *San Fiorenzo*, 36, Captain Sir Harry Burrard Neale, and *Nymphe*, 36, Captain John Cooke (2), discovered two of the French ships engaged in this expedition, the *Résistance*, 40, Captain J. B. M. Laroque, and *Constance*, 22, Captain Purchet, approaching Brest. The British frigates at once bore down, though the Brest fleet of twenty sail could be made out from the masthead, and attacked. The *Résistance* struck after twenty minutes' fight. She had lost her rudder and steered badly.

[1] Or *Tortue*. *See* p. 481, *antea*.

[2] James, ii. 11, gives the date as Jan. 5th, 1797. Log of *Polyphemus*: which ship had one wounded.

[3] James, ii. 89.

[4] *Ib.*, 90. Log of *Andromache*.

[5] Guillon, 'France et l'Irlande,' 297. The name is now spelt Fishguard. Barras, Mémoires,' ii. 345.

The *Constance* offered a stouter resistance, but ended by hauling down her flag ten minutes later. The British *Robust*, 74, and *Triton*, 28, came in sight at the close of the action. The British ships suffered no loss. The French had eighteen killed and fifteen wounded. The *Résistance* mounted 48 guns and measured 1182 tons. She was purchased for the Navy and renamed the *Fishguard*, after the place where she had landed the invading force.[1]

On April 26th, the British *Irresistible*, 74, Captain George Martin (2), and *Emerald*, 36, Captain Velters Cornwall Berkeley, forming part of the squadron blockading Cadiz, chased the Spanish frigates, *Ninfa*, 34, and *Santa Elena*, 34,[2] into Conil Bay, near Cadiz, attacked them at 2.30 P.M., and compelled them to strike ninety minutes later. The *Santa Elena*, however, after striking, cut her cable and went ashore, when her crew escaped. She sank after being got off. The *Ninfa*, purchased for the Navy, was renamed the *Hamadryad*. The Spanish loss was eighteen killed and thirty wounded; the British, one killed and one wounded. The Spanish frigates had treasure on board, but unloaded it into fishing-boats, and despatched it ashore before they were attacked.

On July 16th, Sir John Borlase Warren's frigate squadron, composed of the *Pomone*, 40, *Anson*, 44, *Artois*, 38, *Sylph*, 18,[3] and a cutter, chased a French convoy in charge of the *Calliope*, 28, and two corvettes. The corvettes escaped into Audierne Bay, but the *Calliope* was driven upon the Penmarcks early on the 17th. To prevent the French crew from removing her stores and guns, she was cannonaded, first by the *Anson* and then at close quarters by the *Sylph*. The *Calliope* went to pieces on the 18th. The loss of the *Sylph* in her gallant attack was six wounded.

On August 10th, the *Arethusa*, 38, Captain Thomas Wolley, cruising in the latitude of the Bermudas, fell in with the French corvette *Gaîté*, 20, Enseigne J. F. Guiné.[4] The latter did not

—	Tons.	Guns.	Broadside.	Men.	Killed.	Wounded.	Total.
			Lbs.				
Arethusa . .	938	44	393?	277	1	3	4
Gaîté . . .	514	20	88	186	2	8	10

30 minutes.

[1] James, 91; Troude, 61.
[2] James, 93; Brenton, i. 494.
[3] James, 95; Troude, 70.
[4] Troude, iii. 71; James, 98.

attempt to escape, but fought the heavy British frigate for half an hour and then struck. For his recklessness Guiné was court-martialled and censured.

On August 11th, Warren's squadron of three frigates (*Pomone*, *Jason*, and *Triton*) and one brig-sloop, the *Sylph*, 18, Commander John Chambers White, attacked a French convoy, under the charge of the corvette *Réolaise*, 20, a gunboat and a lugger.[1] The gunboat was destroyed and the corvette a good deal cut up, with a loss to the British ships of three killed and five wounded.

On October 14th, near the Canaries, the French *Ranger*, 12, Captain Hullin, was captured by the *Indefatigable*, 44, Captain Sir Edward Pellew.[2] On the 25th, in the same waters, the same British ship was mistaken by a French privateer for an East Indiaman. The capture of the Frenchman was the result. The vessel proved to be the *Hyène*, 24, a ship taken from Britain by the French in 1793, and commissioned as a privateer.

On December 20th, the *Phœbe*, 36, Captain Robert Barlow, gave chase in the Bay to the French *Néréide*, 36, Captain A. Canon.[3] At 9 P.M. the two were near enough for the *Néréide* to open with her stern-chasers, which inflicted much damage on the *Phœbe's* masts, sails, and rigging. The *Néréide* then suddenly tacked, and the *Phœbe* shot ahead. The *Phœbe*, however, tacked as soon as she could, and seemingly the *Néréide* tacked again, for the two passed on opposite courses exchanging fire. Finally, they closed and fought at three hundred yards for three-quarters of an hour. The *Néréide* once fell on board the *Phœbe*, but the latter easily got clear. At 10.45 P.M. the French ship struck, being in a very battered condition.

—	Tons.	Guns.	Broadside.	Men.	Killed.	Wounded.	Total.
Phœbe . .	926	44	Lbs. 407	261	3	10	13
Néréide . .	892	40	278	330	20	55	75

1¾ hours.

On December 29th, the British frigate *Anson*, 44, Captain Philip Charles Durham, captured without much difficulty the French

[1] James, 96; Troude, 72.
[2] Troude, 73. Log of *Indefatigable*. Osler, 116.
[3] James, 103; Troude, 73.

corvette *Daphné*, 24, Captain Latreyte.[1] The two ships exchanged broadsides, with the result that the *Daphné* lost two killed and five wounded. She was bound for Guadeloupe with dispatches, but had not been able to get clear of the French coast. She was very much inferior in force to the *Anson*.

In January, 1798, the British frigates *Sibylle*, 38, Captain Edward Cook, and *Fox*, 32, Captain Pulteney Malcolm, entered the bay of Manilla, disguised as French frigates, and succeeded in making two hundred prisoners and in capturing seven boats.[2]

On the 22nd, they attacked the Spanish fort of Samboangon in the Philippines, but after a sharp action were repulsed, with the loss of four killed and fifteen wounded. Visiting Pullock Harbour on the 31st, two seamen were killed by the natives and nine carried off. The latter were afterwards restored.

In the same month a number of Swedish merchantmen, freighted with contraband of war, were seized, though under convoy of a Swedish warship, and condemned by the British prize-courts—an act which led to great soreness in Sweden.[3] The value of the property in them was £600,000.

On February 3rd and 4th, the British brig *Speedy*, 14, Commander Hugh Downman, fought a protracted action with a French privateer, the *Papillon*, 14, of very superior metal. She succeeded in driving her enemy off with the loss of four killed and four wounded, but, owing to the failure of her ammunition, could not capture her.

On March 22nd, 1798, the *Canada*, 74, Captain Sir John Borlase Warren, *Anson*, 44, Captain Philip Charles Durham, and *Phaeton*, 38, Captain the Hon. Robert Stopford, chased, off the isle of Aix, the French *Charente*, 36, Captain A. A. M. Bruillac, with a number of French political prisoners on board, destined for Cayenne.[4] Early in the morning of the 23rd the *Phaeton* got within long range of the *Charente*, whereupon the latter turned and ran for the Gironde, exchanging broadsides with the *Canada* in passing. A little later, both the *Charente* and *Canada* ran aground. The former, after throwing her guns overboard, escaped up the river to Bordeaux in a damaged condition. The latter was got off without much difficulty a little later.

[1] James, 105; Troude, 74; Murray, 'Durham,' 42, gives the date as the 23rd.
[2] James, 237.
[3] 'Ann. Register,' 1801, p. 36.
[4] Troude, 124; James, 228.

On April 23rd, the French gunboat *Arrogante*, 6, was captured off Brest by the British frigates *Jason* and *Naiad*.

On April 24th, the *Pearl*, 32, Captain Samuel James Ballard, found the French frigate *Régénérée*, 36, at anchor at Factory Island in the Loss Archipelago, on the west coast of Africa, and attacked her.[1] On this a second French frigate, the *Vertu*, 40, came up to the help of the *Régénérée*, and the latter weighed, and with her companion gave chase to the *Pearl*. The British frigate, though hotly pursued for twenty-four hours, made good her escape to Sierra Leone, with one man mortally wounded.

On May 2nd, the *Flora*, 36, Captain Robert Gambier Middleton, captured the French brig *Corcyre*, 12, off Sardinia.[2] On the 13th, she drove the French brig *Mondovi*, 18, into Cerigo, where late in the night her boats boarded and carried off the enemy with the loss of only one killed and eight wounded.

After the capture of Malta by the French, the frigate *Sensible*, 36, Captain Bourdé, was sent with dispatches and valuables to Toulon, and when on her way thither off Marittimo, was chased by the British *Seahorse*, 38, Captain Edward James Foote.[3] The French ship turned and ran towards Malta, as she had but a very weak crew on board and was not properly equipped. In the night of the 26th–27th, the *Seahorse* gained upon her, and, after a running fight, brought her to close action at 4 A.M. Many of the Maltese galley slaves, who had been placed on board the *Sensible*, deserted their guns at the first broadside, and at the end of eight minutes' action the French captain, having made a vain attempt to board his enemy, hauled down his flag. He was censured by the French Directory for not having offered a more stubborn resistance, but, as a matter of fact, the force opposed to him was very superior, and he was acquitted with honour by a French court-martial on his return to Toulon.

—	Tons.	Guns.	Broadside.	Men.	Killed.	Wounded.	Total.
			Lbs.				
Seahorse . .	984	46	494	292	2	16	18
Sensible . .	946	40	280	300	25	55	80

1 hour ?

[1] James, 246; Troude, 139. [2] James, 250; Troude, 131. Log of *Flora*. [3] James, 234; Troude, 134.

The *Sensible* was purchased for the Navy.

On June 29th, the British frigates *Jason*, 38, Captain Charles Stirling (1), *Pique*, 36, Captain David Milne, and *Mermaid*, 32, Captain James Newman Newman, whilst cruising off the Penmarcks, sighted the French frigate *Seine*, 38, Lieutenant J. G. Bigot, on her way home from Mauritius,[1] with four hundred soldiers on board, in addition to her crew. She was making her landfall, but, when she saw the British ships, turned south for La Rochelle, hotly pursued. The *Mermaid* and *Jason* stretched inshore to cut her off from Lorient. The *Pique* followed her, and, at 9 P.M., began a running fight, ranging alongside at 11 P.M. The two fought broadside to broadside under sail till, two and a half hours later, the *Pique's* main top-mast was shot away. Then the *Jason* came up, and Captain Stirling ordered the *Pique* to anchor, as the land was very close. Instead of so doing she pressed on and ran aground. A very little later the *Jason* shared her fate. The *Seine* drove ashore almost at the same moment. The *Jason's* stern floated, and, as the tide rose, the ship swung round, offering her stern to the *Seine's* raking broadsides. The *Pique* managed to bring some of her guns to bear on the French ship, and then, as the *Mermaid* was coming up fast, the *Seine* struck her colours.

—	Tons.	Guns.	Broadside.	Men.	Killed.	Wounded.	Total.
			Lbs.				
Pique . . .	906	44?	314?	247 n.	2	6	8
Jason . . .	984	46?	494?	277 n.	7	12	19
Seine . . .	1146	42	390	610	170?	100?	270?

The *Seine* was got afloat, but the *Pique* had to be abandoned, after being rendered unserviceable.

On July 15th, to the south-east of Cartagena, the *Lion*, 64, Captain Manley Dixon, engaged four Spanish frigates, the *Pomona*, *Proserpine*, *Sta. Cazilda*, and *Sta. Dorotea*, each of thirty-four guns.[2] The Spaniards formed in a line of battle, the *Lion* holding the weather gage. The *Sta. Dorotea* dropped astern in the line and was attacked by the British ship, whereupon the other frigates tacked to her support, and, passing the *Lion*, each gave and received

[1] James, 247; Troude, 136; Brenton, i. 389. [2] James, 254.

a broadside twice. The *Lion*, however, closed her opponent, and the other three Spanish ships, after a third attempt to give help, stood away for Cartagena. The *Sta. Dorotea*, being very much cut up and quite unable by herself to resist the battleship's crushing fire, struck her colours.

—	Tons.	Guns.	Broadside.	Men.	Killed.	Wounded.	Total.
			Lbs.				
Lion . . .	1374	72?	678?	485 n.	0	2	2
Sta. Dorotea .	958	34	180?	371	20	32	52

The *Sta. Dorotea* was purchased for the Navy.

On July 23rd, the *Resistance*, 44, Captain Edward Pakenham, whilst at anchor in the Straits of Banca, blew up from some unexplained cause.[1] Of the people on board her, 332 were killed and only thirteen survived. These clung to her wreckage, constructed a raft, and set sail for Sumatra, but a sudden storm arising, all but five perished. These five reached Sumatra and were imprisoned by the Malays. Eventually, only one man escaped.

On July 26th, the British *Brilliant*, 28, Captain the Hon. Henry Blackwood, was chased by the French *Vertu*, 36, and *Régénérée*, 36, which she had found at anchor at Tenerife.[2] They slipped, and stood after her. In the evening, though the *Brilliant* cut away boats and anchors, the *Régénérée* came up fast and began a running fight. To extricate herself the *Brilliant* suddenly bore up, and, crossing the hawse of the *Régénérée*, which was to leeward of her, gave her a raking broadside, and, bringing her main top-sail down, ran off on the starboard tack. The *Vertu* took up the chase and opened with her bow-guns. At midnight the wind fell and the *Régénérée* was able to come up again. Matters were looking very bad for the small British frigate when a fresh breeze sprang up and the *Brilliant* drew away, covered by darkness. She suffered no loss and little damage. She was very much the weakest ship, as, allowing her six 24-pr. carronades, her broadside did not exceed 198 lbs. The broadside of the two French ships was 670 lbs. at least.

On the night of August 3rd–4th, the British vessels *Melpomene*, 38, Captain Sir Charles Hamilton, and *Childers*, 14, Commander

[1] James, 245. [2] *Ib.*, 250; Troude, 130.

James O'Bryen,[1] sent in their boats to the harbour of Corréjou, in the Ile de Bas, to cut out the French brig *Aventurier*, 12, Lieutenant R. G. Raffy.[2] The night was dark, stormy, and rainy, and this covered the British approach. At three in the morning the *Aventurier* was surprised and captured after a sharp scuffle, in which the British loss was two killed and four wounded. In spite of the fire of a fort commanding the inlet, the *Aventurier* was carried out of the port.

On August 7th, the British brig-sloop *Espoir*, 14, Commander Loftus Otway Bland,[3] whilst in charge of a convoy in the Mediterranean, was attacked by a large Genoese pirate, the *Liguria*, 26.[4] The two ships began their battle at about 7 P.M. and fought till 11, when the *Liguria* struck. The indiscipline of the pirate's crew is probably the explanation of her easy defeat by a vessel so much her inferior in armament.

—	Tons.	Guns.	Broadside.	Men.	Killed.	Wounded.	Total.
			Lbs.				
Espoir . .	215	14	42	80	1	6	7
Liguria . .	—	26	162	120	7	14	21

4 hours.

On the same day, Captain Sir Edward Pellew, in the *Indefatigable*, 44, cruising in the Bay, fell in with and captured, after a few shots, the French corvette *Vaillante*, 20, Lieutenant La Porte, on her way to Cayenne with political prisoners.[5] The prize was purchased for the Navy and equipped with thirty-four carronades and long guns. She was renamed *Danaë*.

On August 12th, the British sloop *Hazard*, 18, Commander William Butterfield, chased and captured the French armed ship *Neptune*, 10, in the North Atlantic.[6]

On August 18th, the British 50-gun ship *Leander*, Captain Thomas Boulden Thompson, on her way from Alexandria with Nelson's dispatches announcing the victory of the Nile, was sighted by the

[1] Nephew of Murrough, first Marquis of Thomond, and later known as Lord James O'Bryen. He succeeded his eldest brother, as third Marquis, in 1846, and died, a full Admiral, in 1855.—W. L. C.

[2] James, 255; Troude, 140.

[3] A Commander of Oct. 1, 1797. For this action he was posted on Sept. 25, 1798. —W. L. C.

[4] James, 256. [5] James, 258; Osler, 116. [6] James, 259.

French *Généreux*, 74, Captain Lejoille, one of the two French vessels of the line that had escaped with Villeneuve.[1] The *Leander* was short of her proper complement by not fewer than eighty men, had no Marine officer on board, and had had one of her two 12-pr. carronades dismounted at the Nile. She was off the western end of Candia when she was seen. She at once made sail to escape, being vastly inferior in force to the French vessel which was chasing her. A breeze, however, brought up the enemy without reaching the *Leander*, and, at 8 A.M., the *Généreux* was within random shot. Seeing that escape was hopeless, Captain Thompson shortened sail and waited for his powerful antagonist. Soon after nine, the *Généreux* was close enough to the *Leander's* larboard quarter to open fire. A furious action began, the two ships moving slowly before the wind, broadside to broadside. The *Leander* was terribly shattered in her rigging, sails, and yards, of which fact the *Généreux* took advantage by running on board the *Leander's* larboard bow and falling alongside at 10.30. The French then made a determined attempt to board. They were repulsed by the valour and resolution of the *Leander's* Marines, who, though they had no officer to lead or encourage them, poured in a terrible fire upon the French boarding parties. Below, the great guns continued the battle.

A breeze at length sprang up and carried the *Généreux* clear. The *Leander* had been still more crippled by the fall of her mizen-mast, which covered her starboard quarter, of her fore top-mast, which had gone over the larboard bow, and of her yards, which were lying on the booms. Yet, as the *Généreux* took the starboard tack, Captain Thompson managed to place his ship under his enemy's stern, where he delivered a deliberate raking broadside. The two closed once more at the shortest range, with the sea "smooth as glass," and fought thus till 3.30 P.M. Then the *Généreux* paid off and came round across the *Leander's* bow, raking her, whilst the *Leander's* forward guns, masked by the wreck of the fore top-mast, could not fire. In that position, the *Leander* being quite unmanageable, with every mast gone and much shattered in hull, the *Généreux* hailed to know if her enemy had struck. The *Leander* seems to have had no colours flying, and thence the question. A reply was made in the affirmative by waving a French ensign on a pike; and two French officers swam on board, the *Généreux* having no boat that would

[1] James, 259; Troude, 140; Clarke and McArthur, 'Nelson' (Fisher's edition), ii. 175; Hennequin, 'Biographie Maritime,' iii. 293.

float. The *Leander* was thus taken possession of, after a six and a half hours' resistance, famous in history for its gallantry.

In the *Leander* the loss was heavy. Nelson's flag-captain, the gallant Edward Berry, hero of innumerable pitched battles, who was on board as the bearer of dispatches, was wounded by a piece of a man's skull being driven into his arm. Captain Thompson had three serious wounds; three Midshipmen were killed and a fourth, with two Lieutenants,[1] the Master, and a Master's Mate, was wounded. In all, 35 were killed and 57 wounded out of a crew of 282 men, amongst whom were included 14 men wounded at the Nile. The *Généreux* suffered far more heavily, in spite of her thicker and stronger sides. She is said to have had 100 killed besides 188 wounded, out of a crew of 936. Thus each ship lost about one-third of her crew. The *moral* of the *Leander* had doubtless been raised by the great victory of the Nile, or she might have been expected to strike sooner to force so overpowering.

—	Tons.	Guns.	Broadside.	Men.	Killed.	Wounded.	Total.
			Lbs.				
Généreux . .	1926	80	1024	936	100?	188	288
Leander . .	1052	51	432	282	35	57	92

6½ hours.

Troude describes the *Leander* as a 64, and gives her eight 32-pr. carronades. His account is apparently based upon the official letter of Captain Lejoille, who wilfully misrepresented the force of the ship which he had conquered, and pretended that she was a 74. It is, of course, well known and ascertained that the *Leander* carried only fifty-one effective carriage-guns in all, and therefore twenty-three guns must have been added by Lejoille's exuberant imagination.

The behaviour of the captors was disgraceful.[2] They plundered the ship and plundered the prisoners. Captain Thompson had his kit, and Captain Berry a valuable pair of pistols, taken from him. The *Leander's* surgeon was robbed even of his instruments, and was

[1] Bridges Watkinson Taylor and William Swiney (2). The former, a Commander of 1799 and a Captain of 1802, was drowned in the *Apollo* in 1814. The latter retired with the rank of Commander in 1830, and died in 1841.—W. L. C.

[2] Troude cites evidence to the contrary, but it is far from convincing. The statements of the British Consul at Trieste ('Naval Chronicle,' xiv. 10) are unimpeachable, though I cannot find that either Berry or Thompson complained.

not allowed to attend upon Captain Thompson. The wounded seamen were treated with great barbarity; and the prisoners were compelled to aid in refitting the ship, a breach of the established usages of war.

On the way to Corfu, on August 28th, the *Généreux* and her prize were sighted by the British sloop *Mutine*, 16, Captain the Hon. Thomas Bladen Capell, carrying Nelson's duplicate dispatches; and the French made preparations to cast off the prize and abandon her, but, discovering the *Mutine's* real force, did not carry out this intention. At Corfu, after much more ill-usage, the *Leander's* officers were released on parole. Her seamen were detained prisoners, and at a later date an attempt was made by Captain Lejoille to persuade or compel some of them to join the French Navy. The reply of a gallant main top-man, George Bannister, has come down to us over the sea of time: "No, you damned French rascal; give us back our little ship and we'll fight you again till we sink."

On the capture of Corfu by the Russians and Turks on March 3rd, 1799, the *Leander* was restored to England. Captain Thompson was most honourably acquitted by court-martial for the loss of his ship, and, going ashore after the verdict, was cheered by every vessel at Sheerness. He and Berry were knighted for their gallantry.

On August 22nd, the British *Naiad*, 38, Captain William Pierrepont, saw the French *Décade*, 36, Captain Villeneuve, making her landfall off Finisterre, and chased her during the night.[1] Next day the *Magnanime*, 44, Captain the Hon. Michael de Courcy, joined the *Naiad* in her pursuit. At 5 P.M., the *Décade* opened on the leading British ship, the *Naiad*, and the latter, a little more than an hour later, replied. The two fought for about sixty minutes, when, seeing no chance of escape from so superior a force, Captain Villeneuve hauled down his flag. The *Décade* was from Cayenne, where she had left ten of her guns; she was no match for the *Naiad* alone, which mounted forty-six guns, much less for the *Magnanime*, which carried 24-prs., and was a cut-down 64-gun ship.

On October 24th, off the Texel, the British *Sirius*, 36, Captain Richard King (2), fell in with the Dutch vessels *Furie*, 36, Captain Bartholomeus Pletsz, and *Waakzaamheid*, 24, Captain Meindert van Neirop.[2] As these two were some distance apart, the *Sirius* was able to isolate the *Waakzaamheid* and attack her, when at the first shot she struck. A prize crew was placed on board her,

[1] James, 269; Troude, 144.

[2] James, 270.

and then the *Sirius* made sail after the *Furie*, which had taken to her heels. At 5 P.M., the British frigate was close enough to her enemy to open fire, and a running fight ensued. The *Furie* continued a very ill-directed fire for an hour, doing little damage to the *Sirius*, while sustaining serious injury herself. Then the Dutch colours were hauled down. In this action the two Dutch captains displayed singular incapacity, allowing their ships to be separated and beaten in detail.

—	Tons.	Guns.	Broadside.	Men.	Killed.	Wounded.	Total.
			Lbs.				
Sirius . .	1049	44	407	251 n.	0	1	1
Furie . . .	827	36	202	328	8	14	22
Waakzaamheid	504	26	111	222	0	0	0

Both prizes were purchased for the Navy, the *Furie* being renamed the *Wilhelmina*, which had been her original appellation.

On December 3rd, the British brig-sloops *Victorieuse*, 14, Commander Edward Stirling Dickson, and *Zephyr*, 14, Commander William Champain, landed a small force in the West Indian island of Margarita to attack a fort on the river Caribe.[1] This surrendered without any ado, and the brigs sailed for Gurupano, another port in the island. Seventy soldiers and Marines were landed there, and stormed two forts, with a loss of two killed and two wounded. A privateer in the harbour was captured.

On December 14th occurred one of the very few actions in this war which are disgraceful to the British arms.[2] The *Ambuscade*, 32, Captain Henry Jenkins, whilst cruising off the Gironde, expecting to be joined by the *Stag*, 32, sighted a sail approaching. No private signals were made or asked for; a discreditable degree of carelessness prevailed on board, and the men went to breakfast. Suddenly, at about 9 A.M., the stranger, having approached almost within gunshot, went about under a press of sail. She was the French corvette *Bayonnaise*, 24, Lieutenant J. B. E. Richer. The *Ambuscade*, when Captain Jenkins discovered his mistake, hurried in pursuit, and towards noon was near enough to the chase to open fire. The *Bayonnaise* shortened sail and courted battle. The two fought for an hour, when one of the *Ambuscade's* 12-prs. burst, doing much damage to the ship and

[1] James, 230. [2] *Ib.*, 273; Troude, 145; C.M., 90, Aug. 26.

wounding eleven men.[1] Such an incident, as a study of the minor actions proves, has a disastrous effect on the *moral* of the ship wherein it occurs. The only exception to this is in the case of the action between the *Serapis* and *Bonhomme Richard*. The *Bayonnaise* seized the opportunity of the confusion which this occurrence caused in the *Ambuscade* to make off. She was pursued by the *Ambuscade*, which came up to leeward, and shot a little ahead under a press of sail. The French had so far suffered severely. At that juncture they determined to board. They had a much larger crew than had the *Ambuscade*; and serving in the *Bayonnaise* were thirty veteran soldiers of the Alsace regiment. The French ship ran on board the *Ambuscade*, which was becalmed as the French ship wore under her stern, carrying away the tiller ropes, starboard quarter-deck bulwarks, mizen shrouds and mizen-mast, and locking the wheel with her sprit-sail yard, and then dropped under the British vessel's stern, but did not clear her. The French soldiers from the *Bayonnaise's* bowsprit swept the *Ambuscade's* deck, which was not barricaded with hammocks, with a deadly fire. In a few minutes five officers [2] were killed or wounded in quick succession, and the command devolved upon the Purser, Mr. William Bowman Murray. An explosion of cartridges, left on the rudder-head, blew out a portion of the *Ambuscade's* stern, and caused panic amongst her men. Most of the British crew left their quarters. At that moment the French boarders rushed on to the *Ambuscade's* deck and carried it. The British crew was, according to James, an ill-disciplined one, and Captain Jenkins a most indiscreet and incompetent officer. The management of the *Ambuscade* left much to be desired, and, as often is the case, bad management was attended by bad luck. The two explosions, and the great weakness of the British crew, from which not less than thirty-one officers and men had been detached and placed on board a prize, must be taken into account. All the French officers except two were wounded; all the British executive officers killed or wounded. The action shows clearly that superiority of force is useless with a bad or weak captain and an ill-disciplined crew. The French may none the less be proud of their victory.

[1] Nine men, according to a witness at the court-martial.

[2] Lieutenant Dawson Main, mortally wounded; Captain Jenkins, wounded; Lieutenant of Marines, James Sinclair, wounded; Mr. Brown, Master, killed; Lieutenant Joseph Briggs, wounded.—W. L. C.

—	Tons.	Guns.	Broadside.	Men.	Killed.	Wounded.	Total.
			Lbs.				
Bayonnaise .	580?	32	123[1]	250?	30?	30?	60?
Ambuscade .	684	40	268	190	11	39	50

4 hours ?

[1] Troude. According to James, her broadside was 156 lbs. or thereabouts, as he credits her with two 36-pr carronades, and gives good reasons for his statement. Of the *Ambuscade's* 24-pr. carronades some, if not all, were disabled in the action.

Captain Jenkins, whilst still suffering from his wound, was tried and acquitted for the loss of his ship. This fact may explain the verdict. His officers and his crew were likewise acquitted, though the opinion was expressed that all had not behaved with the accustomed courage of British seamen. Lieutenant Richer was promoted two steps for his brilliant success.

On January 4th, 1799, the *Wolverine*, 12, Commander Lewis Mortlock, cruising off Boulogne, was attacked by two strongly-manned French privateers, the *Rusé*, 8, and the *Furet*, 4, but succeeded in repulsing them.[1] The *Wolverine*, though she carried only seventy men, could fight on each side two 18-prs., six 24-pr. carronades, and two, if not three, 12-pr. carronades. She was, therefore, a more formidable ship at close quarters than her rating seemed to show.

On February 1st, the British 28-gun frigate *Proserpine*, Captain James Wallis (1), struck on the Scharhörn Riff, below Neuwerk, at the mouth of the Elbe, in stormy weather, and had to be abandoned.[2] Her crew escaped ashore on the ice with the loss of fourteen frozen to death in the bitterly cold weather.

On February 6th, the British ships *Leviathan*, 74, Captain John Buchanan (1), and *Argo*, 44, Captain James Bowen (1), discovered off Majorca two Spanish frigates, the *Sta. Teresa*, 34, and *Proserpina*, 34.[3] The two latter separated and took different courses. The *Sta. Teresa* was pursued by the *Argo*, but the *Leviathan*, which had dropped behind, did not alter course and chase the *Proserpina*. At midnight the *Argo* closed the *Sta. Teresa* after a running fight, and a broadside brought down the Spanish flag. The Spaniard was no match for the *Argo* alone, much less for the *Argo* and *Leviathan* combined. The prize was purchased for the Navy.

On February 9th, the British *Dædalus*, 32, Captain Henry

[1] James, 353. [2] *Ib.*, 354. [3] *Ib.*, 359.

Lidgbird Ball, cruising in the Indian Ocean, sighted the French *Prudente*, 36, Captain Joliff, with a prize.[1] The *Prudente* had only thirty guns on board, having left eight at Mauritius, and she had already detached seventeen of her officers and men to form the prize crew. She separated from her prize and was soon closed by the *Dædalus*, which engaged her hotly just after noon. The British ship crossed her stern, raked her and luffed, bringing the two broadside to broadside. At 1.21 P.M., the *Prudente* struck in a very shattered condition. According to Troude, she was a privateer and not a warship.

—	Tons.	Guns.	Broadside.	Men.	Killed.	Wounded.	Total.
			Lbs.				
Dædalus . .	703	38	246	212	2	12	14
Prudente . .	920	30	214	301	27	22	49

1 hour 20 minutes.

The *Prudente* was too much damaged to be purchased for the Navy.

On February 22nd, off the Spanish coast,[2] the British sloop *Espoir*, 14, Commander James Sanders, captured the Spanish xebec *Africa*, 14, with a loss of four killed and wounded. The Spanish loss was thirty-seven killed and wounded.

Late in February, the French frigate *Forte*, 40, Captain Beaulieu, arrived in the Bay of Bengal and began to harass British commerce.[3] She was in bad order; the discipline of her crew was not good; and her captain, according to Rear-Admiral Sercey, was too old and feeble for his work. The British cruiser *Sibylle*, 40, Captain Edward Cook, a very fine and powerful vessel, went to look for her, to stop her depredations. In the evening of the 28th, whilst the *Sibylle* was on this quest, vivid flashes were seen to the north-west, and supposed to be lightning. As, however, the flashes went on continuously till nine, and then stopped altogether, Captain Cook began to suspect that they were from guns, and stood towards them, with all lights out, to make certain. At 9.30 he sighted the *Forte* and two prizes lying side by side. Captain Cook manœuvred to gain the weather gage, untroubled by the *Forte*. The French captain saw the *Sibylle*, but was obstinately persuaded that she was

[1] James, 357; Troude, 170. [2] James, 364.
[3] *Ib.*, 365; Troude, 171.

a merchantman, and made no preparations to attack her, though assured by his officers that she was an enemy. The French were on the starboard tack, lying to. The *Sibylle* bore steadily down, until, as she approached, the *Forte* crossed her bows and fired a few random shot at her, to which the British ship made no answer. Then, at 12.45 A.M., the *Sibylle* put her helm up, the *Forte* being abaft her beam, and passed under the enemy's stern, pouring in a most destructive broadside at the very shortest range. She followed this up by closing the *Forte* broadside to broadside, whilst the guns of the French were fired by mistake at one of their prizes. The *Forte* had had to supply crews for seven captures and for this reason was unable to man her forecastle and quarterdeck guns. In consequence, her fire was not very effective. Early in the action Captain Cook[1] was wounded, and Captain Beaulieu was killed an hour after the battle began. At 2.30 the *Forte* had only four guns which could be used. She therefore stopped her fire and endeavoured to make sail and escape. Discovering her intentions, the *Sibylle*, after twice hailing her to strike, resumed her fire and very quickly brought down the *Forte's* masts. On this the French ship struck and was taken possession of. The *Sibylle* was much cut up in her masts and rigging. The *Forte* was in a horrible state, with her starboard side almost beaten in, and three hundred shot in her hull.

—	Tons.	Guns.	Broadside.	Men.	Killed.	Wounded.	Total.
			Lbs.				
Sibylle . .	1091	48[1]	503	371	5	17	22
Forte . . .	1401	52[1]	610	370?	65	80?	145

2½ hours.

[1] The *Sibylle* carried twenty-eight 18-prs., six 9-prs., and fourteen 32-pr. carronades. The *Forte's* armament is variously given:—

—	24-prs. (French).	24-prs. (English).	8-prs.	36-pr. (carronades).
James	28	2	14	8
Troude . . .	28	—	10	4

James has been followed in the text.

[1] This gallant officer, a Captain of 1794, died of his wounds at Calcutta on May 25th, following. 'Nav. Chron.,' ii. 643. James and others spell his name "Cooke"; but the *Navy List* spelling is here followed.—W. L. C.

In the *Sibylle* were 131 officers and men of the Scotch brigade, who fought with great credit. It should be noted that in the general opinion of naval men at that time the *Sibylle* was no match for the *Forte*. The latter's weight of broadside, from long guns only, was 448 lbs., as against the *Sibylle's* 279 lbs. The bad shooting of the *Forte* is partly explained by the fact that her gun-quoins had been planed down three days previously. The *Forte* was purchased for the Navy and rated a 44.

On April 9th, the British *San Fiorenzo*, 36, Captain Sir Harry Burrard Neale, and *Amelia*, 38, Captain the Hon. Charles Herbert (1), were cruising off Belle Isle, where lay three French frigates, the *Cornélie*, 40, *Sémillante*, 36, and *Vengeance*, 40, when a squall carried away the *Amelia's* main top-mast and her two other topgallant-masts.[1] On this the three French ships stood out, and, supported by a gunboat, attacked the frigates. A scrambling distant action of three hours followed, after which the French retired, to the great surprise of the British. The *San Fiorenzo* and *Amelia* were much cut up in their rigging. They had to face not only the French ships but also a battery on Hoëdic Island. The retreat of the French was explained by the fact that they imagined they were dealing with two cut-down ships of the line.

On May 8th, the British polacca *Fortune*, 10, Lieutenant Lewis Davis, cruising on the Syrian coast,[2] was attacked by the French brig *Salamine*, 18. After a three hours' desperate engagement the *Fortune* struck, as three French frigates of Rear-Admiral Perrée's squadron were seen to be coming up. The *Fortune* had the help of a gunboat, the *Dame de Grâce*, which was sunk. Her loss was five.

On June 9th, the boats of the *Success*, 32, Captain Shuldham Peard, cut out an armed Spanish polacca, laden with merchandise, from the harbour of La Selva. The British loss was four killed and eight wounded out of forty-two.

On August 11th, the British sloops, *Pylades*, 16, Commander Adam Mackenzie, and *Espiègle*, 16, Captain James Boorder, with the cutter *Courier*, 10, Lieutenant Thomas Searle, attacked the ex-British brig *Crash*, 12, which was lying between Schiermonnikoog and the Dutch mainland.[3] The *Courier* led, followed by the other two, and after a fifty minutes' action the Dutch flag was hauled down. The British loss was three killed or wounded. On the 12th, the *Crash* and the boats of the other vessels attacked the Dutch

[1] James, 376. [2] *Ib.*, 379. [3] *Ib.*, 382.

schooner *Vengeance*, 6, which was lying under the guns of a battery on Schiermonnikoog. Under a heavy fire the battery was taken and its guns spiked or brought off. The schooner was burnt by her crew. There was no loss on the British side.

On August 20th, the British *Clyde*, 38, Captain Charles Cunningham, was cruising off Rochefort, when she sighted the French ships *Vestale*, 32, Captain M. M. P. Gaspard, and *Sagesse*, 20.[1] The two separated, and the *Vestale* was followed by the *Clyde*. At 1.30 P.M. the latter was within range, and the action began, the *Clyde* and *Vestale* engaging broadside to broadside. The *Clyde* changed from larboard to starboard of the French ship, passing astern and raking her, and repeated this manœuvre several times. The *Vestale's* crew was weak, as thirty or forty men had died in the West Indies of yellow fever; and of those on board many were ill. She had no chance of success against so superior an antagonist. At about 3.20 she struck her flag.

—	Tons.	Guns.	Broadside.	Men.	Killed.	Wounded.	Total.
			Lbs.				
Clyde . . .	1000?	46	425	281	2	3	5
Vestale . .	946	36?[1]	273[1]	230	10	22	32

110 minutes.

[1] James calls the *Vestale* a 36-gun frigate, and gives her a total of thirty-eight carriage-guns. From Troude, and from the number of her complement as detailed in James, she appears to have been a 32 of thirty-six carriage guns.

The *Vestale* was not purchased for the Navy.

On August 25th, off the coast of Guiana, the British *Tamar*, 38, Captain Thomas Western, chased the French corvette *Républicaine*, 28, Captain P. M. Lebozec.[2] The latter during the night escaped into shoal water, whence under cover of darkness she ran for the open sea. At daylight she was seen and pursued. At 5.30 P.M. the *Tamar* came up with her; and, after ten minutes' fighting, the *Républicaine* struck.

—	Tons.	Guns.	Broadside.	Men.	Killed.	Wounded.	Total.
			Lbs.				
Tamar . .	999	46	425	281	0	2	2
Républicaine .	—	36	266	175	9	12	21

10 minutes.

[1] James, 384; Troude, 177. [2] James, 387; Troude, 179.

The *Républicaine's* eight 36-pr. carronades, counted above, were so badly mounted as to be almost unserviceable.

On September 12th, the British sloops *Arrow*, 28, Commander Nathaniel Portlock, and *Wolverine*, 12, Commander William Bolton (1), attacked off Harlingen the Dutch brig *Gier*, 14, and ship, *Draak*, 18.[1] The *Wolverine* secured the surrender of the first without loss on either side, but the *Arrow* had a harder task, as she had to work up to the *Draak* under fire, against tide and wind. When close to her enemy she opened, and in fifteen minutes the *Draak* hauled down her colours. The *Wolverine* was then fast coming up.

—	Tons.	Guns.	Broadside.	Men.	Killed.	Wounded.	Total.
			Lbs.				
Arrow . .	—	28	448	20	1	9	10
Draak . .	?	24?	358?	180	?	?	?

15 minutes.

The *Draak* was destroyed, and the *Gier* purchased for the Navy.

On September 20th, the British vessels *Camel*, armed storeship, Commander John Lee, and *Rattlesnake*, 16, Commander Samuel Gooch, were lying at anchor in Algoa Bay, South Africa,[2] with masts and yards down, and their commanders and about forty-five men serving on shore, when the French *Preneuse*, 36, Captain L'Hermitte, entered the bay and anchored near them, without attacking them, though each British vessel fired a shot at her. At 8.30 P.M., since it appeared from the *Preneuse's* manœuvres that she intended to board the *Rattlesnake*,[3] that vessel opened fire and was supported by the *Camel*.[4] The *Preneuse* at about nine returned the fire, directing her guns mainly upon the *Camel*. The latter ship was hulled below the water-line, and all her crew had to be withdrawn from the guns to the pumps. The *Preneuse*, supposing that the *Camel* was silenced, next turned her fire on the *Rattlesnake*; but at 3.30 A.M., to the surprise of all, she slipped and retreated. The French explanation of this is that the *Preneuse's* crew was very weak, and that she dreaded attack from a supposed British brig—really a prize schooner. The British

[1] James, 388. [2] *Ib.*, 390.

[3] Temporarily commanded by Lieut. William Fothergill.—W. L. C.

[4] Temporarily commanded by Lieut. Charles Shaw (1).—W. L. C.

loss was three killed and thirteen wounded in this action, against very superior force.

On October 9th, the *Jupiter*, 50, Captain William Granger, having arrived in Algoa Bay, sailed in quest of the *Preneuse*, and on the 10th, in a heavy gale, sighted her, and chased her.[1] The *Jupiter* could not open her lower deck ports owing to the sea. A running fight continued during the 10th and 11th till 2 P.M. of the latter day, when the *Jupiter* closed. The sea was still so high that the British ship could not use her 24-prs. The *Preneuse*, though seriously damaged, was handled with great skill. She twice raked her heavier enemy, and at about 5 P.M. so disabled her foe in masts and rigging as to be able to escape. No explanation of the *Jupiter's* failure can be given. As Troude points out, even if her lower-deck guns were useless, she had her twelve 36-pr. carronades with her 6-prs., which gave her a broadside of 228 lbs.

On October 11th, the *Excellent*, 74, Captain the Hon. Robert Stopford, captured off Lorient the French corvette *Aréthuse*, 18, Captain Halgan, after an eight hours' chase.[2]

On October 11th, the British *Révolutionnaire*, 38, Captain Thomas Twysden, captured an exceptionally large and fast French privateer, the *Bordelaise*, 24, on the Irish coast.[3] The *Bordelaise* offered no resistance.

On the 12th, the British *Trincomale*, 16, Commander John Rowe, whilst engaging a French privateer, the *Iphigénie*, 18, in the strait of Bab-el-Mandeb, blew up, all her crew except two perishing.[4]

On October 15th, the British frigate, *Naiad*, 38, Captain William Pierrepont, cruising in the bay, sighted the two Spanish frigates, *Sta. Brigida*, 34, and *Thetis*, 34, with treasure from Mexico on board to the value of £600,000.[5] She at once gave chase, and early next morning saw another ship—a friend, the *Ethalion*, 38, Captain James Young (2), which also joined in the chase. A third British frigate, the *Alcmène*, 32, Captain Henry Digby, and a fourth, the *Triton*, 32, Captain John Gore (2), arrived on the scene after day

[1] James, 392; Troude, 180; Log of *Jupiter*.

[2] Troude, 183; *Gazette*, 1799, p. 1066.

[3] James, 399; Log of *Révolutionnaire*.

[4] Rowe had been a Commander for less than three months. The explosion also sank the *Iphigénie*, about 115 men perishing in her. The British loss was about 98.—W. L. C.

[5] James, 401.

broke. The two Spaniards then separated and took different courses. The *Ethalion* pursued the *Thetis*, passing the *Sta. Brigida* and firing into her. At 11.30, the *Ethalion* brought the *Thetis* to action, and, after a running fight of an hour, captured her.

—	Tons.	Guns.	Broadside.	Men.	Killed.	Wounded.	Total.
			Lbs.				
Ethalion . .	992	46	425	281	0	0	0
Thetis . .	950?	34?	180?	370?	1	9	10

60 minutes.

Meantime the *Sta. Brigida* doubled Cape Finisterre, closely pursued by the *Triton*. The latter was so unfortunate as to strike a reef, but was quickly got off, and at 7 A.M. brought the Spaniard to action. At the same time the *Alcmène*, steering so as to cut off the *Sta. Brigida* from the shore, engaged her on the other side. Thus assailed, the *Sta. Brigida*, after a vigorous resistance, hauled down her flag. All the three frigates and the *Naiad* were amongst the rocks, whence they succeeded in extricating themselves on a breeze springing up opportunely from the shore.

The Spanish frigates and their captors arrived at Plymouth on the 21st and 22nd. The treasure was in due course removed to London, and divided amongst the captors in the following proportion: Captains, £40,730 18*s*. each; Lieutenants, £5091 7*s*. 3*d*.; warrant-officers, £2468 10*s*. 9½*d*.; Midshipmen, £791 17*s*. 0¼*d*.; seamen and Marines, £182 4*s*. 9½*d*. The Spanish frigates were not purchased for the Navy.

On October 20th, off Cape Ortegal, the British *Cerberus*,[1] 32, Captain James Macnamara (2), discovered a large Spanish convoy of eighty sail, under charge of the *Ceres*, 40, *Diana*, *Esmeralda*, *Mercedes*, and an unknown ship, all of 34, besides two brigs. The *Cerberus* at once approached them, closed a frigate, and with extraordinary audacity, attacked her. The Spaniard was unprepared. She probably never expected a single enemy to venture within the reach of so large a squadron; and at 8.30 her guns are said to have been silenced. The other four Spanish frigates then approached and assailed the intruder, the *Cerberus* being at times engaged on both sides; and at 9.30 Captain Macnamara decided to retire. He

[1] James, 404.

succeeded in getting clear of his assailants, and then, at 11 P.M., captured a brig from the convoy and burnt her. The *Cerberus's* loss was only four wounded. That of the Spaniards is unknown.

On the night of October 24th, the boats of the *Surprise*, 28, Captain Edward Hamilton, cut out the ex-British frigate *Hermione*, 32, from the harbour of Puerto Cabello in Venezuela.[1] The enterprise was a desperate one, as batteries mounting about two hundred

ADMIRAL SIR EDWARD HAMILTON, BART.

(From the engraving by Ridley, after the painting by Thompson.)

guns commanded the harbour. Six boats were employed under the lead of Captain Hamilton himself. They were discovered by two Spanish gun-vessels, and fired on long before they reached the *Hermione*; and, when they got alongside her, they found her crew at quarters. None the less they boarded her, and a desperate fight upon her deck ensued. Captain Hamilton was felled by a clubbed musket, and several of the British were wounded. They drove the

[1] James, 405.

Spaniards, however, from the deck, cut the cable, and loosed the foresail and topsails. In spite of a heavy fire from the batteries they carried out their prize with the loss of only 12 wounded. The Spaniards, on the other hand, lost no fewer than 119 killed and 97 wounded out of a crew of 365. This is perhaps the most gallant of the many gallant cutting-out actions of this war, and Captain Hamilton was deservedly knighted for his conduct. The *Hermione* was restored to the Navy under the name first of *Retaliation* and then of *Retribution*.

On November 6th, the British *Speedy*, 14, Commander Jahleel Brenton, whilst waiting for her convoy off Gibraltar, was attacked by twelve Spanish gunboats which endeavoured unsuccessfully to capture two vessels in her charge.[1] She drove them off after a sharp action, with the loss of only two killed and one wounded. She was, however, very much cut up in hull. The batteries of Gibraltar gave her no support; the explanation being, as Brenton discovered, that the governor of Gibraltar had agreed with the governor of Algesiras, that if the gunboats would not fire on the town of Gibraltar, the batteries would not fire on the gunboats.

On November 15th, the British *Crescent*, 36, Captain William Granville Lobb, and *Calypso*, 16, Commander Joseph Baker, with a convoy, fell in with the Spanish *Asia*, 64, *Amfitrite*, 40, and *Galgo*, 16, under Commodore Don F. Montes, bound from San Domingo to Havana.[2] The *Calypso* reconnoitred the Spaniards and stood between them and the British convoy, as also did the *Crescent*. Meantime the convoy had scattered and the *Galgo* was observed to be closing it. On this the *Crescent* made sail from the *Asia* and *Amfitrite*, and in face of them captured and carried off the *Galgo*. The whole convoy reached Jamaica with the loss of only one ship. There must have been the most astonishing incapacity on the part of the Spaniards.

On November 24th, the British *Solebay*, 32, Captain Stephen Poyntz, discovered off San Domingo four French ships, the flûte, *Egyptien*, 18, store-ship, *Eole*, 16, *Lévrier*, 12, and *Vengeur*, 8.[3] They bore away for Cape Tiburon, and were followed by Poyntz,

[1] James, 395; Brenton, i. 487.

[2] James, 413.

[3] James, 415. Not in Troude, so, probably, these vessels were privateers, or hired by privateer companies from the French navy; or else armed ships, with stores on board. (The *Vengeur* was the ex-British schooner *Charlotte*, which had been captured off Cape François, under Lieut. John Thicknesse, earlier in the year.—W. L. C.)

until the four were becalmed and separated, when the *Solebay* attacked them in turn and captured them all. Between them, they mounted fifty-eight guns, and were manned by 431 men. The *Eole*[1] was purchased for the Navy and renamed *Nimrod*.

On December 11th, the French *Preneuse*, 36, Captain L'Hermitte, was chased off Mauritius by the British *Tremendous*, 74, and *Adamant*, 50, and driven ashore.[2] She was boarded by the British boats and burnt.

On December 17th, the British *Glenmore*, 36, Captain George Duff, and *Aimable*, 32, Captain Henry Raper, with a large convoy, fell in with the French *Sirène*, 36, Captain J. M. Renaud, *Bergère*, 18, Captain Bourdichon, and the *Calcutta*, East Indiaman, which the French had just captured, off Madeira.[3] The *Glenmore* mistook the *Calcutta* for a cut-down ship of the line and stood in chase of her and captured her. Meantime the *Aimable* pursued the two French warships, and at 1.30 P.M. was out of sight of her consort. She attacked the *Bergère*, hoping that the *Glenmore* would come up to her aid; but, when this did not happen and the *Sirène* wore and stood towards her, she had to draw off. She remained watching the French ships till nightfall, when she rejoined the convoy.

In December, a Danish frigate in charge of a convoy resisted an attempted search of her convoy by British vessels, and was compelled to accompany the British ships to Gibraltar, but was there eventually released.[4]

On February 5th, 1800, the British sloops *Fairy*, 16, Commander Joshua Sydney Horton, and *Harpy*, 18, Commander Henry Bazely, off St. Malo discovered the French frigate *Pallas*, 38, Captain Jacques Epron.[5] The British vessels stood out to sea and were followed by the *Pallas*, which closed and engaged them. An action

—	Tons.	Guns.	Broadside.	Men.	Killed.	Wounded.	Total.
			Lbs.				
Pallas . .	1028	46	498	362	12 ?	?	12 ?
{ *Fairy* . . .	— }	40?	334?	240	5	11	16
{ *Harpy* . .	367 }						

1¼ hours.

[1] Called *Eolan* in Steel, and *Goelan* (*i.e. Goeland*) in Marshall, i. 753.—W. L. C.
[2] Troude, 184.
[3] James, 416; Troude, 186.
[4] Chevalier, iii. 28.
[5] James, iii. 3; Troude, iii. 202.

of over an hour followed, in which the *Harpy* several times raked her opponent. Then the *Pallas* retired, leaving the *Harpy* and *Fairy* too much damaged to follow her.

Repairing their damage, the *Fairy* and *Harpy* made sail in chase of the *Pallas*, when they sighted, coming up ahead, the British *Loire*, 38, Captain James Newman Newman, *Danaë*, 20, Captain Lord Proby, and *Railleur*, 16, Commander William Turquand. These joined in the chase, and the *Railleur*, at about 7.45 P.M., compelled the *Pallas* to tack off-shore, when she passed the *Loire* and exchanged fire. At 11 P.M. the *Loire* closed her off the Sept Iles, and began a sharp action with her and a battery on shore. The *Railleur*, *Harpy*, and *Fairy* all joined in, and the five ships fought running on the starboard tack till 1.30, when the *Harpy* got under the *Pallas's* stern and gave her several raking broadsides. On this she struck after a brilliant resistance to an overwhelming force. The *Loire* had on board one hundred "volunteers" from prison-ships who showed great cowardice. The British loss in this action was nine killed and thirty-six wounded; the French loss is unknown. The *Pallas*, a remarkably fine frigate, was purchased for the Navy and renamed *Pique*.

On March 20th, the British *Petrel*, 16, Commander Francis William Austen (1), off the Riviera, engaged the French *Cerf*, 14, *Lejoille*, 6, and *Ligurienne*, 14, in charge of a convoy.[1] As the British *Mermaid*, 32, was seen to be coming up, though at a great distance, the French vessels made all sail to escape. The *Ligurienne* was overtaken by the *Petrel*, and after a smart fight, in which the French had the support of a coast battery mounting four heavy guns, struck.

—	Tons.	Guns.	Broadside.	Men	Killed.	Wounded.	Total.
			Lbs.				
Petrel . .	—	20?	96?	89	0	0	0
Ligurienne .	—	16	85	104	2	2	4

1½ hours.

On April 5th, the British ships *Leviathan*, 74, Captain James Carpenter, carrying Rear-Admiral John Thomas Duckworth's flag, *Swiftsure*, 74, Captain Benjamin Hallowell, and *Emerald*, 36, Captain

[1] James, iii. 10; Troude, 203.

Thomas Moutray Waller, off Cadiz discovered a Spanish convoy.[1] Early on the 6th they captured one of its ships, and later in the day a second. Then, seeing six sail in the north-east, the *Leviathan* and *Emerald* stood towards them, and early on the 7th found that two of them were frigates. At dawn the two British ships bore down upon them, and being taken by the Spaniards for vessels of the convoy, were able to get very close. The enemies were hailed to strike, and, thus discovering their mistake, attempted to escape, but were foiled by the *Emerald*, which disabled their sails and rigging. They then struck, and proved to be the *Carmen*, 32, and *Florentina*, 34. They had lost between them twenty-two killed and twenty-six wounded. The British ships apparently suffered no loss. A third Spanish frigate effected her escape.

On June 3rd, the French corvette *Albanaise*, 12, was captured by the British *Phœnix*, 36, and *Port Mahon*, in the Mediterranean.[2]

On the night of June 10th, the boats of Sir John Borlase Warren's frigate-squadron, cruising off the Penmarcks, captured three small French vessels and eight merchantmen in the harbour of St. Croix with a loss of four men.[3] On the night of the 23rd–24th, a party landed from the boats of the same squadron and stormed and destroyed three small batteries and forts at the mouth of the Quimper river. On the night of July 1st–2nd, the boats boarded and destroyed the French armed ship *Thérèse*, 20, lying inside Noirmoutier Island, three other armed vessels, and fifteen merchantmen. On returning, the boats grounded upon a sandbank, and ninety-two officers and men were captured by the French. The remaining one hundred fought their way clear.

On July 7th, the sloop *Dart*, 30,[4] Commander Patrick Campbell, with two gunbrigs,[5] four fireships,[6] and the cutters and boats from the *Andromeda*, 32, and *Nemesis*, 28, ran into Dunquerque Road to capture or destroy four French frigates lying there, the *Poursuivante*, 44, *Carmagnole*, 40, *Désirée*, 38, and *Incorruptible*, 38.[7] The *Dart* answered a hail in French, and arrived abreast of the inmost frigate but one without a shot being fired. The French vessel then opened on her, and she replied with her 32-pr. carronades, passing on

[1] James, iii. 13. [2] Troude, 210. [3] James, iii. 15.

[4] 32-pr. carronades.—W. L. C.

[5] *Biter*, Lieut. William Norman, and *Boxer*, Lieut. Thomas Gilbert.—W. L. C.

[6] *Wasp*, Com. John Edwards (2); *Falcon*, Com. Henry Samuel Butt; *Comet*, Com. Thomas Leef; and *Rosario*, Com. James Carthew.—W. L. C.

[7] James, iii. 17; Troude, 191.

and running on board the innermost enemy. Her men dashed on to the deck of the Frenchman, and in a moment the *Désirée* was carried. She was successfully taken out by her captors and was purchased for the Navy. Meantime the fireships ran up to the other three French frigates, but, though well handled, could not destroy them, and they escaped. The smaller British craft cannonaded the French gunboats. The total British loss in this dashing enterprise was only six killed or wounded.

On the night of July 26th, three boats from Sir Edward Pellew's squadron, under the command of Lieutenant Jeremiah Coghlan (actg.) of the cutter *Viper*, most gallantly cut out the French gun-brig *Cerbère,* 7, from Port Louis.[1] The French crew was found at quarters, but, though two of his boats failed to arrive in time, Coghlan boarded. He was driven back and wounded in the thigh, but, returning to the attack, forced his way in and carried her. She was towed out successfully; and Lord St. Vincent, then in command of the Channel Fleet, was so pleased with Coghlan's conduct that he presented him with a sword and confirmed him as Lieutenant, in spite of his not having served his time.[2]

On August 4th, the British *Belliqueux*, 64, Captain Rowley Bulteel, with six East Indiamen under her charge, sighted the French frigates *Concorde,* 40, Captain J. F. Landolphe, *Franchise,* 36, Captain P. Jurien de La Gravière, and *Medée,* 36, Captain J. D. Coudin, with a prize schooner, off the coast of Brazil.[3] Taking the Indiamen for ships of the line, the French scattered. The British pursued, the *Belliqueux* capturing the *Concorde* after a few shots which hurt no one, and the East Indiamen chasing the *Medée* and the *Franchise* The *Medée* was overtaken by, and after a very short resistance struck to, the Indiamen *Bombay Castle,* John Hamilton, master, and *Exeter,* Henry Meriton, master. The *Franchise* alone escaped.

[1] James, 20; *Navy League Journal,* i. 195; Osler, 131.

[2] Coghlan, who was born in 1775, was made a Commander in 1804, and a Captain in 1810. He died in the latter rank on March 4, 1844. He had been given a C.B. in 1815.—W. L. C.

[3] James, 23; Troude, 193; J. de La Gravière, 'Souvenirs, ii. 23. The names of the French ships were changed purposely in the last-named work. Captain Jurien protested to his senior officer that the supposed ships of the line were only merchantmen, but to no purpose. The *Franchise,* after escaping, cruised for three weeks on the South American coast without seeing a sail. "Was," asks the captain, "the damage which we had caused to commerce worth the loss of two frigates with 700 men? I am far from believing it. . . . I assert that commerce-destruction has only a secondary importance in the general outline of war."

On August 20th, the British *Seine*, 38, Captain David Milne, after a six hours' chase, came up with the French *Vengeance*, 36, Captain Pitot, off the coast of Puerto Rico.[1] At 4 P.M. the French ship opened fire with her stern-chasers. The *Seine* was not able to use her broadside till 11.30, when she opened fire, taking up a position on the *Vengeance's* quarter. The fire of the French directed at the *Seine's* masts caused her to drop behind; but the *Vengeance*, before she escaped from her enemy, lost her foremast and main topmast. Early on the 21st the *Seine* came up again, only to be once more disabled, and once more to refit. At about 9 A.M. she closed the *Vengeance* for the third time and fought the French ship till 10.30, when the latter, with foremast, main topmast, and mizenmast gone, and fearfully shattered in hull, struck her flag. She was quite unmanageable. The *Seine* had her mainmast tottering, but was not greatly injured.

—	Tons.	Guns.	Broadside.	Men	Killed.	Wounded.	Total.
			Lbs.				
Seine . . .	1146	48[1]	498	281	13	29	42
Vengeance .	1180	50[1]	434	326	35?	70?	105?

8–9 hours.

1 Each ship seems to have fought one extra gun at an empty port on the engaged broadside. Troude gives the *Vengeance* forty carriage-guns and a broadside of 377 lbs.

The *Vengeance* was purchased for the Navy, but saw no service.

On September 3rd, eight boats from the *Minotaur*, 74, and *Niger*, flûte, under Commander James Hillyar, of the latter, rowed in to cut out from Barcelona the Spanish corvettes *Esmeralda*, 22, and *Paz*, 22.[2] The British boats on their way in boarded a Swedish merchantman bound into the port, but quitted as soon as she was within range. The boats, as soon as the Spaniards opened fire, dashed at the *Esmeralda*, and carried her, following up their success by rushing the *Paz*. Both ships were carried off in the face of Spanish gunboats and batteries, with a British loss of only three killed and six wounded.

On October 9th, the East Indiaman *Kent*, 26, Robert Rivington, master, after a long and obstinate resistance, was captured in the Bay of Bengal by the French privateer *Confiance*, 26, Robert

1 James, 23; Troude, 215.

2 'Annual Register,' 1801, p. 87; James, iii. 27; Brenton, i. 515.

Surcouf.[1] The *Kent* was not supplied with sufficient muskets to resist the French boarders, who behaved very badly—as, indeed, privateersmen of both nations only too often did. Rivington fell in the action.

On October 22nd, the French corvette *Vénus*, 28, was captured in the Atlantic by the British ships *Indefatigable*, 44, and *Fishguard*, 38.[2]

In the evening of October 27th, the boats, under Lieutenant Francis Beaufort, of the British frigate *Phaeton*, 38, Captain James Nicholl Morris, cut out from under the guns of the fortress of Fuengirola, near Malaga, the Spanish polacca *San Josef*, 14.[3] The Spaniards made a desperate resistance, but could not stand against the valour of the British seamen, whose loss was only one killed and four wounded. The *San Josef* lost nineteen wounded. She was purchased for the Navy, and renamed the *Calpe*.

An action which is important as illustrating the value of non-recoil mountings, was that of November 13th, between the British schooner *Milbrook*, of sixteen 18-pr. carronades, mounted on non-recoil principles,[4] and a large French privateer, the *Bellone*, off Oporto. The *Milbrook*, Lieutenant Matthew Smith (2), fired eleven broadsides to the enemy's three. The *Bellone* was of far superior orce,[5] and succeeded in escaping.

On November 17th, a British squadron, under Captain Sir Richard John Strachan, discovered the French corvette *Réolaise*, 20, running along the Morbihan coast, and attempting to gain the shelter of a battery.[6] She was cut off from it by the *Nile*, cutter, Lieutenant George Argles, and ran aground in Port Navalo, striking her colours. The boats of the squadron approached to cut her out, but she rehoisted her colours, got off the ground, and fired on them. This only postponed her fate, as the boats returned, and,

[1] Norman, 'Corsairs of France,' 353. [Robert Surcouf, one of the greatest of the French corsairs, was born at St. Malo in 1773, and first went to sea, in a merchantman, in 1789. He was engaged in the slave trade, even after the traffic had been formally abolished by the Republic in 1794, and was in consequence arrested, but, escaping, became a privateer. In the East Indies he was extraordinarily successful. He was at length appointed an unattached enseigne in the navy, but did not serve as such; and, after 1802, contented himself with fitting out privateers, until 1806, when he returned to the East Indies, and gained further successes. After the peace he lived as a shipowner and shipbuilder till his death in 1827. Laughton, 'Studies in Nav. Hist.'—W. L. C.]

[2] Troude, 220. [3] James, 33. [4] *Ib.*, iii. 35.

[5] Mounting twenty-four long 8-prs., and six or eight 36-pr. carronades.—W. L. C.

[6] James, 36; Troude, 220.

under a heavy fire, boarded and destroyed her, with the loss of one killed and seven wounded.

On the night of January 3rd, 1801, five boats from the *Melpomene*, 38, Captain Sir Charles Hamilton, crossed the bar of the river Sénégal, and, without being discovered, approached the French brig *Sénégal*, 18, Captain Renou, at anchor in the river.[1] They were close to her when she fired, and sank two of the boats. The others pushed alongside her, boarded her, and carried her after a short struggle. The British boats then proceeded to attack a schooner, which had run under the shelter of a battery, but were repulsed. In taking the *Sénégal* out she grounded on the bar, and no efforts could get her off. She was, therefore, abandoned, and the boats rowed back to the ship. The loss was heavy, as out of a total of ninety-six officers and men engaged, eleven were killed[2] and eighteen wounded. The *Sénégal* was totally lost in the quicksands on which she had struck.

On January 17th, the small British schooner *Garland*,[3] and some boats, the whole under Lieutenants Kenneth M'Kenzie and Francis Peachey, approached the French schooner *Eclair*, at anchor under the batteries of Trois Rivières in the island of Guadeloupe, under the Swedish flag, boarded her, and carried her off with the loss of five men.

On January 20th, the British *Mercury*, 26, Captain Thomas Rogers, in the Mediterranean, fell in with and captured the French *Sanspareille*, 20, Lieutenant G. Renaud, then on her way to Egypt with stores and ammunition for the French army.[4] Some days previously, in the Gulf of Lions, the same British ship had captured fifteen sail of a French convoy.

On January 23rd, the late Spanish *Nuestra Señora de los Dolores*, 1, acting as tender to the British *Abergavenny*, 54, captured in the most gallant way a Spanish preventive schooner, the *Santa Maria*, 6, on the South American coast.[5] The tender chased the Spaniard ashore, followed her and grounded, when a number of British seamen, led by Lieutenant Michael Fitton (actg.), swam off to her, sword in mouth, and carried her. She was then destroyed.

[1] James, 118; Troude, 245.

[2] Including Lieut. William Palmer, Lieut. of Marines William Vyvian, and Midshipman Robert Main.—W. L. C.

[3] Troude, 246; James, 120. [4] James, 119; Troude, 247. [5] James, 123.

On January 26th, the British *Oiseau*, 36, Captain Samuel Hood Linzee, off Cape Ortegal, sighted the French *Dédaigneuse*, 36, Captain Lacroix, on her way from Cayenne to Rochefort.[1] The French ship was in very bad order. Amongst other defects, the bolts of her cut-water had worked loose and given the bowsprit too much play. Other British frigates, the *Sirius*, 36, and *Amethyst*, 36, came into sight, and the *Dédaigneuse* turned and headed for Ferrol. A long chase followed, but late in the night of the 27th-28th the *Sirius* and *Oiseau* began a running fight. Off Ferrol harbour the French vessel was becalmed, whilst the British pursuers were carried down upon her by a breeze from the sea. After four broadsides the *Dédaigneuse's* captain was wounded. The French ship struck, seeing another British frigate, the *Immortalité*, approaching. The British suffered no loss, and very little damage. The French loss is unknown.[2] The *Dédaigneuse* was purchased for the Navy.

On January 29th the British corvette *Bordelaise*, 24, Captain Thomas Manby, off Barbados, found three French vessels standing after her.[3] These were the *Curieux*, 18, Captain G. Radelet, *Mutine*, 16, Captain Reybaud, and *Espérance*, 6, Captain Hamon. The British ship shortened sail and waited. The *Curieux* came up, and was at once attacked, whereupon her two consorts beat a prompt retreat. All but two of the *Bordelaise's* guns were 32-pr. carronades, and those made short work of her audacious assailant. For thirty minutes the two fought at the closest quarters, when the *Curieux* struck, after suffering terrible loss. Her captain paid for his gallantry with the loss of his life. The *Curieux* foundered almost immediately after the action, two British seamen going down in her.

—	Tons.	Guns.	Broadside.	Men.	Killed.	Wounded.	Total.
			Lbs.				
Bordelaise .	625	24	361	195	1	7	8
Curieux . .	—	18	78	168	—	—	about 50

30 minutes.

[1] James, 123; Troude, 248.

[2] "Several killed and seventeen wounded," says the *Gazette* letter with the usual vagueness.

[3] James, 124.

On February 18th, in the Southern Atlantic, the British *Penguin*, 18, Captain Robert Mansel,[1] fought a sharp action with three unknown French ships, one looking like a corvette, and the other two apparently merchantmen.[2] The *Penguin* gave chase, and compelled one of them to strike. On this she was assailed by the corvette, and was so damaged in masts and rigging that she could not pursue her antagonists, who then sheered off. Her foremast went overboard, but her loss was only one man wounded.

On February 19th the British *Phœbe*, 36, Captain Robert Barlow, to the east of Gibraltar, discovered the French frigate *Africaine*, 40, Captain Saunier, steering up the Mediterranean.[3] The *Africaine* was heavily laden, having, besides her crew, four hundred troops for Egypt, six field-guns, and a quantity of arms and ammunition on board. She had parted from the similarly freighted *Régénérée*, 36, some days previously. The *Phœbe* quickly overhauled her enemy, and brought her to close action, steering a parallel course. The French ship had her decks encumbered, and was at a great disadvantage. Her only chance lay in boarding the *Phœbe*, but this Captain Barlow was adroit enough to prevent. The effect of the *Phœbe's* well-directed fire upon the crowded decks of the *Africaine* was deadly in the extreme. After two hours' furious fighting, Captain Saunier and Commander J. J. Magendie, the two French senior officers, were wounded, the ship was on fire in several places, and had five feet of water in her hold, and most of her guns were dismounted. She struck her flag.

—	Tons.	Guns.	Broadside.	Men.	Killed.	Wounded.	Total.
			Lbs.				
Phœbe . .	926	44	407	239	1	12	13
Africaine .	1059	44	334	715 [1]	200	144	344

2 hours.

[1] Including 400 troops, etc.

This action shows clearly the disastrous result of encumbering a warship with soldiers and cargo. The French troops, as a point of honour, insisted on remaining on deck during the action, though their

[1] Mansel had been posted on February 14th, but had not received his commission.—W. L. C.

[2] James, 125; Troude, 249; Log of *Penguin*.

[3] James, 127; Troude, 250; Chevalier, iii. 47; Napoleon's Correspondence, 5514.

presence was useless, and even harmful; and this contributed to the terrific loss. It was only with extreme difficulty that the *Phœbe* carried her prize into Port Mahon. The *Africaine* was purchased for the Navy, and her name changed to *Amelia*. It appears that the bad shooting of the French—who only put three shot into the *Phœbe's* hull—was due to Captain Saunier having planed down the quoins before the day of battle, and to his having actually removed them when the *Phœbe* was in chase of him. Thus the French gunners were compelled to fire high and to endeavour to dismast their enemy. This came to the knowledge of the First Consul, who warned his officers that they were to fire, "not to dismast the enemy, but to do him as much harm as possible."

On March 22nd, the boats of the *Andromache*, 32, and *Cleopatra*, 32, captured a Spanish gunboat on the Cuban coast, but only with heavy loss – nine killed and twelve wounded.[1]

On the night of April 2nd–3rd, the boats of the *Trent*, 36, off the islands of Bréhat, captured a French lugger and her prize as these were making for Paimpol. The British loss was two killed and one wounded.

Early in April the *Speedy*, 14, Commander Lord Cochrane, cruising off the Spanish Mediterranean coast, was decoyed close under the guns of a heavy Spanish xebec disguised as a merchantman.[2] To escape was impossible; to fight, taken unprepared, against such odds, hopeless. Cochrane was sailing under Danish colours. His ship was painted to resemble a Dane; and he placed an officer, who could speak Danish, in Danish uniform at the gangway, and caused him to reply in Danish to the Spaniard's hail. Dissatisfied, the Spaniard sent a boat, which was told that the supposed Dane was from one of the Barbary ports, where the plague was then raging. On this the Spaniards were only too anxious to be off.

On May 6th, the *Speedy* met a large Spanish frigate, the *Gamo*. Sailing under American colours till he was close to his enemy, Cochrane, in spite of two broadsides from the Spaniard, which did him no damage, ran alongside, and fired his guns treble-shotted into the foe. The Spaniards attempted to board, but, as soon as Cochrane heard the order given, he sheered off, continuing his fire. A second and a third attempt on the part of the Spaniards were repulsed. Then, running under her big adversary once more, the

[1] James, 130.

[2] *Ib.*, 132; 'Autobiography of a Seaman' (1890 ed.), 43.

Speedy emptied her whole crew upon the Spaniard's deck, and the *Gamo* was carried, though not without a struggle.

—	Tons.	Guns.	Broadside.	Men.	Killed.	Wounded.	Total.
			Lbs.				
Speedy . .	158	14	28	54	3	8	11
Gamo . .	600	32	190	319	15	41	56

45 minutes.

This is one of the most extraordinary actions of the war, and exhibits in a brilliant light Lord Cochrane's audacity, judgment, and fertility of resource. He carried his big prize safe into harbour, but only with great difficulty.

On May 25th, the boats of the *Mercury*, 28, Captain Thomas Rogers, attempted to cut out the ex-British bomb *Bulldog* from the harbour of Ancona.[1] The British seamen, according to Troude, disarmed suspicion by answering the challenge in French, boarded the *Bulldog*, and carried her without resistance being offered. They then cut the cables which secured her to the mole, and had worked her nearly to the entrance of the harbour when they were attacked by a number of French boats, and forced to abandon their prize. Their loss was two killed and four wounded.

On June 9th, the *Kangaroo*, 18, Commander George Christopher Pulling, and *Speedy*, 14, Commander Lord Cochrane, attacked a Spanish convoy off Oropeso, under the shelter of a Spanish battery, sank a 20-gun xebec and three gunboats, and captured three merchant brigs.[2] On July 3rd, Rear-Admiral Linois' squadron, of three French sail of the line and one frigate, captured the little *Speedy*, 14, in the Strait of Gibraltar.[3]

On the night of July 20th–21st, the boats of the British frigates *Beaulieu*, 40, Captain Stephen Poyntz, and *Doris*, Captain Charles Brisbane, 36, made an attempt to cut out the French corvette *Chevrette*, 20, which was lying in Camaret Bay, but failed to arrive before day had dawned.[4] They retired, but they had been seen, and the *Chevrette* prepared for another attempt by embarking a party of soldiers, which brought her crew up to 339, and by loading her guns to the muzzle with grape. On the following night, the boats of the above frigates with those of the *Uranie*, 38, Captain

[1] James, 135; Troude, 254. [2] James, 135. [3] *Ib.*, 97.
[4] *Ib.*, 137; Troude, 255; 'Nav. Chronicle,' 7, 216.

George Henry Gage, as well, embarked 280 men, and rowed in. Six boats, however, proceeded to chase a French look-out boat, and did not return. The other boats,[1] with 180 men, grew impatient, and dashed at the *Chevrette.* They were received with a heavy fire of great guns and small arms, both from her and from the shore, but pressed on; and the British seamen forced their way on board. A party of topmen, appointed for that purpose, fought their way up her rigging and spread her topsails, and presently the *Chevrette* stood out of the bay. Meantime, the party on deck carried the forecastle and quarter-deck, and drove the Frenchmen down the hatches. As soon as that had been done the other six boats rejoined. The *Chevrette* was carried off, though fired upon by the French batteries. In the affair the British loss was twelve killed or missing and fifty-seven wounded, whilst the French lost ninety-two killed and sixty-two wounded. The gallantry of the British officers and seamen was above all praise. The *Beaulieu's* quartermaster, Henry Wallis, who had been ordered to take the *Chevrette's* helm, fought his way to his post, and continued at it, though badly wounded.

On July 21st, the British hired brig *Pasley*, 16, Lieutenant William Wooldridge (1), fought a sharp action with a Spanish xebec of twenty-two guns. The xebec escaped. The *Pasley's* loss was one killed and two wounded.[2]

On July 31st, the British brig *Sylph*, 18, Commander Charles Dashwood, off Santander, was engaged by a large ship of unknown nationality—probably a French or Spanish privateer—and after eighty minutes' close fighting had to retire.[3] She was not pursued by the strange ship. On August 1st, the *Sylph* saw her enemy at some distance with her foreyard on the deck, and gave chase, but, by reason of the heavy sea and her own injuries, could not close. The *Sylph's* loss was one killed and nine wounded. Having repaired her damage, the *Sylph*, cruising off the coast of Spain on September 28th, again encountered an unknown ship, and fought her for over two hours, when the enemy retired. The *Sylph* only had one man wounded. According to Dashwood, the stranger was the French *Artémise*, 40. We may be permitted to feel the gravest doubt as to this. It is impossible to believe that a large and powerful

[1] Under Lieuts. Keith Maxwell, James Pasley, Martin Neville, and Walter Burke; Lieut. of Marines James Sinclair; and Mids. Robert Warren. Sinclair and Warren were killed, and Burke was mortally wounded.—W. L. C.

[2] James, 149.

[3] *Ib.*, 145; Marshall, vol. ii. pt. i. 454.

French frigate would have failed to inflict far heavier loss on a small brig—if, indeed, she had not captured her. The matter remains a mystery.

On August 18th,[1] the British *Sibylle*, 38, Captain Charles Adam, discovered the French *Chiffonne*, 36, Captain P. Guieysse in Mahé roads with her foremast out. The *Sibylle* prepared for battle, steered in through a narrow intricate passage, and anchored two hundred yards off the Frenchman, with springs on her cables. An action of seventeen minutes followed, during which the *Sibylle* had to take the raking fire of a French battery on the island. Then the *Chiffonne* cut her cable, struck her flag, and drifted on a reef. The *Sibylle* sent a boat to take possession, and another to capture the battery, upon which she turned her guns. The battery then surrendered.

—	Tons.	Guns.	Broadside.	Men.	Killed.	Wounded.	Total.
			Lbs.				
Sibylle . .	1091	48	503	217 n.	2	1	3
Chiffonne .	945	40	370	190	23	30	53

17 minutes.

The *Chiffonne* was taken by surprise, and many of her men were on shore. She was got off, and was afterwards purchased for the Navy.

On September 2nd, the British *Victor*, 18, Commander George Ralph Collier, off the Seychelles, engaged for ninety minutes the French *Flèche*, 18, Captain J. B. Bonamy.[2] The *Victor* had the heavier metal and soon drove her enemy to flight, but, having received serious injury in her masts and rigging, could not pursue closely. The *Victor* followed at a distance till the 5th, when the *Flèche* had disappeared. That afternoon, however, she saw her entering Mahé. The channel was sounded at night, and next day the *Victor* stood in and anchored with springs, taking a raking fire during her approach. A fight of two and a half hours followed, when the *Flèche*, in a sinking condition, cut her cables, drove on shore, and was set on fire by her crew. A British party boarded her, but she fell over and sank.

[1] James, 131, gives the date as April 19th. Troude, 259, gives the date as August 20th. Log of *Sibylle*.

[2] James, 143; Troude, 262.

—	Tons.	Guns.	Broadside.	Men.	Killed.	Wounded.	Total.
			Lbs.				
Victor . .	—	18	262	120	0	2	2
Flèche . .	—	18	78	145	4	?	?

4 hours.

The *Flèche* was eventually raised by the French.

On September 16th, the ex-British bomb *Bulldog* was recaptured off the south coast of Italy by the British frigates *Mercury*, 26, and *Sta. Dorotea*,[1] 36.

For the minor actions of the Revolutionary war we have the aid of the invaluable *Naval Chronicle*, and of the painstaking James, who appears to have carefully collated *Gazette* letters, logs, courts-martial, and what French authorities were accessible in his day.[2] The ship's logs were still kept in a most unsatisfactory way, especially in small craft. For instance, the British frigate *Oiseau* sights the French *Dédaigneuse*, and the log is dumb. But towards the close of the century there is a very distinct improvement, and, as printed forms come into use, more care is exercised.

There is a great similarity about all the minor actions between ships. One vessel sights another, gives chase, maintains a running action, closes, rakes, or attempts to rake, gets the enemy's fire under, and brings down his flag. The same characteristics which prevented the French navy from achieving anything great in the American war are exemplified in the frigate actions of this war, where French ships are concerned. There is the same timidity, the same straining after some ulterior object, the same dislike to damaging the French ship in action, the same firing at the British masts and rigging. To this the loss of at least one action can be

[1] Troude, 263.

[2] The authorities for this war are, besides James and Troude: Brenton, 'Naval History' (2 vols. 1837); Chevalier, 'Marine Française sous la Première République,' and 'Sous le Consulat et l'Empire'; the *Naval Chronicle*, which gives *Gazette* letters, lives of eminent officers and much interesting matter; Schomberg's 'Naval Chronology'; Courts-Martial, Logs, List Books, Captains' Letters and Admirals' Dispatches; the various biographies of great seamen—Nelson (Nicolas), Saumarez (Ross), Pellew (Osler), Dundonald, St. Vincent (Tucker), Keith (Allardyce), Durham (Murray); Marshall's 'Naval Biography'; Ralfe, 'Naval Biography'; 'Dictionary of National Biography,' the naval biographies in which, by Professor Laughton, are full of research. The compiler takes this opportunity of acknowledging the value of the excellent 'Index to James's Naval History,' published by the Navy Records Society, which will be found most useful.

directly traced;[1] to this also are probably due in part the very slight losses of men inflicted on British ships in several hotly fought actions. British crews invariably fired at the hulls of their opponents, and strove to kill the men rather than to disable the ship. Chance, as in all battles, plays a considerable part. Israel Pellew shoots away the *Cléopâtre's* wheel, and greatly contributes to one of the most brilliant victories of the war.[2] The bursting of a gun leads not indirectly to the *Ambuscade's* defeat by an inferior ship.[3]

In this war French ships usually carried large but undisciplined crews and unskilled officers. In these circumstances they were wise to follow Jean Bon Saint André's famous advice[4]—to "disdain evolutions" and "attempt to board." Thus they could best employ their masses of men. If the shooting of the French crews was wretched—and how bad it was these actions show—the spirit and fiery courage of the French sailors—seamen we cannot call them—were above all reproach. They endured enormous losses in innumerable instances before they struck.

It is interesting to develop further the examination of the influence of weight of metal upon the result of actions. In the American war we have seen that there were very few instances indeed in which the weaker broadside won. That is not the case in the Revolutionary war. Taking important and decisive single-ship actions, the results can be tabulated thus—

—	Superior Broadside Wins against.	Inferior Broadside Wins against.
British ships . . .	1	1
French „ . . .	21	7
Spanish „ . . .	4	2
Dutch „ . . .	2	—

But in the French navy the circumstances were quite abnormal, owing to indiscipline, want of seamanship, bad gunnery, and possibly

[1] *Forte* and *Sibylle*.

[2] *Cf.* also Ross, 'Saumarez,' i. 101. The *Réunion's* wheel was shot away in her action with the *Crescent*. The British gunners seem to have regularly aimed at the wheel, rudder and steering-gear.

[3] The Court-martial attributed the loss of the *Ambuscade* "to a rapid succession of the most unfortunate accidents."

[4] Chevalier, ii. 49.

—from a hint contained in one of Napoleon's letters—bad powder.[1] The heavier broadside, even in these exceptional circumstances, usually wins the day; and nothing is more noticeable than the steady increase in the force of frigates, so as to ensure having the heavier broadside. The 28-gun ship practically disappears; the 32, the standard cruiser of the American war, gives way to the 36, 38, 40, or to the cut-down ship of the line. The evolution and development which our own day has seen in the size of ships, progress steadily, if slowly. We find, by the close of the war, such frigates as the *Forte* superior by fifty per cent. in weight of metal to the old 50-gun vessel of the line.

In British frigates the carronade was given a very important place. It became larger in calibre, and to a great extent replaced the small guns—6 and 9-prs.—which had been carried on the forecastle and quarter-deck. In the smaller classes it frequently constituted the entire armament except only for a pair of bow-chasers. Owing to its lightness, ease of handling, and rapidity of fire, it was most efficient in action at short ranges, when pitted against long guns, as the instances of the *Glatton*, *Pelican*, *Wolverine*, and *Milbrook* prove. In the last case, the British ship with non-recoil carronades fired eleven broadsides to her enemy's three. In fact the carronade was a quick-firer of large calibre but very short range. The wonder is that enemies attacked by British ships so armed did not select a longer range, for the carronade was of little value outside four hundred yards. Probably the strong objection to this weapon, which we find expressed by many experienced and able officers, was that it limited our tactics and constrained close action. In French ships of and above the size of frigates, the 36-pr. carronade is regularly carried during this war: in small French craft, however, there are often no carronades. In Spanish vessels 24-pr. carronades are carried.[2]

The two conspicuous instances where British ships were taken after a well-contested action, are those of the *Leander* and *Ambuscade*. The first was overpowered by a ship of more than twice her strength, on which she had inflicted enormous loss; the second was beaten under peculiar circumstances by a ship of inferior force. She had an indifferent Captain and a weak crew: she was surprised and she was boarded.

[1] Correspondence, 5476.

[2] 'Autobiography of a Seaman,' Cochrane, 51. The *Gamo* had two 24-pr. carronades.

Examining the seven important instances in which a French vessel hauled down her flag to an inferior opponent, we find that in three cases there were other British ships at hand. Even where these do not fire a shot, the moral effect must be great. To fight without a chance of success, when the sacrifice of life is productive of no result, demands almost superhuman courage. The other four instances are those of the *Pique*, *Tamise*, *Vestale*, and *Forte*. The *Pique* was raked, and when we know that in the case of the *Réunion* a single raking shot killed or wounded twenty-one men out of a crew of 320,[1] we see what that might mean. She was entangled and held in an awkward position for some minutes under this raking fire. The defeat of the *Tamise* was probably due to the French trick of firing at the masts of the enemy; and, in any case, she was superior to the British ship which captured her by only ten per cent. in weight of broadside. The advantage of the *Vestale* in weight of metal was still smaller, and she was attacked by an exceptionally smart captain, Bowen, the hero of Tenerife. She inflicted heavy loss upon the victor. Lastly, the *Forte* was, if French authorities can be believed, badly manned and most indifferently commanded. She was superior by twenty per cent. to the *Sibylle*, which captured her, but she fired high.

The Spanish instances need not be examined. As a fighting force the Spanish navy was worthless, and it may be doubted whether the hearts of the Spanish officers were in the war. The same may be said of the Dutch in minor actions. The numerous engagements with privateers—which are for the most part omitted in these pages—are not very instructive. From want of discipline a privateer, unless of quite exceptional size, was not formidable to a man-of-war.

There are several remarkable instances wherein powerful French ships were captured after a brisk engagement, in which the British loss was trivial to a degree. The *Crescent*, *Unicorn*, *Révolutionnaire*, and *Indefatigable* each captured an enemy without having a man killed or even seriously wounded. The losses they inflicted were respectively 81, 51, 20, and 42. The first case illustrates the admirable skill in manœuvring and seamanship of the best of our naval officers.[2] The *Crescent's* opponent was virtually equal in force, and was superior in size. Other instances in which the British losses were insignificant and the French losses very heavy are those of the

[1] Ross, 'Saumarez,' i. 111. [2] *Ib.*, i. 112.

Proserpine (9 killed and wounded to 75 killed and wounded in the enemy), *Seahorse* (18 to 80), *Lively* (2 to 41), *Santa Margarita* (5 to 51), *Sibylle* (22 to 145), and *Phœbe* (13 to 344). In this last case the enemy was crowded with troops, and the result was a simple massacre. But to this result contributed the French practice of firing to dismast. A British officer on board the *Crescent* noted that "the enemy (the *Réunion*) fired so high that scarcely any shot struck the hull of the *Crescent*."[1] In the *Africaine*, which the *Phœbe* handled so severely, the French captain had actually removed the quoins of his guns, to compel his men to shoot high.

The skill of the British officers and men is clearly shown by the celerity with which they refitted their ships when damaged in masts and rigging. The famous examples of the *Vanguard* in 1798 and Saumarez's ships after their action with Linois belong to the major operations. In the minor actions the instance of the *Seine* is very striking. After some hours' firing she is so damaged by the French *Vengeance* in her masts that she drops behind. She refits and comes up again, and again is more or less disabled. A second time she refits; a third time she closes and then takes her enemy.

There are several actions in which British merchantmen repulsed the attack of powerful French frigates or privateers; one or two in which they captured French ships through mistake on the part of the latter. Such successes were, however, obtained by few but East Indiamen. They were formidable-looking ships, having at a distance the appearance of frigates or small vessels of the line; and they were usually well commanded, had disciplined crews, and invariably carried a light armament of such guns as 9-pr. carronades and 12-pr. long guns. An East Indiaman, the *Pigot*, repulsed two French privateers, together mounting sixty guns; and five East Indiamen captured these privateers some days later. Five East Indiamen were mistaken by Sercey's squadron for ships of the line and left unmolested. The French *Medée* surrendered to two East Indiamen which she mistook for vessels of the line. In general the merchant ship was too badly manned, too much encumbered, too feebly armed, and too weakly built to have any chance against the privateer, much less against the warship.

Very many of the minor actions took place in *the* Bay, the Bay of Biscay, which was very thoroughly scoured by British cruisers. Taking the year 1796 we find that five 44's, ten 38's, five 36's, five

[1] 'Saumarez,' i. 102.

32's, and eight sloops or brigs were cruising in the Channel and in the Bay.[1] Besides these, eleven small vessels were employed on convoy duty. In the North Sea, off Brest with the Channel fleet, and on the British coast, were yet more frigates and small craft, whilst the List Book gives the strength of 44's, frigates, and small craft on foreign station in January, 1797,[2] thus: 44's, seven; frigates, sixty-four; sloops, etc., forty-four. Of these, most were engaged in convoy duty, commerce protection, and watching the enemy's ports. The total so employed was even larger in 1798–1801 than in 1796, seeing that the Navy steadily expanded.

[1] Schomberg, 4, 532, 533.

[2] —	E. Indies.	Jamaica.	Leeward Is.	Mediterranean.	Nova Scotia.
44's . . .	3	2	1	—	1
Frigates . .	14	10	14	19	7
Small . . .	5	10	14	10	5

APPENDIX TO CHAPTERS XXXV. AND XXXVI.

A.—List of H.M. Ships Taken, Destroyed, Burnt, Foundered or Wrecked during the War of the French Revolution, 1793–1801, and of Losses to the end of 1802.

Year.	Date.	H.M. Ship.	Guns.	Commander. [* Lost his life on the occasion.]	Remarks.
1793	May 27	*Hyæna*	24	Capt. William Hargood.	Taken by *Concorde*, 40, in W. Indies.
	June 1	*Advice*, cutter	4	Lieut. Edward Tyrrel.	Wrecked on Key Bokell, Honduras.
	Oct. 4	*Thames*	32	Capt. James Cotes.	Taken by three French frigates, going to Gibraltar. Retaken, June 7, 1796.
	Nov. 20	*Scipion*	74	..	Accidentally burnt off Leghorn.
	Dec. 16	*Pigmy*, cutter	14	Lieut. Abraham Pulliblank.*	Wrecked on the Motherbank.
	,, 18	*Vigilante*, cutter	4	..	Taken by the French at Toulon.
	,, 18	*Alerte*	14	(Not in commission.)	Taken by the French at Toulon.
	,, 18	*Conflagration*, f.s.	14	Com. John Loring.	Burnt on evacuation of Toulon.
	,, 18	*Vulcan*, f.s.	14	,, Charles Hare.	Expended at Toulon.
	,, 18	*Union*, gunboat	..	..	Blown up at Toulon.
		Vipère, cutter	4	..	Wrecked in Hyères Bay.
1794	Jan. 7	*Moselle*	24	,, Richard Henry Alexander Bennett.	Taken on entering Toulon by mistake.
	,, 30	*Amphitrite*	18	Capt. Anthony Hunt.	Wrecked in the Mediterranean.
	Feb.	*Spitfire*, cutter	6	Com. T. W. Rich.*	Capsized off San Domingo, with all hands.
	Mar. 8	*Convert* (ex *Inconstant*)	32	Capt. John Lawford.	Wrecked on Grand Cayman.
	Apr. 11	*Prosélyte*, floatg. batt.	24	Com. Walter Serocold.	Sunk by batteries at Bastia.
	,,	*Ardent*	64	Capt. Robert Manners Sutton.	Accidentally blown up off Corsica, with all hands.
	May 8	*Placentia*	..	Lieut. Alexander Shippard.	Lost at Newfoundland.
	,, 10	*Castor*	32	Capt. Thomas Troubridge.	Taken by Adm. Nielly's squadron off Cape Clear.
	,,	*Alert*	16	Com. Charles Smith.	Taken by *Unité*, 40, off Ireland.
	June 28	*Rose*	28	Capt. Matthew Henry Scott.	Wrecked on Rocky Point, Jamaica.
	,,	*Speedy*	14	Com. George Eyre.	Taken by French frigates, off Nice.
	,,	*Ranger*, cutter	14	Lieut. Isaac Cotgrave.	Taken by a French squadron, off Brest.
	July 14	*Hound*	16	Com. Richard Piercy.	Taken by *Seine* and *Galatée*, coming from W. Ind.
	Aug. 24	*Impétueux*	74	(Not in commission.)	Accidentally burnt at Portsmouth.
	,,	*Scout*	16	Com. Charles Robinson.	Taken by two French frigates, off Cape Bona.
	Nov. 6	*Alexander*	74	Rear-Adm. Richard Rodney Bligh.	Taken by a French squadron off Sicily.
	,, 26	*Pylades*	16	Com. Thomas Twysden.	Wrecked on Isle of Nest, Shetlands.
	,, 26	*Actif*, brig	10	,, John Harvey (2).	Foundered off Bermuda.
		Espion	16	,, William Hugh Kittoe.	Taken by three French frigates.
	Dec. 22	*Daphne*	20	Capt. William Edward Cracraft.	Taken by two French men-of-war. Retaken, Dec. 28, 1797.
1795	Mar. 7	*Berwick*	74	,, Adam Littlejohn.	Taken by the French fleet in the Mediterranean.
	,, 14	*Illustrious*	74	,, Thomas Lenox Frederick.	Wrecked near Avenza.
	May 1	*Boyne*	98	,, George Grey.	Accidentally burnt at Spithead.
		Mosquito, floatg. batt.	5	Lieut. William McCarthy.*	Lost on coast of France with all hands.
	June	*Flying Fish*, schoon.	6	,, George Seaton.	Taken in W. Ind. by two French privateers.
	Aug. 2	*Diomede*	44	Capt. Matthew Smith (1).	Wrecked near Trincomale.
	Oct. 7	*Censeur*	74	,, John Gore (1).	Taken by a French squadron off C. St. Vincent.
	Nov. 12	*Flèche*	14	Lieut. Charles Came.	Wrecked in San Fiorenzo Bay.
	Dec. 9	*Nemesis*	28	Capt. Samuel Hood Linzee.	Taken by two French men-of-war at Smyrna. Retaken, March 9, 1796.
	,, 11	*Shark*, Dutch hoy	4	Lieut. —— Watson.	Carried by her crew into La Hougue.
	,, 29	*Amethyst*	38	Capt. Thomas Affleck.	Lost at Alderney.
1796	..	*Scourge*	16	Com. William Stap.	Foundered off the Dutch coast.

Year.	Date.	H.M. Ship.	Guns.	Commander. [* Lost his life on the occasion.]	Remarks.
1796	Feb. 11	*Leda*	36	Capt. John Woodley.*	Capsized in a squall.
	„ 12	*St. Pierre* . . .	..	..	Wrecked off Pt. Negro.
	Apr. 4	*Spider*, hired lugger	..	Lieut. James Oswald.	Collided with *Ramillies*.
	„ 11	*Ça Ira*	80	Capt. Charles Dudley Pater.	Accidentally burnt in San Fiorenzo Bay.
	May 13	*Salisbury* . . .	50	„ William Mitchell.	Wrecked near San Domingo.
	June 10	*Arab*	16	Com. Stephen Seymour.*	Wrecked near Point Penmarck.
	July 15	*Trompeuse* . . .	16	„ Joshua Rowley Watson.	Wrecked near Kingsale.
	„	*Active*	32	Capt. Edward Leveson Gower.	Wrecked in the St. Lawrence.
		Sirène	16	Com. Daniel Guerin.*	Wrecked in the Bay of Honduras.
	Aug. 27	*Undaunted* (ex *Aréthuse*). . .	38	Capt. Robert Winthrop.	Wrecked on Morant Keys.
		Bermuda . . .	14	Com. Thomas Maxtone.*	Foundered in Gulf of Florida.
	Sept. 22	*Amphion* . . .	32	Capt. Israel Pellew.	Accidentally burnt in Hamoaze.
	Oct. 2	*Experiment*, brig .	10	Lieut. George Hayes.	Taken by the Spaniards in the Mediterranean.
	„ 3	*Narcissus* . . .	20	Capt. Percy Fraser.	Wrecked off New Providence.
	„ 10	*Malabar*. . . .	54	„ Thomas Parr.	Foundered coming from W. Ind.
	„ 20	*Poulette*	26	Edwards.	Burnt at Ajaccio, as unserviceable.
	„ 20	*Bellette*	24	Com. John Temple.	Burnt at Ajaccio, as unserviceable.
	Nov. 3	*Helena*	14	„ Jermyn John Symonds.*	Foundered on Dutch coast, with all hands.
	„	*Berbice*, brig . .	8	Lieut. John Tresahar.	Wrecked at Dominica.
	„	*Vanneau*, brig . .	8	„ John Gourly.	Wrecked at Porto Ferrajo.
	Dec. 7	*Réunion*. . . .	36	Capt. Henry William Bayntun.	Wrecked in the Swin.
	„ 14	*Vestale*	36	..	Retaken, after capture, on Dec. 13.
	„ 19	*Courageux* . . .	74	„ Benjamin Hallowell.	Wrecked below Ape's Hill.
	„ 21	*Bombay Castle* . .	74	„ Thomas Sotheby.	Wrecked in the Tagus.
	„ 24	*Cormorant* . . .	18	Lieut. Thomas Gott.*	Accidentally blown up at Port au Prince.
	„ 27	*Hussar*	28	Capt. James Colnett.	Wrecked near Isle Bas.
	„ 31	*Curlew*	18	Com. Francis Ventris Field.*	Foundered in the North Sea.
1797	Jan. 2	*Vipère*	..	„ Henry Harding Parker.*	Foundered off the Shannon.
	„	*Hermes*	..	„ William Mulso.*	Foundered at sea.
	„ 14	*Amazon*	36	Capt. Robert Carthew Reynolds.	Wrecked near Isle Bas.
	Feb. 24	*Bloom*, tender . .	14	Lieut. Andrew Congalton.	Taken by the French, off Holyhead.
	„ 24	*Brighton*, tender .	14	..	Taken by the French, off Holyhead.
	Apr. 27	*Albion*, floatg. batt.	60	Capt. Henry Savage.	Wrecked in the Swin.
	„	*Tartar*	28	„ Hon Charles Elphinstone.	Wrecked off San Domingo.
	May 17	*Providence*, discovery ship . .	16	„ William Robert Broughton.	Wrecked in the Pacific.
	„	*Lacedemonian* . .	12	Com. Matthew Wrench.	Taken by the French in the West Indies.
	„	*Port Royal*, schoon.	10	Lieut. Elias Man.	Taken in the West Indies.
	June 15	*Fortune*	16	Com. Valentine Collard.	Wrecked near Oporto.
	July 24	*Fox*, cutter . . .	..	Lieut. John Gibson.*	Destroyed before Santa Cruz.
	„ 31	*Artois*	38	Capt. Sir Edmund Nagle.	Wrecked on the French coast.
	„ 31	*Mignonne* . . .	32	„ Hon. Philip Wodehouse.	Burnt as unserviceable at Porto Ferrajo.
	Sept. 22	*Hermione* . . .	32	„ Hugh Pigot (2).*	Carried by mutinous crew into La Guaira.
	Nov. 16	*Tribune*	32	„ Scory Barker.*	Wrecked off Halifax.
	„	*Hope*, hired lugger.	10	..	Run down in the Channel.
	Dec. 27	*Hunter*	18	Com. Tudor Tucker.	Wrecked on Bog Island, Virginia.
	„	*Growler*	12	Lieut. John Hollingsworth.*	Taken off Dungeness by two French row-boats.
		Swift	18	Com. Thomas Hayward.*	Foundered in the China Seas.
		Pandour . . .	14	Lieut. Samuel Mason.*	Foundered in the North Sea.
		Resolution . . .	14	„ William Huggett.*	Foundered at sea.
		Marie Antoinette, schoon. . . .	10	„ John M'Inerheny.*	Carried by mutinous crew into a French W. I. port.
1798	Jan. 3	*George*	6	„ Michael Mackey.	Taken by two Spanish privateers.
	Feb. 3	*Raven*	18	Com. John William Taylor Dixon.	Wrecked at the mouth of the Elbe.
	Apr. 4	*Pallas*	32	Capt. Hon. Henry Curzon.	Wrecked on Mount Batten Point.
	„ 12	*Lively*	32	„ James Nicoll Morris.	Wrecked near Rota Point, Cadiz.
	May 23	*De Braak* . . .	16	Com. James Drew.*	Capsized in the Delaware.
	June 23	*Rover*	16	„ George Irwin.	Wrecked in the Gulf of St. Lawrence.
	„ 29	*Pique*	36	Capt. David Milne.	Wrecked on the French coast.
	July 18	*Aigle*	38	„ Charles Tyler (1).	Wrecked off Cape Farina.
	„ 24	*Resistance* . . .	44	„ Edward Pakenham.*	Accidentally blown up in the Strait of Banca.
	„ 26	*Garland*. . . .	28	„ James Athol Wood.	Wrecked off Madagascar.
	„	*Princess Royal*, cutter	8	..	Taken by a French privateer.

Year.	Date.	H.M. Ship.	Guns.	Commander. [* Lost his life on the occasion.]	Remarks.
1798	Aug. 15	*Etrusco*, armed transport . . .	24	Com. George Reynolds.	Foundered coming from the West Ind.
	,, 18	*Leander*	50	Capt. Thomas Boulden Thompson.	Taken by the *Généreux*, 74. Retaken, March 3, 1799.
	,, 26	*Crash*	12	Lieut. Bulkley Mackworth Praed.	Taken on the coast of Holland. Retaken, August 11, 1799.
	Oct. 13	*Jason*	38	Capt. Charles Stirling.	Wrecked near Brest.
	Nov. 12	*Petrel*	16	Com. Charles Long.	Taken by three Spanish frigates. Retaken, November 13, 1798.
	,, 26	*Medusa*, armed transport . . .	50	,, Alexander Becher.	Wrecked on the coast of Portugal.
	,,	*Margaret*, tender .	..	Lieut. John Pollexfen.*	Lost off the Irish coast.
	Dec. 3	*Kingfisher* . . .	18	,, Frederick Lewis Maitland (2).	Wrecked on Lisbon Bar.
	,, 10	*Colossus*	74	Capt. George Murray (3).	Wrecked off Sicily.
	,, 14	*Ambuscade* . . .	32	,, Henry Jenkins.	Taken by *Bayonnaise*, 28.
		Hamadryad . .	36	,, Thomas Elphinstone.	Wrecked off the Portuguese coast.
		Neptune, lugger .	6	Gormer.	Run down off Beachy Head.
		Caroline, tender .	..	Lieut. —— Whittle.*	Lost in the East Indies.
1799	Jan. 7	*Apollo*	38	Capt. Peter Halkett.	Wrecked on coast of Holland; crew saved.
	,, 12	*Weazel*	14	Com. Hon. Henry Grey.*	Wrecked in Barnstaple Bay; nearly all lost.
	Feb. 1	*Proserpine* . . .	28	Capt. James Wallis.	Wrecked in the Elbe; nearly all saved.
	,, 2	*Nautilus* . . .	16	Com. Henry Gunter.	Wrecked off Flamborough Head; crew saved.
		Charlotte, schooner	8	Lieut. John Thicknesse.	Taken by the French, off Cape François. Retaken, Nov. 22.
		Mosquito, schooner	6	,, Thomas White.	Taken by Spanish frigates off Cuba.
	,,	*Grampus*, storeship (54)	26	Capt. George Hart.	Wrecked on Barking Shelf; crew saved.
	Mar. 18	*Torride*	2	..	Taken by French, Egypt. Retaken same day.
	Apr. 22	*Brave*, lugger, hired	12	Lieut. Gardiner Henry Guion.	Run down in the Channel; crew saved.
	May 8	*Fortune*	10	,, Lewis Davies.	Taken by French frigates; coast of Syria.
	,, 8	*Dame de Grâce*, gunboat . . .	..	..	Taken by French frigates; coast of Syria.
	,, 23	*Deux Amis* . . .	14	,, Henry Smith Wilson.	Wrecked on the Isle of Wight; crew saved.
	June 6	*William Pitt*, lugger	14	,, —— Haswell.	Taken by Spanish gunboats; Mediterranean.
	July 7	*Penelope*, cutter, hired	18	,, Daniel Hamline.	Taken by *N. S. del Carmen*; Mediterranean.
	Aug. 28	*Contest*	14	,, John Ides Short.	Wrecked on the coast of Holland; crew saved.
	Sept. 28	*Blanche*, storeship (32)	18	Com. John Ayscough.	Wrecked in the Texel; crew saved.
	,, 28	*Fox*	14	Lieut. William Wooldridge (?).	Wrecked in the Gulf of Mexico; crew saved.
	Oct. 9	*Lutine*	36	Capt. Lancelot Skynner.*	Wrecked off Vlieland; nearly all lost.
	,, 12	*Trincomale* . . .	16	Com. John Rowe.*	Blown up in action; crew lost.
	,, 14	*Nassau*, storeship (64)	36	Capt. George Tripp.	Wrecked on coast of Holland; nearly all saved.
	,, 19	*Impregnable* . .	98	,, Jonathan Faulknor (2).	Wrecked near Langstone; crew saved.
	,, 25	*Amaranthe* . . .	14	Com. John Blake.	Wrecked on coast of Florida; 22 lost.
	Nov. 5	*Orestes*	18	,, William Haggitt.*	Foundered in the East Indies; crew lost.
	,, 16	*Espion* (ex *Atalante*), st. sh. (38)	16	,, Jonas Rose.	Wrecked on the Goodwin; crew saved.
	Dec. 5	*Sceptre*	64	Capt. Valentine Edwards.*	Wrecked in Table Bay; 291 lost.
	,, 25	*Ethalion*	38	,, John Clarke Searle.	Wrecked off Penmarch; crew saved.
1800	Jan. 5	*Mastiff*	12	Lieut. James Watson (1).	Wrecked near Yarmouth; nearly all saved.
	,, 21	*Weymouth*, armed transport . . .	26	Com. Ambrose Crofton.	Wrecked on Lisbon Bar; crew saved.
	,, 26	*Brazen*	18	,, James Hanson.*	Wrecked near Brighton; all but one lost.
	Mar. 10	*Repulse*	64	Capt. James Alms (2).	Wrecked off Ushant; nearly all saved.
	,, 17	*Queen Charlotte* .	100	Vice-Adm. Lord Keith. Capt. Andrew Todd.*	Accidentally burnt off Leghorn; nearly all lost.
	,, 17	*Danaë* (ex *Vaillante*)	20	,, Lord Proby.	Carried by mutinous crew into Brest.
	May 17	*Trompeuse* . . .	18	Com. J— Parker Robinson.*	Supposed foundered in Channel; crew lost.
	,, 17	*Railleur*	14	,, John Raynor.*	Supposed foundered in Channel; crew lost.
	,, 17	*Lady Jane*, hired cutter	8	Lieut. W. Bryer.*	Supposed foundered in Channel; crew lost.
	,, 20	*Cormorant* . . .	20	Capt. Hon. Courtenay Boyle.	Wrecked on coast of Egypt; crew saved.
	July 7	*Comet*, f.s. . . .	..	Com. Thomas Leef.	Expended in Dunquerque Road.
	,, 7	*Falcon*, f.s. . . .	..	,, Henry Samuel Butt.	Expended in Dunquerque Road.
	,, 7	*Rosario*, f.s. . .	..	,, James Carthew.	Expended in Dunquerque Road.
	,, 7	*Wasp*, f.s. . . .	..	,, John Edwards (2).	Expended in Dunquerque Road.

Year.	Date.	H.M. Ship.	Guns.	Commander. [* Lost his life on the occasion.]	Remarks.
1800	Aug. 10	*Dromedary*, store-ship	24	Com. Bridges Watkinson Taylor.	Wrecked near Trinidad; crew saved.
	Sept 6	*Stag*	32	Capt. Robert Winthrop.	Wrecked in Vigo Bay; crew saved.
	,, 26	*Hound*	18	Com. William James Turquand.*	Wrecked near Shetland; crew lost.
	,,	*Diligence*	18	,, Charles Bayne Hodgson Ross.	Wrecked near Havana; crew saved.
	Oct. 9	*Chance* (ex *Galgo*)	18	,, George Samuel Stovin.*	Foundered in W. Indies; nearly all lost
	,, 13	*Rose*, hired cutter	10	Lieut. —— Smith.	Taken by the Dutch in the Ems.
	,,	*Martin*	16	Com. Hon. Matthew St. Clair.*	Supposed foundered in N. Sea; crew lost.
	Nov. 4	*Marlborough*	74	Capt. Thomas Sotheby.	Wrecked near Belle Isle; crew saved.
	,, 9	*Havik*	16	Com. Philip Bartholomew.	Wrecked off Jersey; crew saved.
	,, 23	*Albanaise*	14	Lieut. Francis Newcombe.	Carried by mutinous crew into Malaga.
	,,	*Active*, cutter	12	,, J—— Hamilton.	Taken by French and Dutch in the Ems. Retaken, May 16, 1801.
	Dec. 2	*Sir Thomas Pasley*, brig	16	,, C—— J—— Nevin.	Taken by two Spanish gunboats, Mediterranean.
		Urchin, gun vessel.	..	,, Thomas Pearson Croasdaile.	Foundered in Tetuan Bay.
1801	Jan. 1	*Requin*	10	,, Samuel Fowell.	Wrecked near Quiberon; crew saved.
	,, 9	*Constitution*, hired cutter	12	,, William Humphrey Faulknor.	Taken by two French cutters. Retaken same night.
	,, 29	*Incendiary*, f.s.	14	Com. William Dalling Dunn.	Taken by the squadron of M. Gantheaume.
	Feb. 2	*Légère*	18	,, Cornelius Quinton.	Wrecked near Cartagena, S. America; crew saved.
	,, 10	*Sprightly*, cutter	12	Lieut. Robert Jump.	Taken by the squadron of M. Gantheaume.
	,, 13	*Success*	32	Capt. Shuldham Peard.	Taken by the squadron of M. Gantheaume.
	,, 14	*Telegraph*, hired brig	16	Lieut. Cæsar Corsellis.*	Supposed foundered off Cape Ortegal.
	,, 27	*Bulldog*, bomb	18	Com. Barrington Dacres.	Taken by the French at Ancona. Retaken, Sept. 16, 1801.
	,,	*Charming Molly*, cutter	..	D. Sheriff, Master.	Foundered coming from St. Marcou.
	,,	*Lurcher*, hired cutter	12	Lieut. R—— Forbes.	Taken by a French privateer.
	Mar. 16	*Invincible*	74	Rear-Adm. Thomas Totty. Capt. John Rennie.*	Wrecked on Hasborough Sand; nearly all lost.
	,, 23	*Blazer*	12	Lieut. John Tiller.	Taken by the Swedes at Warberg; restored.
	,, 24	*Fulminante*	10	,, Robert Corbett.	Wrecked on coast of Egypt.
	,, 25	*Scout*	18	Com. Henry Duncan (2).	Lost on the Shingles, Isle of Wight; crew saved.
	,,	*Nancy*, hired cutter	6	Lieut. J—— Yames.	Taken by a French privateer.
	June 9	*Meleager*	32	Capt. Hon. Thomas Bladen Capell.	Wrecked on the Triangles, Gulf of Mexico; crew saved.
	,, 24	*Swiftsure*	74	,, Benjamin Hallowell.	Taken by the squadron of M. Gantheaume.
	,,	*Forte*	44	,, Lucius Ferdinand Hardyman.	Wrecked at Jeddah; crew saved.
	,,	*Speedy*	14	Com. Lord Cochrane.	Taken by the squadron of M. Linois.
	July 5	*Hannibal*	74	Capt. Solomon Ferris.	Taken by the squadron of M. Linois.
	,, 7	*Augustus*, gun-vessel	1	Lieut. James Scott.	Wrecked in Plymouth Sound; crew saved.
	,, 21	*Jason*	36	Capt. Hon. John Murray.	Wrecked near St. Malo; crew saved.
	,,	*Iphigenia*	32	Com. Hassard Stackpoole.	Accidentally burnt at Alexandria; crew saved.
	Aug. 11	*Lowestoft*	32	Capt. Robert Plampin.	Wrecked off Inagua, W. Indies; crew saved.
	Sept. 4	*Proselyte*	32	,, George Fowke.	Wrecked off St. Martin, W. Indies; crew saved.
	Oct. 25	*Bonetta*	18	,, Thomas New.	Wrecked on the Jardines, Cuba; crew saved.
	Nov.	*Utile*	16	Com. Edward Jekyll Canes.*	Capsized in the Mediterranean; crew lost.
	,,	*Cockchafer*, hired lugger	8	V—— Philpot.	Foundered off Guernsey; crew saved.
	,,	*Friendship*, gun-vessel	2	..	Foundered off Guernsey; crew saved.
		Babet	20	Capt. Jemmett Mainwaring.*	Supposed foundered in the W. Indies; crew lost.
1802	Mar. 2	*Sensible*	..	Com. Robert Sause.	Wrecked off Ceylon; crew saved.
	,, 29	*Assistance*	50	Capt. Richard Lee.	Wrecked near Dunquerque; crew saved.
		Scout	18	,, Henry Duncan (2).*	Foundered off Newfoundland; crew lost.
		Fly	14	Com. Thomas Duvall.*	Foundered off Newfoundland; crew lost.

LIST OF ENEMY'S MEN-OF-WAR TAKEN, DESTROYED, OR BURNT, AND, SO FAR AS CAN BE ASCERTAINED, WRECKED OR FOUNDERED DURING THE WAR OF THE FRENCH REVOLUTION, 1793–1801.

B.—FRENCH.

Year.	Date.	French national ship. [* Added to the Royal Navy.]	Guns.	Fate. M Medals granted in 1849, in pursuance of *Gazette* notice of June 1st, 1847. M Flag-officers' and Captains' gold medals.
1793	Feb. 15	*Léopard*	74	Foundered in Cagliari Bay.
		Vengeur (supposed)	74	Wrecked near Ajaccio.
	Apr. 16	*Goéland*	14	Taken by *Penelope*, 32, Capt. B. S. Rowley, W. Ind.
	May 21	(Unknown	36	Destroyed by the Spaniards at St. Pietro.
	,, 28	*Prompte**	20	Taken by *Phaeton*, 38, Capt. Sir A. S. Douglas, B. of Biscay.
	June 3	*Curieux*, brig	14	Taken by *Inconstant*, 36, Capt. Aug. Montgomery, W. Ind.
	,, 6	*Vanneau*	6	Taken by *Colossus*, 74, Capt. C. M. Pole, B. of Biscay.
	,, 9	*Eclair**	22	Taken by *Leda*, 36, Capt. Geo. Campbell, Medit.
	,, 18	*Cléopâtre* (* as *Oiseau*)	36	Taken by *Nymphe*, 36, Capt. E. Pellew, off Start. M
	July 25	*Lutine*	12	Taken by *Pluto*, 14, Com. J. N. Morris, Newfoundland.
	Aug. 29	*Commerce de Marseilles**	120	Taken at Toulon by Lord Hood.
	,, ,,	*Pompée**	74	,, ,, ,,
	,, ,,	*Puissant**	74	,, ,, ,,
	,, ,,	*Scipion**	74	,, ,, ,,
	,, ,,	*Arethuse* (* as *Undaunted*)	40	,, ,, ,,
	,, ,,	*Topaze**	36	,, ,, ,,
	,, ,,	*Perle* (* as *Amethyst*)	40	,, ,, ,,
	,, ,,	*Aurore**	36	,, ,, ,,
	,, ,,	*Lutine** as 32	36	,, ,, ,,
	,, ,,	*Alceste*	36	,, ,, ,, (Given to Sardinians.)
	,, ,,	*Poulette**	26	,, ,, ,,
	,, ,,	*Belette**	28	,, ,, ,,
	,, ,,	*Prosélyte**	36	,, ,, ,,
	,, ,,	*Moselle**	20	,, ,, ,,
	,, ,,	*Embroye* (?)	20	,, ,, ,, (Given to Neapolitans.)
	,, ,,	*Mulet*	18	,, ,, ,,
	,, ,,	*Sincère*	18	,, ,, ,,
	,, ,,	*Petite Aurore*	18	,, ,, ,, (Given to Spaniards.)
	,, ,,	*Tarleton*	14	,, ,, ,,
	Sept.	*Convention Nationale*	10	Taken by Commod. John Ford, San Domingo.
	Oct. 11	*Impérieuse**	38	Taken by V.-Ad. John Gell, off Genoa.
	,, 17	*Modeste**	36	Taken by *Bedford*, 74, Capt. R. Man (3), etc., off Genoa.
	,, 20	*Réunion**	36	Taken by *Crescent*, 36, Capt. J. Saumarez, off Cherbourg. M
	Nov. 25	*Inconstante* (* as *Convert*)	36	Taken by *Penelope*, 32, and *Iphigenia*, 32, off San Domingo.
	,, 27	*Blonde*	28	Taken by *Latona*, 38, and *Phaeton*, 38, off Ushant.
	,, 30	*Espiègle**	16	Taken by *Nymphe*, 36, and *Circe*, 28, off Ushant.
	Dec. 18	*Triomphant*	80	Destroyed at the evacuation of Toulon.
	,, ,,	*Destin*	74	,, ,, ,,
	,, ,,	*Centaure*	74	,, ,, ,,
	,, ,,	*Duguay Trouin*	74	,, ,, ,,
	,, ,,	*Héros*	74	,, ,, ,,
	,, ,,	*Liberte* (ex *Dictateur*)	74	,, ,, ,,
	,, ,,	*Suffisant*	74	,, ,, ,,
	,, ,,	*Thémistocle*	74	,, ,, ,,
	,, ,,	*Tricolor* (ex *Lys*)	74	,, ,, ,,
	,, ,,	*Victorieuse*	36	,, ,, ,,
	,, ,,	*Montréal*	32	,, ,, ,,
	,, ,,	*Iris*	32	,, ,, ,,
	,, ,,	*Auguste*	24	,, ,, ,,
	,, ,,	*Caroline*	24	,, ,, ,,
	,, 30	*Sans Culotte*	22	Taken by *Blanche*, 32, Capt. Christ. Parker (2), W. Ind.
	,, ,,	*Révolutionnaire*	20	,, ,, ,, ,,
	,, ,,	*Vengeur*	12	,, ,, ,, ,,
1794	Jan. 12	*Trompeuse**	18	Taken by *Sphinx*, 20, Capt. Rich. Lucas, off C. Clear.
	,, 23	*Vipère**	16	Taken by *Flora*, 36, Capt. Sir J. B. Warren, Channel.
	Feb. 19	*Minerve* (* as *San Fiorenzo*)	38	Taken at San Fiorenzo.
	,, ,,	*Fortunée*	36	Destroyed at San Fiorenzo.
	Mar. 16	*Actif**	16	Taken by *Iphigenia*, 32, Capt. Pat. Sinclair, W. Ind.
	,, ,,	*Espiègle**	12	,, ,, ,, ,,
	,, 17	*Bienvenue* (* as *Undaunted*)	28	Taken by V.-Ad. Sir J. Jervis, at Martinique. M
	,, ,,	*Avenger*	16	,, ,, ,, ,,
	,, 28	*Liberté*	14	Taken by *Alligator*, 28, Capt. Thos. Surridge, Jamaica.
	Apr. 23	*Pomone**	44	Taken by Commod. Sir J. B. Warren, off Isle Bas.
	,, ,,	*Babet**	20	,, ,, ,, ,,
	,, ,,	*Engageante**	36	Taken by *Concorde*, 36, Capt. Sir R. J. Strachan, Channel.

Year.	Date.		French national ship. [* Added to the Royal Navy.]	Guns.	Fate. M Medals granted in 1849, in pursuance of *Gazette* notice of June 1st, 1847. **M** Flag-officers' and Captains' gold medals.
1794	Apr.	23	*Guadeloupe*	16	Taken by V.-Ad. Sir J. Jervis, Guadeloupe.
	May	5	*Duguay Trouin*	28	Taken by *Orpheus*, 32, Capt. Hen. Newcome, E. Ind.
	,,	5	*Atalante* (* as *Espion*)	36	Taken by *Swiftsure*, 74, Capt. Chas. Boyles, near Cork.
	,,	5	*Inconnue*	16	Taken and burnt by Lord Howe.
	,,	21	*Flèche* *	14	Taken at Bastia by Lord Hood.
	,,	23	*Moselle* *	18	Taken by *Aimable*, 32, Capt. Sir H. Burrard, off Hyères.
	,,	,,	*Courier*, cutter	10	Taken and scuttled by Lord Howe, Channel.
	,,	25	*Republicain*	20	Taken and burnt by Lord Howe, Channel.
	,,	29	*Castor* *	32	Retaken by *Carysfort*, 28, Capt. Fras. Laforey, off Land's End. M
	June	1	*Juste* *	80	Taken by Lord Howe, Ushant 150 leagues E. ½ N. } M **M**
	,,	,,	*Sans Pareil* *	80	,, ,, ,, ,,
	,,	,,	*Amerique* (* as *Impétueux*)	74	,, ,, ,, ,,
	,,	,,	*Achille*	74	,, ,, ,, ,,
	,,	,,	*Northumberland*	74	,, ,, ,, ,,
	,,	,,	*Impétueux*	74	,, ,, ,, ,,
	,,	,,	*Vengeur*	74	Sunk ,, ,, ,, ,,
	,,	17	*Sibylle* *	40	Taken by *Romney*, 50, Capt. Hon. W. Paget, at Miconi. M
	,,	18	*Narcisse*, cutter	14	Taken by *Aurora*, 28, Capt. W. Essington, off Shetland.
	Aug.	10	*Melpomène* *	40	Taken by Lord Hood, at Calvi.
	,,	,,	*Mignonne* *	28	,, ,, ,,
	,,	,,	*Auguste*, brig	4	,, ,, ,,
	,,	,,	*Providence*, brig	4	,, ,, ,,
	,,	,,	*Ça Ira*, g.b.	3	,, ,, ,,
	,,	23	*Volontaire*	36	Driven ashore and destroyed, near Penmarck.
	,,	,,	*Alerte*	12	Driven ashore and destroyed, off P. du Raz.
	,,		*Sirène* *	16	Taken by *Intrepid*, 64, and *Chichester*, 44, San Domingo.
			Reprisal	16	Taken by V.-Ad. Sir John Jervis, W. Ind.
	Sept.	7	*Quartidi*	14	Taken by Commod. Sir E. Pellew, off Sicily.
	Oct.	21	*Révolutionnaire* *	44	Taken by Commod. Sir E. Pellew, off Brest.
	,,	30	*Jacobin* (* as *Matilda*)	24	Taken by *Ganges*, 74, and *Montagu*, 74, W. Ind.
			Revenge (* as *Hobart*)	18	Taken by *Resistance*, 44, Capt. Edw. Pakenham, S. Sunda.
	Nov.	30	*Carmagnole*, schooner	10	Taken by *Zebra*, 16, W. Ind.
	Dec.	2	A sloop	..	Taken by *Beaulieu*, 40, Capt. E. Riou, W. Ind.
	,,	27	*Républicain*	110	Wrecked near Brest.
	,,	30	A schooner	..	Taken by *Blanche*, 32, Capt. Robt. Faulknor (3), W. Ind.
1795	Jan.	5	*Duquesne*	36	Taken by *Bellona*, 74, Capt. Geo. Wilson, W. Ind.
	,,	6	*Pique* *	36	Taken by *Blanche*, 32, Capt. Robt. Faulknor (3), W. Ind. M
	,,	8	*Espérance*	22	Taken by *Argonaut*, 64, Capt. A. J. Ball, America.
	,,		*Neptune*	74	Wrecked in Audierne Bay.
	,,		*Scipion*	80	Foundered in a gale.
	,,		*Neuf Thermidor*	80	,, ,,
	,,		*Superbe*	74	,, ,,
	,,		*Duras*	20	Taken by *Bellona*, 74, and *Alarm*, 32, W. Ind.
	Feb.	10	*Iphigénie*	36	Taken by the Spaniards, Medit.
	,,	20	*Requin* *	12	Taken by *Thalia*, 36, Capt. Rich. Grindall, Channel.
	,,	26	*Curieuse*, schooner	12	Taken by *Pomone*, 44, Capt. Sir J. B. Warren, off Groix.
	Mar.	2	*Espion* (* as *Spy*)	18	Taken by *Lively*, 32, Capt. Geo. Burlton, off Brest.
	,,	13	*Tourterelle* *	28	,, ,, ,, ,, off Ushant. M
	,,	14	*Ça Ira* *	80	Taken by V.-Ad. W. Hotham (1), off Genoa } M
	,,	,,	*Censeur* *	74	,, ,, ,, ,,
			Temeraire, cutter	20	Taken by *Dido*, 28, Capt. Geo. Hen. Towry, Medit.
	,,	27	*Républicaine*	22	Taken by R.-Ad. J. Colpoys, Channel.
	,,		*Speedy* *	14	Taken by *Inconstant*, 36, Capt. Thos. Fras. Fremantle, Medit.
	,,	29	*Jean Bart* (* as *Arab*)	18	Taken by *Cerberus*, 32, and *Sta. Margarita*, 36, Channel.
	Apr.	10	*Gloire* *	36	Taken by *Astræa*, 32, Capt. Lord Hen. Paulet, Channel. M
	,,	11	*Gentille* *	36	Taken by *Hannibal*, 74, Capt. John Markham, Channel.
	,,	15	*Jean Bart* (* as *Laurel*)	26	Taken by Commod. Sir J. B. Warren, off Rochefort.
	,,	16	*Expédition*	16	,, ,, ,, off Belle Isle.
	,,	23	*Galatée*	36	Wrecked near Penmarck.
	May	9	*Eclair*, g.v.*	3	Taken by Capt. Sir R. J. Strachan, coast of France.
	,,	,,	*Crache Feu*, g.v.*	3	,, ,, ,, ,,
	,,	17	*Prévoyante*, en flûte (40) *	24	Taken by *Thetis*, 38, and *Hussar*, 28, Chesapeake } M
	,,	,,	*Raison*, en flûte (24) *	18	,, ,, ,, ,,
	,,	28	*Courier Nationale*	18	Taken by *Thorn*, 16, Com. Robt. W. Otway, W. Ind.
	,,	28	*Prompte*	28	
	,,	30	*Liberté*	20	Sunk by *Alarm*, 32, Capt. David Milne, off Puerto Rico.
	June	23	*Tigre* *	74	Taken by Lord Bridport, off Lorient. } M
	,,	,,	*Alexandre* *	74	,, ,, ,,
	,,	,,	*Formidable* (* as *Belleisle*)	74	,, ,, ,,
	,,	24	*Minerve* *	40	Taken by *Lowestoft*, 32, and *Dido*, 28, Medit. M
	,,		*Perdrix* *	24	Taken by *Vanguard*, 74, Capt. Simon Miller, off Antigua.
	July	3	*Vesuve*, g.v.*	4	Taken by *Melampus*, 36, and *Hebe*, 38, off St. Malo.
	,,	13	*Alcide*	74	Struck to Ad. Hotham, but accidentally blew up, Medit.
			Echoué	28	Run ashore and destroyed on Rhé by *Phaeton*, 38, Capt. Hon. R. Stopford.

Year.	Date.		French national ship. [* Added to the Royal Navy.]	Guns.	Fate. M Medals granted in 1849, in pursuance of *Gazette* notice of June 1st, 1847. M Flag-officers' and Captains' gold medals.
1795	Aug.	16	*Résolue*	10	Taken by Commod. H. Nelson, Alassio Bay.
	,,	,,	*République*, g.b.	6	,, ,, ,, ,,
	,,	,,	*Constitution*, galley	5	,, ,, ,, ,,
	,,	,,	*Vigilante*, galley	5	,, ,, ,, ,,
	,,	31	*Suffisante* *	14	Taken by Ad. Duncan, off the Texel.
	,,	,,	*Victorieuse* *.	14	,, ,, ,, ,,
	Sept.	2	*Assemblée Nationale*	22	Driven ashore by *Diamond*, 38, Capt. Sir W. S. Smith, off Treguier.
	,,	,,	*Rude*, g.v.	12	Burnt by *Pomone*, 44, Capt. Sir J. B. Warren, coast of France.
	,,	3	*Vigilante*, cutter	6	Taken by *Childers*, 14, Com. Rich. Dacres, off St. Brieux.
	,,	22	*Sans Culotte*	18	Burnt by *Aimalle*, 32, Capt. Chas. Sydney Davers, W. Ind.
	Oct.	10	*Superbe*	22	Taken by *Vanguard*, 74, Capt. Simon Miller, W. Ind.
	,,	10	*Brutus*	10	Taken by *Mermaid*, 32, and *Zebra*, 16, W. Ind.
	,,	14	*Républicain* *	18	,, ,, ,, ,,
	,,	15	*Eveillé*	18	Taken by Commod. Sir J. B. Warren, off Rochefort.
	Nov.		*Droits du Peuple*	36	Wrecked off Trondhjem.
	Dec.	1	*Pandore* (* as *Pandour*)	14	Taken by *Caroline*, 36, Capt. Wm. Luke, North Sea.
1796	Mar.	9	*Nemesis* *.	28	Taken by *Egmond*, 74, Capt. John Sutton, and consorts, off Tunis.
	,,	,,	*Sardine* *.	22	,, ,, ,, ,,
	,,	10	*Bonne Citoyenne* *	20	Taken by *Phaeton*, 38, Capt. Hon. Robt. Stopford, Cape Finisterre.
	,,	10	*Aspic*, cutter	..	Taken by the *Quebec*, St. George's Channel.
	,,	18	*Etourdie*	16	Burnt by *Diamond*, 38, Capt. Sir W. S. Smith, off Cape Fréhel. M {*Diamond* *Liberty* *Aristocrat*
	,,		*Favorite*	22	Taken by *Alfred*, 74, Capt. Thos. Drury, off Cape Finisterre.
	,,		*Marsouin*.	26	Taken by *Beaulieu*, 44, Capt. Lancelot Skynner, W. Ind.
	,,	20	*Etoile*, armed storeship	28	Taken by Commod. Sir J. B. Warren, coast of France.
			Alerte	14	Taken by *Cormorant*, 18, Com. Joseph Bingham, W. Ind.
			Mutine, brig	..	Taken by frigates in the Bay.
	Apr.	13	*Unité* *	36	Taken by *Révolutionnaire*, 38, and consorts, coast of France.
	,,	15	*Robuste* (* as *Scourge*)	22	Taken by Commod. Sir J. B. Warren, off the Saintes.
	,,	20	*Unité* (* as *Surprise*)	28	Taken by *Inconstant*, 36, Capt. Thos. Fras. Fremantle, Medit.
	,,	21	*Perçante* (* as *Jamaica*)	26	Taken by *Intrepid*, 64, Capt. Hon. Chas. Carpenter, W. Ind.
	,,	22	*Virginie* *	40	Taken by squadron of Sir E. Pellew, off the Lizard. M (*Indefatigable*.)
	,,		*Aurore*	10	Taken by *Cleopatra*, 32, Capt. Chas. Rowley, America.
	,,	27	*Ecureuil*, lugger	18	Burnt by boats of *Niger*, 32, Capt. E. J. Foote, off Penmarck.
	May	2	*Abeille*, cutter	14	Taken by *Dryad*, 36, Com. John King Pulling (actg.), off Lizard.
	,,	4	*Volcan*	12	Taken by *Spencer*, 18, Com. And. Fitzherbert Evans, off Bermuda.
	,,	7	*Cygne*, cutter	14	Taken by *Doris*, 36, Capt. Hon. Chas. Jones, off Scilly.
	,,	8	*Athénienne* *.	14	Taken by *Albacore*, 16, Com. Robt. Winthrop, off Barbados.
	,,	31	*Genie*, ketch	3	Taken by Commod. H. Nelson, at Oneglia.
	,,	,,	No. 12, g.b.	1	,, ,, ,, ,,
	June	8	*Tribune*	36	Taken by *Unicorn*, 32, Capt. Thos. Williams (4), Ireland. } M
	,,	8	*Tamise* (* as *Thames*)	32	(Ex Brit. *Thames*). Retaken by *Sta. Margarita*, 36, Capt. T. Byam Martin, Ireland. } M
	,,	10	*Utile*	24	Taken by *Southampton*, 32, Capt. Jas. Macnamara (2), off Hyères. M
	,,	11	*Trois Couleurs*, brig	10	Taken by Commod. Sir E. Pellew, off Ushant.
	,,	,,	*Blonde*, brig	16	,, ,, ,, ,,
	,,	13	*Proserpine* (* as *Amelia*)	40	Taken by *Dryad*, 36, Capt. Lord Amelius Beauclerk, off C. Clear. M
	,,	22	*Légère* *	22	Taken by *Apollo*, 36, and *Doris*, 36, off Scilly.
	July	12	*Renommée* *	36	Taken by *Alfred*, 74, Capt. Thos. Drury, off San Domingo.
	Aug.	19	*Alerte*	16	Taken by *Carysfort*, 28, Capt. Thos. Alexander, E. Ind.
	,,	22	*Andromaque*.	36	Destroyed by Commod. Sir J. B. Warren, near Arcachon.
	,,	28	*Elisabeth*	36	Taken by V.-Ad. Geo. Murray (2), N. Amer.
	Oct.	18	*Eliza*	10	Taken by *Fury*, 16, Com. Hy. Evans, W. Ind.
	Nov.	1	*Cerf Volant*	18	Taken by *Magicienne*, 32, Capt. Wm. Hy. Ricketts, off San Domingo.
	,,	13	*Etonnant*.	18	Destroyed by *Minerva*, 44, and *Melampus*, 36, off Barfleur.
	,,	,,	*Etna* (* as *Cormorant*).	18	Taken by *Melampus*, 36, and *Childers*, 14, coast of France.
	,,	27	*Décius*.	28	Taken by *Lapwing*, 28, Capt. Robt. Barton, W. Ind. (destroyed Nov. 28th). } M
	,,	,,	*Vaillant*, brig	4	Destroyed by *Lapwing*, 28, Capt. Robt. Barton, W. Ind. } M

Year.	Date.	French national ship. [* Added to the Royal Navy.]	Guns.	Fate. M Medals granted in 1849, in pursuance of *Gazette* notice of June 1st, 1847. **M** Flag-officers' and Captains' gold medals.
1796	Dec. 3	*Africaine*	18	Taken by *Quebec*, 32, Capt. John Cooke (2), off San Domingo.
	„ 10	*Général Leveau*	16	Taken by *Mermaid*, 32, and *Resource*, 28, off San Domingo.
	„ 13	*Vestale*	36	Taken by *Terpsichore*, 32, Capt. Rich. Bowen.
	„ 16	*Séduisant*	74	Wrecked near Brest.
	„ 30	*Scévola*	44	Foundered off Ireland.
	„ „	*Impatiente*	44	Wrecked near Mizen Head.
	„ 31	*Amaranthe**	14	Taken by *Diamond*, 38, Capt. Sir R. J. Strachan, off Alderney.
	„	*Justine*, st. ship, en flûte	44	Lost off Irish Coast.
1797	Jan. 5	*Tortue** (later *Ariane*)	40	Taken by *Polyphemus*, 64, Capt. Geo. Lumsdaine, off Ireland.
	„ 7	*Ville de Lorient*, en flûte	36	Taken by *Doris*, 36, *Unicorn*, 32, and *Druid*, 32, off Ireland.
	„ 8	*Suffren*, st. ship	44	Sunk by *Majestic*, 74, *Dædalus*, 32, and *Incendiary*, 14, off Ushant.
	„ 10	*Atalante**	16	Taken by *Phœbe*, 36, Capt. Robt. Barlow, off Scilly.
	„ 12	*Allègre*, st. ship	..	Taken by *Spitfire*, 16, Com. Michael Seymour (1), off Ushant.
	„ 13	*Droits de l'Homme*	74	Wrecked in action with *Indefatigable* and *Amazon*, off Penmarck. M
	„	*Surveillante*	36	Scuttled in Bantry Bay.
	Feb. 13	A schooner	2	Taken by *Matilda*, 28, Capt. Hy. Mitford, off Barbados.
	Mar. 9	*Résistance* (* as *Fishguard*)	40	Taken by *San Fiorenzo*, 44, and *Nymphe*, 36, off Brest. } M
	„ „	*Constance**	22	„ „ „ „ } M
		Modeste	20	Taken by *Fox*, 32, Capt. Pulteney Malcolm, off Vizagapatam.
	Apr. 17	*Hermione*	36	Destroyed by *Thunderer*, 74, and *Valiant*, 74, off San Domingo.
	May 13	*Jalouse**	18	Taken by *Vestal*, 28, Capt. Chas. White, North Sea.
	„ 29	*Mutine**	14	Cut out by boats of *Minerve* and *Lively* (Lieut. T. M. Hardy), Santa Cruz. M
	June 12	*Harriette*	6	Taken by *Aigle*, 32, Capt. Chas Tyler, off Lisbon.
	July 17	*Calliope*	36	Destroyed by Commod. Sir J. B. Warren, coast of France.
	„ „	*Freedom*, en flûte	8	Taken and burnt by Commod. Sir J. B. Warren, coast of France.
	Aug. 11	A ship corvette	22	Taken and bilged „ „ „
	„ „	A brig, g.v.	12	Taken and sunk „ „ „
	„ 20	*Gaïeté**	20	Taken by *Arethusa*, 38, Capt. Thos. Wolley, Atlantic.
	„ 23	*Egalité*, chasse-marée	8	Taken by Commod. Sir J. B. Warren, coast of France.
	„ 27	*Petit Diable*, cutter	18	Taken and bilged by Commod. Sir J. B. Warren, coast of France.
	Sept. 10	*Espoir**	16	Taken by *Thalia*, 36, Capt. Lord Hy. Paulet, Medit.
	Oct. 9	*Decouverte*	18	Taken by *Unité*, 36, Capt. Chas. Rowley, Channel.
	„ 14	*Ranger**	14	Taken by *Indefatigable*, 44, Capt. Sir Ed. Pellew, off Tenerife; retaken.
	Nov. 6	*Venturier* (ex *Ranger*)*	14	Retaken by *Galatea*, 32, Capt. Geo. Byng.
	„ 12	*Epervier*	16	Taken by *Cerberus*, 32, Capt. John Drew (2), off Ireland.
	„	*Méduse*	40	Foundered on passage from America.
	Dec. 22	*Néréide**	36	Taken by *Phœbe*, 36, Capt. Robt. Barlow, off Scilly. M
	„ 28	*Daphné** as 20	30	Retaken by *Anson*, 44, Capt. P. C. Durham, B. of Biscay.
	„	*République Triomphante*	14	Taken by *Severn*, 44, and *Pelican*, 18, W. Ind.
1798	Jan. 5	*Chéri*	26	Taken by *Pomone*, 44, Capt. Robt. Carthew Reynolds, B. of Biscay, and foundered.
	„ 16	*Désirée*	6	Taken by pinnace (Lt. Saml. Pym) of *Babet*, 20, W. Ind.
	Feb. 16	*Scipion*	20	Taken by *Alfred*, 74, Capt. Thos. Totty, Guadeloupe.
	„ 26	*Souris*, chasse-marée	16	Taken by *Badger*, 4, Lt. Chas. Papps Price, and consorts, St. Marcou.
	Apr. 5	*Sainte Famille*, chasse-marée.	..	Taken by *Impétueux*, 78, and *Sylph*, 16.
	„ 19	*Arrogante*, g.v.*	6	Taken by *Jason*, 36, Capt. Chas. Stirling (1), off Brest.
	„ 21	*Hercule**	74	Taken by *Mars*, 74, Capt. Alex. Hood, off Bec du Raz. M
	May 1	*Quatorze Juillet*	74	Accidentally burnt at Lorient.
	„ 7	*Flibustier*	..	Taken during attack on St. Marcou. M {*Badger*. *Sandfly*.
	„ 13	*Mondovi**	16	Cut out by boats (Lt. Wm. Russell) of *Flora*, 36, at Cerigo.
	„ 31	*Confiante*	36	Run ashore and destroyed by *Hydra*, 36, Capt. Sir Fras. Laforey, near Le Hâvre.
	June 22	*Corcyre*	16	Taken by *Flora*, 32, Capt. Robt. Gambier Middleton, off Sicily.
	„ „	*Egalité*	20	Destroyed by *Aurora*, 28, Capt. Hy. Digby, B. of Biscay.
	„ 27	*Sensible*	36	Taken by *Seahorse*, 36, Capt. E. J. Foote, Medit.
	„ 30	*Seine**	40	Taken by *Jason*, 36, Capt. Chas. Stirling (1), and *Pique*, 36, Capt. David Milne.
	Aug. 1	*Orient*	120	Burnt in action with R.-Ad. Sir H. Nelson.
	„ „	*Franklin* (* as *Canopus*)	80	Taken in Aboukir Bay by R.-Ad. Sir H. Nelson. } M **M**
	„ „	*Tonnant**	80	„ „ „ „ } M **M**
	„ „	*Timoléon*	74	Destroyed by her crew after action with R.-Ad. Sir H. Nelson. } M **M**

Year.	Date.		French national ship. [* Added to the Royal Navy.]	Guns.	Fate. M Medals granted in 1849, in pursuance of *Gazette* notice of June 1st, 1847. M Flag-officers' and Captains' gold medals.
1798	Aug.	1	*Guerrier*	74	Taken in Aboukir Bay by R.-Ad. Sir H. Nelson, and burnt.
	,,	,,	*Spartiate* *	74	Taken in Aboukir Bay by R.-Ad. Sir H. Nelson.
	,,	,,	*Conquérant* *	74	,, ,, ,,
	,,	,,	*Aquilon* (* as *Aboukir*) . .	74	,, ,, ,,
	,,	,,	*Heureux*	74	,, ,, ,, and burnt. M
	,,	,,	*Mercure*	74	,, ,, ,, and burnt.
	,,	,,	*Souverain Peuple* (* as *Guerrier*)	74	,, ,, ,,
	,,	,,	*Artemise*	36	Burst after action with R.-Ad. Sir H. Nelson.
	,,	,,	*Sérieuse*	36	Sunk in action with R.-Ad. Sir H. Nelson.
	,,	3	*Aventurière*	14	Cut out by boats (Lt. Thos. Geo. Shortland) of *Melpomène* and *Childers*, Corigiou.
	,,	7	*Vaillante* (* as *Danaë*) . .	20	Taken by *Indefatigable*, 44, Capt. Sir E. Pellew, B. of Biscay.
	,,	,,	*Liguria* (Genoese)	26	Taken by *Espoir*, 16, Com. Loftus Otway Bland, Medit. M
	,,	11	*Fortune* (* as 10)	18	Taken by *Swiftsure*, 74, Capt. Benj. Hallowell, coast of Egypt; retaken May 5th, 1799.
	,,	12	*Neptune*	20	Taken by *Hazard*, 16, Com. Wm. Butterfield, coast of Ireland.
	,,	22	*Légère*,* g.v..	6	Taken by *Alcmene*, 32, Capt. Geo. Hope (1), off Alexandria.
	,,	24	*Décade* *	36	Taken by *Magnanime*, 44, and *Naiad*, 38, off Finisterre.
	,,	25	*Torride*,* ketch	7	Taken by boats (Lt. Wm. Debusk) of *Goliath*, off Aboukir; retaken Mar. 18th, 1799.
	Sept.	1	*Réunion*	6	Taken by *Oiseau*, 36, Capt. Chas. Brisbane, E. Ind.
	,,	2	*Anémone*, g.v.	4	Destroyed off Damietta by *Seahorse*, 38, and *Emerald*, 36.
	Oct.	12	*Hoche* (* as *Donegal*) . . .	74	Taken by Commod. Sir J. B. Warren, coast of Ireland.
	,,	,,	*Embuscade* (* as *Ambuscade*).	36	,, ,, ,, ,, M
	,,	,,	*Coquille*	36	,, ,, ,, ,,
	,,	,,	*Bellone* (* as *Proserpine*) . .	36	,, ,, ,, ,,
	,,	13	*Résolue* *	36	Taken by *Melampus*, 36, Capt. Graham Moore, coast of Ireland.
	,,	18	*Loire* *	40	Taken by *Anson*, 44, Capt. P. C. Durham, and *Kangaroo*, 18, Com. Ed. Brace, Ireland.
	,,	20	*Immortalité*	40	Taken by *Fishguard*, 38, Capt. Thos. Byam Martin, off Brest. M
	,,	29	*Fulminante*, cutter	8	Taken by *Espoir*, 16, Capt. Loftus Otway Bland, Medit.
	Nov.	17	*Fouine*, lugger	8	Taken by *Sylph*, 16, Com. John Chambers White, off Brest.
	,,	20	*Hirondelle*	20	Taken by *Phaeton*, *Ambuscade*, and *Stag*, Channel.
	Dec.	28	*Wilding*, armed transport . .	14	Taken by *Spitfire*, 20, Com. Michael Seymour, B. of Biscay.
1799	Feb.	9	*Prudente*	36	Taken by *Dædalus*, 32, Capt. Hy. Lidgbird Ball, Cape of Good Hope.
	,,	28	*Forte* *	44	Taken by *Sibylle*, 44, Capt. Edward Cook, Bengal. M
	Mar.	1	*Marianne*	4	Taken by Commod. Sir W. S. Smith, coast of Syria.
	,,	3	*Leander* *	50	Taken by Russians and Turks at Corfu; restored to Brit.
	,,	,,	*Brune*	28	Taken by Russians and Turks at Corfu.
	,,	18	*Hirondelle*	16	Taken by *Telegraph*, 16, Lt. Jas. And. Worth, off Isle Bas. M
	,,	,,	*Négresse* *	6	Taken by Commod. Sir W. S. Smith, coast of Syria.
	,,	,,	*Foudre*	8	,, ,, ,, ,,
	,,	,,	*Dangereuse* *	6	,, ,, ,, ,,
	,,	,,	*Marie Rose*	4	,, ,, ,, ,,
	,,	,,	*Dame de Grâce* *	4	,, ,, ,, ,,
	,,	,,	*Deux Frères*	4	,, ,, ,, ,,
	,,	,,	*Torride*	2	,, ,, ,, ,,
			Courier	16	Taken by *Zealous*, 74, Capt. Saml. Hood (2), Medit.
	Apr.	4	*Sans Quartier*	14	Taken by *Danaë*, 20, Capt. Lord Proby, coast of France.
	,,	27	*Rebecca*, chasse-marée . . .	16	Taken by *Black Joke*, 10, Lt. Jas. Nicolson, off Ushant.
	,,		A corvette	16	Taken by *Lion*, 64, Capt. Manley Dixon, Medit
	June	18	*Junon* (* as *Princess Charlotte*)	38	Taken by squadron under Capt. John Markham, Medit.
	,,	,,	*Alceste* *	36	,, ,, ,, ,,
	,,	,,	*Courageuse* *.	36	,, ,, ,, ,,
	,,	,,	*Salamine* (* as 16) . . .	18	,, ,, ,, ,,
	,,	,,	*Alerte* (* as *Minorca*) . . .	14	,, ,, ,, ,,
	Aug.	20	*Vestale*	36	Taken by *Clyde*, 36, Capt. Chas. Cunningham, mouth of Garonne.
	,,	,,	*Hussard* (* as *Surinam*) . .	18	Taken by V.-Ad. Lord Hugh Seymour, Surinam.
	,,	26	*Républicaine*	28	Taken by *Tamer*, 32, Capt. Thos. Western, off Surinam.
	Sept.	13	*St. Jacques*	6	Taken by *Triton*, 32, Capt. John Gore (2), off Lorient.
	Oct.	10	*Aréthuse* (* as *Raven*) . . .	18	Taken by *Excellent*, 74, Capt. Hon. Robt. Stopford, off Lorient.
	,,	12	*Iphigenie*	24	Blown up in action with *Trincomale*, 16, Com. John Rowe, Red Sea.
	Nov.	10	*Charente*	36	Wrecked off Lorient.

Year.	Date.		French national ship. [* Added to the Royal Navy.]	Guns.	Fate. M Medals granted in 1849, in pursuance of *Gazette* notice of June 1st, 1847. **M** Flag-officers' and Captains' gold medals.
1799	Nov.	22	*Egyptienne*, en flûte, 44	20	Taken by *Solebay*, 32, Capt. Steph. Poyntz, off San Domingo.
	,,	,,	*Eole* (* as *Nimrod*)	16	,, ,, ,, ,,
	,,	,,	*Lévrier*	12	,, ,, ,, ,,
	,,	,,	*Vengeur* (ex Brit. *Charlotte*)	8	,, ,, ,, ,,
	Dec.	11	*Preneuse*	36	Destroyed by boats (Lt. Ed. Grey) of *Tremendous* and *Adamant*, off Port Louis.
1800	Jan.	7	*Brule Gueule*	20	Wrecked off Brest.
	Feb.	6	*Pallas* (* as *Pique*)	38	Taken by *Loire*, *Danaë*, and consorts, coast of France. M *Fairy* *Harpy*
	,,	9	A polacre (Genoese)	14	Driven ashore and destroyed by *Pearl*, 32, Capt. Sam. Jas. Ballard, Medit.
	,,	10	*Vedette*	14	Taken by *Triton*, 32, Capt. John Gore (2), coast of France.
	,,	18	*Généreux* *	74	Taken by R.-Ad. Lord Nelson, Medit.
	,,	,,	*Ville de Marseille*, st. ship	..	,, ,, ,,
	,,	19	No. 57, g.v.	1	Taken by *Aristocrat*, 18, Lt. Corbet Jas. d'Auvergne, C. Fréhel.
	Mar.	21	*Ligurienne*	16	Taken by *Petrel*, 16, Com. Fras. Wm. Austen (1), near Marseilles. M
	,,	30	*Guillaume Tell* (* as *Malta*)	80	Taken by *Lion*, 64, *Foudroyant*, 80, and *Penelope*, 36, Medit. M *Penelope*. *Vincejo*.
	Apr.	13	*Diligente*	6	Taken by cutter (Master Buckley) of *Calypso*, 16, W. Ind.
	,,		*Neptune*, schooner	4	Taken by *Mayflower*, privateer, Jas. Le Blair, coast of France.
	May	5	*Dragon*	14	Taken by *Cambrian*, 40, and *Fishguard*, 44, Channel.
	,,	20	*Prima*, galley	2	Taken by boats under Com. Philip Beaver, Genoa.
	,,	31	*Légère*, lugger	3	Taken by *Netley*, 16, Lt. Fras. Godolphin Bond, Medit.
	June	1	*Cruelle* *	16	Taken by *Mermaid*, 32, Capt. Robt. Dudley Oliver, off Toulon.
	,,	6	*Insolente*	18	Burnt by boats (Lt. John Pilfold) of *Impétueux*, 78, B. of Biscay.
	,,	11	*Nochette*, g.b.	2	Taken by boats of squadron of Sir J. B. Warren, off Penmarck.
	,,	,,	A chasse-marée	10	,, ,, ,, ,,
	,,	,,	A chasse-marée	6	,, ,, ,, ,,
	,,		*Diligente*	12	Taken by *Crescent*, 36, Capt. Wm. Granville Lobb, W. Ind.
	,,	17	*Revanche*	4	Taken by *Phœnix*, 36, Capt. Laurence Wm. Halsted, Medit.
	July	2	*Thérèse*	20	Taken and burnt by boats (Lt. Hy. Burke) of *Renown*, *Fishguard*, and *Defence*, Bourgneuf Bay.
	,,	,,	A lugger	12	,, ,, ,, ,,
	,,	,,	A gunboat	6	,, ,, ,, ,,
	,,	,,	A gunboat	6	,, ,, ,, ,,
	,,	,,	A cutter	6	,, ,, ,, ,,
	,,	8	*Désirée*	38	Taken by *Dart*, 30, Com. Pat. Campbell, Dunquerque road. M
	,,	29	*Cerbère*	7	Cut out by boat (Lt. Jeremiah Coghlan, actg., of *Viper*), of *Impetueux*, Port Louis. M
	,,		*Boudeuse*	..	Destroyed to provide fuel, Valetta.
	Aug.	5	*Concorde*	40	Taken by *Belliqueux*, 64, Capt. Rowley Bulteel, and consorts, off Rio.
	,,	,,	*Médée*	36	Taken by Indiamen *Bombay Castle* and *Exeter*, off Rio.
	,,	24	*Diane* (* as *Niobe*)	40	Taken by *Northumberland*, *Généreux*, and *Success*, off Malta.
	,,	25	*Vengeance*	40	Taken by *Seine*, 38, Capt. David Milne, in Mona Passage. M
	Sept.	1	*Capricieuse*	6	Taken by *Termagant*, 18, Com. Wm. Skipsey, off Corsica.
	,,	4	*Athénien* * (Maltese)	64	Taken at the surrender of Valetta.
	,,	,,	*Dégo* (Maltese)	64	,, ,, ,,
	,,	,,	*Cartagénoise*	36	,, ,, ,,
	Oct.	8	*Quid pro Quo*	8	Taken by *Gipsy*, 10, Lt. Coryndon Boger, off Guadeloupe.
	,,	22	*Vénus*	28	Taken by *Indefatigable*, 44, and *Fishguard*, 44, off Portugal.
	Nov.	17	*Réolaise*	20	Driven ashore by *Nile*, 16, Lt. Geo. Argles, and burnt by boats (Lt. Wm. Hennah) of squadron.
1801	Jan.	3	*Sénégal*	18	Cut out and destroyed by boats (Lt. Thos. Dick), of *Melpomène*, 38, Sénégal.
	,,	18	*Aurore* *	16	Taken by *Thames*, 32, Capt Wm. Lukin, Channel.
	,,	,,	*Eclair* (* as 12)	4	Cut out by *Garland*, tender, Lt. Kenneth Mackenzie, Guadeloupe.
	,,	20	*Sans Pareille*	20	Taken by *Mercury*, 28, Capt. Thos. Rogers, off Sardinia.
	,,	28	*Dédaigneuse* *	36	Taken by *Oiseau*, 36, *Sirius*, 36, and *Amethyst*, 36, off Portugal.
	,,	29	*Curieuse*	18	Taken by *Bordelais*, 24, Capt. Thos. Manby, off Barbados; foundered.
	,,		*Bombarde*, g.v.	1	Taken by *Boadicea*, 38, Capt. Rich. Goodwin Keats, off Brest.

Year.	Date.	French national ship. [* Added to the Royal Navy.]	Guns.	Fate. M Medals granted in 1849, in pursuance of *Gazette* notice of June 1st, 1847. M Flag-officers' and Captains' gold medals.
1801	Feb. 16	*Furieuse*, xebec	6	Taken by *Minorca*, 16, Com. Geo. Miller, Medit.
	,, 19	*Africaine* *	40	Taken by *Phœbe*, 36, Capt. Robt. Barlow, Medit. M
	,, 20	*Arc*, cutter	..	Taken by boats of *Excellent*, 74, Quiberon Bay.
	Apr. 9	*Général Brune*	14	Taken by *Amethyst*, 36, Capt. John Cooke (1), Channel.
		Laurette	26	Taken by *Arrogant*, 74, Capt. Edw. Oliver Osborn, E. Ind.
	May 27	*Corvesse* (?) disp. vessel	1	Taken by *Corso*, 18, Com. Wm. Ricketts, Medit.
	,, 28	*Egypte*	16	Taken by *Heureux*, 24, Capt. Loftus Otway Bland, off Barbados.
	June 23	*Tigre* (suspected pirate)	8	Taken by boats of *Mercury*, 28, and *Corso*, 18, G. of Venice.
	July 12	*St. Antoine*	74	Taken by R.-Ad. Sir James Saumarez, off Gibraltar. M
	,, 22	*Chevrette*	20	Cut out by boats (Lt. Keith Maxwell) of *Beaulieu*, *Doris*, *Uranie*, and *Robust*, near Brest. M
	,, 25	A corvette	10	Taken by *Déterminée*, 24, Capt. John Clarke Searle, off Alexandria.
	Aug. 3	*Carrère* *	38	Taken by *Pomone*, 40, Capt. Ed. Leveson Gower, etc., off Elba.
	,, 10	*Eveillé*, lugger	2	Taken by cutter (Mid. Fras. Smith) of *Atalante*, 16, Quiberon Bay.
	,, 19	*Chiffonne* *	36	Taken by *Sibylle*, 38, Capt. Chas. Adam, off Seychelles.
	,, 21	4 howitzer-boats . . . each	1	Taken or destroyed by boats (Lt. James John Charles Agassiz) of Capt. Jonas Rose's squadron, near Etaples.
	Sept. 2	*Succès* (* as *Success*)	32	Retaken by *Pomone*, 44, *Phœnix*, 36, and *Minerve*, 44, off Vado.
	,, ,,	*Bravoure*	36	Driven ashore ,, ,, ,, ,,
	,, ,,	*Causse*	64	Taken at capitulation of Alexandria; delivered to Turkey.
	,, ,,	*Egyptienne* *	44	,, ,, ,, retained.
	,, ,,	*Justice*	40	,, ,, ,, delivered to Turkey.
	,, ,,	*Régénérée* *	36	,, ,, ,, retained.
	,, ,,	Unknown (Venetian)	32	,, ,, ,, delivered to Turkey.
	,, ,,	Unknown (Venetian)	32	,, ,, ,, retained.
	,, 7	*Flèche*	18	Sank after capture by *Victor*, 18, Com. Geo. Ralph Collier, E. Ind.
	,, 16	*Bulldog* *	18	Retaken by *Champion*, 24, Capt. Lord Wm. Stuart, near Gallipoli.

C.—DUTCH.

Year.	Date.	Ships of the Batavian Republic. [* Added to the Royal Navy.]	Guns.	Fate.
1795	Aug. 18	*Willemstad* (* as *Princess*)	26	Taken by V.-Ad. Sir G. K. Elphinstone, Simon's Bay.
	,, ,,	*Ster*, armed brig	14	,, ,, ,, ,,
	,, 20	*Brak* (* as *De Braak*)	14	Detained by *Fortune*, 16, Com. Fras. Wooldridge, Falmouth.
	,, 22	*Alliantie* (* as *Alliance*, 20)	36	Taken by *Stag*, *Réunion*, *Isis*, and *Vestal*, off Norway.
	,, 28	*Komeet* (* as *Penguin*)	18	Taken by *Unicorn*, 32, Capt. Thos. Williams (4), Irish station.
	Oct. 22	*Overijssel* *	64	Taken by *Polyphemus*, 64, Capt. Geo. Lumsdaine, Queenstown.
	,,	*Maria Louise*	14	Taken by *Rattlesnake*, 16, Com. Edw. Ramage, C. of Good Hope.
1796	Jan.	*Harlingen* (* as *Amboyna*)	10	Taken by R.-Ad. Peter Rainier (1), E. Ind.
	Mar.	*Zefir* (* as *Eurus*)	36	Detained by *Andromeda*, *Ranger*, and *Kite*, Firth of Forth.
	,, 4	*Zeeland* (* as *Zealand*)	64	Taken by V.-Ad. Rich. Onslow, at Plymouth.
	,, ,,	*Brakel* *	54	,, ,, ,, ,,
	,, ,,	*Tholen* (* as *Thulen*)	40	,, ,, ,, ,,
	,, ,,	*Meermin* (* as *Miermin*)	16	,, ,, ,, ,,
	,, ,,	*Pijl* *	16	,, ,, ,, ,,
	Apr. 22	*Vlugheid*	12	Taken by Adm. Duncan, coast of Norway.
	,, 23	*Thetis*	24	Taken by Commod. Thos. Parr at Demerara.
	,, ,,	*Zeemeeuw*	12	,, ,, ,, ,,
	May 12	*Argo* (* as *Janus*)	36	Taken by *Phœnix*, 36, Capt. Lawrence Wm. Halsted, etc., N. Sea.
	,, ,,	*Echo*	12	Driven ashore by *Pegasus*, 28, Capt. Ross Donnelly, Vriesland.
	,, ,,	*Gier*	12	,, ,, ,, ,,
	,, ,,	*Mercurius* (* as *Hermes*)	12	Taken by *Sylph*, 16, Com. John Chambers White, off the Texel.
	June 8	*Jason* (* as *Proselyte*)	36	Brought into Greenock by mutinous crew.
	July 6	*Bataaf*	12	Taken by *Roebuck*, 44, Com. Alex. Saunderson Burrowes, off Barbados.

Year.	Date.		Ships of the Batavian Republic. [* Added to the Royal Navy.]	Guns.	Fate. M Medals granted in 1849, in pursuance of *Gazette* notice of June 1st, 1847. M Flag-officers' and Captains' gold medals.
1796	Aug.	17	*Dordrecht* (* as *Dortrecht*)	64	Surrendered to V.-Ad. Sir G. K. Elphinstone, Saldanha Bay.
	"	"	*Revolutie* (* as *Prince Frederick*)	64	" " " "
	"	"	*Maarten Harpertzoon Tromp* (* as *Van Tromp*)	54	" " " "
	"	"	*Castor* (* as *Saldanha*)	44	" " " "
	"	"	*Brave* (* as *Braave*)	40	" " " "
	"	"	*Bellona* (* as *Vindictive*)	24	" " " "
	"	"	*Sirene* (* as *Laurel*)	26	" " " "
	"	"	*Havik* (* as *Havick*)	18	" " " "
	"	"	*Vrouw Maria*	16	" " " "
1797	Oct.	11	*Vrijheid* *	74	Taken by Adm. Adam Duncan in the battle off Camperdown. M M
	"	"	*Jupiter* (* as *Camperdown*)	72	" " "
	"	"	*Haarlem* *	68	" " "
	"	"	*Admiraal Tjerk Hiddes De Vries* (* as *Admiral Devries*)	68	" " "
	"	"	*Gelijkheid* *	68	" " "
	"	"	*Wassenaar*	64	" " "
	"	"	*Hercules* * (later *Delft*)	64	" " "
	"	"	*Delft*	54	" " " sank.
	"	"	*Alkmaar* *	56	" " "
	"	"	*Monnikendam*	44	" " " lost.
	"	"	*Embuscade*	32	" " " retaken.
			Yonge Frans (?)	10	Taken by *Resistance*, 44, Capt. Edw. Pakenham, E. Ind.
			Yonge Lansier (?)	10	" " " "
			Wakker (?)	10	" " " "
			Limbi	8	" " " "
			Ternate	4	" " " "
			Resource (?)	6	" " " "
			Juno	4	" " " "
1798	Oct.	24	*Waakzaamheid* *	24	Taken by *Sirius*, 36, Capt. Rich. King (2), North Sea.
	"	"	*Furie* (* as *Wilhelmina*)	36	" " " "
1799	Apr.	26	*Helena*	8	Taken by *Virginie*, 44, Capt. Geo. Astle, E. Ind.
	"	"	*Helena*	12	" " " "
	"	"	*Brak*	12	" " " "
	May	24	A brig	6	Taken by *Arrogant* and *Orpheus*, E. Ind.
	Aug.	11	*Crash* *	12	Retaken by *Pylades*, 16, Com. Adam Mackenzie, and consorts, off Groningen. M
	"		A schuyt (* as *Undaunted*)	2	Taken by " " " "
	"	14	*Weerwraak*, g.v.	6	Burnt by " " " "
	"	20	*Kemphaan* (* as *Camphaan*)	16	Taken by V.-Ad. Lord Hugh Seymour, Surinam.
	"	28	*Verwachting*	64	Taken by V.-Ad. Andrew Mitchell, Nieuwe Diep, Texel.
	"	"	*Broederschap*	54	" " " "
	"	"	*Hector* (* as *Pandour*)	44	" " " "
	"	"	*Duif*	44	" " " "
	"	"	*Expeditie*	44	" " " "
	"	"	*Belle Antoinette*	44	" " " "
	"	"	*Constitutie*	44	" " " "
	"	"	*Unie*	44	" " " "
	"	"	*Heldin* *	28	" " " "
	"	"	*Minerva* (* as *Braak*)	24	" " " "
	"	"	*Venus* (* as *Amaranthe*)	24	" " " "
	"	"	*Valk*	24	" " " "
	"	"	*Alarm*	24	" " " "
	"	30	*Washington* (* as *Princess of Orange*)	70	Surrendered to V.-Ad. Andrew Mitchell, in the Vlieter, Texel.
	"	"	*Gelderland* *	64	" " " "
	"	"	*Admiraal De Ruijter* (* as *De Ruyter*)	64	" " " "
	"	"	*Utrecht*	64	" " " "
	"	"	*Cerberus* (* as *Texel*)	64	" " " "
	"	"	*Leijden* *	64	" " " "
	"	"	*Beschermer* *	56	" " " "
	"	"	*Batavier* *	56	" " " "
	"	"	*Amphitrite* *	44	" " " "
	"	"	*Mars* (* as *Vlieter*) rasée	44	" " " "
	"	"	*Embuscade* *	32	" " " "
	"	"	*Galatée* *	16	" " " "
	Sept.		*Valk*	20	Taken by V.-Ad. Andrew Mitchell, Zuijder Zee, but lost Nov. 10th, 1799.
	"	12	*Draak*	24	Taken by *Arrow*, 28, Com. Nath. Portlock, and *Wolverine*, 13, Com. Wm. Bolton (1), off Vlie. M
	"	"	*Gier* *	14	" " " "
	"	15	*Dolfijn* (* as *Dolphin*)	24	Surrendered to " " " "
	Oct.	9	*Lijnx*	12	Taken by boats of *Circe*, 28, Capt. Robt. Winthrop, River Ems.
	..	..	*Perseus*	8	" " " "

Year.	Date.	Ships of the Batavian Republic. [* Added to the Royal Navy.]	Guns.	Fate.
1799	Oct.	4 gunboats . . . . each	4	Cut out by boats of *Dart*, *Hasty*, *Defender*, *Cracker*, and *Isis*, coast of Holland.
1800	Aug. 23	A brig (* as *Admiral Rainier*)	16	Taken by *Dœdalus*, *Centurion*, *Braave*, and *Sibylle*, E. Ind.
	Oct. 28	5 gunboats	..	Burnt by *Admiral Rainier*, 16, Lt. Wm. Hugh Dobbie (1), Carawang River.
	,, 30	3 gunboats	..	Taken ,, ,, ,, ,,

D.—SPANISH.

Year.	Date.	Ships of the Spanish Royal Navy. [* Added to the Royal Navy.]	Guns.	Fate. M Medals granted in 1849, in pursuance of *Gazette* notice of June 1st, 1847. **M** Flag-officers' and Captains' gold medals.
1796	Sept. 16	*Princesa*	16	Detained by *Seahorse*, 38, Capt. Geo. Oakes, off Corunna.
	Oct. 13	*Mahonesa* *	34	Taken by *Terpsichore*, 32, Capt Rich. Bowen, off Cape de Gata. M
	Nov. 2	*San Pio*	18	Taken by *Regulus*, 44, Capt. Wm. Carthew, Atlantic.
	,, 23	*Galgo*	18	Taken by *Alarm*, 32, Capt. Edw. Fellowes, off Grenada.
	Dec. 2	*Corso* *	18	Taken by *Southampton*, 32, Capt. Jas. Macnamara (2), off Monaco.
	,, 20	*Santa Sabina*	40	Taken by *Minerve*, 38, Capt. Geo. Cockburn, Medit.; retaken Dec. 21st, 1796. M
1797	Feb. 14	*Salvador del Mundo* * . . .	112	Taken by the fleet of Adm. Sir John Jervis, K.B., off C. St. Vincent. M **M**
	,, ,,	*San Josef* *	112	,, ,, ,, ,,
	,, ,,	*San Nicolas* *	80	,, ,, ,, ,,
	,, ,,	*San Ysidro* *.	80	,, ,, ,, ,,
	,, 17	*San Vincente*	80	Burnt to prevent capture by R.-Ad. Hy. Harvey (1), Trinidad.
	,, ,,	*Arrogante*	74	,, ,, ,, ,,
	,, ,,	*Gallardo*	74	,, ,, ,, ,,
	,, ,,	*Santa Cecilia*	34	,, ,, ,, ,,
	,, ,,	*San Damaso* *	74	Taken by R.-Ad. Hy. Harvey (1), Trinidad.
	Mar. 12	*Los Magellanes*	4	Taken by *Dover*, 44, Lt. Hy. Kent, coast of Portugal.
	Apr. 26	*Ninfa* (* as *Hamadryad*) . .	34	Taken by *Irresistible*, 74, Capt. Geo. Martin (2), Lisbon station.
	,, ,,	*Santa Elena*.	34	Destroyed by *Irresistible*, 74, Capt. Geo. Martin (2), near Cadiz.
	May 24	*Nuestra Señora del Rosario* (* as *Rosario*).	20	Taken by *Romulus*, 36, and *Mahonesa*, 34, off Cadiz.
	June 21	*San Francisco*	14	Taken by *Santa Margarita*, 36, Capt. Geo. Parker, off Ireland.
	Nov. 14	*Bolador*	16	Taken by *Majestic*, 74, Capt. Geo. Blagden Westcott, Lisbon station.
1798	May	*San Antonio*, packet . . .	6	Taken by *Endymion*, 44, Capt. Sir Thos. Williams (4), off Ireland.
	,, 8	*Receviso*	6	Taken by *Aurora*, 28, Capt. Hy. Digby, Lisbon station.
	July 15	*Santa Dorotea* *	34	Taken by *Lion*, 64, Capt. Manley Dixon, off Cartagena. M
	Sept. 16	*Velosa Aragonesa*, en flûte .	30	Taken by *Aurora*, 28, Capt. Hy. Digby, off the Azores.
	Nov. 13	*Petrel*.	16	Retaken by *Argo*, 44, Capt. Jas. Bowen (1), Medit.
	,, 15	A brig on the stocks (* as *Port Mahon*).	..	Taken at the capture of Minorca.
	,, ,,	14 gunboats	..	,, ,, ,,
	,, 28	*San Leon*	16	Taken by *Sta. Dorotea*, *Stromboli*, *Perseus*, and *Bulldog*, Lisbon station.
1799	Jan. 2	*Valiente*, packet.	12	Taken by *Cormorant*, 20, Capt. Lord Mark Robt. Kerr, off Malaga.
	Feb. 6	*Santa Teresa* *	34	Taken by *Argo*, 44, Capt. Jas. Bowen (1), off Majorca.
	,, 22	*Africa*, xebec	14	Taken by *Espoir*, 16, Com. Jas. Sanders, Medit.
	Mar. 16	*Guadalupe*	34	Driven ashore by *Centaur*, 74, and *Cormorant*, 20, Medit.
	,,	*Urca Cargadora*	12	Burnt by *Prompte*, 20, Capt. Thos. Dundas, W. Ind.
	,, 19	*Vincejo* *	18	Taken by *Cormorant*, 20, Capt. Lord Mark Robt. Kerr, Medit.
	,, 24	*Golondrina*, packet. . . .	4	Taken by *Mermaid*, 32, and *Sylph*, 14, off Corunna.
	May	*Pájaro*, packet	4	Taken by *Alarm*, 32, Capt. Robt. Rolles, G. of Florida.
	June 23	*San Antonio*	14	Taken by *Terpsichore*, 32, Capt. Wm. Hall Gage, Medit.
	July	*Feliz*	14	Taken by *Alarm*, 32, Capt. Robt. Rolles, W. Ind.
	,,	*Sandoval* (?)	4	Taken by *York*, 64, and consorts, W. Ind.
	Aug. 6	*Infanta Amalia* (* as *Porpoise*)	12	Taken by *Argo*, 44, Capt. Jas. Bowen (1), coast of Portugal.
	Sept.	A gunboat	2	Taken by *Mayflower*, privateer, Medit.
	,,	A packet	8	,, ,, ,,
	Oct. 17	*Thetis*	34	Taken by *Ethalion*, 38, Capt. Jas. Young (2), and consorts, off Ferrol.
	,, 18	*Santa Brigida*	34	Taken by *Naiad*, 38, *Alcmene*, 32, and *Triton*, 32, off C. Finisterre.

Year.	Date.		Ships of the Spanish Royal Navy. [* Added to the Royal Navy.]	Guns.	Fate. M Medals granted in 1849, in pursuance of *Gazette* notice of June 1st, 1847. M Flag-officers' and Captains' gold medals.
1799	Oct.	25	*Hermione* (* as *Retribution*, 32)	34	Cut out of Puerto Cabello by boats of *Surprise*, 32, Capt. Edw. Hamilton. M M
	Nov.	15	*Galgo**	16	Taken by *Crescent*, 36, Capt. Wm. Granville Lobb, Atlantic.
1800	Jan.	26	*N.S. del Carmen*	16	Taken by *Penelope*, 36, Capt. Hon. Hy. Blackwood, Medit.
	Feb.		*Cuervo*	4	Taken by *Alarm*, 32, Capt. Robt. Rolles, W. Ind.
	Apr.	7	*Carmen** (as 36)	34	Taken by R.-Ad. John Thos. Duckworth, off Cadiz.
	,,	,,	*Florentina** (as 36)	34	,, ,, ,, ,,
	June	22	*Cortez*	4	Taken by *Flora*, 36, Capt. Robt. Gambier Middleton, Lisbon station.
			N.S. del Carmen, felucca	2	Destroyed by *Bonetta*, 18, Com. Hy. Vansittart, W. Ind.
	,,	29	*Gibraltar*, g.b.	10	Taken by *Anson*, 44, Capt. Phil. Calderwood Durham off Gibraltar.
	,,	,,	*Salvador*, g.b.	10	,, ,, ,, ,,
			A gunboat	2	Taken by *Rattler*, 16, Com. John Mathias Spread, W. Ind.
	July	27	*Cántabro*	18	Taken by *Apollo*, 36, Capt. Peter Halkett, off Havana.
	Aug.	20	*Veloz*	4	Taken by *Clyde*, 38, Capt. Chas. Cunningham, Channel.
	Sept.	3	*Concepción* (alias *Esmeralda*)	22	Cut out by boats (Com. Jas. Hillyar) of *Minotaur*, 74, and *Niger*, 32, Barcelona.
	,,	,,	*Paz*	22	,, ,, ,, ,,
	,,	30	*Vivo*	14	Taken by *Fishguard*, 44, Capt. Thos. Byam Martin, coast of Spain.
	Oct.	27	*San Josef*, polacca	8	Cut out by boats (Lt. Fras. Beaufort) of *Phaeton*, 38, near Malaga. M
	Nov.	10	*Resolución*	18	Taken and destroyed by *Apollo*, 36, Capt. Peter Halkett, G. of Mexico.
1801	Jan.	6	*Reina Luisa*	2	Taken by *Hind*, 28, Capt. Thos. Larcom, off Jamaica.
	May	6	*Gamo*, xebec	30	Taken by *Speedy*, 14, Com. Lord Cochrane, near Barcelona. M
	,,	16	*Alcudia*	..	Cut out by boats of *Naiad*, 38, and *Phaeton*, 38, near Pontevedra.
	,,	,,	*Raposo*	..	,, ,, ,, ,,
	June	8	*Duides*, cutter	8	Taken by *Constance*, 24, Capt. Zachary Mudge, off Vigo.
	,,	9	A xebec	20	Sunk in action by *Kangaroo*, 18, and *Speedy*, 14, under a battery, Oropesa.
	,,	,,	2 gunboats	..	,, ,, ,, ,,
	July	5	5 gunboats	..	Sunk in action by R.-Ad. Sir Jas. Saumarez, Algeciras.
	,,	12	*Real Carlos*	112	Burnt in action with R.-Ad. Sir Jas. Saumarez, S. of Gibraltar. M
	,,	,,	*San Hermenegildo*	112	,, ,, ,, ,, M
			Perla	24	Sunk after action ,, ,, ,, M
	Aug.	20	*Neptuno* (pierced for 20)	..	Taken by boats of *Fishguard*, 44, *Diamond*, 38, and *Boadicea*, 38, Corunna.
	,,	,,	A gunboat	1	,, ,, ,, ,,
	Sept.	24	*Limeño*	18	Taken by *Chance*, privateer, 16, coast of Peru.

DANISH.

Year.	Date.		Ships of the Danish Royal Navy. [* Added to the Royal Navy.]	Guns.	Fate. M Medals granted in 1849, in pursuance of *Gazette* notice of June 1st, 1847.
1801	Apr.	2	*Sjælland*	74	Taken and burnt by V.-Ad. Lord Nelson, Copenhagen. M
	,,	,,	*Holsteen**	60	Taken by ,, ,, ,, M
	,,	,,	*Infædstretten*	64	Taken and burnt by ,, ,, ,, M
	,,	,,	*Dannebrog*	62	Blew up after action with ,, ,, M
	,,	,,	*Prævesteen*	56	Taken and burnt by ,, ,, ,, M
	,,	,,	*Valkyrien*	48	Taken and burnt by ,, ,, ,, M
	,,	,,	*Jylland*	48	Taken and burnt by ,, ,, ,, M
	,,	,,	*Charlotte Amalie*	26	Taken and burnt by ,, ,, ,, M
	,,	,,	*Kronborg*	20	Taken and burnt by ,, ,, ,, M
	,,	,,	*Rendsborg*	20	Driven ashore and burnt by ,, ,, M
	,,	,,	*Nyborg*	20	Sank after action with ,, ,, ,, M
	,,	,,	*Sværdfisken*	20	Taken and burnt by ,, ,, ,, M
	,,	,,	*Haien*	20	Taken and burnt by ,, ,, ,, M
	,,	,,	*Aggershuus*	20	Sank after action with ,, ,, ,, M
	,,	,,	*Sæhesten*	18	Taken and burnt by ,, ,, ,, M

CHAPTER XXXVII.

VOYAGES AND DISCOVERIES, 1793–1802.

SIR CLEMENTS MARKHAM, K.C.B., F.R.S.

Broughton to the Pacific—Phillip and Hunter to Botany Bay—Matthew Flinders—George Bass—Voyage of Flinders in the *Investigator*—Wreck of the *Porpoise*—French bad faith.

LANTERN CRANK. 18TH CENT.

WHEN Lieutenant William Robert Broughton left the *Chatham* in 1793, and took home Vancouver's dispatches, crossing Mexico from San Blas to Vera Cruz, it was under consideration whether another surveying and exploring expedition should not be sent to the North Pacific. Captain James King had observed that the navigation of the sea between Japan and China offered the largest field for discovery; and his remark had received attention from the Lords of the Admiralty. The result was that Lieutenant Broughton[1] was appointed to the *Providence* with secret orders, on October 3rd, 1793. This vessel was a sloop of war of 400 tons, carrying 16 guns, with a complement of 115 men. She had just returned from the service of conveying bread-fruit plants from Tahiti to the West Indies, under the command of Captain William Bligh. Broughton had three Lieutenants under him, Zachary Mudge, George Forbes Freeman Young, and James Giles Vashon; Mr. John Crossley shipped as astronomer, William Chapman was the Master, and John Cawley, Master's Mate. On October 21st, 1794, the *Providence* sailed from St. Helens, reached Sydney in August, 1795, and arrived at Tahiti in the end of November.

Memories of Cook were dear to the Tahitians, who gave every assistance to English ships and supplied them amply with fresh provisions. After rating the chronometers at Point Venus, Broughton

[1] Broughton was made a Commander in Jan. 1795, and a Captain on Jan. 28th, 1797.—W. L. C.

shaped a course for the Sandwich Islands. On December 17th, 1795, he discovered a low island covered with trees, which he named Caroline after the daughter of Sir Philip Stephens, Secretary to the Admiralty. On January 8th, 1796, he anchored in Karakakoa Bay. There the error and rate of chronometers was again ascertained, and uniform kindness and goodwill were displayed by the natives. The murder of Captain Cook, in a moment of blind rage, was deeply deplored, for he had been loved and respected by them. At that time Kamehameha I. had made himself sovereign of all the islands but Kauai. From Hawaii the *Providence* went to Lahaina in Maui, and thence to Waikiki Bay in Oahu, where Kamehameha was preparing for the conquest of Kauai. Captain Broughton left the Sandwich Islands on February 2nd, 1796, arriving at Nootka Sound on the 15th of March; and, after some stay in the Strait of Juan de Fuca, anchored at Monterey in June. He then, with the advice of his officers, decided upon a plan to survey the coast of Asia from the island of Saghalien to the Nankin river, with the Kurile and Japan islands, thinking that such survey would complete a knowledge of the North Pacific, and would be very acceptable to geographers.

Returning to the Sandwich Islands, the vessel was steered thence to the westward, and sighted the Japanese island of Yesso on the 12th of September. Broughton anchored in Endermo Bay, in the island of Yesso, examined the whole western coast of Niphon, and passed through the Strait of Sangaar into the Gulf of Tartary. On November 11th, the *Providence* was off the entrance to the Bay of Tokio, and soon afterwards had a glorious view of Fusi-yama, towering above the high land and covered with snow. In December she arrived at Macao, where Commander Broughton purchased a small schooner to assist him in the work of surveying. He took on board fifteen months' provisions, and completed a thorough refit. All the men were in good health, and the work was recommenced with the brightest prospects in April, 1797.

But within a month the circumstances had entirely altered. Broughton was navigating among the islands to the east of Formosa. In the evening of May 17th white water was reported to Lieutenant Vashon, the officer of the watch, ahead and on both bows. Directly afterwards the ship struck upon a coral reef: the helm having been put up, and the sails being all full. When Captain Broughton came on deck his opinion was that, if the helm had been put a-lee on seeing the danger, the ship would have cleared it. Vashon was tried by court-martial, and dismissed his ship.[1] The wind freshened, the sea began to break with great force, and the leak rapidly increased on the pumps. There was no hope of saving the vessel, which fell over on her broadside; and the people were all got into the boats. They made sail, with the schooner, to the S.W., and were very hospitably received on the island of Typing, or Myako-sima, by the inhabitants. Returning to Canton, arrangements were made for passages home, for officers and men, in the East India Company's ships.

Captain Broughton continued the survey in the small schooner, with a select body of officers and men. His operations embraced an examination of the Pescadores and Lu-Chu Islands, and of the southern and eastern coasts of Japan; and in August, 1797, he was again off the island of Yesso. Passing through the Strait of Sangaar, the little schooner was taken up the east coast of Yesso and Saghalien to latitude 52° N. Captain Broughton came to the conclusion that he would be unable to pass through the narrow strait into the sea beyond. On September 16th, therefore, he turned to the south, along the western side of the Gulf of Tartary, a name given by Broughton on the 24th. He examined the coast of Corea, and anchored in the harbour of Chosan, where he was able to learn something of Corea and its inhabitants. Proceeding southwards in October, Broughton found himself among the cluster of islands off the south coast of Corea, one of which is Port Hamilton; and he surveyed the large island of Quelpart. The only chart he had on board was that by Van Kuelen, which was of little use as a guide; and his surveys were laid down without aid from other sources. The little schooner returned from her adventurous voyage, and anchored safely in Macao Roads on November 27th, 1797. Captain Broughton and his officers then took passages to England, arriving in February, 1799, after an absence of four years. The narrative of his voyage was published in 1804.

The most important results of Captain Cook's voyages of discovery, were the colonisation of Australia and New Zealand, and the establishment of large civilised communities of English race in the southern hemisphere. On January 19th, 1788, nine years after the great navigator's death, Captain Arthur Phillip arrived at Botany Bay in H.M. brig *Supply*, followed by Captain John Hunter

[1] He was also dismissed the service, but was reinstated, and reached the rank of Captain on May 28th, 1802.—W. L. C.

in the *Sirius*, with six transports and three store ships.[1] Soon afterwards they removed to Port Jackson, a much better harbour three leagues to the northward, where the town of Sydney was founded. Captain Phillip was the first Governor of New South Wales. Early in 1795, Captain Hunter arrived at Sydney with H.M.S. *Reliance* and *Supply*, to relieve Captain Phillip. On board the *Reliance* there was a young Midshipman whose ardour for discovery secured

CAPT. MATTHEW FLINDERS, R.N.

for him the illustrious position of the foremost maritime explorer of Australia.

The name of this Midshipman was Matthew Flinders. Born in 1774 at Donington, near Boston, in Lincolnshire, where his father was a medical man, young Flinders was filled with a longing to go

[1] Phillip flew a broad pennant as Commodore of the expedition, and left England in the *Sirius*, with Hunter as his Captain, Lieut. Henry Lidgbird Ball commanding the *Supply*; but on Nov. 25th, 1787, Phillip shifted his broad pennant to the *Supply*, and proceeded, leaving Hunter, in the *Sirius*, to follow. The six transports were the *Scarborough*, *Lady Penrhyn*, *Friendship*, *Charlotte*, *Prince of Wales*, and *Alexander*, having on board convicts guarded by Marines. The three store ships were the *Golden Grove*, *Fishburn*, and *Borrowdale*.—W. L. C.

to sea by having read 'Robinson Crusoe.' The boy succeeded in learning navigation, and at length he was allowed to join the Navy in 1790, on board the *Scipio*, 64, Captain Thomas Pasley, at Chatham. He served in the *Providence* with Bligh, in the second voyage to Tahiti, to transport plants of the bread-fruit to the West Indies, and he was in the *Bellerophon* at the battle of the 1st of June, 1794. Arriving at Port Jackson in the *Reliance* in September, 1795, Flinders soon found that there was no survey of the coast, beyond Captain Cook's general chart. He at once conceived a project to supply the deficiency. In Mr. George Bass, the surgeon of the *Reliance*, he had the good fortune to find a friend whose ardour for discovery was equal to his own. Flinders and Bass determined to complete the examination of the coast of New South Wales, by all such opportunities as the duties of the ship, and the means at their disposal, would admit.

The plans of the young explorers were discouraged by the authorities. They, however, had resolution and perseverance. All official help and countenance were withheld. But they managed, by their own unaided exertions, to equip a small boat called the *Tom Thumb*,[1] and they sailed in her with a crew consisting of themselves and one boy. In their first voyage they explored for a considerable distance the George River, which falls into Botany Bay. Their second enterprise was to examine a large river, which was said to fall into the sea to the south of Botany Bay.

Leaving Port Jackson on March 25th, 1795, Flinders and Bass sailed along the coast until, in the first watch of the 29th, a gale of wind sprang up from the south. In a few minutes the waves began to break. The danger to which the little boat was exposed, was increased by the darkness of the night, and the uncertainty of finding any place of shelter. Flinders steered with an oar, and it required the utmost care to prevent the boat from broaching to. A single wrong movement, or a moment's inattention, would have sent them to the bottom. Bass kept the sheet in his hand, drawing in a few inches occasionally when he saw a particularly heavy sea following. The boy was kept constantly at work baling out. After running for a hour in this critical situation, some breakers were distignuished ahead. The boat's head was brought to the wind at a favourable moment, sail and mast were got down, and the oars were got out. Pulling towards the reef during the intervals of the

[1] She was but eight feet long. *Nav. Chron.* xxxii. 181.—W. L. C.

heaviest seas, they found that it terminated in a point, and in a few minutes they were in smooth water, under its lee. Such were the perils that the ardent explorers gallantly faced in the cause of geographical discovery.

In 1798, Bass undertook a voyage to the southward of Port Jackson in a whale boat, with a crew of five convicts. He explored six hundred miles of coast line. In this open boat, exposed during the greater part of the time to very tempestuous weather, Bass persevered until he had discovered the entrance to the strait which now bears his name, separating Australia from Tasmania. This feat has few equals in the annals of maritime enterprise. The zeal of Flinders[1] and Bass was at length rewarded. The Governor of New South Wales gave them the use of the *Norfolk*, a sloop of twenty-five tons, with authority to complete the discovery of Bass's Strait. They had a good crew of eight naval volunteers, and twelve weeks' provisions. Sailing from Port Jackson on the 7th of October, 1798, they thoroughly explored the coasts of Tasmania and the adjacent islands, where seals and birds abounded. Bass landed on one islet where he had to fight his way with the seals up the hill side; and, when he arrived at the top, he was obliged to make a path with his club amongst the albatrosses. These birds were sitting on their nests, and covered the surface of the ground. Flinders made regular astronomical observations throughout this very important voyage, and he returned to Port Jackson on the 11th of January, 1799. The main result of the voyage was the complete examination of the strait between Australia and Tasmania. At the special request of young Flinders, it received, from Governor Hunter, the name of Bass's Strait. Flinders made one more exploring voyage to the northward of Port Jackson, before returning to England on board the *Reliance* in 1800.

When the charts based on the discoveries of Flinders and Bass were published, men of science were strongly impressed with the great importance of completing the work, and making a thorough examination of all the coasts of Australia. Sir Joseph Banks, the President of the Royal Society, submitted a plan to the Government; and it was decided that such a voyage should be undertaken. The right man was selected to do the work. Young Flinders was appointed to the command.

[1] Flinders was made a Lieut. in 1798, a Commander on Feb. 16th, 1801, and a Captain on May 7th, 1810.

In January, 1801, Flinders took command of the *Investigator*,[1] a north country built ship of 334 tons, closely resembling the vessels employed in Captain Cook's voyages. Crowds of volunteers eagerly came forward for the service. The instructions were to examine first the south coast of Australia from King George's Sound to Bass's Strait, then the north-west coast, then the Gulf of Carpentaria and the coast to the westward. The instructions were signed by Lord St. Vincent, Captain Thomas Troubridge, and Captain John Markham. They were accompanied by extracts from a memoir by Mr. Alexander Dalrymple[2] on the winds and weather. A passport was also granted by the French Government, promising protection to a voyage undertaken solely for the advancement of science. There were two lieutenants on board, one being Samuel William Flinders, the Commander's brother. The Master was John Thistle, and there were eight Midshipmen, including the future Sir John Franklin. The astronomer was John Crossley, and the botanist was Robert Brown, so well known afterwards, in the scientific world, as the "Princeps Botanicorum." On the 18th of July, 1801, the expedition sailed from Spithead, and, using Vancouver's chart, the *Investigator* was anchored in King George's Sound on the 9th of December.

The voyage was continued along the south coast of Australia in January, 1802, and a careful survey was made from King George's Sound to Port Phillip. The new discoveries included the great gulfs of Spencer and St. Vincent; and the surrounding coasts, which were all laid down with remarkable accuracy. It was near Thistle Island, at the entrance of Spencer Gulf, that Mr. Thistle the Master, and a young Midshipman named Taylor, were lost by the capsizing of a cutter. Commander Flinders deplored the death of the Master, who had served with him in his previous voyage round Tasmania, and was a most valuable officer. The numerous Lincolnshire names, including Donington and Spilsby the birthplaces of Flinders and Franklin, given to points on the coast, show from what county the Commander hailed. On April 27th, the *Investigator* anchored at Port Phillip, which had been discovered and named ten weeks earlier by Lieutenant James Murray, who had come from Port Jackson in the *Lady Nelson*, brig. Flinders, however, made a complete examination of this great sheet of water.

The *Investigator* arrived at Port Jackson on the 9th of May, 1802, all on board being in better health and spirits than when they

[1] Ex-*Xenophon*. [2] The Hydrographer.

left Spithead; for Flinders promoted the happiness of the men by strict discipline combined with kindly sympathy and consideration; and health was preserved by closely following the system of Captain Cook—cleanliness, wholesome food, and free circulation of air in the messing and sleeping place. An observatory was temporarily established at Port Jackson, where young Franklin was appointed assistant. The brig, *Lady Nelson*, commanded by Lieutenant Murray, was placed under the orders of Commander Flinders at Port Jackson.

In July, 1802, the examination of the coast to the northward was commenced, as well as of the Barrier Reef, of which Flinders wrote an interesting description. In October, he proceeded onwards to Torres Strait and the Gulf of Carpentaria; but the ship was in a most unseaworthy condition. It was found that most of the timbers were rotten, and that, even with fine weather, she would not hold together for more than six months. Nevertheless Flinders continued the survey for some time longer, as far along the north coast of Australia as Melville Bay. In June, 1803, he returned to Port Jackson.

The *Investigator* was quite unfit for further use. Old, crazy, and leaky when she was bought, she was a vessel such as, in our days, would not be deemed fit for the business of a collier. It was a school of hardship and rough work, yet full of interest for an ardent young sailor. It was in discovering many a reef and island, and many a mile of coast line, that John Franklin's mind became imbued with that sincere love of geographical discovery which marked his career through life. Flinders was the example, and the Australian survey was the nursery which reared one of the greatest of our Arctic navigators, the discoverer of the North-West Passage. Able, brave, and modest, Flinders was exactly the man to awaken similar qualities in his officers.

The *Investigator* was condemned, and a small vessel named the *Porpoise* was hired to take the officers and men to England. On the 10th of August, 1803, she sailed from Port Jackson, homeward bound, with two other vessels in company, the *Bridgewater* and *Cato*. In the evening of the 17th, all the ships being still in company, and going about eight knots under double-reefed topsails, breakers were seen ahead from the forecastle of the *Porpoise*. The helm was immediately put down, but she missed stays, and in another minute was carried among the breakers. Striking upon a coral reef, she took a fearful heel over on her beam ends, the foremast going over the side at the second or third shock. Soon the hold was full of water, but luckily she went over with the upper deck away from the surf. The *Cato* struck on the reef about two cables' length from the *Porpoise*, fell over towards the surf, and her masts went by the board. The *Bridgewater* escaped, and her dastardly master—his name was Palmer—made sail, leaving his consorts to their fate.

During the night Commander Flinders and his first Lieutenant, Robert Merrick Fowler, employed the people in making a raft and securing water and provisions on it. The *Cato*, having fallen over to windward, with her deck exposed to the waves, the decks were torn up and everything was washed away. The only safe place for the unfortunate crew was in the port fore chains, where they were all crowded together. In this situation, some clinging to the chain plates and dead eyes, others holding to one another, they passed the night. With daylight there appeared a dry sandbank about half a mile distant, sufficiently large to receive the shipwrecked people and such provisions as could be saved. The *Porpoise's* boats were brought as near to the *Cato* as possible, the crew jumping from the fore chains and swimming to them through the surf. All got safe to the boats except three young lads, who were drowned. All next day the people worked hard, landing water and provisions on the sandbank. The ships soon broke up, but two boats were saved.

Commander Flinders took command of the combined ships' companies. He resolved to lay down two decked boats, capable of conveying all the shipwrecked people to Port Jackson, and also to send the cutter for assistance. The latter service would be one of great danger, and Flinders, therefore, resolved to perform it himself. He started on the 25th of August with a crew of fourteen men, and, after a perilous voyage of 750 miles in an open boat, he safely reached Port Jackson on September 8th. The ship *Rolla*, bound to China, was engaged to call at the reef, and take the shipwrecked people on board. This was successfully done; and young Franklin was one of those who went home by Canton.

Flinders was anxious to return to England direct, with his charts and notebooks. He was supplied with a smaller schooner of twenty-nine tons, called the *Cumberland*. Passing through Torres Strait the little vessel sprang a leak, and Commander Flinders was obliged to put into Mauritius. There he was perfidiously made a prisoner of war by the French governor, contrary to the established usage of civilised nations, and to the written promise of the French government. The governor, whose name was Decaen, used the quibble that the passport was for the *Investigator*, not the *Cumberland*.[1] Surveyors and explorers, whose work is intended to benefit the whole world, are allowed to pass free in time of war, and this Decaen disgraced his country and himself by detaining Flinders. He was kept a prisoner for nearly seven years. It broke his heart. Released at length in June, 1810, he returned to England in the following October. He was three years preparing the narrative of his voyage in two quarto volumes and an atlas, which were published in 1814. His work finished, the great surveyor died on July 19th of the same year. Flinders had extraordinary natural gifts as a surveyor. He was one of the first to investigate the deviation caused by the iron in ships. He it was who first suggested the name of *Australia*. He was a man of remarkable talent, but modest and unassuming, and though he was a strict disciplinarian, he was beloved by all who served under him.

With the voyage of Flinders ended the long and glorious labours of naval discoverers, which had been continuous for forty years. From 1764 to 1804, Byron, Wallis, Carteret, Cook, Phipps, Vancouver, Broughton and Flinders had advanced geographical science, and made discoveries, the results of which are incalculable. They created and trained a school of marine surveyors, but they also trained Nelson, Riou, Vashon, and others, the heroes of Trafalgar and many other sea fights, and the saviours of their country. After 1804 there was a pause for some years, though, even during that time of stress, surveying was not entirely neglected. In 1818, Great Britain was once more aroused to a sense of her duties, as the leader of exploration and discovery among the nations of the earth.

[1] He also charged Flinders with being an impostor. *Nav. Chron.* xiv. 332.—W. L. C.

PUNT: 18TH CENT.

Publisher's note

In the original edition the four photogravure plates and three full-page illustrations faced the text pages as listed on page XI. In this edition these illustrations are collected on the following pages in the order in which they appeared in the first edition. The original position indicators have been retained.

Walter L. Colls. Ph. Sc.

Admiral Sir Samuel Hood, Viscount Hood, Bart. K.B.
Governor of Greenwich Hospital.

From the Mezzotint by J. Jones, after the Portrait by Reynolds.

THE "BRUNSWICK" AND THE "VENGEUR," JUNE 1ST, 1794.

(From W. Ellis's lithograph, after the drawing by N. Pocock.)

[To face p. 234.

COMMODORE NELSON'S SQUADRON CHASED BY THE FRENCH. OFF SAN FIORENZO. JULY 8TH, 1795.

(From a drawing by Pocock, after a sketch by W. H. R., an officer who was present.)

[To face p. 274.

Walter L. Colls, Ph. Sc.

Sir John Jervis, Earl St. Vincent, K.B.

Admiral of the Fleet.

From the Mezzotint by C. Turner, after the Painting by Sir W. Beechey.

Walter L. Colls. Ph. Sc.

Admiral Adam, Viscount Duncan.

From the Mezzotint by C. Turner, after the Painting by D. Orme

Walter L. Colls. Ph. Sc.

Admiral Sir James Saumarez, Lord de Saumarez, Bart. K.B. D.C.L.
Vice Admiral of Great Britain.

From the Mezzotint by C. Turner, after the Painting by Carbonier.

CAPTURE OF THE "CLÉOPÂTRE" BY THE "NYMPHE," JUNE 18TH, 1793.

(From T. Medland's engraving, after the drawing by N. Pocock.)

[*To face p.* 476.

INDEX.

VOLUME IV.

NOTE—*British naval officers in the following are described as of the rank to which they attained upon the completion of their active service.*